Lecture Notes of the Institute for Computer Sciences, Social Informatics and Telecommunications Engineering 396

More information about this series at http://www.springer.com/series/8197

Xianbin Wang · Kai-Kit Wong · Shanji Chen ·
Mingqian Liu (Eds.)

Artificial Intelligence for Communications and Networks

Third EAI International Conference, AICON 2021
Xining, China, October 23–24, 2021
Proceedings, Part I

 Springer

Editors
Xianbin Wang 🆔
The University of Western Ontario
London, ON, Canada

Kai-Kit Wong 🆔
University College London
London, UK

Shanji Chen
Qinghai University for Nationalities
Xining, China

Mingqian Liu 🆔
Xidian University
Xi'an, China

ISSN 1867-8211   ISSN 1867-822X (electronic)
Lecture Notes of the Institute for Computer Sciences, Social Informatics
and Telecommunications Engineering
ISBN 978-3-030-90195-0   ISBN 978-3-030-90196-7 (eBook)
https://doi.org/10.1007/978-3-030-90196-7

This Springer imprint is published by the registered company Springer Nature Switzerland AG
The registered company address is: Gewerbestrasse 11, 6330 Cham, Switzerland

Preface

We are delighted to introduce the proceedings of the second edition of the European Alliance for Innovation (EAI) International Conference on Artificial Intelligence for Communications and Networks (AICON 2021), which was held in Xining, China, October 23–24, 2021. This conference aims to stimulate debate and provide a forum for researchers working on related problems to exchange ideas and recent results (both positive and negative ones) in applying artificial intelligence to communications and networks. The artificial intelligence based approach may offer some new design approaches for traditionally difficult information and signal processing tasks in wireless communication, networking, and computing.

The technical program of AICON 2021 consisted of 81 full papers, including the five best papers, in oral presentation sessions at the main conference tracks: Track 1: Deep Learning/Machine Learning on Information and Signal Processing; Track 2: Artificial Intelligence in Wireless Communications and Satellite Communications; Track 3: Artificial Intelligence in Electromagnetic Signal Processing; Track 4: Artificial Intelligence Application in Wireless Caching and Computing; Track 5: Artificial Intelligence Application in Computer Network; and Track 6: Advances in AI and Their Applications in Information, Circuit, Microwave and Control. Aside from the high-quality technical paper presentations, the technical program also featured three keynote speeches given by Nan Zhao from the Dalian University of Technology, China, Yunfei Chen from the University of Warwick, UK, and Jie Tang from the South China University of Technology, China.

Coordination with the steering chairs, Imrich Chlamtac, Xuemai Gu, and Cheng Li, was essential for the success of the conference. We sincerely appreciate their constant support and guidance. It was also a great pleasure to work with such an excellent organizing committee team for their hard work in organizing and supporting the conference. In particular, the Technical Program Committee, who completed the peer-review process for technical papers and put together a high-quality technical program. We are also grateful to Conference Manager Aleksandra Sledziejowska for her support and to all the authors who submitted their papers to the AICON 2021 conference.

We would like to express our thanks to all members of the organizing committee and all the volunteer reviewers who worked so hard, day and night, for this conference. We would like also to express our gratitude for the sponsorship from various sources. Finally, we are grateful to EAI for sponsoring this conference.

October 2021

Xianbin Wang
Kai-Kit Wong

Organization

Steering Committee

Imrich Chlamtac   University of Trento, Italy
Xuemai Gu   Harbin Institute of Technology, China
Cheng Li   Memorial University of Newfoundland, Canada

Organizing Committee

General Chair

Gang Wang   Qinghai Nationalities University, China

General Co-chairs

Xianbin Wang   Western University, Canada
Kai-Kit Wong   University College London, UK
Shanji Chen   Qinghai Nationalities University, China

Technical Program Committee Co-chairs

Mingqian Liu   Xidian University, China
Tiankui Zhang   Beijing University of Posts and
     Telecommunications, China
Gongliang Liu   Harbin Institute of Technology, China

Sponsorship and Exhibit Chair

Ying Ma   Qinghai Nationalities University, China

Local Chair

Lingfei Zhang   Qinghai Nationalities University, China

Workshops Chair

Bo Li   Harbin Institute of Technology, China

Publicity and Social Media Chair

Guilian Feng   Qinghai Nationalities University, China

Publications Chair

Weidang Lu   Zhejiang University of Technology, China

Web Chair

Zhutian Yang   Harbin Institute of Technology, China

Posters and PhD Track Chair

Qian Lin   Qinghai Nationalities University, China

Tutorials Chair

Tao Wang   Qinghai Nationalities University, China

Technical Program Committee

Jin Li	Xidian University, China
Junlin Zhang	Xidian University, China
Junfang Li	Xi'an Aeronautical University, China
Nan Qu	Xidian University, China
Bodong Shang	Virginia Tech, USA
Fangfang Liu	Beijing University of Posts and Telecommunications, China
Yang Yang	Beijing University of Posts and Telecommunications, China
Yu Xu	Beijing University of Posts and Telecommunications, China
Guangyu Zhu	Beijing University of Posts and Telecommunications, China
Yuanpeng Zheng	Beijing University of Posts and Telecommunications, China
Qihang Cao	Harbin Institute of Technology, China
Yangfei Liu	Harbin Institute of Technology, China
Mingyi Wang	Harbin Institute of Technology, China
Ziqi Sun	Harbin Institute of Technology, China
Jianrui Lu	Harbin Institute of Technology, China
Hang Yuan	Xidian University, China
Ke Yang	Xidian University, China
Lei Jin	Xidian University, China
Jiakui Wang	Xidian University, China
Zhiyang Gao	Xidian University, China
Yaqi Fan	Xidian University, China
Han Zhu	Xidian University, China

Huigui Cheng	Xidian University, China
Sihao Qin	Xidian University, China
Meng Cao	Xidian University, China
Yuanpo Cai	Xidian University, China
Zhenju Zhang	Xidian University, China
Chen Fan	Xidian University, China
Tianming Yang	Xidian University, China
Yifan Zhang	Xidian University, China
Hongyi Zhang	Xidian University, China
Xinge Bao	Xidian University, China
Yi Wang	Xidian University, China

Contents – Part I

**Artificial Intelligence in Wireless Communications and Satellite
Communications**

Artificial Intelligence in Electromagnetic Signal Processing

Artificial Intelligence Application in Wireless Caching and Computing

Contents – Part II

**Advances in AI and Their Applications in Information, Circuit,
Microwave and Control**

Deep Learning/Machine Learning on Information and Signal Processing

Federated Learning Based Distributed Algorithms for RF Fingerprinting Extraction and Identification of IoT Devices

Weiwei Wu[1], Su Hu[1(✉)], Yuan Gao[2], and Jiang Cao[2]

[1] University of Electronic Science and Technology of China, Chengdu, China
husu@uestc.edu.cn
[2] Academy of Military Science of the PLA, Beijing, China

Abstract. With the development of Internet of things (IoT), exponential data growth and diversified functions and services have dramatically enhanced the importance of user authentication for data access. As a solution to the problem of user authentication, we study the deep-learning based methods for the radio frequency (RF) fingerprinting recognition of mobile devices in this paper. In consideration of the distributed storage of RF signals in practice, instead of using the deep learning algorithms for centralized data training, we employ the federated learning algorithms for distributed RF fingerprinting recognition, where the data of RF signals are distributed in multiple mobile devices for storage and recognition. To reduce the impact of uneven data distribution among mobile devices on the performance of federated learning algorithms, we propose the dynamic sample selection based federated learning algorithms to train the data. In comparison with the traditional federated learning algorithms, our proposed algorithm can improve the system accuracy as well as reduce the computation time.

Keywords: RF fingerprinting · Federated learning · IoT devices

1 Introduction

The amount of data has dramatically increased in the era of Internet of Things (IoT) with the development of sensors, mobile devices, etc. By the forecast of CISCO company, more than 25 billion devices will be connected in the communication systems by 2021 [1]. Because of their inherent nature, mobile devices are vulnerable to malicious attacks when these devices are under untrusted environments. When a mobile device is required to be authenticated, a few traditional authentication methods, e.g., digital signature are not applicable since they are vulnerable to various key-hacking attacks, e.g., invasive attacks, side channel attacks, etc. Also a few mobile devices cannot support high-complexity computation, and thus the traditional authentication methods by using IP or MAC addresses for authentication are not efficient [2].

As a promising authentication method, radio frequency (RF) fingerprinting can identify the unique features of a mobile device by analyzing its transmitted signals, and thus

© ICST Institute for Computer Sciences, Social Informatics and Telecommunications Engineering 2021
Published by Springer Nature Switzerland AG 2021. All Rights Reserved
X. Wang et al. (Eds.): AICON 2021, LNICST 396, pp. 3–18, 2021.
https://doi.org/10.1007/978-3-030-90196-7_1

effectively prevent the impersonation of a mobile device for security credentials. The features of mobile devices which can be extracted from transmitted signals are primarily caused by the difference of RF components in the process of manufacturing, including the imperfections of power amplifiers, the errors of magnitude and phase, carrier frequency differences, phase offset, and clock offset, etc. [3].

Based on the original signals and the extracted features, we can use either machine-learning based algorithms or deep-learning based algorithms to identify mobile devices [4]. With machine-learning based RF fingerprint technologies, we preprocess the collected signals by denoising and normalization, extract various fingerprint features, and identify the mobile devices by analyzing the fingerprint features. In comparison, the deep-learning based radio frequency fingerprint recognition technology does not require the extraction of features from the signals. After the preprocessing, the predicted label is directly compared with the label registered in the fingerprint library in the deep neural network to identify different communication devices. Deep learning method relies on a large amount of data to train a model with existing fingerprints.

Either machine-learning based algorithms or deep-learning based algorithms need to train a large amount of data on the original signals as well as the extracted features. However, the traditional data processing method which needs to load all the data into a centralized node is no longer applicable. Instead, we need to use distributed machine-learning or deep-learning algorithms, e.g., federated learning algorithms. Under the federated learning based distribution architecture, we can train the data in separate nodes instead of performing centralized computations with an aggregation model.

In this paper, we discuss the design of federated learning based RF fingerprinting extraction and identify mobile devices under the distribution architecture. In the following, we overview the RF Fingerprinting and its applications in identifying mobile devices. We then present the design of federated learning based RF Fingerprinting extraction and device identification algorithms. Finally, we discuss a few comparative study results and conclude the paper.

2   Related Work of RF Fingerprinting Recognition

Based on the types of signals, the studies on the RF fingerprinting recognition can be classified as transient signal recognition and steady-state signal recognition, and the primary studies are summarized in Table 1.

A.   RF fingerprinting recognition methods for transient signals.

The relevant literature mainly studies on transient signals when the communication process starts or finishes. A transmitter emits transient signals in an unstable working state in which the transmit power fluctuates between approaching zero and rated power when turning on or down transmit power [5]. Transient signal only shows the hardware characteristics of a transmitter, and does not carry any data information. The RF fingerprinting recognition based on the transient signals is independent from data, so it is one of the most commonly studied method in the field of RF fingerprinting recognition Fig. 1.

Table 1. Studies of RF fingerprinting recognition

	Authors	Type of communications	Methods	Key features
Transient signals	Bihl [5]	VHF FM	Wavelet	Wavelet coefficients
	Zhuo [6]	Wavelet	Wavelet	Statistical and power density characteristics
	Li [7]	VHF FM	Time-frequency analysis	Multi-segment fractal dimension
	Xiao [8]	VHF FM	Time-frequency analysis	Complex envelope, instantaneous amplitude, instantaneous phase and instantaneous frequency
	Shi [9]	VHF FM	Time-frequency analysis	Amplitude and phase characteristics
	Polak [10]	IEEE 802.11b	Wavelet	Transient signal amplitude, phase, in-phase component, quadrature component, power and discrete wavelet transform (DWT) coefficients, etc.
	Wang [11]	433 MHz	Wavelet	Signal duration, normalized amplitude variance, peak number of carrier signal, discrete wavelet transform coefficients of the first signal extracted, and the difference between the average and maximum normalized amplitude
Steady-state signals	Demers [12]	UMTS	FFT	Preamble spectrum

(*continued*)

Table 1. (*continued*)

	Authors	Type of communications	Methods	Key features
	Patel [13]	IEEE 802.11a/g	FFT	Power spectral density of preambles
	Reising [14]	IEEE 802.11b	FFT	Frequency offset, preamble correlation, I/Q offset, amplitude error and phase errors
	Knox [15]	MIMO	FFT	Error vector magnitude, carrier center frequency deviation, OFDM pilot phase deviation, symbol clock deviation, I/Q offset, I/Q phase rotation, I/Q gain imbalance, and preamble correlation
	Yuan [16]	IEEE 802.15.4	FFT	Phase information of the demodulated baseband signal

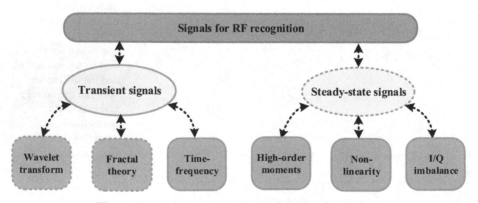

Fig. 1. Signal characteristics for RF fingerprinting analysis

Due to the short duration of a transient signal, it is necessary to determine the starting point of the transient signal in order to obtain the information from the signal. Typical methods of detecting the starting points primarily rely on the comparison of transient signals and noises, and the specific methods include amplitude threshold detection, Bayesian step-start detection, Bayesian rising-point detection, as well as variance estimation detection [6]. Basic principles primarily include Wavelet transform, fractal theory, and time-frequency analysis.

(1) Research on the wavelet transform.

By analyzing transient signals, Li et al. propose a self-recognition method, and it builds neural network models on the non-cooperative radar signals by using wavelet transform features [7]. Aimed at the wireless signals intercepted by a receiver, Li et al. extract the wavelet features of transient signals, and propose the time-frequency information from the signals through wavelet decomposition to identify different signal sources. However, the result shows extremely high signal-to-noise ratio. Through multi-scale and multi-resolution analysis of the signals in the actual environment, Li et al. [7] can achieve a fairly high resolution in the time-frequency domain and high accuracy of classifications. Wavelet analysis reflects the individual characteristics of radiation sources by increasing the number of decomposition layers, at the high cost of time computation.

(2) Research on the fractal theory.

Fractal geometry is a new and emerging geometry theory recently in the field of complex graphs. Xiao et al. [8] study the extraction of multiple dimensions from wireless signals as RF fingerprint features to identify different transmitters, achieving a fairly good recognition performance. Fractal features lack a description of time-varying characteristics of transient signals, and thus the signals with significantly different instantaneous characteristics may have the same fractal complexity. This situation may result in partial misjudgment of RF fingerprinting recognition and reduce the accuracy of recognition. At the same time, due to the different computation methods in different fractal dimensions, we cannot achieve a consistent recognition rate. Xiao et al. [8] analyze the recognition performance when various values of fractal dimensions are used as feature vectors. The testing results show that the recognition performance of the methods with multiple dimensions outperforms the other methods.

(3) Research on the time-frequency analysis.

In the time-frequency analysis of transient signals, Hilbert transform is always used to extract the instantaneous amplitude and phase from the signals. A nonlinear model for transient signal transmission and reception is established, and the characteristics of signal amplitude and phase distortion are used to identify different transmitters [9]. However, in practical applications, the complexity of nonlinear model is extremely high and thus it is difficult to establish with a nonlinear model. Bradford W. Polak et al. construct a kernel function to improve the classification performance, apply time-frequency analysis into the recognition of transmitters, and achieve fairly good recognition performance [10].

But it is worth noting that the RF fingerprinting recognition technology based on transient signals requires extremely high accuracy of the recognition instrument, and the signal energy is quite weak at the receive end [11]. Intercepting the transient signal from the received signal is also the difficulty of transient-signal recognition technology. RF fingerprinting features of transient signals include signal duration, transient spectrum, etc. The transient signal duration is extremely short, and the channel environment (e.g., noise, temperature, etc.) has a great impact on the transient signals. All the above-mentioned factors may influence the performance in practice.

B.   RF fingerprinting recognition methods for steady-state signals.

In addition to a few transient signals, most wireless signals are steady-state signals. In the steady-state part of a signal, the transmitter is typically stable throughout the communication process, and the information part is easy to be separated from the received signal. Therefore, researchers start to study the RF fingerprint recognition on the steady-state signals.

(1)   Research on high-order moments and high-order spectra.

A high-order moment feature recognition method is designed on envelope features, but its recognition rate cannot meet the actual demand [12]. Specifically, the recognition method uses the power spectral density of a preamble sequence as feature vectors to identify different transmitters. However, the default signals of conventional second-order cumulants follow Gaussian distribution, which is always assumed in practical applications. Patel et al. in [13] propose a method of computing the rectangular integral bispectrum of a signal, and it can achieve fairly good recognition performance. With higher-order spectral features, Patel et al. can achieve high performance by extracting the RF fingerprinting features from non-Gaussian signals.

(2)   Research on the non-linearity of devices.

Due to the appearance of a large number of non-linear devices such as power amplifiers, researchers employ non-linear characteristics for RF fingerprinting recognition [14]. Specifically, a method of nonlinear dynamics is proposed to spatially reconstruct the received signal, and the results show that spatial reconstruction has a good identification performance for weakly nonlinear devices. Also fractal geometry is used to characterize the nonlinearity of a steady-state signal, and the results show that different transmitters have different fractal characteristics [15].

(3)   Research on the imbalance of I/Q signals.

Researchers study the use of frequency estimation to identify different transmitters with instantaneous frequency as the characteristic parameter [16]. By extracting the signal's frequency offset, phase offset, IQ offset, and preamble-related modulation errors, the proposed method can identify different transmitters, and the experimental results show that the proposed method can achieve high anti-noise capability and strong robustness. The study uses IQ imbalance to identify the relay system, and the results show that this method has greatly improved the recognition performance [16].

3   Deep Learning Based RF Fingerprinting Recognition Algorithms

In the process of recognition, we can classify the methods of extracting RF fingerprinting features into two types (see Fig. 2). The former is a traditional machine-learning recognition technology, while the latter is a deep-learning recognition technology.

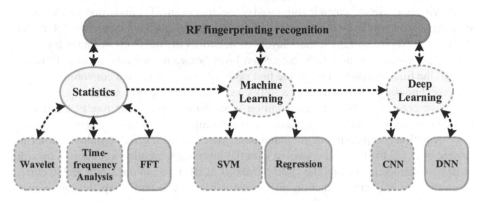

Fig. 2. Types of algorithms for RF fingerprinting recognition

Before 2018, the research on RF fingerprinting focuses on using machine learning algorithms, e.g., support vector machines (SVM) to recognize the identity document (ID) of each mobile device. A few studies employ multiple SVM algorithms to recognize the ID of mobile devices, including the Platt's Minimization Optimization (SMO) algorithm, the PolyKernel algorithms, the Pearson VII Universal Kernel (PuK) algorithms [17]. Typically, the PuK algorithms are more effective in RF Fingerprinting recognition, attaining high performance in recognition and dramatically reducing the computation time. The traditional machine-learning RF fingerprinting recognition technology first preprocesses the collected signals, including power normalization, noise reduction, and label setting. Then, with different algorithms to extract RF fingerprinting features from the pre-processed signal data, we can store the marked features into the fingerprint library. Finally, the extracted RF fingerprint features are used to identify the mobile devices. In the traditional machine-learning recognition technology, the key is to select appropriate signal characteristics from RF fingerprints.

After 2018, the study of using deep learning in the field of RF fingerprinting recognition has gradually appeared. Sankhe et al. in [18] propose to use a 2-layered convolution neural networks (CNN) to train the RF fingerprinting data from 16 of X310 USRP SDRs. Wu et al. in [19] employ a deep neural network (DNN) with rectified linear units (ReLU) to run the training model for the RF fingerprinting recognition of 12 Ettus USRP N210. Also Wu et al. in [19] propose an incremental learning based neural networks to train the data in multiple stages and modify the learning model with new-arrival data to accelerate the process of training. Compared with traditional machine learning algorithms, deep-learning based radio frequency fingerprinting recognition technology does not require the procedure of feature extraction. After preprocessing, we directly compare the predicted labels with the labels registered in the fingerprint library in a deep learning network to identify different mobile devices. Deep learning relies on a large number of data to train the models with existing RF fingerprints.

As the most successful artificial intelligence method in the field of computer vision, CNN has been widely used in classification, recognition, etc. In our research of RF fingerprinting recognition, we load the original signals from various mobile devices into a CNN model for RF fingerprinting recognition. Specifically, we design the CNN model by referring to LeNet-5, which is composed of the operations of convolution and pooling. By using 2 groups of convolution and pooling, we can build up a 5 layered CNN model as Fig. 3. As shown in Fig. 3, the 5 layers of networks include 2 convolution layers, 2 pooling layers, as well as 1 fully connected layer before output. The input data flows through the first convolution layer, the first pooling layer, the second convolution layer, the second pooling layer, as well as a fully connected layer before output.

As the core of a CNN, the convolution layer primary plays the role of extracting RF features from the original signals, and it is composed of a few kernels to operate the convolution computation on the input data. Specifically, a kernel employs a filter in the size of 2×2 to slide and convolve with the input data, creating a feature map with the dimension determined by the sliding interval of the filter. In our CNN architecture, we employ an activation function on the elements of a feature map through a pre-determined transformation, and a typical activation function includes sigmoid, tanh, etc. In our model, we use a rectified linear unit (ReLU) to compose CNN networks, and a ReLU represents the maximum between the input value and zero, i.e. setting each of the negative values to be 0.

In the CNN model for RF fingerprinting recognition, the input data are 2×128 I/Q samples of RF signals. The first convolution layer is in the size of $50 \times 1 \times 3$ with the kernel of ReLU, the first pooling layer is a Max pooling layer, the second convolution layer is in the size of $50 \times 2 \times 3$ with the kernel of ReLU, the second pooling layer is also a Max pooling layer, the last layer is a fully-connected layer with the kernel of Softmax. The output is the ID of a mobile device for recognition.

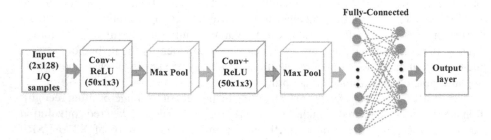

Fig. 3. CNN model for RF fingerprinting recognition

4 Federated Learning Based RF Fingerprinting Recognition

A. Preprocessing data.

The input data of a training model is a sequence of I/Q samples, and usually it represents a time-series of collected data through Rayleigh fading channels. Before we can train raw data, we need to preprocess these data. First, we need to use the channel estimation methods with the objective of minimum mean square error (MMSE), and then normalize the data valued in a range of [0,1]. Before we load the whole sequence of data into the training model, we need to partition data into a few subsequences. Assume that the length of input I/Q sequence is T and each of the subsequences is t, then the number of partitioned subsequences is $M = T/t$. Also we set a window with the length of t, and slide the window over the I/Q sequence with the length of T.

Instead of loading the sequence of I/Q samples with the length of T into our training model, we put multiple subsequences into the model one by one. It is critical but difficult to select the length of subsequence, since a short subsequence can result in a low variance within a subsequence but high bias between subsequences, while a long subsequence can lead to a high variance within a subsequence but low bias between subsequences. In practice, we need to balance the variance within a subsequence and the bias between subsequences when selecting the length of subsequences.

In view of the variation of wireless channels, we can assume that the channels are invariant when the duration of a subsequence is short, i.e. the length of subsequence is small. Thus, we select fairly short subsequences of input samples to train the model and it can simplify the estimation of coefficients in the wireless channels. Specifically, we train the real part and the imaginary part of the I/Q subsequences in a 2×1 vector, respectively.

B. RF Fingerprinting recognition.

In this section, we establish a federated learning based distributed computing model, in which each mobile device trains its own sample data and one server is used to finalize the model by collecting the parameters from each device and modifying the model at each of the device end. In the following, we first present the federated learning based distributed computing model. Then, we present the potential impact of unbalanced amount of sample data on the recognition performance of federated learning. Finally, we address the method of dynamic sample gradient to mitigate the impact of unbalanced amount on the decrease of recognition performance and save the computation time.

(1) Federated learning based heterogeneous data computing model.

Based on the distributed computing model of federated learning, different amount of data is distributed to different devices for computation, and a server is used to coordinate with multiple devices. Each of the devices can update its own federated learning model based on local data, and communicate with the server regularly to achieve the global minimum of learning loss. The flow chart of model training for federated learning is shown in Fig. 4. The federated learning process is composed of three steps: encrypted sample alignment, encrypted models training, and incentive effect. Encrypted sample alignment refers to the use of encryption-based sample alignment to find the common samples of two parties on the premise that each device does not disclose data in order to combine the characteristics of these samples for modeling; encryption model training refers to using the distribution of public keys, intermediate encryption effects, and model updating to establish learning models; effect incentive refers to recording the effects of the established model through a permanent data recording mechanism such as blockchain to further optimize the parameters in the federated-learning model.

The distributed computing model based on federated learning is designed to enable the server to aggregate the updates of all the mobile devices. The goal of optimization in the model is defined as the overall learning loss, which equals to the weighted average of learning loss of each mobile device and the weight is the proportion of samples trained at each device.

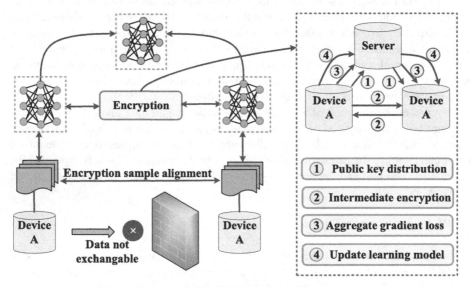

Fig. 4. Flow chart of training in federated learning model

The process of solving the above-mentioned optimization problem can be summarized as follows: we first select n_k mobile devices and use federated learning to train the data distributed at each device. Given the learning rate of η, we can locally compute the average gradient $g_k = \nabla F_k(w_k)$ at each device and send the computation results to the server. For mobile device k, it can update the weight as $w_{t+1}^k \leftarrow w_t^k - \eta g_k$.

In federated learning, when data is heterogeneously distributed at each mobile device, it may cause a few devices to take long time to compute the data, incapable of completing the local update and uploading to the server within the allowed time. In view of the unbalanced distribution of data among heterogeneous mobile devices, we need to quantify the amount of data into several levels for the analysis of federated learning performance. By setting a few thresholds to scale the data amount of mobile devices, we can differentiate the devices which need to handle huge amount of data with those which only need to process small amount of data. Assume that the capacity of all the mobile devices is almost the same and the sample size of each mobile device can be arranged in an ascending order as $\{n_1, n_2, \cdots, n_k\}$, then the local update time at each mobile device can be computed as $t_1 \leq t_2 \leq \cdots \leq t_k$, since the local update time is linearly increasing with the sample size.

Data is independently generated at each of the distributed mobile devices. The data from different devices have different distribution characteristics, and the amount of training data used when performing local learning is very unbalanced. We intend to use a dynamic sample selection algorithm to mitigate the impact of unbalanced data distribution on the performance of learning model. This method allocates processing tasks according to the data processing capabilities of heterogeneous devices. By guaranteeing the accuracy of learning model, the running efficiency of model can be dramatically improved.

(2) Dynamic sample selection algorithm model.

Mobile devices have different data processing capabilities. When a few devices need to process a large amount of data, they may lead to a dramatic increase in time consumption when performing local update. Previous studies have shown that the use of dynamic sample selection algorithms can meet the challenges of heterogeneous mobile devices to handle large amount of data, and accelerate the convergence rate of data processing algorithms at mobile devices.

Specifically, the dynamic sample selection algorithm computes the estimation of variance obtained by batch gradient to increase the training sample size. The algorithm can dynamically increase the training sample size when setting the initial size to be a small value, and achieve a relatively low computation cost while guaranteeing the expected accuracy of our algorithm. For the local sample set S_k established at device k, the objective function of our dynamic sample selection algorithm can be characterized as the average loss function $l(f(w, x_k), y_k)$ at each device k, given w to be the algorithm parameters, x_k to be the input data and y_k to be the output data.

In the first iteration, we select a data set in a relatively small size and determine whether the sample size can optimize the objective function. If the sample set can enhance the value of an objective function, the sample set is maintained in the next iteration, and new samples in the same size are selected to complete the iteration. Conversely, if the sample set does not increase the value of an objective function, the algorithm will increase the sample size and reselect a new sample based on a higher value to perform the next iteration. In the gradient descent process of a dynamic sample selection algorithm, the vector $\nabla J_S(w)$ represents the descent direction of our objective function J with the parameter w. In order to achieve the convergence of our objective function, we can represent the deterministic conditions as $\|\nabla J_S(w) - \nabla J(w)\|_2 \leq \theta \|\nabla J_S(w)\|_2$.

When the amount of data to be processed by a mobile device is large, the iteration cost in our federated learning algorithm is high. If all the local samples are trained on a single mobile device, we have to experience a high cost of updating our model in each round of iteration. To solve the above-mentioned problem, we intend to use the dynamic sample selection strategy. First, we use a small number of samples to train the model, and then increase the sample size gradually to achieve a higher model accuracy. The process is summarized in Algorithm 1, where K represents the set of mobile devices, D_k represents the threshold between the size of a large data set and the size of a small data set, N represents the total number of iterations, t represents the iteration round, η represents the iterative learning rate.

Algorithm 1 Dynamic sample selection algorithm (DASA)

Input K, D_k, N, η

Output ω_{t+1}

Initialize ω_0, D_k

for $t = 1, \cdots N$ do

    select S_t where $S_t \subset K$

        for $k \in S_t$ in parallel do

            $\omega_{t+1}^k = DeviceUpdate(k, \omega_t, D_k)$

        end for

        $\omega_{t+1} = \sum_{k=1}^{K} \dfrac{n_k}{n} \omega_{t+1}^k$

end for

function $DeviceUpdate(k, \omega_t, D_k)$

    Initialize n_k

    If $n_k > D_k$

        Initialize $S_0 \subset \{1, \cdots, n_k\}$

        for $i = 1, \cdots N$ do

            $g_k = -\nabla J_S(\omega_t^k)$

            $\omega_{t+1}^k = \omega_t^k - \eta g_k$

            $i = i + 1$

            Compute the sample variance

        end for

    else

        for $i = 1, \cdots N$ do

            $\omega_{t+1}^k = \omega_t^k - \eta g_k$

        end for

    end if

    return ω_{t+1}^k

end function

In Algorithm 1, the server sends D_k to each of the mobile devices, and each device compares its own sample size n_k with D_k. If $n_k \le D_k$, we can use all the sample resources without any adjustment and perform the local gradient descent process based on the stochastic gradient algorithm. Otherwise, a few mobile devices can be selected to adjust their gradient descent parameters. The sample size at each iteration is determined by the estimation of variance obtained by the computation of batch gradient. The complexity of this algorithm can be denoted as $F = O(\omega/\varepsilon)$, where ε refers to the allowed computation error, ω represents the data processing task allocation among mobile devices.

5 Simulation Results

In the federated learning based RF fingerprinting algorithm, we first consider the convergence of our proposed algorithm (shown in Algorithm 1), and compare it with the convergence of a distributed training model without dynamic sample selection, i.e., using the whole set of data at a local mobile device as training data. Also we consider the accuracy of our proposed algorithm with different parameters in the model.

We complete the distributed RF fingerprinting recognition task based on the experiment shown in Fig. 5, which contains the records of I/Q samples from 4 of X310 USRP SDRs as the transmitters and a X310 USRP SDR as the receiver through a Rayleigh fading channel with the signal noise ratio (SNR) of 5 dB. The records are received at the rate of 5 M/s around the frequency of 2.45 GHz, and the total amount of data is 20 million recored in the PXIE 8840 for one mobile device [20].

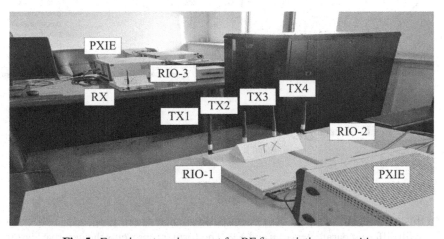

Fig. 5. Experiment environment for RF fingerprinting recognition

A. Convergence Analysis.

Based on the collected data in our experiment, we set the learning rate as 0.2, and set the number of mobile devices to be 50, 100, and 200, respectively. Figure 6 (a) shows the learning loss of the dynamic sample selection algorithm (DASA) in Algorithm 1 and the fixed gradient algorithm (FGA) [21] in which no sample selection is used. In comparison with the FGA, our proposed DASA can effectively reduce the learning loss with different numbers of mobile devices. In addition, the learning loss of both algorithms increases with the rise of the number of mobile devices, which indicate that the performance gap between the distributed learning algorithms and the centralized algorithm dramatically increases with the number of mobiled devices rising. This is the cost of distributed learning algorithms when loading and training data in the memory of a single device is not applicable.

Figure 6 (b) shows the accuracy of RF fingerprinting recognition in the DASA algorithm (Algorithm 1) and the FGA algorithm. Compared with the FGA algorithm, the DASA algorithm can achieve higher recognition accuracy with different numbers of mobile devices. In addition, the DASA algorithm can converge to the final accuracy results in 400–600 rounds of iterations, while the FGA algorithm needs to complete the convergence after 1000 rounds of iterations. This shows that the DASA algorithm can accelerate the convergence process, reduce the computation cost, as well as guarantee the accuracy of recognition.

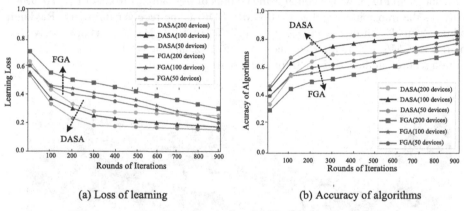

(a) Loss of learning   (b) Accuracy of algorithms

Fig. 6. Accuracy of federated learning based recognition algorithms

B.   Performance Evaluation.

In this section, we compare the system performance of our proposed DASA algorithms with different parameters of η and N_K. The former represents the iterative learning rate, while the later represents the number of mobile devices in the set of K.

As shown in Fig. 7, the recognition accuracy decreases with the rise of iterative learning rate η. The internal rationale of this result is that when we enhance the learning rate η, the gradient parameters $\omega_{t+1}^k = \omega_t^k - \eta g_k$ in each iteration changes at a high speed, and thus has a high risk of missing the optimum of $\nabla J_S(w)$. Once the optimal $\nabla J_S(w)$ is not achieved, the accuracy of the recognition will be reduced.

Also shown in Fig. 7, the recognition accuracy decreases with the rise of N_K. In other words, it is more difficult to recognize the mobile devices when more devices are required to identify. With the subtle differences of RF signals emitted by mobile devices, the process of RF fingerprinting recognition is difficult to complete.

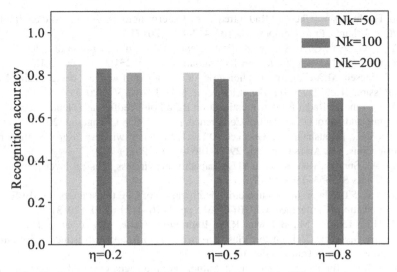

Fig. 7. Accuracy of federated learning algorithms with different parameters

6   Conclusion

To solve the problem of user authentication, we study the federated learning algorithms for the RF fingerprinting recognition of mobile devices in this paper. In consideration of the impact of uneven data distribution on the performance of federated learning algorithms, we propose a dynamic sample selection algorithm to train the RF signals. In comparison with fixed-gradient federated learning algorithms, our proposed algorithm can improve the system accuracy by 10%–20%, while converging to the solution at a higher speed.

Acknowledgements. This work was supported by Sichuan Science and Technology Program, and supported by the Fundamental Research Funds for the Central Universities (no. ZYGX2019J076).

References

1. Li, S., Xu, L.D., Zhao, S.: 5G Internet of Things: a survey. J. Ind. Inf. Integr. **10**, 1–9 (2018)
2. Li, Y.S., Xie, F.Y., Chen, S.L., et al.: Feature Extraction and Recognition of Radio Frequency Fingerprint Signal Suitable for Terminal. Commun. Technol. **251**(001), 63–66 (2018)
3. Zhao, F., Jin, Y.: An optimized radio frequency fingerprint extraction method applied to low-end receivers. In: International Conference on Communication Software and Networks, pp. 753–757 Chongqing (2019)
4. Ding, G., Huang, Z., Wang, X.: Radio Frequency Fingerprint Extraction Based on Singular Values and Singular Vectors of Time-frequency Spectrum. In: International Conference on Signal Processing, pp. 1–6 (2018)
5. Bihl, T.J., Bauer, K.W., Temple, M.A.: Feature selection for RF fingerprinting with multiple discriminant analysis and using ZigBee device emissions. IEEE Trans. Inf. Forensics Secur. **11**(8), 1862–1874 (2016)

6. Zhuo, F., Huang, Y., Chen, J.: Radio frequency fingerprint extraction of radio emitter based on I/Q imbalance. Proc. Comput. Sci. **107**, 472–477 (2017)
7. Li, Y.S., Xie, F.Y., Chen, S.L., et al.: Feature extraction and recognition of radio frequency fingerprint signal suitable for terminal. Commun. Technol. **251**(1), 63–66 (2018)
8. Shi, Y., Jensen, M.A.: Improved radiometric identification of wireless devices using MIMO transmission. IEEE Trans. Inf. Forensics Secur. **6**(4), 1346–1354 (2011)
9. Xiao, Z., Yan, Z.: Radar Emitter Identification Based on Feedforward Neural Networks. In: Electronic and Automation Control Conference, pp. 555–558 Chongqing (2020)
10. Polak, A.C., Dolatshahi, S., Goeckel, D.L.: Identifying wireless users via transmitter imperfections. Sel. Areas Commun. **29**(7), 1469–1479 (2011)
11. Wang, W., Sun, Z., Ren, K., et al.: User capacity of wireless physical-layer identification. IEEE Access **5**, 3353–3368 (2017)
12. Demers, F., ST-Hilaire, M.: Radiometric identification of LTE transmitters. In: IEEE Global Communications Conference (GLOBECOM), pp. 4116–4121. IEEE (2013)
13. Patel, H.J., Temple, M., Baldwin, R.O.: Improving ZigBee device network authentication using ensemble decision tree classifiers with radio frequency distinct native attribute fingerprinting. IEEE Trans. Reliab. **64**(1), 221–233 (2015)
14. Reising, D.R., Temple, M., Jackson, J.: Authorized and rogue device discrimination using dimensionally reduced RF-DNA fingerprints. IEEE Trans. Inf. Forensics Secur. **10**(6), 1180–1192 (2015)
15. Knox, D.A., Kunz, T.: Wireless fingerprints inside a wireless sensor network. ACM Trans. Sens. Netw. **11**(2), 1–30 (2015)
16. Yuan, Y., Huang, Z., Wang, F., et al.: Radio Specific Emitter Identification based on nonlinear characteristics of signal. In: IEEE International Black Sea Conference on Communications and Networking (BlackSeaCom), pp. 77–81. IEEE (2015)
17. Hu, S., et al.: Machine learning for RF fingerprinting extraction and identification of soft-defined radio devices. In: Liang Q., Wang W., Mu J., Liu X., Na Z., Chen B. (eds) Artificial Intelligence in China. LNEE, vol. 572, pp. 189–204. Springer, Singapore (2020). https://doi.org/10.1007/978-981-15-0187-6_22
18. Sankhe, K., Belgiovine, M., Zhou, F., et al.: Oracle: Optimized radio classification through convolutional neural networks. In: IEEE INFOCOM 2019-IEEE Conference on Computer Communications, pp. 370–378. IEEE (2019)
19. Wu, Q., Feres, C., Kuzmenko, D., et al.: Deep learning based RF Fingerprinting for device identification and wireless security. Electron. Lett. **54**(24), 1405–1407 (2018)
20. Sankhe, K., Belgiovine, M., Zhou, F., Riyaz, S., Ioannidis, S., Chowdhury, K.R.: ORACLE: optimized radio classification through convolutional neural networks. In: IEEE INFOCOM, Paris (2019)
21. McMahan, H., et al.: Communication-efficient learning of deep networks from decentralized data. In: International Conference on Machine Learning (ICML) (2017)

Fast Beam Switching Based on Machine Learning for MmWave Massive MIMO Systems

Kean Chen[1], Danpu Liu[2](✉), and Xingwen He[3]

[1] Beijing Laboratory of Advanced Information Networks, Beijing, China
[2] Beijing Key Laboratory of Network System Architecture and Convergence, Beijing, China
dpliu@bupt.edu.cn
[3] Beijing University of Posts and Telecommunications, Beijing 100876,
People's Republic of China
hexingwen@bupt.edu.cn

Abstract. Millimeter wave (mmWave) and massive multiple-input-multiple-output (MIMO) systems are two key technologies for 5G. Beamforming based on massive MIMO can produce high directional beams with array gain, and thus effectively compensate for the high path loss of mmWave. As the number of antennas increases, the beams become increasingly narrow, resulting in large overhead and high latency in the initial access and handover of the beams. For high-speed mobile scenarios, beam switching becomes more challenging since the traversal search among a large number of beams cannot be completed in a short period of time. To address this problem, this paper proposes a method based on machine learning to predict the optimal Base Station (BS) and the optimal beam pair at the successive instant for the User Equipment (UE) in motion. More specifically, a Random Forest (RF) classification model is trained to learn the channel's features in a multi-cell scenario, and complete the nonlinear modeling of the propagation environment. Furthermore, this model is used to predict the future optimal BS and the optimal beam pair for a moving UE based on the present UE's location, BS beam index and RSRP value. The simulation results show that the prediction accuracy is greater than 90% in most situations, thus the latency and the consumption of signaling resources for beam switch is reduced significantly while the loss in spectral efficiency is little.

Keywords: 5G mobile communication · Beam switching · Machine learning · Random forest

1 Introduction

mmWave is an important frequency band that will be used in 5G communication. To compensate the high attenuation of mmWave, massive MIMO and beamforming technologies are used in the 5G system to generate a highly directional beam and provide high beamforming gain. As the antenna scale increases, the number of candidate beams at the transceiver also increases, and the beams become narrower. Since beams have

X. Wang et al. (Eds.): AICON 2021, LNICST 396, pp. 19–29, 2021.
https://doi.org/10.1007/978-3-030-90196-7_2

strong directivity, User Equipment (UE) is accompanied by frequent beam switching as they move. However, the traditional method to find the optimal beam in next time step is to perform exhaustive searching among all candidate beams, which results in high beam sweeping complexity and signaling overhead in massive MIMO scenario. Moreover, if the UE moves too quickly and the beam switches not fast enough, the beam after switching is not the optimal beam pair at the current location. This beam misalignment inevitably results in the loss of spectral efficiency. Therefore, quicker and more accurate beam switching methods in high-speed scenario are needed.

Many approaches to improve the speed and efficiency of beam switching have been proposed. These algorithms can be divided into three categories. In the first category, the beam search process combined with codebook design is optimized. More specifically, a fast beam search algorithm based on a new codebook [1] is proposed to improve the speed of the beam search, and a hierarchical beam search algorithm [2] is proposed to simplify the complexity of the beam search. Besides, a dynamic iterative beam search algorithm is proposed in [3] to reduce the time delay of the beam search. In [4], the features of the Poisson distribution are used before and after the beam is blocked, and a scheme of dynamic beamforming is proposed. The second approach is to perform beam switching based on location information. Owing to the development of positioning technology, the UE's location can be obtained when the UE moves from one location to another; and the search range of the beam can be greatly narrowed down with the help of location information. For example, GPS positioning data is used in [5], and demonstrates good performance in the absence of line-of-sight propagation. A beamforming method based on image tracking and positioning in the LOS scenario is proposed in [6]. In [7], the Extended Kalman Filter is used to predict the location which is used to optimize beamforming. In [8], a 3D beamforming technology based on positioning assistance in mobile scenario is proposed to improve the beam switching speed and spectrum efficiency. Besides, both channel and location information are used to estimate the DOA angle in [9]. This method is more suitable for UAV beam switching scenarios with three-dimension (3D) mobility and rapid velocity changes. The third approach is to use machine learning methods to optimize beam management. In [10], a deep neural network is utilized, and the optimal beam combination can be output by inputting the channel vector with transmit power. In [11], the gNB learns the UE mobility information, signal-to-noise ratio and current beam information, and predicts whether the beams are aligned or not. In addition, Q-Learning is used for beam selection in NLOS scenarios in [12].

In most communication scenarios, the location of scatters such as buildings and vegetation are relatively fixed, and the line-of-sight path also exists, which will result in the correlated channel between adjacent time steps. However, the correlation between channels is nonlinear and difficult to be analyzed by deterministic mathematical models. Machine learning is well suited to deal with nonlinear problems, it can accomplish the prediction by extracting nonlinear information from a large amount of data. More specifically, the nonlinear features of the channel are expressed by some information obtained by the receiver easily, such as the received signal strength, the beam direction, and UE's location. With these available information, the channel features of the current moment can be extracted through machine learning, and further used to accurately predict the channel features of the next moment. Therefore, it is possible to achieve a much faster beam switching owing to the removal of time-consuming beam search.

Based on above consideration, we propose a method to optimize beam switching speed in high-speed mobile scenario by using a Random Forest (RF) multi-classification model in this paper. The model is firstly trained to learn the nonlinear features of the channel, and then it can quickly predict which beam pairs are optimal for the UE to switch to at next moment. Based on the results obtained by simulation, the model proposed in this paper successfully predicts the desired beam to switch to for each UE in a short time with a high prediction accuracy above 90% in most situations. Moreover, although the beam predicted by the model is not always the optimal, nearly the same spectral efficiency can be achieved. In addition, in order to make a compromise between the training cost and the prediction accuracy, several combinations of features are tested and the most suitable one for the scenario is found out. To sum up, the method proposed in this paper reduces complex signaling interactions, and improves the beam switching efficiency greatly in high-speed mobile scenario.

2 System Model

2.1 Scenario Description

Figure 1 shows a mobile mmWave communication scenario. A number of cars, i.e., the UEs are moving within an area consisting of multiple cells, and each cell is served by one Base Station (BS). Both BSs and the UEs are equipped with multiple antennas, each BS has Nt antennas, each UE has Nr antennas, and there is only one RF link between each BS and each UE. That means analog beamforming is applied at both BS and UE, and each UE is only served by one BS at each time slot. The analog precoder and combiner are composed of a set of phase shifters, which can offset the phase of the input signal [13].

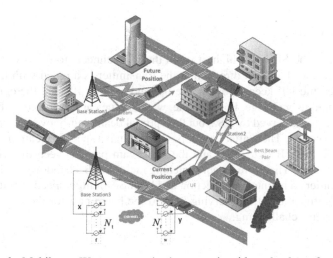

Fig. 1. Mobile mmWave communication scenario with analog beamformer.

In this paper, we focus on the downlink, so the signal is sent at the k-th BS and received at the served u-th UE. The received signal at the u-th UE can be expressed as [14]:

$$y_u = w_u^H H_{u,k} f_{u,k} x_u + w_u^H n_u \tag{1}$$

where x_u denotes the transmitted signal from the BS to the u-th UE, and its average power is $P_t = E\{|x_u|^2\}$. $f_{u,k}$ denotes the analog beamforming vector with $N_t \times 1$ dimension, $H_{u,k}$ denotes the channel matrix with $N_r \times N_t$ dimension between the u-th UE and the k-th BS, w_u denotes the analog combination vector with $N_r \times 1$ dimension at the u-th UE, n_u denotes Gaussian white noise with $N_r \times 1$ dimension.

In practice, w_u and $f_{u,k}$ are codewords selected from a DFT beam codebook, which is a pre-defined matrix. To facilitate the traversal search among a combination of candidate beams, the beam direction is usually quantized into a vector in the beam codebook, and each column in the codebook corresponds to a beam direction. The values in each vector in the codebook represent the phase shift applied to each antenna. The expression for the DFT codebook [15] is defined as:

$$W(m, n) = exp(i\frac{2\pi mn}{N}), n = 0, 1, ..., N - 1; m = 0, 1, ..., M - 1, \tag{2}$$

where M is the number of antennas and N is the number of beams. Generally, $M = N$ in the DFT codebook because the beam vectors generated in this way are orthogonal to each other.

Given the received signal at the UE in (1), the Spectral Efficiency (SE) is defined as:

$$SE = log_2\left(1 + \frac{P_t}{\delta_{nu}^2} \frac{w_u^H H_{u,k} f_{u,k} f_{u,k}^H H_{u,k}^H w_u}{w_u^H w_u}\right) \tag{3}$$

where δ_{nu}^2 is the power of Gaussian white noise.

2.2 Beam Switching

As shown in (3), the SE is the highest when the UE connects to the BS with the best channel quality and the beam direction at the transmitter is aligned with the receiver. However, when the UE keeps moving, the optimal serving BS and the optimal beam pair may continuously change. For example, when a blue car moves along the blue line in Fig. 1, initially it is served by BS2, but the optimal beam pair between them will vary with the car's location. Then, after the car passes through a specific location, the optimal BS will change from BS2 to BS1, and the best beam pair between the UE and BS1 will continue to vary. Therefore, beam switching including BS handover will frequently take place in order to maintain connection and high SE in high-speed mobile scenario, and how to identify the optimal serving BS and the beam pair for the UE in time and efficiently becomes challenging.

3 Beam Switching Based on Machine Learning

3.1 Feasibility of Machine Learning Prediction

As we all know, exhaustive beam sweeping method leads to high beam searching over-head which hardly meet the low latency requirements in high-speed scenario, hence it is necessary to design faster and accurate beam switching algorithms to ensure the optimal communication quality. In a given scenario, the locations of many scatters such as buildings, vegetation, and ground are fixed as well as line-of-sight path exists, which makes the channel correlated between adjacent time steps. The channel features can-not be directly measured, but indirectly reflected by measurable information, such as the received signal strength, beam index, BS and UE's locations, etc. This provides the possibility to predict the channel features of the next moment by the channel features of the previous moment. However, the correlation between channels is nonlinear, and it is difficult to extract the nonlinear features of channels by deterministic mathematical modeling methods. Given the outstanding advantage of machine learning for dealing with nonlinear problems, we attempt to use this approach to extract the nonlinear fea-tures of the channel and complete the prediction of the BS index, BS beam index and UE beam index at the next moment. With respect to the model for machine learning, the Random Forest (RF) Multi-Classification model is chosen owing to its good performance at multi-classification tasks with simple logic and extremely fast training speed.

3.2 Beam Prediction Based on RF

The RF algorithm is a bagging ensemble learning algorithm whose base evaluator is a decision tree [16]. RF increases the differences between each classification model (decision tree) by constructing different training sets, thus improving the prediction performance of the combined training model (forest). It can be used to complete multi-classification tasks [17]. As shown in Fig. 2. the procedure of RF algorithm is as follows: firstly, n sample sets $[T_1, T_2, ..., T_n]$ are selected from the original training set T using bagging sampling; secondly, n decision tree models $[h_{T_1}, h_{T_2}, ..., h_{T_n}]$ are built for each of the n sample sets; thirdly, the same validation data x are used to test each of the n decision tree models to obtain n classification results $[R_1(x), R_2(x), ..., R_n(x)]$. Finally, the final classification is voted on according to the n classification results, following the principle of majority rule. The flow of RF model can be represented by the following equation:

$$H(x) = arg \max_Y \sum_{i=1}^{n} I\left(h_{T_n}(x) = Y\right) \tag{4}$$

where $H(x)$ represents the final classification results from the vote, $I(°)$ represents a schematic function, h_{T_n} represents a single decision tree classification model, x represents the validation set, and Y represents output classification.

When the RF model is used to predict the optimal BS and beam pair for the next moment, the prediction process can be expressed specifically as:

$$f[\theta, x_{test}] = \left[(I_{BS})_{opt}, \left(I_{beam}^{BS}\right)_{opt}, \left(I_{beam}^{UE}\right)_{opt}\right] \tag{5}$$

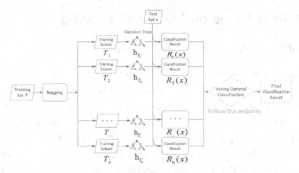

Fig. 2. RF processing flow

where θ represents some parameters of the model, such as the number of decision trees, the number of samples per node, etc. x_{test} represents the feature of validation data on the model input. Considering the difficulty of feature acquisition and the influence of each feature on the prediction effect, we investigate six candidate features, which are UE's location (L_{UE}); the beam index of the BS (I_{beam}^{BS}); the RSRP value of the received signal ($RSRP_{rx}$); the distance between the UE and the BS (d_{UE}^{BS}); the BS index (I_{BS}); the beam index of the UE (I_{beam}^{UE}) [18]. Some of these features may contain similar nonlinear channel features, so the contribution of certain features to the model prediction accuracy may be the same, thus, the combination of some features in the feature set can be selected to reduce the training cost. The effect of different feature combinations on the model prediction accuracy is tested through simulation, and the feature combinations that correspond to higher prediction accuracy and smaller number of features are found out. Specifically, the combination of L_{UE}, I_{beam}^{BS}, $RSRP_{rx}$ performs better. The output of the model includes three prediction targets, i.e., the optimal BS index ($(I_{BS})_{opt}$), the optimal BS beam index ($(I_{beam}^{BS})_{opt}$), and the optimal UE beam index ($(I_{beam}^{UE})_{opt}$). These three targets will be transmitted to the BS and the UE, and used in the following beam switching process.

3.3 Generation of Data Sets

In order to complete the training and testing of the RF model, a large number of channel-related data sets are needed. Given that real channel measurement data during communication is difficult to obtain, some theoretical channel models are applied to generate channel samples close to real scenarios. Currently, there are two main approaches for mmWave channel modeling: Extended Saleh-Valenzuela (eSV) channel modeling and ray tracing channel modeling. The eSV channel model adopts the statistical modeling method and takes into account the clustering characteristics of mmWave and multi-antenna array structure, while the ray-tracing method calculates the amplitude, phase, delay, and polarization of each ray based on electromagnetic wave propagation theory. Given that the ray tracing modeling method is closer to the actual communication environment, Wireless Insite simulation software based on ray-tracing is used in this paper to generate the data sets of channel samples. Specifically, the data sets consist of numerical values, each data including six candidate features and three labels. All the BSs and all beam directions between BS and UE are traversed at each location of the UE, and the beam pair corresponding to the maximum RSRP at the UE is selected as the optimal beam pair which is used as the label of the dataset. To generate the data sets as close as possible to the real scenario, a random positioning error within 10 m is added to each L_{UE} sample.

4 Simulation Results

4.1 Simulation Scenario

Figure 3 shows a 2D view of the simulation scenario, which contains many buildings, 5 BSs and 4 UE's movement paths. The 5 BSs are located in the four corners and the center of the scenario, and 4 movement paths of the UE are randomly generated. Considering the UE's moving direction influences the choice of beam pairs, the UE's moving trajectory covers the main streets in both directions. The red triangles in the Fig. 3 indicate the sampling points during the UE's movement. The sampling interval is 1 s, i.e., the channel information is measured every second. Considering a downlink scenario, we set different BS transmitted power (P_t) in the interval of -20 dBm to 20 dBm in steps of 5 dBm. A total of 25000 data samples were generated under one P_t. Given the 9 P_ts of the BS, data set includes a total of 225000 data samples, of which the validation set accounted for 30% and the training set accounted for 70%. The UE's movement paths of the validation set and the training set are the same. However, due to the randomness of the noise and the positioning error, the $RSRP_{rx}$ and the L_{UE} are different in each piece of training or validation data. The other parameters are detailed in Table 1.

Fig. 3. A 2D view of the simulation scenario

Table 1. Simulation parameters

Parameter name	Value
Carrier type	Sine wave
Carrier frequency	28 GHz
Antenna number of base stations	128
Antenna number of users	32
Number of base stations	5
Number of user movement paths	4
User movement speed	15 m/s(54 km/h)
Sampling interval	15 m
Channel bandwidth	100 MHz
Antenna array	ULA
Noise power	−90 dBm

4.2 Results and Analysis

The performance metrics of the proposed method mainly include the model's prediction accuracy and the spectral efficiency (SE). Prediction accuracy is defined as:

$$Prediction\ accuracy = \frac{\sum_{k=1}^{N(Validationset)} I_k\{(index)_{pre} = (index)_{opt}\}}{N(Validation\ set)} \tag{6}$$

where $N(Validation\ set)$ represents the size of validation set. $I_k\{\}$ is an indicative function of the k-th sample of validation set, where 1 represents the conditions in the brackets are met, and 0 otherwise. $(index)_{pre}$ represents RF model's predicted index, $(index)_{opt}$ represents optimal index acquired by traversal, both of which include three prediction targets, as expressed in Eq. (5).

At first, we investigate the effect of different channel feature combinations on the model's prediction accuracy, where $(I_{beam}^{BS})_{opt}$ is selected as the prediction target of the model. From Fig. 4, it can be seen that no matter which combination of features is chosen, model's prediction accuracy is improved with the increase of the P_t. Moreover, the more features selected for training, the better the prediction performance of the model. However, the difficulty of learning and training time will greatly go up with the increase of the number of the used features. Therefore, it is necessary to make a compromise between training cost and prediction accuracy. As shown in the figure, the model trained with the feature combination $(L_{UE}, I_{beam}^{BS}, RSRP_{rx})$ or the feature combination containing the triplet demonstrates the highest accuracy, while the prediction accuracy is lower for the feature combination without the beam index. That indicates the beam index contains the majority information of channel nonlinear characteristics. However, prediction accuracy is also very low if there are only $(I_{BS}, I_{beam}^{BS}, I_{beam}^{UE})$ in the combination. That indicates the diversity of the features also needs to be considered. Therefore, the triple feature combination $(L_{UE}, I_{beam}^{BS}, RSRP_{rx})$ is used in the following simulations.

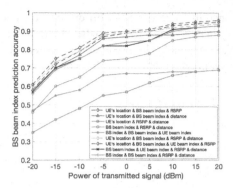

Fig. 4. Combinations of features

Figure 5 shows that prediction accuracy of more than 90% for 3 prediction targets when the P_t of BS is greater than 5_dBm. When the P_t is low, i.e., the signal-to-noise ratio (SNR) is low, a small increase of the P_t is a great boost to the prediction accuracy. However, when the P_t becomes higher, this boost effect gradually wears off. Among the three prediction targets, the model demonstrates the highest prediction accuracy for the $(I_{BS})_{opt}$ because the total number of categories for the I_{BS} is the least. On the contrary, the $\left(I_{beam}^{BS}\right)_{opt}$ prediction is the least accurate because it has the highest number of categories. The prediction accuracy of the $\left(I_{beam}^{UE}\right)_{opt}$ is in the middle. In addition, the size of the training set affects the performance. The prediction accuracy increases with the increasing size of training data and stabilizes at over 90% with more than 40,000 samples.

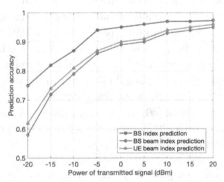

Fig. 5. The prediction accuracy for $(I_{BS})_{opt}$, $\left(I_{beam}^{BS}\right)_{opt}$, and $\left(I_{beam}^{UE}\right)_{opt}$

Figure 6 shows that the average SE corresponding to the beam pair via traversal search and RF-based prediction. Given a specific noise power, with the increase in P_t, the SE of the proposed method gradually approximates the optimal beam. Furthermore, the SE gap between the proposed method and the exhaustive beam sweeping is small, although the accuracy of prediction at low P_t is not very high as shown in Fig. 5. These results are reasonable since the received SNR difference between the suboptimal and optimal beam pairs is tiny in many cases owing to the narrow beam-width and clustering characteristics of mmWave channel. The prediction based on RF may be not optimal, but still suboptimal and supports a relatively high received SNR.

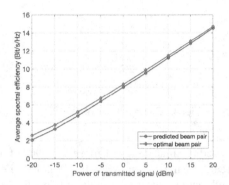

Fig. 6. Average SE comparison

To sum up, the accuracy of the model in predicting the beam depends mainly on the signal strength and the combination of features used to train the model. Moreover, although the predicted beam pair are not optimal at low transmit power, the achieved SE is still quite close to the upper bound.

5 Conclusion

In this paper, we propose a method to optimize the efficiency of beam switching in high-speed mobile scenarios by using a RF model. The core idea is to learn the nonlinear features of the channel by machine learning based on the correlation between the adjacent time steps of the channel in the fixed scenario. Therefore, the beam pair at the next moment can be predicted based on the information of the previous moment.

Simulation results show that the spectral efficiency of the proposed method is close to the upper bound, and the prediction accuracy can reach more than 90% within a typical BS transmitted power range. What's more, the proposed method reduces frequent signaling interaction to determine the optimal beam pair, and improves the efficiency of beam switching with extremely short time delay.

Acknowledgement. This work is supported by Beijing Natural Science Foundation under Grant No. L202003, the National Natural Science Foundation of China under Grant No. 61971069, 61801051, and the Open Project of A Laboratory under Grant No. 2017XXAQ08.

References

1. Weixia, Z., Chao, G., Guanglong, D., Zhenyu, W., Ying, G.: A new codebook design scheme for fast beam searching in millimeter-wave communications. China Communications **11**(6), 12–22 (June 2014)

2. Yang, L., Ma, S., Yang, H., Tan, H.: A hierarchical beam search algorithm with betterperformance for millimeter-wave communication. In: 2019 2nd World Symposium on Communication Engineering (WSCE), pp. 16–20, Nagoya (2019)
3. Lin, J., An, W.: A New Initial Beam Search Scheme in 5G New Radio. In: 2019 3rd International Conference on Electronic Information Technology and Computer Engineering (EITCE), pp. 182–186, Xiamen (2019)
4. Lin, F., Yang, J., Wang, Y., Li, J.: Dynamic Beam Search Scheme for Mobile Scenarios in Millimeter Wave Communication. In: ICC 2020 - 2020 IEEE International Conference on Communications (ICC), pp. 1–6, Dublin (2020)
5. Maiberger, R., Ezri, D., Erlihson, M.: Location based beamforming. In: 2010 IEEE 26-th Convention of Electrical and Electronics Engineers in Israel, pp. 000184–000187, Eliat (2010)
6. Chen, X., Wei, Z., Zhang, X., Sang, L.: A beamforming method based on image tracking and positioning in the LOS scenario. In: 2017 IEEE 17th International Conference on Communication Technology (ICCT), pp. 1628–1633, Chengdu (2017)
7. Talvitie, J., et al.:Positioning and location-based beamforming for high speed trains in 5G NR networks. In: 2018 IEEE Globecom Workshops (GC Wkshps), pp. 1–7, Abu Dhabi (2018)
8. Lu, Y., Koivisto, M., Talvitie, J., Valkama, M., Lohan, E.S.: Positioning-aided 3D beamforming for enhanced communications in mmWave mobile networks. IEEE Access **8**, 55513–55525 (2020)
9. Miao, W., Luo, C., Min, G., Wu, L., Zhao, T., Mi, Y.: Position-Based Beamforming Design for UAV Communications in LTE Networks. ICC 2019 - 2019 IEEE International Conference on Communications (ICC), pp. 1–6, Shanghai (2019)
10. Kwon, H.J., Lee, J.H., Choi, W.: Machine learning-based beamforming in K-user MISO interference channels. Access IEEE **9**, 28066–28075 (2021)
11. Na, W., Bae, B., Cho, S., Kim, N.: Deep-learning Based Adaptive Beam Management Technique for Mobile High-speed 5G mmWave Networks. In: 2019 IEEE 9th International Conference on Consumer Electronics (ICCE-Berlin), pp. 149–151, Berlin (2019)
12. Wang, R., et al.: Reinforcement learning method for beam management in millimeter-wave networks. In: 2019 UK/ China Emerging Technologies (UCET), Glasgow (2019)
13. Hao, Y.: Research on beam management technology based on millimeter wave distributed antenna array. In: Master's thesis of Beijing University of Posts and Telecommunications, June 2019
14. Zhaoqiang, L.: Research on beam search algorithm in hybrid beamforming system. In: Master's thesis of Beijing University of Posts and Telecommunications, March 2018
15. Yang, D., Yang, L.L., Hanzo, L.: DFT-based beamforming weight vector codebook design for spatially correlated channels in the unitary precoding aided multiUE downlink. In: Proc. IEEE International Conference Communications, vol. 1, pp. 1–5, Cape Town (2010)
16. Breiman, L.: Random forests. Machine learning **45**(1), 5–32 (2001)
17. Cutler, A., Cutler, D.R., Stevens, J.R.: Random forests[M]//Ensemble machine learning, pp. 157–175. Springer, US (2012)
18. Ekman, B.: Machine Learning for Beam Based Mobility Optimization in NR. Thesis of Linkoping University, Swedn (2017)

Study on Pixel Level Segmentation and Area Quantification of Highway Slope Cracks

YunLing Zhang[1,2], Pei Guo[1,2], Pengyu Liu[3,4,5(✉)], Yaoyao Li[3,4,5], and Shanji Chen[6]

[1] Research and Development Center of Transport Industry of Spatial Information Application and Disaster Prevention and Mitigation Technology, Beijing 100097, China
[2] China Highway Engineering Consultants Corporation, Beijing 100097, China
[3] Faculty of Information Technology, Beijing University of Technology, Beijing 100124, China
liupengyu@bjut.edu.cn
[4] Beijing Laboratory of Advanced Information Networks, Beijing 100124, China
[5] Beijing Key Laboratory of Computational Intelligence and Intelligent System, Beijing University of Technology, Beijing 100124, China
[6] School of Physics and Electronic Information, Qinghai Nationalities University, Xining 810007, China

Abstract. Highway slope disasters show obvious stage characteristics before the occurrence, and cracks are the early symptoms of most highway slope disasters. Computer vision is widely used in crack detection because of its advantages of high efficiency and low cost. In view of the shortage of traditional crack actual area calculation methods and poor effect, this paper proposes a slope crack pixel level segmentation method based on deep convolutional neural network, so as to generate accurate segmentation of crack morphology. Then, according to the binary segmentation mask, the checkerboard mapping method is proposed to calculate the actual crack area. Finally, the effectiveness and superiority of the proposed checkerboard mapping method are verified and evaluated with a self-made data set of highway crack image. The experimental results show that this method can effectively detect the actual crack area, and the relative error is small. The calculated results can be used as a reference for slope disaster warning.

Keywords: Crack · Pixel area · Actual area

1 Introduction

China is a country with frequent geological hazards, and the serious hazard of highway slope is related to economic development, traffic, production and the safety of people's life and property. The occurrence of slope disasters not only depends on the rock quality and environment of the slope, but also depends on the cracks in the rock mass to a great extent. Cracks are the early symptoms of most slope disasters, and the increase, expansion and evolution of cracks are the direct reflection of slope instability. By capturing the change of cracks, this small change can be used as an important reference for real-time monitoring of slope state. How to capture the change of fracture is an urgent problem to

© ICST Institute for Computer Sciences, Social Informatics and Telecommunications Engineering 2021
Published by Springer Nature Switzerland AG 2021. All Rights Reserved
X. Wang et al. (Eds.): AICON 2021, LNICST 396, pp. 30–41, 2021.
https://doi.org/10.1007/978-3-030-90196-7_3

be solved, and the accurate calculation of the actual area change of fracture is the key to solve the problem.

At present, the surface cracks of highway slope are mainly observed by artificial high-power telescope. Although this observation method is convenient to operate, it has shortcomings such as incomplete detection and careless observation. In order to make the detection method more safe, efficient and comprehensive, and to meet the needs of highway slope crack detection, some scholars proposed a slope crack detection method based on computer vision, which made up for the shortcomings of traditional detection methods. The research on slope crack detection algorithm based on computer vision has become a hot topic of academic attention. In [1], Weixing Wang et al. studied a crack extraction method based on the standard deviation of local window gray scale and the standard deviation of connected area distance. This method has a good detection effect on pavement cracks, and the detection accuracy can reach 96%. In [3], Zhang Haichuan put forward a kind of based on UNet++ and conditions against network (CGAN) road crack detection of image segmentation method, including the generator and the discriminant, through repeated game of generator and the discriminant training, the crack detection and segmentation algorithm makes the generator to generate highly close to the real image segmentation, and generator to achieve the effect of the crack detection. In [4], Zhang Yuefei et al. proposed an improved pavement crack detection algorithm of Mask RCNN, which adopted an adaptive loss function with weight and paid more attention to the characteristics of cracks. In [5], Youfa Cai et al. proposed a crack detection method based on computer vision technology and coordinate mapping. The crack measurement system integrated a high-power mirror image acquisition system, a two-dimensional electric pan-head device and a laser ranging system, which could automatically locate the measured crack within 16 s. In [7], Yana Xiao et al. proposed a crack detection method based on the fusion of penetration algorithm and adaptive Canny operator, which extracted more abundant edge information. In [9], Sadia Mubashshira et al. proposed a pavement threshold detection method based on road color histogram analysis, which achieved satisfactory results when detecting and locating cracks in the image by the algorithm. It can effectively remove noise and retain edges, which is very useful for obtaining better accuracy.

The calculation of crack area is an important link in slope disaster monitoring, but how to calculate the actual crack area from the pixel area of the crack is still a difficult problem. In [2], Wang Lei proposed the threshold segmentation based on the maximum inter-class variance method to extract cracks, calculate the crack area of highway, and realize the calculation of crack area. In [6], X. Jiang et al. proposed an improved phased array ultrasonic absolute time of arrival (AATT) technique, which used the absolute position of tip diffraction echo and angular reflection echo in the S-scan image of ultrasonic phased array to estimate the height and dip Angle of the crack. In [8], X. Xi et al. selected deep granite in a gold mine and studied the sample with pre-crack thickness of 0.3 mm by acoustic emission (AE) sensor and digital image correlation system, and finally obtained the change law of crack morphology and crack length through numerical simulation. In [10], Cherryl O. Tayo et al. used digital image processing to analyze the image, and the experimental results showed that the calculation accuracy of the developed crack width calculation device reached 96.93%. In [11],

Diana A A et al. proposed a computer vision method based on ripple changes to detect concrete hot cracks, and used ripple changes to detect hot cracks of different concrete grades and different temperature profile durations. In [12], Zhao et al., based on the Timoshenko beam model, proposed the expression of the transfer matrix method to solve the natural frequency and mode shape of vibration, simulated various types of cracks in the cantilever beam with the finite element method, and compared the solution method with the transfer matrix method. The difference between the results can be used to detect the size and location of the crack.

In view of this, this paper proposes a method of slope crack detection and crack area quantification based on computer vision. Firstly, FsNet network was designed to segment the cracks at pixel level. Based on the generated binary segmentation mask, the chessboard mapping method is proposed to calculate the actual crack area, and the effectiveness of the proposed method is fully verified by taking the self-made data set of highway crack image as an example.

2   Crack Image Preprocessing

Highway slope is generally in the outskirts of barren mountains, slope images often have some shadows, strong light, dark light, etc., which will cause a large noise in the crack detection of highway slope, affecting the effect of crack detection of highway slope. The existence of noise will lead to the characteristics of the highway slope crack detection is not obvious, which will affect the calculation of the crack area, so it is necessary to pre-process the highway slope crack image, that is, image grayscale processing, image equalization processing. The original image of the fracture is shown in Fig. 1.

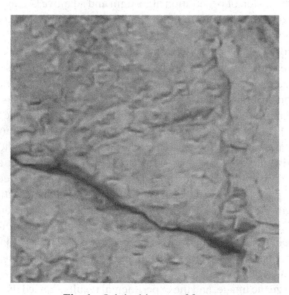

Fig. 1. Original image of fracture

The grayscale of the image is to change the color image of the RGB three-channel data into the grayscale image of the single-channel data. The grayscale processing of the image can make the image containing only brightness information, without color information, which is convenient for further processing of the image. The image gray conversion formula is as follows:

$$Gray = \sqrt[2.2]{\frac{R^{2.2} + (1.5G)^{2.2} + (0.6B)^{2.2}}{1 + 1.5^{2.2} + 0.6^{2.2}}} \tag{1}$$

Where, Gray represents the grayscale value in the grayscale image. R, G, and B represent the component values of the basic colors of red, green, and blue in the original color image.

Grayscale image of cracks is shown in Fig. 2.

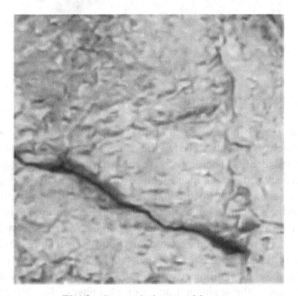

Fig. 2. Grayscale image of fracture

Image equalization is used to enhance the image. After image equalization correction, the gray distance of the image can be widened and the gray distribution can be uniform, so as to increase the contrast, make the image details clear, and achieve the purpose of enhancement. The equalized image is shown in Fig. 3, and it can be seen that the image becomes clearly clearer.

Fig. 3. Image equalization processing

3   Crack Image Segmentation

The main purpose of crack image segmentation is to facilitate further image analysis and processing. The crack of highway slope has the characteristics of crisscross direction and difficult to locate and identify. Therefore, it is necessary to design an algorithm with high identification accuracy and a crack identification model that is easy to deploy and apply. At present, image segmentation methods are mainly divided into traditional methods and deep learning-based segmentation methods. With the continuous optimization and improvement of deep learning algorithms, image segmentation based on deep learning is applied more and more, which has the advantages of obvious feature extraction and high accuracy. In view of the characteristics of cracks and the development of deep learning technology, an image segmentation network FSNET based on deep learning is designed in this paper to achieve the segmentation of crack images. The image segmentation framework is shown in Fig. 4.

After the crack image is preprocessed, the image segmentation network FSNET is used to train the preprocessed image. In the process of training, increasing the network depth can capture richer and more complex features. However, the greater the network depth is, the better it is. Excessive network depth will cause the problem of gradient disappearance. The crack output image after segmentation is shown in Fig. 5.

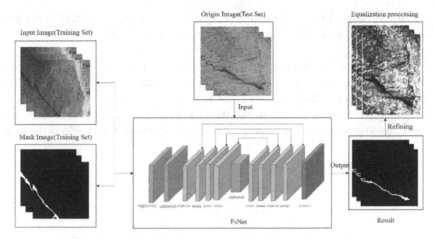

Fig. 4. Image segmentation framework

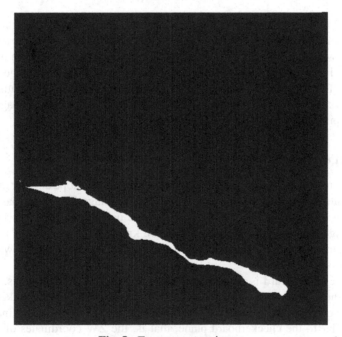

Fig. 5. Fracture output image

4 Actual Fracture Area Calculation

4.1 Crack Pixel Area Calculation

The result of FsNet network segmentation is a relatively ideal binary image (white represents the crack and black represents the background). The number of white pixels in the image is counted by digital image processing technology to calculate the pixel area of the crack automatically. The specific process is as follows:

(1) Image preprocessing: first, the combined operation of morphological corrosion and expansion is used to eliminate the noise such as isolated points in the output binary image, and then the discontinuous crack fragments are Mosaic processed through the connected domain operation, and then the threshold of the connected domain area is set to determine the number of continuous and complete cracks in the image N_C.

$$f \ominus b = \left\{ x, y | (b)_{xy} \subseteq f \right\} \tag{2}$$

$$f \oplus b = \left\{ x, y | (b)_{xy} \cap f \neq \emptyset \right\} \tag{3}$$

Where: f is the set of image pixels to be operated (etched or inflated); B is structural element; (x,y) is the position coordinate of any pixel point in set F.

(2) Calculation of crack pixel area: The pixel statistical method is used to calculate the coverage area of cracks in the image. The digital matrix of the binary image is traverse with a pixel point as a unit. The total number of pixels with a statistical value of 1 is the crack area S_c. If there are $N_c > 1$ cracks in the image, to get the area S_c^n of the N th crack, it is necessary to conduct pixel traversal statistics in the N th marked connected domain. The pixel area in the crack output image in Fig. 5 is 6256 pixels.

4.2 Actual Fracture Area Calculation

The calculation of the actual crack area is an important part of slope disaster monitoring, but it is difficult to measure the actual crack area from an image. The chessboard mapping method is proposed in this paper. The chessboard is used as the calibration plate, and the actual length and width of the chessboard are known according to the principle of keyhole imaging, and crack length is measured by length ratio and known length of the reference object.

Firstly, a checkerboard is placed on the plane where the test plane is. When the system is in the condition of small distortion, the checkerboard plane is taken as the X plane in the world coordinate system, then the ZW axis of the world coordinate system is perpendicular to the checkerboard plane, that is, the ZW coordinates of all feature points on the plane are 0.

$$\begin{bmatrix} \mu \\ \nu \\ 1 \end{bmatrix} = K \begin{bmatrix} x_w \\ y_w \\ 1 \end{bmatrix} \tag{4}$$

Where, K is the homography matrix between the world coordinates on the plane and the pixel coordinate system; (μ, ν) is the ideal pixel coordinate without distortion, and (x_w, y_w) is the actual coordinate of the plane where the checkerboard is located.

The specific steps are as follows:

(1) Use a professional camera to photograph M rows and N columns of alternating black and white checkerboard. And record the height, distance, camera elevation when shooting. As shown in Fig. 6, this checkerboard is 1 cm by 1 cm.

Fig. 6. Checkerboard.

(2) Binary processing was carried out on the captured checkerboard image, and the combined operation of morphology etching and expansion was used to eliminate the noise such as isolated points in the output binary image, and then the discontinuous crack fragments were stitched through the connected domain operation. The checkerboard preprocessed image as shown in Fig. 7 is obtained. The pixel area of the checkerboard preprocessed image is 1764 pixels.

Fig. 7. Checkerboard preprocessing.

(3) Will Fig. 6 checkerboard placed in the cracks of the image above, using distance, height and elevation of the same camera checkerboard, if cracks of the pixel fall within one of checkerboard grid, known fracture pixel area, checkerboard pixel area and the actual area of checkerboard, according to the laws of the map to the actual area of the cracks.

5   The Example Analysis

Please note that the first paragraph of a section or subsection is not indented. The first paragraphs that follows a table, figure, equation etc. does not have an indent, either. The above image processing method was used to obtain the crack area of the highway slope, and the above image processing method was verified by taking the highway crack as an example. A certain section of pavement with cracks was selected. The experimental data were 300 highway crack images collected by professional cameras, and the image pixel size was 3000 * 4000px. Ten images with cracks were selected to calculate the pixel area of cracks. At the same time, the crack area of the road surface was measured by the crack area observation instrument and compared with the calculated actual crack area. Absolute error refers to the error between the measured value x and the true value x, which is the difference between the measured value and the true value. Relative error refers to the ratio between the absolute error Δx and the true value X, which can reflect the reliability of the measurement.

The calculation formula of absolute error is as follows:

$$\Delta x = x - X \tag{5}$$

The relative error is calculated by the following formula

$$E_r = \frac{\Delta x}{X} \times 100\% \tag{6}$$

The comparison results are shown in Table 1. It can be seen from Table 1 that the recognition accuracy of this image detection method is high.

Table 1. Correct rate of slope crack image area detection

Number	Theoretical value/mm^2	The measured values/mm^2	Absolute error/mm^2	The relative error/%
1	5.136	8016	0.592	13.02%
2	12.688	20065	−1.313	11.54%
3	10.773	19848	0.479	4.25%
4	9.03	17657	0.98	9.79%
5	11.91	21714	0.4	3.25%
6	8.1125	13579	−0.4145	5.38%
7	6.54	12947	0.8	10.89%
8	6.156	11970	0.63	9.28%
9	6.68	12383	0.34	4.84
10	5.8104	9380	−0.4924	9.58

The test data verify the validity of the calculation of the actual fracture area. It can be seen from Table 1 that the identification accuracy of the actual area calculation of the fracture is good, and the relative errors of each test image are all less than 15%. The method adopted satisfies the calculation requirements of the fracture variation trend.

6 Conclusion

According to the characteristics of slope cracks, this paper realized the pixel-level detection of slope cracks based on deep learning and digital image processing technology, showing that deep learning has great advantages in crack detection. At the same time, the chessboard mapping method is proposed, and combined with the self-made data set of highway crack, the simulation scene is constructed and the comparative experiment is set, and the actual area of slope crack is calculated. The results show that the method is feasible for the detection of crack area. Although board mapping method can well solve the problem of actual slope crack area computation, but there is still a homemade checkerboard recognition accuracy, but the next step will continue to improve the method for calculating the actual highway slope cracks, improve the detection of highway slope fracture area as a result, improve the reliability and accuracy of the algorithm.

Citations. Funding Statement: This paper is supported by the following funds: Basic Research Program of Qinghai Province under Grants No. 2021-ZJ-704 and Advanced information network Beijing laboratory (PXM2019_014204_5000 29).

Conflicts of Interest: The authors declare that they have no conflicts of interest to report regarding the present study.

References

1. Wang, W., Li, L., Han, Y.: Crack detection in shadowed images on gray level deviations in a moving window and distance deviations between connected components. Constr. Build. Mater. **271**, 121885 (2021). https://doi.org/10.1016/j.conbuildmat.2020.121885
2. Lei, Z.: Research on Detection Technology of Highway Pavement Crack Based on Image Processing. Mach. Des. Manuf. Eng. **46**(2), 87–90 (2017)
3. Haichuan, Z., Bo, P., Weiqiang, X.: Road crack detection based on UNET ++ and conditional generated adversance network. Comput. Appl. **40**(S2), 158–161 (2020)
4. Yue-fei, Z., Jing-fei, W., Bin, C., Tao, F., Zhi-yi, C.: Highway crack detection algorithm based on improved mask R-CNN. Comput. Appl. **40**(S2), 162–165 (2020)
5. Cai, Y., Fu, X., Shang, Y., Shi, J.: Methods for long-distance crack location and detection of concrete bridge structures. In: 2018 IEEE 3rd International Conference on Image, Vision and Computing (ICIVC), pp. 576–580, Chongqing(2018). https://doi.org/10.1109/ICIVC.2018.8492764.
6. Jiang, X., Jia, J., Mao, X., Han, Q.: Simulation of modified absolute arrival time technique for measuring surface breaking cracks. In: 2018 IEEE Far East NDT New Technology and Application Forum (FENDT), pp. 170–174, Xiamen (2018). https://doi.org/10.1109/FENDT.2018.8681956.
7. Xiao, Y., Li, J.: Crack detection algorithm based on the fusion of percolation theory and adaptive canny operator. In: 2018 37th Chinese Control Conference (CCC), pp. 4295–4299, Wuhan (2018). https://doi.org/10.23919/ChiCC.2018.8482676.
8. Xi, X., Wu, X., Guo, Q., Cai, M.: Experimental investigation and numerical simulation on the crack initiation and propagation of rock with pre-existing cracks. IEEE Access **8**, 129636–129644 (2020). https://doi.org/10.1109/ACCESS.2020.3009230

9. Mubashshira, S., Azam, M.M., Masudul Ahsan, S.M.: An unsupervised approach for road surface crack detection. In: 2020 IEEE Region 10 Symposium (TENSYMP), pp. 1596–1599, Dhaka (2020). https://doi.org/10.1109/TENSYMP50017.2020.9231023
10. Tayo, C.O., Linsangan, N.B., Pellegrino, R.V.: Portable Crack Width Calculation of Concrete Road Pavement Using Machine Vision. In: 2019 IEEE 11th International Conference on Humanoid, Nanotechnology, Information Technology, Communication and Control, Environment, and Management (HNICEM), pp. 1–5, Laoag (2019). https://doi.org/10.1109/HNICEM48295.2019.9072731.
11. Diana A.A., Anand, N., Prince, A.G.: A novel approach for thermal crack detection and quantification in structural concrete using ripplet transform. Struct. Control Health Monit. **27**(11) (2020)
12. Zhao, D.: Analysis on the vibration of cracked cantilever beams with application on crack detection. J. Phys. Conf. Series **1631**(1), 012086 (2020)

LSTM-Based Prediction of Airport Aircraft in and Outflow

Baoqiang Li, Jin Huang$^{(\boxtimes)}$, Yamei Duan, and Yuan Zhao

Civil Aviation Flight University of China, Guanghan 618300, China

Abstract. The prediction of airport inbound and outbound traffic is a hot research direction in civil aviation air traffic management. Using the historical data of air traffic as the data source of the traffic prediction model, the traffic data are processed and machine learning algorithm models such as Support Vector Machine (SVM) linear regression, LSTM (Long Short-Term Memory) recurrent neural network, and BP neural network are used to predict the air traffic. The experiments, analysis, and generalization of relevant machine learning algorithms for air traffic flow prediction are conducted. The experiments show that the prediction results are based on historical airspace traffic data, the LSTM model has the highest accuracy, the SVM linear regression has the second-highest prediction effect, and the BP neural network has a poor prediction effect and insufficient stability. The experimental results demonstrate that the LSTM-based inbound and outbound traffic prediction model can achieve airport traffic prediction based on historical traffic data. The usability and accuracy of the LSTM-based prediction results are illustrated by comparing different algorithms, proving that the LSTM model can be used for future urban air traffic flow prediction. It is demonstrated that the LSTM model can be used for future urban air traffic flow prediction. It provides a theoretical and reference basis for the future air traffic flow management of intelligent urban transportation systems.

Keywords: Airport traffic forecasting · Long and short-term memory networks (LSTM) · Support vector machines (SVM) · Machine learning

1 Introduction

In the coming years, airport construction will intensify, air routes will become more complex and airport traffic will continue to grow. However, the rapid development of China's civil aviation transport and the air traffic management system load-bearing limit of the conflict between the increasingly prominent, airspace congestion and extensive delays have become commonplace. The study of air traffic flow forecasting is of great importance.

Research on airspace traffic forecasting algorithms in China's national airspace began relatively late. The current airspace traffic forecasting algorithms in China's civil aviation industry are divided into short-term traffic forecasting algorithms and medium- and long-term traffic forecasting algorithms. Most of the research focuses on the prediction

X. Wang et al. (Eds.): AICON 2021, LNICST 396, pp. 42–54, 2021.
https://doi.org/10.1007/978-3-030-90196-7_4

of air cargo throughput and terminal passenger flow. For medium and long-term traffic forecasting, common models include multiple regression function fitting, artificial neural network, grey prediction, and other traffic forecasting methods. Short-term forecasts are generally chosen from autoregressive integrated moving average (ARIMA) forecasting models or models such as HoltWinters [1, 2].

Due to the intensive air traffic, the flow increases and causes delays. At the same time, air traffic flow changes are non-linear and time-series in nature. The prediction accuracy of traditional forecasting methods is low. The intelligent technology represented by the neural network has been more widely used in the field of prediction, but the method is influenced by the complexity of the network structure and the sample dimension, thus sometimes the learning or generalization ability is too low.

The core of the time series forecasting problem is to mine time-series data from the data for trends that keep changing over time and use these trend patterns to make predictions about future data [3]. Machine learning-based forecasting methods refer to the use of multiple machine learning methods for forecasting data in time series and are effective in dealing with non-linear time series data. Takashi K [4] used a deep belief network (DBN) consisting of a multilayer restricted Boltzmann machine (RBM) for feature capture of time series, which can be used for approximate or short-term forecasting. Rohitash Cl [5] used Elman neural networks to predict complex time series after decomposing them, which improved the prediction accuracy. Xiao Fan [6] used wavelet transform to decompose the time series and subsequently used a support vector machine to predict and fuse the sets of wavelet coefficients.

In this paper, the LSTM-based model for forecasting airport throughput time-series traffic data is proposed. After obtaining data such as population, short-term traffic data, annual total traffic data, and production values of each industry at the local airport, the data are pre-processed by correlation factor analysis, normalization, and other pre-processing operations, L2 regularisation terms are introduced into the LSTM network model, and the appropriate number of LSTM network layers and the number of hidden neurons in the feedforward network layers are explored experimentally, which can make accurate forecasts of airport throughput.

2 Traffic Data Pre-processing

The airport of a provincial capital city in China was selected as the object of the study by checking relevant information. Through the Tushar package that comes with python, a crawler program was used to select the historical data published in the airport production bulletin to crawl according to the prescribed format, combined with data from the ADS-B airport take-off and landing traffic statistics (Excel format) on the official website of flightradar24. Data for each industry was obtained by compiling information from visits to the annual economic development reports. The basic data include: GDP index, number of local people in passenger traffic, and industrial output as significant factors affecting passenger throughput, and the correlation between each influencing factor and passenger throughput is calculated using the grey correlation method.

Step 1: The significance factors were homogenized and the results were obtained in the following table. (Table 1)

Table 1. Results for each relevant factor

Year	Passenger traffic	GDP	Number of local people	Industrial output
2014	6271701	11218200	3946.91	6077587
2015	7339228	13830700	5250.42	7336821
2016	8746034	17103100	6344.21	9206999
2017	10472589	20854000	6820	11550000
2018	12525537	24975300	7730	14127000
2019	14598527	30265800	8749.18	17198500
Average value	9992269	19707850	6473.453	10916151

Step 2: Remove each of the original series from the above mean values to obtain the averaged series. The averaging is done separately for each indicator in each year.

Step 3: Using the mean value series derived in step 2, calculate the absolute difference between the passenger throughput and the number of passengers, the city's annual GDP, the local population, and the industrial output respectively for the same period. Similarly, the absolute difference between the indicators for each of the remaining years is calculated separately, and the maximum and minimum values are then found from the final results. The maximum value is $\Delta max = 0.287443784$ and the minimum value is $\Delta min = 0.001913079$.

Step 4: Calculate the correlation coefficient by taking the resolution factor $\rho = 0.5$ and calculating the formula as follows,

$$\xi_\sigma(t) = \frac{\Delta(min) + 0.5\Delta(max)}{\Delta_{oi}(t) + 0.5\Delta(max)} = \frac{0.001913079 + 0.5 * 0.287443784}{\Delta_{oi}(t) + 0.5 * 0.287443784} = \frac{0.145634971}{\Delta_{oi}(t) + 0.14372189}$$

The results of calculating the correlation factors are as follows (Table 2):

Table 2. Relevance factor table

Year	ζ_{01}	ζ_{02}	ζ_{03}	ζ_{04}
2014	0.543969907	0.693844356	0.903049781	0.630949904
2015	0.818740287	0.55229239	0.932667747	0.680083667
2016	0.905959100	0.485204959	0.725522172	0.905162326
2017	0.679300508	0.414776189	0.583754289	0.733389278
2018	0.562927338	0.708439884	0.410303886	0.767843817
2019	0.513227692	0.845412192	0.661525638	0.898629578

3 The Inbound and Outbound Traffic Forecasting Model

3.1 LSTM Neural Network Prediction Model

RNNs (recurrent neural networks) are commonly used to analyze predictive sequence data [7], but research has shown that as time increases, RNNs forget information about previous states. Therefore, this paper introduces LSTM (Long-Short-Time Recurrent Neural Network). LSTM temporal recurrent neural networks have the property of being suitable for processing and predicting important events with long intervals and delays in time series and have been outstanding in many fields in recent years.

The LSTM model is an improved model based on an RNN model that can solve the correlation problem between short and long-term time series by using the hidden layer as a memory unit. Figure 1 gives a diagram of the structure of the memory unit, with the storage unit located at the core of the entire memory unit, indicated by a red circle. The input is the known data, while the output is the predicted result. There are three gates in the memory cell, the input gate, the forgetting gate, and the output gate, identified by the green circles in the diagram. The blue dots represent the convergence points and the dotted lines are the previous state functions. After being gated by different functions, the LSTM memory unit can capture complex correlation properties in both short and long-term time series, with significantly improved performance compared to the RNN model.

In this paper, LSTM networks are applied to data prediction. To optimize the LSTM network prediction effect, this paper focuses on exploring the appropriate number of layers of LSTM networks and the number of hidden neurons in its feedforward network layers to study an effective LSTM prediction network model. The LSTM network model with a different number of layers is used to analyze and forecast the traffic data of a domestic airport from 2014 to 2019 by comparing the real values with the predicted values. Through the experiments, we eventually arrive at the optimal parameters for the LSTM-based airport traffic prediction model.

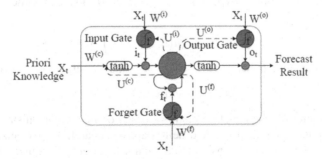

Fig. 1. LSTM model schematic diagram

3.2 SVM Linear Regression Prediction Model

In the 1990s scientists, Vapnik et al. proposed a support vector machine (SVM) algorithm, based on structural risk minimization to find inductive statistical design models to achieve minimum risk generalization, using kernel functions to map data from low-dimensional to high-dimensional space. Dimensional catastrophe and computational complexity are reduced [8].

SVM   model   input   linearly   separable   training   set. T $=$ $\{(x_1, y_1), (x_2, y_2), \ldots, (x_M, y_M)\} y_i \in \{-1, 1\}, i = 1, 2, \ldots, M$

SVM model construction steps.

Step 1, constructing the constrained optimization problem

$$\min_{\alpha} \frac{1}{2} \cdot \sum_{i=1}^{M} \alpha_i \alpha_j y_i y_j (x_i \cdot x_j) - \sum_{i=1}^{M} \alpha_i \tag{1}$$

$$s.t. \sum_{i=1}^{M} \alpha_i y_i = 0$$

$$0 \leq \alpha_i \leq c, i = 1, 2, \ldots M$$

In step 2, the SMO algorithm is used to solve the optimization problem above to obtain values of the vectors $\alpha*$.

In step 3, the value $w*$ of the w vector is then calculated using the following equation.

$$w^* = \sum_{i=1}^{M} \alpha_i^* y_i x_i \tag{2}$$

In step 4, find the support vector point $(x_S, y_S), s = 1, 2, \ldots, S$ that satisfies $0 < \alpha_S^* < c$ the corresponding support-vector, and use the following equation to calculate b the value b^*.

$$b^* = \frac{1}{S} \sum_{s=1}^{S} [y_s - w^* \cdot x_s] \tag{3}$$

In step 5, the segmentation hyperplane $w^* \cdot x + b^* = 0$ and the classification decision function are obtained from $w^* b^*$:

$$h(x) = sign(w^* \cdot x + b^*) \tag{4}$$

Output segmentation hyperplane $w^* x + b^* = 0$ and classification decision function:

$$h(x) = sign(w^* x + b^*) \tag{5}$$

Traditional time-series prediction methods based on mathematical statistics do not have self-learning, self-organizing and self-adaptive capabilities, especially for data types with multiple feature dimensions that cannot be effectively fitted and functionally expressed [8, 9]. Support vector machine SVM, as a machine learning method based on statistical learning theory [10, 11], is mainly based on VC dimensional theory and structural risk minimization principles [12] and is also a machine learning algorithm based on geometric distance. Therefore SVM models are sensitive to missing data in the dataset when the sample size is very large. SVMs are prone to lag when the computational volume is too large. The experiments in this paper use the sklearn. SVM module in the Python package library to implement the SVM linear regression model.

3.3 Flow Prediction Model with BP Neural Network

In 1986, Rumelhart first proposed an error backward-corrected multilayer feedback network based on BP neural network, which has good pattern classification ability and multidimensional function mapping ability, and has wide application prospects. BP neural network is mainly divided into three layers: input layer, implicit layer, and output layer, and uses empirical risk minimization and gradient descent methods to calculate the optimal value of the objective function in the form of an approximate function representation.

The BP neural network structure is shown in Fig. 2:

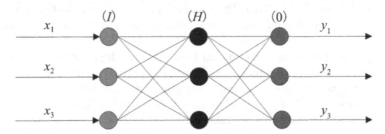

Fig. 2. BP neural network structure

where (I) is the input layer, (H) is the implicit layer, and (0) is the output layer. $\{x_1, x_2, x_3 \ldots x_n\}$ represent the n-dimensional model input units, $\{y_1, y_2, y_3 \ldots y_n\}$ represent the model outputs, and the forward and backward propagation parameters are adjusted with the corresponding weights w and bias terms b of the inputs and outputs. BP neural network as a machine learning algorithm has the advantages of self-learning, self-adaptive and scalable. However, BP neural networks face the complex problem of optimizing the output of the neuron of the objective function to approximate the true value. It is easy to fall into local optimality, and its network structure and neuron requirements are artificially set, so the predictive ability and scalability of BP neural networks need to be further improved.

4 Experimental Studies

The overall experimental procedure was as follows.

(1) Data download: Historical statistics of air traffic on the FR24 website using ADS-B observation-based statistics.
(2) Data pre-processing: The raw data obtained may have disordered and missing values, which need to be interpolated and sorted to obtain regular time-series data.
(3) Data noise reduction: Since the data contains noise due to unstable observation methods, the pywt library in python is used to remove the noise from the data.
(4) Data normalization: As multiple parameters with too large values are fed into the model as feature values at the same time, it is not possible to show a large proportion of influence on the prediction results just because the values of certain indicators are too large, so the feature series need to be normalized.

(5) Fine-tuning of parameters: The network framework structure and the values of the regularisation term parameters in the LSTM layer are continuously adjusted during the training process of the model until the best prediction results are achieved.

4.1 Experimental Procedure

4.1.1 LSTM Neural Network Construction

The GPU version of the Keras framework was built under the Linux operating system. Keras framework is highly encapsulated, modular, simple, easy to extend, and fine-tuning steps, etc. Its core data structure contains two models: one is the Sequential model, and the other is called the Model model. The Sequential model is a series of network layers in a sequential stack, with single input and a single output, and only adjacency between layers.

This experiment uses the Model model to build single-layer and two-layer LSTM network models to analyze and predict future traffic respectively. The model's prediction performance evaluation metrics are used to compare the experimental results using root mean square error (RMSE), mean absolute error (MAE), and model prediction accuracy (accuracy). The RMSE and MAE are calculated by the following equations.

$$RMSE = \sqrt{\frac{1}{N} \sum_{t=1}^{N} (X_{pridiction,t} - X_{real,t})^2} \tag{6}$$

$$MAE = \frac{1}{N} \sum_{i=1}^{N} |X_{pridiction,i} - X_{real,i}| \tag{7}$$

For the predicted LSTM model, to improve the model generalization, this experiment uses the following two ways to avoid overfitting.

First: the experiment uses dropout regularization, in which a portion of the units are randomly selected to be deactivated at a certain deactivation rate in each update of the network training, including input connections and recursive connections, which can effectively prevent overfitting. If a deep LSTM network is used, deactivation regularization can be applied between each layer at the same time, so there are three deactivation parameters in each layer of the network.

Second: the experiment uses the early stop method, dividing the training samples into training and validation sets. In each iteration, the loss values of the training and validation sets are calculated separately, and if the loss value of the validation set no longer decreases within step k, the training is stopped and the model parameters with the lowest validation loss value are returned.

In this paper, two layers of the LSTM neural network are used, so there are six deactivation parameters. In the training set, 80% of the samples are used as the training set, 20% of the samples are used as the validation set, and the number of steps k is set to 50. To observe the prediction effects of different prediction methods for the short, medium, and long term, the last 20, last 60, and last 250 parity data of the overall data set of each index are taken as the test set for short, medium, and long term prediction respectively in this paper, and the test set is excluded as the corresponding training set.

Experiment 1 used the data from 2014–2016 as the training set and the data from 2017–2018 as the test set. After several tests, we set the number of hidden neurons in the feedforward network layer to 10 after weighing the amount of computation against the prediction accuracy of the model. To avoid the overfitting phenomenon, the experiments used L2 regularization terms and the dropout mechanism to improve the generalization ability of the model.

Experiment 2 built a two-layer LSTM network and a fully connected layer model, where the number of hidden neurons in the first LSTM layer was the same as in Experiment 1. Experiment 2 used the same input values and test values as in Experiment 1, and finally, it was compared and analyzed with the prediction results of Experiment 1, which led to good or bad prediction performance.

4.1.2 Tuning of Linear SVM Model Parameters

According to the prediction principle of the support vector machine model, it is known that SVM model parameters mainly include kernel function type, penalty coefficient c, and insensitivity coefficient ε. The determination of this parameter has a great impact on the accuracy of the SVM model, which is a difficult and hot issue in the current support vector machine model research, and this experiment uses grid search which is an exhaustive idea based on the specified parameter value search method.

As the primary means of machine learning models, grid search is optimized by cross-validating the parameters of the estimation function. After selecting the grid search to train each machine learning model for fitting all possible parameter combinations, the phenotype of the model is evaluated using cross-validation to finally obtain the combination of parameters under optimal performance.

In this experiment, comparing the optimization results of the grid search, the efficiency performance of the model is not significantly improved under the optimization of the random search method. Therefore, the grid search method, which is faster in computation, was finally chosen in this paper. The experiments in this paper use the Grid-SearchCV module in the Python package library sklearn.model_selection to implement grid search.

4.1.3 Parameter Selection for the BP Neural Network Prediction Model

The pre-processed data were divided into training samples p-train and T-train and input to the three-layer BP neural network model, with the transfer functions "transit", "login", "purely", "trail" and "learned". "purely", the training function is "trail" and the learning function is "learned". After repeated training of the BP neural network model, it was found that the best results were obtained when the number of nodes in the hidden layer was 5, the learning rate was 0.8, the number of training times was 500, and the training target error was 0.01.

4.2 Experimental Results and Analysis

4.2.1 Experimental Analysis

The accuracy of the LSTM predicted models varies due to the number of different iterations set. The figure below shows the box plots of the RMSE errors for the LSTM models at 50, 100, 150, 200, 250, 300, 350, and 400 iterations in the experiment. The box plot shows that the mean value of the RMSE at 350 iterations is 19.991, which sets this parameter as the optimal parameter for the LSTM model (Table 3) (Fig.3).

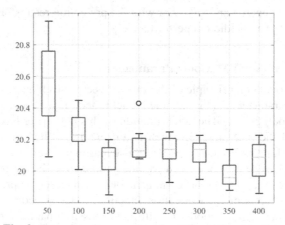

Fig. 3. Box plot of error values for different iteration times

Table 3. Comparison of the results of the improved LSTM algorithm for flight traffic prediction with the traditional single-layer LSTM regression algorithm

Actual flow/sortie	Predicted value		Prediction error/%		Actual flow/sortie	Predicted value	
	Traditional single-layer LSTM	Improved model	Traditional single-layer LSTM	Improved model		Traditional single-layer LSTM	Improved model
156	176	152	12.8	2.5	156	176	152
134	114	136	14.9	1.5	134	114	136
185	195	182	5.4	1.6	185	195	182
247	207	240	16.2	2.8	247	207	240
278	248	287	10.8	3.2	278	248	287
290	261	285	10	1.7	290	261	285

The single-layer LSTM network and fully-connected layer model built-in Experiment 1 to predict throughput, based on separate 2014 and 2015 annual data, with 2014 data as the training set and 2015 data as the test set, was debugged and tested several times in the experiments, and the number of hidden neurons in the feedforward network layer was set to 10 after weighing the computational effort against the prediction accuracy of the model. In Experiment 1, it was mainly demonstrated that the single-layer LSTM network is capable of making predictions, and the model error performance results of its experiments are shown below (Table 4) (Fig. 4)

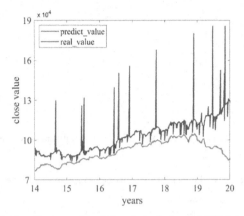

Fig. 4. Prediction diagram of traditional single-layer LSTM network model

Table 4. Prediction results of single-layer LSTM network models

Performance	RMSE	MAE	Accuracy
Numerical values	2.58	1.74	0.44

From the comparative validation in Table 5, it can be intuitively seen that the prediction effect of the single-layer LSTM is not satisfactory, even though the flow prediction results are consistent with the actual trend, but only the trend is judged, and the gap with the actual flow still exists, the prediction value is generally high, and it is necessary to further improve its prediction performance.

Experiment 2 built a two-layer LSTM network and a fully connected layer model, where the number of hidden neurons in the first LSTM layer was the same as in Experiment 1, and the same input and test values were used as in Experiment 1. After pushing to the model for training and testing, the prediction performance was compared and analyzed with that of Experiment 1, and the experimental results are shown in Fig. 5:

By analyzing the results of Experiment 2, it can be found that the two-layer LSTM network model has been greatly improved in terms of prediction performance, and from the above graph comparing the LSTM prediction model's 2018–2020 annual traffic forecast curve with the real airport traffic curve, there is a high degree of fit between the predicted and actual values. The RMSE and MAE values are reduced by 2.12 and 1.632 respectively for the two-layer LSTM compared to the single-layer model, and the prediction accuracy of Experiment 2 is improved by approximately 30% compared to Experiment 1. This shows that the LSTM network model has a clear advantage in the processing of traffic sequence data.

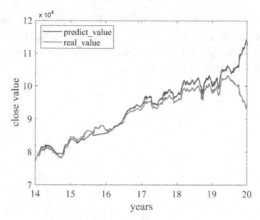

Fig. 5. Two-layer LSTM network model prediction graph

Table 5. Two-layer LSTM network model prediction results

Performance	RMSE	MAE	Accuracy
Numerical values	0.46	0.108	0.78

Furthermore, analysis of the literature shows that as the number of layers increases, the effectiveness of feature extraction improves, as does the prediction accuracy [13]. However, the three-layer LSTM network is not significant in improving the prediction accuracy, only 0.002%, indicating that a continuous increase in the training depth of the network does not consistently improve the prediction performance and may even lead to computational redundancy. Because of the above findings, prediction performance and computational effort must be considered together. Based on the comparative analysis, this paper concludes that the two-layer LSTM network model is suitable for the prediction of airport inbound and outbound traffic.

4.2.2 Comparison of Experimental Results

A comparison of the graphs below shows that there is a significant lag in the prediction results of the SVM linear prediction model. the SVM linear model is unstable and can be partially good or bad, and the BP neural network is worse than the other two algorithms due to the tendency of the BP neural network to over-fit the training set, lose generalization and also under-fit to achieve good prediction results. The blue line shows the LSTM prediction model with relatively good results and a good fit to the true values.

Among the three machine learning prediction models, BP neural network prediction SVM support vector machine prediction LSTM, LSTM neural network prediction model is the most effective, SVM support vector machine prediction is the second most effective, while the traditional BP neural network prediction is the least effective. This shows that LSTM has a clear advantage in air traffic flow prediction (Table 6) (Figs. 6, 7).

Table 6. Forecast comparison table

Year	Actual value	BP neural networks		Support vector machines		LSTM model	
		Predicted value	RE (%)	Predicted value	RE (%)	Predicted value	RE (%)
2017	101076	119613	18.34	119593	18.32	112568	11.37
2018	107930	126375	17.09	117611	8.97	121863	12.91
2019	108275	125003	15.45	119221	10.11	121116	11.86
Average relative error			15.09		12.98		10.75

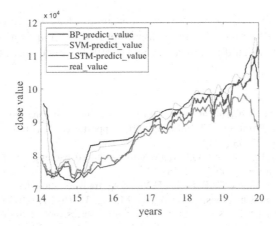

Fig. 6. Comparison of prediction results

Fig. 7. Prediction accuracy analysis based on machine learning algorithms

5   Conclusion

In this paper, an optimized LSTM deep learning neural network is developed to predict airport traffic by analyzing the intrinsic causal links between airport traffic and its influencing factors. By collecting data related to the throughput of an international airport in China, the local GDP index of a city, and the production value index of various industries into the established LSTM model, the feasibility and accuracy of the LSTM model in airport traffic forecasting is verified by comparing the real values of airport traffic with the traffic forecasting values of various machine learning models such as linear SVM and LSTM. The establishment of the traffic prediction model is affected by various factors, so in future work, instead of simply considering the influence of multiple factors on the traffic prediction results, the interrelationship between various factors should be considered to build a more perfect and accurate traffic prediction model. In 2020, the predicted values deviated significantly from the true values due to the occurrence of a worldwide epidemic 2020, which the authors were unable to take into account due to their limited level.

This study provides example proofs and a basis for ideas for subsequent studies of airport traffic forecasting models. It has important research implications for modeling and simulation of aircraft traffic forecasting and controller and airspace load forecasting.

References

1. Jing, L., Lulu, X.: Comparison and analysis of research hot trend prediction models based on machine learning algorithms-BP neural network, support vector machine, and LSTM model. Modern Inf. **39**(4), 23–33 (2019)
2. Yuanhui, L., Xia, L., Zhipeng, O.: ARIMA model-based passenger traffic forecasting for Sanya airport. Software **7**, 50–55 (2018)
3. Dantas, T.M., Oliveira, F.L.C., Repolho, H.M.V.: Air transportation demand forecast through Bagging Holt-Winters methods. J. Air Transp. Manag. **3**, 116–123 (2017)
4. Takashi, K., Shinsuke, K., Kunikazu, K., et al.: Time series forecasting using a deep belief network with restricted Boltzmann machines. Neurocomputing **137**, 47–56 (2014)
5. Rohitash, C., Mengjie, Z.: Cooperative coevolution of Elman recurrent neural networks for chaotic time series prediction. Neurocomputing **86**, 116–123 (2012)
6. Fan, X., Jiezhong, M., Lankun, R.: Time series prediction based on wavelet analysis and support vector machines. Aviation Computing Technology **41**(6), 49–52 (2011)
7. Li, J., Lin, Y.F.: Time-series data prediction based on multi-timescale RNN. Computer Applications and Software **35**(7), 33–37 (2018)
8. Cristianini, N.: Introduction to Support Vector Machines = An Introduction to Support Vector Machines and Other Kernel-Based Learning Methods. Electronic Industry Press, Cambridge (2004)
9. Xuegong Z.: Introduction to statistical learning theory and support vector machines. J. Automation (2000)
10. Vapnik, V.N.: The Nature of Statistic Learning Theory. Springer, New York (2000)
11. Wapnik, X.J., Zhang, X.G.: Statistical Learning Theory: Statistical Learning Theory. Electronic Industry Press, Cambridge (2009)
12. An Introduction to Support Vector Machines. Recent Advances and Trends in Nonparametric Statistics **32**(8), 3–17 (2002)
13. Chen, K., Zhou, Y., Dai, F.: A LSTM- based method for stock returns prediction: a case study of China stock market. In: IEEE International Conference on Big Data, pp. 2823–2824 (2015)

Micro-motion Classification of Rotor UAV and Flying Bird via CNN and FMCW Radar

Xiaolong Chen[1](✉), Jian Guan[1], Jiefang Li[2], and Weishi Chen[3]

[1] Naval Aviation University, Yantai, China
[2] East China Normal University, Shanghai, China
[3] China Academy of Civil Aviation Science and Technology, Airport Research Institute, Beijing, China

Abstract. Aiming at the problem that it is difficult to recognize flying birds and rotary-wing UAVs by radar, a micro-motion feature classification method based on multi-scale convolutional neural network (CNN) is proposed in this paper. Using the K-band frequency modulated continuous wave (FMCW) radar, data acquisition is performed on the rotor UAV and flying bird targets in indoor and outdoor scenes, and then the feature extraction and parameterization of the micro-Doppler signal are performed using time-frequency analysis technology to construct the radar feature dataset. A novel type of multi-scale CNN is designed, which can extract the global and local information of the target's micro-Doppler features and improve the classification accuracy. Validation of measured data shows that the classification probability of rotary-wing drones and flying bird targets can reach higher than 98% by using the proposed algorithm, which provides a new technical and practical approach for the identification of low and slow small targets.

Keywords: Radar target classification · Micro-motion · Flying bird · Rotor UAV · FMCW radar · CNN

1 Introduction

Bird strikes refer to incidents of aircraft taking off or landing or colliding with birds during flight. It is a traditional security threat in the takeoff and landing phase of flights. Recently, "low, slow and small" aircraft represented by small UAVs, i.e., drones, have been developing rapidly [1]. There have been successive incidents of "black flying" of drones in many airports. Illegal flying of drones has become a new problem together with the "bird strike", which may threaten the safety of flights around the airport's clear area. At present, the surveillance of drones and flying birds, especially the identification, is still lacking effective technology and means [2]. The "black flight" is still very common.

This work was supported by Shandong Provincial Natural Science Foundation, grant number ZR202102190211, National Natural Science Foundation of China, grant number U1933135, 61931021, Major Science and Technology Project of Shandong Province, grant number 2019JZZY010415.

Once used by terrorists to carry dangerous weapons, it will seriously threaten public safety.

Both the drone and the bird are non-rigid targets. The rotation of the drone's rotor and the flapping of the bird's wings will introduce additional modulation sidebands near the Doppler frequency of the radar echo generated by the translation of the main body. It is called the micro-Doppler (m-D) effect. Due to the faster rotation speed of the UAV's rotor, its micro-motion period is much faster than that of the bird, but its strength is weaker than the bird's micro-Doppler [3, 4]. In addition, the irregular wing flapping caused by the bird's maneuvering makes the m-D feature more complex. The echo of the rotor drone is the superposition of the Doppler signals of the main body and the rotor components. The rotation of the rotor produces the modulation characteristics of the echo, which is time-varying and periodic, and has the characteristics of micro-motion. Different types and numbers of rotors are different. Therefore, the m-D characteristics are good solution for the classification of UAVs and flying birds and will improve the radar's fine description and recognition abilities of target motion.

At present, for the m-D feature recognition of targets, methods based on neural network algorithms show high recognition accuracy [5–7]. Compared with methods based on empirical mode decomposition (EMD), principal component analysis (PCA), and linear discriminant analysis, methods based on deep convolutional neural networks (DCNN) can directly learn and obtain effective features from the original data. It has received great attention in the field of pattern recognition and is widely used. CNN as an important part of deep learning, has been widely used in image recognition and classification [8]. It has two important properties, local connection and weight sharing, and can directly learn the image automatically and extract the features of the target, so as to realize the high-precision recognition of the image.

The current models based on CNN classification use the convolution operation of the convolution kernel and learn features from the information of the input layer according to the characteristics from coarse to fine. This kind of method is very easy to make the network model learn some useless feature information for multi-target motion states and complex environments, which will lead to over-fitting problem. And the generalization ability would become worse. Therefore, how to fully develop a feature information that can learn the target at a finer granularity, while retaining the useful feature information and suppressing the invalid feature information, will play an important role in improving the feature extraction and classification capabilities of complex moving targets.

In this paper, the classification of flying bird and rotary-wing UAV is analyzed based on the m-D features. Based on the K-band frequency-modulated continuous wave (FMCW) radar [9], the target micro-motion signal measurement experiment was carried out, and radar dataset was constructed. A multi-scale CNN model is proposed for the learning and classification of micro-movement features of different types of targets, which can extract global and local information of m-D features. The measured data verifies the effectiveness of the algorithm. Section 2 introduced the micro-motion measurement of drones and flying bird based on K-band FMCW radar. M-D classification of flying bird and UAV target via multi-scale CNN is introduced in detail in Sect. 3, including the CNN model structure, m-D classification method, and classification results analysis. The last section concludes the paper and presents its future research direction.

2 Micro-motion Measurement of Drones and Flying Bird Based on K-Band FMCW Radar

2.1 Description of K-Band FMCW Radar

When the FMCW radar is working, a voltage-controlled oscillator (VCO), a phase-locked loop (PLL) and a modulator together generate a FMCW signal, and then through a power divider or a coupler, a part of the generated signal is amplified and sent to the transmitting antenna and transmitted. The other part is sent to the mixer, where it is mixed with the received signal processed by the low-noise power amplifier to obtain the difference frequency signal. After the digital conversion, it is sent to the digital signal processing equipment for further processing. Finally, the digital signal processing equipment can calculate the relevant information of the difference frequency signal, including the frequency information and phase information of the signal, and then combine the modulation law of the signal to further obtain the target's distance, speed, azimuth and other information.

The K-band FMCW radar system used in this paper is mainly composed of four parts: radio frequency module, control module, acquisition module and software module. The radio frequency module realizes the transmission of FMCW signals, and mixes, filters and amplifies the received echo signals; the control module is responsible for receiving commands from the computer, generating control signals, and further filtering and amplifying the echo signals; the acquisition module is responsible for collecting echoes and transmitting the original echo signal to the computer; the software module completes the information display and the setting of the radar core parameters. The main technical parameters of the K-band FMCW radar are shown in Table 1.

Table 1. Main parameters of K-band FM continuous wave radar.

Parameters	Value
Working frequency	23.7 GHz
Modulation bandwidth	10 MHz–2000 MHz
Modulation period	0.2 ms–10 ms
Repetition frequency	100 Hz–5000 Hz
−3 db beam range	Azimuth: 16° Elevation: 12°
−10 db beam range	Azimuth: 30° Elevation: 20°

Figure 1 shows the data acquisition and signal processing flowchart of K-band FMCW radar. Firstly, set the working mode, system parameters, and processing parameters in turn. Then set the relevant parameters for m-D analysis (pulse number, time window, frequency window) according to the time-frequency method. By means of fast Fourier transformation (FFT), moving target indication (MTI), short-time Fourier transform (STFT) and other related processing methods, the one-dimensional range profile, range-pulse image, and time-frequency image are obtained. Then adjust the time-frequency parameters online and observe the time-frequency diagram of the target. If the result is not good as expected, readjust the radar parameters; otherwise start data collection.

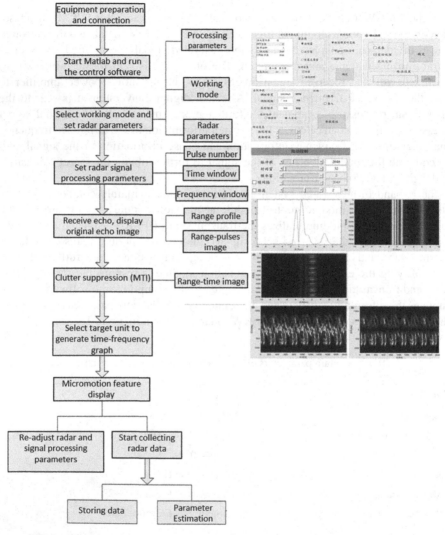

Fig. 1. Data acquisition and signal processing flowchart of K-band FMCW radar.

2.2   Data Collection and Micro-motion Analysis

2.2.1   UAV Target Data Collection and M-D Analysis

The MAVIC Air 2 and Inspire 2 rotary-wing drones of DJI company were selected for the outdoor drone acquisition experiment, the experimental scene is shown in Fig. 2. The height of the drone and the distance of the radar are adjusted and the m-D features of real-time observation are carried out. Taking into account the relatively weak scattering characteristics of outdoor UAV rotor blades, clutter suppression may cause the loss of target information. Therefore, when analyzing the influencing factors of m-D characteristics, MTI clutter suppression processing is not performed on the echo signal. Figure 3 shows the m-D images of the two drone targets respectively. According to the measured m-D characteristic image of the rotor drone, it can be seen that the echo intensity at zero frequency and its surroundings is very strong. The m-D characteristics of the "Inspire 2" UAV have clearer m-D features than those of the "MAVIC Air 2" in Fig. 3(a).

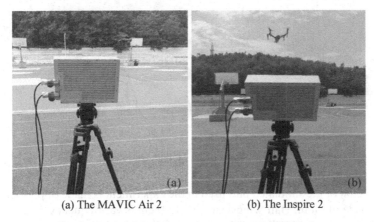

(a) The MAVIC Air 2   (b) The Inspire 2

Fig. 2. Scene of drone experiment using FMCW Radar.

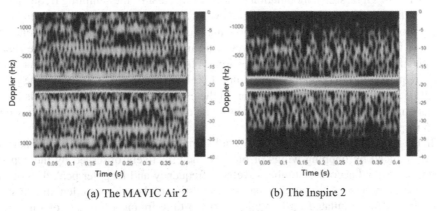

(a) The MAVIC Air 2   (b) The Inspire 2

Fig. 3. Micro-Doppler feature of different drone targets.

2.2.2 Flying Birds Data Collection and M-D Analysis

Due to seasonal influences, it is difficult to grasp the routines of flying birds, which makes the outdoor experiment more difficult. To solve this problem, this experiment uses a simulated bird that highly simulates the flapping flight of real birds. The subjects of the experiment are a single bird and two birds that perform flapping wings. The experimental scene of flying birds using FMCW radar is shown in Fig. 4.

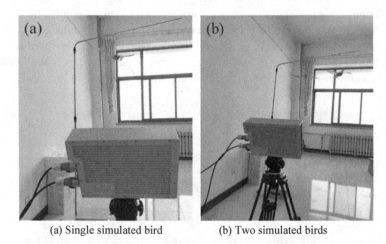

(a) Single simulated bird   (b) Two simulated birds

Fig. 4. The experimental scene of flying birds using FMCW radar

The skeleton of the simulated bird used in the experiment is made of plastic, and the wings are made of cloth. Half wingspan $L = 42.0$ cm, swat frequency $f_{flap} = 3.5$ Hz. The parameters of the FMCW radar are set as follows: signal modulation bandwidth $B = 200$ MHz, sampling frequency (distance dimension) $f_s = 500$ kHz, carrier frequency is 23.7 GHz, signal modulation period is 1 ms, that is, the sampling frequency of periodic dimension is 1000 Hz. Number of cycles $N = 2048$, time window length is 32, observation distance $R = 2$ m, observation angle is 35°. As for the sampling frequency, the radar used in this experiment involves two sampling frequencies, one is the signal sampling frequency in the distance dimension (500 kHz), and the other is the signal sampling frequency in the periodic dimension (1000 Hz), which is equivalent to the pulse repetition frequency (PRF) in pulse radar. In the experiment, the m-D characteristics of the flapping wings of a single simulated bird and a pair of simulated birds are shown in Fig. 5 respectively.

In the time-frequency domain of the single-simulated bird, it can be found that m-D effect produced by flapping wings of bird can be effectively observed by the experimental radar. And according to the waveform frequency and Doppler peak data of the m-D characteristic in the figure, we can further estimate the wingspan length and swat frequency of the simulated bird. While from the time-frequency image of Fig. 5(b), it is found that when simulating the side-by-side flapping movement of two birds, the micro-motion characteristics in the time-frequency domain may be overlapped.

Based on the echo signal acquisition and feature extraction and analysis of the indoor simulated bird, the simulated bird experiment is brought to the outdoor environment for micro-motion signal acquisition. The simulated bird does not make any changes, only the radar parameters are appropriately adjusted. The signal modulation period is set to

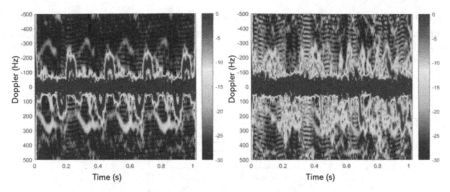

(a) Micro-Doppler of a single simulated bird (b) Micro-Doppler of two simulated birds

Fig. 5. The micro-Doppler characteristics of the flapping wings of birds.

0.4 ms, the observation distance is 2 m, and other parameters remain unchanged. The obtained m-D characteristics of simulated bird flight are shown in Fig. 6. According to the time-frequency image, the m-D effect produced by the experimental radar on the flapping wings of birds can still be observed.

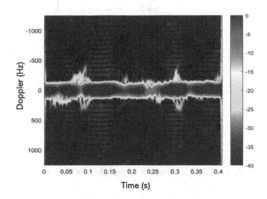

Fig. 6. Micro-Doppler characteristics of outdoor simulated birds.

3 Micro-doppler Classification of Flying Bird and UAV Target via Multi-scale CNN

3.1 Novel Multi-scale CNN Model

At present, for the target recognition methods based on m-D features, many CNN classification models are shallow structures, and cannot be applied in case of the smaller data samples or the complex signals. The target features cannot be effectively learned. This paper proposed a target m-D feature classification method based on a novel multi-scale CNN, which uses multi-scale splitting of the hybrid connection structure. The output of the multi-scale module contains a combination of different receptive field sizes, which is conducive to extracting the global feature information and the local information of the target.

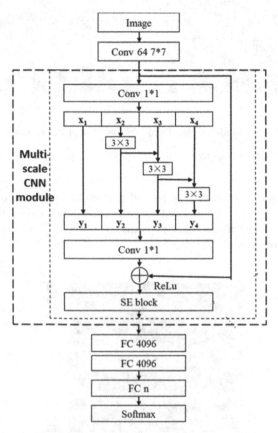

Fig. 7. The proposed multi-scale CNN model.

The structure of the novel multi-scale CNN model is shown in Fig. 7, which is based on the residual network module. The feature map after 1×1 convolution, assuming that there are n channels, replace n with a filter bank with a convolution kernel size of 3×3. The feature map after 1×1 convolution of two channels is divided into s feature map subsets, and each feature map subset contains n/s number of channels. Except for the first feature map subset that is directly passed down, the rest of the feature map subsets are followed by a convolutional layer with a convolution kernel size of 3×3, and the convolution operation is performed. The second feature map subset is convoluted, a new feature subset is formed and passed down in two lines. One line is passed down directly; and the other line is combined with the third feature map subset using a hierarchical arrangement connection method and sent to the convolution to form a new feature map subset. And then the new feature map subset is divided into two lines, one is directly passed down, and the other line is still connected with the fourth feature map subset using hierarchical progressive arrangement and sent to the convolutional layer to obtain another new feature map subsets. Repeat the above operations until all feature map subsets have been processed. Each feature map subset is combined with another feature map subset after passing through the convolutional layer. This operation makes the equivalent receptive field of each convolutional layer gradually increase, so as to complete the extraction of information at different scales.

Use $K_i()$ to represent the 3×3 output of the convolution kernel, and x_i represents the divided feature map subsets, where $i \in \{1, 2, ..., s\}$ and s represents the number of feature map subsets divided by the feature map. The above process can be expressed as follows

$$
\begin{aligned}
y_1 &= x_1 \\
y_2 &= K_2(x_2) \\
y_3 &= K_3(x_3 + y_2) = K_3(x_3 + K_2(x_2)) \\
y_4 &= K_4(x_4 + y_3) = K_4(x_4 + K_3(x_3 + K_2(x_2)))
\end{aligned}
\tag{1}
$$

Then the output y_i can be expressed as

$$
y_i = \begin{cases}
x_i & i = 1; \\
K_i(x_i) & i = 2; \\
K_i(x_i + y_{i-1}) & 2 < i \le s
\end{cases}
\tag{2}
$$

According to the network structure and the above formula, it can be seen that this split hybrid connection structure can make the output of the multi-scale module include a combination of different receptive field sizes. This structure is beneficial to extracting global and local information. After the above-mentioned multi-scale structure is mixed and connected, the processed feature map subsets are combined by a splicing method, and then a convolutional layer with a convolution kernel size of 1×1 is used to fuse the spliced feature map subsets. Then the information fusion of s feature map subsets is realized. After that the multi-scale residual module is combined with the identity mapping $y = x$ to form a multi-scale residual module.

Finally, a three-layer fully connected layer is added after the multi-scale model structure. On the one hand, the effective features learned by the multi-scale model structure are mapped to the label space of the sample; the second advantage is to increase the depth of the network model so that it can learn more deeply hierarchical abstract features. Compared to the use of global average pooling, the fully connected layer can obtain faster convergence speed and higher recognition accuracy for the recognition of micro-motions.

3.2 Micro-motion Classification Method

This paper proposes a classification method for flying birds and rotary-wing UAVs based on the proposed multi-scale CNN structure. The flowchart is shown in Fig. 8, which is consisted of four parts, radar echo data processing, m-D dataset construction, model training and model testing.

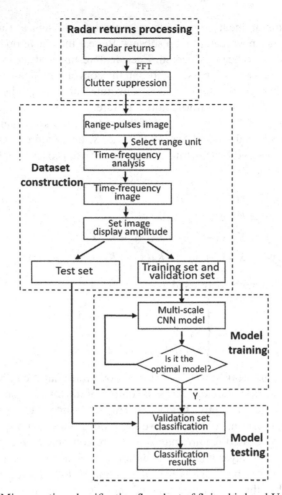

Fig. 8. Micro-motion classification flowchart of flying bird and UAV target.

Step 1: Radar echo data preprocessing. Fast Fourier transform (FFT) is used to obtain the Doppler spectrum of the target micro-motion for different ranges, and the MTI technology is used to perform pulse-to-pulse cancellation on the echo range-pulses data to obtain the echo data after clutter suppression.

Step 2: M-D dataset construction. Select the appropriate target range unit from the range-pulses profile, and use the time-frequency analysis method to extract the m-D features of the target to obtain the time-frequency image. The time-frequency image is reshaped for edge clipping and size normalization. The processed dataset is randomly divided into training data and test data, and the training data is divided into training set and validation set according to the preset ratio.

Step 3: CNN model training. Input the constructed time-frequency image dataset into the multi-scale CNN model for feature learning. The feature learning of the multi-scale

CNN model is to perform an iterative training on the training set, and then verify and analyze the network model on the verification set, and continuously optimize and adjust the network parameters until the expected recognition accuracy rate is reached on the verification set. At this time, the parameters of the multi-scale CNN model are saved, and the optimal network model is obtained.

Step 4: Target classification (Model testing). Input the test data not involved in training and verification into the optimal network model to verify the effectiveness and generalization ability of the multi-scale CNN model. The verification of the validity and generalization ability of the multi-scale CNN model is to calculate the ratio of the number of correctly classified samples of the test data set to the total number of samples in the entire test set. Finally the target classification results are obtained.

3.3 Classification Results Analysis

The dataset is composed of training data and test data. At the same time, the training data is randomly divided into training data set and verification data set according to the ratio of 8:2. The test data is composed of data that has not participated in training and verification, as shown in Table 2.

Table 2. Target recognition classification dataset composition.

Category	Training data	Testing data
Flying birds	900	69
Rotor UAV	900	69
Total	1800	138

The number of training is 50, the number of training batches is 120, and the number of iterations of the training set is 600 (($1440 \div 120$) $\times 50 = 600$), and the number of iterations of the validation set is 150. Based on the proposed multi-scale CNN network model, high recognition accuracy is obtained in the category recognition of flying birds and rotary-wing UAVs, as shown in Fig. 9. It is found that as the number of iterations increases, the classification accuracy rate quickly reaches 100% and remains unchanged, and the loss value is infinitely close to zero, indicating that the multi-scale CNN structure has fast convergence ability and high classification accuracy.

Finally, the generalization ability of the network model is verified on the test set, and the experimental results are shown in Table 3. It can be seen from the confusion matrix that the total recognition probability of the multi-scale network model can reach 99.51%, and the recognition probability of each target is not less than 98.55%. By analyzing the classification results, it is found that the rotation of the dual-rotor and dual-blade of the UAV is similar to the m-D features produced by the dual simulated bird flapping motion. Therefore, the network model is misjudged as the same category.

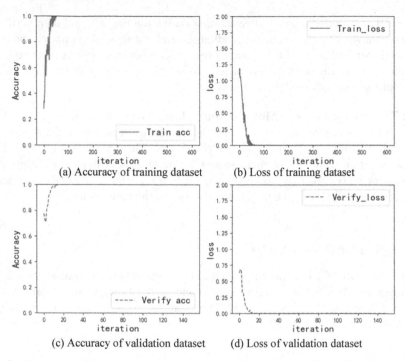

Fig. 9. Accuracy and loss of target recognition classification on training and validation sets

Table 3. Confusion matrix of classification result.

	Flying birds	Rotor UAV
Flying birds	100.0%	0
Rotor UAV	1.45%	98.55%

4   Conclusions

In this paper, the classification of flying bird and rotary-wing UAV is analyzed based on the m-D features. Based on the K-band FMCW radar, the target micro-motion signal measurement experiment was carried out, and radar dataset was constructed. A multi-scale CNN model is proposed for the learning and classification of micro-movement features of different types of targets, which can extract global and local information of m-D features. The measured data verifies the effectiveness of the algorithm. In the future, more radar detection experiment for different types of flying birds and rotor UAVs will carry out.

References

1. Chen, X., Chen, W., Rao, Y., et al.: Progress and prospects of radar target detection and recognition technology for flying birds and unmanned aerial vehicles. J. Radars **9**(5), 803–827 (2020)
2. Taha, B., Shoufan, A.: Machine learning-based drone detection and classification: state-of-the-art in research. IEEE Access **7**, 138669–138682 (2019)
3. Li, T., Wen, B., Tian, Y., Li, Z., Wang, S.: Numerical simulation and experimental analysis of small drone rotor blade polarimetry based on RCS and Micro-Doppler signature. IEEE Antennas and Wireless Propag. Lett. **18**(1), 187–191 (2019)
4. Chen, X., Guan, J., Chen, W., Zhang, L., Yu, X.: Sparse long-time coherent integration–based detection method for radar low-observable maneuvering target. IET Radar, Sonar Navig. **14**(4), 538–546 (2020)
5. Kim, B.K., Kang, H., Park, S.: Experimental analysis of small drone polarimetry based on Micro-Doppler signature. IEEE Geosci. Remote Sens. Lett. **14**(10), 1670–1674 (2017)
6. Gong, J., Yan, J., Li, D., Chen, R., Tian, F., Yan, Z.: Theoretical and experimental analysis of radar Micro-Doppler signature modulated by rotating blades of drones. IEEE Antennas Wirel. Propag. Lett **19**(10), 1659–1663 (2020)
7. Singh, A.K., Kim, Y.: Automatic measurement of blade length and rotation rate of drone using w-band Micro-Doppler radar. IEEE Sens. J. **18**(5), 1895–1902 (2018)
8. Kim, B.K., Kang, H., Park, S.: Drone classification using convolutional neural networks with merged Doppler images. IEEE Geosci. Remote Sens. Lett. **14**(1), 38–42 (2017)
9. Shin, D., Jung, D., Kim, D., Ham, J., Park, S.: A distributed FMCW radar system based on fiber-optic links for small drone detection. IEEE Trans. Instrum. Meas. **66**(2), 340–347 (2017)

Transformer-Based Few-Shot Learning
for Image Classification

Tao Gan$^{(\boxtimes)}$, Weichao Li, Yuanzhe Lu, and Yanmin He

School of Information and Software Engineering, University of Electronic Science and
Technology of China, Chengdu 610054, China
gantao@uestc.edu.cn

Abstract. Few-shot learning (FSL) remains a challenging research endeavor.
Traditional few-shot learning methods mainly consider the distance relationship
between the query set and the support set, while the context information between
different support sets are not fully exploited. This paper proposes a Transformer-
based few-shot learning method (TML). By taking advantage of the self-attention
mechanism of Transformer, TML effectively exploits the correlation between support sets so as to learn highly discriminative global features. Furthermore, in order
to cope with the overfitting problem introduced by the increase of model complexity, we introduce a classification loss into the total loss function as a regularization term. To overcome the limit of traditional cross-entropy loss, a label
refinement method is used to refine the label assignment for classification. The
experimental results show that TML improves the ability of learning hard samples
and achieves higher classification accuracy than existing state-of-the-art few-shot
learning methods.

Keywords: Few-shot learning · Classification · Transformer · Regularization

1 Introduction

Few-shot Learning (FSL) is a new machine learning paradigm which aims to learn from a
limited number of examples with supervised information. To make best use of the limited
data available, different methods have been proposed. Ravi et al. [1] raise the episodic
training idea and propose a meta-learning approach in which an embedding model is
learned so that the base learner minimizes generalization error through the distribution
of tasks with few training examples. Lee et al. [2] investigate linear classifiers as the base
learner for a meta-learning based approach for few-shot learning. Another category of
methods addresses the problem with data augmentation by distorting the labeled images
or synthesizing new images/features based on the labeled ones [3]. Alternatively, the
third group of methods resort to enhance the discriminability of the feature representations such that a simple linear classifier learned from a few labeled samples can reach
satisfactory classification results. Snell et al. [4] proposes the prototypical networks that
learn a metric space in which classification can be performed by computing distances

X. Wang et al. (Eds.): AICON 2021, LNICST 396, pp. 68–74, 2021.
https://doi.org/10.1007/978-3-030-90196-7_6

to prototype representations of each class. Le et al. [5] introduce a category traversal module to extract feature dimensions most relevant to each task, by looking the context of the entire support set. Simon et al. [6] uses a dynamic subspace classifier to calculate a subspace of the feature space for each category, and then project the feature vector of the query sample into the subspace.

Our proposed method falls into the feature enhancement based category. Intuitively, the objective for the classification task is to optimize the feature space in which samples of the same class should be close by in the learned manifold, while samples of a different class should be far away. However, in few-shot setting, the work of [7] shows that optimizing feature distances may not necessarily lead to performance gains. Inspired by the work of [5], we attempt to improve the classification performance by considering the context information between different support sets within the whole task. Furthermore, we try to investigate more powerful techniques to exploit the relation between support sets than that used in [5].

Recently, self-attention-based architectures, in particular Transformer [8], have become the model of choice in natural language processing (NLP) and Transformer has started to be studied in computer vision [9]. The powerful feature representation ability of Transformer just fits the need of our task. Moreover, for the sake of computational efficiency, we do not apply Transformer directly on samples of support sets. Instead, we first employ prototypical network [4] to extract prototype features of original samples and then fed the obtained prototype feature embeddings to Transformer. Since there is one feature embedding for one support, we can keep the computational complexity in low level.

Furthermore, the introduction of Transformer may increase the risk of overfitting. Inspired by the work of [10], we cope with the overfitting problem by regularizing the loss function. To do so, we calculate the classification loss and add it into the total loss function as a regularization term. Meanwhile, to overcome the limit of traditional cross-entropy loss, we refine the label assignment for classification. This is achieved by using a label refinement procedure in which the similarities between the query and support sets are used to refine the label assignment information.

To conclusion, we propose a Transformer-based few-shot learning method (TML). In this method, we integrate the prototypical network and Transformer to train a better feature space and at the same time, we mitigate the risk of overfitting by regularizing the loss function. Our main contributions are as follows:

1. We introduce Transformer into few-shot learning to efficiently exploit the relation between support sets.
2. Incorporated with modified loss function, the proposed method improves the ability of learning hard samples and achieves higher classification accuracy than existing state-of-the-art few-shot learning methods.

2 Methodology

2.1 Overview

In few-shot learning, the model usually trained in episode fashion. An episode corresponds to one task and the categories contained in support sets between episodes may be different. For n-way k-shot image classification problem, we aim to build a complex classifier $f(\cdot)$ which reduces the average error rate in different episode as much as possible. The problem can be formulated as

$$f^* = arg \min_f \sum_{(x_{test}, x_{test}) \in D_{test}} \ell(f(x_{test}; D_{train}), y_{test}) \tag{1}$$

where D_{train} represents the training set for episode training and D_{test} represents the verification set for the same task as the training set $\ell(\cdot)$ is a loss function which measures the differences between the ground-truth labels and the predicted ones. In our method, the image is generally embedded into one feature space by an embedding function ϕ and a nearest neighbor classifier is used on that space. The classifier can be formulated as

$$y_{test} = f\left(\phi_{x_{test}}; \{\phi_x, \forall(x, y) \in D_{train}\}\right) \propto exp\left(sim\left(\phi_{x_{test}}, \phi_x\right)\right) y, \forall(x, y) \in D_{train} \tag{2}$$

The proposed TML model consists of three principle modules: prototypical network, transformer and label refinement. Firstly, images in both support sets and query set are input into the prototypical network and the prototype feature embeddings of corresponding sets are obtained. Then the transformer and label refinement modules are designed for computing the distance loss and classification loss, respectively. The total loss is the combination of the distance loss and classification loss calculated. The system structure is illustrated in Fig. 1. In the following sections, we describe the proposed transformer and label refinement modules in detail.

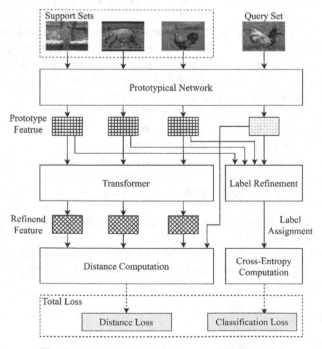

Fig. 1. The overview of the proposed TML model.

2.2 Transformer

The Transformer is a network model designed to process machine translation. It consists of encoder and decoder modules, each of which has multiple encoders or decoders of the same architecture. Each encoder consists of a self-attention layer and a feed-forward network. Each decoder consists of a self-attention layer, a codec attention layer and a feed-forward network.

The traditional few-shot image classification models, such as prototypical networks, obtain the feature embeddings of input images only by independently feeding them into convolutional neural networks. Thus the obtained feature embeddings of one support set contains no information about the that of others. In the proposed TML model, the output features of prototypical networks are fed into Transformer for feature re-extraction. Thus the embedded function ϕ in formula (1) can be expressed as

$$\{\psi_x; \forall x \in X_{train}\} = T(\{\phi_x; \forall x \in X_{train}\}) \tag{3}$$

where $T(\cdot)$ represents the function of Transformer and ψ_x represents features after transformed.

2.3 Label Refinement

As mentioned above, to mitigate the risk of overfitting, we resort to introduce the classification loss to regularize the loss function. However, the traditional classification loss function, e.g., cross-entropy, may not be appropriate for few-shot image classification task. Since when each sample is classified independently, it is possible that two images of the same class have two distant embeddings that both allow for a correct classification. Here we attempt to refine the classification information that used for calculating cross-entropy so as to make the classification loss contain ingredient that reflects distances between samples.

Towards this end, we introduce a label refinement method. This is an iterative procedure that uses the similarities between the query and support sets to refine the label assignment information. The structure of label refinement is shown in Fig. 2, where the similarity matrix and label matrix contains information of similarity and label assignment, respectively.

Consider a n-way k-shot image classification problem. Suppose W represents a $n + 1 \times n + 1$ matrix of pairwise similarity and $X = (x_{i\lambda})$ represents a $n + 1 \times n$ matrix of image label assignments. The label refinement procedure consists of the following steps:

(1) For all pairs of prototype feature embeddings of the query set and support sets, generate a similarity matrix W by computing similarities among them. The similarity measure used is the Pearson's correlation coefficient:

$$\omega(i, j) = \frac{Cov[\varphi(I_i), \varphi(I_j)]}{\sqrt{Var[\varphi(I_i)], Var[\varphi(I_j)]}} \tag{4}$$

(2) Initialize X with the result of softmax computation of all prototype feature embeddings.

(3) Define the support matrix $\prod = (\pi_{i\lambda}) \in R^{n \times m}$ as

$$\prod = WX \tag{5}$$

Given the initial assignment matrix $X(0)$, the algorithm refines it using the following update rule:

$$x_{i\lambda}(t+1) = \frac{x_{i\lambda}(t)\pi_{i\lambda}(t)}{\sum_{\mu=1}^{m} x_{i\lambda}(t)\pi_{i\lambda}(t)} \tag{6}$$

where the denominator represents a normalization factor which guarantees that the rows of the updated matrix sum up to one.

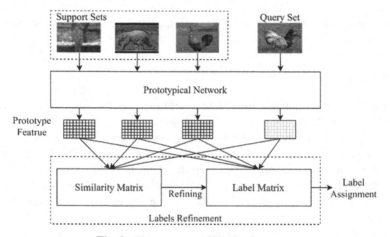

Fig. 2. The structure of label refinement.

3 Experiments

Below we evaluate our method on Mini ImageNet datasets. This dataset is a subset of 100 classes selected from the ImageNet. All images on are $84 \times 84 \times 3$ and the number of samples per class is 600. We build datasets for 5-way 1-shot and 5-way 5-shot classification tasks. We train the method in 200 epochs with each epoch has 1000 images. We use Adam optimizer which has an initial learning rate of 0.0002 and decays by 0.5 for every 10 strides. In addition, the momentum of the optimizer is set to 0.9, and the weight decay is set to 0.0005.

We randomly construct 600 tasks for testing. The performance of our proposed TML is compared to that of other state-of-the-art few-shot methods, including ProtoNets [1], MetaOpnet [2], CTM [5], AFHN [3] and DSN-MR [6]. The classification accuracy results of these methods are presented in Table 1.

Table 1. Comparison of classification accuracy results

Method	1-shot	5-shot
ProtoNets	60.37 ± 0.83	78.02 ± 0.57
MetaOpnet	62.64 ± 0.61	78.63 ± 0.46
CTM	64.12 ± 0.82	80.51 ± 0.13
AFHN	62.38 ± 0.72	78.16 ± 0.56
DSN-MR	64.60 ± 0.72	79.51 ± 0.50
TML	66.75 ± 0.20	82.05 ± 0.14

It can be seen that TML provides best performance among all methods for both 1-shot and 5-shot cases. Especially, TML performs much better than ProtoNets, with 10.57% and 5.17% gains in accuracy for 1-shot and 5-shot, respectively. This can be attributed to the fact that TML build its model on the basis of ProtoNets and the superior performance is achieved by introducing Transformer as well as label refinement modules. In additional, we observe that the superiority of TML is more noticeable for 1-shot than 5-shot, indicating TML is more robust for difficult task.

It is worth noting that like TML, state-of-art MetaOptNet and CTM are methods that consider the context information of support sets within the entire task. TML still yields results that are superior to MetaOptNet and CTM for both 1-shot and 5-shot cases. This indicates that Transformer can exploit the correlation between support sets so as to learn highly discriminative features embeddings.

4 Conclusion

This work has presented a few-shot learning method based on Transformer. Incorporate with the prototypical network, Transformer exploits the relation between support sets effectively and efficiently. In addition, in order to cope with the overfitting problem introduced by the increase of model complexity, a classification loss is introduced into the total loss function as a regularization term. Experiments demonstrate the superiority of the proposed method over existing state-of-the-art few-shot learning methods.

References

1. Ravi, S., Larochelle, H.: Optimization as a model for few-shot learning. In: Proceeding International Conference Learning Representation (ICLR) (2017).
2. Lee, K., et al.: Meta-learning with differentiable convex optimization. In: Proceeding IEEE Conference Computer Vision and Pattern Recognition (CVPR) (2019).
3. Li, K., Zhang, Y., Li, K., et al.: Adversarial feature hallucination networks for few-shot learning. In: Proceedings of the IEEE/CVF Conference on Computer Vision and Pattern Recognition, pp. 13470–13479 (2020)
4. Snell, J., Swersky, K., Zemel, R.: Prototypical networks for fewshot learning. In: Proceeding Neural Information Processing Systems (NIPS), pp. 4077–4087 (2017).

5. Li, H., Eigen, D., et al.: Finding task-relevant features for few-shot learning by category traversal. In: Proceeding IEEE Conference Computer Vision and Pattern Recognition (CVPR) (2019)
6. Simon, C., Koniusz, P., Nock, R., et al.: Adaptive subspaces for few-shot learning. In: Proceedings of the IEEE/CVF Conference on Computer Vision and Pattern Recognition, pp. 4136–4145 (2020)
7. Liu, B., et al.: Negative margin matters: understanding margin in few-shot classification. In: Vedaldi, A., Bischof, H., Brox, T., Frahm, J.-M. (eds.) ECCV 2020. LNCS, vol. 12349, pp. 438–455. Springer, Cham (2020). https://doi.org/10.1007/978-3-030-58548-8_26
8. Vaswani, A., et al.: Attention is all you need. In: Proceeding Neural Information Processing Systems (NIPS), pp. 5998–6008 (2017)
9. Dosovitskiy, A., et al.: An image is worth 16x16 words: transformers for image recognition at scale. arXiv preprint arXiv:2010.11929 (2020)
10. Elezi, I., Vascon, S., et al.: The group loss for deep metric learning. arXiv preprint arXiv: 1912.00385 (2019)

Fractional Time-Frequency Scattering Convolution Network

Jiabin Zheng[1]([⊠]), Jun Shi[2], Gong Chen[2], Weiping Chen[1], and Zhenya Geng[3]

[1] MEMS Center, Harbin Institute of Technology, Harbin 150001, China
chenwp@hit.edu.cn
[2] Communication Research Center, Harbin Institute of Technology,
Harbin 150001, China
junshi@hit.edu.cn
[3] Department of Control Science and Engineering, Harbin Institute of Technology,
Harbin 150001, China
zhenya.geng@hit.edu.cn

Abstract. The wavelet scattering convolution network (SCN) have recently developed as a kind of effective feature extractor, which has achieved a great performance in signal and image processing applications. Unfortunately, as feature extractor, SCN is not appropriate to mimic the visual system of mammals in image classification tasks, so that STFT-based time-frequency scattering convolution network (TFSCN) is proposed. However, TFSCN is limited by a major drawback: it is only available for stationary signals'analysis but not for non-stationary ones, since STFT can viewed as linear translation-invariant filters in the FT domain intrinsically. The aim of this paper is to overcome this weakness using the short-time fractional fourier transform (STFRFT) which is a bank of linear translation-variant bandpass filters and thus may be used for non-stationary signal analysis. First, We present the fractional time-frequency scattering transform based upon the STFRFT. Then a generalization of TFSCN's structure dubbed FRTFSCN is illustrated. The significant performance of FRTFSCN are shown via experiment simulations.

Keywords: Time-frequency scattering · Scattering network · Short-time fractional fourier transform · Non-stationary signal analysis · Translation-variant filtering

1 Introduction

In recent years, the wavelet scattering convolution network [1–3] (SCN) introduced by Mallat has drawn extensive attention in various field, and has led to state-of-the-arts results in a wide range of classification tasks including handwritten digit recognition [2], musical genre classification [3], audio classification [4], texture discrimination [5], art authentication [6], astronomy [7], chemical [8],

© ICST Institute for Computer Sciences, Social Informatics and Telecommunications Engineering 2021
Published by Springer Nature Switzerland AG 2021. All Rights Reserved
X. Wang et al. (Eds.): AICON 2021, LNICST 396, pp. 75–81, 2021.
https://doi.org/10.1007/978-3-030-90196-7_7

biomedical science [9,10], and time-frequency representations [11]. It is pioneering in mathematical analysis of feature extractors generated by DCNNS [1,2]. Furthermore, Li et al. developed time-frequency scattering convolution network (TFSCN) [11] by combing Mallats scattering transform framework with short-time fourier transform (STFT) with Gaussian window to make sense to mimic the visual system of mammals for designing a feature extractor in image classification. Theoretically, TFSCN provides a translation and rotation-invariant and deformation-stable representation by cascading Gabor filters and modulus nonlinearities, and performs well in practice e.g. image classification. Unfortunately, TFSCN still suffers from a major drawback: it is only appropriate for stationary signals'analysis but not for non-stationary ones, for the reason that the STFT is intrinsically a set of linear time-invariant bandpass filters in the Fourier transform (FT) domain, which indicates that TFSCN does not work well when analyzing non-stationary signals. Thus, it is desirable to impart a certain degree of time-varying behavior to these networks. Our objective of this paper is to propose a new structure for TFSCN dubbed fractional TFSCN (FRTFSCN) by employing the short-time fractional fourier transform (STFRFT) which is a generalization of the conventional short-time fourier transform (STFT) in the fractional FT (FRFT) domain. We first define fractional time-frequency scattering transform based on STFRFT, then fractional time-frequency scattering convolution network is constructed using STFRFT-based scattering transform, which includes the STFT-based TFSCN as a special case. Finally, a practical application of the FRTFSCN in image classification is discussed.

2   Fractional Time-Frequency Scattering Convolution Network

In this section, the formulation of the FRTFSCN is described. We start by introducing the definition of the STFRFT. Then, a STFRFT-based scattering transform is proposed. In the following, the FRTFSCN is constructed according to STFRFT-based scattering transform.

2.1   The Definition of STFRFT

According to [12], *Shi et al.* define a novel STFRFT of a function $f(t) \in L^2(\mathbb{R})$ with respect to a given window $g(t)$ as

$$\text{STFRFT}_f^\alpha(t, u) = \int_R f(\tau) g_{\alpha,t,u}^*(\tau) d\tau \tag{1}$$

with its kernel given by

$$g_{\alpha,t,u}(\tau) \triangleq g(\tau - t) e^{-j\frac{\tau^2 - t^2}{2}\cot\alpha + j\tau u \csc\alpha} \tag{2}$$

then based on the definition of the fractional convolution [13]:

$$f(t) *_\alpha g(t) = \int_{\mathbb{R}} f(\tau) g(t - \tau) e^{-j\frac{t^2 - \tau^2}{2}\cot\alpha} d\tau \tag{3}$$

then (1) can be rewritten as the form of fractional convolution, that is

$$\text{STFRFT}_f^\alpha(t, u) = e^{-jtu\csc\alpha}\left[f(t) *_\alpha \left(g^*(-t)e^{jtu\csc\alpha}\right)\right]. \tag{4}$$

Note that, when $\alpha = \pi/2$, STFRFT reduces to STFT.

2.2 STFRFT-Based Scattering Transform

In this operation, a scattering transform computes nonlinear invariants from fractional short-time fourier coefficients by modulus operator performed as a nonlinear pooling operator on the ground that it could preserve the signal energy [11]. As for the signal $x(t) \in L^2(\mathbb{R})$, the STFRFT-modulus coefficients, considered as the translation-invariant coefficients, are built from the STFRFT by the modulus operator defined as:

$$U[p]x = |x *_\alpha f_p|, \quad p \in \mathbb{P} \tag{5}$$

and STFRFT-based scattering transform is defined as

$$S[p]x = U[p]x *_\alpha f_0, \quad p \in \mathbb{P} \tag{6}$$

where $f_p(t) = f_0(t)e^{jpt}$, $p \in \mathbb{P}$ and f_0 form a frame dubbed as a fractional uniform covering frame, that is $\mathfrak{F} = \{f_0\} \cup \{f_p : p \in \mathbb{P}\}$ satisfying

$$|F_0(u\csc\alpha)|^2 + \sum_{p \in \mathbb{P}} |F_p(u\csc\alpha)|^2 = 1 \tag{7}$$

where $F_0(u\csc\alpha)$ and $F_p(u\csc\alpha)$ denote the FT (with their argument scaled by $\csc\alpha$) of $f_0(t)$ and $f_p(t)$, respectively. In addition, Eq. 7 implies that $\mathfrak{F}$ is a semi-discrete Parseval frame [14] for all $x(t) \in L^2(\mathbb{R})$,

$$\|x *_\alpha f_0\|^2 + \sum_{p \in \mathbb{P}} \|x *_\alpha f_p\|^2 = \|x\|^2 \tag{8}$$

More fractional STFRFT-modulus coefficients can be obtained by further iterating on the STFRFTs and the modulus operator along any path $p \in \mathbb{P}^k$ and $k \in \mathbb{N}$, then we associate $p \in \mathbb{P}^k$ with the fractional scattering propagator $U[p]$:

$$U[p]x = \begin{cases} x, & \text{if } p \in \mathbb{P}^0 \\ |x *_\alpha f_p|, & \text{if } p \in \mathbb{P} \\ U[p_k]U[p_{k-1}] \cdots U[p_1]x, & \text{if } p = (p_1, p_2, \ldots, p_k) \in \mathbb{P}^k \end{cases} \tag{9}$$

then STFRFT-based scattering transform with association $p \in \mathbb{P}^k$, $S[p]$, is a vector-valued operator

$$S[p]x = \{U[p]x *_\alpha f_0 : \quad p \in \mathbb{P}^k, k = 0, 1, 2, \cdots\} \tag{10}$$

which is fractional time-frequency scattering transform, the generalization of the conventional time-frequency scattering transform.

2.3   The Construction of FRTFSCN

Based on the results obtained above, we now introduce the fractional time-frequency scattering convolution network (FRTFSCN), which can be viewed as an iterative process over a one-step fractional scattering propagator. Similar to the DCNNs [15], the FRTFSCN is built upon a building block comprised of a FRFT-domain filtering followed by a modulus nonlinearity. Let us recursively construct the FRTFSCN. The first layer collects all the results of the STFRFTs with respect to $k = 0$, i.e.,

$$S[p]x = \{U[p]x *_\alpha f_0 : \quad p \in \mathbb{P}^k, k = 0\} = x *_\alpha f_0 \tag{11}$$

The m-th layer of the FRTFSCN is constructed by taking all the possible STFRFTs of level $m - 1$, i.e., $S[p]x$ with $p \in \mathbb{P}^{m-1}$, where $\mathbb{P}^{m-1}$ is the set of all the paths p of length $m - 1$. Note from (9) that for any given path $p \in \mathbb{P}^{m-1}$ and m-th path element $p_m \in \mathbb{P}$, we can derive a m-length path set $\mathbb{P}^m$ satisfying $\mathbb{P}^m = \{\mathbb{P}^{m-1}, p_m\}$ and $p_m \in \mathbb{P}$. Then we can derive that m-th layer of the FRTFSCN satisfying

$$\begin{aligned} U[p']x &= U[p_m]U[p]x, \quad p' = (p, p_m), p \in \mathbb{P}^{m-1} \\ &= U[p_m]U[p_{m-1}] \cdots U[p_1]x. \end{aligned} \tag{12}$$

Moreover, it follows that

$$S[p']x = U[p']x *_\alpha f_0 \tag{13}$$

therefore, we can iteratively compute the nodes of the FRTFSCN by first recursively calculating the fractional scattering propagators $U[p]$ for all level m up to the pre-determined maximum depth of the FRTFSCN. Then, all the nodes value can be extracted by computing the STFRFTs. A graphical representation of the proposed FRTFSCN is shown in Fig. 1. As can be seen from the figure, the proposed FRTFSCN is a fully connected network which has the similar structure of CNNs [15]. Compared with the conventional TFSCN, FRTFSCN is performed from the perspective of fractional filtering and remain some basic properties in fractional domain, like rotation and translation-invariant and deformation stability. Furthermore, note that, when $\alpha = \pi/2$, the FRTFSCN reduce to TFSCN,

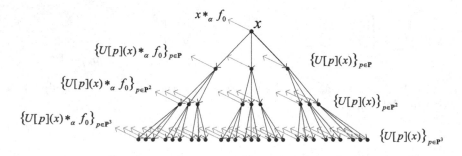

Fig. 1. The architecture of FRTFSCN.

which implies that TFSCN is a special case of the FRTFSCN. The FRTFSCN has a free parameter α and thus is more flexible than the conventional TFSCN.

3   The Application of FRTFSCN

In this section, we give a potential application of the proposed FRTFSCN. Since both the FRTFSCN and TFSCN the similar properties like rotation and translation-invariant and deformation stability, it means the FRTFSCN could provide a translation- and rotation-invariant fractional time-frequency scattering representation which is stable to small deformations. These properties determine that FRTFSCN is useful in image classification tasks. So, we apply the proposed FRTFSCN in a texture classification to illustrate its significant performance.

3.1   Texture Database

The database constructed by merging UMD [16] and ALOT [17], which contains 9 classes of images, as illustrated in Fig. 2, and there are 40 images in each class. As can be seen from the Fig. 2, there are some non-stationary textures in those sample images, which implies FRTFSCN would perform better compared with the conventional TFSCN when selecting an appropriated angle.

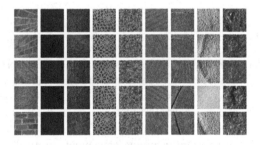

Fig. 2. Sample images from the UMD [16] and ALOT [17] databases.

3.2   Classification Results

In classification stage, the images in each class are divied into two groups randomly. One group of images is labled for training, and the other group is for testing. As aforementioned, the FRTFSCN has a free parameter $\alpha \in [0, \pi/2]^d$, on which the classification performance depends. For image analysis, we set $d = 2$ and $\alpha = (\alpha_1, \alpha_2)$. According to [18], we fix one element of α to $\pi/2$, and let the other vary from 0 to $\pi/2$ with a step of $\pi/20$ to accelerate the computation of the FRTFSCN. Hereby, the angle pair $(9\pi/10, \pi/2)$ is chosen to calculate fractional time-frequency scattering coefficients which fed into PCA classifier for classification. The results of classification are shown in Table 1 which gives a comparison of the FRTFSCN and several well-known networks (e.g., the conventional SCN

[1], the time-frequency scattering network (TFSN) [11], and the CNN [15]). To illustrate the results of experiments, the third row of Table 1 is taken as an example, in which each class containing 40 images, 10 sample images are randomly chosen for training, and the remaining 30 images are used for testing. In order to obtain statistical results, we calculate the mean and variance of classfication errors for the FRTFSCN with $(9\pi/10, \pi/2)$ over 1000 experiments. As can be observed from Table 1, the FRTFSCN with angle pair $(9\pi/10, \pi/2)$ yields the minimum classification error, and even with small size of training, its performance is always best. Particularly, when the size of training is extremely small (i.e. training samples = 2), the FRTFSCN still exhibits best performance.

Table 1. Classification errors using different networks.

Training samples	FRTFSCN $(9\pi/10, \pi/2)$	TFSCN	SCN	CNN
2	**0.13 ± 0.05**	0.23 ± 0.03	0.24 ± 0.02	0.45 ± 0.08
5	**0.05 ± 0.03**	0.13 ± 0.04	0.13 ± 0.04	0.35 ± 0.09
8	**0.02 ± 0.02**	0.09 ± 0.02	0.08 ± 0.03	0.34 ± 0.12
10	**0.02 ± 0.02**	0.07 ± 0.02	0.07 ± 0.02	0.30 ± 0.11
15	**0.01 ± 0.01**	0.05 ± 0.02	0.04 ± 0.01	0.18 ± 0.07
20	**0.01 ± 0.01**	0.04 ± 0.01	0.02 ± 0.01	0.12 ± 0.05

4 Conclusion

This paper aims to overcome the drawback of the TFSCN based upon the STFRFT, which are suitable to analysis non-stationary signal as a bank of linear translation-variant bandpass filters. First, a STFRFT-based scattering transform is proposed, then we construct FRTFSCN based on fractional time-frequency scattering transform. Eminent numerical performance of the FRTFSCN is presented to illustrate its advantage in image classification application.

References

1. Mallat, S.: Group invariant scattering. Commun. Pure Appl. Math. **65**(10), 1331–1398 (2012)
2. Bruna, J., Mallat, S.: Invariant scattering convolution networks. IEEE Trans. Pattern Anal. Mach. Intell. **35**(8), 1872–1886 (2013)
3. Andén, J., Mallat, S.: Deep scattering spectrum. IEEE Trans. Signal Process. **62**(16), 4114–4128 (2014)
4. Andén, J., Lostanlen, V., Mallat, S.: Joint time-frequency scattering. IEEE Trans. Signal Process. **67**(14), 3704–3718 (2019)
5. Sifre, L., Mallat, S.: Rigid-motion scattering for texture classification. Appl. Comput. Harmon. Anal. **00**, 1–20 (2014)
6. Leonarduzzi, R., Liu, H., Wang, Y.: Scattering transform and sparse linear classifier for art authentication. Signal Process. **150**, 11–19 (2018)

7. Allys, E., et al.: The RWST, a comprehensive statistical description of the non-Gaussian structures in the ISM. A&A **629**(A115), 1–21 (2019)
8. Hirn, M., Mallat, S., Poilvert, N.: Wavelet scattering regression of quantum chemical energies. Multiscale Model. Simul. **15**(2), 827–863 (2017)
9. Chudáček, V., Andén, J., Mallat, S., Abry, P., Doret, M.: Scattering transform for intrapartum fetal heart rate variability fractal analysis: a case-control study. IEEE Trans. Biomed. Eng. **61**(4), 1100–1108 (2014)
10. Oyallon, E., et al.: Scattering networks for hybrid representation learning. IEEE Trans. Pattern Anal. Mach. Intell. **41**(9), 2208–2221 (2019)
11. Czaja, W., Li, W.: Analysis of time-frequency scattering transforms. Appl. Comput. Harmon. Anal. **47**, 149–171 (2019)
12. Shi, J., Zheng, J., Liu, X., Xiang, W., Zhang, Q.: Novel short-time fractional fourier transform: theory, implementation, and applications. IEEE Trans. Signal Process. **68**, 3280–3295 (2020)
13. Shi, J., Sha, X., Song, X., Zhang, N.: Generalized convolution theorem associated with fractional Fourier transform. Wirel. Commun. Mob. Comput. **14**(13), 1340–1351 (2014)
14. Chui, C.K., Shi, X.: On a Littlewood-Paley identity and characterization of wavelets. J. Math. Anal. Appl. **177**(2), 608–626 (1993)
15. Krizhevsky, A., Sutskever, I., Hinton, G.E.: ImageNet classification with deep convolutional neural networks. Adv. Neural Inform. Process. Syst. **25**(2), 1097–1105 (2012)
16. http://users.umiacs.umd.edu/~fer/website-texture/texture.htm
17. http://aloi.science.uva.nl/public_alot/
18. Liu, L., Wu, J., Li, D., Senhadji, L., Shu, H.: Fractional wavelet scattering network and applications. IEEE Trans. Biomed. Eng. **66**(2), 553–563 (2019)

Fault Prediction Analysis of Communication Optical Fiber Based on SVM Algorithm

Pengfei Li$^{(\boxtimes)}$ (iD)

Qinghai Minzu University, Xining, Qinghai, China

Abstract. Optical fiber is the basis of communication network, carrying a huge network traffic, the impact of the cable failure is significant. As a result, the fiber fault prediction is a hot research topic. In this paper, based on the basic parameters and fault information of optical fiber, Support Vector Machine (SVM) model is adopted to classify the faults. Since the cable fault is a small probability event, there is an imbalance in the distribution of the data sample. Use Synthetic Minority Oversampling Technique (SMOTE) algorithm to treat the imbalance data, and then analyze and study by using the SVM classification model.

The results show that the overall classification accuracy of the prediction model is 79.8%, and the prediction sensitivity of the fault fiber is 62.2%. The results show that the model has a good effect, and it can provide a certain auxiliary role for the operation and maintenance of communication fiber.

Keywords: Optical cable fault · SVM algorithm · SMOTE algorithm

1 Introduction

Optical fiber has the advantages of large communication capacity, long distance and strong anti-electromagnetic interference ability, it is widely used in communication network [1]. Multiple optical fibers are combined into optical cables, which are laid in the form of overhead, pipeline, and ground, etc., thus establishing the foundation of the whole communication network. The environment of optical cable laying is complex, once the fault causes interruption, it will have a great impact on the communication network. Therefore, the prediction of optical cable fault is the difficulty and key to the operation and maintenance of communication system, this problem is widely researched [2].

At present, in order to deal with optical cable failure, a series of technologies have been developed, such as optical fiber automatic protection switching

Supported by The research innovation team of the multi-source data fusion and application of Qinghai Minzu University, and Qinghai Minzu University 2018 University-level Science and Technology Research Project under Grant 2018XJQ04.

technology. Optical cable online monitoring system is also widely used, it uses optical time domain reflectometer and other equipment to monitor the running state of optical cable for a long time to realize the functions of optical cable fault warning, analysis, positioning and so on, and provides guarantee for the safe and efficient operation of optical cable network [3,4].

In the main research methods of optical cable fault prediction at present, data mining algorithms are also beginning to be applied, based on the optical power data to carry out the analysis of a large amount for a long time, according to the mathematical characteristics of light power on the time series, optical power time series of high-frequency random factor and trend of low frequency factor analysis using wavelet transform method, optical power trend analysis and forecasting, fiber optical line state warning system [5]. The above methods are expensive to implement and require special hardware and software platforms, which can only be realized by collecting a large amount of data for a long time.

The main contribution of this article is a novel framework for optical cable fault prediction. We propose a method, based on data mining algorithm based on optical fiber cable directly basic parameters and history fault information, with cable length, type, installation, usage and so on as the input features, using SMOTE completion algorithm does not balance data, fault classification training SVM model, prediction results can be a preliminary screening failure probability higher cable, with very low cost for cable operation maintenance efficiency.

The rest of this article is organized as follows. How to select the valuable features form basic data of optical cable is described in Sect. 2. Section 3 solve the problem of data type imbalance. In Sect. 5, we use SVM algorithm to find the optical cable failure, the experimental results are presented. At last, Conclusions are in Sect. 6.

2   Data and Feature Selection of Optical Cable

Based on the basic parameters and historical fault data of all optical cables in the power communication network of a province, this paper carry out the training and verification of the prediction model. There is a total of 1652 optical cables, 121 of them have faults, and the fault samples only account for 7.9% of the normal samples, this is a typical unbalanced data set.

According to the characteristics of the fiber optic cable, delete parts of the features which has nothing to do with the cable fault variables, ultimately determine the input characteristics of the prediction model has: the total number of fiber in the cable, the number of optical fibers already in use, the manufacturer, the fiber length, the laying type, the user, the construction completion time. The model of predicting output is fault state (0 indicates normal, 1 failure).

3   SMOTE Algorithm Processes Unbalanced Data

At present, logistic regression, support vector machine, neural network, K-nearest neighbor, decision tree and other mainstream classification algorithms in machine learning require the quantity distribution of all categories to be balanced. When the above algorithm is directly applied to unbalanced data samples, the effect is going to be very bad, such as events with low probability such as default, illness, disqualification, failure, etc., which are often classified into most classes, but rare samples with low probability are exactly what the prediction is really concerned about [5–7].

To solve the above problems, it is necessary to add a small number of sample data to improve the model effect. SMOTE is an approach to the construction of classifiers from imbalanced datasets is described. It can add the new sample to the data set artificially according to the Minority samples, which solve the overfitting problem of the model caused by the over-sampling algorithm adopting the strategy of simply copying the samples [8].

The basic principle of SMOTE algorithm: in the Euclidean space of the data point, for each minority sample xi, choose a sample xj randomly from its nearest neighbor, and then choose a randomly selected point on the line between the two points as the newly composed minority sample [9].

In this paper, on the basis of 121 fault optical cable data, 1413 fault data are supplemented by SMOKE algorithm, and the original 1652 optical cable data are expanded to 3065, among which fault and normal account for 50% respectively, providing a balanced data sample for the prediction model.

4   SVM Algorithm

SVM is a class of supervised learning that carries out binary classification of data in the generalized linear classifier, whose decision boundary is the maximum margin hyperplane that can be solved for the learning sample [10]. SVM is first proposed by Cortes and Vapnik in 1995, has shown many unique advantages in solving small sample sizes, nonlinear and high-dimensional pattern recognition and can be generalized to other machine learning problems such as function fitting [11].

SVM method is based on statistical learning theory based on VC dimension theory and structure risk minimum principle, according to the limited sample information in the complexity of the model (i.e. the specific learning Accuracy of training samples, Accuracy) and learning ability to seek the best compromise between, in order to get the best generalization ability [12]. Therefore, SVM is very suitable to solve the problem of optical cable fault prediction in our study.

5   Analysis of Classification Results

Using Scikit-learn machine learning framework [13], we set up a multi-layer perceptron neural network model, the SMOKE algorithm adds balance after 3065 cable data, random selection of 80% of the data samples constitute the training sample, the remaining 20% of the data form the test samples, according to the result of training to determine the suitable network convergence threshold and weights, the SVM model uses the gaussian kernel function, the test data is used to test the model predictions, the effect as shown in Table 1:

Table 1. List of notation

Real value/Predicted	Normal	Fault
Normal	293	5
Fault	119	196

The accuracy rate is a good and intuitive evaluation index to measure the quality of the classification algorithm, but sometimes the high accuracy rate does not mean that the algorithm can solve problems. In this paper, there are only two fault categories of optical cable: 0 means normal, 1 means failure. In the operation and maintenance of optical cable, it is more concerned about whether faults can be found. The omission of faults is more serious than the false detection of normal optical cable. Therefore, the prediction sensitivity of optical cable faults (also known as recall rate [14]) is more important, that is, the proportion of the actual fault samples predicted as faults. According to Table 1, the prediction classification results of the cable fault warning model are calculated as follows:

$$Precision = (293 + 196) / (293 + 5 + 119 + 196) = 79.8\%$$
$$Recall = 196 / (196 + 119) = 62.2\%$$

The classification effect of this model has an overall accuracy rate of 79.8%, and the recall of the fault optical cable reaches 62.2%, with relatively high accuracy. Obviously, the optical cable fault probability model established in this study can provide a certain auxiliary role for the operation and maintenance of optical cable.

6 Conclusion

In this paper, the optical cable fault warning model is proposed, and the operation and fault data of the optical cable in a provincial power communication network are selected for example analysis. The SVM algorithm is used to predict the fault based on the key operation indexes such as the length, type and laying mode of the optical cable. By analyzing, it is found that the traditional classification algorithm has a poor classification effect on this kind of unbalanced data. Therefore, SMOTE algorithm is selected for the balance treatment of the sample test data, and the predicted effect after treatment is better. In this study, under the condition of not increasing the cost of hardware and software, the cable fault warning model is used to predict, and the cable fault possibility is preliminarily screened to strengthen the maintenance in advance to reduce the fault, promoting the cable operation and maintenance work from the empirical type to the analysis type, engaged in the passive type to advance the active type transformation.

In the following work, more variable characteristics can be added to the cable fault warning model for research, such as optical receiving power, optical transmission power, machine room operating parameters, cable off-line type, etc., to further improve the prediction sensitivity of the model, better guide the cable operation and maintenance work.

References

1. Keiser, G.: Optical Fiber Communications. Wiley Encyclopedia of Telecommunications (2003)
2. Wang, Z., Zhang, M., Wang, D., et al.: Failure prediction using machine learning and time series in optical network. Opt. Exp. **25**(16), 18553–18565 (2017)
3. Shaneman, K,, Gray, S.: Optical network security: technical analysis of fiber tapping mechanisms and methods for detection & prevention. In: IEEE MILCOM 2004. Military Communications Conference, 2004, vol. 2, pp. 711-716. IEEE (2004)
4. Zhang, H., Dai, G.L.: Design of optical fiber communication network monitoring and detection system based on address resolution protocol cheats. Optik **127**(23), 11242–11249 (2016)
5. Tao, Q., Wu, G.W., Wang, F.Y., et al.: Posterior probability support vector machines for unbalanced data[J]. IEEE Transactions on Neural Networks **16**(6), 1561–1573 (2005)
6. Searle, S R.: Linear Models for Unbalanced Data. John Wiley & Sons, New York (2006)
7. Mani, I., Zhang, I.: kNN approach to unbalanced data distributions: a case study involving information extraction. In: Proceedings of Workshop on Learning from Imbalanced Datasets, vol. 126. United States: ICML (2003)
8. Chawla, N.V., Bowyer, K.W., Hall, L.O., et al.: SMOTE: synthetic minority oversampling technique. J. Artif. Intell. Res. **16**, 321–357 (2002)
9. Fernández, A., Garcia, S., Herrera, F., et al. : SMOTE for learning from imbalanced data: progress and challenges, marking the 15-year anniversary. J. Artif. Intell. Res. **61**, 863–905 (2018)
10. Joachims, T.: Making large-scale SVM learning practical[R]. Technical report (1998)
11. Schuldt, C., Laptev, I., Caputo, B.: Recognizing human actions: a local SVM approach. In: Proceedings of the 17th International Conference on Pattern Recognition, 2004 (ICPR 2004), vol. 3, pp. 32–36. IEEE (2004)
12. Leslie, C., Eskin, E., Noble, W.S.: The spectrum kernel: a string kernel for SVM protein classification. Biocomputing **2001**, 564–575 (2002)
13. Pedregosa, F., Varoquaux, G., Gramfort, A., et al.: Scikit-learn: machine learning in python. J. Mach. Learn. Res. **12**, 2825–2830 (2011)
14. Davis, J., Goadrich, M.: The relationship between Precision-Recall and ROC curves. In: Proceedings of the 23rd International Conference on Machine Learning, pp. 233–240 (2006)

RSEN-RFF: Deep Learning-Based RF Fingerprint Recognition in Noisy Environment

Zhaonan Du[1(✉)], Di Liu[1], Jiawen Zhang[2], Di Lin[1], Yuan Gao[3], and Jiang Cao[3]

[1] School of Information and Software Engineering, The University of Electronic Science and Tecnology of China (UESTC), Chengdu, People's Republic of China
201922090507@std.uestc.edu.cn
[2] National Key Laboratory of Science and Technology on Communications, University of Electronic Science and Technology of China (UESTC), Chengdu, People's Republic of China
[3] Military Academy of Sciences, Beijing, China

Abstract. As an emerging technology of Internet of Things security, radio frequency (RF) fingerprint identification technology can be used to identify wireless devices and meet the needs of the Internet of Things regarding user access control. Machine learning and deep learning have been applied to recognize a mobile device by extracting and analyzing its RF fingerprinting characteristics due to their powerful feature learning and representational abilities. However, the performance and accuracy of the learning algorithm will degrade dramatically in the circumstances of high-intensity noise (low signal-to-noise ratio, low SNR). To address this problem, this paper proposes an attention-based residual network algorithm, named RSEN-RFF, to train and recognize the RF fingerprint characteristics of lightweight mobile devices, and compared the proposed algorithm with classic convolutional neural networks (LeNet5, etc.), which are the most widely used algorithms for IoT device identification. Unlike other machine learning methods based on feature engineering, deep models use neural networks to solve the characterization of RF fingerprint features without the need for a process of feature extraction based on professional knowledge. The results show that the fitting speed and recognition accuracy of proposed algorithm are better than those of the previous algorithm under the condition of low SNR.

Keywords: RF fingerprint recognition · IoT security · Deep learning

1 Introduction

In recent years, with the rapid development of wireless networks, artificial intelligence and big data analysis technology, all kinds of Internet of things applications continue to emerge, becoming one of the three major application scenarios in the fifth-generation mobile communication network (5G) [1]. Online mobile devices and sensor deployments explosive growth. According to Cisco's forecast, there will be more than 25 billion terminal devices connected to each other through the Internet of Things in 2021 [2]. With the continuous expansion of the application scope of the Internet of Things and the rapid growth of the number of devices, its security issues have become increasingly prominent. At present, the identification technology of wireless devices mainly includes traditional password-based methods. These methods mainly use IP, MAC addresses, etc. as the basis for identification [3], or use complex mathematical operations, protocols to generate keys, passwords, digital signatures, etc. to complete the identification work between users [4]. However, this method has hidden dangers such as key information leakage and tampering. Nowadays, the continuous improvement of computer capabilities has also made the ability to decipher passwords continuously enhanced, thus threatening the effectiveness of password-based identification methods. In addition, the Internet of Things devices includes a large number of lightweight devices, whose computing power cannot meet this complex identification method. Therefore, the method of purely using encryption becomes no longer reliable, and it is necessary to find a more stable and secure wireless device identity authentication method. In this context, RF fingerprint technology has become an emerging identity authentication method. It can identify the unique characteristics of the mobile device by analyzing the signal sent by the mobile device, thereby effectively preventing malicious parties from fake identity to obtain security credentials.

In a practical application scenario, there are various noises and interferences, such as multi-user co-channel interference and multipath interference. In a low SNR environment, the decay of SNR will conceal the small differences between devices, causing the fingerprint recognition rate of the device to drop significantly. Existing machine learning algorithms may not be suitable for radio frequency fingerprint identification with a low signal-to-noise ratio. Therefore, radio frequency fingerprint identification algorithms based on traditional machine learning or convolutional networks may reduce about 10%–20% at a signal-to-noise ratio of 5 dB performance [5]. This paper focuses on the research of radio frequency fingerprint recognition under the conditions of high-intensity electromagnetic noise. Based on the attention mechanism in deep learning that has been widely used in recent years, the residual module is introduced at the same time, and the cross-layer identity path of the residual network is adopted to alleviate the training difficulty of the deep network and improve the representation feature learning ability of the recognition model. In addition, the soft threshold function noise reduction algorithm in communication is used for reference, and the corresponding processing process is added to the model to eliminate the influence of SNR decay as much as possible. While improving the recognition accuracy, the overall generalization ability of the model is improved.

The rest of this paper is arranged as follows. Section 2 reviews the field of RF fingerprinting recognition and related learning methods. Section 3 describes the internal hardware impairments and channel models that lead to signal differences. Section 4 presents our methodology on RSEN-RFF based algorithm, followed by Sect. 5 which reports the simulation results. Section 6 concludes with a discussion of the results and suggestions for future research.

2 Related Work

The mainstream RF fingerprint identification technology mainly includes two research directions: one is feature-based RF fingerprint identification, and the other is data-based RF fingerprint identification. Feature-based RF fingerprint identification requires the combination of feature engineering and professional communication knowledge to extract appropriate device fingerprints, and then use the feature similarity between devices for identification. Specifically, traditional machine-learning algorithms are used to recognize the devices based on the device's unique fingerprint. Data-based RF fingerprint identification uses deep learning algorithms, which can automatically train the raw data of the signal to identify mobile devices.

Before 2018, the research of radio frequency fingerprint identification mainly focused on the use of machine learning algorithms, e.g., the support vector machines (SVM) algorithms are used to recognize the identity document (ID) of each mobile device. Some studies employ multi-core SVM algorithms to identify the ID of mobile devices, including Platt's Minimization Optimization (SMO) algorithms, the poly-kernel algorithms,and the Pearson-VII Universal Kernel (PuK) algorithms [6]. Generally, the PuK algorithms are more effective in RF fingerprint identification, obtains higher recognition performance, and greatly reduces calculation time. The traditional machine-learning RF fingerprinting identification technology first preprocesses the collected signals, including power normalization, noise reduction and label set. Then, the RF fingerprint characteristics are extracted from the pre-processed signal data through different algorithms, and the marked characteristics are stored in the fingerprint library. Finally, the extracted RF fingerprint features are used to identify the mobile devices. In the traditional machine-learning recognition technology, the key is to select appropriate signal characteristics from RF fingerprints.

After 2018, research on the application of deep learning in the field of RF fingerprint identification has gradually emerged. Sankhe et al. in [7] proposed to use a 2-layered convolution neural network (CNN) to train the RF fingerprinting data from 16 X310 USRP SDRs. Wu et al. in [8] employ a deep neural network (DNN) with a rectified linear units (ReLU) to run the training model for the RF fingerprint identification of 12 Ettus USRP N210. In addition, Wu et al. [8] proposed a neural network based on incremental learning to train data in multiple stages, and use new-arrival data to modify the learning model to speed up the training process. Compared with traditional feature extraction algorithms based on machine learning, RF fingerprint identification based on deep learning does not require feature extraction. After preprocessing, the predicted label is directly compared with the label registered in the fingerprint library in the deep learning network to identify different mobile devices.

In this paper, we use deep learning algorithms instead of machine learning to identify mobile devices. The RF signal of the device is represented by the original I/Q data. Assuming that we choose to use traditional machine learning algorithms, we must go through a complex feature selection process to construct a series of mathematical and statistical indicators. This process is time-consuming, and a lot of information can be lost. Therefore, we finally use deep learning algorithms to build learning models to distinguish transmission devices.

3 The Mechanism of RF Fingerprint Generation

3.1 RF Impairments and I/Q Imbalance

RF fingerprints are mainly caused by differences in hardware during the manufacturing process, including power amplifier defects, amplitude and phase errors, carrier frequency differences, phase offsets and clock offsets, etc. [9]. I/Q imbalance is a phenomenon that occurs in direct down-conversion radio frequency receivers, which directly down-converts the RF signal to the baseband. The conversion process from baseband digital signals to radio frequency analog signals will have a unique impact on radio frequency signals. Therefore, individual identification of wireless devices can be realized based on these inherent, stable and unique signal characteristics. In this section, we will introduce and study the mechanism of the RF fingerprint generated by the modulator. By using different modulation schemes, subtle differences in modulator hardware can be collected.

3.2 I/Q Imbalance on Different Channel

Although most modern communication systems are affected by frequency-dependent IQ imbalance, for simplicity, frequency independence is usually assumed in the existing literature [10]. This article first assumes that IQ imbalance has nothing to do with frequency, and the modulated signal is transmitted through different channels (e.g., additive white Gaussian noise channel, AWGN), as follows:

Denote the ideal signal s(t) at the transmitter as:

$$s(t) = cos(2\pi f_0 t)x_i(t) - j \cdot sin(2\pi f_0 t)x_q(t) \tag{1}$$

where $x_i(t)$ and $x_q(t)$ are baseband signals respectively in the I and Q path, f_0 is the fixed carrier frequency.

Due to the different degrees of damage to the hardware, compared with the ideal signal s(t), the actual signal ŝ(t) modulated by different devices may have slight differences in amplitude and phase. Hence, the baseband signals which through IQ imbalance modulator can be denoted as:

$$\hat{s}(t) = (1 + \Delta) \, cos \, (2\pi f_0 t + \theta)x_i(t) - j \cdot sin(2\pi f_0 \, \Delta \, t)x_q(t) \tag{2}$$

the transmitter's gain imbalance is represented by Δ, and the transmitter's phase imbalance is represented by θ, such that the ideal transmitter, with no IQ imbalance, has $\Delta = 0$ and $\theta = 0$.

In this paper, we use additive white Gaussian noise to simulate training samples that pass through the AWGN channel, as follows:

$$y(t) = \hat{s}(t) + n(t) \tag{3}$$

where n(t) is a zero-mean white Gaussian noise process.

For Rayleigh fading channels, this paper uses the form of circular complex Gaussian random variables to model the tap coefficients as follows:

$$\alpha_k = A + j \cdot B \tag{4}$$

where α_k is the path index, A and B are zero mean iid Gaussian random variables with variance σ^2 [11] as follows:

$$\sigma^2 = \frac{1}{2}\left\{\left[1-exp(\frac{-T_s}{T_{rms}})\right]exp(\frac{-kT_s}{T_{rms}})\right\} \tag{5}$$

where T_s is the sampling period and T_{rms} is the Root-Mean-Squared (RMS) delay spread of the channel [11], and the Rayleigh channel model is defined as:

$$h(t, \tau)=\sum_{k=1}^{L} \alpha_k\delta(t - \tau_k T_s) \tag{6}$$

where τ_k is the delay of the k-th path normalized by T_s[12]. In summary, the modulated signal after passing through the Rayleigh fading channel is as follows:

$$r(t) = \hat{s}(t) * h(t, \tau) + n(t) \tag{7}$$

where $*$ denotes convolution.

In the following, we will use the subtle difference between the ideal signal and the actual signal as the internal features of mobile devices to identify them. We use different channel conditions, e.g. (3), (6) and (7) to simulate the real environment, and using the amplitude difference and phase difference in (2) to distinguish between different devices, which will be shown in Sect. 6.

4   Network Structure

In this section, the design and training approaches of the Residual Squeeze-and-Excitation Networks for the RF fingerprint (RSEN-RFF) are introduced. The RSEN-RFF network in this paper trains IQ samples of radio frequency signals to identify IoT devices. It is an improved residual network based on the channel attention mechanism. It consists of typical components, such as a convolutional layer, batch normalization (BN), rectification linear unit (ReLU), global average pool (GAP), fully connected layer (FC). The innovation of this article in the deep network is mainly reflected in the residual building unit (RSBU) we proposed with reference to the residual-based channel attention mechanism. The structure of RSEN-RFF is shown in Fig. 1.

4.1   Design of Essential Architectures of RSEN-RFF

The most important component of a convolutional neural network is the filter that performs convolution operations in the convolutional layer. Because the convolution operation can describe image features well, it is widely used in image recognition tasks. In this paper, the convolutional layer is used to abstract RF fingerprint features, by calculating the convolution between the input initial I/Q sample and the convolution kernel, the convolution layer is used to abstract and extracts the RF fingerprint features, which can compress the input data size to reduce the space complexity of the model. RSBU is the core of the RSEN-RFF model, which can suppress noise components by using dynamic thresholds. Generally, RSBU consists of one layer of BN, one convolutional layer with

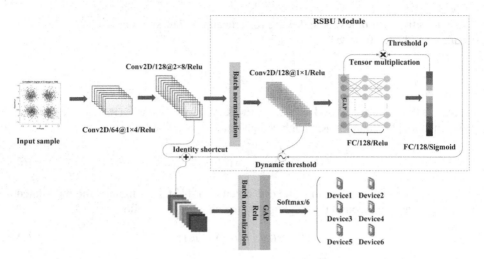

Fig. 1. The overall architecture of RSEN-RFF

rectifier linear unit, one layer of GAP, three layers of FC. Among all fully connected layers, the first two use the ReLU activation function, and the third layer uses the sigmoid activation function. BCR includes three components, namely batch normalization (BN), rectifier linear unit (ReLU) and convolutional layer unit. BCR assumes the role of nonlinear transformation, improves the deep abstraction ability of the network, and further expands the characterization of the RF fingerprint characteristics in I/Q samples. The GAP layer calculates the mean value of the characteristic channel as the input of the channel weight calculation.

4.2 Dynamic Threshold

Soft thresholding is often used as a key step in many signal denoising methods. Usually, the original signal will be scaled, and then soft thresholding will be applied to convert the features close to zero into zero. However, the setting of the soft threshold has always been a challenging problem. Deep learning provides a new way to solve this problem. Deep learning can use the gradient descent algorithm to automatically learn the filter threshold, instead of artificially setting the threshold by expert experience. Therefore, the integration of soft thresholds and deep learning can be a promising method to eliminate noise-related information and build highly discriminative features. The function of the soft threshold can be expressed as:

$$y = \begin{cases} x - \rho, & x > \rho \\ 0, & -\rho \le x \le \rho \\ x + \rho, & x < -\rho \end{cases} \tag{8}$$

where x represents the features of input I/Q signals, y represents the output features, and ρ represents a dynamic threshold which is usually a positive parameter. Different from the ReLU activation function, the soft threshold setting is not to set the negative feature to zero, but to set the feature close to zero, so that the useful negative feature can be retained.

The used in the RSBU is expressed as follows:

$$\rho = \omega \triangle mean[|x|] \tag{9}$$

where $mean[|x|]$ represents the mean of input x, and ω represents the scaling parameter, which is expressed as:

$$\omega = (1 + e^{-t})^{-1} \tag{10}$$

where t represents the output of fully connected networks.

4.3 The Structure of RSBU

RSBU is an improvement based on SENet [13] and residual network. It uses a dynamic threshold method to suppress noise components and inserts the dynamic threshold as a nonlinear conversion layer into the building unit. In addition, the threshold can be trained in the building unit, which will be described below.

As shown in Fig. 1, In the RSBU module, the input data is IQ samples that have been convolved twice, and the output data is the data that has undergone a dynamic threshold filtering operation and a residual cross-layer identity shortcut operation. First, the input data by BN layer, in order to address after two convolution data distribution changes, in order to prevent the disappearance or explosion gradient, speed up the training. Then there is a convolutional layer to further abstract the channel features of the feature map. Since this layer performs a residual cross-layer identity shortcut operation with the input data after dynamic threshold filtering, the size of the feature map here needs to be aligned. Common alignment methods include a 1×1 convolution kernel and zero paddings. This paper uses a 1×1 convolution kernel for feature map alignment. The following is the generation and filtering of dynamic thresholds. The feature map obtains a one-dimensional vector of the channel average value through the GAP layer. Then, the one-dimensional vector is propagated to the three-layer full-path network, and a sigmoid function is applied at the end of the full-path network to scale the scaling parameter ω to the range of $(0,1)$. The scaling parameter is as shown in formula (10) above. The scaling parameter is multiplied by the channel average value to obtain the dynamic threshold ρ vector, as in the above formula (9). Finally, use the dynamic threshold vector to filter the feature map, and output the data after the cross-layer identity shortcut operation.

After being processed by the RSBU module, the sample data has been greatly abstracted and noise suppressed. The conventional BCR layer and Softmax function can be used to classify and identify the device.

5 Simulation Experience

5.1 Data Sampling Platform

We built a data sampling platform in a static indoor office environment, as shown in Fig. 2. The IQ sequences used in this paper, including the training data and the test data, are collected from Universal Software Radio Peripherals (USRPs). Our hardware platform consists of NI-PXIe 1085 devices and two USRP-RIO-2943. NI-PXIe 1085 is a computer-based platform for data transmission and graphic display. All transmitters of the RIO2 are bit-similar and emit IEEE 802.11a standards compliant frames generated via a MATLAB WLAN System toolbox. We use the open-source GNU Radio companion (GRC) to transmit standard-compliant IEEE 802.11a data packets through the SDR. Using set_iq_balance() and set_dc_offset() functions in GRC, these two separate complex correction factors can be set to intentionally introduce required level of impairments in the radio. By the above methods, we simulate six different transmitters that need to be identified; The other USRP RIO-2943 (RIO1) is a fixed receiver, responsible for receiving signals from the six transmitters. As for the transmitters, their hardware differences can lead to amplitude difference and phase difference. We will set the parameters as follows: signal impairment transmitter only has an offset 1 in amplitude, a signal transmitter 2 only has offset damage in phase, the remaining transmitter mode offset exists in amplitude and phase.

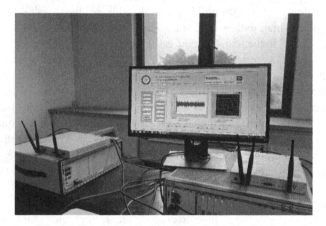

Fig. 2. Signal sampling platform for data collection.

5.2 Data Pre-process

The data samples sent to the network in the past are all original I/Q two-way signals, in which the signals are generated by modulating different phases and amplitudes according to a randomly generated bitstream. In training and testing above 15 db, the order of the bitstream has little effect on the recognition result, and training using the original I/Q two-way signal is text-independent. However, under the condition of a low SNR, the obvious text correlation appears during training, that is, the effect of training and testing with different batches of bitstreams is not good. In order to eliminate the influence of the sequence under the condition of a low SNR, consider rearranging the original I/Q two-way signals and then sending them to the network for training. Taking QPSK modulation as an example, we can separate the four I/Q signals representing 00 01 10 11, and then sort them, and rearrange the original $2 \times N$ size I/Q signals into $8 \times N/4$ format. The schematic diagram of QPSK modulation rearrangement is shown in Fig. 3:

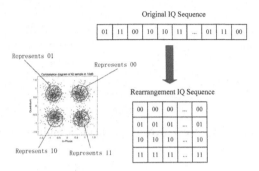

Fig. 3. IQ data sample rearrangement diagram

5.3   Experiment I: Effects of Different Modulation Identification Rearrangement

In this experiment, we compared the impact of the rearrangement preprocessing method under different modulation methods on the recognition accuracy under the AWGN channel. As shown in Fig. 4, the overall recognition accuracy after rearrangement can be improved by about 5%−20%. In addition, in PSK modulation, as the phase point increases, the accuracy of the radio frequency fingerprint will decrease to a certain extent, but the rearrangement preprocessing can effectively solve this problem. In Fig. 4, without pre-processing, the recognition accuracy difference between BPSK, QPSK and 8PSK modulation methods is about 5%–10%. This gap can be reduced to 1%–3% after rearrangement and preprocessing. Rearrangement is a key step to eliminate the relevance of text content. All results are executed based on the RSEN-RFF algorithm, which shows that our network is robust to the reordering pre-processing under the modulation mode. According to the results of the experiment, the rearrangement preprocessing of IQ samples can effectively improve the recognition accuracy of the network and is not affected by the modulation method.

5.4   Experiment II: Effect of Different Conditions Identified Rayleigh Channel

Multipath seriously affects the performance of a wireless communication network, because destructive interference will produce a plurality of reflected signals received at the receiver. This is the main problem between 802.11a wireless transceivers in the indoor environment [14]. The paper simulates the Rayleigh fading channel model to collect IQ sample data in the indoor multipath environment. At this time, there are one or more paths without a line path. The Rayleigh fading channel model is a standard method for predicting IEEE 802.11a WiFi modulation performance in a wireless multipath environment. Multipath is characterized by the time delay associated with each reflection path and is called delay spread. The delay spread varies based on the type

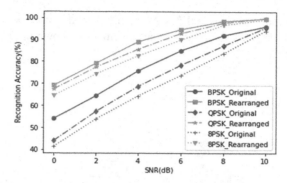

Fig. 4. Accuracy comparison of different modulation identification rearrangement

of indoor environment. For example, the delay spread is lower than 50 ns in a home multipath environment, and about 100 ns in an Office environment. The modeling of the Rayleigh fading channel is represented by the above formula (4)–(7).

In order to test the robustness of the model under complex conditions, we designed and simulated a set of parameters under different Rayleigh fading channel conditions, as shown in Tables 1 and 2, where the channel conditions become worse as the number of paths increases. The channel estimation adopts the least-squares (LS) channel estimation, and the channel equalization adopts the minimum mean square error (MMSE) equalization.

Table 1. Delay selection of different paths $T_{RMS} = 100$

Path delay

L	50	100	150	200	250	300	350	400	450	500	550	600	650	700	750
3	√	--	√	--	√	--	--	--	--	--	--	--	--	--	--
5	√	--	√	--	√	--	√	--	√	--	--	--	--	--	--
7	√	√	--	√	√	--	√	--	√	--	√	--	--	--	--

Table 2. A normalized variance of fading coefficients for different paths $T_{RMS} = 100$

Path variances (σ_k^2)

L	50	100	150	200	250	300	350	400	450	500	550	600
3	0.6652	--	0.2447	--	0.0900	--	--	--	--	--	--	--
5	0.6364	--	0.2341	--	0.0861	--	0.0317	--	0.0117	--	--	--
7	0.4153	0.2519	--	0.0927	0.0562	--	0.0207	--	0.0076	--	0.0028	--

By evaluating the recognition accuracy of the RF fingerprint feature in the Rayleigh fading channel, as shown in Fig. 5, the average recognition accuracy fluctuates within 7% under different Rayleigh fading channel conditions, indicating that the RSEN-RFF algorithm has a good generality. It can overcome the influence of signal fading in the actual environment on the accuracy of radio frequency fingerprint identification. At the same time, when the signal-to-noise ratio is greater than 6 dB, the average recognition accuracy of the RSEN-RFF algorithm on the Rayleigh fading channel test samples can reach more than 85%.

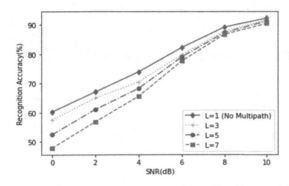

Fig. 5. Accuracy comparison of different conditions identified Rayleigh channel

5.5 Experiment III: The Proposed RSEN-RFF V.S. LeNet5

In this experiment, we compare the convergence speed and accuracy of RF fingerprint identification with LeNet5 and our RSEN-RFF algorithm. As shown in Fig. 6, the average recognition accuracy of the RSEN-RFF algorithm is higher than that of LeNet5 by about 15%–20%. In terms of convergence speed, as shown in Fig. 7, when the SNR is greater than 6 dB, RSEN-RFF needs 8–9 epochs to achieve AWGN channel convergence, while LeNet5 requires 18–20 epochs to achieve convergence.

In addition, when the SNR is less than 6 dB, it takes more than 12 epochs to achieve the convergence of the Rayleigh channel in RSEN-RFF, and 20 epochs to converge in LeNet5. The reason is that, compared with the AWGN channel, the Rayleigh fading channel is affected by the multipath effect, so it needs more time to learn the characteristics of the signal.

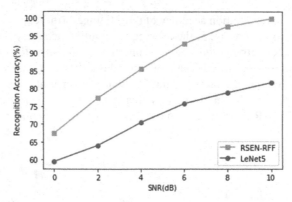

Fig. 6. Accuracy comparison of RSEN-RFF and LeNet5

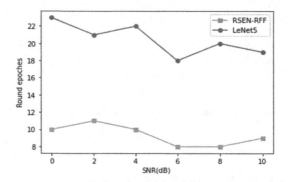

Fig. 7. Convergence and round epochs comparison of RSEN-RFF and LeNet5

6   Conclusion

In this paper, we propose RSEN-RFF, which is a novel algorithm to identify IoT devices via RF fingerprint analysis. RSEN-RFF can effectively overcome low SNR settings in some IoT scenarios. Specifically, our algorithm incorporates a dynamic shrinkage threshold to improve the accuracy of device recognition. In addition, compared to traditional methods, RSEN-RFF can accelerate the training process of model learning. Detailed analysis and extensive experiments have proved the robustness of RSEN-RFF in various SNR scenarios. Finally, the actual deployment of the six-device network shows that in terms of recognition accuracy and running time, RSEN-RFF is overall better than the typical CNN network LeNet5, thus meeting the security requirements in real-time IoT scenarios. In order to further improve the robustness of the network in complex situations, we plan to extend the scope of research to the case of small-scale sampling data, in which case the amount of data is insufficient for model training. In actual situations, the number of RF signals collected by a single device may be unbalanced.

Acknowledgement. Partially Funded by Science and Technology Program of Sichuan Province (2021YFG0330), partially funded by Grant SCITLAB-0001 of Intelligent Terminal Key Laboratory of SiChuan Province, and partially Funded by Fundamental Research Funds for the Central Universities (ZYGX2019J076).

References

1. Li, S., Xu, L.D., Zhao, S.: 5G Internet of Things: a survey. J. Ind. Inf. Integr. **10**, 1–9 (2018)
2. Zhang, K., et al.: Sybil attacks and their defenses in the internet of things. IEEE Internet of Things J. **1(5)**, 372–383 (2014)
3. He, D., Zeadally, S.: An analysis of RFID authentication schemes for internet of things in healthcare environment using elliptic curve cryptography. IEEE Internet Things J. **2**(1), 72–83 (2014)
4. Zhao, F., Jin, J.: An optimized radio frequency fingerprint extraction method applied to low-end receivers. In: 2019 IEEE 11th International Conference on Communication Software and Networks (ICCSN). IEEE (2019)
5. Peng, L., et al.: Deep learning based RF fingerprint identification using differential constellation trace figure. IEEE Trans. Veh. Technol. **69**(1), 1091–1095 (2019)
6. Hu, S., et al.: Machine learning for RF fingerprinting extraction and identification of soft-defined radio devices. In: Liang, Q., Wang, W., Mu, J., Liu, X., Na, Z., Chen, B. (eds.) Artificial Intelligence in China. Lecture Notes in Electrical Engineering, vol. 572, pp. 189–204. Springer, Singapore (2020). https://doi.org/10.1007/978-981-15-0187-6_22
7. Sankhe, K., et al.: ORACLE: optimized radio classification through convolutional neural networks. In: IEEE INFOCOM 2019-IEEE Conference on Computer Communications. IEEE (2019)
8. Wu, Q., et al.: Deep learning based RF fingerprinting for device identification and wireless security. Electr. Lett. **54**(24), 1405–1407(2018)
9. Ding, G., Huang, Z., Wang, X.: Radio frequency fingerprint extraction based on singular values and singular vectors of time-frequency spectrum. In: 2018 IEEE International Conference on Signal Processing, Communications and Computing (ICSPCC). IEEE (2018)
10. Wong, L.J., Headley, W.C., Michaels, A.J.: Emitter identification using CNN IQ imbalance estimators. arXiv preprint arXiv:1808.02369 (2018)
11. O'hara, B., Petrick. A.: IEEE 802.11 Handbook: A Designer's Companion. IEEE Standards Association, Piscataway (2005)
12. Hijazi, H., Ros, L.: Polynomial estimation of time-varying multipath gains with intercarrier interference mitigation in OFDM systems. IEEE Trans. Veh. Technol. **58**(1), 140–151 (2008)
13. Hu, J., Shen, L., Sun, G.: Squeeze-and-excitation networks. In: Proceedings of the IEEE Conference on Computer Vision And Pattern Recognition (2018)
14. Fadul, M., et al.: Preprint: using RF-DNA fingerprints to classify OFDM transmitters under rayleigh fading conditions. arXiv preprint arXiv:2005.04184 (2020)

Q-Learning Based Optimum Relay Selection for a SWIPT-Enabled Wireless System

Haojie Wang$^{(\boxtimes)}$ ⓘ and Bo Li ⓘ

Harbin Institute of Technology, Weihai 264209, Shandong, China
18S130269@stu.hit.edu.cn, libo1983@hit.edu.cn

Abstract. This paper exploits q-learning to solve the optimization of relay resource allocation in a SWIPT system in order to maximize the overall source nodes communication rate. The traditional method based on greedy strategy search can find the current optimal relay. However, this method does not adapt to the changes of the dynamic network and is easy to fall into the local optimum. In q-learning, agents are driven to intelligently switch strategies to obtain rewards for complex dynamic environments. A multi-source node competition relay environment is created. Our proposed scheme treats the optimised objective as an environmental reward and models the process of relay selection as a Markovian decision process. After experimental simulations and comparisons, the proposed scheme improves the overall throughput and resource utilisation in an environment where multiple source nodes compete with each other, and performs significantly better than the greedy strategy.

Keywords: Simultaneous wireless information and power transfer ·
Reinforcement learning · Relay selection

1 Introduction

Q-Learning is one of the most widely used off-policy algorithms in reinforcement learning and is a model-free reinforcement learning method that has the advantage of being simple to train and does not depend on the current environment model [1].

Simultaneous wireless information and power transfer (SWIPT) is a new type of wireless network that has received extensive attention recently, which could prolong the living time of energy-restrained nodes [2, 3].

In order to implement energy harvesting and information transmission, this paper considers the use of time switching and power splitting [4], two accepted technical criteria. The working modes of relay nodes are divided into regenerative and non-regenerative, and amplified forwarding under non-regeneration is considered in this paper [5, 6].

In Paper [7], the optimal relay selection is treated as an external optimisation condition, and a greedy strategy is used to give the best relay selection strategy. However, the above work does not consider complex multi-node scenarios, which are computationally difficult to solve, so we come up with the idea of using reinforcement learning to

X. Wang et al. (Eds.): AICON 2021, LNICST 396, pp. 100–107, 2021.
https://doi.org/10.1007/978-3-030-90196-7_10

settle the issue. Multiple source nodes bring many time-varying effects to the relays, and inappropriate relay selection can have many detrimental consequences for the network. The combination of relay selection and reinforcement learning is an advanced method to cope with changes in the network environment [8]. We consider running Q-learning independently for each source node to achieve overall optimization [9, 10].

In this paper, we first establish a multi-source node environment and emphasise the problem of competition, followed by a formulation of the problem, incorporating features of Q-learning bar modelling the problem as a Markovian decision process, which can be handled by reinforcement learning.

The rest is ordered as follows. A relay resource competition SWIPT communication model is depicted mathematically in Sect. 2. Section 3 describes the solution idea of maximizing the overall communication rate of all source nodes using Q-learning, while Sect. 4 delivers the simulation results and analysis. Last but not least, the conclusion is placed.

2 System Model and Problem Formulation

2.1 System Model

We model a communication system where the relay nodes and the end point are available for energy harvesting. As depicted in Fig. 1, this comprises N source nodes S, K relay nodes R and a destination node D. The relay nodes operate in an amplified forwarding mode. Special emphasis needs to be placed on the possibility of competing relays between the source nodes, as we assume that the relay nodes can only serve one source node at a time. It is assumed that there is no data interaction between the source nodes. Each source node runs the Q-learning algorithm independently and chooses which one relay node to attach. In addition, to streamline the problem, we also suppose that there is no mutual interference between the source nodes and that the information is delivered in a one-way communication direction from the source to the end. This is a two-hop relay network and we will give evaluations of the two steps.

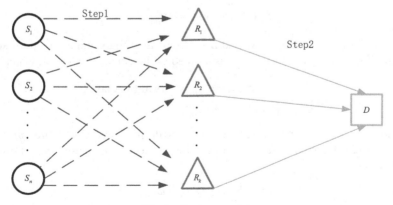

Fig. 1. System model.

The process from one source is first given as a formula, and then the case of multiple source nodes competing is discussed.

For the first step, the effective signal-to-noise ratio received by the relay are

$$\gamma_{TS}^{(1)} = \frac{P_S |g_k|^2}{\sigma_\eta^2 + \sigma_d^2},$$ (1)

and

$$\gamma_{PS}^{(1)} = \frac{(1 - \lambda) P_S |g_k|^2}{(1 - \lambda)\sigma_\eta^2 + \sigma_d^2},$$ (2)

where σ_η^2 is the variance of additive white Gaussian noise, σ_d^2 is the noise variance generated by the circuit baseband, $|g_k|$ represents the channel gain, λ is power splitting ratio, and P_S is the transmission power at the source.

The effective signal-to-noise ratio received by the ending node for the second step can be indicated as

$$\gamma_{TS}^{(2)} = \frac{|w_k|^2 |m_k|^2 |g_k|^2 P_S}{|w_k|^2 |m_k|^2 \sigma_k^2 + \sigma_\eta^2 + \sigma_d^2},$$ (3)

and

$$\gamma_{PS}^{(2)} = \frac{(1 - \lambda)|w_k|^2 |m_k|^2 |g_k|^2 P_S}{(1 - \lambda)(|w_k|^2 |m_k|^2 \sigma_k^2 + \sigma_\eta^2) + \sigma_d^2},$$ (4)

where $|m_k|$ is the amplification factor of the selected relay k, $|w_k|$ is the significance of the channel gain among the relay R_k and the end node, and σ_k^2 is the variance of the noise during this period.

The user rate received by the destination node can be indicated as

$$R_{TS} = \frac{B}{2}(1 - \mu) \log_2(1 + \gamma_{TS}^{(2)}),$$ (5)

and

$$R_{PS} = \frac{B}{2} \log_2(1 + \gamma_{PS}^{(2)}),$$ (6)

where μ is time switching ratio, and B is bandwidth. To extend to the multi-source node scenario, a binary variable $\varphi_{n,k}(t)$ is defined as the connection factor, which is

$$\varphi_{n,k}(t) = \begin{cases} 1, & \text{if source } S_n \text{ is served by relay } R_k \\ 0, & \text{otherwise} \end{cases}.$$ (7)

Because a relay can only serve one source node in a time slot, source and relay connections are valid in the absence of congestion. Hence, the total user rate for multiple source nodes is

$$R_U = \sum_{n \in N} R_{n(TS/PS)} \cdot \varphi_{n,k}(t).$$ (8)

2.2 Problem Formulation

The target is to select a strategy that will optimise the relay selection to maximise the overall channel capacity. The issue was instituted as

$$P1: \max \sum_{n \in N} R_{n(TS/PS)} \cdot \varphi_{n,k}(t)$$

$$s.t. \ C1: \varphi_{n,k}(t) \in \{0, 1\} \tag{9}$$

$$C2: 0 \le R_{n(TS/PS)} \le \max R_{n(TS/PS)}.$$

where C2 expresses the fact that there is actually an upper limit to the communication rate of each source node in order to satisfy the minimum energy harvesting request.

3 Q-Learning Based Solution

3.1 Markov Decision Process

For a conventional single Agent Markov decision process, it consists of a quadruple M $=< S, A, P, R>$, where S denotes the collection of states the Agent is in, A denotes the collection of possible actions the Agent can choose, P is the transfer probability between states, and R denotes the payoff function. Assume that the Agent is in state S the Agent can take an action and move to the next state with a certain probability P. Then, Agent moves from the environment to the next state. Through this action, the Agent receives a payoff R from the environment, and through iterative learning maximizes the cumulative payoff to obtain the most appropriate decision for itself.

3.2 State, Action, Transition and Reward

In the following, MDP quadruple is specified in the time slot of the system under consideration.

State: For each source node, $S_t = [\Psi_1, \Psi_2, \Psi_3]$ where Ψ_1 represents the current access status of that source node, Ψ_2 represents the congestion of the current relay accessed by that source node, and Ψ_3 indicates the value corresponding to the current service level of that source node. Each source node can adjust its decision based on the access status of the relay and the perceived relevant environment.

Action: In the system under consideration, we use discrete numbers to indicate which relay node the source node has chosen to communicate with.

Transition: The transition function is the probability distribution of the next state given the current state of the Agent and the joint action, the transfer of the considered scenario state is determined as

$$\Pr\left\{s'|s_t, a_t\right\} = \begin{cases} 1, & \text{if } s' = s_{t+1} \\ 0, & \text{otherwise} \end{cases}, \tag{10}$$

Reward: The reward function reflects the Optimisation target, which for this problem is to increase the overall user channel rate. The payback function can therefore be defined as

$$r_t(s_t, a_t) = \sum_{n \in N} R_{n(TS/PS)} \cdot \varphi_{n,k}(t) \cdot \Psi_3, \tag{11}$$

3.3 Q-Learning Method

Q-Learning is used to guide the intelligence in its decision making through the Q-table, which can be used as a guide for action decisions once the training has converged. The Q-table value can be written as

$$Q(s_t, a_t) = E\left[\sum_t^T \theta r(s_t, a_t) | s_t, a_t\right], \tag{12}$$

Input: MDP quadruple
1:   Random selection of actions in the current state, Q value initialized to 0
2:
    Repeat (Selecting action based on ε-greedy strategy)
3:       **if** exploration **then**
4:           Random selection of actions in the current state
5:       **else**
6:
        Choose an action $a^* = \arg\max_a Q^*(s,a)$
7:
        Execute chosen a_t, observe reward and next state s_{t+1}
8:
        $Q(s_t, a_t) \leftarrow \kappa r(s_t, a_t) + \kappa \theta \max_{a_{t+1}} Q^*(s_{t+1}, a_{t+1}) + (1 - \kappa)Q(s_t, a_t)$
9:
        Let $s_t \leftarrow s_{t+1}$
10:     **Until** (Completion of a specific number of steps or convergence of all Q values)
Output: Relay selection strategy

Fig. 2. Q-learning algorithm.

where the θ is discount parameter and $0 \le \theta \le 1$. In order to obtain the optimal value function $Q^*(s_t, a_t)$, the Bellman optimality equation is utilised as

$$Q^*(s_t, a_t) = r(s_t, a_t) + \theta \max_{a_{t+1}} Q^*((s_{t+1}, a_{t+1}) | s_t, a_t), \tag{13}$$

where a_{t+1} and s_{t+1} is the source node state and action in the next time slot. In the following, we assume that each source node is an agent and runs the Q-learning code independently. Q-learning algorithm is shown in the figure attached below, where κ is the learning rate. We also introduce an exploration rate e to control the probability of exploring non-optimal actions during the training process, which is different from the greedy strategy. Normally, the learning system will choose the action with the largest value of the value function, but there may be some good actions that have not been performed yet. By setting the size of the exploration rate, we can control the probability that the learning system can explore these good actions.

4 Simulation Results and Discussion

Table 1. Key simulation parameters.

Notations	Description	Value
P_S	transmitted power at the source	5 dBW
$|g_k|$	channel gain	0.3
B	bandwidth	1 MHz
N	number of the sources	1–5
K	number of the relays	5
$R_{PS\,max}$	Maximum communication rate for a single source meeting minimum energy harvesting (PS)	0.5 bits/s
$R_{TS\,max}$	Maximum communication rate for a single source meeting minimum energy harvesting (TS)	0.4 bits/s
κ	learning rate	0.5
θ	Discount factor	0.8

The key simulation metrics can be found in the table above. In addition, to emphasize the issue of source node competition, we have set up a relay node in which the quality of the relay channel is significantly greater than that of the other relays. For a single source node, this relay will inevitably be the one they will contest. If each source node uses a greedy strategy to compete for this relay, it will certainly lead to a waste of relay resources. The simulation shows that after 2000 iterations and updates, individuals with high priority tasks will use the optimal relay, while others will get very little reward for competing with network congestion, which will make them give up the greedy optimal relay and go for the second-best relay. The results are presented in Fig. 3, where we choose the perspective of a particular node to observe the change in its strategy. It is clear that the reward from the greedy strategy decreases as the probability of disruption increases, but that q-learning is able to adjust the strategy and withdraw from the competition after interacting with the environment.

In Fig. 4, we give a comparison of the total communication rate. As the quantity of source nodes rises, so does the number of competing individuals, while the greedy strategy leads to a large increase in congestion. To summary, reinforcement learning has two major advantages over greedy strategies, the first is the ability to interact with the environment in pursuit of greater reward, and the other is the ability to rationally allocate

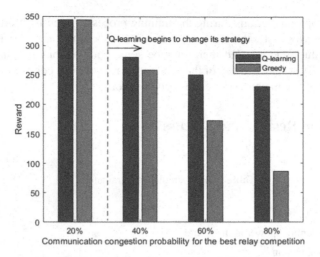

Fig. 3. Single node action and reward observation.

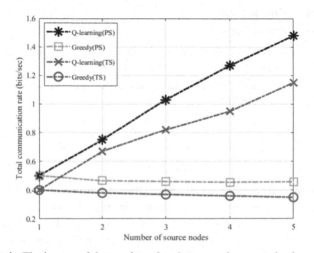

Fig. 4. The impact of the number of nodes on total communication rate.

resources, as in our experiments, after a period of training, the best relay is not only not wasted, but also serves tasks with as high a priority as possible.

5 Conclusion

In order to establish an intelligent relay selection strategy for multiple source nodes in a SWIPT system, a relay selection strategy using q-learning algorithms is proposed, where each source node is an intelligent body capable of selecting the appropriate strategy based on environmental interaction funding. Specifically, maximising the overall communication rate under the TS and PS criteria is used as the goal, and machine learning is used to solve the corresponding problem. A comparative analysis with a greedy strategy is performed, and simulations reveal that the proposed method has significant advantages.

References

1. Sutton, R.S., Barto, A.G.: Reinforcement Learning: An Introduction. MIT Press, Cambridge (1998)
2. Liu, L., Zhang, R., Chua, K.C.: Wireless information transfer with opportunistic energy harvesting. IEEE Trans. Wireless Commun. **12**(1), 288–300 (2013)
3. Huang, K., Larsson, E.: Simultaneous information and power transfer for broadband wireless systems. IEEE Trans. Sig. Process. **61**(23), 5972–5986 (2013)
4. Krikidis, I., Timotheou, S., Nikolaou, S., Zheng, G., Ng, D., Schober, R.: Simultaneous wireless information and power transfer in modern communication systems. IEEE Commun. Mag. **52**(11), 104–110 (2014)
5. Cover, T., Gamal, A.E.: Capacity theorems for the relay channel. IEEE Trans. Inf. Theory **25**(5), 572–584 (1979)
6. Laneman, J.N., Tse, D.N.C., Wornell, G.W.: Cooperative diversity in wireless networks: efficient protocols and outage behavior. IEEE Trans. Inf. Theory **50**(12), 3062–3080 (2004)
7. Gautam, S., Ubaidulla, P.: Relay selection and transceiver design for joint wireless information and energy transfer in cooperative networks. In: IEEE Vehicular Technology Conference (VTC). Sydney, Australia (2017)
8. Wei, J., Schotten, H.D.: A simple cooperative diversity method based on deep-learning-aided relay selection. IEEE Transactions on Vehicular Technology, p. 1 (2021)
9. Busoniu, L., Babuska, R., De Schutter, B.: A comprehensive survey of multiagent reinforcement learning. IEEE Trans. Syst. Man Cybern. Part C (Appl. Rev.) **38**(2), 156–172 (2008)
10. Tan, M.: Multi-agent reinforcement learning: independent vs. cooperative agents. In: Proceedings of the Tenth International Conference on Machine Learning, pp. 330–337. Morgan Kaufmann (1993)

Power Quality Prediction of Active Distribution Network Based on CNN-LSTM Deep Learning Model

Liang Hua[✉] [iD]

Zhejiang Business College, Hangzhou 310023, China

Abstract. Aiming at the sequential and non-linear characteristics of power quality data over a long time span, a set of PQ evaluation and early warning system with DG distribution network based on deep learning is proposed. The intelligent power distribution network power quality monitoring and early warning system aims to realize the monitoring and forecasting and early warning functions of multiple indicators of power quality in the distribution network. First, use the sliding window to convert the power quality data into a number of square graphs with time as the scale; second, use the feature extraction advantages of the (Convolutional Neural Network, CNN) to extract the features of each square graph sample and extract it The characteristic information of is transformed into the input of (Long Short Term Memory, LSTM) in a time series sequence; Finally, according to the output of CNN, LSTM is used to complete the power quality data prediction of the active distribution network. Through an IEEE-13 node active distribution network simulation example with distributed power sources, this method decouples the feature extraction analysis and prediction tasks of power quality data, and simplifies the prediction work. Compared with the selected control model, it is significantly Improve the prediction accuracy.

Keywords: Deep learning · Convolutional neural network (CNN) · Long-term and short-term memory network (LSTM)

1 Introduction

A complete power quality (PQ) information prediction and early warning system is the key to timely discovering power quality problems in distribution networks and improving power quality. Countries around the world are actively seeking to use environmentally friendly and renewable energy sources. Among them, distributed new energy sources represented mainly by wind power and photovoltaic power generation are attracting more and more attention. A distribution network with the ability to combine control of various DGs, energy storage, controllable loads, etc.-Active Distribution Network (ADN) has become one of the most important development models of smart distribution networks in the future [1]. However, due to the wide access of DGs and the flexible operating characteristics of the active distribution network, each node of the active distribution

X. Wang et al. (Eds.): AICON 2021, LNICST 396, pp. 108–122, 2021.
https://doi.org/10.1007/978-3-030-90196-7_11

network will inevitably face severe power quality problems such as voltage fluctuations and flicker, harmonic distortion, and over voltage [2]. The grid connection of a large number of distributed power sources will bring a more severe test to power quality. The realization of high-performance power quality situation prediction, evaluation and early warning is a prerequisite for effective power quality active control.

Regarding the problem of power quality prediction, although experts at home and abroad have carried out active explorations, systematic in-depth research and consensus results have been few. So far, there are relatively few research literatures on power quality prediction. Literature [3] proposed a combined forecasting model based on linear regression method (LR), random time series method (RTA) and gray model (GM), which improved the prediction accuracy of a single method, but improved the weight determination and modeling The difficulty. Literature [4] combined autoregressive moving average (ARIMA) model and BP neural network to predict power quality indicators, using their respective good performance in handling non-stationary series and high-dimensional nonlinear problems, but their time-dependent data time correlation The ignorance of this will significantly reduce the accuracy of medium and long-term forecasts. Literature [5] uses a combination of discrete Fourier decomposition and time series autoregressive (AR) to predict. Because it removes part of the frequency domain components, there is a defect that the prediction results are lacking as a whole. Literature [6] proposed a prediction method based on dynamic time warping (DTW) and MonteCarlo algorithm. This method introduces clustering ideas to effectively improve the prediction performance, but the randomness introduced by the Monte Carlo algorithm will lead to a certain degree of power quality prediction results. Uncertainty. Literature [7] proposed a random forest model (RF) prediction method with better prediction effect by quantifying the relationship between power quality indicators and temperature, energy storage battery status, but because it needs to consider specific lines, equipment parameters and operation Information is only applicable to certain specific occasions. Literature [8] puts forward a power quality prediction method based on improved KPCA and GA-BP neural network by taking environmental factors, load and historical power quality data as input. Although this method has good prediction results, the method used the algorithm tools are complicated, and the prediction accuracy of BP neural network is limited, which is not suitable for high-complexity target prediction. Literature [9] first reconstructed the phase space of the power quality data by using the chaos theory, and then used the particle swarm algorithm to optimize the prediction parameters of the least square support vector machine, so that the prediction model has a faster convergence speed. And higher prediction accuracy, but considering that support vector machines are generally only suitable for small data volume predictions, they have certain limitations in use. The methods proposed in the above documents have their own characteristics, but under the background of the active distribution network with high DG penetration in the future, they face the high-dimensional and non-linear correlation characteristics between the multiple influencing factors of system power quality and the data of various indicators of power quality. How to better achieve the prediction performance of power quality index items in a longer period of time is still very challenging.

In recent years, in order to solve traditional load clustering methods that require manual setting of load characteristic indicators and the inability to consider load timing characteristics, multiple deep learning models such as recurrent neural network (RNN), convolutional neural network (CNN) and deep confidence network (DBN) and other artificial intelligence models have been vigorously developed and applied in the field of power quality forecasting [10], especially the Long Short-Term Memory (LSTM) model in load forecasting and other time series forecasting applications. Get the attention of the industry. Literature [11] proposed a load forecasting method based on the CNN-LSTM hybrid neural network model. First, a convolutional neural network (CNN) is used to extract feature vectors from a continuous feature map constructed by load influencing factors, and then use the previously extracted feature vectors Establish the LSTM model, and finally carry out the corresponding load forecast [12]. LSTM deep learning has unique network characteristics and its powerful memory function. It can not only realize good memory but also deeply mine the time correlation of massive multi-dimensional time series data in a long time span [13, 14]. The time series prediction function is very strong.

This paper proposes a method for predicting steady-state power quality indicators of active distribution networks based on convolutional neural networks (CNN) and LSTM network deep learning models. First, the structure of the CNN-LSTM model is introduced. Secondly, the obtained data set is preprocessed and segmented according to the model requirements, and load and power quality data are selected as the prediction target to establish a load training and test set that meets the deep learning model. Power quality training and test set; then, use the training set and test set obtained by data segmentation to train and test the respective CNN-LSTM models of load and power quality, and optimize the parameters of CNN and LSTM to select training The model with the best effect; then, use the selected optimal model to complete the forecast of the electricity load in the future period; then, according to the environmental variables in the future period and the predicted load, complete the forecast of the power quality in the future period; finally, pass The IEEE-13 node simulation example of an active distribution network with distributed power sources analyzes and verifies the effectiveness and advancement of the proposed method for predicting the steady-state index of active distribution network power quality (Fig. 1).

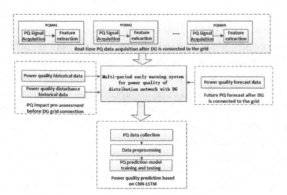

Fig. 1. System framework of PQ prediction based on clustering and LSTM model

2 The Overall Framework of the Hybrid Deep Learning Predictive Model

The system framework of the power quality prediction model of DG active distribution network based on convolutional neural network (CNN) and LSTM deep learning network model, mainly including PQ data set preparation, PQ data preprocessing, CNN-LSTM model training and testing, PQ Data prediction has four functional modules.

The main tasks of each functional module:

1) PQ data set preparation: According to the forecast demand of power quality steady-state index data, arrange environmental variable monitoring devices, load monitors, and load monitors at suitable locations in the active distribution network with three distributed energy sources including photovoltaics, wind power, and fuel cells. Intelligent instruments such as power quality monitors can obtain system light intensity, temperature and other environmental factor data, load data, and corresponding power quality common steady-state indicator data in a long time span, and associate and save them based on the same time mark. As a data source for predictive model training and performance evaluation.

2) PQ data preprocessing; preprocessing and segmenting the acquired data set according to model requirements. And select the load and power quality data as the prediction target to establish the load forecasting training and testing set and the power quality forecasting training and testing set that meet the deep learning model.

3) CNN-LSTM model training and testing: build a CNN-LSTM deep learning network model, use the training set and test set obtained by data segmentation to train and test the respective CNN-LSTM models of load and power quality, and test CNN and LSTM The parameters are tuned to select the model with the best training effect; then, the selected optimal model is used to complete the forecast of electricity load in the future period.

4) PQ data prediction: Obtain the environmental factor forecast data and load forecast data of the target power grid in a certain period in the future, and implement clustering to determine its category; use it as input data, and call the CNN-LSTM network of the corresponding category that has been trained The model makes predictions, and the output of the model is the predicted data of the target grid power quality steady-state index items to be obtained.

3 CNN-LSTM Hybrid Depth Model

3.1 Convolutional Neural Network (CNN) Model

Convolution Neural Network (CNN), as a feedforward neural network, is one of the most popular and widely used models in the field of deep learning in recent years [15–19]. It consists of one or more convolutional layers and pooling layers, as well as associated weights and a fully connected layer at the top. Through the convolutional layer and pooling layer in its structure, CNN can make full use of the two-dimensional characteristics of the original data, and can automatically extract the local features of the original data and make effective representations in the form of a combination of a single convolutional layer and a single pooling layer. At the same time, through the information transfer between each combined layer, CNN can establish a condensed and complete feature vector for the top fully connected layer. Therefore, this paper uses this superior feature of CNN to extract features of the data. For the input, the characteristic information format transfer is shown in Fig. 2. In the figure, N is the abbreviation of Node, and (N, 32, 32) is the node matrix.

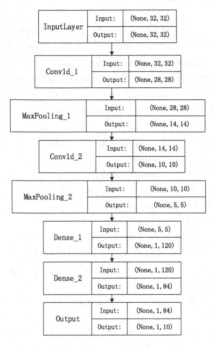

Fig. 2. Convolutional neural network information transfer format

3.2   Long Short-Term Memory (LSTM) Neural Network

LSTM neural network is an improved deep learning algorithm based on time recurrent neural network (RNN). Because of its unique design structure, LSTM is particularly suitable for processing tasks with very long time intervals and delays. As a nonlinear model, LSTM is very suitable for constructing larger deep neural networks.

LSTM has a form structure of a chain of repeated modules of a neural network [20]. Compared with a single neural network layer of (RNN), LSTM has four layers that interact in a very special way. The repeating module chain of LSTM neural network is also called LSTM cell unit, as shown in Fig. 3. In the entire LSTM network structure, the cell state of the LSTM unit is the most critical. They are like a conveyor belt on the production line, which transmits information from the previous cell unit to the next cell unit. The linear correlation with the elements in the current cell unit is low, and the efficiency of information transmission is low. Very high. The LSTM network deletes information or adds information to the unit state through a structure called "gate" [18]. "Gate" is a structure that controls the selective passage of information. It is composed of an output value in the [0, 1] interval to activate the function Sigmoid and pointwise multiplication operations. Each LSTM cell unit contains a forget gate, an input gate, and an output gate. The forget gate is responsible for deciding to keep part of the unit state from the previous moment to the unit state at the current moment; the input gate is responsible for deciding to keep the proportion of the unit state from the current moment input to the current moment; the output gate is responsible for deciding the proportion of the unit state output at the current moment.

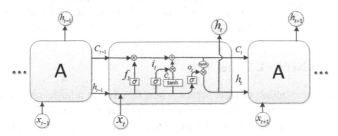

Fig. 3. Structure of LSTM cell

The first step of the LSTM neural network needs to solve the problem of discarding part of the information in the cell state. This function is realized by the forget gate. The forget gate is a Sigmoid function with the output of the previous cell unit and the input of this cell unit as input. It generates a value in [0, 1] for each item in it to control the state of the previous cell unit the degree of being forgotten. In Fig. 3, f_t is the output sequence of the Sigmoid function:

$$f_t = \sigma\left(W_f \cdot \left[h_{t-1}, x_t\right] + b_f\right) \tag{1}$$

Where σ is the Sigmoid activation function, W_f is the weight coefficient matrix, and b_f is the bias term.

The input gate and a hyperbolic tangent function tanh cooperate to update the control information. The activation function creates a new candidate value vector $\tilde{C}_t$, and the input gate $\tilde{C}_t$ generates a value in [0, 1] for each item, determines how much new information is added, and updates the state of the unit:

$$i_t = \sigma\left(W_i \cdot \left[h_{t-1}, x_t\right] + b_i\right) \tag{2}$$

$$C_t = f_t \cdot C_{t-1} + i_t \cdot \tilde{C}_t \tag{3}$$

$$\tilde{C}_t = \tanh\left(W_c \cdot \left[h_{t-1}, x_t\right] + b_c\right) \tag{4}$$

The output gate is used to determine the last part of the information output. First, the Sigmoid activation function is used to determine which part of the cell state will be output to the next unit, and then we process the cell state through the tanh function to generate a value in [0, 1] for each item, and compare it with the Sigmoid function The output results are multiplied, and finally, the degree to which the control unit status is filtered:

$$o_t = \sigma\left(W_o \cdot \left[h_{t-1}, x_t\right] + b_o\right) \tag{5}$$

$$h_t = o_t \cdot \tanh(C_t) \tag{6}$$

Where i_t, $\tilde{C}_t$, o_t and f_t have the same form, but their respective weight coefficient matrices $\{W_i, W_c, W_o\}$ and bias terms $\{b_i, b_c, b_o\}$ are completely different from each other; Sigmoid and functions are used to "compress" the input continuous real value to where is a certain range between [0, 1] and [−1, 1].

3.3 CNN-LSTM Network Model

For the regression prediction of time series, when faced with a large-scale data set with multiple features, it is often difficult for a simple LSTM model to achieve high-precision prediction results. The main reason is that its temporal structural characteristics make it difficult to extract Go to the global feature information. However, for CNN, one of its characteristics is that it can extract the local features of the input data and generate high-level features through layer-by-layer combination abstraction. This feature completes the high-level mapping of the global features of the input data and solves the feature extraction of the LSTM model. Of inadequacy. Therefore, through the combination of CNN and LSTM network models, adding the CNN feature extraction layer before the LSTM model, on the one hand, it can decouple the two tasks of feature extraction and time series prediction that a separate LSTM model needs to do. First, use CNN for data set The feature extraction and flattening the extracted feature information as the input of the LSTM model, and then use LSTM to complete the time series prediction. On the other hand, it can also reduce the complexity of the single LSTM model and effectively improve the prediction accuracy of the model. For complex data The regression prediction of the set is of great significance. The CNN-LSTM network model is shown in Fig. 4.

In order to evaluate the prediction performance of the model, select the Mean Square Error (MSE), Root Mean Square Error (RMSE), and Mean Absolute Percentage Error (Mean Absolute Percentage Error) in the evaluation indicators of the regression prediction algorithm. MAPE) is used as an evaluation index item. For the MAPE index, if there is 0 item in the true value of the data, then the index is no longer suitable as an evaluation item.

The calculation formula of each index is as (7)–(9):

$$\varepsilon_{MAE} = \frac{1}{n} \sum_{i=1}^{n} \left|y_i - \hat{y}_i\right| \tag{7}$$

$$\varepsilon_{RMSE} = \sqrt{\frac{1}{n} \sum_{i=1}^{n} \left[y_i - \hat{y}_i\right]^2} \tag{8}$$

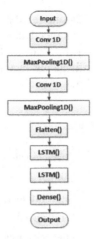

Fig. 4. CNN-LSTM network model structure

$$\varepsilon_{MAPE} = \frac{1}{n} \sum_{i=1}^{n} \left| \frac{y_i - \hat{y}_i}{y_i} \right| \times 100\% \tag{9}$$

In the formula: y_i and $\hat{y}_i$ are the true value and predicted value of the time data respectively; n are the total number of predictions.

4   Power Quality Prediction Model Based on CNN-LSTM

4.1   PQ Influencing Factors and Data Set Construction

For the Active Distribution Network (ADN), it often contains a variety of distributed power (DG), including wind power (WP), photovoltaic power (Photovoltaic power, PV), fuel cell (FC), biomass power (Biomass power, BP), etc., among which wind power, photovoltaic power and fuel cells are the most commonly used. For DG, the principle is nothing more than converting a certain form of energy into electrical energy through corresponding devices. Common methods include wind energy to electrical energy, light energy to electrical energy, and biochemical energy to electrical energy. Therefore, environmental factors affect DG. Working status is very important. When the DG is connected to the ADN, the working status of each DG is closely integrated with the working status of the active distribution network. When external environmental factors affect the work of the DG, it will also indirectly affect the ADN. The power quality of the ADN is bound to be Will be affected, so environmental factors are one of the influencing factors of ADN power quality. In the active distribution network, in addition to a large number of DGs, a large number of different types of electrical loads will definitely be connected. These loads play the role of power consumption in the ADN. Therefore, when the load fluctuates, its fluctuations It will also become one of the influencing factors of ADN power quality changes. At the same time, in addition to the above two ADN power quality influencing factors, by adding appropriate prior knowledge in the training of the neural network model, that is, predicting the data at the current time of the target, using single-step or multi-step historical target data as Entering one of the characteristic variables can effectively improve the performance of the model. Therefore, the ADN power quality data itself is also an influencing factor of ADN power quality changes [14]. The influencing factors of ADN power quality changes are shown in Table 1.

Table 1. Summary of factors affecting power quality.

Influencing factors	Characteristic variable	Unit
Envirnmental factor	**Temperature**	/°C
Envirnmental factor	**Light intensity**	W/m
Envirnmental factor	**Wind speed**	m/s
The fuel cell	**Fuel cell capacity**	/AH
Load factor	**Load type curve**	/W
Historical data	*Voltage deviation*	/
Historical data	*Frequency deviation*	/
Historical data	*Voltage three-phase unbalance*	/

According to the influencing factors of power quality, the input of deep learning model training can be constructed, in the form of a two-dimensional vector containing multiple features, the ordinate represents the feature vector, and the abscissa represents the time span of this input.

Thereafter, in order to evaluate the power quality prediction performance of the obtained LSTM model, a considerable amount of specific historical data is also required for testing and evaluation. Therefore, after selecting the historical data set used to determine the power quality LSTM prediction model, it needs to be data segmented. Based on general principles, this article divides the used power quality historical data set into training set and test set in chronological order, and their magnitudes account for about 70% and 30% of the total historical data set, respectively. In this way, it can not only ensure that the LSTM prediction model can fully learn the relevance and regularity of the input variables and output index items in the historical data set, but also can fully guarantee the effectiveness of the obtained prediction model performance evaluation.

4.2 Data Preprocessing

1) Abnormal data processing

There are many factors influencing power quality prediction. In the process of acquiring and counting power quality data, load data and environmental data, there will be abnormal data due to model operation errors and negligence. Their existence will affect the training model to a certain extent. Accuracy, so you need to exclude them. There are 4 common outlier processing methods, which are to delete the records containing outliers; to treat the abnormal values as missing values and hand them over to the missing value processing methods; use the average value to correct them; not to process them. The above several methods can be selected and used according to the actual situation to improve the data set.

2) Data standardization

Considering that each characteristic variable that affects power quality has different dimensions, and each characteristic variable has a large numerical span within each dimension, in addition, analyze the input and output range of the nonlinear activation function in the cell unit in the LSTM deep learning model, In order to prevent the neurons in the LSTM model from falling into a saturated state, and to ensure that all variables can equally affect the change prediction of power quality, it is necessary to standardize all variables and power quality indicators.

Characteristic variables such as temperature, light, wind speed, electricity load, fuel cell capacity, historical power quality, etc. are all standardized, and they are linearly converted to [0, 1] using formula (10). Correspondingly, the predicted data of the power quality index items obtained by the LSTM model are also standardized data. In order to obtain the power quality data with actual physical significance, it needs to be de-standardized using formula (11):

$$x' = \frac{x - x_{min}}{x_{max} - x_{min}} \tag{10}$$

$$x = x' * (x_{max} - x_{min}) + x_{min} \tag{11}$$

In the formula, x, x' respectively represent the value of the variable or index item before and after normalization; x_{max}, x_{min} select the maximum and minimum limits of each variable or index item in the historical data set.

3) Data set segmentation

For a given data set, in order to obtain a CNN-LSTM deep learning model that can realize the power quality prediction function, it is first necessary to determine the input object and output target according to the data set to form a supervised learning sequence, and secondly, a large amount of specific input variable historical data and Output power quality target historical data for supervised learning training to obtain the internal parameters of the CNN-LSTM network model. Finally, in order to evaluate the power quality prediction performance of the obtained CNN-LSTM model, a proper amount of specific historical data is required for testing and evaluation. Therefore, based on general principles, the data set containing characteristic variables and power quality target data is divided into training set and test set in chronological order, and their magnitudes account for approximately 70% and 30% of the total data set, respectively. In this way, it can not only ensure that the CNN-LSTM prediction model can fully learn the relevance and regularity of each input variable and output target item in the historical data set, but also can fully guarantee the effectiveness of the obtained prediction model performance.

4) Set the input step size of the training and test sets

As the feature extraction part of the CNN-LSTM model, CNN has one of the advantages of its application in that it can directly extract feature information from the numerical matrix. Therefore, after the data is divided, it is necessary to specify the step size n_steps (single step corresponding to a time point) of the single input data when training and testing the model, and then form the input matrix. In addition, the selection of n_steps can refer to the value of the feature variable. In general, its value should be selected as the number of feature variables to form a square matrix with the same rows and columns to facilitate subsequent CNN feature extraction.

4.3 Power Quality Prediction Based on CNN-LSTM

After the data is preprocessed, the power quality prediction model based on CNN-LSTM can be trained and tested according to historical power quality data and power quality influencing factor data. Then, by using the load forecast in the future period completed in 3.4, the complete power quality influencing factor data in the future period can be obtained, and finally the power quality forecast data in the future period can be obtained according to the input of the influencing factors.

5   Power Quality Prediction Results and Comparative Analysis

In order to verify the superiority of the CNN-LSTM prediction model proposed in this article, the typical methods of time series prediction are selected as references, mainly including differential autoregressive movement translation (ARIMA) model, BP neural network, CNN and LSTM.

For the prediction of power quality in the future, use CNN-LSTM to model the PQ training set and use the test set for testing, and select Voltage Deviation (VD) as a case. The test results are shown in Table 2. At the same time, using the predicted load of the next two days to predict the power quality of the next two days, and compare with the reference model, the results are as follows (Fig. 5).

Table 2. Comparison of MAE, RMSE, MAPE prediction results of each model.

VD	ARIMA	BP	CNN	LSTM	CNN-LSTM
MAE	2.08	0.92	0.53	0.53	0.38
RMSE	2.91	1.60	0.67	0.89	0.50
MAPE	187.1%	27.4%	10.4%	10.5%	7.6%

Through the observation and analysis of Table 2, Fig. 7, and Fig. 8, we can know that in terms of MAE and RMSE indicators, BP, ARIMA, LSTM, CNN, and CNN-LSTM are in a decreasing state, and the CNN-LSTM model corresponds to the smallest value. It shows that the actual situation of the error between the predicted value and the actual value of the CNN-LSTM model on the test set is the best. It also shows that the deviation between the predicted value and the actual value on the test set is the smallest, and the model prediction is the most stable; just MAPE In terms of indicators, ARIMA, BP, LSTM, CNN, and CNN-LSTM are in a decreasing state. The minimum MAPE index of

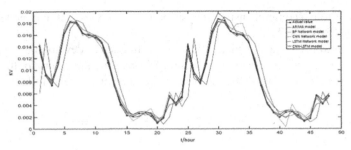

Fig. 5. Comparison of VD prediction curves and actual curves of each model in the next two days

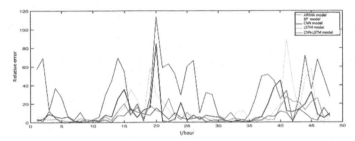

Fig. 6. Comparison of relative errors of VD prediction results of each model in the next two days

the CNN-LSTM model is only 1.8%, which is the closest to 0, indicating the predicted value of the CNN-LSTM model on the test set. The relative error with the actual value is the smallest, and the model's prediction accuracy is the highest; for the load forecast in the next two days, the CNN-LSTM model has the smallest forecast fluctuation, and the relative error is kept within 6%, which fits the actual value as a whole; CNN, LSTM model The overall volatility is good, but the LSTM model fluctuates too much at individual points; BP performs the worst, with nearly half of the points exceeding 4%. Although the performance of ARIMA is much better than BP, the prediction effect is still poor. The main reason for the above situation is that the BP neural network uses the fully connected layer as the hidden layer, and the feature extraction ability under multivariate is weak, and it does not have the ability to learn sequence dependence on a long time span. Therefore, the data forecast for future periods will fluctuate greatly.; The ARIMA model is complicated in order and is not suitable for large-volume data prediction. In essence, it can only capture linear relationships. In addition, it uses time as the only variable to target prediction, so that its predictive indicators MAE and RMSE are better, but it does not have time. The learning ability of the sequence dependence relationship fluctuates greatly at some prediction points, and the index MAPE is correspondingly large; the CNN model has a better feature extraction ability, but it is difficult to learn the dependence relationship of the target sequence over a long time span; LSTM model It can well memorize the dependence of the target sequence in a long time span, but for multi-feature variable data sets, the feature extraction ability is poor; the CNN-LSTM model makes full use of the advantages of the CNN and LSTM models. For multiple features, generally It can give full play to its advantages and has the best prediction performance. From a comprehensive analysis point of view, the optimal model for load forecasting is CNN-LSTM.

In addition to the voltage deviation indicators, frequency deviation and harmonics are selected as the prediction objects. The comparison of the indicators for the next two days and the results of the prediction curve and the time curve are as follows (Fig. 8).

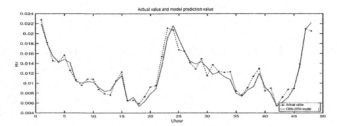

Fig. 7. Comparison of frequency deviation prediction curve and actual curve of CNN-LSTM model in the next two days

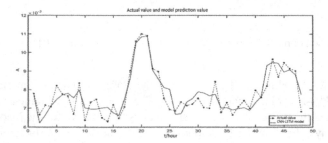

Fig. 8. Comparison of harmonic prediction curves and actual curves of CNN-LSTM model in the next two days

For the two indicators of frequency deviation and harmonics, analyze the prediction of the two steady-state indicators. From above figures, it can be seen that the MAPE indicator of the CNN-LSTM prediction model is similar to that of the voltage deviation prediction, and the predicted value is According to the actual value change curve, the CNN-LSTM model has performed a good fit to the power quality indicators. Overall, the CNN-LSTM deep learning model is the best choice for power quality prediction in active distribution networks.

6 Conclusion

In response to the increasing demand for power quality situational awareness in future DG-containing active distribution networks and considering the limitations of traditional prediction algorithms, this paper proposes a power quality prediction method based on the CNN-LSTM deep learning model. This method takes advantage of the two deep learning models of convolutional neural network and long-short-term memory network.

It not only solves the problem of difficult extraction of massive and complex power quality data features, but also solves the lack of correlation information for time series in traditional forecasting algorithms. Considerations. Finally, the comparison of calculation examples shows that the prediction model of the early warning system has good accuracy and is suitable for the power quality data prediction of today's active distribution network with DG.

In subsequent work, it is necessary to use more effective algorithm tools to further improve the data cleaning and processing tasks, and at the same time add more factors to the power quality influencing factors, such as seasonal changes, holidays, and emergencies, so as to further improve the performance. Improve the universality and accuracy of prediction models.

References

1. Gao, Y., Zhang, W., Gao, S., et al.: Intelligent power distribution network status monitoring technology based on big data. Commun. Power Technol. **36**(5), 259–260 (2019)
2. Mo, Y., Zhang, Y.: Optimal selection of power utilization reliability improvement objects for intelligent distribution network based on variable weight gray correlation. Power Syst. Prot. Contr. **47**(5), 26–34 (2019)
3. Ding, Z., Liu, P., Sen, O., Zeng, J., Huang, R.: Power quality prediction and early warning mechanism and its application. J. Electr. Power Syst. Autom. **27**(10), 87–92 (2015)
4. Su, W., Ma, S., Qi, L.: Power quality steady-state index prediction based on ARIMA and neural network. Comput. Technol. Develop. **24**(03), 163–167 (2014)
5. Cui, X., Ma, Z., Xu, Z., Wen, C.: AR prediction method of power quality unbalance index based on discrete Fourier decomposition. Modern Electr. Power **30**(06), 38–42 (2013)
6. Bai, J., Gu, W., Yuan, X., Li, Q., Xue, F., Wang, X.: Power quality prediction, early warning, and control for points of common coupling with wind farms. Energies **8**(9), 1–18 (2015)
7. Vantuch, T., Mišák, S., Ježowicz, T., Buriánek, T., Snášel, V.: The power quality forecasting model for off-grid system supported by multiobjective optimization. IEEE Trans. Ind. Electron. **64**(12), 9507–9516 (2017)
8. Weng, G., Huang, F., Tang, Y., Yan, J., Nan, Y., He, H.: Fault-tolerant location of transient voltage disturbance source for DG integrated smart grid. Electr. Power Syst. Res. **144**, 13–22 (2017)
9. Martins, V.F., Borges, C.L.T.: Active distribution network integrated planning incorporating distributed generation and load response uncertainties. IEEE Trans. Power Syst. **26**(4), 2164–2172 (2011)
10. Liu, J., Liu, Y., Feng, C., Li, J., Zhang, Y.: Research on steady-state power quality early warning threshold based on k-center point clustering. Electr. Meas. Instr. **55**(23), 41–45 (2018)
11. Bian, Y., Zhao, Q., Hu, S., Xu, H., Cao, L., Zhou, N.: Research and application of smart distribution network power quality monitoring and early warning based on cloud platform. Huadian Technol. **43**(01), 31–37 (2021)
12. Lu, J., Sun, Y., Xie, X., Zheng, L., Xu, B., Wu, Y.: Research on power quality early warning based on improved combined forecasting. New Technol. Electr. Eng. Energy **39**(09), 65–73 (2020)
13. Bedi, J., Toshniwal, D.: Empirical mode decomposition based deep learning for electricity demand forecasting. IEEE Access **6**, 49144–49156 (2018)
14. Liu, Y., Dong, S., Lu, M., Wang, J.: LSTM based reserve prediction for bank outlets. Tsinghua Sci. Technol. **24**(01), 77–85 (2019)

15. Fang, C.: The simulation and analysis of quantum radar cross section for three-dimensional convex targets. IEEE Photonics J. **10**(1), 1–8 (2018)
16. Fang, C., et al.: The calculation and analysis of the bistatic quantum radar cross section for the typical 2-D plate. IEEE Photonics J. **10**(2), 1–14 (2018)
17. Fang, C.: The analysis of mainlobe-slumping quantum effect of the cube in the scattering characteristics of quantum radar. IEEE Access **7**, 141055–141061 (2019)
18. Fang, C.: The closed-form expressions for the bistatic quantum radar cross section of the typical simple plates. IEEE Sens. J. **20**(5), 2348–2355 (2020)
19. Fang, C.: Multistep cylindrical structure analysis at normal incidence based on water-substrate broadband metamaterial absorbers. Z. Naturforsch A. **0**(0), 4–6 (2018)
20. Tomas, V., Stanislav, M., Tomas, J., et al.: The power quality forecasting model for off-grid system supported by multi-objective optimization. IEEE Trans. Ind. Electr. **64**(12), 9507–9516 (2017)

Artificial Intelligence in Wireless Communications and Satellite Communications

System Simulation and Coverage Analysis of 5G NR Communication System Based on 700 MHz Frequency Band

Zhongqiu Xiang[1]([✉]), Xuemin Huang[1], Pei Zhao[1], Xiaohui Zhang[2], Shumin Jiang[1], Tiankui Zhang[3], Li Peng[4], Ruibiao Niu[5], Yunjing Wang[1], Yiming Yu[1], Bowei Pu[6], and Fan Chen[1]

[1] China Mobile Group Design Institute Co., Ltd., A16, DanLing Street, HaiDian District, Beijing, China
xiangzhongqiu@cmdi.chinamobile.com

[2] Air China Co., Ltd., No. 30, Tianzhu Road, Tianzhu Airport Economic Development Zone, Beijing, China

[3] Beijing University of Posts and Telecommunications, A10, XiTuCheng Road, HaiDian District, Beijing, China

[4] China Mobile Group Design Institute Co., Ltd., Guangdong Branch, TianHe District, Guangzhou, China

[5] China Mobile Group Design Institute Co., Ltd., Neimenggu Branch, Mengnailun Square, Huhehaote, China

[6] China Mobile Group Design Institute Co., Ltd., Hebei Branch, Chang'an District, Shijiazhuang, China

Abstract. 700 MHz is the golden frequency band recognized by the global communications industry and the main frequency band of 5G for global operators. Currently, countries around the world are seizing 5G opportunities and deploying networks on a large scale. Due to the characteristics of low 700 MHz spectrum, wide coverage, and low cost of network construction, it will play an important role in the construction of 5G networks. As a refined network planning and forecasting method, the ray tracing transfer model has been provided by foreign manufacturers for a long time, such as Aster in France and WinProp in Germany. This paper proposes a ray tracing propagation model LiShuttle based on stereo space search, and applies it to the system simulation in the 700 MHz frequency band. Compared with other ray tracing models, LiShuttle can complete direct, reflected, and diffracted path searches by emitting full-dimensional and omni-directional rays, and has the characteristics of flexible configuration and accurate simulation. Based on the LiShuttle ray tracing propagation model, this paper has carried out 700 MHz link budget, outdoor remote simulation, area coverage simulation and building stereo simulation, and comprehensively analyzes its coverage capability, which is full of reference value and guiding significance for the planning and optimization of 5G NR network.

Keywords: 700 MHz · Ray tracing · LiShuttle · System simulation · Coverage analysis

X. Wang et al. (Eds.): AICON 2021, LNICST 396, pp. 125–137, 2021.
https://doi.org/10.1007/978-3-030-90196-7_12

1 Introduction

700 MHz is not only considered to be the golden frequency band of 5G, but this frequency band has always been called the "digital dividend" in the wireless communication system. Due to its low frequency spectrum, long coverage, and strong deep coverage, this frequency band is suitable for large-area network coverage and has the lowest networking cost. On March 19, 2020, at the 87th access network plenary meeting of 3GPP, the China Radio and Television 700 MHz frequency band 2 * 30/40 MHz technical proposal was adopted and included in the 5G international standard, becoming the world's first 5G low frequency band (Sub-1 GHz) The large bandwidth 5G international standard, numbered TR38.888, NR format is n28. With the release of the 700 MHz "digital dividend", countries around the world are seizing the opportunity of 5G construction, and the global 700 MHz frequency band industry chain is developing rapidly.

The Ministry of Industry and Information Technology of China has issued the "Notice of the Ministry of Industry and Information Technology on Adjusting the Plan for the Use of the 700 MHz Frequency Band" on April 1, 2020, and made adjustments to the plan for the use of the 700 MHz frequency band, clearly changing the frequency of the 702–798 MHz band. Use planning adjustment for mobile communication systems, and use 703–743/758–798 MHz frequency band planning for frequency division. On January 26, 2021, China Mobile and China Radio and Television signed a "5G Strategy" cooperation agreement in Beijing, officially launching the joint construction and sharing of 700 MHz 5G networks.

Domestic and foreign experts have also conducted related research on the 700 MHz frequency band and 5G NR system. In this paper, the related research on 700 MHz is carried out. The literature mainly introduces the necessity of cooperation between 700 MHz and 2.6 GHz [1]. In addition, the literature mainly elaborated the 700 MHz network technical architecture from three aspects of the wireless access network, bearer network and core network, and analyzed the advantages and disadvantages of the 700 MHz frequency band [2]. There is also a paper that analyze the application of different propagation models in different scenarios, such as the close-in (CI) free space reference distance model, the floating intercept model (FI), and the alpha-beta-gamma (ABG) model [3].

Based on the LiShuttle ray tracing propagation model, this paper conducts system simulation and coverage analysis of 700 MHz. Through simulation and analysis, it can guide the planning, construction, maintenance and optimization of 5G NR in the 700 MHz frequency band. In addition, a performance comparison was made with the lower 2.6 GHz of the 5G NR mid-band.

2 The System Simulation and Frequency Analysis of 700 MHz

2.1 5G System Simulation Based on LiShuttle Ray Tracing Model

Network Simulation and Propagation Model
The purpose of wireless network system simulation is to evaluate wireless network coverage and capacity indicators through simulation calculations to achieve the purpose of simulating actual network characteristics. Then, the rationality of network construction can be analyzed based on the simulation results. At the same time, it provides references

for site deployment location, broadcast weight optimization, RF parameter optimization, etc. It is an important means of network evaluation and prediction. The general flow of the simulation is shown in Fig. 1.

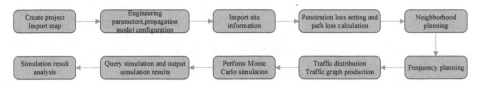

Fig. 1. Wireless network simulation flow chart

In the above process, the setting of the propagation model is the most important link, which has the greatest impact on the simulation results. The propagation model needs to calculate the propagation loss of radio waves under a certain environment or propagation path. In terms of research methods, the communication models currently used are mainly divided into two categories: one is a statistical model based on a large amount of test data, also called an empirical model. The common ones are Okumura-Hata, Cost231-Hata, Lee, Spm, Uma, etc. The other type is a deterministic model calculated based on electromagnetic theory. The most representative one is the three-dimensional ray tracing model. The common ray tracing models in the industry mainly include Aster in France, Volcano in France, and WinProp in Germany [4].

LiShuttle Ray Tracing Model

This paper proposes a new three-dimensional ray tracing propagation model LiShuttle, which is based on geometric optics principles and three-dimensional space search, which can accurately simulate the direct, reflection, diffraction, and transmission phenomena of electromagnetic waves in space propagation. It is a refined propagation prediction model that can accurately reflect the coverage of wireless signals on the existing network. The realization of the LiShuttle ray tracing model is mainly divided into two major steps: path search and loss calculation.

In the path search, the macro cell, micro cell, and mini cell must be judged first. Then, determine the type of multipath that needs to be calculated according to the cell type. The main types of multipath calculated by this ray tracing model are: direct radiation, horizontal reflection, roof diffraction, horizontal plane diffraction and transmission. The flowchart of LiShuttle path search is shown in Fig. 2, then Tx is used here to refer to transmitter.

After completing the path search in the calculation area, it is necessary to calculate the path type of each grid in the area to calculate the path loss. This model takes into account all factors such as base station parameters, terminal parameters, ground features, and multipath loss when calculating. The specific calculation formulas are formula 1 and formula 2:

$$PL = K_0 + K_{near} \log(d_{3d}) + 20 \log(f_c) + \Delta K_{farf}(d_{2d}) + \partial_{\text{ref}} PL_{ref} + \partial_{dif} PL_{dif} \quad (1)$$

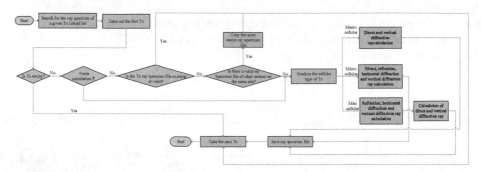

Fig. 2. The flow chart of LiShuttle's path search

In formula 1,

$$f(d_{2d}) = \begin{cases} 0 & d_{2d} <= d'_{bp} \\ \log \dfrac{d_{3d}}{\sqrt{d'_{bp}+(h_{bs}-h_{ut})^2}} & d_{2d} > d'_{bp} \end{cases} \qquad (2)$$

In the formula, K_0 is the fading constant, K_{near} is the coefficient of the near field, K_{far} is the coefficient of the far field, ∂_{dif} is the coefficient of diffraction, ∂_{ref} is the coefficient of reflection.

After the path loss is calculated, the signal level value at the receiving point is obtained by the following formula, which is calculated according to formula 3:

$$P_r = P_t + G - PL - L_{body} - SFM - FFM - OTA \qquad (3)$$

In formula 3, P_r is the received signal level value, P_t is the transmitted signal level value, G is the antenna gain, PL is the path loss, L_{body} is the human body loss, SFM is the shadow fading margin, FFM is the fast fading margin, OTA is the Over-the-Air loss.

2.2 Analysis of 700 MHz Frequency Characteristics

Analysis of Electromagnetic Wave Propagation Loss in Free Space

The propagation of electromagnetic waves in free space can be derived from the Friisian transmission equation [5]. The Friesian transmission equation is:

$$P_r = \frac{P_t G_t G_r \lambda^2}{(4\pi)^2 d^2} \qquad (4)$$

In formula 4, P_r is the received power, P_t is the transmit power, G_t and G_r represents the transmit antenna gain and the receive antenna gain, λ s the carrier wavelength, d is the distance between the transmitting and receiving antennas.

From the above formula, it can be concluded that the propagation loss of electromagnetic waves in free space is:

$$PathLoss = 10\log(\frac{P_t}{P_r}) = 10\log(\frac{4\pi d}{\lambda})^2$$
$$= 32.45 + 20\lg f + 20\lg d \qquad (5)$$

In formula 5, *PathLoss* is the free space propagation loss, f is the operating frequency of electromagnetic waves.

It can be seen from formula 1.5 that the lower the frequency of the 700 MHz electromagnetic wave signal is, the smaller the space loss will be.

Analysis of Wavelength and Diffraction Ability
The formula between wavelength and frequency:

$$\lambda = \frac{c}{f} \tag{6}$$

c: Speed of light, unit: m/s, the speed of light is a constant, approximately equal to 3×10^8 m/s in vacuum.
f: Frequency, unit: Hz.
λ: wavelength, unit: m.

According to the relationship between the wavelength and frequency of electro-magnetic waves, the wavelength λ is inversely proportional to the frequency f. If the frequency is lower, the wavelength is longer, the diffraction ability is stronger, and the coverage area is wider. Compared with other 5G frequency bands such as 2.6 GHz, 3.5 GHz, 4.9 GHz, the 700 MHz frequency band has a huge wavelength advantage and a wider coverage. Under the goal of achieving full wireless communication network coverage, fewer base stations are required to use this frequency band, which can greatly reduce network construction and operating costs.

Analysis of the Doppler Effect
Mobile communication customers will suffer from the inconvenience caused by the phenomenon of "Doppler frequency offset" under high-speed operating environment. This effect will cause a serious deviation of the frequency received by the terminal, which will affect the demodulation performance of the receiver [6].

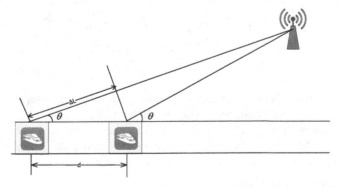

Fig. 3. Schematic diagram of Doppler frequency offset in the high-speed rail scenario

Analyze the Doppler frequency deviation according to the high-speed rail Doppler diagram in Fig. 3. Assuming that the speed of the high-speed rail is v, the angle between the train and the signal transmission direction is θ, and after a certain period of time Δt, the train's running distance is d, then the distance difference between the signals received by the user can be calculated as ΔL is:

$$\Delta L = d\cos\theta = v \cdot \Delta t\cos\theta \tag{7}$$

Then the phase change of the received signal is:

$$\Delta\varphi = \frac{2\pi\,\Delta L}{\lambda} = \frac{2\pi v\Delta t}{\lambda}\cos\theta \tag{8}$$

From the above analysis, it can be concluded that the Doppler frequency shift is:

$$f_d = \frac{1}{2\pi} \cdot \frac{\Delta\varphi}{\Delta t} = \frac{v}{\lambda} \cdot \cos\theta = \frac{f}{c} \cdot v \cdot \cos\theta \tag{9}$$

In formula 9, c is the speed of light, and the value is 3×10^8 m/s. It can be seen from the formula that the faster the speed and the higher the frequency, the greater the Doppler frequency deviation. According to the calculation, the relationship between the speed of the high-speed rail and the frequency bands of the 5G network can be obtained, as shown in Table 1.

Table 1. The influence of train speed and frequency on Doppler frequency deviation

Speed (km/h)	700M Frequency deviation (Hz)	1.8G Frequency deviation (Hz)	2.6G Frequency deviation (Hz)	3.5G Frequency deviation (Hz)
200	259	667	963	1296
250	324	833	1204	1620
300	389	1000	1444	1944
350	454	1167	1685	2268
400	518	1333	1926	2592
450	583	1500	2166	2916
500	648	1666	2407	3240

It can be seen from Table 1 that under the same frequency, the faster the train speed is, the greater the Doppler frequency deviation will be; if the train speed is the same, the higher the frequency is, the greater the Doppler frequency deviation will be. Therefore, choosing the 700 MHz frequency band can effectively reduce the Doppler frequency offset when deploying base stations in high-speed rail scenarios.

Small Delay in FDD Duplex Mode
In 5G, the duplex mode includes two modes: FDD and TDD. FDD receives and transmits on two separate symmetric frequency channels, and uses guard bands to separate the receive and transmit channels; TDD, time division duplex, uses time to Separate the

receive and transmit channels. It is carried out in one channel [4]. In a TDD mobile communication system, different time slots of the same frequency carrier are used for reception and transmission as channel bearers, and time resources are allocated in two directions. In TDD mode, some uplink data feedback needs to wait for the corresponding uplink time slot. Generally, the TDD system allocates fewer time slots to the uplink, so the feedback waiting time of TDD is longer than FDD.

The 700 MHz frequency band adopts the FDD standard, while other 5G frequency bands such as 2.6G, 3.5G and 4.9G all adopt the TDD standard. When only the air interface delay is considered, the air interface delay of the 700 MHz frequency band is theoretically less than Other 5G frequency bands.

3   Analysis of 700 MHz Simulation Coverage

3.1   Simulation Parameter Configuration

Introduction to the Simulation Area
The selected area for this simulation is the Zhujiang New Town area of Guangzhou, which is a super dense scene with an area of 6.12 Km^2. The distribution of wireless base stations in the Zhujiang New City area: 242 cells with a total of 99 base stations of 2.6 GHz; 68 cells with a total of 27 base stations of 700 MHz.

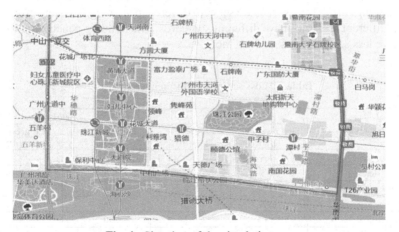

Fig. 4. Situation of the simulation area

Simulation Parameters
The map used in this simulation is a planet electronic map with the precision of 5 m. The propagation model is the LiShuttle ray tracing model. In the simulation, the constant K_0 is set to 28, the near field coefficient K_{near} is set to 22, the far field coefficient K_{far} is set to 40, and the maximum number of reflections is 4. The maximum diffraction order is 2. The parameters of this system simulation are shown in Table 2.

Table 2. Parameter setting of LiShuttle propagation model

NR parameters	2.6G	700M	Impact index	Parameter Description
Propagation model	LiShuttle Ray tracing model		Indicators of each dimension	Propagation model accuracy affects simulation accuracy
map	5m precision three-dimensional electronic map		Indicators of each dimension	Electronic map affects simulation accuracy
bandwidth （MHz）	100	30	rate	Cell bandwidth
Subcarrier spacing (kHz)	30	15	rate	Subcarrier spacing
Uplink and downlink timeslot ratio	2:8	/	rate	Uplink and downlink frame ratio
Maximum number of reflections	4	4	RSRP	Maximum number of reflections for ray search
Maximum diffraction order	2	2	RSRP	Maximum diffraction number of ray search
Base station antenna transceiver number	64trx	4T4R	rate	Number of transmitting and receiving antennas on the base station side
Terminal transmit power （dBm）	16.85	20.9	RSRP、 rate	Maximum transmit power of terminal
Number of terminal antennas	2T4R	1T2R	rate	Number of terminal transmitting and receiving antennas

In order to improve the accuracy of the simulation, when building-level simulation is performed, the buildings are divided into eight typical scenes. Based on on-site measurements, buildings in different scenes are set with different penetration loss and progressive loss, and different scenarios have different standards. The building penetration loss and progressive loss settings are shown in Table 3.

Table 3. Loss settings in different scenarios.

Scenes	2.6G		700M	
	First layer loss （dB）	Progressive loss(dB)	First layer loss （dB）	Progressive loss(dB)
Hospital	11.5	1.2	6	1
Hotel	10.5	1.5	6	1
Office building	11.5	1.8	6	1.2
Residential area	13.5	1.5	6	1
School	13	1.2	6	1
Shopping mall	13.5	1.5	6	1.2
Transportation hub	20	1.8	12	1.2
Large venue	20	1.8	12	1.2

3.2   Analysis of Simulation Results

Link Budget Simulation
Ten co-located cells in Zhujiang New Town are selected randomly, and the link budgets of 2.6 GHz and 700 MHz are compared and analyzed under the same conditions of transmission power, antenna and propagation model.

The results are shown in Table 4:

Table 4. Link budget results

The name of the base station cell	2.6GHz	700MHz	Difference between two means
Zhumeila Apartments	154.1267	139.7513	14.37535
Northwest of New Axis Plaza	143.5671	129.2682	14.29886
Pearl River Dijing Apartment_1	136.3937	123.1116	13.28211
Feiyu Hotel	143.9388	129.9341	14.00461
Yuancun South Street	150.0634	135.6127	14.45062
Cuihu Villa (Relocation)_1	143.5218	128.0173	15.50449
Pearl River Dijing Apartment_2	121.4908	108.7548	12.73604
Yuexiu CPPCC (relocation)	114.8379	100.7843	14.05365
Cuihu Villa (Relocation)_2	137.1835	121.7174	15.46604
South Gate of the Zoo	133.5832	118.1363	15.44695

By comparing the link calculation results of 2.6 GHz band and 700 MHz band, in the single residential area, the coverage gain of 700 MHz band is 14–15 db relative to 2.6 GHz band. At the same time, four residential areas in Table 5 are selected and the results of path loss are rendered. As shown in Fig. 5, the picture on the left is the result of 2.6 GHz, and the picture on the right is the result of 700 MHz. Then, the blue legend represents the path loss is smaller, and red represents the greater the path loss. Through the comparison of rendering diagram, it can be seen clearly that the path loss of 700 MHz is obviously less than the loss of 2.6 GHz. It can be concluded that under the same conditions, the smaller the path loss is, the better the coverage effect will be.

Outdoor Remote Simulation
Zhumeila apartments base station cell in Zhujiang New Town area is selected to simulate the outdoor remote coverage of 2.6 GHz and 700 MHz. The electrical level of 700 MHz is reduced to −110 dBm at 1.94 km, and the electrical level of 2.6 GHz is reduced to −110 dBm at 1.48 km. The outdoor remote range of 700 MHz per cell is better than 2.6 GHz, which is more than 30%.

Region Coverage Simulation
The ray tracing simulations of 2.6 GHz and 700 MHz were carried out in this area, and the simulation results are shown in Fig. 7.

The statistical results are shown in Table 5:

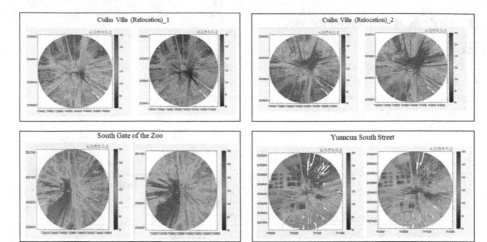

Fig. 5. Path loss rendering results

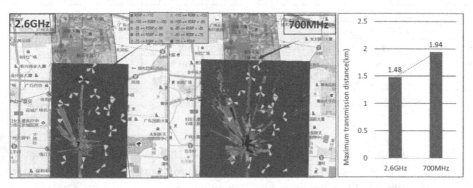

Fig. 6. Comparison of 700 MHz and 2.6 GHz outdoor remote coverage

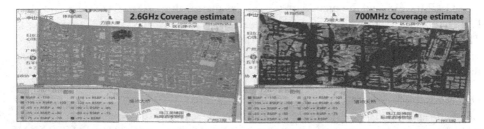

Fig. 7. 3D ray tracing simulation results

Table 5. Statistical results of regional coverage indicators.

Simulated frequency band	Average RSRP (dBm)	RSRP (>=-93dBm) coverage percentage	SINR (>=-3db) compliance rate percentage	RSRP (>=-93dBm) coverage rate percentage and SINR (>=-3db) compliance rate percentage
2.6GHz	-76.02	94.3	54.6	50.1
700MHz	-73.52	93.5	70.6	63.4

According to the simulation results, the prediction effect of 700 MHz area coverage is far better than that of 2.6 GHz. When 700 MHz base stations account for 28% of the number of 2.6 GHz base stations, the coverage effect of 2.6 GHz can be reached and exceeded.

Stereoscopic Building Simulation

Based on LiShuttle ray tracing propagation model and Plannet electronic map, three-dimensional simulation and rendering of buildings in this area are carried out, which using open source 3D rendering technology Cesium. This rendering adopts two methods: floor average and edge average. The floor average rendering is based on the average value of all grid field strength of each floor to render the building, and the edge average method is based on the grid field strength of the building contour to render the building. The results of building stereoscopic simulation are shown in Fig. 8.

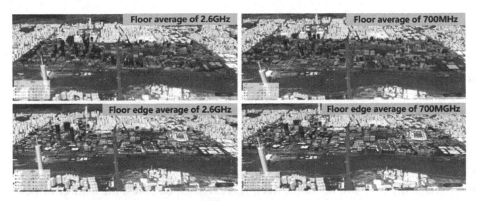

Fig. 8. Building stereoscopic simulation results

It can be seen from the simulation results that the indoor coverage effect of 700 MHz through the outdoor macro base station is obviously better than that of 2.6 GHz. Although in some areas, there are deviations due to the distribution of base stations. By analyzing the simulation results of the buildings in this area, among the total number of the buildings in the area which is 1069, there are 736 buildings with 700 MHz resulting better than bulidings with 2.6 GHz in terms of indoor average and 727 bulidings resulting better than buildings with 2.6 GHz with respect to edge average, accounting for 68.8% and 68.1% respectively.

The typical building Greater China International Trading Market in this area is selected for analysis. The simulation results are shown in Fig. 2, 3, 4, 5 and 6. The average floor RSRP of the building is −96.4 dBm and the average indoor RSRP of 700 MHz is −81.2 dBm. Therefore, the RSRP of 700 MHz is about 15 dBm higher than that of 2.6 GHz (Fig. 9).

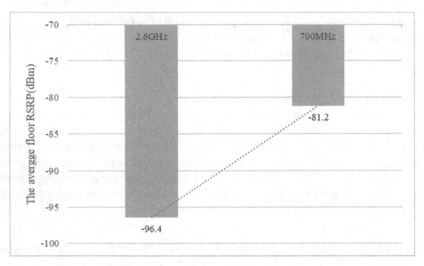

Fig. 9. Results of typical building statistics

4 Conclusion

Based on the traditional ray tracing propagation model LiShuttle, this paper explores the simulation and coverage capability of 5G NR system in 700 MHz frequency band under ultra dense scene, and conducts the comparative analysis with the lowest 5G frequency band 2.6 GHz allocated by our country. According to the simulation analysis, it can be seen that the 700 MHz frequency band link budget will produce significant gains, its coverage distance will be longer when it is extended outdoors, the number of base stations will be greatly reduced to achieve the same coverage effect, and the building can have an excellent coverage effect. All in all, it will have a very big advantage in the future 5G base station construction.

References

1. Tang, X., Mo, R.: Study on the Necessity of 700M and 2.6G cooperation. Electr. Technol. Softw. Eng. (05), 3–4 (2021). (in Chinese)
2. Wang, T., Zhang, J., Li, C.: Radio and TV 700M 5G network networking architecture and business development strategy research. In: China Federation of Journalists. Proceedings of China Federation of Journalists' Annual Conference 2020. China Federation of Journalists, p. 7 (2020). (in Chinese)
3. Rodriguez, I., Sun, S., Rappaport, T.S., et al.: Investigation of prediction accuracy, sensitivity, and parameter stability of large-scale propagation path loss models for 5G wireless communications. IEEE Trans. Veh. Technol. **65**(5), 2843–2860 (2016)
4. Chao, X.: Research on deep coverage technology of mobile communication wireless network. In: 2019 7th International Conference on Machinery, Materials and Computing Technology (ICMMCT 2019), pp. 228–231 (2019)
5. Ai, Q., Feng, W., Wu, W., et al.: Design of power wireless private network coverage prediction system. In: The 3rd International Conference on Mechatronics Engineering and Information Technology, pp. 335–342 (2019)

6. Peng, J.: Application scenario and key technology analysis of 5g communication technology based on optical fiber transmission network. In: 2019 4th International Industrial Informatics and Computer Engineering Conference (IIICEC 2019), pp. 25–28 (2019)
7. Shu, Y., Zhu, F.: Green communication mobile convergence mechanism for computing self-offloading in 5G networks. Peer-to-Peer Netw. Appl. **12**(6), 1511–1518 (2018). https://doi.org/10.1007/s12083-018-0704-7
8. Othman, A., Nayan, N.A.: Efficient admission control and resource allocation mechanisms for public safety communications over 5G network slice. Telecommun. Syst. **72**(4), 595–607 (2019). https://doi.org/10.1007/s11235-019-00600-9
9. Khalid, N., Abbasi, N.A., Akan, O.B.: Statistical characterization and analysis of low-THz communication channel for 5G Internet of Things. Nano Commun. Netw., 22100258 (2019). https://doi.org/10.1016/j.nancom.2019.100258

The Influence of Navigation and Remote Sensing LEO Satellite Attitude on BDS Augmentation

Li Tian[1,2][✉], Wei Zhang[1,2], Shuangna Zhang[2], and Qijia Dong[2]

[1] Tianjin Zhong Wei Aerospace Data System Technology Co., Ltd., Tianjin 300301, China
[2] Space Star Technology Co., Ltd., Beijing 100086, China

Abstract. In remote sensing tasks, LEO satellites need to adjust the attitude. The influence of the LEO satellite attitude on the augmentation of BDS is researched. In the paper, an on-orbit test scenario is built based on MATLAB and STK simulation software. The number and PDOP values of BDS satellites received by the LEO satellite receiver are analyzed under the three common satellite attitudes of LEO satellites: stable coordinate axis, cruising to the sun, and staring at the target area. In addition, a LEO satellite on ascending orbit and descending orbit was evaluated for two times. The results show that in the telemetry mission, the LEO satellite passes through the same target area, and the satellite attitude has a greater impact on the LEO satellites receiver to receive BDS satellites. Comparing the simulation data with the on-orbit telemetry data, the satellite receiver receives the BDS satellites basically the same, which verifies the reliability of the simulation data and provides support and reference for the on-orbit test.

Keywords: LEO satellite · BDS augmentation · Satellite attitude

1 Introduction

The satellite navigation system as an important national space infrastructure can provide any weather, any time, high-precision positioning, navigation and timing services. It occupies an increasingly important position in the field of national defense and the national economy. Navigation and remote sensing are the most important applications of civil satellites, and they are also an important part of our country's space-based information system. The two are different in constellation configurations, signal structures, and application modes, so that it is difficult to achieve complete integration. LEO satellite serves as the supplement and backup of the current four major satellite navigation systems (GPS, GLONASS, BDS and Galileo). It is in a stage of rapid development, providing development space for navigation and synesthesia integration.

The orbital height of LEO satellites is 500–2000 km. The LEO satellites, compare with medium and high orbit satellites are lighter in weight and lower in orbit. They can be launched by multiple satellites with one arrow. The research and development costs of satellites and rocket launch costs are lower. The LEO satellites have high ground dynamics, downlink wireless signal Doppler is large, and navigation signals have fast

X. Wang et al. (Eds.): AICON 2021, LNICST 396, pp. 138–152, 2021.
https://doi.org/10.1007/978-3-030-90196-7_13

ambiguity resolution and convergence. It is suitable for fast positioning and precision augmentation of navigation on the ground. In addition, the LEO satellites are close to the ground, suitable for the detection and information acquisition of the earth and celestial bodies, data transmission assistance, and remote sensing data analysis and processing, and can perform fine synthesizing detection of ground targets.

At present, the LEO navigation augmentation technology has become a hot direction of research institutions at home and abroad. Design the LEO navigation to enhance satellite constellation, and give the results that the influence of the constellation configuration, orbit height, and orbit inclination on the ground coverage. The LEO satellites combine with GNSS can improve the geometric accuracy [1, 2]. The new constellation configuration design proposed [3]. A LEO satellite navigation augmentation system with integrated communication and navigation is designed, which is based on LEO communication technology to achieve navigation augmentation [4]. The analysis of the attitude control of the remote sensing satellite telemetry mission is analyzed, but did not analyze the impact on the navigation performance [5–7]. There is no article for analyzing the influence that the attitudes of the LEO satellite in the remote sensing mission affect the navigation and positioning. Orienting to engineering, this article analyzes that the influence of navigation and remote sensing integrated LEO satellite attitude on BDS augmentation.

2 Navigation and Remote Sensing LEO Satellite Augmentation System

2.1 Features and Research Goals of Navigation and Remote Sensing LEO Satellite

At present, remote sensing satellites are developing in the direction of LEO satellites. Satellite navigation and positioning are the basis for remote sensing data analysis and calibration, such as remote sensing satellite positioning and remote sensing target positioning. LEO satellites are close to the ground and have a finer remote sensing resolution compared with medium-high orbit satellites. The following Table 1 gives a summary. However, in the process of telemetry missions, the satellite attitude is in a maneuvering state, which has a greater impact on the satellite receivers to receive BDS satellites. It is showed by Table 1.

In the remote sensing tasks, LEO satellite integrated with navigation and remote has the phenomenon of adjusting its attitudes. The LEO satellite attitudes will have a certain impact on the number of BDS satellites received by the satellite receiver. On the one hand, the LEO satellite attitudes affect the orbit determination performance. Due to the satellite attitude adjustment, the receiver channel frequently changes satellites, which affects the positioning accuracy. On the other hand, the LEO satellite attitudes affect the augmentation capabilities of users. Because the satellite transmitter broadcasts the effective ephemeris of the BDS satellites visible to the satellite receiver, and the LEO satellite attitude affects the generation of the effective ephemeris. In this paper, LEO satellite attitudes including stable coordinate axis, cruising to the sun, and staring at the target area, have an effect on satellites receiver to receive BDS satellites and PDOP values. It can support the on-orbit test.

Table 1. Comparison of medium, high and low orbit satellites.

System type		Resolution
GEO remote sensing satellite	U.S. meteorological satellite GOES	Kilometer level
	Europe GEO-Oculus	Meter level
	China GF-4	Optical imaging 50 m
HEO remote sensing satellite	Electronic weather satellite	Kilometer level
	Amber 4K remote sensing satellite	Meter level
MEO remote sensing satellite	U.S. 8X satellite	Optical imaging SAR 1 m
	French MEO satellite	Optical imaging SAR 1 m
LEO remote sensing satellite	KH-12	Optical imaging SAR 1 m
	Lacrosse	Microwave SAR 0.3 m
	GF-2	Optical imaging SAR 0.8 m
	GF-3	Microwave SAR 1 m

2.2 System Composition

The system is mainly composed of BDS satellites, navigation and remote sensing integrated LEO satellite, and users. The remote sensing integrated LEO satellite includes a satellite receiver, satellite BDS signal receiving antenna, a satellite transmitter, and satellite transmitting antenna. It is showed by Fig. 1.

The receiver receives the BDS satellite signal through the receiving antenna, and performs orbit prediction and clock error prediction based on BDS observation data and navigation messages. The satellite transmitter receives orbit forecast and clock error forecast results, and generates LEO navigation augmentation information. The IF module in the satellite transmitter modulates the pseudo code and enhanced information to generate an intermediate frequency signal. The RF module in the satellite transmitter is up-converted, and the intermediate frequency signal is generated into the RF signal. Then the satellite transmitter sends to users via telemetry antenna. The clock module is used for time synchronization between the satellite receiver and t the satellite transmitter.

The workflow figure is showed by Fig. 2.

2.3 Satellite Attitudes

The satellite attitudes are the direction of the space when it is moving on the orbit. The satellite attitudes are represented by three variables: yaw, roll and pitch in the orbital coordinate system. The origin O (x_0, y_0, z_0) of the orbital coordinate system is located on the satellite. The Z_0 axis points to the center of the earth, which is the yaw direction. The X_0 axis is along the tangential direction of the track surface and is perpendicular to the Z_0 axis, which is the rolling direction. The Y_0 axis is perpendicular to the track surface and forms a right-handed system with the X_0 axis and Y_0 axis, which is the pitch

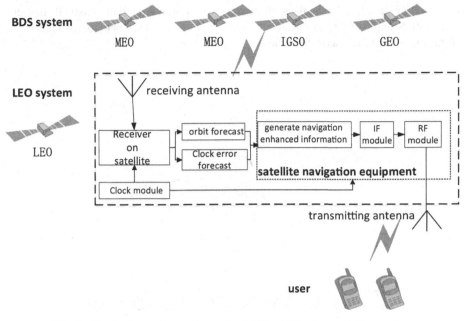

Fig. 1. Navigation and remote sensing LEO satellite augmentation system

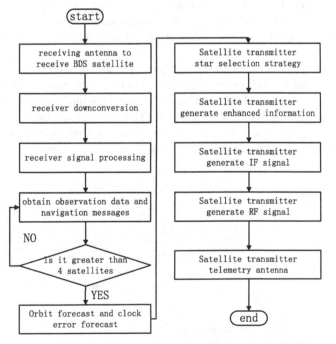

Fig. 2. LEO with navigation and remote integrated enhanced BDS system.

direction. Yaw (pitch) refers to the attitude angle of rotation around the z axis. Roll refers to the attitude angle of rotation around the x-axis. Pitch (yaw) refers to the attitude angle of rotation around the y-axis. Show in the Fig. 3 below.

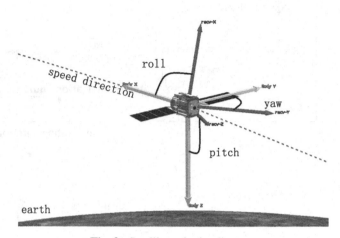

Fig. 3. Satellite attitudes diagram.

With the gradual deepening of the exhibition of remote sensing technology applications, satellite will adopt different attitude modes according to the tasks performed during orbit, such as stable coordinate axis, cruising to the sun, and s staring at the target, etc.

The mode of staring at the target has become one common attitude of remote sensing satellites, which enables the satellite platform to continuously observe hotspot areas. In this attitude mode, the ground station adjusts the satellite attitude. A coordinate axis of the imaging system or optical axis of optical load on the satellite platform always point to the targets. So as to continuously obtain the dynamic information of the target area, it has high engineering application value. Show in the Fig. 4 below.

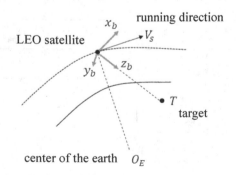

Fig. 4. Staring at the target schematic diagram.

The mode of stable coordinate axis is a stable attitude relative to the spin of the satellite. It means that the satellite body is stable in the three directions of X, Y, and Z, and maintains a certain attitude relationship with the earth. This attitude adapts to most satellite applications, easy to meet the directional requirements of the payload, and easy to achieve orbit control. In the orbital plane of LEO, the $+Z_0$ axis direction always points to the center of the earth, and the $+X_0$ axis direction is along the forward tangential direction. Show in the Fig. 5 below.

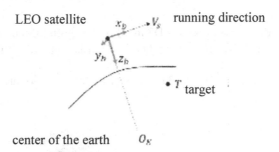

Fig. 5. Stable coordinate axis schematic diagram.

Cruising to the sun is one of the commonly used attitude control mission modes for satellites. It sets the desired attitude of the satellite so that the solar array plane of the satellite is fully aligned with the sun to provide sufficient energy. For example, the $+z0$ axis of the low-orbit satellite points to the sun. Show in the Fig. 6 below.

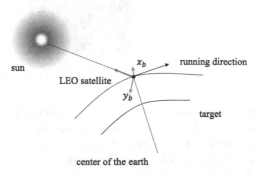

Fig. 6. Cruising to the sun schematic diagram.

3   System Simulation and Verification

3.1   Verification Scenario

In order to verify the influence of navigation and remote sensing LEO satellite attitude on BDS augmentation, a test verification platform was built based on MATLAB and

Table 2. LEO satellite attitude.

Number	LEO satellite attitude	Detailed settings
1	Staring at the targets	$+Z_0$ axis stares at Beijing
2	Stable coordinate axis	$+Z_0$ axis always points to the center of the earth; $-X_0$ axis is along the tangential direction of advancement
3	Orienting toward the sun	$-Y_0$ axis orients to the sun

STK software. The BDS system is the BD3 in orbit. The ground station is Beijing. And the orbital height of the LEO satellite is 500 km. The LEO satellite attitude is shown in the Table 2.

STK software simulates the above 3 types of attitudes scenarios are as follows in the Fig. 7:

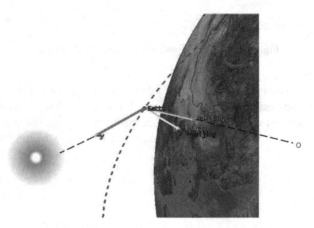

Fig. 7. LEO satellite 3 types of attitude schematic diagram.

In different attitudes, the sensitivity of the satellite receiver is −163 dBW. The receiving antenna is installed at the same position on the satellite, and it points differently as the satellite attitude changes. For example, when the satellite is in a stable coordinate axis attitude, the receiving antenna is located −Z axis deviates from −X axis direction 30° in the satellite body coordinate system.

The return period of the satellite is about 24 h, and the simulation time is selected as 2020.8.31 00:00:00-2020.09.01 04:00:00. There are 6 time periods when the LEO satellite transits the target area of Beijing, as shown in the following Table 3:

The trajectory of LEO satellite includes ascending orbit and descending orbit. The orbits numbered 1, 2, 5, and 6 are satellite ascending orbits, and this orbit is the process from low latitude to high latitude. The orbits numbers 3 and 4 are the descending orbit, and this orbit is the process from high latitude to low latitude. Select 2 sets of ascending orbits (No. 1 and No. 2) and 2 sets of descending orbits (No. 3 and No. 4) to analyze the performance of navigation and remote sensing LEO satellite attitude on BDS augmentation.

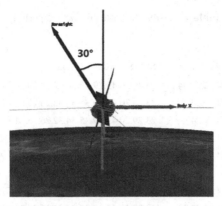

Fig. 8. The relationship between antenna pointing and satellite body coordinate system.

Table 3. LEO and target area Beijing visible time.

Number	Visible time	Visible length of time
1	2020-8-31 09.06.07-09:17:30	682
2	2020-8-31 10:40:35-10:49:17	522
3	2020-8-31 19:42:49-19.53.20	631
4	2020-8-31 21:16:12-21:26:57	645
5	2020-9-1 08:44:42-08:55:37	654
6	2020-9-1 10:18:32-10:28:35	603

3.2 Validation Results

Under the three attitudes of stable coordinate axis, cruising to the sun, and staring at the target area, LEO satellite passes through the target area of Beijing. The receiving antenna on the LEO satellite receives BDS satellites every 30 s. The number of BDS satellites during the 4 time periods is shown in the following Table 4, 5, 6 and 7. It can be seen that the PDOP value of number of BDS satellites changes with time, as shown in the Figs. 9, 10, 11, 12.

Table 4. Visible satellites in the 1rd period

	Time	Visible satellite PRN		
		Staring at the target area	Stable coordinate axis	Cruising to the sun
1	09.06.07	29.20.43.19.34.32.26.24	23.29.20.43.19.35.34.32.26.25.24	29.20.43.19.34.32.26.24
2	09:06:30	29.20.43.19.34.26.24	23.29.20.43.19.35.34.32.26.25.24	29.20.43.19.34.26.24
3	09:07:00	29.20.43.19.34.26.24	23.29.20.43.19.35.34.32.26.25.24	29.20.43.19.34.26.24
4	09:07:30	29.20.43.19.34.26.25.24	23.29.20.43.19.35.34.32.26.25.24	29.20.43.19.34.26.25.24
5	09:08:00	29.20.43.19.34.26.25.24	23.29.20.43.19.35.34.32.26.25.24	29.20.43.19.34.26.25.24
6	09:08:30	29.20.43.19.34.25.24	23.29.20.43.19.35.34.32.26.25.24	29.21.20.43.19.34.26.25.24
7	09:09:00	29.20.43.19.34.25.24	23.29.20.43.19.35.34.32.26.25.24	29.21.20.43.19.34. 25.24
8	09:10:30	29.21.20.43.19.34.25.24	23.29.20.43.19.35.34.32.26.25.24	29.21.20.43.19.34.25.24
9	09:11:00	29.21.20.43.19.34.25.24	29.20.43.19.35.34.32.26.25.24	29.21.20.43.19.34.25.24
10	09:11:30	29.21.20.43.19.34.25.24	29.20.43.19.35.34.32.26.25.24	29.21.20.43.19.34.25.24
11	09:12:00	29.21.20.43.19.34.25.24	29.20.21.43.19.35.34.32.26.25.24	29.21.20.43.19.34.25.24
12	09:12:30	29.21.20.43.19.34.25.24	29.20.21.43.19.35.34.32.26.25.24	29.21.20.43.19.34.25.24
13	09:13:00	29.21.20.43.19.34.25.24	29.20.21.43.19.35.34.32.26.25.24	29.21.20.43.19.34.25.24
14	09:13:30	29.21.20.43.19.34.25.24	29.20.21.43.19.35.34.32.26.25.24	29.21.20.43.19.34.25.24
15	09:14:00	29.21.20.43.19.34.25.24	29.20.21.43.19.35.34.32.26.25.24	29.21.20.43.19.34.25.24
16	09:14:30	29.21.20.43.19.34.25.24	29.20.21.43.19.35.34.26.25.24	29.21.20.43.19.34.25.24
17	09:15:00	29.21.20.43.19.34.25.24	29.20.21.43.19.35.34.26.25.24	29.21.20.43.19.34.25.24
18	09:15:30	29.21.20.43.19.34.25.24	29.20.21.43.19.35.34.26.25.24	29.21.20.43.19.34.25.24
19	09:16:00	29.21.20.43.19.34.25.24	29.20.21.43.19.35.34.26.25.24	29.21.20.43.19.34.25.24
20	09:16:30	29.21.20.43.19.34.25.24	29.20.21.43.19.35.34.26.25.24	29.21.20.46.43.19.34.25.24
21	09:17:00	29.21.20.46.43.19.34.25.24	29.20.21.43.19.35.34.26.25.24	29.21.20.46.43.19.34.25.24
22	09:17:30	29.21.46.43.19.34.25.24	29.20.21.43.19.35.34.26.25.24	29.21.20.43.19.34.25.24
23	09:10:30	29.21.46.43.19.34.25.24	29.20.21.43.19.35.34.26.25.24	29.21.20.43.19.34.25.24

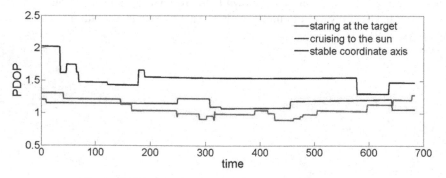

Fig. 9. Visible BDS satellite PDOP value in the 1rd period.

Table 5. Visible satellites in the 2rd period

	Time	Visible satellite PRN		
		Staring at the target area	Stable coordinate axis	Cruising to the sun
1	10:40:35	23.21.20.43.19.35.34.26	23.21.20.44.43.19.37.35.34.26.24	23.21.20.43.19.35.34.26
2	10:41:00	23.21.20.43.19.35.34.26	23.21.20.44.43.19.37.35.34.26.24	23.21.20.43.19.35.34.26
3	10:41:30	23.21.20.43.19.35.34.26	23.21.20.44.43.19.37.35.34.26.24	23.21.20.43.19.35.34.26
4	10:42:00	23.21.43.19.35.34.26	23.21.20.44.43.19.37.35.34.26.24	23.21.43.19.35.34.26
5	10:42:30	23.21.43.19.35.34.26.24	23.21.20.44.43.19.37.35.34.26.24	23.21.43.19.35.34.26.24
6	10:43:00	23.21.43.19.35.34.26.24	23.21.20.44.43.19.37.35.34.26.24	23.21.43.19.35.34.26.24
7	10:43:30	23.21.43.19.35.34.26.24	23.21.20.44.43.19.37.35.34.26.24	23.21.43.19.35.34.26.24
8	10:44:00	21.43.19.35.34.26.24	23.21.20.44.43.19.37.35.34.26.24	21.43.19.35.34.26.24
9	10:44:30	22.21.43.19.35.34.26.24	23.21.20.44.43.19.37.35.34.26.24	22.21.43.19.35.34.26.24
10	10:45:00	22.21.43.19.35.34.26.24	23.21.20.44.43.19.35.34.26.24	22.21.43.19.35.34.26.24
11	10:45:30	22.21.43.19.35.34.26.24	23.21.20.44.43.19.35.34.26.24	22.21.43.19.35.34.26.24
12	10:46:00	22.21.43.19.35.34.26.24	23.21.20.44.43.19.35.34.26.24	22.21.43.19.35.34.26.24
13	10:46:30	22.21.43.19.35.34.26.24	23.22.21.20.44.43.19.35.34.26.24	22.21.43.19.35.34.26.24
14	10:47:00	22.21.43.19.35.34.26.24	23.22.21.20.44.43.19.35.34.26.24	22.21.43.19.35.34.26.24
15	10:47:30	22.21.43.19.35.34.26.24	23.22.21.20.44.43.19.35.34.26.24	22.21.43.19.35.34.26.24
16	10:48:00	22.21.43.19.35.34.26.24	23.22.21.20.44.43.19.35.34.26.24	22.21.43.19.35.34.26.24
17	10:48:30	22.21.43.19.35.34.26.24	23.22.21.20.44.43.19.35.34.26.24	22.21.43.19.35.34.26.24
18	10:49:00	22.21.43.19.35.34.26.24	23.22.21.44.43.19.35.34.26.24	22.21.43.19.35.34.26.24

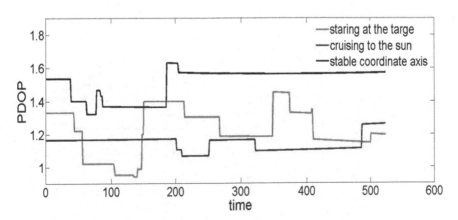

Fig. 10. Visible BDS satellite PDOP value in the 2rd period.

Table 6. Visible satellites in the 3rd period

	Time	Visible satellite PRN		
		Staring at the target area	Stable coordinate axis	Cruising to the sun
1	19:43:00	23.42.41.33.26.24	23.22.28.27.44.42.41.35.33.32.26.24	23.42.41.33.26.24
2	19:43:30	23.42.41.33.26.24	23.22.28.27.44.42.41.35.33.32.26.24	23.42.41.33.26.24
3	19:44:00	23.42.41.33.26.24	23.22.28.27.44.42.41.35.33.32.26.24	23.42.41.33.26.24
4	19:44:30	23.42.41.33.26.24.25	23.28.27.44.42.41.35.33.32.26.24	23.42.41.33.26.25.24
5	19:45:00	23.42.41.33.26.24.25	23.28.27.44.42.41.35.33.32.26.24	23.42.41.33.26.25.24
6	19:45:30	23.42.41.33.26.24.25	23.28.27.44.42.41.35.33.32.26.24	23.42.41.33.26.25.24
7	19:46:00	23.42.41.33.26.24.25	23.28.27.44.42.41.35.33.32.26.24	23.42.41.33.26.25.24
8	19:46:30	23.42.41.33.26.24.25	23.30.28.27.44.42.41.35.33.32.26.24	23.42.41.33.26.25.24
9	19:47:00	23.42.41.33.26.24.25	23.30.28.27.44.42.41.35.33.32.26.24	23.42.41.33.26.25.24
10	19:47:30	23.42.41.33.26.24.25	23.30.28.27.44.42.41.35.33.32.26.24	23.42.41.33.26.25.24
11	19:48:00	23.42.41.33.26.24.25	23.30.28.27.44.42.41.35.33.32.26.24	23.42.41.33.26.25.24
12	19:48:30	23.42.41.33.26.24.25	23.30.28.27.42.41.33.32.26.24	23.42.41.33.26.25.24
13	19:49:00	42.41.33.26.24.25	23.30.28.27.42.41.33.32.26.24	42.41.33.26.25.24
14	19:49:30	42.41.33.26.24.25	23.30.28.27.42.41.33.32.26.24	42.41.33.26.25.24
15	19:50:00	42.41.33.26.24.25	23.30. 27.42.41.33.32.26.24	42.41.33.26.25.24
16	19:50:30	42.41.33.26.24.25	23.30. 27.42.41.33.32.26.24	42.41.33.26.25.24
17	19:51:00	41.33.32.26.24.25	23.30. 27.42.41.33.32.26.24	41.33.32.26.25.24
18	19:51:30	41.33.32.26.24.25	23.30. 27.42.41.33.32.26.24	41.33.32.26.25.24
19	19:52:00	41.33.32.26.24.25	23.30. 27.42.41.33.32.26.24	41.33.32.26.25.24
20	19:52:30	41.33.32.26.24.25	23.30. 27.42.41.33.32.26.24	41.33.32.26.25.24

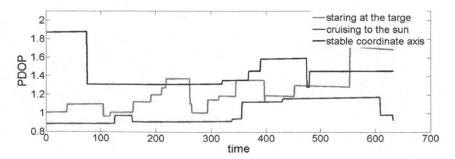

Fig. 11. Visible BDS satellite PDOP value in the 3rd period.

Table 7. Visible satellites in the 4rd period

	Time	Visible satellite PRN		
		Staring at the target area	Stable coordinate axis	Cruising to the sun
1	21:16:30	23.41.37.33.32.26	23.30.28.27.44.42.41.37.33.32.26	23.41.37.33.32.26
2	21:17:00	23.41.37.33.32.26	23.30.28.27.20.44.42.41.37.33.32.26	23.41.37.33.32.26
3	21:17:30	23.41.37.33.32.26	23.30.28.27.20.44.42.41.37.33.32.26	23.41.37.33.32.26
4	21:18:00	23.41.37.33.32.26	23.30.28.27.20.44.42.41.37.33.32.26	23.41.37.33.32.26
5	21:18:30	23.41.37.33.32.26	23.30.28.27.20.44.42.41.37.33.32.26	23.41.37.33.32.26
6	21:19:00	23.41.37.33.32.26	23.30.28.27.20.44.42.41.37.33.32.26	23.41.37.33.32.26
7	21:19:30	23.41.37.33.32.26	23.30.28.27.20.44.41.37.33.32.26	23.41.37.33.32.26
8	21:20:00	23.41.37.33.32.26.24	23.30.28.27.20.44.41.37.33.32.26	23.41.37.33.32.26.24
9	21:20:30	23.41.37.33.32.26.24	23.30.28.27.20.44.41.37.33.32.26	23.41.37.33.32.26.24
10	21:21:00	23.41.37.33.32.26.24	23.30.28.27.20.44.41.37.33.32.26	23.41.37.33.32.26.24
11	21:21:30	23.41.37.33.32.26.24	23.30.28.27.20.44.41.37.33.32.26	23.41.37.33.32.26.24
12	21:22:00	23.41.37.33.32.26.24	23.30.29.28.27.20.44.41.37.33.32.26	23.41.37.33.32.26.24
13	21:22:30	23.41.37.33.32.26.24	23.30.29.28.27.20.44.41.37.33.32.26	23.41.37.33.32.26.24
14	21:23:00	23.41.37.33.32.26.24	23.30.29.27.20.41.37.33.32.26	23.41.37.33.32.26.24
15	21:23:30	23.41.33.32.26.24	23.30.29.27.20.41.37.33.32.26	23.41.33.32.26.24
16	21:24:00	23.41.33.32.26.24	23.30.29.27.20.41.37.33.32.26	23.41.33.32.26.24
17	21:24:30	23.41.33.32.26.24	23.30.29.27.20.41.37.33.32.26	23.41.33.32.26.24
18	21:25:00	23.41.33.32.26.24	23.30.29.20.41.37.33.32.26	23.41.33.32.26.24
19	21:25:30	23.41.33.32.26.24	23.30.29.20.41.37.33.32.26	23.41.33.32.26.24
20	21:26:00	23.41.32.26.24	23.30.29.20.41.37.33.32.26	23.20.41.32.26.24
21	21:26:30	23.41.32.26.24.20	23.30.29.20.41.37.33.32.26	23.20.41.32.26.24

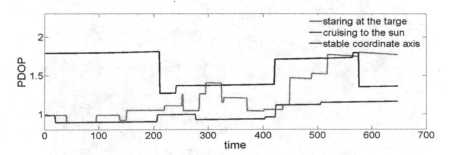

Fig. 12. Visible BDS satellite PDOP value in the 4rd period.

When the LEO satellite is in the ascending orbit through the target area, Table 4 and Table 5 show the PRN of the visible satellites that received by the LEO satellite receiver. When the LEO satellite is in descending orbit through the target area, Table 6 and Table 7 show the PRN of the visible satellites that received by the LEO satellite receiver. From the data in the table, the number of satellites received by the satellite receiver is more than 4, which can achieve positioning. It can be seen that the satellite PRN number is not exactly the same in different attitudes.

Figure 9 and Figure 10 are graphs that show PDOP values of visible satellites received by LEO satellite receiving antenna when the LEO satellite is in the ascending orbit. The simulation results show that the order of the navigation and positioning performance of the LEO satellite from high to low is: staring at the target > cruising to the sun > three-axis stability.

Figure 11 and Figure 12 are graphs that show PDOP values of visible satellites received by LEO satellite receiving antenna when the LEO satellite is in the ascending orbit. The simulation results show that the order of the navigation and positioning performance of the LEO satellite from high to low is: staring at the target > cruising to the sun > three-axis stability.

In summary, when the LEO satellite is in the attitude of staring at the target and orienting toward the sun, the number of BDS satellites is received more. When the LEO satellite is in the attitude of three-axis stable, the number of BDS satellites received by the LEO satellite receiver is small.

4   On-Orbit Evaluation

In order to verify the simulation results, this paper conducts two on-orbit evaluations on a LEO satellite. In order to verify the adequacy of the experiment, the selection target area is visible for a longer period of time, and the satellite trajectory includes ascending orbit and descending orbit. According to the telemetry data of the LEO satellite receiver, the PRN and the number of satellites visible to the satellite receiver are counted and compared with the simulation results (Fig. 13).

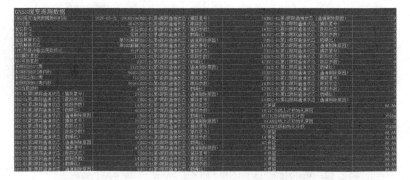

Fig. 13. LEO satellite 3 types of attitude schematic diagram.

Table 8. Visible time of LEO satellite passing through target area Beijing.

Number	Visible time	Visible satellite orienting toward the sun
1	2021-08-31 09:06:56	23.29.20.43.19.35.34.32.26.25.24
2	2021-08-31 09:07:28	23.29.20.43.19.35.34.32.26.25.24
3	2021-08-31 09:08:00	23.29.20.43.19.35.34.32.26.25.24
4	2021-08-31 09:09:04	23.29.20.43.19.35.34.32.26.25.24
5	2021-08-31 09:10:08	23.29.20.43.19.35.34.32.26.25.24
6	2021-08-31 09:11:12	29.20.43.19.35.34.32.26.25.24
7	2021-08-31 09:12:16	29.20.21.43.19.35.34.32.26.25.24
8	2021-08-31 09:13:20	29.20.21.43.19.35.34.32.26.25.24
9	2021-08-31 09:14:24	29.20.21.43.19.35.34.26.25.24
10	2021-08-31 09:15:28	29.20.21.43.19.35.34.26.25.24
11	2021-08-31 09:16:32	29.20.21.43.19.35.34.26.25.24

On August 31, 2020, the LEO satellite is in the ascending orbit. The visible time that LEO satellite passing through the target area was 09:06.07–09:17:30. The time was on the day, and the LEO satellite attitude was cruising to the sun. The telemetry data of the receiver on the LEO satellite is shown in the following Table 8:

On August 31, 2020, the LEO satellite is in the descending orbit. The visible time that LEO satellite passing through the target area was 19:42:49–19:53:20. The time was in the night, and the LEO satellite attitude was three-axis stability. The telemetry data of the receiver on the LEO satellite is shown in the following Table 9:

Table 9. Visible time of LEO satellite passing through target area Beijing.

Number	Visible time	Visible satellite three-axis stability
1	2021-08-31 19:43:56	23.42.41.33.26.24
2	2021-08-31 19:44:28	23.42.41.33.26.24.25
3	2021-08-31 19:45:00	23.42.41.33.26.24.25
4	2021-08-31 19:46:04	23.42.41.33.26.24.25
5	2021-08-31 19:47:08	23.42.41.33.26.24.25
6	2021-08-31 19:48:12	41.33.32.26.24.25
7	2021-08-31 19:49:16	41.33.32.26.24.25
8	2021-08-31 19:50:20	41.33.32.26.24.25
9	2021-08-31 19:51:24	41.33.32.26.24.25
10	2021-08-31 19:52:28	41.33.32.26.24.25

Comparing Table 8 and Table 4, Table 9 and Table 6, the results show that the on-orbit telemetry data is basically the same as the simulation data, except for the low elevation angle and low carrier-to-noise ratio satellites.

The reason for the difference is the complex environment in orbiting space and the influence of ground control satellite attitude maneuverability. The complex environment in orbiting space includes ionosphere and troposphere etc. The simulation results provide support and reference for the on-orbit test.In addition, when there is no telemetry mission it is recommended to use a three-axis stable attitude at night and a cruise attitude toward the sun on the day.

5 Conclusion

This article introduces the composition of the navigation and remote sensing LEO satellite augmentation system. Compare and analyze characteristics of three LEO typical satellite attitudes: staring at the targets, cruising to the sun, and three-axis stability. In order to obtain the simulation data of the influence of navigation and remote sensing LEO satellite attitude on BDS augmentation, a test verification platform is built based on MATLAB and STK software. In the verification platform, the trajectory of LEO satellite includes ascending orbit and descending orbit, the number and the PDOP value of BDS visible satellites received by LEO satellite receiver is verified. Finally, the reliability of the simulation data is verified by on-orbit telemetry data.

References

1. Tian, Y., Zhang, L., Bian, L.: Design of LEO satellites augmented constelliation for navigation. Chinese Space Sci. Technol. **39**(6), 55–61 (2019)
2. Tian, R., Cui, Z., Zhang, S., Wang, D.: Navigation positioning & timing **1**(8), 66–81 (2021)
3. Shen, Y., Zhang, Y.: Design for LEO satellite navigation augmentation system based on integrated communication and navigation. In: Academic Exchange Center of China Satellite Navigation System Management Office. Proceedings of the 11th China Satellite Navigation Annual Conference 2020. LNCS, vol. 9999, pp. 25–29 (2020)
4. Li, Q., Deng, Z., Wang, Y., Wang, J.: Quasi-sun-pointing oriented attitude for solar power satellites. J. Astronaut. **40**(01), 29–40 (2019)
5. Shen, D., Meng, Y., Bian, L.: A global navigation augmentation system based on LEO communication constellation. J. Terahertz Sci. Electron. Inf. Technol. **17**(02), 209–215 (2019)
6. Wang, L., Li, D., Chen, R., et al.: Low earth orbiter (LEO) navigation augmentation: opportunities and challenges. Strat. Study CAE **22**(2), 144–152 (2020)
7. Pan, L., Wang, S., Yuan, J., et al.: Design and simulation of LEO remote sensing satellite. Spacecraft Eng. **30**(01), 52–56 (2021)

LEO-Assisted Beidou B1C Signal Acquisition Algorithm and On-Orbit Verification

Wei Zhang[1,2(✉)], Qijia Dong[2], Shuangna Zhang[2], Li Tian[1,2], Kun Liu[1,2], and Jinshan Liu[1,2]

[1] Tianjin Zhong Wei Aerospace Data System Technology Co., Ltd., Tianjin 300301, China
[2] Space Star Technology Co., Ltd., Beijing 100086, China

Abstract. In the occlusion and electromagnetic interference environment, the GNSS navigation signal is seriously attenuated, and traditional GNSS receivers are difficult to capture. For direct capture of weak signals, long-time coherent integration and non-coherent integration can be used to improve the signal-to-noise ratio (SNR) of the signal. However, coherent integration time is limited and bit flipping, and non-coherent integration has a square loss, resulting in a significant increase in the SNR. Taking into account the advantages of LEO satellites with low orbital height and large landing power, this paper proposes a LEO-assisted acquisition algorithm. The code phase and Doppler frequency estimates can be obtained through the assistance of LEO satellites, which can extend the coherent integration time. This method can effectively improve the anti-interference ability of the B1C signal and reduce the average acquisition time. The on-orbit test results show that under the condition of 80 ms coherent integration and 2 times incoherent, B1C anti-interference ability can be improved by 14 dB.

Keywords: LEO-assisted · Acquisition · Anti-interference · On-orbit

1 Introduction

On July 31, 2020, the BDS-3 global satellite navigation system was officially opened for use, which can provide users around the world with all-day, continuous and uninterrupted navigation and positioning services, and is widely used in military and civilian fields. Although BDS-3 has been built, due to the inherent shortcomings of the satellite navigation system, BDS, like GPS and other global navigation satellite systems (GNSS), naturally has shortcomings. Moreover, with the gradual expansion of satellite navigation applications and the continuous improvement of users' demand for service accuracy, especially in the fields of autonomous driving, homeland survey, military and national defense, the vulnerability of GNSS navigation signals has become more prominent [1, 2]. GNSS satellite orbit height is above 20000 km. On the one hand, due to the limitation of the energy on the satellite, it cannot transmit high-power signals; on the other hand, the navigation signal undergoes radio frequency attenuation and electromagnetic interference during long-distance propagation, and the signal is already very

© ICST Institute for Computer Sciences, Social Informatics and Telecommunications Engineering 2021
Published by Springer Nature Switzerland AG 2021. All Rights Reserved
X. Wang et al. (Eds.): AICON 2021, LNICST 396, pp. 153–164, 2021.
https://doi.org/10.1007/978-3-030-90196-7_14

weak when it reaches the ground, only about −160 dbW [3]. Moreover, in practical applications, GNSS navigation signals are widely used in weak signal environments, including urban indoors, forests, mountains, canyons, tunnels, underground garages, etc. The carrier to noise ratio (CN0) of satellite signals in these environments is about 15 dB lower than that in an open outdoor environment. The acquisition sensitivity of traditional receivers is difficult to meet the acquisition requirements of weak signals in these complex environments.

For weak signal capture technology, coherent integration and non-coherent integration are the classic weak signal capture methods [4] The coherent integration method can obtain the maximum signal-to-noise ratio gain. However, the coherent integration is limited by the influence of the navigation data bit flip, and the coherent integration time usually cannot exceed the length of one navigation data bit. Although the non-coherent integration method can overcome the impact of bit jumps, its disadvantage is that there is a square loss. In view of the shortcomings of the above-mentioned direct acquisition method, this paper proposes a LEO satellite to assist BDS B1C weak signal acquisition algorithm, through the LEO satellite to obtain code phase estimates and doppler estimates to extend the coherent integration time, improve the weak signal capture ability.

2 System Model

With the continuous development of navigation application requirements such as artificial intelligence, Internet of Things, and autonomous driving, LEO satellites have become a hot issue in the construction of satellite navigation systems in recent years due to their excellent signal characteristics and application potential. LEO satellites can enhance satellite navigation signals as an enhancement and supplement to GNSS. They can also broadcast independent ranging signals through the integration of communication systems and navigation systems to form backup positioning and navigation capabilities. Iridium in the United States has realized the integration and development of GPS systems, providing users with STL (Satellites Time and Location) services, which can back up and enhance GPS capabilities [5]. China has also built and deployed its own low-orbit navigation constellation, the "ongYan" constellation constructed by China Aerospace Science and Technology Corporation, the "HongYun" project planned by China Aerospace Science and Industry Corporation, and the "LuoJia-1" scientific experiment satellite developed by Wuhan University [6] and many more.

Compared with the current networked medium and high orbit satellite navigation system, the application of LEO satellite signals in navigation and positioning has the following advantages: First, the orbital height of LEO satellites is lower, which is about 5% of that of conventional GNSS satellites. One part, the free propagation loss of the signal is small, so the signal received on the ground is stronger; second, the LEO satellites are faster, the Doppler change is fast, and the geometric pattern changes quickly, which is conducive to the use of Doppler for positioning [7, 8]. Third, the research and development cost of LEO satellites and rocket launch costs are relatively low, and they can be launched by multiple satellites with one rocket (Fig. 1).

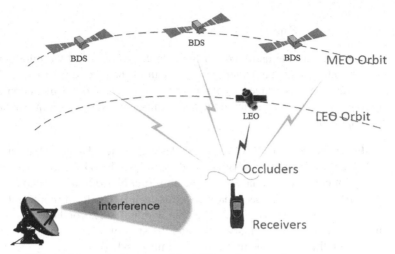

Fig. 1. Schematic diagram of the LEO navigation enhancement system

The LEO navigation enhancement system designed in this paper includes GNSS constellations, LEO satellites and ground navigation enhancement terminals.

The GNSS constellation transmits GNSS navigation signals. LEO satellites carry navigation enhancement payloads, forward the ephemeris of BDS satellites, and broadcast navigation enhancement signals. First, the LEO satellite receives and processes the GNSS navigation signal, and completes its own positioning based on the GNSS satellite signal, and at the same time obtains the ephemeris information of the BDS satellite. Then the ephemeris information of the BDS satellite is modulated into the LEO navigation enhancement signal and broadcasted to the ground navigation enhancement terminal.

The ground navigation enhancement terminal firstly performs independent positioning and timing by receiving the navigation enhancement signal of the LEO satellite. Then obtain the ephemeris of the forwarded BDS satellite through decoding. Finally, the auxiliary information is obtained by calculation, including the Doppler estimation value and code phase estimation value of the B1C signal, which assists in the realization of the B1C weak signal acquisition and completes more accurate positioning and timing services.

3 Algorithm Model

3.1 B1C Signal Model

Signal Structure. Compared with the BPSK single-channel signal system of BDS-2, the BDS-3 B1C signal adopts a new BOC modulation method, and at the same time, it has also been improved from a traditional single data channel to a data and pilot dual-channel structure. The data channel modulates a navigation message containing ranging information, while the pilot channel does not contain any data information. The baseband signal expression is as follows [3]:

$$S_{B1c\_Data}(t) = A_1 D(t) C_{Data}(t) sc_{Data}(t) \tag{1}$$

$$S_{B1c\_Pilot}(t) = A_2 C_{Pilot}(t) sc_{Pilot}(t) \tag{2}$$

Where, A_1 and A_2 are the amplitude of the data component and the pilot component respectively; $D(t)$ is the navigation message data of the B1C signal; $C_{Data}(t)$ and $C_{Pilot}(t)$ are the ranging code sequences of the data component and the pilot component respectively; $sc_{Data}(t)$ is the subcarrier of the data component; $sc_{Pilot}(t)$ is the subcarrier of the pilot component.

Ranging Code Structure.   The B1C ranging codes are the tiered codes which are generated by XORing the primary codes with secondary codes. The B1C primary codes (for both data and pilot components) have the same chip rate of 1.023 Mcps, and have the same length of 10230 chips. The secondary code for each B1C pilot component has the length of 1800 chips. As shown in Fig. 2, The chip width of the secondary code has the same length as one period of a primary code, and the start of a secondary code chip is strictly aligned with the start of the first chip of primary code (Fig. 2).

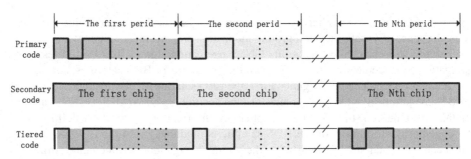

Fig. 2. Timing relationships of the primary code and secondary code

3.2 Algorithm Design

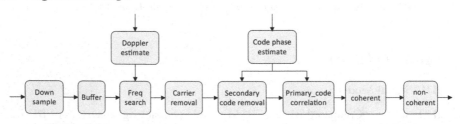

Fig. 3. Schematic diagram of the B1C acquisition algorithm assisted by LEO

Since the landing power of LEO satellites is generally 10-30dB higher than that of BDS satellites, ground terminals can still receive LEO navigation enhancement signals normally under B1C signal obstruction or interference. Considering the advantages and disadvantages of coherent integration and non-coherent integration, this paper designs a LEO-assisted B1C acquisition algorithm for weak B1C signals, which is shown in Fig. 3. The algorithm uses the assistance of LEO satellites to achieve the acquisition of weak B1C signals by extending the coherent integration time as the main method and non-coherent as the auxiliary method.

According to Sect. 3.1, the data component of the B1C signal and the signal of the pilot component are synchronized. Moreover, the pilot component does not modulate the navigation message, so only capturing the pilot component can complete the capture of the B1C signal. Although the pilot component does not modulate the navigation message, it modulates the secondary code. This article uses LEO's auxiliary information to strip the secondary code of the pilot component to achieve long-term coherent integration.

Get auxiliary information. First, the ground navigation enhancement terminal uses the LEO navigation enhancement signal to independently complete coarse positioning and coarse timing, and at the same time obtain the retransmitted ephemeris of the visible BDS satellite. Taking into account the low orbital height of LEO and the large Doppler frequency deviation (usually around ± 40 kHz), the LEO signal is captured using a parallel code algorithm, the frequency search step is set to 400 Hz, and the total integration accumulation time is 2 ms, so that the capture time can be Within 1 s.

Then, according to the results of coarse positioning and coarse timing and the transmitted ephemeris of the visible BDS satellite, comprehensively considering the receiver clock offset, clock drift and other factors, the Doppler and code phase estimates of the BDS B1C visible satellite are calculated.

Acquisition of weak B1C signals by auxiliary information. As shown in Fig. 3, the LEO-assisted B1C capture algorithm includes Down sample, Buffer, Freq search, Carrier removal, Secondary code removal, Primary_code correlation, coherent, non-coherent and so on. The ground navigation enhancement terminal uses the Doppler estimate to reduce the frequency search range when searching for frequencies. Using the code phase estimation value, on the one hand, the secondary code is stripped before the correlation operation, eliminating the limitation of "bit flip", and long-time coherent integration; on the other hand, the code phase search range is reduced during the main code correlation operation, saving hardware resources.

In order to improve the efficiency of acquisition, a parallel code acquisition method based on DBZP (Double Block Zero Padding) and FFT is used in the FPGA acquisition design. After the signal is mixed and down-converted to baseband, the received sequence is double-filled by the double-block zero-filling method, and then correlated with the local sequence. The correlation operation is realized by the FFT/IFFT module of the classic acquisition method of PCS (parallel code search), and then the correlation operation results are stored in RAM. For long-time coherent integration, the segment correlation accumulation operation is adopted to accumulate and store the correlation results of the same code phase. Then the stored coherent accumulation results are sequentially read out, and the IFFT operation is performed. Finally, the result is modulated and accumulated to complete the incoherent integration, and the peak value is compared with the threshold to complete the acquisition.

In addition, although the aiding information from LEO can narrow the search range of frequency and code phase, the longer the coherent integration time, the smaller the frequency search step. Under the same Doppler frequency offset, the number of frequency grids to be searched increases, which will increase the acquisition time to a certain extent. Moreover, after long-time coherent integration is used, the data sampling time is the main part of the acquisition time. In order to reduce the acquisition time and improve the acquisition efficiency, this paper designs the use of a large-capacity buffer to store the amount of data required to complete a acquisition in advance, reducing the subsequent sampling time.

3.3 Determination of Integration Time

In order to enhance the filtering effect, reduce noise and improve sensitivity, the longer the coherent integration time, the better for improving the capture sensitivity. However, the determination of the coherent integration time requires comprehensive consideration from the following aspects:

(1) As the coherent integration time is lengthened, the crystal noise of the receiver will accumulate as a frequency deviation, which will cause the attenuation of the integral gain;
(2) The longer the coherent integration time, the greater the frequency error caused by the frequency stability of the receiver clock and the satellite clock, and the greater the coherent integration loss;
(3) The longer the coherent integration time, the smaller the frequency search step and the greater the amount of calculation;
(4) In order to maintain the dynamic response performance of the receiver, including the dynamics of satellite motion and clock noise, the integration result of the coherent integration needs to leave a certain bandwidth, and the coherent integration time cannot be too large.

After Matlab simulation analysis, with the assistance of LEO satellites, this article uses 80 ms coherent integration time and 2 non-coherent integrations to capture, which can take into account the noise and dynamic performance of the receiver, while balancing the coherent integration gain and the amount of calculation.

4   On-Orbit Verification

4.1   Testing Platform

In order to verify the effectiveness of the LEO-assisted B1C acquisition algorithm for improving the anti-jamming performance, this paper carried out an on-orbit test for experimental verification and analysis. The equipment required for the ground test verification platform mainly includes GNSS and LEO receiving antennas, anti-jamming navigation receivers, interference generators, combiners, computers, etc. GNSS and LEO receiving antennas are used to receive GNSS navigation signals and LEO navigation enhancement signals. The anti-jamming navigation receiver receives and processes the GNSS/LEO signal to complete the acquisition, tracking, positioning and calculation. The interference generator generates interference signals and sends them to the combiner for anti-interference testing. The combiner combines the signal received by the antenna with the interference signal to transmit the anti-jamming navigation receiver. The computer displays the test results and stores the test data.

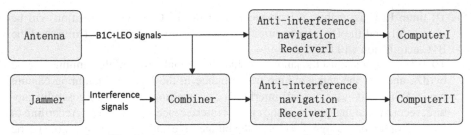

Fig. 4. On-orbit test equipment connection diagram

In order to verify the anti-jamming characteristics, this paper designed a ground test platform for on-orbit tests, as shown in Fig. 4. Receiver I is a non-interference on-orbit test, only receiving navigation signals, using the normal acquisition mode without assistance, as a reference and result comparison. Receiver II is an anti-jamming in-orbit test. Before LEO enters the test site, Receiver II uses the normal acquisition mode without assistance. The purpose is to test the anti-jamming performance of the acquisition algorithm without external assistance. When the LEO enters the visual range of the test site, the acquisition mode of the Receiver II is switched to the anti-jamming acquisition mode, in order to test the anti-jamming performance of the acquisition algorithm assisted by the LEO.

4.2 Testing Process

For the test platform shown in Fig. 4, the corresponding test process is designed in this section. Assume that T0 is the entry time of the LEO in orbit. For Receiver I, it only needs to be turned on 15 min before the entry of LEO, and use the normal mode to capture B1C. The test results of the Receiver I, including the captured satellite's PRN, CN0, Doppler, etc. And they will be used as the benchmark standard for the Receiver II. In order to verify the performance of LEO-assisted B1C acquisition, the test procedure of Receiver II is specifically designed as follows:

(1) T0–15 min time: Turn on Receiver II and keep the jammer off. The B1C signal works in the normal acquisition mode, and it is expected that multiple visible satellites will be successfully acquired.
(2) T0–12 min: Turn on the jammer and set a high-power jamming signal to ensure that the B1C signal is out of lock and cannot be positioned.
(3) T0–10 min: Adjust the jammer, reduce the signal power of the jamming signal by dB, and test the anti-jamming performance of the B1C normal capture mode. When B1C successfully captures using the normal capture mode, it records the signal power of the current interference signal. According to the calibration of the signal power in the budget, the anti-interference threshold of the normal mode is calculated.
(4) T0–5 min time: adjust the jammer and set high-power jamming signal to ensure that the B1C signal is out of lock and cannot be positioned.

(5) T0 time: LEO is visible, it is expected that the LEO signal acquisition will be successful, and the Doppler positioning will be completed within 1 min, and the B1C acquisition will be guided.

(6) T0 + 1 min time: adjust the jammer, reduce the signal power of the jamming signal by dB, and test the anti-jamming performance in the B1C anti-jamming capture mode. When B1C uses the anti-interference acquisition mode to successfully capture, record the signal power of the current interference signal power. According to the calibration of the signal power in the budget, the anti-jamming threshold of the anti-jamming mode is calculated.

Since the LEO satellite can be seen for about 10 min, the time is very short. During the on-orbit test, the test process of steps (3) and (6) is relatively time-consuming. Therefore, before the on-orbit test, the anti-interference ability of the terminal using GNSS and LEO signal simulation sources was used to conduct a threshold test. It only needs to test near the threshold.

The test process using GNSS/LEO signal simulator is the same as above. Without the aid of LEO satellites, test the acquisition situation of the anti-jamming receiver under different interference power conditions in the normal acquisition mode. After testing, the terminal capture interference signal ratio (ISR) threshold is 28 dBc. Under LEO-assisted conditions, test the anti-jamming terminal's anti-jamming mode under different interference power conditions. After testing, the terminal positioning ISR threshold is 42 dBc, compared with no LEO satellite guidance, anti-jamming The ability is increased by 14 dB.

4.3   On-Orbit Test and Results

On December 9, 2020, in Beijing, China, a ground receiving test was conducted on a LEO satellite signal in orbit. The visible time range of the LEO test satellite is 21:03:07–21:12:07, and the duration is 540 s.

LEO Signal Power Test. Normally and continuously LEO signals were received within the visible time. After successful acquisition and stable tracking, as shown in the Fig. 5, the satellite's elevation angle to the ground varies from 9° to 35°, and the statistical CN0 is from 47 dB-Hz to 63 dB-Hz. According to the positive correlation between the channel CN0 and the elevation angle, the CN0 will be even greater when the LEO satellite passes from the top, about 70 dB-Hz. In the Fig. 5, the start time of the time count on the horizontal axis is 21:03:59, which corresponds to 52 s after the entry of the LEO satellite. The elevation angle of the BDS satellite to the ground varies between 5° and 90°, and the CN0 is generally between 37 dB-Hz and 50 dB-Hz. It can be verified that the CN0 of LEO is about 10–20 dB higher than that of GNSS satellites, which is feasible for assisting B1C weak signal acquisition.

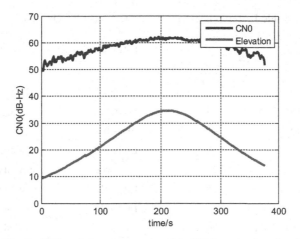

Fig. 5. CN0 and elevation angle of the LEO navigation signal

Anti-interference Ability Test. The anti-jamming capability test will begin 15 min before the LEO test satellite becomes visible. The test process and recorded results are shown in Table 1. In a non-interference scenario, anti-jamming Receiver I and Receiver II normally receive signals from 8 BDS satellites. The satellites are PRN23, PRN 24, PRN 25, PRN 34, PRN 39, PRN 40, PRN 43, and PRN 44.

The meanings of some abbreviations in Table 1 are as follows:
ACQ_OK: successful acquisition.
TRK_POS_OK: stable tracking and complete positioning.
LOSE_LOCK: the signal is in lock-out and recapture state.
AACQ: LEO is assisting B1C acquisition.
At 20:51:07, the interference value configuration of Receiver II is performed by the method described in Sect. 4.2, and ISR is set to 50 dbc. After the interference is turned on, the successfully captured satellites all lose lock, and the terminal enters the non-positioning state. When the interference signal power is adjusted and ISR is set to 28 dbc, the B1C acquisition in normal mode successfully captures multiple BDS satellites, indicating that the anti-jamming capability of the B1C acquisition without assistance in the orbit test is 28 dbc.

At 20:58:07, the anti-jamming test assisted by LEO is ready to be carried out, the ISR is set to 50dbc, and the successfully captured satellites lose lock again, and the Receiver II is in a non-positioning state. At 21:03:07, LEO can be seen, and the anti-jamming Receiver II starts to capture, track and Doppler single-satellite positioning of LEO. At 21:06:35, the positioning accuracy reached the level of guiding B1C, and the B1C acquisition began to be guided. At 21:07:42, when the ISR is set to 42 dbc, the B1C acquisition in anti-jamming mode successfully captured 6 satellites, indicating that the anti-jamming capability of B1C capture with the assistance of LEO in the orbit test is 42 dbc.

Table 2 shows the statistics of CN0 and elevation angle of BDS satellites captured by Receiver I without interference and Receiver II with interference.

Table 1. Test process and record results of Receiver II.

Time	Jammer		LEO	BDS B1C
	State	ISR (dbc)		
20:48:07	OFF	---	Invisible	Power on
20:48:53	OFF	---	Invisible	ACQ_OK
20:49:45	OFF	---	Invisible	TRK_POS_OK
20:51:07	ON	50	Invisible	LOSE_LOCK
20:51:15	Power down	29	Invisible	LOSE_LOCK
20:53:07	Power down	**28**	Invisible	ACQ-OK
20:58:07	Power up	50	Invisible	LOSE_LOCK
21:03:07	Power hold	50	Visible	LOSE_LOCK
21:03:15	Power hold	50	ACQ_OK	LOSE_LOCK
21:03:59	Power hold	50	TRK_POS_OK	LOSE_LOCK
21:06:35	Power hold	50	AACQ	LOSE_LOCK
21:06:50	Power down	43	AACQ	LOSE_LOCK
21:07:42	Power down	**42**	AACQ	ACQ_OK
21:08:27	Power hold	42	AACQ	TRK_POS_OK
21:12:07	Power hold	42 dbc	Invisible	TRK_POS_OK

Table 2. Comparison of B1C acquisition results with or without interference scenes

PRN	Receiver I		Receiver II		
	CN0 (dB-Hz)	Elevation (°)	CN0 (dB-Hz)	Elevation (°)	ISR (dbc)
23	48.3	53.34	36.6	60.72	28.5
24	36.1	14.74	25.8	8.69	39
25	48.6	70.83	35.8	63.66	29
28	---	---	27.0	18.31	38
34	48.4	58.59	---	---	---
37	---	---	23.0	9.77	42
39	38.2	22.29	24.8	18.07	40
40	46.8	64.86	---	---	---
43	48.2	61.99	---	---	---
44	35.9	7.51	---	---	---

In a non-interference scenario, Receiver I captures 8 satellites, of which PRN28 and PRN37 are not captured. According to the results captured by Receiver II, the elevation angles of the two satellites to the ground are small, and the signal CN0 is also small, which is limited by the acquisition sensitivity and probability of capture, so Receiver I failed to capture them.

In the interference scenario, the anti-interference acquisition mode captures 6 satellites, the elevation angle of PRN37 is 9.77°, the CN0 is 23.0 dB-Hz, the ISR is 42 dBc. And the CN0 of the remaining 5 satellites is higher than 23 dB.It should be noted that the PRN34, PRN40, PRN43, and PRN44 satellites were successfully captured in the non-interference scenario, but the anti-interference acquisition mode capture in the interference scenario failed to capture. After analyzing the forwarding strategy of satellite selection on the satellite, affected by factors including the validity of the ephemeris and the upper limit of the forwarding ephemeris, the above-mentioned satellites could not be forwarded to the ground by LEO, so the anti-jamming mode could not be captured.

In summary, the BDS satellites forwarded by LEO are visible to the ground. The ground anti-jamming receiver can complete the acquisition of the weak B1C signal according to the LEO forwarding BDS satellite ephemeris. In the non-interference scenario, the anti-interference ability of the normal acquisition mode is 28 dbc, and in the interference scene, the anti-interference ability of t anti-interference acquisition mode is 42 dbc. It shows that the anti-jamming performance of the LEO-assisted B1C acquisition algorithm proposed in this paper is very effective. The on-orbit test shows that the anti-jamming ability of the LEO-assisted B1C acquisition algorithm is improved by 14 dB.

5   Conclusion

This article analyzes the vulnerability of GNSS under occlusion and interference environments, and compares the effects of coherent integration and incoherent integration on the signal processing gain. Considering the development and advantages of LEO satellites, it is concluded that the acquisition algorithm that increases the coherent integration time with the aid of the low-orbit navigation enhancement signal is more effective for the acquisition of B1C signals under the condition of low SNR. Based on this, this paper designs a low-orbit navigation enhancement system, and proposes a LEO-assisted B1C acquisition algorithm, and analyzes the effectiveness and feasibility of the LEO-assisted acquisition algorithm from various aspects such as system design and algorithm principles. Finally, through the on-orbit test analysis of an on-orbit test satellite, it is obtained that the anti-jamming capability of the B1C signal with the assistance of LEO can be increased by 14 dB, which is of great significance for improving the anti-jamming performance of the GNSS signal.

References

1. Zhao, Yu.: Brief probe on application of compass navigation satellite system in the fields of sea, land and air. In: Proceedings of 2017 2nd International Conference on Materials Science, Machinery and Energy Engineering, pp. 212–217.Dalian, China (2017)

2. Yang, Y.: Concepts of comprehensive PNT and related key technologies. Acta Geodaetica et Cartographica Sinica **45**(5), 505–510 (2016)
3. BeiDou Navigation Satellite System Signal in Space Interface Control Document Open Service Signal B1C (Version 1.0). http://www.beidou.gov.cn. Accessed 21 Apr 2021
4. Yang, C., Miller, M., Blasch, E., Blasch, E.: Comparative study of coherent non-coherent and semi-coherent integration schemes for GNSS receivers. Proc. ION GNSS **1**(2), 572 (2007)
5. Satelles-White-Paper-Final.   https://satelles.com/wp-content/uploads/pdf/Satelles-White-Paper-2019.pdf. Accessed 21 Apr 2021
6. Tian, R., Cui, Z.-y., Zhang, S., Wang, D.: Navigation positioning & timing **1**(8), 66–81 (2021)
7. Zhizhong, L., Yu, Z., Xueli, Z., Yan, C.: Research and simulation of single star positioning algorithm based on low earth orbit satellite. In: Proceeding of 9th China Satllellite Navigation Conference. Ha'er bin China (2018)
8. Qin, H., Tan, Z., Cong, L., Zhao, C.: Positioning technology based on IRIDIUM signals of opportunity. J. Beijing Univ. Aeronaut. Astronaut. **45**(09), 1691–1699 (2019)

Research on Ship Target Detection in SAR Image Based on Improved YOLO v3 Algorithm

Yang Chen[✉], Shaojie Zhu, Xiuwen Xu, Hui Ye, Yang Liu, and Yuchuan Xu

Shanghai Institute of Satellite Engineering, Shanghai, China

Abstract. Synthetic aperture radar (SAR) has the characteristics of all-weather, all day and multi-application observation. In recent years, ship target detection based on SAR image has been widely concerned by relevant researchers. In this paper, based on the object detection method of deep learning algorithm, the detection performance of ship target in SAR image is studied by using YOLOv3 algorithm. In order to solve the problem of increasing error rate of ship target detection in complex background, YOLOv3 algorithm is improved. By adding a preprocessing layer in the front of the input layer, the accuracy of the ship detection is improved from 92.17% to 95.80%. The algorithm can be applied to other target detection in SAR image.

Keywords: Deep learning · YOLOv3 · Ship detection · SAR image

1 Introduction

Synthetic aperture radar (SAR) has the characteristics of all-weather, all-day and multi-purpose observation. It can make high-resolution imaging of the observation area, and has a wide range of applications in environmental protection, disaster monitoring, marine observation, resource exploration, precision agriculture, geological mapping and other fields [1]. Therefore, for SAR images, it is particularly important to achieve fast and accurate target detection.

With the rapid development of global economy and society, the trade between countries is increasing, the demand for shipping is growing rapidly, and ships are getting bigger and faster. Safety has become an important research content in the field of modern ship research [2]. With the increase of the number of ships, the increase of ship size and tonnage, the risk of ship navigation is also increasing. In March 2021, "Ever Given", a super large freighter of Taiwan Evergreen Marine Corp, ran aground in the Suez Canal. It led to the whole river blocked for several days, resulting in huge economic losses. Therefore, it is of great significance to realize the ship target detection in SAR image for ship monitoring (Fig. 1).

With the continuous progress of SAR imaging technology, the ability to obtain high-resolution and massive data has been greatly improved. Ship target detection based on SAR image has been paid more and more attention by relevant researchers and engineers, and has become one of the important research contents in the field of marine remote sensing technology [3].

© ICST Institute for Computer Sciences, Social Informatics and Telecommunications Engineering 2021
Published by Springer Nature Switzerland AG 2021. All Rights Reserved
X. Wang et al. (Eds.): AICON 2021, LNICST 396, pp. 165–176, 2021.
https://doi.org/10.1007/978-3-030-90196-7_15

Fig. 1. The "Ever Given" stranded in Suez Canal

2 Current Situation of Ship Target Detection

Object detection is one of the basic researches in the field of computer vision. In recent years, with the continuous improvement of computer computing ability, the research of object detection based on deep learning has developed rapidly. The target detection algorithm has also changed from the traditional algorithm based on artificial features to the deep neural network detection technology. In just a few years, many excellent algorithm technologies have emerged in the top-level conference of machine vision. From R-CNN and OverFeat proposed in 2013 to the following Fast R-CNN, SSD and YOlO series, the network structure has changed from two levels to one level, and the algorithm performance has changed from PC oriented to mobile oriented (Fig. 2). The object detection algorithm based on deep learning shows strong detection effect and performance [4].

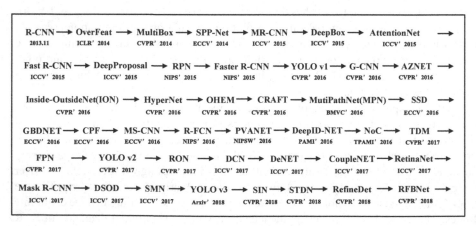

Fig. 2. The history of object detection

The core of ship target detection research is image technology. Through the acquisition of the ship target image, the object detection technology is used to recognize the ship target in the complex environment. The existing methods are mainly divided into two categories: traditional image processing technology or artificial intelligence deep learning technology. Different methods are different in the specific processing process [3], but these methods have general characteristics. The details are shown in the figure below (Fig. 3).

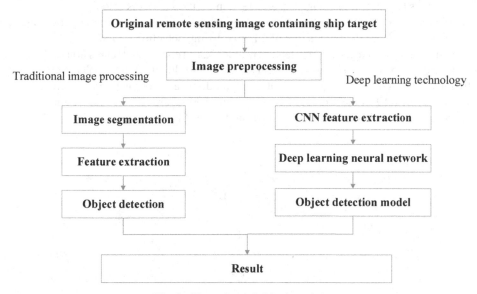

Fig. 3. Flow chart of ship detection

The method of target detection based on deep learning uses convolution neural network or other deep learning models to extract the deep features of the image. Then the network structure is used to transfer the feature map layer by layer to complete the accurate prediction of the target location. In this paper, YOLOv3 algorithm based on deep learning is used to detect ship targets in SAR images. More than 1000 SAR images are trained and tested in SSDD dataset, and the detection effect was evaluated by calculating mAP(mean Average Precision). At the same time, through the improvement of yolov3 algorithm, the detection performance is improved.

3 YOLO v3 Algorithm

The target detection methods based on convolution neural network can be divided into two categories, one is two-stage detection method, the other is single-stage detection method. The two-stage target detection usually starts with region proposal correction and background elimination, and then carries out region proposal classification and bounding box regression; The single-stage target detection algorithm integrates the two processes, and achieves the framework by anchor points and classification refinement [4].

Each of the two methods have their own advantages and disadvantages. The two-stage detection has some advantages in detection accuracy and performance, but its speed and real-time performance are still far behind the single-stage detection. The single-stage detection method only needs one feed-forward network calculation, which greatly improves the detection speed and it is more conducive to the on orbit application in the case of limited satellite resources.

YOLO is the first single-stage target detection method and it is also the first method to realize real-time target detection. The detection speed can reach 45 frames per second, and the mAP is more than twice that of other real-time detection systems.

YOLO algorithm regards the detection problem as an end-to-end regression problem, so the process of image processing is very simple and direct. In 2018, YOLO v3 was officially proposed. On the basis of YOLO v2, it adopts a deeper network structure and extends darknet-19 to darknet-53. The model has 106 layers of network. The network structure of Yolo V3 is shown in the following figure (Fig. 4):

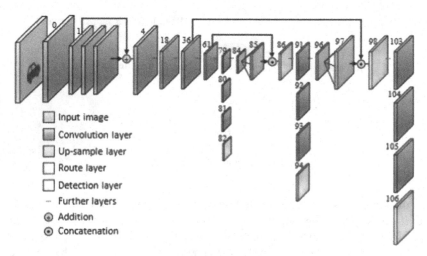

Fig. 4. The network structure of YOLO v3

As shown in the figure above, the number represents the number of layers, and its network structure includes Input layer, Convolution layer (including residual bloack), Up-sample layer, Route layer and Detection layer. As can be seen from the figure, YOLO v3 model realizes three kinds of different scale detection in the detection layer, which are located in the 82nd, 94th and 106th layers. The characteristic maps are 13 × 13, 26 × 26 and 52 × 52, which can detect targets of different sizes.In addition, YOLO v3 uses a total of nine anchor boxes, and each anchor box has three sizes, which can predict more frames [4]. In YOLO v3, the loss functions of predicted and true values are calculated as follows:

$$
\begin{aligned}
loss = & \sum_{i=0}^{S^2} \sum_{j=0}^{B} I_{ij}^{obj} \left[\left(\sigma(t_x)_i^j - \sigma(\hat{t}_x)_i^j \right)^2 + \left(\sigma(t_y)_i^j - \sigma(\hat{t}_y)_i^j \right)^2 \right] \\
& + \sum_{i=0}^{S^2} \sum_{j=0}^{B} I_{ij}^{obj} \left[\left(t_{w_i^j} - \hat{t}_{w_i^j} \right)^2 + \left(t_{h_i^j} - \hat{t}_{h_i^j} \right)^2 \right] \\
& + \sum_{i=0}^{S^2} \sum_{j=0}^{B} I_{ij}^{obj} \left(C_i^j - \hat{C}_i^j \right)^2 \\
& + \sum_{i=0}^{S^2} \sum_{j=0}^{B} \sum_{C \in classes} I_{ij}^{obj} \left(p_i^j(c) - \hat{p}_i^j(c) \right)^2
\end{aligned}
\tag{1}
$$

Where S2 is the number of grids, and B is the number of bounding boxes in each grid. The means that when the jth bounding box of the ith grid is responsible for predicting the target. If the target is detected, the, otherwise it is 0. The first term in the formula represents the loss of the center point of the bounding box, the second term represents the loss of the width and height of the bounding box. The parameter C is the confidence score. The p is the probability of ship class.

4 Ship Detection in SAR Image Based on YOLOv3

4.1 Experimental Environment

In order to verify the ability of YOLOv3 algorithm in ship target detection of SAR image. In this paper, the framework of deep learning is Tensorflow2.4.0. Tensorflow is a widely used framework developed and maintained by Google for deep learning. It has a training visualization component Tensorboard, which can visualize the network structure and training process, and it is convenient for long-term and large-scale training of the network. Our framework was developed on Windows 10 operating system and Intel (R) core (TM) processor i5-8400cpu@2.80 Ghz. The GPU version is NVIDIA GTX 1060 which contains 5G RAM. The memory capacity is 8G and the programming language is python.

4.2 Experimental Dataset

The common dataset called SSDD used in this paper contains 1160 SAR images and 2456 ship targets. The dataset contains ship targets under various conditions, which is commonly used in this field (Fig. 5).

The dataset in this article uses the same format as the PASCOL VOC dataset, which store the data content in three folders called Annotation、JPEGImages and ImageSets.

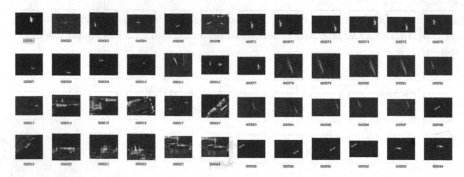

Fig. 5. The SSDD dataset

```
- <annotation verified="no">
    <folder>JPEGImages</folder>
    <filename>000001</filename>
    <path>/home/ljw/FRCN_ROOT/data/VOCdevkit2007/VOC2007/JPEGImages/000001.jpg</path>
  - <source>
      <database>Unknown</database>
    </source>
  - <size>
      <width>416</width>
      <height>323</height>
      <depth>1</depth>
    </size>
    <segmented>0</segmented>
  - <object>
      <name>ship</name>
      <pose>Unspecified</pose>
      <truncated>0</truncated>
      <difficult>0</difficult>
    - <bndbox>
        <xmin>208</xmin>
        <ymin>50</ymin>
        <xmax>273</xmax>
        <ymax>151</ymax>
      </bndbox>
    </object>
  </annotation>
```

Fig. 6. The Label data format

The JPEGImages folder is used to store images, and the Annotation folder is used to store label files corresponding to each image. The XML file format is shown in the following figure (Fig. 6):

The label content includes the category (name) of the target in the bounding box, as well as the width, height and position (x_{min}, x_{max}, y_{min}, y_{max}) of the bounding box. The dataset is divided into training set, validation set and test set according to the ratio of 8:2:1.6.

4.3 Model Training

The weight adjustment method of model training is gradient descent method. The training batchsize value is 4, epoch value is 100, the initial learning rate value is 0.01, and the attenuation weight of learning rate value is 0.0001. The training generates CKPT model file and node file, which saves the weights in the network structure. The weight parameter file occupies about 240 MB of storage capacity. The figures below show the process of the loss value changing with the number of iterations in the training process. With the increase of training times, the training error gradually decreases, and the network fitting effect is getting better and better (Fig. 7).

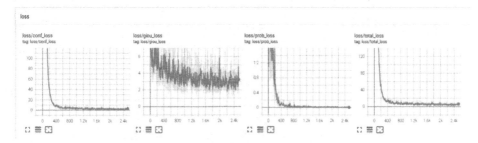

Fig. 7. The process of loss reduction in training

4.4 Experimental Results Analysis

In this paper, mAP (average precision) is used as the measurement index. Since the data only contains lable like ship, the AP value of the ship is mAP value of the experimental results, and the calculation formula is as follows:

$$AP = \int_0^1 P(R)dR \tag{2}$$

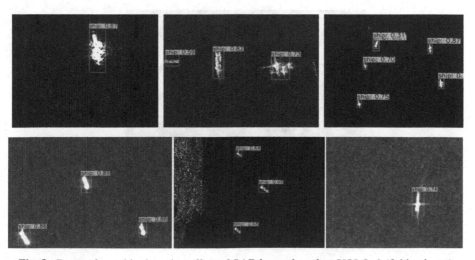

Fig. 8. Research on ship detection effect of SAR image based on YOLOv3 (fishing boats)

The parameter P represents the accuracy rate and the parameter R represents the recall rate.

The ship target detection algorithm based on YOLO v3 has achieved good results on SSDD dataset. The test set contains 188 images, including 348 ship targets, with an average accuracy of 92.17%. The specific test results are shown in the figure below (Fig. 8 and Fig. 9).

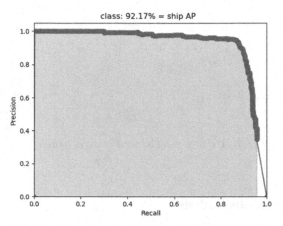

Fig. 9. P-R curve of test results (accuracy 92.17%)

However, the effect of this algorithm is not good in the detection of complex background, and it is easy to mistakenly detect the background as a ship, as shown in the figure below (Fig. 10).

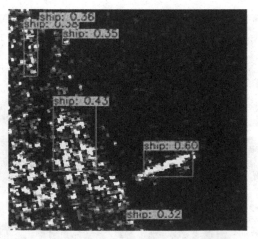

Fig. 10. Weak detection in complex background

5 Ship Detection in SAR Image Based on Improved Algorithm

5.1 Algorithm Improvement

Because there are a lot of coherent noises in SAR images, especially in complex background, it is easy to cause interference to the network, which leads to the false detection of the background as the target and reduces the accuracy. To solve this problem, this paper adds a preprocessing layer before the input layer of the network structure (Fig. 11).

Fig. 11. Improved network structure

Before network training, median filtering is performed on the preprocessing layer. Median filtering is a non-linear smoothing technique, which sets the gray value of each pixel to the median value of all pixels in the neighborhood window. If the filter window length value L is equal to 2N + 1, the calculation formula of window filter output is as follows:

$$y(i) = Med[x(i - N), \cdots, x(i), \cdots, x(i + N)] \qquad (3)$$

Median filter is very effective for removing salt and pepper noise, while preserving the edge details of the image. The figures below show a comparison of SAR image before and after median filtering (Fig. 12).

It can be seen from the above figure that the filtered SAR image effectively suppresses the background noise, and the target is more prominent. After preprocessing all training images, the network model is retrained according to the settings in Sect. 4.3. The experimental results have been effectively improved.

5.2 Experimental Results Analysis and Comparison

Meanwhile, 188 images in the testset of SSDD are used to test the improved algorithm model in this paper. The average accuracy value was 95.80%. Compared with single YOLO network, the accuracy is improved by 3.63%. The specific test results are shown in the figure below (Figs. 13 and 14).

It can be seen from the above figures that the proportion of correct prediction is significantly improved after median filtering, which indicates that the network can better identify the image target after preprocessing and the proportion of the correct predicted quantity value has been greatly increased. Especially in the complex background, the accuracy of the method has been greatly improved (Fig. 15).

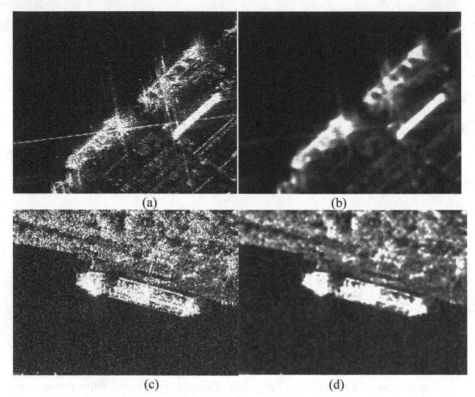

(a)   (b)

(c)   (d)

Fig. 12. Comparison of SAR image (Cargo Ship) before and after median filtering: (a) and (c) original image, (b) and (d) after median filtering image

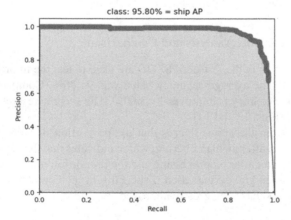

Fig. 13. The P-R curve of the improved algorithm (accuracy 95.80%)

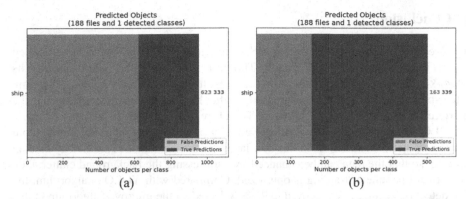

Fig. 14. The proportion change of correct prediction number before and after the improvement of the algorithm: (a) The correct proportion number of the original algorithm; (b) The correct proportion number of the improved algorithm

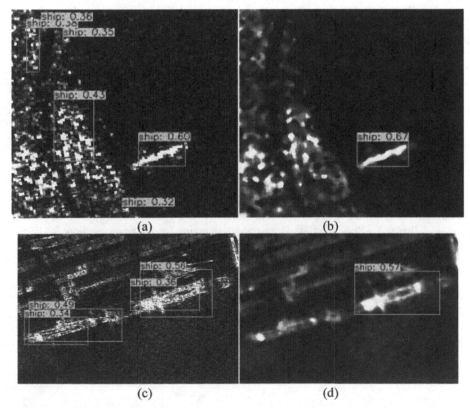

Fig. 15. Comparison of detection results before and after improved algorithm model: (a) and (c) The detection results of the original algorithm; (b) and (d) The detection results of the improved algorithm

6 Conclusion

To solve the problem of ship detection in SAR image, the YOLOv3 algorithm is applied to detect ship targets in SSDD dataset. Through the training and optimization of its network parameters, the accuracy of the test results only reached 92.17%. According to the specificity analysis, the main reason for the decrease of detection accuracy is the interference of complex sea background. Therefore, in this paper the network structure of YOLO v3 is improved. Specifically, we add a preprocessing layer before the input layer of the network structure. In this new layer, the image data is processed by median filtering, so that the data can be enhanced by suppressing the background clutter, then the network parameter training is optimized. Compared with YOLOv3 algorithm, the ship detection accuracy is improved to 95.80% based on the improved algorithm in this paper. The algorithm can be applied to other target detection in SAR images.

References

1. Qingjun, Z., Xiaolei, H., Jie, L.: Technology progress and development trend of spaceborne synthetic aperture radar remote sensing. Spacecraft Eng. **26**(6), 1–7 (2017). (in Chinese)
2. Wei, S.: Overview of ship detection technology based on remote sensing image. Telecommun. Eng. **60**(9),1126–1132 (2020) (in Chinese)
3. Li, J.W., Qu, C.W., Peng, S.J., Deng, B.: Ship detection in SAR images based on convolutional neural network. Syst. Eng. Electr. **40**(9), 1953–1959 (2018). (in Chinese)
4. Peng, D., Ming, C., Hua, S.T.: Deep Learning and Object Detection. Publishing of Electronics Industry, Beijing, March 2020
5. Redmon, J., Divvala, S., Girshick, R.: et al.: You only look once: unified, real-time object detection. In: IEEE Conference on Computer Vision and Pattern Recognition, pp. 779–788 (2016)
6. Redmon, J., Farhadi, A.:Yolov3: an incremental improvement. arXiv preprint arXiv:1804. 02767 (2018)
7. An, Q., Pan, Z., You, H.: Ship detection in Gaofen-3 SAR images based on sea clutter distribution analysis and deep convolutional neural network. Sensors **18**(2), 1345–1357 (2018)
8. He, K., Zhang, X., Ren, S., et al.: Deep residual learning for image recognition. In: IEEE Conference on Computer Vision and Pattern Recognition, pp. 770–778 (2016)

Energy Efficiency Optimization for Plane Spiral OAM Mode-Group Based MIMO-NOMA Systems

Jie Tang[1,2](✉), Yan Song[1], Chuting Lin[1], Wanmei Feng[1], Zhen Chen[1], Xiuying Zhang[1], and Kai-kit Wong[3]

[1] School of Electronic and Information Engineering,
South China University of Technology, Guangzhou, China
{eejtang,chenz,zhangxiuyin}@scut.edu.cn, songyan1222@whut.edu.cn,
eewmfeng@mail.scut.edu.cn
[2] The National Mobile Communications Research Laboratory, Southeast University,
Nanjing, China
[3] Department of Electronic and Electrical Engineering, University College London,
London, UK
kai-kit.wong@ucl.ac.uk

Abstract. In this paper, a plane spiral orbital angular momentum (PS-OAM) mode-groups (MGs) based multi-user multiple-input-multiple-out-put (MIMO) non-orthogonal multiple access (NOMA) system is studied, where a base station (BS) transmits date to multiple users by utilizing the generated PSOAM beams. For such scenario, the interference between users in different PSOAM-mode groups can be avoided, which leads to a significant performance enhancement. We aim to maximize the energy efficiency (EE) of the system subject to the total transmission power constraint and the minimum rate constraint. This design problem is non-convex by optimizing the power allocation, and thus is quite difficult to tackle directly. To solve this issue, we present a bisection-based power allocation algorithm where the bisection method is exploited in the outer layer to obtain the optimal EE and a power distributed iterative algorithm is exploited in the inner layer to optimize the transmit power. Simulation results validate the theoretical findings and demonstrate the proposed system can achieve better performance than the traditional multi-user MIMO system in terms of EE.

Keywords: Energy efficiency (EE) · Plane spiral orbital angular momentum (PSOAM) · Non-orthogonal multiple access (NOMA)

1 Introduction

The rapid development of Internet-of-Things (IoTs) applications has caused the exponential growth of wireless devices. Consequently, the sixth generation (6G) wireless networks face particular challenges to meet the further requirements in

X. Wang et al. (Eds.): AICON 2021, LNICST 396, pp. 177–188, 2021.
https://doi.org/10.1007/978-3-030-90196-7_16

terms of reliable data connectivity and ultra-high data-rate. In addition, the data rates of devices are severely limited by the insufficient spectrum resources. These trends make spectral efficiency (SE) to become the main indicator of mobile communication networks. On the other hand, a massive number of connected devices also leads to enormous energy consumption, and thus energy efficiency (EE) has become an important and global topic from both environmental and economic reasons.

Orbital angular momentum (OAM) can provide a new degree of freedom for improving the SE due to its orthogonality, thus it can meet the requirements of high data rate [1,2]. However, the main practice challenge for applying such technology into the electromagnetic (EM) filed is the beam divergence and phase singularity caused by the OAM modes and long-distance transmission. To solve this issue, S. Zheng *et al.* proposed a new form of OAM waves called plane spiral orbital angular momentum (PSOAM), which propagates along the transverse plane intelligently, and thereby avoiding the aforementioned issues of phase singularity and the diversity [3]. The authors further analysed the PSOAM beams and put forward the concept of PSOAM mode-groups (MGs), which had the promising prospect in spatial modulation multiple-input-multiple-output (SM-MIMO), smart antenna and MIMO [4]. To demonstrate the performance of PSOAM MGs, the authors in [5] applied PSOAM MGs into a single-user system, where the partial arc sampling receiving (PASR) method was adopted to de-multiplex the PSOAM-MGs-carrying data streams due to its low complexity.

On the other hand, non-orthogonal multiple access (NOMA) is viewed as a key technique to enhance SE in the beyond fifth generation (B5G) communication networks [6]. It can simultaneously serve a large amount of users with the same physical resource via superposition coding (SC), where different users are distinguished with different power levels and the successive interference cancellation (SIC) is used to cancel the multi-user interferences [7]. It has been proved that NOMA can obtain better behaviours from the perspective of SE compared with orthogonal multiple access (OMA).

In fact, the combination of PSOAM MGs and NOMA can greatly improve the SE while considering the interference among all users. Previous works on OAM systems mainly focused on maximizing the spectral efficiency in a PSOAM MGs system [5,8], and NOMA-based wireless networks [9,10]. However, seldom works have been studied in EE optimization for the PSOAM MGs based multi-user MIMO-NOMA system. In this paper, a downlink PSOAM-MGs based multi-user MIMO-NOMA system is investigated, where the transmit power is optimized to achieve the maximum EE of the system. The resultant optimization problem considering the constraints of the transmit power and minimum required data rate of users, is non-convex and NP-hard, which cannot be solved directly. To tackle this problem, by applying the fractional programming and the first order Taylor approximation, the original problem is equivalently reformulated as a convex maximization problem, which can be solved by the Lagrange dual method. Particularly, we propose a bisection-based power allocation algorithm, where the bisection method is exploited in the outer layer to obtain the optimal EE and a power distributed algorithm is adopted to optimize the transmit power in the

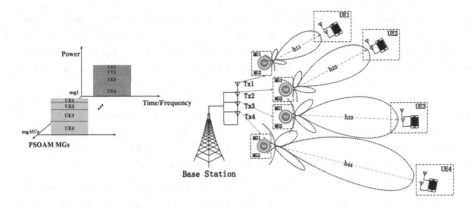

Fig. 1. System model of PSOAM-MGs based multi-user MIMO-NOMA.

inner layer. Simulation results illustrate that the proposed algorithm can achieve the optimal EE in the proposed PSOAM MGs system. In addition, numerical results also demonstrate that the EE achieved in the proposed PSOAM MGs system is superior compared with the conventional multi-user MIMO system.

2   System Model and Problem Formulation

2.1   System Model

In Fig. 1, the PSOAM MGs based multi-user MIMO-NOMA system includes one base station (BS) with N_t antennas is deployed to serve K users. The K users are randomly distributed in a fan-shaped area and the antenna spacing is ζ. At the transmitting side, each antenna only sends data streams to its corresponding user, in which two superposed PSOAM MGs waves are radiated into the free space. Supposing there are G PSOAM waves in one MG and the equivalent PSOAM MGs phase slope can be calculated by the smallest and the biggest modes [5]. At the receiver, each user is equipped with N_r receiving antennas, which are placed within the main lobe of the superposed PSOAM MGs waves.

The total transmit power is restricted to P_{max} and in the mg^{th} mode group, the signal transmitted to user k can be written as

$$X_{k,mg} = p_{k,mg} \cdot x_{k,mg}, \tag{1}$$

where $p_{k,mg}$ denotes the power allocation of the mg^{th} PSOAM mode group at the kth user. Let φ_0^k as the initial phase of user k and for the mg^{th} mode group, the link of channel gain $h_{k,nr,nt,mg}$ between the nt^{th} transmitting antenna and the nr^{th} receiving antenna can be written as

$$
\begin{aligned}
h_{k,nr,nt,mg} &= \beta_{k,nt} \frac{\lambda}{4\pi d_{k,nr,nt}} e^{-j\frac{\lambda}{2\pi} d_{k,nr,nt}} \frac{1}{\sqrt{G^{mg}}} \sum_{g^{mg}=1}^{G^{mg}} e^{-jl_{g^{mg}}^{mg} \varphi_{k,nr,nt}} \\
&= \beta_{k,nt} \frac{\lambda}{4\pi d_{k,nr,nt}} e^{-j\frac{\lambda}{2\pi} d_{k,nr,nt}} \frac{1}{\sqrt{G^{mg}}} e^{-jl_{eq}^{mg} \varphi_{k,nr,nt}},
\end{aligned}
\tag{2}
$$

where $d_{k,nr,nt}$ represents the distance between the nt^{th} transmitting antenna and the nr^{th} receiving antenna of user k. Importantly, $\beta_{k,nt} = \sqrt{G_t G_r}$ is a constant related to the antenna gain of the nt^{th} transmitting antenna at the nr^{th} receiving antenna. Specifically, G_t can be determined by the distribution of the users and the interference of the minor lobe.

In addition, $\varphi_{k,nr,nt}$ represents the phase between the nt^{th} transmitting antenna and the nr^{th} receiving antenna of user k. For the two PSOAM MGs based system and to calculate the phase $\varphi_{k,nr,nt}$, there are two conditions that should be considered. One is the initial phase $\varphi_0^k > 0$ and the other is $\varphi_0^k < 0$. For the condition $\varphi_0^k > 0$, three cases are discussed as follows:

Case 1 $k = nt$. We define the vertical distance between the center of the two receiving antennas of user k and the corresponding transmitting antenna as d_k. The radius of the arc is marked as R_{ad}. The distance between the nr^{th} receiving antenna and the nt^{th} transmitting antenna can be calculated by $d_{k,nr,nt,cor} = \sqrt{d_k^2 + (\frac{R_{ad}}{2})^2}$ and the phase φ_k between d_k and $d_{k,nr,nt,cor}$ can be regarded as $\varphi_k = (-1)^{nr} \cdot \arctan(\frac{R_{ad}}{2d_k})$, where the radius of the receiving antennas R_{ad} is fixed regardless of the transmission distance, which can be calculated by $R_{ad} = 2D \tan \left(\frac{\pi}{2|l_{eq}^{mg1} - l_{eq}^{mg2}|} \right)$ and D is the relative distance. Thus, the radius of the receiving antennas R_{ad} is fixed regardless of the transmission distance [5] and the phase $\varphi_{k,nr,nt,cor}$ is calculated by $\varphi_k + \varphi_0^k$.

Case 2 $k < nt$. According to the cosine theorem, we can calculate the distance between the nr^{th} receiving antenna of the non-intended user k and the nt^{th} transmitting antenna as follows

$$d_{k,nr,nt} = \sqrt{((nt - k) \cdot \zeta)^2 + d_{k,nr,nt,cor}^2 - \Theta}, \qquad (3)$$

where $\Theta = 2 \cdot d_{k,nr,nt,cor} \cdot \zeta \cdot (nt - k) \cdot \cos(\frac{\pi}{2} + \varphi_{k,nr,nt,cor})$. In addition, the azimuthal angle of the nr^{th} receiving antenna of user k to the nt^{th} transmitting antenna can be defined as

$$\varphi_{k,nr,nt} = \frac{\pi}{2} - \omega, \qquad (4)$$

where

$$\omega = \arccos(\frac{((nt - k) \cdot \zeta)^2 + d_{k,nr,nt}^2 - d_{k,nr,nt,cor}^2}{2 \cdot d_{k,nr,nt} \cdot ((nt - k) \cdot \zeta)}). \qquad (5)$$

Case 3 $k > nt$. Similarly, we can calculate $\varphi_{k,nr,nt}$ according to case 2.

For the condition $\varphi_0^k < 0$, the related angle and distance can be calculated the same as the condition $\varphi_0^k > 0$. Considering the mutual interferences among users within one PSOAM MG, NOMA-SIC is applied to the whole system. In the mg^{th} PSOAM MG, if each transmitting antenna sends MGs PSOAM mode groups, the corresponding channel gain from the lth transmitting antenna to the kth user is indicated as $h_{kl,mg}$. Note that if $k \neq l$, the channel gain of the $h_{kl,mg}$ is regarded as the interference signal. The channel model can be denoted as a $MGs \times MGs$ matrix written as $\boldsymbol{H}$ and we use singular value decomposition

(SVD) to obtain singular values, denoted as $\lambda_{kl,mg}$. Considering the channel gains in one PSOAM mode group of all users satisfy the following condition: $\lambda_{11,mg} \leq \lambda_{22,mg} \leq \ldots \leq \lambda_{KK,mg}$. To obtain the capacity upper bound, the decoding order of NOMA users is set to $\{1, 2, \ldots, K\}$. As a result, for the mg^{th} PSOAM mode group, the data rate of user k, $1 \leq k \leq (K-1)$, is given by

$$R_{k,mg} = Blog_2 \left(1 + \frac{p_{k,mg} \cdot \lambda_{kk,mg}^2}{\sum\limits_{l=k+1}^{K} p_{l,mg} \lambda_{kl,mg}^2 + \sigma^2} \right). \tag{6}$$

Further, the total rate of all K users can be formulated as

$$R_{total} = \sum_{mg=1}^{MGs} R_{k,mg} = \sum_{k=1}^{K} R_k. \tag{7}$$

In general, the power consumption of the PSOAM MGs based multi-user MIMO-NOMA system consists of transmit power and circuit power, which is defined as follows

$$PC_{total} = \alpha \sum_{k=1}^{K} \sum_{mg=1}^{MGs} p_{k,mg} + N_t \cdot P_{ic}, \tag{8}$$

where α indicates the power amplifier drain efficiency and P_{ic} represents the circuit power consumption of system hardware.

2.2 Problem Formulation

The work aims to maximize the EE of the PSOAM MGs based multi-user MIMO-NOMA system with the constraint of the minimum required data rate of each user and the total transmit power as well. Therefore, the EE optimization problem is expressed as follows

$$\max_{p_{k,mg}} \frac{\sum\limits_{k=1}^{K} \sum\limits_{mg=1}^{MGs} Blog_2 \left(1 + \frac{p_{k,mg} \cdot \lambda_{kk,mg}^2}{\sum\limits_{l=k+1}^{K} p_{l,mg} \lambda_{kl,mg}^2 + \sigma^2} \right)}{\alpha \sum\limits_{k=1}^{K} \sum\limits_{mg=1}^{MGs} p_{k,mg} + Nt \cdot Pic} \tag{9}$$

$$s.t. C1 : log_2 \left(1 + \frac{p_{k,mg} \cdot \lambda_{kk,mg}^2}{\sum\limits_{l=k+1}^{K} p_{l,mg} \lambda_{kl,mg}^2 + \sigma^2} \right) \geq \frac{R_{req}}{B}, \forall k \in \mathcal{K}, \forall mg \in \mathcal{MG}, \tag{10}$$

$$C2 : \sum_{k=1}^{K} \sum_{mg=1}^{MGs} p_{k,mg} \leq P_{max}, \tag{11}$$

$$C3 : p_{k,mg} \geq 0, \forall k \in \mathcal{K}, \forall mg \in \mathcal{MG}, \tag{12}$$

where $\mathcal{K} = \{1, 2, \ldots, K\}$ represents the set of users, $\mathcal{MG} = \{mg1, mg2, \ldots, MGs\}$ denotes the set of all PSOAM mode groups. $C1$ guarantees the constraint of the minimum rate requirement of each user, which is denoted as R_{req}. $C2$ guarantees that the total transmit power is limited to P_{max}. In $C3$, the power of each PSOAM MG of user k is $p_{k,mg}$, which ought to be a positive number and $mg \in \mathcal{MG}$ for any $k \in \mathcal{K}$ is requested.

3   Proposed Iterative Resource Allocation Scheme

The optimization problem (9) is non-convex with respect to the power vector $\boldsymbol{P}$, and it is hard to be solved directly. Fortunately, the optimization problem can be converted into a generalized fractional programming problem. We assume that $R_{k,mg}(\boldsymbol{P}) > 0$ and $PC_{total}(\boldsymbol{P}) > 0$. The optimal EE can be denoted as γ_{EE}^* and the optimal power allocation of the considered problem is expressed as $\boldsymbol{P}^*$. We can get the following equation

$$\gamma_{EE}^* = \max_{\boldsymbol{P} \in \{C1, C2, C3\}} \frac{R_{total}(\boldsymbol{P})}{PC_{total}(\boldsymbol{P})} = \frac{R_{total}(\boldsymbol{P}^*)}{PC_{total}(\boldsymbol{P}^*)}. \tag{13}$$

Furthermore, according to generalized fractional programming, and let

$$\Upsilon(\gamma_{EE}) = \max_{\boldsymbol{P} \in \{C1, C2, C3\}} [R_{total}(\boldsymbol{P}) - \gamma_{EE} PC_{total}(\boldsymbol{P})], \tag{14}$$

where Υ is a function and γ_{EE} is the independent variable.

Theorem 1. Problem *(14) is strictly monotonically decreasing with respect to the* γ_{EE}.

Therefore, the optimal EE can be tackled by the bisection method and the detailed information of the method is presented in Table 1.

For a given γ_{EE}^i, the optimization problem turns to be

$$\max_{\boldsymbol{P}} \quad R_{total}(\boldsymbol{P}) - \gamma_{EE}^i PC_{total}(\boldsymbol{P})$$
$$\text{s.t.} \quad C1, C2, C3. \tag{15}$$

To solve the problem (15), $\Upsilon(\gamma_{EE}^i)$ can be transformed as follows

$$R_{total}(\boldsymbol{P}) - \gamma_{EE}^i PC_{total}(\boldsymbol{P}) = F(\boldsymbol{P}) - H(\boldsymbol{P}), \tag{16}$$

where different PSOAM MGs can be regarded as the sub-channels paralleling to each other, and

$$F(\boldsymbol{P}) = f_{mg1}(\boldsymbol{P_{mg}}) + f_{mg2}(\boldsymbol{P_{mg}}) + \cdots + f_{mgMGs}(\boldsymbol{P_{mg}}), \tag{17}$$

$$H(\boldsymbol{P}) = h_{mg1}(\boldsymbol{P_{mg}}) + h_{mg2}(\boldsymbol{P_{mg}}) + \cdots + h_{mgMGs}(\boldsymbol{P_{mg}}). \tag{18}$$

Table 1. Proposed bisection-based power allocation algorithm.

1: **Initialization**
Set iteration index $i = 0$ and termination precise $\varepsilon > 0$.
Set γ_{EE}^{min} and γ_{EE}^{max} , let $\gamma_{EE}^{min} \leq \gamma_{EE}^{*} \leq \gamma_{EE}^{max}$.
2: **repeat**
3:    $\gamma_{EE}^{i} = (\gamma_{EE}^{max} + \gamma_{EE}^{min})/2$.
4:    Solve (13) with a given γ_{EE}^{i} and get $\boldsymbol{P}^{i}$.
5:    **if** $\mid \Upsilon\left(\gamma_{EE}^{i}\right) \mid = \mid R_{total}(\boldsymbol{P}^{i}) - \gamma_{EE}^{i}P_{total}(\boldsymbol{P}^{i}) \mid \leq \varepsilon$
then$\boldsymbol{P}^{*} = \boldsymbol{P}^{i}$ and $\gamma_{EE}^{*} = R_{total}(\boldsymbol{P}^{i})/P_{total}(\boldsymbol{P}^{i})$
6:     break.
7:   **else**
8:     **if** $\Upsilon\left(\gamma_{EE}^{i}\right) < 0$, then
9:      $\gamma_{EE}^{max} = \gamma_{EE}^{i}$.
10:    **else**
11:     $\gamma_{EE}^{min} = \gamma_{EE}^{i}$.
12:    **end if**
13:   **end if**
14:   $i = i + 1$.
15: **until** $\mid \Upsilon\left(\gamma_{EE}^{i}\right) \mid = \mid R_{total}(\boldsymbol{P}^{i}) - \gamma_{EE}^{i}P_{total}(\boldsymbol{P}^{i}) \mid \leq \varepsilon$.

For each PSOAM MG, we can obtain the expression of the function $f_{mg}(\boldsymbol{P_{mg}})$ and $h_{mg}(\boldsymbol{P_{mg}})$ as follows

$$f_{mg}(\boldsymbol{P_{mg}}) = \sum_{k=1}^{K} Blog_2(\sum_{l=k}^{K} p_{l,mg}\lambda_{kl,mg}^2 + \sigma^2) - \gamma_{EE}^{i} \cdot (\alpha \sum_{l=k}^{K} p_{k,mg} + \frac{N_t \cdot P_{ic}}{MGs}),$$

(19)

$$h_{mg}(\boldsymbol{P_{mg}}) = \sum_{k=1}^{K} Blog_2(\sum_{l=k+1}^{K} p_{l,mg}\lambda_{kl,mg}^2 + \sigma^2).$$

(20)

Besides, the non-convex constraint $C1$ in problem (15) is transformed into an equivalent convex linear form mathematically as follows

$$C1' : (1 - 2^{\frac{R_{req}}{B}})\left(\sum_{l=k+1}^{K} p_{l,mg}\lambda_{kl,mg}^2 + \sigma^2\right) + p_{k,mg}\lambda_{kk,mg}^2 \geq 0, \forall k, \forall mg.$$

(21)

Now, the considered problem (15) is equivalent to

$$\max_{\boldsymbol{P}} \quad F(\boldsymbol{P}) - H(\boldsymbol{P})$$

$$\text{s.t.} \quad C1', C2, C3.$$

(22)

Table 2. Power allocation algorithm based on PDIA.

1):   **Initialization**
Set the iteration index $q = 0$.
Set the termination precise $\epsilon > 0$.
Set the initial transmit power $\boldsymbol{P}^{(0)}$.
Calculate $I^0 = F(\boldsymbol{P}^0) - H(\boldsymbol{P}^0)$.
2):   **repeat**
3):   Solve (13) to get the optimal transmit power $\boldsymbol{P}^*$
4):   Set $q = q + 1$, and $\boldsymbol{P}^q = \boldsymbol{P}^*$.
5):   Calculate $I^q = F(\boldsymbol{P}^q) - H(\boldsymbol{P}^q)$.
6):   **until** $\mid I^q - I^{q-1} \mid = \mid \Xi \mid \leq \epsilon$.

Although the constraints of the optimization problem (22) are convex sets, (9), (15) and (22) remain to be the NP-hard problem. We define the expression pairs in (16) as f minus h. Each expression pair is regarded as two concave functions. Therefore, the corresponding optimization problem is non-convex. To solve this issue, we can obtain $\boldsymbol{P}^q$ through an iterative power allocation algorithm at the qth iteration. Then, the first-order Taylor expansion at $\boldsymbol{P}^q$ is expressed by

$$h_{mg}(\boldsymbol{P}^q_{mg}) + \nabla h^T_{mg}(\boldsymbol{P}^q_{mg})(\boldsymbol{P}_{mg} - \boldsymbol{P}^q_{mg}), \tag{23}$$

where $\nabla h_{mg}(\boldsymbol{P}_{mg})$ represents the gradient of $h_{mg}(\boldsymbol{P}_{mg})$, $\boldsymbol{P}_{mg} = \boldsymbol{P}((mg-1)K + 1, mg \cdot k)$ and the optimization problem (22) can be further transformed into

$$\max_{\boldsymbol{P}} \sum_{mg=1}^{MGs} \left(f_{mg}(\boldsymbol{P}_{mg}) - [h_{mg}(\boldsymbol{P}^q_{mg}) + \nabla h^T_{mg}(\boldsymbol{P}^q_{mg})(\boldsymbol{P}_{mg} - \boldsymbol{P}^q_{mg})^T]) \right)$$

$$\text{s.t.}\quad C1', C2, C3. \tag{24}$$

Fortunately, (24) is a standard convex optimization problem, which can be tackled effectively using Lagrange duality algorithm [11]. The detail information of the power distribution iterative algorithm (PDIA) is presented in Table 2.

4   Simulation Results

In this section, simulation results are presented to validate the behaviour of the proposed bisection-based power allocation scheme. To study the EE performance, we employ a channel with a carrier frequency operating at 10 GHz [5]. The channel noise power σ^2 is set to 1×10^{-5}W. The power amplifier drain efficiency is set to $\alpha = 2$; P_{ic} is set to 6W; In particular, we consider $K = 4$ users randomly distributed in a fan-shaped area, which is 30m away from the BS and the degree of the area ranges from –60 °C to 60 °C. The system we proposed is composed of uniform linear arrays (ULAs) with 4 antennas at the transmitter and

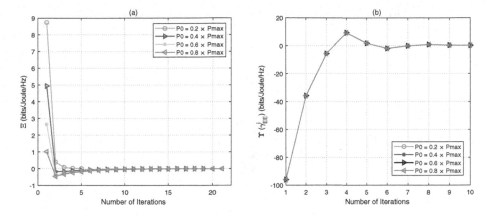

Fig. 2. An example of the convergence behaviour of the proposed bisection-based power allocation algorithm in a PAOAM-MGs based multi-user MIMO-NOMA system. (a) The proposed power resources allocation, (b) The proposed bisection-based EE optimization algorithm.

the element spacing is $\zeta = 7\lambda$. The selected PSOAM MGs of each transmitting antenna are $mg^1 = \{1, 2, 3, 4, 5, 6, 7, 8\}$ and $mg^2 = \{9, 10, 11, 12, 13, 14, 15, 16\}$. When the relative distance is $100\,\mathrm{m}$, the R_{ad} under the PASR method is about $0.7\,\mathrm{m}$. The bandwidth of the system is normalized $1\,\mathrm{Hz}$. According to the algorithm we proposed, the termination precises are set to $\varepsilon = \epsilon = 10^{-3}$ and $\gamma_{EE} \in$ [0,5] bit/Joule/Hz. It is worth noting that the parameters in this system are selected to prove the the performance of EE as an example and can be replaced by other reasonable parameters according to the specific scenarios.

First, the convergence behaviour of the proposed bisection-based power allocation algorithm is evaluated by demonstrating how the Ξ and Υ behave with the number of iterations. We set $P_{max} = 2\mathrm{W}$, $R_{req} = 1$ bit/s/Hz. As seen in Fig. 2(a) that the inner layer of the proposed algorithm on Ξ can converge to zero, and the P_0 affects the convergence rate of the proposed algorithm. Specifically, Ξ converges to zero after six iteration when $P_0 = 0.2P_{max}$, $0.4P_{max}$, $0.6P_{max}$, $0.8P_{max}$. Moreover, in Fig. 2.(b), the outer layer of the proposed algorithm on Υ can also converge to zero at approximately eight iterations, which proves that our proposed two-layer algorithm converges to a stable value. This result demonstrates the stability and validity of the proposed algorithm.

Next, we show the γ_{EE}^* of the presented bisection-based power allocation algorithm with different transmit power P_{max} and minimum required data rate R_{req}. To demonstrate the effectiveness of our proposed method, we apply the algorithms in the PSOAM MGs based multi-user MIMO-NOMA system and the conventional multi-user MIMO system [12] for comparison. We set $P_{max} = 2\mathrm{W}$. In Fig. 3, the γ_{EE}^* obtained by all the algorithms are monotonically decreasing with the increase of R_{req}. For the proposed bisection-based power allocation algorithm, a significant drop occurs when the minimum data rate of users is

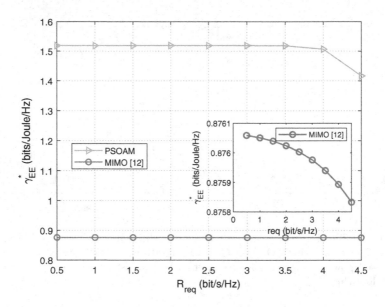

Fig. 3. The γ_{EE}^* vs different minimum rate requirement constraints.

larger than 4 bit/s/Hz. This is due to the fact that the limitation of transmit power cannot satisfy the QoS requirement of each user.

Finally, we investigate the γ_{EE}^* of the proposed solution with various transmit power P_{max} as well as different number of users. We set $R_{req} = 1$ bit/s/Hz. In Fig. 4, the γ_{EE}^* obtained by the two approaches are monotonically non-decreasing under the constraint of P_{max}. Specifically, the γ_{EE}^* increases swiftly with a lower P_{max}, and then achieves an asymptotic value when the balance between the available rates and the energy consumption is obtained. Additionally, higher P_{max} is required to achieve the stable γ_{EE}^* when the number of users increases in the system network. Compared with the traditional multi-user MIMO system, our proposed solution can achieve a significant performance gain in terms of EE due to the degree of freedom provided by PSOAM MGs and NOMA techniques.

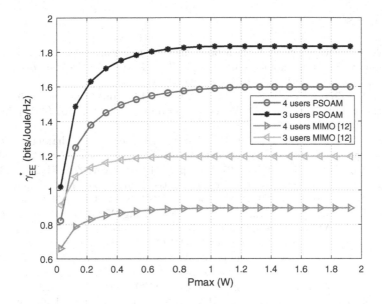

Fig. 4. The γ_{EE}^* vs different entire transmit power constraints.

5 Conclusions

This paper explores the optimization problem of EE for a PSOAM MGs based multi-user MIMO-NOMA system. We aim to maximize the EE while meeting several constraints of total transmit power and minimum required data rate of each user. The corresponding problem of maximizing EE is NP-hard and cannot be tackled directly. Particularly, we obtain the optimal EE in the outer layer via the bisection-based power allocation algorithm and achieve the optimal power allocation in the inner layer through the power distribution iterative algorithm. Numerical results validate the superiority of the PSOAM MGs based multi-user MIMO-NOMA system in EE compared with the conventional multi-user MIMO system. In general, it is worth to further study the joint power resources allocation of EE and SE in the PSOAM MGs based multi-user MIMO-NOMA system in the future.

Acknowledgement. This work has been supported in part by Nation Key Research and Development Project under Grant 2019YFB1804100, in part by the National Natural Science Foundation of China under Grant 61971194, in part by Key Research and Development Project of Guangdong Province under Grant 2019B010156003, in part by the Natural Science Foundation of Guangdong Province under Grant 2019A1515011607, in part by the Open Research Fund of National Mobile Communications Research Laboratory, Southeast University (No. 2019D06), in part by the Fundamental Research Funds for the Central Universities under Grant 2019JQ08, and in part by the Research Fund Program of Guangdong Key Laboratory of Aerospace Communication and Networking Technology under Grant 2018B030322004.

References

1. Edfors, O., Johansson, A.J.: Is orbital angular momentum (OAM) based radio communication an unexploited area? IEEE Trans. Antennas Propag. **60**(2), 1126–1131 (2012). https://doi.org/10.1109/TAP.2011.2173142
2. Cheng, W., Zhang, W., Jing, H., Gao, S., Zhang, H.: Orbital angular momentum for wireless communications. IEEE Wireless Commun. **26**(1), 100–107 (2019). https://doi.org/10.1109/MWC.2017.1700370
3. Zheng, S., Hui, X., Jin, X., Chi, H., Zhang, X.: Transmission characteristics of a twisted radio wave based on circular traveling-wave antenna. IEEE Trans. Antennas Propag. **63**(4), 1530–1536 (2015). https://doi.org/10.1109/TAP.2015.2393885
4. Wang, Z., et al.: Structure radio beam construction in azimuthal domain. IEEE Access. **8**, 9395–9402 (2020). https://doi.org/10.1109/ACCESS.2020.2964833
5. Xiong, X., Zheng, S., Zhu, Z., Yu, X., Jin, X., Zhang, X.: Performance analysis of plane spiral OAM mode-group based MIMO system. IEEE Commun. Lett. **24**(7), 1414–1418 (2020). https://doi.org/10.1109/LCOMM.2020.2981086
6. Chen, Z., Ding, Z., Dai, X., Zhang, R.: An optimization perspective of the superiority of NOMA compared to conventional OMA. IEEE Trans. Signal Process. **65**(19), 5191–5202 (2017). https://doi.org/10.1109/TSP.2017.2725223
7. Ding, Z., Yang, Z., Fan, P., Poor, H.V.: On the performance of non-orthogonal multiple access in 5G systems with randomly deployed users. IEEE Signal Process. Lett. **21**(12), 1501–1505 (2014). https://doi.org/10.1109/LSP.2014.2343971
8. Zhang, Z., Zheng, S., Jin, X., Chi, H., Zhang, X.: Generation of plane spiral OAM waves using traveling-wave circular slot antenna. IEEE Antennas Wireless Propag. Lett. **16**, 8–11 (2017). https://doi.org/10.1109/LAWP.2016.2552227
9. Liu, G., Wang, Z., Hu, J., Ding, Z., Fan, P.: Cooperative NOMA broadcasting/multicasting for low-latency and high-reliability 5G cellular V2X communications. IEEE Internet Things J. **6**(5), 7828–7838 (2019). https://doi.org/10.1109/JIOT.2019.2908415
10. Xu, Y., et al.: Coordinated direct and relay transmission with NOMA and network coding in Nakagami-m fading channels. IEEE Trans. Commun. **69**(1), 207–222 (2021). https://doi.org/10.1109/TCOMM.2020.3025555
11. Li, Y., Sheng, M., Wang, X., Zhang, Y., Wen, J.: Max–min energy-efficient power allocation in interference-limited wireless networks. IEEE Trans. Veh. Technol. **64**(9), 4321–4326 (2015). https://doi.org/10.1109/TVT.2014.2361920
12. Tang, J., So, D.K.C., Zhao, N., Shojaeifard, A., Wong, K.: Energy efficiency optimization with SWIPT in MIMO broadcast channels for internet of things. IEEE Internet Things J. **5**(4), 2605–2619 (2018). https://doi.org/10.1109/JIOT.2017.2785861

Energy Efficient Resource Allocation for UCA-Based OAM-MIMO System

Jie Tang[1,2]($\boxtimes$), Chuting Lin[1], Yan Song[1], Yu Yu[1], Zhen Chen[1], Xiuying Zhang[1], Daniel K. C. So[3], and Kai-Kit Wong[4]

[1] School of Electronic and Information Engineering,
South China University of Technology, Guangzhou, China
{eejtang,chenz,zhangxiuyin}@scut.edu.cn, songyan1222@whut.edu.cn
[2] The National Mobile Communications Research Laboratory, Southeast University,
Nanjing, China
[3] Department of Electronic and Electrical Engineering, University of Manchester,
Manchester, UK
d.so@manchester.ac.uk
[4] Department of Electronic and Electrical Engineering, University College London,
London, UK
kai-kit.wong@ucl.ac.uk

Abstract. The combination of orbital angular momentum (OAM) and multi-input multi-output (MIMO) is identified as an effective solution to improve energy efficiency (EE) in the next-generation wireless communication. According to the orthogonality of OAM, we adopt uniform circular array (UCA) to establish the transmitter and receiver of the OAM-MIMO system in this paper. Our goal is to maximize the EE of the system whilst satisfying the maximum total transmit power and the minimum capacity requirement of each mode. Due to the inter-interference of different UCA at the same mode, the optimization problem involving the power allocation of modes is non-convex, thus is difficult to solve directly. To tackle this problem, the optimization problem is transformed into two sub-problems by using the fractional programming. Then we develop a dual-layer iteration algorithm where the nonconvex power allocation problem is transformed into a convex problem by exploiting the the first-order Taylor approximation in the inner layer, and the dichotomy is used to update EE in the outer layer. Simulation results confirm the effectiveness of the proposed solution, and demonstrate the superiority of the OAM-MIMO system over the conventional MIMO system from the perspective of EE.

Keywords: Energy efficiency (EE) · Orbital angular momentum (OAM) · Multi-input multi-output (MIMO) · Power allocation

1 Introduction

With the phenomenal increase of connected devices, there is the massive growth rate in data traffic and energy consumption in wireless communication. However,

X. Wang et al. (Eds.): AICON 2021, LNICST 396, pp. 189–200, 2021.
https://doi.org/10.1007/978-3-030-90196-7_17

the available spectrum resources are far from enough to support the communication systems with the increasing demand for high data rate. To alleviate this problem, orbital angular momentum (OAM) technology is proposed to improve spectrum efficiency of the wireless communication system [1]. Due to the orthogonality of different OAM modes, OAM can ensure the independence of each channel and increase the degree of freedom of the channel, which is also known as mode division multiplexing [2]. Thus it can greatly improve the transmission rate of point-to-point wireless communication [3]. Recently, OAM has been developed continuously on the way of multiplexing, the transmission distance and the antenna structures of generating OAM [4–6]. Since the antenna structure based on uniform circular array (UCA) is more flexible in the multipexing of OAM, multiple UCAs are applied to enhance the freedom of the antenna radius and alleviate the divergence of OAM beam [7]. It is proved that the OAM-MIMO system based on UCAs is a potential solution for the future communication system, which has aroused great interest gradually. In [8], the authors studied the transmission characteristics of multiplexing three-OAM-mode based on Butler phase shift and UCA in microwave frequency band. The work in [9] achieved 100 Gbit/s data transmission in the OAM-MIMO multiplexing system based on UCAs in 28 GHz band for the first time, with 11 multiplexed signals and a transmission distance of 10 m. The experience achieved gigabit-class wireless transmission, which enhanced the communication rate.

However, previous research works mostly focused on the optimization of system capacity, which is rarely associated with EE [10–12]. With the requirement of green wireless communication, EE is regarded as an important role in the wireless communication system to balance the total power consumption and the achievable capacity. Motivated by this, the power allocation problem of the OAM-MIMO system based on UCAs is proposed to achieve the maximum EE in this paper. The considered EE optimization problem is nonconvex, due to involving the power allocation of multiple modes on multiple UCAs. To tackle nonconvex optimization problem, we reformulate the objective function into an equivalent subtraction form based on fractional programming accordingly. Based on this, a dual-layer iterative algorithm is proposed, where the power allocation is optimized based on first order Taylor approximation and Lagrange duality method in inner layer, and the optimal EE is obtained by the dichotomy in the outer layer. The simulation results confirm the convergence of the proposed EE maximization algorithm. Besides, we also demonstrate that the proposed EE maximization algorithm can achieve significant performance gain, compared with the traditional point-to-point MIMO algorithm.

2   System Model and Problem Formulation

2.1   UCA-Based OAM-MIMO Model

The OAM-MIMO system with multiple UCAs is considered, as shown in Fig. 1. The azimuthal angle of the tth transmit antenna and the rth receive antenna are denoted by $\phi_t = \frac{2\pi(t-1)}{T}$ and $\vartheta_r = \frac{2\pi(r-1)}{R}$ respectively, where T and R are the number of antenna. To transmit and receive of the multiplexing OAM beams, the transmitter and receiver consist of the Butler matrix and UCAs. We set the number of multiplexed modes on each UCA as L, thus the Butler matrix of the nth UCA at the transmitter is $o_n = [e^{jl\phi_t}]^H \in C^{T \times L}$ and the Butler matrix of the mth UCA at the receiver is $o_m^H = [e^{jl\vartheta_r}]^H \in C^{L \times R}$. Therefore, the Butler matrix of the transmitter and receiver are denoted as $O = diag\{o_1, ..., o_N\}$ and $O^H = diag\{o_1^H, ..., o_M^H\}$, where N and M are the number of UCAs at the transmitter and receiver, respectively. The channel matrix between the nth UCA of transmitter and the mth UCA of receiver can be expressed as $H_{m,n} = [h_{mr,nt}] \in C^{R \times T}$, where $h_{mr,nt}$ is the channel gain from the tth antenna on the nth UCA of transmitter to the rth antenna on the mth UCA of receiver under free space propagation. It can be expressed as

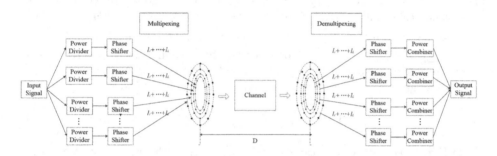

Fig. 1. The system model of the considered OAM-MIMO system based on UCAs.

$$h_{mr,nt} = \beta \frac{\lambda}{4\pi d_{mr,nt}} e^{\frac{-j2\pi d_{mr,nt}}{\lambda}}, \qquad (1)$$

where β denotes the antenna gain and λ is wavelength. The distance between the tth transmit antenna on the nth UCA and the rth receive antenna on the mth UCA is

$$d_{mr,nt} = \sqrt{D^2 + S_n^2 + S_m^2 - 2S_n S_m cos(\vartheta_r - \phi_t)}, \qquad (2)$$

where D is the vertical distance between the transmit UCA and the receive UCA center. S_n and S_m denote the radius of the nth transmit UCA and the mth receive UCA. According to $\sqrt{(1-x)} \approx 1 - \frac{x}{2}$, $d_{mr,nt}$ is given by

$$d_{mr,nt} \approx \sqrt{D^2 + S_n^2 + S_m^2} - \frac{S_n S_m cos(\vartheta_r - \phi_t)}{\sqrt{D^2 + S_n^2 + S_m^2}}. \qquad (3)$$

Combining (1) with (3), we have

$$h_{mr,n,l} = \sum_{t=1}^{T} \frac{\beta \lambda e^{-j\frac{2\pi\sqrt{D^2+S_n^2+S_m^2}}{\lambda}}}{4\pi D\sqrt{T}} e^{jl_n\phi_t} \cdot exp\{\frac{j2\pi S_n S_m cos(\vartheta_r - \phi_t)}{\lambda\sqrt{D^2 + S_n^2 + S_m^2}}\}. \qquad (4)$$

By utilizing the l-order Bessel function $J_l(\alpha) = \frac{j^l}{2\pi} \int_0^{2\pi} e^{jl\varphi} e^{j\alpha \cos \varphi} d\varphi$ and defining $\phi_t = \theta + \vartheta_r$, the channel gain $h_{mr,n,l}$ in (4) is converted to

$$h_{mr,n,l} \approx \frac{\beta \lambda \sqrt{T} e^{-j\frac{2\pi\sqrt{D^2+S_n^2+S_m^2}}{\lambda}}}{4\pi D j^l} e^{jl_n\vartheta_r} \cdot J_l\left(\frac{2\pi S_n S_m}{\lambda\sqrt{D^2 + S_n^2 + S_m^2}}\right). \quad (5)$$

By turning $e^{jl_n\vartheta_r}$ into continuous $e^{jl_n\vartheta}$, we can get the channel gain before spatially sampling. Thus, (5) can be written as follow

$$h_{mn,l} = \frac{\beta \lambda \sqrt{T} e^{-j\frac{2\pi\sqrt{D^2+S_n^2+S_m^2}}{\lambda}}}{4\pi D j^l} \cdot J_l\left(\frac{2\pi S_n S_m}{\lambda\sqrt{D^2 + S_n^2 + S_m^2}}\right). \quad (6)$$

The multiplexed signal can be recovered based on the zero-forcing successive interference cancellation algorithm [13]. We denote $\sum_{m,n} = o_m^H H_{mn} o_n$. The lth diagonal element of $\sum_{m,n} \in C^{L \times L}$ is set as $\delta_{l,m,n}$ and $\sum_l = [\delta_{l,m,n}] \in C^{M \times N}$. $W_l = (\sum_l^H \sum_l)^{-1} \sum_l^H \in C^{N \times M}$ denotes the filter coefficient of the lth OAM mode. Since the number of UCA is N, we calculate W_l for N times to obtain the channel gain of the lth mode, denoted by G_l. Then, we have

$$W_l^n = \left(\sum_l^n\right)^+, \sum_l^n \in C^{N \times N}, \quad (7)$$

where W_l^n is the nth calculations of W_l, $\sum_l^n$ is the nth processing of $\sum_l$ and $(.)^+$ is pseudo inverse. We denote $k_n = arg\min_j ((W_L)_l^n)_j$ to choose the minimum value except zero of $(W_L)_l^n$, where $((W_L)_l^n)_j$ is the jth value of $(W_L)_l^n$ and $(W_L)_l^n = [\|(W_l^n)_1\|^2, ..., \|(W_l^n)_N\|^2]$. After finding the value of k_n, we set the values of the k_n columns of the matrix $\sum_l^n$ to zero, which is expressed as $\sum_l^{n+1} = (\sum_l^n)_{\bar{k}_n}$. Based on the pseudo-inverse of $\sum_l^{n+1}$, $W_l^{n+1} = (\sum_l^{n+1})^+$ is obtained. Then, we denote $(W_{LS})_l^n = [\|(W_l^n)_{k_1}\|^2, ..., \|(W_l^n)_{k_{N-1}}\|^2, \|(W_l^n)_{k_N}\|^2]$. For the lth mode, we can get the channel gain G_l. It can be shown as

$$G_l = \begin{pmatrix} \frac{1}{\|(W_{l^1})_{k_1}\|^2} & \frac{1}{\|(W_{l^1})_{k_2}\|^2} & \cdots & \frac{1}{\|(W_{l^1})_{k_N}\|^2} \\ \frac{1}{\|(W_{l^2})_{k_1}\|^2} & \frac{1}{\|(W_{l^2})_{k_2}\|^2} & \cdots & \frac{1}{\|(W_{l^2})_{k_N}\|^2} \\ \vdots & \vdots & & \vdots \\ \frac{1}{\|(W_{l^n})_{k_1}\|^2} & \frac{1}{\|(W_{l^n})_{k_2}\|^2} & \cdots & \frac{1}{\|(W_{l^n})_{k_N}\|^2} \end{pmatrix}. \quad (8)$$

2.2 Problem Formulation

According to the UCAs with the same modes, these OAM beam links are sorted, the first mode of the first UCA is set as link $i = 1$, and then the second mode of the first UCA represents link $i = N + 1$. The total transmit power and the total power consumption from the system hardware can be expressed as $P = \sum_{i=1}^{N_L} P_i$

and $PC_{tot} = \sum_{n=1}^{N} PC_n$ respectively. Hence, the total power consumption P_{tot} can be written as follows [14]

$$P_{tot}(\boldsymbol{P}) = \alpha \sum_{i=1}^{N_L} P_i + PC_{tot}, \tag{9}$$

where N_L is the number of miltiplexing OAM channels.

Then, i-th link of the SINR γ_i is written as

$$\gamma_i(\boldsymbol{P}) = \frac{P_i(\boldsymbol{G}_l)_{i' i'}}{\sum_{j=i+1}^{Q} P_i(\boldsymbol{G}_l)_{i' j'} + \sigma^2}, \tag{10}$$

where $i' = i - ((i-1)/N)N$, $j' = j - ((j-1)/N)N$, $l = (i-1)/N + 1$ and $Q = (1 + (i-1)/N)N$. In addition, $(i-1)/N$ represents the integer part of the quotient. From the above conversion, the total capacity C_{tot} can be rewritten as

$$C_{tot}(\boldsymbol{P}) = \sum_{i=1}^{N_L} C_i(\boldsymbol{P}) = \sum_{i=1}^{N_L} \log_2(1 + \frac{P_i(\boldsymbol{G}_l)_{i' i'}}{\sum_{j=i+1}^{Q} P_i(\boldsymbol{G}_l)_{i' j'} + \sigma^2}), \tag{11}$$

where C_i is the capacity of ith link. Based on (9) and (11), the EE is written as follows

$$\lambda_{EE} \triangleq \frac{C_{tot}}{P_{tot}} = \frac{\sum_{i=1}^{N_L} \log_2(1 + \frac{P_i(\boldsymbol{G}_l)_{i' i'}}{\sum_{j=i+1}^{Q} P_i(\boldsymbol{G}_l)_{i' j'} + \sigma^2})}{\sum_{i=1}^{N_L} P_i + PC_{tot}}. \tag{12}$$

According to (12), we can obtain the EE optimization problem

$$\max_{\boldsymbol{P}} \quad \lambda_{EE}(\boldsymbol{P}) \tag{13a}$$

$$\text{s.t.} \quad C1: C_i \geq R_{req}, \forall i, \tag{13b}$$

$$C2: P_i \geq 0, \forall i, \tag{13c}$$

$$C3: P^{max} \geq \sum_{i=1}^{N_L} P_i, \forall i. \tag{13d}$$

where $C1$ is the minimum capacity constraints of each link, $C2$ guarantees the effectiveness of link i and $C3$ is the total transmitting power constraint.

3   The EE Maximization Algorithm

Due to the inter-interference from different UCA at the same mode, the objective function of the proposed problem is not concave about power vector $\boldsymbol{P}$. Since it is the ratio of two real valued functions, the proposed optimization problem is a generalized fractional programming problem. In order to tackle the optimization problem, the objective function is converted into a concave function. Then, the maximum EE λ_{EE}^{opt} is expressed as follows

$$\lambda_{EE}^{opt} = \frac{C_{tot}(\boldsymbol{P}^{opt})}{P_{tot}(\boldsymbol{P}^{opt})} = \max_{\boldsymbol{P}} \frac{C_{tot}(\boldsymbol{P}^{opt})}{P_{tot}(\boldsymbol{P}^{opt})}. \tag{14}$$

According to (14), we define $F(\lambda_{EE}) = \max C_{tot}(\boldsymbol{P}) - \lambda_{EE}P_{tot}(\boldsymbol{P})$. When $\boldsymbol{P} = \boldsymbol{P}^{opt}$, EE reaches the optimal value. It is clear that $F(\lambda_{EE}) = 0$ and $F(\lambda_{EE})$ is a continuous strictly decreasing convex function about λ_{EE}. Hence, we adopt dichotomy to obtain λ_{EE}^{opt} of $F(\lambda_{EE}^{opt}) = 0$. The corresponding optimal power can be obtained by the following problem with given λ_{EE}^z, where λ_{EE}^z is the initial EE of the zth loop.

$$\max_{\boldsymbol{P}} \quad C_{tot}(\boldsymbol{P}) - \lambda_{EE}^z P_{tot}(\boldsymbol{P}) \tag{15a}$$

$$\text{s.t.} \quad C1, C2, C3. \tag{15b}$$

Obviously, (11) can be transformed into the difference between two concave functions about $\boldsymbol{P}$. We turn the objective function of (15) into the following

$$C_{tot}(\boldsymbol{P}) - \lambda_{EE}^z P_{tot}(\boldsymbol{P})) = U(\boldsymbol{P}) - V(\boldsymbol{P}), \tag{16}$$

$$U(\boldsymbol{P}) = \sum_{i=1}^{N_L} log_2 \left(\sum_{j=i}^{Q} P_j(G_l)_{j'\,j'} \right) - \lambda_{EE}^z \left(\sum_{i=1}^{N_L} P_i + PC_{tot} \right), \tag{17}$$

$$V(\boldsymbol{P}) = \sum_{i=1}^{N_L} log_2 \left(\sum_{j=i+1}^{Q} P_j(G_l)_{i'\,j'} + \sigma^2 \right). \tag{18}$$

Therefore, the optimization problem (15) can be rewritten as follows

$$\max_{\boldsymbol{P}} \quad U(\boldsymbol{P}) - V(\boldsymbol{P}) \tag{19a}$$

$$\text{s.t.} \quad C1', C2, C3. \tag{19b}$$

$$C1' : P_i(G_l)_{i'\,i'} + (1 - 2^{R_{req}})(\sum_{j=i+1}^{Q} P_i(G_l)_{i'\,j'} + \sigma^2) \geq 0, \tag{19c}$$

where the feasible set of constraints $C1'$, $C2$ and $C3$ is convex. Here, the objective function of the problem (19) is the difference between two concave functions. Hence, it can not be determined to be concave or convex, thus the problem (19) is difficult to be proved as a convex optimization problem. To address it, we turn $V(\boldsymbol{P})$ into an affine function by the first order Taylor approximation method. Since the objective function is transformed into a concave function minus an affine function, it is approximated to a concave function. Therefore, the problem (19) is transformed into a convex optimization problem.

Assuming that $\boldsymbol{P}^k$ is the transmit power vector of N_L links in the kth step, the first order Taylor expansion of $V(\boldsymbol{P})$ at $\boldsymbol{P}^k$ is given by $V(\boldsymbol{P}^k) + \nabla V^T(\boldsymbol{P}^k)(\boldsymbol{P} - \boldsymbol{P}^k)$, and $\nabla V(\boldsymbol{P})$ refers to the gradient of $V(\boldsymbol{P})$ as follows

$$\nabla V(\boldsymbol{P}) = \sum_{i=1}^{N_L} \nabla V_i(\boldsymbol{P}) = \sum_{i=1}^{N_L} \frac{1}{\sum_{j=i+1}^{Q} P_i(G_l)_{i'\,j'} + \sigma^2} e_i, \tag{20}$$

Table 1. The proposed EE optimization algorithm.

1: Initialize the iteration index z, the stopping criterion ε, and the boundary values of λ_{EE}
2: **repeat**
3: $\quad \lambda_{EE}^{z} = \frac{\lambda_{EE}^{max} + \lambda_{EE}^{min}}{2}$
4: $\quad$ **The power allocation scheme**
$\qquad$ 1):Initialize the iteration index k, the stopping criterion ϵ for the inner loop, and the initial value of transmit power $\boldsymbol{P}^{(0)}$ calculate $I^0 = U(\boldsymbol{P}^0) - V(\boldsymbol{P}^0)$
$\qquad$ 2):repeat
$\qquad$ 3):Solve the optimization problem (32) to obtain $\boldsymbol{P}^*$, where is the optimal transmit power
$\qquad$ 4):Then $k = k + 1$, $\boldsymbol{P}^k = \boldsymbol{P}^*$ and calculate $I^k = U(\boldsymbol{P}^k) - V(\boldsymbol{P}^k)$
$\qquad$ 6):until$\| I^k - I^{k-1} \| \le \epsilon$
5: $\quad$ Let $\boldsymbol{P}^z = \boldsymbol{P}^k$
6: $\quad$ **if** $\| F(\lambda_{EE}^z) \| = C_{tot}(\boldsymbol{P}^z) - \lambda_{EE}^z P_{tot}(\boldsymbol{P}^z) \le \varepsilon$ then, $\boldsymbol{P}^{opt} = \boldsymbol{P}^z$ and $\lambda_{EE}^{opt} = \frac{C_{tot}(\boldsymbol{P}^z)}{P_{tot}(\boldsymbol{P}^z)}$
7: $\qquad$ break;
8: $\quad$ **else**
9: $\qquad$ **if** $F(\lambda_{EE}^z) < 0$, then
10: $\qquad\quad \lambda_{EE}^{max} = \lambda_{EE}^z$
11: $\qquad$ **else**
12: $\qquad\quad \lambda_{EE}^{min} = \lambda_{EE}^z$
13: $\qquad$ **end if**
14: $\quad$ **end if**
15: $\quad$ Update iteration index $z = z + 1$
16: **until** $\| F(\lambda_{EE}^z) \| = C_{tot}(\boldsymbol{P}^z) - \lambda_{EE}^z P_{tot}(\boldsymbol{P}^z) \le \varepsilon$

where $e_i \in C^{N \times 1}$ is a column vector. When $j' \ge i'$, we have $e_i(j') = \frac{(G_l)_{i',j'}}{ln2}$; otherwise $e_i(j') = 0$. Then, the optimization problem can be transformed into the following

$$\max_{\boldsymbol{P}} \quad U(\boldsymbol{P}) - [V(\boldsymbol{P}^k) + \nabla V^T(\boldsymbol{P}^k)(\boldsymbol{P} - \boldsymbol{P}^k)] \tag{21a}$$

$$\text{s.t.} \quad C1', C2, C3, \tag{21b}$$

where the objective function is concave and the constraint set of the optimization problem (21) is convex. Therefore, it is obvious that the problem (21) is a convex optimization problem. However, the considered EE optimization problem is still hard to solve directly. Here, we adopt Lagrange duality method to deal with the problem. The Lagrange function of the optimization problem (21) can be given by

$$\mathcal{L}(\boldsymbol{P}, \boldsymbol{\mu}, \boldsymbol{\nu}, \psi) = U(\boldsymbol{P}) - [V_i(\boldsymbol{P}^k) + \nabla V_i^T(\boldsymbol{P}^k)(\boldsymbol{P} - \boldsymbol{P}^k)] + \psi \left(P_{max} - \sum_{i=1}^{N_L} P_i \right)$$

$$+ \sum_{i=1}^{N_L} \nu_i (P_i) + \sum_{i=1}^{N_L} \mu_i \left(P_i(G_l)_{i'i'} + (1 - 2^{R_{req}})(\sum_{j=i+1}^{Q} P_i(G_l)_{i'j'} + \sigma^2)) \right),$$

$$(22)$$

where $\boldsymbol{\mu} \geq \boldsymbol{0}$, $\boldsymbol{\nu} \geq \boldsymbol{0}$ and $\psi \geq \boldsymbol{0}$ denote the lagrangian multipliers of $C1'$, $C2$ and $C3$ respectively. Based on (22), the dual objection function is shown as

$$g(\boldsymbol{\mu}, \boldsymbol{\nu}, \psi) = \max_{\boldsymbol{P}} \mathcal{L}(\boldsymbol{P}, \boldsymbol{\mu}, \boldsymbol{\nu}, \psi). \qquad (23)$$

Therefore, the dual optimization problem can be expressed as the following

$$\min_{\boldsymbol{\mu}, \boldsymbol{\nu}, \psi} \quad g(\boldsymbol{\mu}, \boldsymbol{\nu}, \psi) \qquad (24a)$$

$$\text{s.t.} \quad \boldsymbol{\mu} \geq \boldsymbol{0}, \ \boldsymbol{\nu} \geq \boldsymbol{0} \ and \ \psi \geq 0. \qquad (24b)$$

It is obvious that problem (24) is a convex optimization problem, which can be solved to obtain λ_{EE}^{opt} by CVX. The detailed implementation steps are described in Table 1.

4   Simulation Results

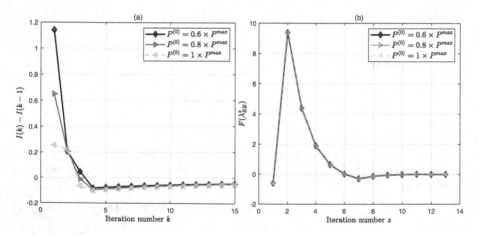

Fig. 2. Convergence performance. (a) the value of $I^k - I^{k-1}$ vs the number of iteration, (b) $F(\lambda_{EE}^z)$ vs the number of iteration.

Simulation experiment are carried out to show the performance of the EE maximization algorithm in this section. We assume that the vertical distance D is 10 m, propagation environment is free space scene and the channel noise is

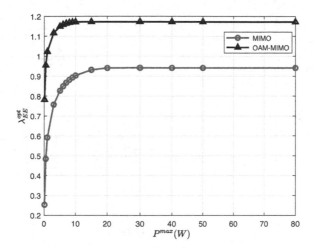

Fig. 3. The EE trend of the OAM-MIMO system and the MIMO system with the variation of P^{max}.

AWGN with power $\sigma^2 = 1 \times 10^{-5}W$. The static circuit power of per antenna is set to 3 W and the drain efficiency of the power amplifier is set to 1.5. In addition, termination accuracy ε and ϵ are set to 0.001. Whereas, the upper and lower limits of EE are considered as $\lambda_{EE}^{max} = 2$ and $\lambda_{EE}^{min} = 0$ [15]. The transmitter with 4 UCAs is considered whereas the radius are 0.24 m, 0.36 m, 0.48 m and 0.6 m respectively [7]. Moreover, the number of antenna arrays on each UCA is set to 16.

Firstly, the convergence performance of the power allocation scheme is investigated. We assume that one mode of vortex electromagnetic wave is transmitted from each UCA and the value of mode is 1 in Fig. 2. In addition, P^{max} and R_{req} are set to 5 W and 1 bits/s/Hz respectively. As shown in Fig. 2, we observe that the value of $I(k) - I(k-1)$ is approaching to zero gradually with any value of P^0 to obtain the corresponding optimal power allocation vector $\boldsymbol{P}$ for given λ_{EE}. Obviously, the result is in consistant with our theoretical analysis, which proves that the power allocation scheme is efficient and convergent. In the next simulation, the convergence of the EE maximization algorithm is demonstrated and the influence of P^0 on the iteration number required to reach the stable value is studied. It can be seen from Fig. 2 that the stable value can achieve converge under different values of P^0. In other words, the convergence of the proposed EE maximization algorithm is not affected by the initial value of P^0, which verifies the convergence and effectiveness of the EE maximization algorithm.

We then compare the performance of the proposed EE maximization algorithm on the OAM-MIMO system with the traditional point-to-point MIMO system in Fig. 3 and Fig. 4. In this simulation, the multiplexed modes on each UCA is within the range of $l \in [-6, 6]$. For fairness comparison, we set the MIMO system the same antennas as the OAM-MIMO system. In addition, the area

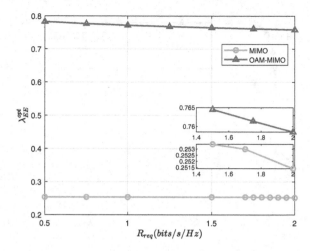

Fig. 4. The EE trend of the OAM-MIMO system and the MIMO system with the variation of R_{req}.

covered by all antennas of the MIMO system is the same as the area covered by the UCA with largest radius in the OAM-MIMO system. In order to ensure that the channels can reach the minimum capacity requirement, we select the channel with relatively large eigenvalues after singular value decomposition of the channel matrix in the MIMO system, which means the relatively superior channel [16].

In the following simulation, the performance of the proposed EE optimization algorithm in two systems is studied, with the variation of the total transmit power budget within a range of $0.1\,\mathrm{W} \leq P^{max} \leq 80$ W. In addition, we set $R_{req} = 0.5$. From Fig. 3, when P^{max} is relatively low, λ_{EE}^{opt} increases sharply with the increase of P^{max} until large than 20 W. It reveals that the extra power budget no longer constitutes the extra gain of λ_{EE}^{opt}, leading to a balance between the total capacity and the total power consumption. Figure 4 shows the variation trend of λ_{EE}^{opt} with the minimum capacity constraint R_{req} varying from 0.2 to 1. P^{max} is fixed as $1 \times 10^{-1}W$ in this simulation. As R_{req} increases, it can be observed that λ_{EE}^{opt} decreases continuously. From Fig. 3 and Fig. 4, we can observe that the stability values of the OAM-MIMO system is higher than the MIMO system. This is because different OAM mode of the OAM-MIMO system are mutually orthogonal, resulting in the lower interference of channel compared with the MIMO system.

5   Conclusions

In this paper, we investigate the EE optimization problem of the OAM-MIMO system with aligned UCAs. The corresponding optimization problem involves power allocation of multiple modes, which is non-convex. To obtain a feasible solution, we propose a dual-layer iterative EE optimization algorithm. The optimal power allocation scheme is obtained by convex programming based on first order Taylor approximation in inner layer and the optimal EE is obtained by the dichotomy in the outer layer. Simulation results demonstrate the validity of the EE optimization proposed algorithm.

Acknowledgement. This work has been supported in part by Nation Key Research and Development Project under Grant 2019YFB1804100, in part by the National Natural Science Foundation of China under Grant 61971194, in part by Key Research and Development Project of Guangdong Province under Grant 2019B010156003, in part by the Natural Science Foundation of Guangdong Province under Grant 2019A1515011607, in part by the Open Research Fund of National Mobile Communications Research Laboratory, Southeast University (No. 2019D06), in part by the Fundamental Research Funds for the Central Universities under Grant 2019JQ08, and in part by the Research Fund Program of Guangdong Key Laboratory of Aerospace Communication and Networking Technology under Grant 2018B030322004.

References

1. Edfors, O., Johansson, A.J.: Is orbital angular momentum (OAM) based radio communication an unexploited area? IEEE Trans. Antennas Propag. **60**(2), 1126–1131 (2012)
2. Opare, K.A., Kuang, Y., Kponyo, J.J.: Mode combination in an ideal wireless OAM-MIMO multiplexing system. IEEE Wireless Commun. Lett. **4**(4), 449–452 (2015)
3. Dong, J., et al.: Capacity analysis of orbital angular momentum multiplexing transmission system. In: 2020 IEEE International Conference on Communications Workshops (ICC Workshops), pp. 1–5, June 2020
4. Yagi, Y., Sasaki, H., Yamada, T., Lee, D.: 200 Gbit/s wireless transmission using dual-polarized OAM-MIMO multiplexing with uniform circular array on 28 Ghz band. In: IEEE Antennas Wireless Propagation Letters, pp. 1–1 (2021)
5. Zheng, S., Hui, X., Jin, X., Chi, H., Zhang, X.: Transmission characteristics of a twisted radio wave based on circular traveling-wave antenna. IEEE Trans. Antennas Propag. **63**(4), 1530–1536 (2015)
6. Gong, Y., et al.: Generation and transmission of OAM-carrying vortex beams using circular antenna array. IEEE Trans. Antennas Propag. **65**(6), 2940–2949 (2017)
7. Lee, D., et al.: Demonstration of an orbital angular momentum (OAM) multiplexing at 28 GHz. In: IEICE General Conference, B-5-90. p. 381, March 2018
8. Wangjoo-Lee, Kim, J., Song, M.S.: Experimental results of triply multiplexed microwave orbital angular momentum mode transmission. In: 2016 International Conference on Information and Communication Technology Convergence (ICTC), pp. 765–767, October 2016
9. Sasaki, H., et al.: Experiment on over-100-Gbps wireless transmission with OAM-MIMO multiplexing system in 28-GHz band. In: 2018 IEEE Global Communications Conference (GLOBECOM), pp. 1–6, December 2018
10. Lee, D., et al.: An experimental demonstration of 28 Ghz band wireless OAM-MIMO multiplexing. In: 2018 IEEE 87th Vehicular Technology Conference (VTC Spring), pp. 1–5, June 2018

11. Yuan, Y., Zhang, Z., Cang, J., Wu, H., Zhong, C.: Capacity analysis of UCA-based OAM multiplexing communication system. In: 2015 International Conference on Wireless Communications Signal Processing (WCSP), pp. 1–5, October 2015
12. Jing, H., Cheng, W., Xia, X., Zhang, H.: Orbital-angular-momentum versus MIMO: orthogonality, degree of freedom, and capacity. In: 2018 IEEE 29th Annual International Symposium on Personal, Indoor and Mobile Radio Communications (PIMRC), pp. 1–7, September 2018
13. Saito, S., Suganuma, H., Ogawa, K., Maehara, F.: Performance analysis of OAM-MIMO using sic in the presence of misalignment of beam axis. In: 2019 IEEE International Conference on Communications Workshops (ICC Workshops), pp. 1–6, May 2019
14. Tang, J., Luo, J., Liu, M., So, D.K.C., Alsusa, E., Chen, G., Wong, K., Chambers, J.A.: Energy efficiency optimization for NOMA with SWIPT. IEEE Journal of Selected Topics in Signal Processing **13**(3), 452–466 (2019)
15. Chen, R., Tian, Z., Zhou, H., Long, W.: OAM-based concentric spatial division multiplexing for cellular IOT terminals. IEEE Access **8**, 59659–59669 (2020)
16. Cho, Y.S., Kim, J., Yang, W.Y., Kang, C.G.: MIMO-OFDM Wireless Communications with MATLAB. IEEE (2010)

Experimental Study on Target Localization for DTMB-Based Passive Bistatic Radar

Jiachuan Qian[1,2(✉)], Haijie Li[3], and Huijie Zhu[1,2]

[1] Science and Technology on Communication Information Security Control Laboratory,
Jiaxing 314033, China
jiachuanqian@sina.com

[2] The 36th Research Institute of China Electronics Technology Group Corporation,
Jiaxing 314033, China

[3] Huaxin Consulting and Designing Institute Co., Ltd., Hangzhou, China

Abstract. This paper introduces the target localization experiment using the digital television terrestrial broadcasting (DTMB) signal. Firstly, the feasibility and advantages of DTMB signal as an external illumination source signal are analyzed. Then the ambiguity function of DTMB signal is analyzed, as well as its distance and Doppler resolution. ECA algorithm is introduced to suppress direct wave and multipath clutter. In order to obtain the positioning results of target, the array antenna is used as the direction-finding antenna to measure the azimuth angle of target. Finally, the target localization experiment based on DTMB signal is designed, and the localization information of target is determined by combining the actual position of TV Tower and receiver in two dimensions.

Keywords: DTMB · Passive radar · Clutter suppression · Direction-finding · Location

1 Introduction

The passive bistatic radar (PBR) [1] system uses a non-cooperative illumination source to detect targets within the coverage area. Now that the spectrum resources are very limited, how to use the electromagnetic spectrum resources in a complex environment to carry out the target location of external radiation sources is a new research hotspot. The PBR has many advantages over the traditional detection system. It does not need a large-volume transmitter, which reduces the cost. Moreover, it does not emit signals and has good concealment capabilities. And bistatic station layout has certain anti stealth ability. The non-cooperative illumination source is generally TV [2], broadcast [3] or base station signals [4], and the wide distribution of the signals ensures the feasibility of target localization.

Digital Television Terrestrial Multimedia Broadcasting (DTMB) is a digital television standard with independent intellectual property rights proposed by China in 2006. DTMB innovatively uses Time Domain Synchronous Orthogonal-Frequency Division Multiplexing (TDS-OFDM) [5] modulation technology. The pseudo-random sequence

© ICST Institute for Computer Sciences, Social Informatics and Telecommunications Engineering 2021
Published by Springer Nature Switzerland AG 2021. All Rights Reserved
X. Wang et al. (Eds.): AICON 2021, LNICST 396, pp. 201–211, 2021.
https://doi.org/10.1007/978-3-030-90196-7_18

is used in the signal frame head, and the frame synchronization sequence of time-domain orthogonal coding is periodically inserted in each OFDM guard interval. Under this system, the spectrum efficiency is increased by 10% compared with the European Digital Video Broadcasting-Terrestrial (DVB-T) [6] standard, and there is more than 20 dB synchronization protection gain. At the same time, it is convenient for reliable synchronization and channel estimation, and can be extended for base station identification and terminal location. Relevant literature analyzes the feasibility of DTMB as an external illumination source for target detection, and designs related experiments to verify it. Many studies [7–11] mainly focus on the direct wave and multipath suppression of the received signal and the subsequent Range-Doppler processing results. However, there are relatively few studies on the localization of the target in space.

Aiming at the problem of target location, the receiver is improved in this paper. Usually, the PBR system contains two receiving antennas, a reference antenna and a monitoring antenna, so that direct wave and multipath suppression can be performed at the receiving end. The array antenna is used as the target monitoring antenna in this paper. First, the extended cancellation algorithm (ECA) [12] is used to suppress the direct wave and multipath for each subarray. Then the results are processed by Range-Doppler with the reference antenna signal to obtain the correlation. And the correlation of each subarray is input as the direction signal to get the direction. Finally, according to the results of direction and distance, the motion trajectory of target is obtained by combining the actual position of TV Tower and receiving station.

2   DTMB Signal Ambiguity Function

Ambiguity function [13] is an important tool for signal research in radar systems, and it is also suitable for DTMB-Based PBR. The auto-ambiguity function describes the joint characteristics of the time-frequency domain of the signals, and can reflect the distance and Doppler resolution of the target. Its calculation formula is defined as:

$$|\chi(\tau, f_{\mathrm{d}})| = \left| \int_{-\infty}^{\infty} s(t)s^*(t+\tau)e^{-j2\pi f_{\mathrm{d}}t}dt \right| \tag{1}$$

Where $s(t)$ represents DTMB signal; τ represents delay; f_d represents Doppler frequency.

The frame header form of the DTMB signal frame is shown in Fig. 1. The signal frame consists of 420 symbols and consists of a pre-synchronization sequence of length 82, a PN255 sequence and a post-synchronization sequence of length 83. Pre-synchronization and post-synchronization are defined as cyclic extensions of PN sequences. And the inserted frame header between each signal frame is the same. Therefore, when calculating its autocorrelation function, these repeated PN sequences will lead to the secondary peak of the ambiguity function.

In order to solve the above problems, the most direct method is to correlate the echo signal with the locally known PN sequence at the receiving end, find the frame head in the echo signal and remove it before Range-Doppler processing. However, for the actual environment considered in this paper, both the bistatic distance difference and Doppler frequency of the target are within the position of the secondary peak. Figure 2 shows

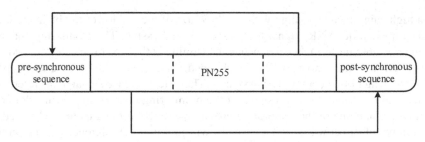

| pre-synchronous sequence | PN255 | post-synchronous sequence |

Fig. 1. DTMB signal frame header structure

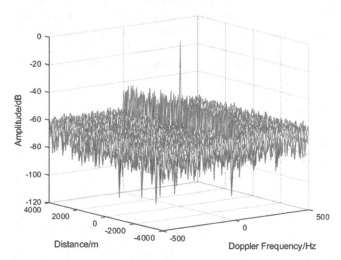

Fig. 2. The ambiguity function of the DTMB signal, where the bandwidth is 7.56 MHz, and the coherent integration time is 0.1 s.

the ambiguity function of the DTMB signal, where the bandwidth is 7.56 MHz, and the coherent integration time is 0.1 s.

The origin of the ambiguity function has a gain of about 40 dB compared to other points, showing an ideal pin shape. At the same time, the distance resolution is defined as:

$$\delta_d = \frac{c}{B} \tag{2}$$

Where c is the speed of light and B is the bandwidth of the signal. After calculation, the range resolution of the DTMB external radiation source radar is about 40 m. Therefore, DTMB signal is feasible as an external illumination source.

3   Key Technologies of DTMB-Based PBR

3.1   The Main Process of DTMB-Based PBR

Figure 3 shows the main flow of DTMB-Based PBR in this paper. There are two channels at the receiving end: monitoring channel and reference channel. The reference channel uses a high gain antenna to align with the direction of the TV tower to obtain the high signal-to-noise ratio (SNR) signal for subsequent processing. The monitoring channel uses an array antenna as the receiving antenna, aiming at the area to be detected, and the angle of arrival of the echo signal can be obtained. At the receiving end, the data is pre-processed to filter out other interfering signals. Then the reference signal of the reference channel is aligned with the echo signal of the monitoring channel in the time domain. Although the antenna of the monitoring channel is aimed at the area to be detected, a large number of direct waves and multipaths will mix into the reference channel in the complex urban environment, so the suppression of direct waves and multipath clutter is essential. Then perform range-Doppler processing between the suppressed residual signal and the reference signal, and extract the peak point. Each subarray can get peak points, and these points are used for interferometer direction-finding to obtain direction information. According to the actual positions of the TV Tower and the receiving station, the two-dimensional motion trajectory of the target is obtained by converting to the same coordinate system.

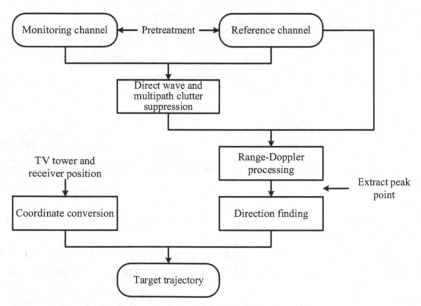

Fig. 3. The main flow of DTMB-Based PBR in this paper.

3.2 Direct Wave and Multipath Clutter Suppression

In the PBR system, the target echo signal is far lower than the direct wave and multipath clutter. Direct range-Doppler processing is not an ideal result, so the suppression of direct waves and multipath clutter is essential. Commonly used direct waves and clutter suppression include Least Mean Square (LMS) [14] algorithm, Recursive least squares (RLS) [15] algorithm and Extended Cancellation Algorithm (ECA) algorithm, etc. As an open-loop algorithm, ECA algorithm does not need iterative calculation, and the suppression effect is better. So, we choose ECA to deal with the problem in this paper. The main idea of ECA algorithm is that the reference signal and its time delay constitute a subspace, and calculate the projection coefficient of the echo signal on this subspace. Because of the Doppler frequency between the target and the clutter, it is usually considered that the target echo signal and the clutter are uncorrelated. Therefore, when the echo signal subtracts the reference signal and the subspace weighting composed of its delay, the echo target signal in the echo signal is considered to be unaffected, while the direct wave and multipath clutter are suppressed.

The antenna of the reference channel is aligned with the TV tower to sample and the reference signal is recorded as ref. The echo signal obtained by the monitoring channel aiming at the target area to be detected is denoted as s. The echo signal includes the direct signal of the TV tower, the multipath signal of the building, the reflection signal of the target and the noise. ECA algorithm is used to suppress the direct wave and multipath clutter in the echo, and the subspace composed of the reference signal and its delay can be expressed as:

$$
\mathbf{V} = \begin{bmatrix} ref\,(1) & 0 & \cdots & 0 \\ ref\,(2) & ref\,(1) & \cdots & 0 \\ \vdots & \vdots & \vdots & \vdots \\ ref\,(L) & ref\,(L{-}1) & \cdots & ref\,(L{-}K) \end{bmatrix} \tag{3}
$$

Where L represents the length of the signal, and K represents the order of canceling multipath clutter.

Finding the projection coefficient of the echo signal in the subspace is a convex optimization problem:

$$
w = \arg\min_{w} \|s - \mathbf{V}w\|_2^2 \tag{4}
$$

The gradient of the objective function is obtained by deriving w in the above formula. Let the gradient be 0, that is:

$$
\frac{\partial (\|s - \mathbf{V}w\|_2^2)}{\partial w} = 0 \tag{5}
$$

We can get the weight vector:

$$
w = (\mathbf{V}^H \mathbf{V})^{-1} \mathbf{V}^H s \tag{6}
$$

The residual signal after clutter suppression can be obtained by subtracting the product of the sliding matrix and the weight vector from the echo signal. It can be expressed as:

$$
echo = s - \mathbf{V}w = s - \mathbf{V}(\mathbf{V}^H \mathbf{V})^{-1} \mathbf{V}^H s \tag{7}
$$

The accuracy of the weight vector obtained by ECA is related to the data length and K value of the signal. The smaller the K is, the less obvious the effect of multipath elimination is. However, the larger the K is, the larger the computation will be. So, in data processing, the appropriate K is determined by considering the influence of multipath in the environment.

3.3 Direction-Finding Algorithm

The target echo signal is still weak, and the noise in the echo signal is still greater than the target echo signal after clutter suppression. It is necessary to perform Range-Doppler processing to improve the SNR of the signal. The calculation formula can be expressed as:

$$|\chi(\tau, f_d)| = \left| \int_0^T echo(t)s^*(t+\tau)e^{-j2\pi f_d t} dt \right| \tag{8}$$

After Range-Doppler processing, the peak point (τ_m, f_{dm}) can be searched as the corresponding target information. So far, we get the speed and distance information of the target. However, there is still a lack of direction information to locate the target, which needs further processing to get the direction-finding results of the array antenna.

The essence of interferometer [16] direction-finding is to use the phase difference formed by the radiation signal on the receiving antenna to determine the direction of the signal. Based on the phase received by element 1 in the M-element antenna array, the phase difference between element M and reference element can be expressed as $\varphi(m - 1)$ (see Fig. 4).

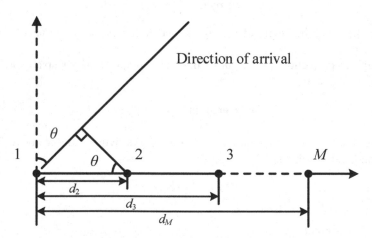

Fig. 4. Principle of interferometer direction-finding.

Where $m = 2,3 \ldots M$ can form a phase difference vector $\boldsymbol{\varphi} = [\varphi(1), \varphi(2), \ldots, \varphi(M - 1)]$. According to the geometric relationship of the linear array, the relationship between the phase and the direction of arrival can be obtained:

$$\varphi(m - 1) = \frac{2\pi \cdot d_{m-1}}{\lambda} \sin \theta \tag{9}$$

Where d_m represents the distance between the m-th subarray and the (m + 1)-th subarray.

If the azimuth θ traverses 2π at a certain step angle, several pairs of the above-mentioned corresponding relations can be expressed as $u(\theta,\varphi)$. The phase difference vector φ corresponding to these azimuth θ is the original phase difference sample. Correlation processing is the process of matching the observation samples generated by the signal response received by the array antenna with the standard samples. Therefore, the cost function of interferometer direction-finding can be expressed as:

$$F(\theta, \varphi) = \frac{v^T u(\theta, \varphi)}{\sqrt{(v^T v)}\sqrt{u^T(\theta, \varphi)u(\theta, \varphi)}} \tag{10}$$

Where v represents the observed phase difference vector of the actual antenna.

In the actual environment, even if the ECA algorithm suppresses most of the direct wave and multipath clutter, the residual clutter and noise are still larger than the target echo. If the residual signal is directly used to calculate the observed phase difference vector, there will be a large error. In this paper, the peak points obtained from the above Range-Doppler processing are used as the basis for observing the phase difference vector rather than the phase of the residual signal. In this way, not only the original phase of the echo signal can be preserved, but also the SNR can be improved.

4   Experiments and Results

The experiment was conducted on the top of a building with latitude and longitude of $(30.768933°, 120.73015°)$. Jiaxing DTMB TV Tower is located in the northeast of the building with latitude and longitude of $(30.776908°, 120.741528°)$. NI USRP2955 is used as the acquisition device in the experiment, which adopts superheterodyne receiving system. It has a maximum instantaneous bandwidth of 80 MHz, 10 MHz–6 GHz RF tuning capability and four channel synchronous acquisition capability. In the experiment, the target is a flying unmanned aerial vehicle (UAV), its model is Dajiang mavic2, and its deployment size is $322 \times 242 \times 84$ mm. The antenna for receiving the direct wave signal is facing the direction of the TV Tower, and its gain is about 15 dBi, which is connected with the collector channel 3. The linear array antenna used for direction-finding has three subarrays, and the distance are [0, 0.28, 0.7] m. It is connected to channel 0, channel 1 and channel 2 of the collector respectively, and the gain is about 7dBi. In the experiment, the linear array is placed in the same direction as the east-west direction, and the east direction is the positive direction of x-axis, and the north direction is the positive direction of y-axis.

The position of each point in the experimental scene is shown in Fig. 5 (ignoring the height information). The origin O is the location of the receiving antenna, and the P (x_0, y_0) point is the location of the TV Tower. The UAV flies in an east-west direction on the south side of the antenna, as shown by the line $y = -r$ in Fig. 5, and r is about 15m. Assuming that after data processing, we can get the bistatic distance difference $d = d_1 + d_2 - d_3$, and the angle θ, then the position of the UAV can be expressed as:

$$x = -\frac{d^2 + 2dd_3}{2d + 2d_3 + 2x_0 \sin\theta + 2y_0 \cos\theta} \sin\theta$$

$$y = -\frac{d^2 + 2dd_3}{2d + 2d_3 + 2x_0 \sin\theta + 2y_0 \cos\theta} \cos\theta \qquad (11)$$

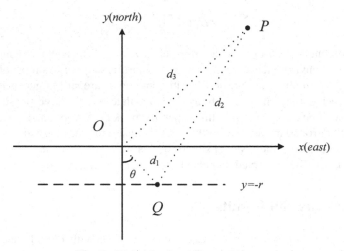

Fig. 5. Diagram of experimental scene.

In the data preprocessing part, the reference signal and the echo signal are aligned in the time domain (see Fig. 6). It can be seen that in urban environment, multipath effect is obvious, direct wave and multipath clutter suppression is essential.

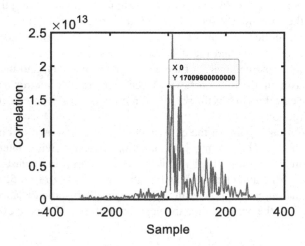

Fig. 6. Correlation of reference signal and echo signal in time domain.

Figure 7 shows the average power of each frame of echo signal in time domain before and after clutter suppression by ECA. It can be seen that most of the signals are suppressed.

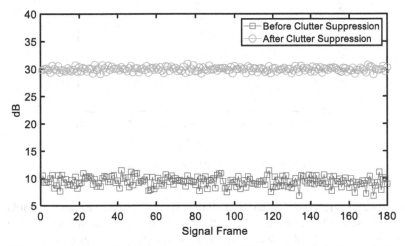

Fig. 7. The average power of each frame of echo signal in time domain before and after clutter suppression.

The distance and Doppler frequency information of UAV can be obtained by Range-Doppler processing of the residual signal and reference signal after suppressed, and the Coherent accumulation time is 100 ms. Figure 8 shows the Range-Doppler processing results of the three channels at a certain time. Because the distance between the subarrays is much smaller than the range resolution, the position of the peak point should be the same.

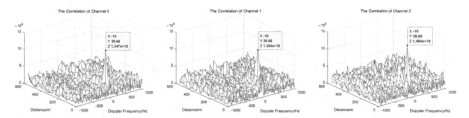

Fig. 8. Range-Doppler processing results of the three channels.

Extracting the peak value for the input of direction-finding of correlation interferometer. The direction-finding results in continuous time are shown in Fig. 9. And there is no obvious correlation peak in the position of $-20°$. This is because the bistatic range is the smallest at this time, and the Doppler frequency of the UAV changes positively and negatively, which leads to the increase of the correlation between the UAV echo signal and the reference signal, which is suppressed by ECA.

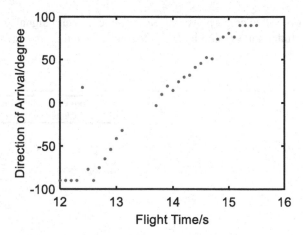

Fig. 9. Result of UAV direction-finding.

Substituting the results of direction finding and ranging into the above formula (11), the two-dimensional trace of the UAV in the x-y plane can be obtained (see Fig. 10). This shows that the UAV flies westward, and its trajectory is roughly the same as the actual scene. However, it is worth noting that the linear array used can only measure the azimuth without the pitch information, so the error caused by the altitude information is ignored. The error of linear array direction-finding results at the edge ($\pm 90°$) is large.

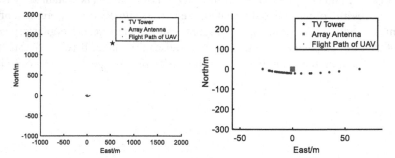

Fig. 10. UAV location experiment results

5   Conclusion

This paper briefly introduces the DTMB signal and analyzes its ambiguity function. In order to be able to be used for target location, the direct wave and multipath suppression algorithm and direction-finding algorithm are studied. On this basis, the UAV location experiment based on DTMB PBR is designed. After data processing, the flight trajectory of UAV in two-dimensional plane is obtained. Further research is carried out on how to further improve the positioning accuracy of UAV location.

References

1. Howland, P.E.: Target tracking using television-based bistatic radar. **146**(3), 166–174 (1999)
2. Griffiths, H.D., Long, N.R.W.: Television-based bistatic radar. IEE Proc. F-Commun. Radar Signal Process. **133**(7), 649–657 (2008)
3. Howland, P.E., Maksimiuk, D., Reitsma, G.: FM radio based bistatic radar. IEE Proc. Radar Sonar Navig. **152**(3), 107–115 (2005)
4. Tan, D., Lu, K.P., et al.: Passive radar using Global System for Mobile communication signal: theory, implementation and measurements. **152**(3), 116–123 (2005)
5. Wang, J., Yang, Z.X., Pan, C.Y., et al.: Iterative padding subtraction of the PN sequence for the TDS-OFDM over broadcast channels. IEEE Trans. Consum. Electron. **51**(4), 1148–1152 (2005)
6. Sun, Z., Wang, T., Jiang, T., et al.: Analysis of the properties of DVB-S signal for passive radar application. In: International Conference on Wireless Communications & Signal Processing, pp. 1–5. IEEE (2013)
7. Wan, X.R.: An overview on development of passive radar based on the low frequency band digital broadcasting and TV signals. J. Radars **1**(2), 109–123 (2012). (in Chinese)
8. Cardinali, R., Colone, F., Ferretti, C., et al.: Comparison of clutter and multipath cancellation techniques for passive radar. 469–474 (2007)
9. So, C.F., Ng, S.C., Leung, S.H.: RLS lattice algorithm using gradient based variable forgetting factor. In: IEEE, pp. 1168–117 (2003)
10. Ansari, F., Taban, M.R.: Implementation of sequential algorithm in batch processing for clutter and direct signal cancellation in passive bistatic radars. In: Electrical Engineering, pp. 1–6. IEEE (2013)
11. Meller, M.: Cheap cancellation of strong echoes for digital passive and noise radars. IEEE Trans. Signal Process. **60**(5), 2654–2659 (2012)
12. Colone, F., O'Hagan, D.W., Lombardo, P., et al.: A multistage processing algorithm for disturbance removal and target detection in passive bistatic radar. IEEE Trans. Aerosp. Electron. Syst. **45**(2), 698–722 (2009)
13. Saini, R., Cherniakov, M.: DTV signal ambiguity function analysis for radar application. **152**(3), 133–142 (2005)
14. Xu, Y.J., Tao, R., Wang, Y., et al.: Using LMS adaptive filter in direct wave cancellation. J. Beijing Inst. Technol. (Engl. Ed.) **12**(4), 425–428 (2003)
15. Dhiman, J., Ahmad, S., Gulia, K.: Comparison between Adaptive filter Algorithms (LMS, NLMS and RLS) (2013)
16. Lee, J.H., Woo, J.M.: Interferometer direction-finding system with improved df accuracy using two different array configurations. IEEE Antennas Wirel. Propag. Lett. **14**, 719–722 (2015)

Application of Artificial Intelligence in the Planning of Navigation Satellite in Orbit Reconstruction Tasks

Lingling Chen[✉], Zhimei Yang, and Wenwen Zhao

China Academy of Space Technology (Xi'an), Xi'an 710100, China

Abstract. The basic system of Beidou-3 has been completed and started to provide global services so far. This system is composed of 24MEO+3GEO+3IGSO, and 80% of products have refactoring functions. In view of the potential load function upgrade needs in the future, as well as the reliability upgrade and maintenance of the system, there is a need for the reconstruction of the entire network of satellites in orbit. Analyze the characteristics of the three types of satellites and break through the traditional reconstruction schemes. Most of them are reconstructed through the ground measurement and control and operation control channels. The speed is low and the timeliness is poor. A new reconstruction idea is proposed, and the IGSO satellite Ka high-speed ground link is used to transfer the program. Make a bet, and then distribute the reconstructed data through the laser inter-satellite link. According to the Beidou satellite's full-satellite redundant backup feature, the three types of satellite mission characteristics are learned through artificial intelligence, and the redundant satellites are met while meeting the positioning requirements. Performing reconstruction upgrades, this method can greatly improve the timeliness of reconstruction and shorten the impact on the system's service performance interruption.

Keywords: Artificial intelligence · On-orbit reconstruction · Mission planning

1 Introduction

In December 2018, the basic system of Beidou-3 completed the construction and began to provide global services, following the development law of navigation system construction, following the incremental thinking, solidifying the engineering technology status in stages, and the key software has the ability to be flexible, reconfigurable and expandable on orbit. At present, 80% of spaceborne stand-alone aircraft have reconfigurable functions. Whether it is software upgrades for a better user experience or software upgrades for system maintenance, it involves the upgrade of a large number of satellites. At present, most of the on-orbit reconstruction schemes are carried out from the operation control/measurement control channel through the L/S frequency band. The above note is that the timeliness is poor. The upload time of the FPGA configuration data for 1 piece of 5.5 million gates is about 600 min [3]. Every system upgrade is faced with a

X. Wang et al. (Eds.): AICON 2021, LNICST 396, pp. 212–219, 2021.
https://doi.org/10.1007/978-3-030-90196-7_19

reconstruction task of 30 satellites, which will greatly affect the system. The continuity of the orbit service, therefore, it is urgent to find a time-efficient reconstruction plan in the system upgrade, and it is necessary to plan the reconstruction task of 30 satellites according to the working status of the satellites.

2 Path of Transmission in Reconstruction

On-orbit reconstruction is a process in which the on-ground injection system transmits configuration data to the spacecraft in a certain format through a wireless channel, and then is parsed by the spacecraft's remote receiving device and sent to the FPGA module that needs to be reconstructed. The process is mainly composed of three parts: the uplink injection station that reconstructs the configuration file, the device that receives and parses the reconstructed configuration file, and the reconfigurable target FPGA; the transmission process can be divided into two stages, the first stage is The satellite-to-ground transmission phase, that is, how to ensure that the configuration file is quickly and reliably uploaded from the injection station to the remote analysis device. The second stage is the intra-satellite transmission stage, that is, how the file is transferred from the remote analysis device to the FPGA module that needs to be reconstructed [3]. The influencing factors of the reliability and timeliness of transmission in these two stages are specifically analyzed, and the focus is on how to realize the rapid reconstruction of the entire constellation.

2.1 Satellite-To-Earth Transmission

Currently available transmission channels are: ground measurement and control, operation and control channels, business channels and dedicated channels.

1) Ground measurement and control, operation control channel
   The ground-based measurement and control channel is independent of the application of the satellite's payload, ensuring that the satellite is always in a controllable state. However, the current measurement and control channel mostly uses the S-band for betting, and the transmission rate is relatively low and the transmission time will be relatively long. The amount of configuration data is generally relatively large. Regardless of the resource consumption of the program preparation phase and the program reloading process, only the transmission speed is considered, and the engineering cost of performing a reconstruction is very large. To solve this problem, a certain algorithm can be used to compress the configuration file. The mainstream compression algorithms currently available include arithmetic coding, Huffman coding, and dictionary-based LZ series compression algorithms [4, 6], which will inevitably reduce its reliability during the compression process., Reduce the bit error rate.
2) Business channel
   The configuration file that needs to be reconstructed is transmitted through the service channel, the configuration data and the remote control command are combined, and the "enter reconstruction state" is sent through the remote control command chain

to start the reconstruction function. Since the communication channel has a certain communication error rate limit, once the program has an error code, it cannot be loaded normally, which will inevitably affect the communication interruption of the service channel.

3) Dedicated channel

Using an independent dedicated channel, the channel supports a higher transmission rate, is independent of business instructions and measurement and control instructions, has less interference, high rate and high reliability.

2.2 Intra-satellite Transmission

After the ground remote control sending center formats the configuration data, it is packaged by the remote control communication protocol and sent to the satellite, it also needs to be transmitted within the satellite. It mainly includes three aspects: 1) Data distribution process: the spacecraft remote control receiving device parses it and gives the correct configuration data, and distributes it to the next-level processing unit according to the extracted target processor ID. 2) Data loading process: The control processing unit writes the configuration data to the configuration register (DSP or FPGA) through a dedicated configuration interface. 3) Result feedback: After the processing module configuration is loaded, the configuration result identification will be returned. Finally, the interface processing unit feeds back the configuration and loading status information and other tasks, and completes the information interaction with the dedicated ground station system.

Due to the different positions of the FPGA that needs to be reconstructed in the spaceborne system, the transmission path is also different. The configuration bus used in the spacecraft is generally 1553B bus, RS422 bus, LVDS bus and high-speed data transmission TLK2711 bus. The maximum transmission rate of 1553B bus is 1Mb/s, and the maximum transmission rate of RS422 bus is 10Mb/s. The transmission rate of LVDS bus is: 10 Mb/s–1 Gb/s (recommended maximum 655 Mbps), TLK2711 bus 1.6Gb/s–2.7 Gb/s. In order to ensure the effectiveness of the transmission, in the long-term reconstruction process, if there is an error in the transmission, it needs to be reconstructed again. For this reason, the configuration file will be formatted in sections in the system design, and all the correct points will be received on the satellite. After the segment data, the overall configuration file assembly and storage are finally completed in the spacecraft. In the system design, the EDAC check is performed in segments, and the telemetry of whether the reception is correct or not is provided in the segmented data, and the data blocks with transmission errors can be reconstructed separately. In addition, the system design has also designed the "Breakpoint Resume" function. Once a power failure occurs, the data that has been noted is valid, and it will be continuously transmitted from the breakpoint when the power is turned on again.

In terms of reliability, the configuration data is stored on the satellite for operations such as the configuration of reconfigurable FPGAs, reloading after power-off reset, and SEU refresh prevention. Its correctness is critical. For long-life spacecraft, long-term storage of data generally requires anti-radiation design and reliability design measures to ensure data availability. On the one hand, the reliability and radiation resistance of the memory chip must meet the requirements, and non-volatile memory such as EEPROM and Flash is generally selected. On the other hand, it is necessary to deal with the single event flip effect that occurs in the space environment and generate data on the memory. There are two common methods for error-tolerant design: Error Detection And Correction (EDAC) and Trip Module Redundancy (TMR) + regular refresh [7].

3 New Type of Navigation Satellite On-Orbit Reconstruction

The Beidou-3 satellite navigation system is composed of 24MEO+3GEO+3IGSO satellites. Its constellation is shown in Fig. 1. All three types of satellites have basic navigation loads, Ka inter-satellite links and laser inter-satellite links, which can pass through each other. The inter-satellite link is built with the characteristics of "one satellite connects to all Netcom". Among them, IGSO satellites have their unique services, namely Ka high-speed ground link and Ka high-speed ground link. 300 M/bps. The betting rate is fast, the reliability is strong, and the timeliness is good.

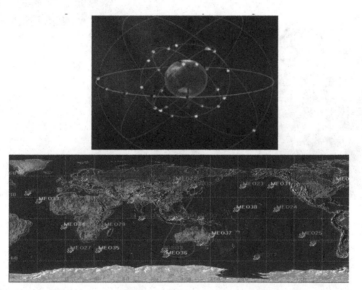

Fig. 1. The constellation composition and sub-satellite trajectory diagram of BDS-3 navigation system

According to the characteristics of the three types of satellites of the Beidou system, an on-orbit reconstruction scheme is proposed. The scheme is based on the IGSO satellite with large-capacity data storage space and the high-speed ground link load with Ka-band to achieve a large number of laser inter-satellite links. The characteristics of the satellite-to-ground high-speed uplink and downlink transmission of data. On the one hand, the satellite-to-ground high-speed link is used as the channel for program reconstruction. On the other hand, the satellite adopts a local dynamic reconstruction scheme. Without affecting other FPGA areas, the FPGA automatically rebuilds a pre-defined area. Configuration. The block diagram of the reconstruction principle is as follows: complete the annotation, verification and file integrity check of the reconstruction program, and give the corresponding response to the corresponding FPGA. The EDAC check bit should be added to the data written in FLASH to improve the reliability of data storage, and it can read back and check the reconstructed files on the note. The reconfiguration refresh control FPGA uses ACTEL's anti-fuse FPGA. The reconstructed program is uploaded at high speed through Ka high-speed ground link, and then the reconstructed program is distributed through the laser inter-satellite link (Fig. 2).

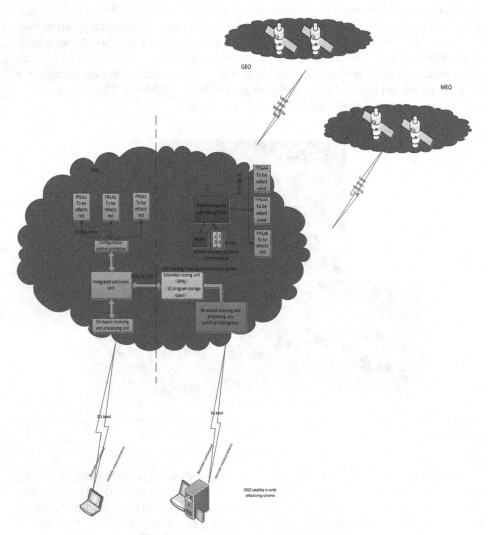

Fig. 2. New on-orbit reconstruction scheme

Program loading is controlled by ACTEL FPGA. The same programs are stored in Zone 1 and Zone 2 as mutual backup to improve the reliability of on-track. The left side of the figure is the traditional reconstruction scheme, which only supports independent reconstruction of one satellite by one star, and the right side is the new reconstruction scheme, which can make full use of the "resumed transmission" function to carry out the whole network satellite when the satellite is idle Refactoring.

On-board receiving and processing unit: receiving remote control information sent by the ground station, receiving uplink configuration data, real-time monitoring of configuration loading status information fed back by the interface processing unit, and completing the information interaction with the dedicated ground station system, and receiving through the ground The status and mission information of other satellites, the information after intelligent processing on the ground, interact with the satellites, and plan reconstruction tasks by learning the status of other satellites.

Extended routing unit: It has a large-capacity storage capacity (1T), which is used to store the data of the laser inter-satellite link, and the space used to store the program is 1G. It mainly completes the verification, analysis, and distribution of configuration data, and sends the correct configuration data frame to the corresponding processor for configuration loading according to the extracted frame type, target processor ID and other identification information.

Refresh control module: complete the power-on configuration and online reconfiguration of the subband exchange FPGA, where the online reconfiguration is determined by the corresponding remote control command. After the configuration is successfully completed, switch to refresh mode, and refresh the subband switching FPGA periodically, with a refresh cycle of 3.5 min $\pm$ 30 s (5 MHz working clock). The configuration refresh program includes the default program (prom) and the reconstruction program (flash). The mode selection is determined by the corresponding remote control command.

4 Application of Artificial Intelligence in Reconstruction Task Planning

The ground station classifies and preprocesses the telemetry information transmitted by the satellite, performs statistics on the information attributes, establishes a model, and initially learns and memorizes it. Then, according to the changes of external factors, it collects the change information of the satellite, and through in-depth analysis, Find the most relevant characteristic indicators and human factors related to the target, form an in-depth understanding of the mission of each satellite, and form a corresponding decision-making system. The decision-making system is combined with the intelligent decision-making model library formed in the previous design process to form According to the decision report under the current situation, the mission characteristics of the satellites are identified. As the Beidou satellite system achieves more than 6-fold coverage worldwide, it forms a backup relationship with each other on the premise of meeting the positioning requirements. The topological structure of the satellite is performed through artificial intelligence. In planning, the satellites that need to be reconstructed are scheduled at the right time, and reconstructed to reduce the interruption of service continuity and do not affect the use of users (Fig. 3).

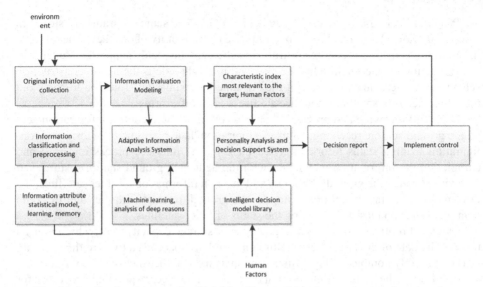

Fig. 3. Application process of artificial intelligence in reconstruction mission planning

5   Verification and Conclusion

In order to verify the reliability and timeliness of the Ka-to-ground link, the engineering test was performed on the ground space by simulating the on-orbit state, and the on-board reconfigurable FPGA was reconstructed. Among them, the upload speed of the Ka-band link is 300 Mbps, and the satellite receiving processing unit receives the configuration data and distributes it to the extended routing unit. The extended routing unit distributes to each module using the LVDS bus, and the designed transmission speed is 20 M/s (Table 1).

Table 1. Statistics of configuration data scale and transmission time of FPGA under different schemes

Serial number	FPGA model	FPGA scale	Configuration data volume/bit	Storage space/Mbit	Transmission time of raditional solution (rate is 4 kbit/s)	Transmission time of the new scheme (rate is 300 Mbit/s)
1	XQ2VR3000	3 million gate	10494368	16	2900	10
2	XQR4VSX55	5.5 million gate	22744832	32	6000	25
3	XC5VFX130T	13 million gate	49234944	49	13000	43

The traditional reconstruction scheme is injected through the uplink S measurement and control\operation control channel. For larger programs, the satellite-to-ground transmission rate limits the timeliness of reconstruction. The Beidou global networking system has been completed. Once needed On-orbit reconstruction requires a lot of time and interrupts the continuity of on-orbit services. The Ka dedicated channel is designed for betting, which can effectively improve the timeliness of betting, and for this star, betting can be completed in minutes. In addition, the on-board program adopts dual backup storage mode, and is equipped with a regular refresh function. The on-board program is refreshed with a 3.5 s refresh cycle, which improves the reliability of the program on orbit, and the timeliness of uploading is greatly improved compared with the traditional reconstruction scheme.. Using artificial intelligence to learn the current state of the satellites, find the operating characteristics between the three types of satellites, and plan out the corresponding reconstruction plan. When the system is upgraded, the impact on the continuity of satellite services is shortened as much as possible. duration.

References

1. Liu, J.: Research and implementation of FPGA remote control system based on embedded Web. Beijing University of Technology (2010)
2. Pang, B.: An engineering realization of SRAM-FPGA on-orbit reconstruction. Spacecraft Eng. 10 (2017)
3. Wang, Z., Zhai, S.: Research on on-orbit reconstruction technology of on-board processing equipment software. Space Electron. Technol. **2013**(1), 7–13 (2013)
4. Gu, H., Li, L., Xu, J., et al.: Lossless configuration bit stream compression for virtex FPGAs. J. Comput. Res. Dev. **43**(5), 940–945 (2006). (in Chinese)
5. Xu, Y., Li, K., Feng, G., et al.: An FPGA on-orbit reconfiguration configuration data compression algorithm. Spacecraft Eng. **24**(6), 75–78 (2015)
6. Guo, H., Wang, W., Luo, Y., et al.: Challenges facing the research of single event effects in new microelectronics technology **33**(7), 538–542 (2010)
7. Xilinx.Std.Zynq-7000 All Programmable SoC Technical Reference Manual. ug585 (v1.6) (2013). www.Xilinx.com
8. Liu, S.L., Du, Z.D., Tao, J.H., et al.: Cambricon: an instruction set architecture for neural networks. In: Proceedings of the ACM/ IEEE 43rd Annual International Symposium on Computer Architecture, pp. 393–405. IEEE, Washington (2016)

Coordinated Beamforming Optimization with Interference Suppressing for Massive MIMO Systems

Huayu Wang, Yaxuan Xing🆔, Jing Lv, and Yinghui Zhang$^{(\boxtimes)}$🆔

College of Electronic Information Engineering, Inner Mongolia University,
Hohhot 010021, China
zhangyinghui@imu.edu.cn

Abstract. To meet the growing demand for high-data rate applications, massive multiple-input multiple-output (MIMO) has been identified to provide better coverage and throughput. Note that the energy efficiency and throughput of massive MIMO system is sensitive to pilot reuse factor, number of antennas and inter-cell interference, which should be accounted when designing a system. In this paper, dynamic division of area coordinated beamforming (DDA-CoBF) algorithm is proposed by suppressing inter-cell interference. Meanwhile, pilot reuse factor, number of antennas and channel state information are investigated for obtaining the optimal energy efficiency and throughput for massive MIMO system. Considering the actual application, we also especially analyze the systems based on imperfect CSI, proving the strong robustness for the proposed DDA-CoBF algorithm. Numerical analysis and simulation indicate that the proposed DDA-CoBF algorithm satisfies the higher energy efficiency and throughput. Moreover, this work provides a potential design scheme for large-scale MIMO multicell systems.

Keywords: Coordinated beamforming · Energy efficiency · Imperfect CSI · Interference suppression · Massive MIMO · Throughput

1 Introduction

With exponentially growing of mobile-data demand, the capacity of wireless communication networks must be increased, so that it can ensure the quality-of-service (QoS) requirements of the mobile applications [1]. In order to satisfy the various applications of 5G wireless communication systems, massive multiple-input multiple-output (MIMO) has been recognized as a promising technology

---

This work was supported in part by the National Natural Science Foundation of China (NSFC) under Grant 61761033 and Grant 62071257, supported by the Natural Science Foundation of Inner Mongolia Autonomous Region of China under Grant 2019MS06033, and supported by the High Education Research Project of Inner Mongolia Autonomous Region of China under Grant NJYT-20-A11.

X. Wang et al. (Eds.): AICON 2021, LNICST 396, pp. 220–234, 2021.
https://doi.org/10.1007/978-3-030-90196-7_20

for increasing network capacity and achieving extremely high spectral efficiency [2]. Many antennas can obtain spatial diversity and multiplexing which can be used to improve performance of wireless communication system. Nevertheless, one of the major drawbacks for adopting large-scale antennas is the associated complexity of using a separate RF chain for each antenna, which also results in a significant increase in energy consumption [3]. Therefore, the critical problem and goal is to design the higher energy efficiency(EE) schemes for massive MIMO systems. Whether large-scale system can outperform systems with fewer antennas in terms of EE is a worthwhile and significant research [4].

Coordinated multiple points is a key technology in Long Term Evolution Advanced (LTE-A), which not only can break the limitation of the SE of single-point transmission, but also can reduce inter-cell interference and improve throughput of the cell edge and whole system [5]. Coordinated beamforming (CoBF) is more effective because of only sharing CSI, especially in massive MIMO system [6]. BS allocates resource blocks according to the CSI of the user location and neighboring cells to avoid the interference. Therefore, CoBF can improve the QoS at the inner and outer edges of the cell [7].

Recently, the EE analysis of massive MIMO systems has been well researched. CoBF is more effective and plays an important role in improving EE especially in massive MIMO system. In [8], aiming at optimize EE for the multi-cell massive MIMO system, the authors provided explicit formulas for the optimal number of antennas for BS with conjugate beamforming. In [9], a dual-layer CoBF scheme was proposed to maximize the EE in a multi-cell massive MIMO system while meeting QoS requirements. In [10], a resource allocation scheme was proposed for wireless power transfer in the case of multi-user massive MIMO system with imperfect CSI. In [11], an efficient algorithm for maximizing the ratio between the system-weighted sum rate and the total power consumption was proposed, considering utility function is constrained by QoS and power of each BS. In [12], an CoBF design was proposed as a cascade of the low-complexity analog beam selection mechanism and a robust digital design. In [13], a beamforming scheme was proposed to minimize the transmission power for a large-scale MIMO channel. In [14], a low-complexity power allocation for beamforming and maximizing the EE of massive MIMO system was developed while guaranteeing the requirement of information transmission quality. Many existing CoBF researching focus on minimizing the transmit power, ignoring the static circuit power consumption to improve EE. The total power consumption is assumed to be the radiation transmission power with a constant or neglected circuit power consumption. This model might be very misleading with many RF chains in which circuit power is comparable to the transmit power.

Therefore, in the actual deployment, the circuit power consumption needs to be considered comprehensively, especially massive MIMO system. Moreover, some beamforming for optimal EE was studied in massive MIMO system under the condition fixed cooperative division of areas [15], In [16], a new full-pilot zero-forcing (ZF) scheme that actively suppresses inter-cell interference in a fully distributed coordinated beamforming was proposed in which partially suppresses strong interference from neighbor cells.

Differing from existing research, we propose dynamic division of area coordinated beamforming (DDA-CoBF) algorithm in which more degrees is adopted to suppress the interference either at all edge users (UEs) in the neighboring cells or UEs close to the BS coverage area. Furthermore, to improve the system EE and throughput, this paper comprehensively considers the influence of the pilot reuse factor, optimal number of antennas and CSI, which are useful insights on the whole optimal system design.

The main contributions are summarized below.

- Suppress interference and improve the EE are explored with considering the neighboring UEs at the cell edge. Exploring the more degrees to serve UEs with a few spatial dimensions to suppress interference.
- DDA-CoBF algorithm are proposed, and the best division of cooperative areas are obtained.
- Simulation results show that the proposed DDA-CoBF algorithm are superior to some existing CoBF. The performance comparisons are used considering the pilot reuse factor number of antenna and imperfect CSI accounting for the power amplifier power and circuit power.

2   System Description

2.1   System Model

We consider the downlink of a massive MIMO system. BS is equipped with M antennas, serving $K(K \leq M)$ single antenna users. Rayleigh small-scale fading and time-division duplexing (TDD) are considered in this work. Therefore, the channels are static within time-frequency coherence blocks of $U = BT$ symbols, where B is the coherence bandwidth and T is the coherence time. A square coverage model is used to facilitate the calculation of interference in this paper, but our proposed algorithm is also applicable to cellular hexagons.

For the sake of ensuring the quality of data transmission and the fairness of the service, we adopted the power distribution to force all users to have the same rate R in a single-layer homogeneous network. User k in the cell where BS i is located can be denoted by $U_{i,k}^{In} \in \mathbb{R}^2$. The j neighbor user of the neighbor cell outside the cell is defined as $U_{i,j}^{Out} \in \mathbb{R}^2$. The set of UE physical locations associated with BS i is denoted by $U_i \in \mathbb{R}^2$. It is assumed that the distribution of the UEs in the cell obeys the homogeneous Poisson point process. Since users are deployed through a round-robin [17], the distribution can be distributed randomly with the distribution $f(x)$, which determines the distribution shape and density of the user, where x represents the distance BS to user.

It is assumed that the cell is affected by the interference of 24 external cells and only non-line-of-sight (NLOS) propagation will be considered in the multi-cell model [17]. When a cooperative area is adopted with pilot reuse factor $F = 1$. The interference calculation formula is given by

$$I_{jik} = \sum_{j=1, j \neq i}^{24} \frac{\sum_{s=1}^{K} p_{js} \left| x_{jik}^H w_{js} \right|^2}{r_{jik} \|w_{js}\|^2} \tag{1}$$

where r_{jik} and x_{jik} is the pass loss and small-scale fading vector from BS j to UE k in cell i. $p_{js} \geq 0$ is the transmission power from BS j to UE s. According to (1), we can obtain the interferences from the different color cells are 0.0540, 0.0202, 0.0043, 0.0028, 0.0011. Therefore, 24 neighboring cells is selected because the interference of other further cells is very small and can be ignored.

Since only NLOS propagation is considered, so the closest distance between the UE and the BS is defined as $d^U_{\min} = 35m$ in a cell.

The BS obtains the CSI of a cooperative user through the training phase, reduces the interference of the local cell to the cooperative user by sacrificing spatial freedom, and improves the rate of the cooperative user. In TDD system, it is assumed that the BS obtains CSI through uplink transmission. Moreover, the user must periodically send relevant information to the BS because of the handover.

2.2   Channel Model

It is assumed that the antennas widely separated to avoid mutual coupling when the BS communicates with the user. In this network, we assume that the channels on Rayleigh fading considering the path loss, which is suitable for both large and small arrays. In the single cell, channel vector is defined as $h_k = [h_{k1}, h_{k2}, ..., h_{kM}]^T \in C^{M \times 1}$, where $\{h_{km}\}$ represents the instantaneous propagation channel between the m-th antenna and k-th UE. The channel matrix H is expressed as $H = [h_1, h_2, ..., h_K]$. Extended to multiple cells, channel vector is defined as $h_{ijk} = \left[h^1_{ijk}, h^2_{ijk}, ..., h^M_{ijk} \right]^T$, where $\left\{ h^m_{ijk} \right\}$ represents the instantaneous propagation between the m-th antenna of BS i and the k-th user in cell j. Then, the channel matrix H_i from BS i and the related K UEs can be expressed as

$$H_i = R_i X_i \tag{2}$$

$$X_i = [x_{ii1}, x_{ii2}, ..., x_{iiK}]^H \tag{3}$$

where $x_{iik} \sim \mathcal{CN}(0_M, I_M)$ is the small-scale fading vector between the i-th BS and the k-th UE in i-th cell. $R_i = diag \{r_{ii1}, r_{ii2}, ..., r_{iiK}\}$ is the channel fading matrix, r_{iik} is the path loss from BS i to the UE k in cell , which is given by

$$r_{iik} = r_{\min} d^{-\alpha}_{iik} \tag{4}$$

where d_{iik} is the distance from BS i to the UE k in cell i, α is the path loss exponent, and $r_{\min} > 0$ is the channel attenuation at $d^U_{\min} = 35m$.

On account of the distance between the UE and the BS is much greater than that between the antennas, the large-scale fading between the antennas of the same user and the BS are assumed to be the same. Because of the system capacity is interference limited for massive MIMO networks [12], the effects of thermal noise are ignored in this paper.

2.3 Channel Estimation and Pilot Reuse

Exploiting channel reciprocity, the BS forms an estimate of the channel between the antennas and the UEs in the uplink, and then the BS transmits data to the UE in the downlink. Accurate CSI is necessary to compensate channel-fading during power allocation. CSI can be obtained from the uplink pilot transmission of each time-frequency coherent block. Based on TDD reciprocity, we can obtain the downlink CSI. Meanwhile, the CSI of extended cooperative users outside the cell can be achieved from the training because some resource blocks will be used for pilot transmission training [18].

As the number of users continue to increase, frequency resources increase sharply, and the allocation of pilots also has the problem of shortage. Therefore, it is necessary to divide the cells into multiple sets. The same pilot is used in the cells. The pilot contamination must be further suppressed in massive MIMO systems, so some researchers have proposed pilot-reuse schemes. The most vulnerable users avoid pilot interference by making pilots of neighboring cells orthogonal to each other.

In this paper, we divide 24 neighbor cells into multiple sets, and the number of sets is pilot reuse factor F. According to the above definition $U = BT$, the transmission bandwidth $B = 180$ kHz and the coherence time is $T = 10$ ms in the TDD protocol [16].

According to the TDD protocol

$$U = (\tau^{ul} + \tau^{dl})K + (L^{ul} + L^{dl}) \tag{5}$$

where $\tau^{ul} \geq 1$, $\tau^{dl} \geq 1$ are the respective lengths of the uplink and downlink pilots, to ensure that all users can obtain an orthogonal pilot. L^{ul} and L^{dl} are respectively the uplink and downlink data transmission [19].

The more pilots, the less data transmission. Therefore, it is necessary to select an appropriate pilot reuse factor. When the pilot reuse factor is set to $F = 4(\tau^{ul} = \tau^{dl} = 4)$, then 24 neighbor cells are divided into four sets, and the BS of each cell serves more than 100 users simultaneously.

In this paper, the estimated small-scale fading $\hat{x}_{iik}$ between BS i and UE k in cell i is defined as

$$\hat{x}_{iik} = \sqrt{1 - \beta_{iik}^2} x_{iik} + \beta_{iik} n_{iik} \tag{6}$$

where $n_{iik} \sim \mathcal{CN}(0_M, I_M)$ is the independent normalized estimation noise, and $\beta_{iik}^2 \in [0, 1]$ is the error variance, which represents the accuracy of the estimated fading channel $\hat{x}_{iik}$, that is, $\beta_{iik}^2 = 0$ corresponds to ideal CSI, while $\beta_{iik}^2 = 1$ corresponds to no CSI. By using MMSE estimation, CSI error variance of UE can be written as

$$\beta_{iik}^2 = 1 - \frac{r_{iik}}{\sum_{l \in \Phi} r_{ilk}} \tag{7}$$

where Φ represents the set of BSs using the same pilot as UE k in cell i. Therefore, the estimated channel matrix at BS i can be written as

$$\hat{H}_i = R_i \hat{X}_i \tag{8}$$

3   Energy Efficiency Optimization

3.1   Cell Association and Cooperative Scheme

In [15], each BS does not suppress the interference of neighboring UEs close to the coverage area. Instead, we specifically target the UEs on the cell edge, which is vulnerable for the neighbor BS. We propose cooperative area division algorithm. The user of a non-local cell in the cooperative range is defined as an extended cooperative user. The extended cooperative users are most vulnerable to interference from the local cell, which are neighbor users outside the cell.

For the proposed DDA-CoBF algorithm, the density function of the distribution can be expressed as

$$
f_s(x) = \begin{cases} \frac{1}{4(d_s^2 - d_{\min}^2)}, & d_s \geq x \geq d_{\min} \\ 0, & otherwise \end{cases} \tag{9}
$$

where $d_{\min}$ and d_s are the nearest distance from the BS to the edge of the cell and from the BS to the edge of the cooperative area. x represents distance between BS to user.

3.2   Traditional ZF Precoding

In traditional ZF precoding, all spatial degrees of freedom are used for multiplexing. The estimated channel matrix can be written as

$$
\hat{H}_i = \left[\hat{h}_{ii1}, \hat{h}_{ii2}, ..., \hat{h}_{iiK} \right] \tag{10}
$$

where $\hat{h}_{iik}$ is the estimated channel vector between the i-th BS and the k-th UE in the cell.

The precoding vector with the i-th BS for user k is defined as

$$
w_{ik} = (\hat{H}_i^H \hat{H}_i)^{-1} \hat{h}_{iik} \tag{11}
$$

Then, the signal V_{ik} of receiver k in cell i is given by

$$
V_{ik} = p_{ik} h_{iik}^H w_{ik} + \sum_{s=1, s \neq k}^{K} p_{is} h_{iik}^H w_{is} + \sum_{j=1, j \neq i}^{24} \sum_{s=1}^{K} p_{js} h_{jik}^H w_{js} \tag{12}
$$

where $p_{ik} \geq 0$ is the downlink transmission power of the i-th BS to the k-th user, and downlink power amplifier (PA) (watts) is defined as the consumption of the PA at the BS. h_{iik} is defined as the channel matrix between BS i and the k-th UE in cell i. The first item in (12) is the data transmission signal from BS i to user k. The second item of Vik is the signal received by user k when BS i transmits to other users in the cell. The third item is the transmission information of the other 24 neighbor cells received by user k. Then, the transmission rate of user k in cell i is given by

$$R_{ik} = B \log \left(1 + \frac{p_{ik} \frac{|h_{iik}^H w_{ik}|^2}{\|w_{ik}\|^2}}{\sum_{s=1, s \neq k}^{K} p_{is} \frac{|h_{iik}^H w_{is}|^2}{\|w_{is}\|^2} + I_{jik} + \sigma^2} \right) \tag{13}$$

where σ^2 is the noise variance and I_{jik} is the interference of user k from cell j to cell i in Eq. (1).

3.3 Proposed DDA-CoBF

All spatial degrees of freedom are used for user multiplexing in traditional ZF precoding. However, some spatial freedom is used to suppress the interference of cell-edge users in the proposed DDA-CoBF, under which the BS increases the transmission power so that users in the cell cause less interference to neighboring-cell users. Inter-cell interference can be effectively suppressed, and the total EE and throughput of the network are significantly improved with DDA-CoBF algorithm.

Then, the precoding vector between BS i to the user k in cell i is defined as

$$\hat{w}_{ik} = \left(\sum_{l=1}^{K} \hat{h}_{iil} \hat{h}_{iil}^H + \sum_{\bar{l}=1}^{N} \hat{h}_{ii\bar{l}} \hat{h}_{ii\bar{l}}^H \right)^{-1} \hat{h}_{iik} \tag{14}$$

where $\hat{h}_{iil}$ is the estimated channel matrix between the i-th BS and the l-th UE in cell i, $\hat{h}_{ii\bar{l}}$ is the estimated channel matrix between the i-th BS and the $\bar{l}$-th neighbor UE outside the cell, $\bar{l}$ indicates that a user is outside the cell where BS j is located. $\hat{h}_{iik}$ is the estimated channel matrix between the i-th BS and the k-th UE in cell i, N is the number of users lying in the cooperative area. These users are most vulnerable to interference outside the cell, and they cause the most serious interference to users in the cell. Therefore, the influence of users in the cell of BS i on the users of other cells can be effectively suppressed after the edge user information is added. After adding an extended cooperative CSI in the precoding vector, the extended cooperative user sets the data in cell i into zero space to improve the SINR of the extended cooperative users. Meanwhile, BS i does not transmit data to these extended cooperative users.

Compared with the traditional precoding, the signal $\hat{V}_{ik}$ at the receiver for user k in cell i with the DDA-CoBF algorithm can be written as

$$\hat{V}_{ik} = p_{ik} h_{iik}^H \hat{w}_{ik} + \sum_{s=1, s \neq k}^{K} p_{is} h_{iik}^H \hat{w}_{is}$$
$$+ \sum_{j=1, j \neq i}^{24} \sum_{s=1}^{K} p_{js} h_{jik}^H \hat{w}_{js} \tag{15}$$

The transmission rate of user k is given by

$$\hat{R}_{ik} = B \log \left(1 + \frac{p_{ik} \frac{|h_{iik}^H \hat{w}_{ik}|^2}{\|\hat{w}_{ik}\|^2}}{\sum_{s=1, s \neq k}^{K} p_{is} \frac{|h_{iik}^H \hat{w}_{is}|^2}{\|\hat{w}_{is}\|^2} + \hat{I}_{jik} + \sigma^2} \right) \tag{16}$$

where $\hat{R}_{ik}$ is the rate of user k in the cell i, $\hat{I}_{jik}$ is the inter-cell interference and can be written as

$$\hat{I}_{jik} = \sum_{j=1,j\neq i}^{24} \frac{\sum_{s=1}^{K} p_{js} \left| x_{jik}^{H} \hat{w}_{js} \right|^2}{r_{jik} \|\hat{w}_{js}\|^2} \tag{17}$$

If the k-th user in cell j is an extended cooperative user of other cells, then the k-th user sets the data transmission information of the other cells in a null space at the downlink data receiving. Since the calculation of inter-cell interference is too complicated in a massive MIMO multi-cell system, we treat CSI error as noise during SINR calculation. Then, the transmission rate [19] can be rewritten as

$$\hat{R}_{ik} = B \log \left(1 + \frac{\rho^2 K \tau (M - K)}{1 + \rho K + \rho K \tau} \right) \tag{18}$$

where τ is the uplink pilot of user k, M is the number of antennas of the cell, and K is the number of UEs in cell j. $\rho \geq 0$ is proportional to SINR. Then, SINR [20] can be expressed as

$$SINR = \rho (M - K) \tag{19}$$

3.4   Energy Efficiency and Throughput Analysis

In this section, we analyze the downlink data rates and the EE of a massive MIMO system. The power consumption model at the BS in each channel can be expressed as

$$P_{BS} = P_{TX}^{(dl)} + P_{CP} \tag{20}$$

where $P_{TX}^{(dl)}$ is the power consumed by the power PAs, and P_{CP} is the circuit power. Then,

$$P_{BS} = P_{TX}^{(dl)} + P_{FIX} + P_{TC} + P_{CE} + P_{C/D} + P_{BH} + P_{LP} \tag{21}$$

where P_{FIX} is constant accounting for the fixed power consumption required for site-cooling, control signaling, and load-independent power of backhaul infrastructure and baseband processors. P_{TC}, P_{CE}, $P_{C/D}$, P_{BH} and P_{LP} are power consumption of transceiver chains, channel estimation, coding and decoding, backhaul, and linear processing, respectively. Taking every part of the circuit power consumption into consideration, we can finally get

$$P_{CP} = a + bM + c \log \left(1 + \rho(M - 1) \right) \tag{22}$$

where a, b, c are constants,

$$a = 2P_{syn} + P_{\ln a} + P_{mix} + P_{ifa} + P_{filr} + P_{adc} \tag{23}$$

$$b = P_{dac} + P_{mix} + P_{filt} \tag{24}$$

$$c = P_{cod} + P_{dec} + P_{bt} \tag{25}$$

where P_{syn}, $P_{\ln a}$, P_{ifa}, P_{filr}, P_{adc}, P_{dac}, P_{mix}, P_{filt}, P_{cod}, P_{dec}, P_{bt} are the power consumption values for the frequency synthesizer, the low-noise amplifier, the intermediate frequency amplifier, the active filters at the receiver side, the ADC, the DAC, the mixer, the active filters at the transmitter side, coding, decoding, and backhaul traffic, respectively. Then, EE can be written as

$$EE = \frac{\sum_{k=1}^{K} R_k^{dl}}{P_{TX}^{dl} + P_{CP}} \tag{26}$$

where R_k^{dl} is the downlink users rate.

Most of the literature define $P_{CP} = P_{FIX}$. However, the system model with constant circuit power is not accurate. The more antennas, the higher the user rate and system EE for fixed PA power. Then we consider a more complete circuit power model to solve the problem, and obtain the best antenna deployment for massive MIMO systems.

Throughput is also an important measure of system performance in massive MIMO multi-cell systems. In this paper, the throughput is defined as

$$R_t = \frac{\sum_{k=1}^{K} R_k^{dl}}{4 d_{\min}^2} \tag{27}$$

where $d_{\min}$ is the closest distance from the BS to the edge of the cooperative area.

The parameters involved in Eq. (21) are given in Table 1.

Table 1. Key parameters.

Parameter	Value
The power dissipation from a DAC: P_{DAC}	15.6 mW
The power dissipation from a transmission filter: P_{FIT}	20 mW
The power dissipation from a mixer: P_{MIX}	30.3 mW
The power dissipation from the frequency synthesizer: P_{syn}	50 mW
Power required for the active filters at the transmitter side: P_{flit}	2.5 mW
Power required for the active filters at the receiver side: P_{flir}	2.5 mW
Power required for backhaul traffic: P_{bt}	0.25 W/(Gbit/s)
Power required for decoding: P_{dec}	0.8 W/(Gbit/s)
Power required for coding: P_{cod}	0.1 W/(Gbit/s)

4   Numerical Results and Discussion

This section presents numerical simulations to verify the accuracy of our analysis of the proposed DDA-CoBF algorithm. First, the performance of the DDA-CoBF algorithm and the traditional algorithm are simulated and compared.

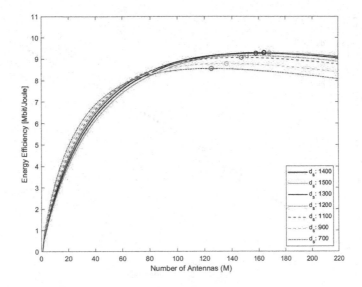

Fig. 1. Energy efficiency for different numbers of BS antennas and different cooperative areas.

Afterwards, the proposed DDA-CoBF algorithm based on cooperative areas is studied respectively. Meanwhile, the respective cooperative area division algorithm for the best EE and throughput are obtained, and the algorithm are compared and discussed. Finally, we analyze the robustness of the DDA-CoBF algorithm, considering the impact of CSI error and pilot reuse factor.

This paper assumes that the number of antennas M, the number of users K, and the rate R in each cell are the same. At the same time, the cell shape and signal propagation conditions are also the same according to the principle of symmetry, which means that the interference in the uplink and downlink is consistent. Suppose that each cell is a cell coverage of $5 \times 10^2 \times 5 \times 10^2$ m^2, the neighbors are the surrounding 24 cells, pilot reuse factor $F = 4$. In this system, under the condition of satisfying $M > K$, antenna arrays ($M = 220$) are deployed at the BS.

Figure 1 shows the EE comparison with different cooperative areas for the DDA-CoBF algorithm. We can see that the EE only slightly increases after the side length of the cooperative area exceeds 1100 m, which reaches the optimum when the side length is 1400 m. The EE does not increase in proportion to the length of the cooperative area, due to the non-uniform user deployment and hardware circuit power limitations. In Fig. 1, the optimal EE of DDA-CoBF algorithm with the longer edge of the cooperative area is relatively low, and not as high as 1400 m, since the inter-cell interference is relatively small when the number of antennas and users are low, the power consumption at the BS is greater than the user gain.

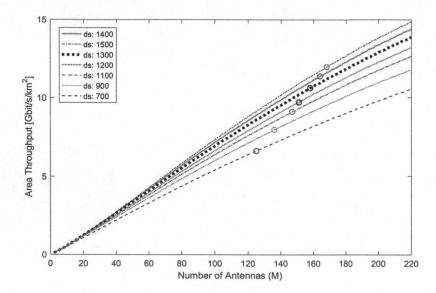

Fig. 2. Area throughput for different numbers of BS antennas with different cooperative areas.

Figure 2 shows the throughput with different cooperative areas and numbers of antennas on the BS. Different from the trend of EE, the throughput increases as the side length of the cooperative area. This is because the proposed algorithm suppresses the interference at the cost of increasing the total PA power, so the EE cannot increase indefinitely. However, the user rate continuously increases without considering the energy consumption, so the throughput of the system gradually increases as the side of the cooperative area from 700 to 1500 m. Therefore, it is not possible to enlarge the cooperative area without limit, because the PA power will increase by a multiple, and the overall EE will be greatly reduced. Therefore, a larger cooperative area should be selected to increase the throughput with the similar EE to further improve the system performance.

The pilot contamination caused by the shortage of frequency bands in massive MIMO systems have a serious impact on system performance. Therefore, we analyze the performance of the cooperative area is set as $9 \times 10^2 \times 9 \times 10^2$ m^2 in the case of pilot contamination. Figure 3 illustrates the EE varying with the number of antennas under different pilot reuse factors (1, 2 and 4). Note that the influence of pilot contamination is serious, as shown in Fig. 3. However, the DDA-CoBF algorithm maintains the higher EE than the traditional algorithm. Moreover, the more serious the pilot contamination is, the more obvious the improvement.

Figure 4 shows the variation of system throughput under different pilot reuse factors. It can be seen the throughput of the system is reduced obviously when the pilot reuse factor is reduced, especially for the traditional algorithm. However, the system throughput of the proposed DDA-CoBF algorithm is always

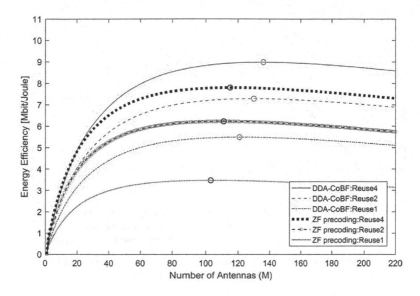

Fig. 3. EE under the influence of pilot reuse factor.

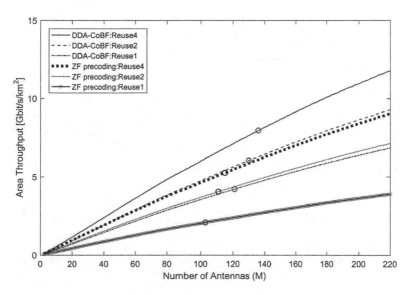

Fig. 4. Area throughput with DDA-CoBF algorithm under the influence of pilot reuse factor.

higher than ZF precoding regardless the pilot reuse factor. Meanwhile, the proposed algorithm also can obviously improve throughput when the pilot reuse factor is 2 or 4.

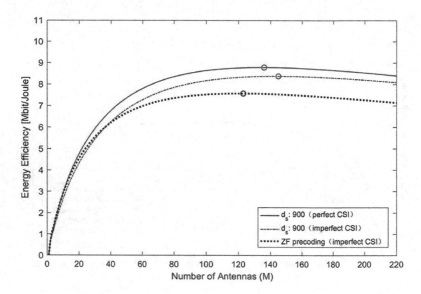

Fig. 5. EE under the influence of imperfect CSI.

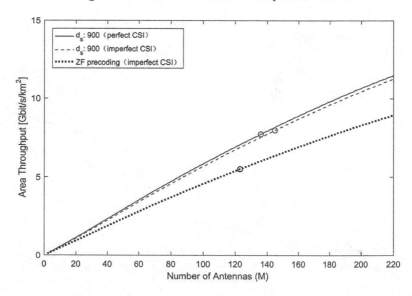

Fig. 6. Area throughput with DDA-CoBF algorithm under the influence of imperfect CSI

Figure 5 depicts the effect of imperfect CSI on the EE with the traditional algorithm and the proposed DDA-CoBF algorithm, which as the function of the number of BS antennas. We can see that the system EE has declined for both the traditional algorithm and DDA-CoBF algorithm. Furthermore, the system with imperfect CSI can also effectively improve the optimal EE when BS antennas are deployed more than 40 with the proposed DDA-CoBF algorithm. The more antennas are deployed, the more obvious the advantages for the proposed algorithm. Therefore, the proposed DDA-CoBF algorithm is particularly well adapted in the massive MIMO systems.

Figure 6 shows the change in system throughput as the number of antennas with and without CSI errors. The system throughput with the proposed DDA-CoBF algorithm slightly decreases with the influence of an imperfect CSI, that is, the CSI error has a relatively small influence on the system throughput than EE. Furthermore, the system with the proposed DDA-CoBF algorithm has a very stable throughput, so the proposed algorithm exhibits greater robustness under the influence of CSI error.

5   Conclusions

In this paper, the proposed DDA-CoBF algorithm by suppressing interference is proposed. This paper analyzes how to select the cooperative area to maximize the EE in multi-user massive MIMO systems. In contrast to existing work, we suppressed the interference of cell-edge users to improve network performance by exploiting and using the spatial degrees of the massive MIMO systems. The algorithm focuses mainly on users at the edge of a cell that are most vulnerable to interference, that is, suppressing the interference of extended cooperative users. By adjusting the cooperative area, we have obtained the optimal EE and throughput with the proposed DDA-CoBF algorithm. Therefore, we can deploy the BS antenna according to the number of served users and improve the performance of the system by selecting an appropriate cooperative scheme and cooperative regions. Finally, we explored the effect of pilot reuse factor and CSI error on the system performance. Numerical results show that the proposed DDA-CoBF algorithm is more robust to pilot contamination and CSI errors, and more suitable for massive MIMO systems.

References

1. Choi, J., Cho, Y., Evans, B.L.: Quantized massive MIMO systems with multicell coordinated beamforming and power control. IEEE Trans. Commun. **69**(2), 946–961 (2021)
2. You, L., Xiong, J., Zappone, A., Wang, W., Gao, X.: Spectral efficiency and energy efficiency tradeoff in massive MIMO downlink transmission with statistical CSIT. IEEE Trans. Signal Process. **68**, 2645–2659 (2020)
3. Xue, X., Wang, Y., Yang, L., Shi, J., Li, Z.: Energy-efficient hybrid precoding for massive MIMO mmWave systems with a fully-adaptive-connected structure. IEEE Trans. Commun. **68**(6), 3521–3535 (2020)
4. Khan, T.A., Yazdan, A., Heath, R.W.: Optimization of power transfer efficiency and energy efficiency for wireless-powered systems with massive MIMO. IEEE Trans. Wirel. Commun. **17**(11), 7159–7172 (2018)

5. Hu, Z., Zhang, W.: High-mobility CoMP massive MIMO uplink transmissions: channel PSD analysis and doppler spread suppression. IEEE Access **8**, 5787–5796 (2020)
6. Bai, J., Dong, T., Zhang, Q., Zhang, X., Lin, Y.: Multi-cell processing and artificial noise for secure transmission in downlink multi-cell MIMO systems under imperfect CSI. In: Proceedings IEEE International Symposium Personal, Indoor and Mobile Radio Communications (PIMRC), pp. 1–6 (2019)
7. Bai, J., Dong, T., Zhang, Q., Wang, S., Li, N.: Coordinated beamforming and artificial noise in the downlink secure multi-cell MIMO systems under imperfect CSI. IEEE Wirel. Commun. Lett. **9**(7), 1023–1026 (2020)
8. H. Yang, T. L. Marzetta: Energy efficient design of massive MIMO: how many antennas? In: Proceedings of 2015 IEEE 81st Vehicular Technology Conference (VTC Spring), pp. 1–5 (2015)
9. Mei, J., Zhao, L., Zheng, K., Wang, X.: Energy-efficient dual-layer coordinated beamforming scheme in multi-cell massive multiple-input-multiple-output systems. IET Commun. **11**(1), 30–38 (2017)
10. Chang, Z., Wang, Z., Guo, X., Han, Z., Ristaniemi, T.: Energy-efficient resource allocation for wireless powered massive MIMO system With imperfect CSI. IEEE Trans. Green Commun. Netw. **1**(2), 121–130 (2017)
11. Marzetta, T.L.: Noncooperative cellular wireless with unlimited numbers of base station antennas. IEEE Trans. Wirel. Commun. **9**(11), 3590–3600 (2010)
12. Xu, G., Lin, C., Ma, W., Chen, S., Chi, C.: Outage constrained robust hybrid coordinated beamforming for massive MIMO enabled heterogeneous cellular networks. IEEE Access **5**, 13601–13616 (2017)
13. Zhang, C., Huang, Y., Jing, Y., Yang, L.: Energy efficient beamforming for massive MIMO public channel. IEEE Trans. Veh. Technol. **66**(11), 10595–10600 (2017)
14. Nguyen, L.D., Tuan, H.D., Duong, T.Q., Poor, H.V.: Beamforming and power allocation for energy-efficient massive MIMO. In: Proceedings of 2017 22nd International Conference on Digital Signal Processing (DSP), pp. 1–5 (2017)
15. Yu, H., Wang, H., Liu, C.: The analysis of power allocation of base station cooperation in massive MIMO. In: International Symposium on Intelligent Signal Processing and Communication Systems (ISPACS), pp. 822–826 (2017)
16. Björnson, E., Larsson, E.G., Debbah, M.: Massive MIMO for maximal spectral efficiency: how many users and pilots should be allocated? IEEE Trans. Wirel. Commun. **15**(2), 1293–1308 (2016)
17. Björnson, E., Sanguinetti, L., Hoydis, J., Debbah, M.: Designing multi-user MIMO for energy efficiency: when is massive MIMO the answer? In: Proceedings of 2014 IEEE Wireless Communications and Networking Conference (WCNC), pp. 242–247 (2014)
18. Yang, H., Geraci, G., Quek, T.Q.S., Andrews, J.G.: Cell-edge-aware precoding for downlink massive MIMO cellular networks. IEEE Trans. Signal Process **65**(13), 3344–3358 (2017)
19. Björnson, E., Sanguinetti, L., Hoydis, J., Debbah, M.: Optimal design of energy-efficient multi-user MIMO systems: is massive MIMO the answer? IEEE Trans. Wirel. Commun. **14**(6), 3059–3075 (2015)
20. Auer, G., Giannini, V., Desset, C., Godor, I.: How much energy is needed to run a wireless network? IEEE Wirel. Commun. **18**(5), 40–49 (2011)

Mobile Load Balancing for 5G RAN Slicing in Mobile Network

Hong Xu[1], Liushan Zhou[2,3], Hong Shen[1], and Tiankui Zhang[2](✉)

[1] China Telecom Co., Ltd., BeiJing Branch, Beijing 100010, China
{xuhong.bj,shenhong.bj}@chiantelecom.cn
[2] Beijing University of Posts and Telecommunications, Beijing 100876, China
zhouliushan@bupt.edu.cn
[3] China Mobile Communications Co., Ltd., HeNan Branch, Henan 450008, China

Abstract. With the rapid development of mobile Internet, network slicing is defined as one of key technologies to deal with the issue of differentiated requirements of diversified services. The introduction of network slicing brings many challenges to the implementation of Radio Access Network (RAN). Considering Mobile Load Balancing (MLB) for RAN slicing, a mobile load balancing algorithm based on Deep Reinforcement Learning (DRL) is proposed. First of all, we propose a system utility model to measure the satisfaction of the system. And a mobile load balancing strategy for RAN slicing is proposed, including slice-level load control realized by adjusting the proportion of radio resource allocated to slice by Radio Remote Unit (RRU), and cell-level load balancing based on handoff. In order to improve the system satisfaction and maximize the system utility, the joint optimization problem of system satisfaction and utility function is proposed. The DRL is used to solve these optimization problems. The simulation results show that the proposed algorithm can effectively reduce the total number of handoffs in the system and bring less balancing overhead. In addition, the proposed algorithm can effectively reduce the number of unsatisfied users and achieve higher system satisfaction.

Keywords: RAN · Network slicing · SLA · Mobile load balancing

1 Introduction

Network slicing has been identified as one of the enabling technologies of 5G, and it will play an important role in future mobile networks [1]. A network slice can be regarded as an independent virtual network to provide services, which meets the diversified communication requirements of users by providing flexible and on-demand network services [2]. By exploiting network slicing technology, the network capabilities in terms of capacity, delay, transmission rate, etc., could be dramatically improved due to the high flexibility and efficiency of resource allocation [3].

In addition to these significant benefits, the introduction of network slicing also brings many challenges to RAN, including network function virtualization,

X. Wang et al. (Eds.): AICON 2021, LNICST 396, pp. 235–250, 2021.
https://doi.org/10.1007/978-3-030-90196-7_21

network resource allocation, and mobility management [3,4]. In particular, MLB is very important to guarantee the service requirements of users while communication environment changes (e.g. channel conditions of different access points, slice resources allocation). It is not only related to ensuring Service Level Agreement (SLA) requirements of users, but also has a significant impact on both slice deployment and radio resource management [5]. Compared with traditional networks, mobile load balancing for RAN slicing is more complicated, which faces the following challenges:

Network Architecture Changes. Specifically, User Equipment (UE) should be accessed with an RAN slicing via a specific RRU, forming a UE-RRU-RAN Slicing three-layer association architecture. Therefore, the load of cell and slice, service type and Reference Signal Receiving Power (RSRP) should be considered simultaneously to guarantee slices' SLA and improve user's service experience.

The Granularity of Load Information Changes. In related specification of MLB enhancement, some slice-related content has been introduced. For example, a slicing load control mechanism is proposed to help to guarantee slicing SLA by using Network Data Analysis Function (NWDAF) for slicing level analysis [6]. At the same time, it is clear that the influence of network slicing should be considered in the mechanism of MLB enhancement [7].

Mobile Load Balancing Strategy Changes. To solve MLB for RAN slicing, cell-level load balancing and slice-level load control need to be considered at the same time. Different from the traditional mechanism, there are several types of balancing strategies, for example, only adjusting the resources of slices, switching between RRUs, or switching between slices and RRUs, or even applying for deploying a new slice. Different types of balancing strategies may lead to different balancing costs. For example, adjusting resource of slices only needs to exchange signaling in the same RRU, which means lower balancing cost, while switching both slice and RRU needs higher cost.

With the development of technology, Reinforcement learning (RL), which is one class of machine learning methods that can adapt to unknown environments by learning from the environmental feedbacks, has already been applied in load balancing [8–10]. These successes envision a bright future to exploit DRL in realizing adaptive and autonomous large-scale load balancing under complex ultradense networks. However, this paradigm still remains to be explored. Some studies have been carried out on the handoff mechanism for RAN slicing, Y. Sun et al. [11] proposed a multi-agent reinforcement learning based smart handoff policy with data Sharing, to reduce handoff cost while maintaining user QoS requirements in RAN slicing. However, many existing researches have not considered how to achieve mobile load balancing based on Network slicing architecture.

Considering mobile network architecture for RAN slicing, we propose a mobile load balancing algorithm based on DRL. First of all, a system satisfaction model is proposed to measure the satisfaction of UEs' requirements. At the same time, the MLB strategy for RAN slicing is proposed, including slice-level load control realized by adjusting the proportion of radio resource allocated to slice by RRU, and cell-level load balancing based on handoff. In order to improve the system satisfaction and maximize the system utility, the joint optimization problem of system satisfaction and user utility function is proposed in slice-level load control and cell-level load balancing respectively. The Deep Q Network (DQN) is used to solve these optimization problems.

2   System Model

We consider a mobile network architecture based on slicing shown in Fig. 1, which consists of multiple network slices, RRUs and UEs. These slices share the physical resources in the Core Network (CN) and the RAN [12]. Each slice is composed of different network function modules (e.g. mobility management, access control, security, etc.) to provide secure and differentiated services for UE.

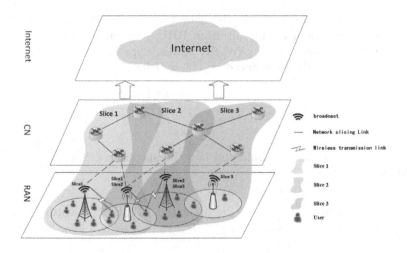

Fig. 1. RAN model based on network slicing.

2.1   Radio Access Network Model

We consider RAN model with multiple RRUs and slices shown in Fig. 1. Let $\mathcal{J} = \{1 \ldots, J\}$, $\mathcal{N} = \{1, \ldots, N\}$ and $\mathcal{U} = \{1, \ldots, U\}$ be the set of RRUs, RAN slices and UEs. N RAN slices are deployed on demand in a mobile network consisting of J RRUs. Multiple RAN slices are deployed on a unified physical infrastructure. Radio resources are allocated according to the requirements of slices. Let $R_u^{\min}$ be the UE's minimum service rate, which represents SLA requirements of UE. Let $\mathcal{T} = \{T_1, T_2, \ldots, T_m\}$ be the set of all service types, and $\varphi_u \in \mathcal{T}$ be the service type of UE u. When the service type can meet the SLA requirements of UE, $\varphi_u = T_m$.

Let $c_{j,n}$ denote the proportion of radio resources allocated to slice by RRU, leading to the constraint

$$\sum_{n \in \mathcal{N}} c_{j,n} = 1 \tag{1}$$

When the RRU j is not in the coverage area of slice n, $c_{j,n}=0$.

Two elements $(T_n, \mathbf{C}_n)$ are used to determine a specific slice. For slice n, T_n is the type of service that slice n can provide, and $\mathbf{C}_n$ is a vector representing the proportion of radio resources allocation of slice n from all RRUs, where $c_{j,n}$ is the j element of vector $\mathbf{C}_n$. In Fig. 1, UE can access slice 1 via RRU 1 and RRU 2. The connection indication variable is defined as $x^u_{j,n}$, when UE accesses the network through slice n of RRU j, $x^u_{j,n}= 1$, otherwise, $x^u_{j,n}= 0$. Each UE can only access a slice through one RRU, leading to the constraint

$$\sum_{n \in \mathcal{N}} \sum_{j \in \mathcal{J}} x^u_{j,n} = 1 \tag{2}$$

Let L^u_j be the pathloss between RRU j and UE u, h^u_j and P^u_j are the channel gain and allocated power of the link from RRU j to UE u, respectively. σ^2 is Additive White Gaussian Noise (AWGN) power. Express Signal to Interference plus Noise Ratio (SINR) experienced by UE u of RRU j as

$$\text{SINR}^u_{j,n} = \frac{P^u_j L^u_j |h^u_j|^2}{\sigma^2 + \sum_{i \in \mathcal{J}, i \neq j} P^u_i L^u_i |h^u_i|^2} \tag{3}$$

According to Shannon formula and (3), the spectrum efficiency can be calculated as

$$e^u_{j,n} = \log_2 \left(1 + \text{SINR}^u_{j,n}\right) \tag{4}$$

If $x^u_{j,n}= 1$, radio resources will be allocated to UE u. According to UE's minimum service rate requirement $R^{\min}_u$, the radio resource allocated to UE u on RRU j can be calculated as

$$w^u_{j,n} = \frac{R^{\min}_u}{B \times e^u_{j,n}} \tag{5}$$

where B is the bandwidth of the subcarrier.

Assuming that each RRU has the same total amount of radio resources, Let W_{total} be the maximum amount of radio resources that can be provided to UE, leading to the constraint

$$\sum_{n \in \mathcal{N}} \sum_{u \in \mathcal{U}} x^u_{j,n} w^u_{j,n} \leq W_{total} \tag{6}$$

Moreover, the radio resource utilization of RRU j can be expressed as

$$\Omega_j = \frac{\sum_{n \in \mathcal{N}} \sum_{u \in \mathcal{U}} x^u_{j,n} w^u_{j,n}}{W_{total}}, \forall j \in \mathcal{J} \tag{7}$$

2.2 System Satisfaction Model

In order to measure the system satisfaction, Let Sat_u be the satisfaction of UE u with the slice's SLA requirement. The satisfaction on rate of UE u is calculated with sigmoid function as follows

$$\mathrm{Sat}_u = \frac{1}{1+e^{-\varphi(\Gamma_u - R_u^{\min})}} \tag{8}$$

where Γ_u is the achievable data rate of UE u. If the value of Sat_u is greater than 0.5, UEs are said to be satisfied, and not satisfied otherwise. Based on satisfaction of UE, satisfaction of slice can be calculated as

$$\lambda_n = \frac{\sum_{u=1}^{|U_n|} \mathrm{Sat}_u}{|U_n|} \tag{9}$$

where U_n is the total number of UEs accessing the network via slice n. We consider the worst result achieved by slices for system satisfaction, the system satisfaction is defined as

$$\lambda = \min\{\lambda_n\} \tag{10}$$

3 Mobile Load Balancing Strategy for RAN Slicing

Due to the different arrival locations of users, some RRU will be overloaded, while some RRU will be lightly loaded, resulting in radio resources can not be used effectively, and the satisfaction of UEs can not be well guaranteed. Therefore, it is necessary to judge whether mobile load balancing is necessary according to the current network state and the coverage range of RAN slices, so as to ensure the service experience and SLA requirements of UEs.

Ensuring the SLA requirements of users and realizing the load balancing of the whole network are the key standards to verify the MLB algorithm, and MLB will also affect radio resource allocation and slice deployment scheme in mobile network. Therefore, this paper defines a MLB strategy for RAN slicing, which includes both cell-level load balancing and slice-level load control.

First of all, slice-level load control and cell-level load balancing are performed by monitoring system satisfaction. For slice-level load control, the proportion of radio resources allocated by RRU to the slice needs to be adjusted by analyzing the radio resource utilization of slice from each RRU. For cell-level load balancing, once the overload threshold is met, UE selects the target RRU and slice to switch by analyzing the load of neighbor cells and slice coverage. Slice-level load control and cell-level load balancing will be introduced in detail.

3.1 Slice-Level Load Control

When $c_{j,n} \neq 0$, $\rho_{j,n}$ is used to represent the load of slice n on RRU j, which is defined as

$$\rho_{j,n} = \frac{\sum_{u \in \mathcal{U}} x_{j,n}^u w_{j,n}^u}{c_{j,n} W_{total}} \tag{11}$$

(11) is expressed as the ratio of the sum of radio resources required by UEs to access network via slice n on RRU j to the sum of radio resources allocated to slice n by RRU j. When $\rho_{j,n} < 1$, the radio resources allocated to slice n by RRU j have not been fully utilized; when $\rho_{j,n} = 1$, radio resources allocated to slice n by RRU j are exactly able to meet the SLA requirements of UEs; when $\rho_{j,n} > 1$, it indicates that radio resources allocated by RRU j to slice n are insufficient, some UEs' SLA requirements will not be met.

Therefore, the load of slice can be measured by the number of UEs whose SLA requirements are not met, and satisfaction of slice can be calculated by (9). According to the achievable data rate of UE can, we can also calculate the satisfaction of UE by (8).

If RRU j is not overloaded, but radio resources allocated to slice n are insufficient, the additional radio resources that slice n needs to obtain from RRU j can be expressed as

$$c_{j,n}^{addition} = \rho_{j,n} - 1 \tag{12}$$

The RRU j dynamically updates the proportion of radio resources allocated to each slice by analyzing its own radio resource utilization Ω_j. According to (11), the radio resources utilization of slices on RRU j is analyzed, radio resources allocated to slice with low radio resource utilization are reduced, and the proportion of radio resources allocated to slice n is increased.

Therefore, we define the balancing strategy for slice-level load control as M_{NS}: adjusting the proportion of radio resources $c_{j,n}$.

3.2   Cell-Level Load Balancing

Similar to the method of calculating slice-level load, the load of RRU can be defined by the radio resource utilization of the RRU j, and the load of the RRU j is defined as

$$\rho_j = \Omega_j = \frac{\sum\limits_{n \in \mathcal{N}} \sum\limits_{u \in \mathcal{U}} x_{j,n}^u w_{j,n}^u}{W_{total}}, \forall j \in \mathcal{J} \tag{13}$$

When $\rho_j < 1$, the sum of radio resources required by all UEs accessed to RRU j is less than total radio resources that RRU j can provide, RRU j is not overloaded; when $\rho_j = 1$, RRU j is just fully loaded; when $\rho_j > 1$, RRU j is overloaded. Based on the above analysis, the load that RRU j needs to transfer can be calculated as

$$\rho_z = \rho_j - \varsigma \tag{14}$$

where ς is overload threshold.

The load that each neighbor cell can accept can be calculated as

$$\rho_i = \varsigma - \rho_j, \forall i \in \mathcal{J}, i \neq j \tag{15}$$

For cell-level load balancing, once the overload threshold is met, UE selects target RRU and slice to switch by analyzing the load of neighbor cells and slice coverage. Therefore, we define three types of balancing strategies for cell-level load:

1) M_{BS}: switching between RRUs, UE switches between RRUs under the same slice coverage;
2) M_{NS-BS}: switching both slice and RRU, slices' SLA need to be considered;
3) M_{New}: deploying a new slicing on the light load RRU, which is a special handoff for RAN slicing.

4 Problem Formulation and Algorithm

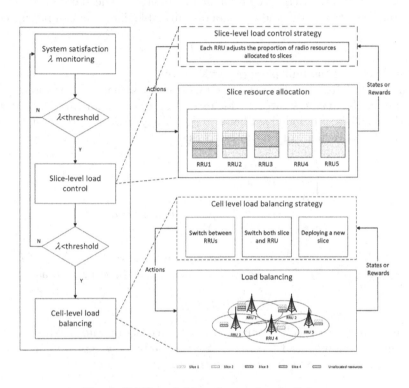

Fig. 2. RAN model based on network slicing.

Based on proposed MLB strategy for RAN slicing, a solution of mobile load balancing for 5G RAN slicing is proposed, as shown in Fig. 2. By monitoring the system satisfaction, the slice-level load control is performed first if system satisfaction does not meet the requirements, the proportion of radio resources allocated by each RRU to slices is adjusted to balance the radio resource utilization and satisfaction of each slice, so as to improve the satisfaction of the system. If the system satisfaction is effectively improved after slice-level load control, the system satisfaction will be continuously monitored; otherwise, cell-level load balancing will be performed, edge users of overloaded RRUs select target RRU and slice to switch to ensure slice performance and users' SLA requirements, and improve the system satisfaction.

4.1   Problem Formulation

In the process of MLB for RAN slicing, it's necessary to consider the system overhead, such as signaling exchange and delay. Therefore, the objective of this paper is to optimize network through slice-level load control and cell-level load balancing, so as to ensure users' SLA requirements and slices' performance, as well as reduce the balancing overhead.

The utility of UE adopting the balancing strategy is composed of achievable data rate and overhead caused by balancing strategy. The data rate of UE is related to the system state, and the gain of achievable data rate can be expressed as

$$g^u = \delta \times \Gamma_{j,n}^u \tag{16}$$

where δ represents the unit price of service rate.

In addition, RRU and slice associated with UE will change after adopting the corresponding balancing strategy, which resulting in the balancing cost. According to the analysis of mobile load balancing strategy in Sect. 3, the cost function generated by balancing can be expressed as

$$\eta^u = \begin{cases} 0, x_{j',n'} = x_{j,n} \\ \beta_{NS} \cdot e^{\rho_j}, x_{j',n'} = x_{j,n}, C'_n \neq C_n \\ \beta_{BS} \cdot e^{\rho_{j'}}, x_{j',n'} \neq x_{j,n}, j' \neq j, n' = n \\ \beta_{NS-BS} \cdot e^{\rho_{j'}}, x_{j',n'} \neq x_{j,n}, j' \neq j, n' \neq n \\ \beta_{New} \cdot e^{\rho_{j'}}, n' \notin \mathcal{N} \end{cases} \tag{17}$$

where, β_{NS}, β_{BS}, β_{NS-BS} and β_{New} are the unit cost of M_{NS}, M_{BS}, M_{NS-BS} and M_{New} respectively. Then the utility function can be expressed as

$$r^u = g^u - \eta^u \tag{18}$$

In this paper, we expect to improve system satisfaction and maximize system utility through mobile load balancing. So we combine system satisfaction and system utility as objective function, which can be expressed as

$$\max_{x,c,\lambda} \lambda \times \sum_{u \in \mathcal{U}} r^u \tag{19}$$

$$s.t. \sum_{n \in \mathcal{N}} \sum_{j \in \mathcal{J}} x_{j,n}^u = 1, \forall u \in \mathcal{U} \tag{19a}$$

$$\sum_{n \in \mathcal{N}} c_{j,n} \leq 1, \forall j \in \mathcal{J} \tag{19b}$$

$$\sum_{n \in \mathcal{N}} \sum_{u \in \mathcal{U}} x_{j,n}^u w_{j,n}^u \leq W_{total}, \forall j \in \mathcal{J} \tag{19c}$$

$$\rho_j < \varsigma, \forall j \in \mathcal{J} \tag{19d}$$

$$\rho_{j,n} \leq 1, \forall j \in \mathcal{J}, \forall n \in \mathcal{N} \tag{19e}$$

Constraint (19a) ensures that each UE can only access a slice via one RRU. Constraint (19b) indicates that the sum of the proportion of radio resource allocated to each slice by this RRU cannot be greater than 1. The total radio resource of each RRU is limited in constraint (19c). Constraint (19d) implies that the load of each RRU cannot exceed overload threshold. Constraint (19e) indicates that the SLA requirements of UEs associated with slice must be met.

Considering the aforementioned challenges including the three layer architecture, SLA guaranteeing as well as different balancing costs, DRL that incorporate information on surrounding environment could be used to design a smart MLB mechanism dedicated for RAN slicing.

4.2 Deep Reinforcement Learning

In this article, We solve mobile load balancing for RAN slicing with DRL. Specifically, DRL aims at maximizing a cumulative reward by selecting a sequence of optimal actions under different system states in a stochastic unknown environment. We denote the state-value function of an arbitrary policy at the time t as follows:

$$V_\pi(s) = E_\pi \left[\sum_{t=0}^{\infty} \gamma^t r(s, a) \right] \tag{20}$$

where s represents the state, a represents the action, π represents the policy, $r(s, a)$ is the reward function, which reflects the learning goal, and $\gamma \in [0, 1]$ is the discount factor, indicating the attenuation degree of the reward. According to the dynamic programming equation, there is at least one optimal strategy π^* that makes the following equation

$$V_\pi^*(s) = \max_a \left(r(s, a) + \gamma \sum_{s' \in \mathcal{S}} \mathcal{P}_{ss'}^a V_\pi^*(s') \right) \tag{21}$$

where s' is the next state when the environment state changes, $\mathcal{P}_{ss'}^a$ is the a stationary transition probability.

In DRL-based algorithm, the objective of the agent is to find the optimal policy π^* that maximizes the Q-function $Q(s, a)$. The optimal Q-function is used to measure the performance of the agent. Based on the Bellman equation, the optimal policy can be selected according to the following equation

$$Q(s, a) = \omega + \gamma \max_{a'} Q(s', a') \tag{22}$$

where ω is the weight parameter of Q-Network.

4.3 Slice-Level Load Control Based on DQN

For slice-level load control, the system satisfaction will be improved by adjusting the proportion of radio resources allocated to each slice by RRU. When system satisfaction is decrease, the load control decision is made according to the state. For slice-level load control, the optimization problem reduce in (19) to

$$\max_c \lambda \times \sum_{u \in \mathcal{U}} r^u \, s.t. \, (19a) \, (19b) \, (19e) \tag{23}$$

At each step, the agent will adjust the proportion of radio resource as the conditions of the slices keep changing. We begin to formulate the Markov decision process (MDP) by defining states, actions, reward, and next state as follows.

State: $s^n \in \mathcal{S}^\mathcal{N}$ represents the network slicing state ($\mathcal{S}$ is a set of all states). We define the state s^n of slice n, as a tuple $s^n = \{\lambda_n, c_{1,n}, \ldots, c_{j,n}, \rho_{1,n}, \ldots, \rho_{j,n}\}$, where λ_n is satisfaction of slice n, which can be calculated by (9); $c_{j,n}$ is the proportion of radio resources allocated to slice n by RRU j; $\rho_{j,n}$ is the load of slice n on RRU j, which is calculated by (11).

Action: Based on states, the agent learns an optimal radio resource allocation for each slice by selecting an action a^n based on state s^n. The action set of a slice is defined as the proportion of radio resources allocated to slice by RRU, $a^n = \{-0.6, -0.4, -0.2, 0, 0.2, 0.4, 0.6\}$. If the selected action is negative, it means that radio resources of slice should be reduced by this percentage, otherwise, it means that an increase proportion of radio resource of this slice, and a value of zero means the radio resource of slice remains the same.

Reward: When actions is selected from the action set, the reward function is also needed to judge the merits of the selected actions. The objective of slice-level load control should take into consideration several variables as the reward for the learning. We define the reward function as the product of the system satisfaction and the sum of the system utility. If the selected action does not satisfy the constraints (19a), (19b) and (19e), the reward function is set to -1 .

$$r^n = \begin{cases} \lambda \times \sum_{u \in \mathcal{U}} r^u, C \, (19a) \, , C \, (19b) \, C \, (19e) \\ -1, \text{otherwise} \end{cases} \tag{24}$$

Next State: After receiving the reward for the selected action, it will enter into the next state. The proportion of radio resource allocated to slice, the satisfaction of slice, and the load of slice will be changed. The next state parameters are affected by the action taken on the slice. After updating the parameters, they are stored in memory and used to predict possible actions during training.

The proportion of radio resource of slice will be updated at the decision step. It can be calculate as

$$c'_{j,n} = \begin{cases} c_{j,n}, \text{if} \, a_j = 0 \\ (1 + a^n) \, c_{j,n}, \text{otherwise} \end{cases} \tag{25}$$

Where a^n is the action taken on the radio resource of slice. It should be noted that these values are updated at each decision step in order to update the radio resources of slice. Finally, the slice allocates the resource to its users. The whole process of the DQN algorithm is given in Algorithm 1.

Algorithm 1. DQN Based Slice-Level Load Control

Input: A replay memory D, action-valuefunction Q, The status information of RAN slices, $s^n = \{\lambda_n, c_{1,n}, \ldots, c_{j,n}, \rho_{1,n}, \ldots, \rho_{j,n}\}$.

Output: Action a^n

 1: **while** $s = s^n$ **do**
 2:     Select action at satisfying $a = \arg\max_{a \in \mathcal{A}} Q_\pi^*(s, a)$
 3:     Update $c_{j,n}$ by (25) and observe reward by (24) and new state
 4:     Update the proportion of radio resource allocation of slices according to the selected action
 5:     Store experience $\{s, a, r, s'\}$ in the replay memory D
 6:     Calculate output Q-values
 7:     Update target Q-value of action by (22)
 8:     Train Q Network using a loss function as the mean squared error of output and target
 9:     Update $t = t + 1$
10: **end while**

4.4   Cell-Level Load Balancing Based on DQN

Similarly, the DRL is also used to solve cell-level load balancing. Target RRU and slice are selected to switch by observing the surrounding environment. We aim to achieve load balancing in a long time and improve the system capacity. For cell-level load balancing, the optimization problem can be expressed as

$$\max_x \lambda \times \sum_{u \in \mathcal{U}} r^u, \text{s.t.} : (19a)\,(19c)\,(19d) \tag{26}$$

Its agent, state, action and reward function are defined as follows. Specifically, the whole process of algorithm is given in Algorithm 2.

State: $s \in \mathcal{S}^{\mathcal{N}}$ represents state of network ($\mathcal{S}$ is a set of all states). The state is composed of the load of RRU j and the fraction of the edge users, as a tuple $s_t = [\rho_1, \ldots, \rho_j, \ldots, \rho_J, E_1, \ldots, E_j, \ldots, E_J]$. Where ρ_j is the load of the RRU, which can be calculated by (13), E_j is the fraction of the edge users. Here, we categorize the edge users according to their downlink SINRs to the corresponding serving RRU and the neighboring RRUs.

Action: An action means selecting both target RRU and RAN slicing when a handoff occurs. In detail, we denote the action taken by UE to access slice via RRU can be expressed as $a = (j, n)$, where j and n is the target RRU and RAN slicing respectively.

Reward: The achievable data rate of UE is affected by balancing strategy. Therefore, the reward function is defined as the joint optimization of system satisfaction and utility function, where the utility function is composed of the achievable data rate of UE after taking action and balancing overhead. Similarly, if the selected action does not satisfy the constraints (19a), (19c) and (19d), the reward function is set to –1.

$$r = \begin{cases} \sum\limits_{u \in \mathcal{U}} r^u, \mathrm{C}\,(19\mathrm{a})\,, \mathrm{C}(19\mathrm{c}), \mathrm{C}\,(19\mathrm{d}) \\ -1, \mathrm{otherwise} \end{cases} \tag{27}$$

Next State: When enter into the next state, the load of RRU and the satisfaction of system will be changed. The next state parameters are affected by the action taken on the slice. After updating the parameters, they are stored in memory and used to predict possible actions during training.

Algorithm 2. DQN Based Cell-Level Load Balancing

Input: A replay memory D, action-valuefunction Q, The status information, $s_t = [\rho_1, \ldots, \rho_j, \ldots, \rho_J, E_1, \ldots, E_j, \ldots, E_J]$.
Output: Action $a = (j, n)$
 1: **while** $s = s_t$ **do**
 2:     Select action at satisfying $a = \arg\max_{a \in \mathcal{A}} Q_\pi^*\,(s, a)$
 3:     Observe reward by (27) and new state
 4:     Select both target RRU and slicing, excute $a = (j, n)$
 5:     Store experience $\{s_t, a, r, s_{t+1}\}$ in the replay memory D
 6:     Calculate output Q-values
 7:     Update target Q-value of action by (22)
 8:     Train Q Network using a loss function as the mean squared error of output and target
 9:     Update $t = t + 1$
10: **end while**

---

5   Performance Evaluation

In this section, we conduct simulation on Python platform and TensorFlow tool to evaluate the performance of proposed mobile load balancing algorithm. We evaluate the performance in terms of system satisfaction and the total number of handoff.

Table 1. Simulation Parameters

Parameters	Value
Number of RRUs	7
Distance between RRUs	1000 m
Number of slices	4
Bandwidth	30 MHz
Transmit power	46 dBm
Noise power	-174 dBm/Hz
UE noise figure	9 dB
Pathloss	$37.6\log_{10}\left(d\,[km]\right) + 128.1$ dB
Overload threshold	0.95
Learning rate	0.2
Discount factor	0.1

In order to improve the accuracy and universality of the simulation, the number of RRU is fixed. And some users move randomly in the area, so that the overloaded cells will not be damaged due to the mobility of users. We also consider comparing proposed algorithm with only slice-level load control and only cell-level load control. The specific simulation parameter are shown in Table 1.

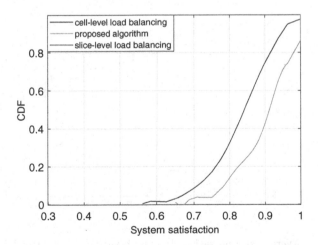

Fig. 3. CDF of system satisfaction.

It is necessary to consider both cell-level load balancing and slice-level load control for the introduction of RAN slicing. Figure 3 shows the distribution of system satisfaction in different situations. It can be seen that the system satisfaction with slice-level load control is distributed between [0.35,1], and the system satisfaction with cell-level load balancing only is distributed between [0.56,1]. The system satisfaction with the proposed algorithm can be effectively improved, which is distributed between [0.65,1]. It indicates that it is important to consider both slice-level load control and cell-level load balancing. In addition, it proves the effectiveness of the proposed algorithm in improving the system satisfaction.

Figure 4 illustrates the average system satisfaction with an increasing number of users. In general, as users increasing, the system satisfaction has decreased obviously. For slice-level load control, it only adjusts the radio resources allocated to slices by each RRU at each decision step. However, the radio resources of each RRU are limited. For overloaded cell, the system satisfaction cannot be effectively improved by adjusting radio resources of slices. For cell-level load balancing, if target RRU and slice are found, user will switch to the target RRU and slice; otherwise, a new slice needs to be deployed in the target RRU, which may resulting in large overhead. After adopting balancing strategy, if the gain of achievable data rate is less than overhead, handoff will not be carried out, so it can not effectively improve the system satisfaction. It can be seen that the performance of the proposed algorithm is always better than the other two cases, which also reflects the superiority of the proposed algorithm.

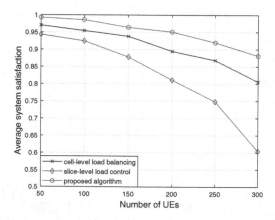

Fig. 4. Average system satisfaction with varying number of UEs.

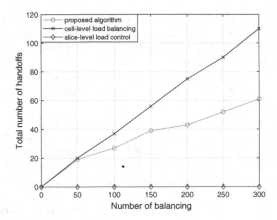

Fig. 5. Total number of handoffs with varying number of balancing.

Number of handoffs with an increasing number of balancing is shown in Fig. 5. As shown in the Fig. 5, the number of handoffs of proposed algorithm is less than cell-level load balancing, except that there is no handoff in slice-level load control. It can be obtained that if proposed algorithm can effectively improve the system satisfaction by slice-level load control, cell-level mobile load balancing will not be performed, the total number of handoffs and overhead will be effectively reduced.

6   Conclusion

To handle with mobile load balancing problem in 5G RAN slicing, we proposed the mobile load balancing strategy and a mobile load balancing algorithm based on DQN. The simulation results show that the proposed algorithm can effectively reduce the total number of handoff in the system and bring less balancing overhead. In addition, the proposed algorithm can effectively reduce the number of unsatisfied users and achieve higher system satisfaction.

References

1. Rost, P., Mannweiler, C., Michalopoulos, D.S., et al.: Network slicing to enable scalability and flexibility in 5G mobile networks. IEEE Commun. Mag. **55**(5), 72–79 (2017)
2. TR 22.864, Feasibility Study on New Services and Markets Technology Enablers - Network Operation, 3GPP, V15.0.0, 09 2016
3. Foukas, X., Patounas, G., Elmokashfi, A., Marina, M.K.: Network slicing in 5G: survey and challenges. IEEE Commun. Mag. **55**(5), 94–100 (2017)
4. Zhang, H., Liu, N., Chu, X., Long, K., Aghvami, A.-H., Leung, V.C.M.: Network slicing based 5G and future mobile networks: mobility, resource management, and challenges. IEEE Commun. Mag. **55**(8), 138–145 (2017)

5. Zhou, L., Zhang, T., Li, J., et al.: Radio resource allocation for RAN slicing in mobile networks. In: IEEE/CIC International Conference on Communications in China (ICCC) 2020, LNCS, pp. 1280–1285. IEEE, China (2020). https://doi.org/10.1109/ICCC49849.2020.9238905
6. TR 23.700, Study on enhancement of network slicing, 3GPP (2020)
7. RP-182105, Study on RAN-centric data collection and utilization for LTE and NR, 3GPP, 09 2018
8. Muñoz, P., Barco, R., Ruiz-Avilés, J.M., de la Bandera, I., Aguilar, A.: Fuzzy rule-based reinforcement learning for load balancing techniques in enterprise LTE Femtocells. IEEE Trans. Veh. Technol. 62(5), 1962–1973 (2013)
9. Mwanje, S.S., Schmelz, L.C., Mitschele-Thiel, A.: Cognitive cellular networks: a Q-learning framework for self-organizing networks. IEEE Trans. Netw. Serv. Manage. 13(1), 85–98 (2016)
10. Xu, Y., Xu, W., Wang, Z., Lin, J., Cui, S.: Load balancing for ultradense networks: a deep reinforcement learning-based approach. IEEE Internet Things J. 6(6), 9399–9412 (2019)
11. Sun, Y., Jiang, W., Feng, G., et al.: Efficient handover mechanism for radio access network slicing by exploiting distributed learning. IEEE Trans. Netw. Serv. Manage. 17(4), 2620–2633 (2020)
12. An, X., et al.: On end to end network slicing for 5G communication systems. Trans. Emerg. Telecommun. Technol. 28(4), e3058 (2016)

Dynamic Communication and Computation Resource Allocation Algorithm for End-to-End Slicing in Mobile Networks

Hong Xu[1], Zhou Tong[2,3], Hong Shen[1], and Tiankui Zhang[2(✉)]

[1] China Telecom Co., Ltd., BeiJing Branch, Beijing 100010, China
[2] Beijing University of Posts and Telecommunications, Beijing 100876, China
[3] China Mobile Research Institute, Beijing 100053, China

Abstract. In the mobile network, to support business diversity and meet the differentiated needs of vertical industries, network slicing technology has emerged. Network slicing is required in both the core network and the radio access network, that is, to achieve end-to-end network slicing. Most of the current network slicing service requirements are dynamic, in end-to-end network slicing, a deep Q network (DQN)-based two-stage joint allocation algorithm for communication and computation resource is proposed to solve the problem of dynamic changes of network slicing data queues, radio channel status, and physical network topology. The dynamic resource allocation model of end-to-end slicing is constructed, and the dynamic joint allocation of communication and computation resource is carried out to maximize the overall utility of the network on a long-term scale. The dynamic migration of virtualization network function (VNF) and the flexible allocation of virtual network resources are realized according to the service state and quality of service (QoS) requirements of virtual network users. The simulation results show that the proposed algorithm can optimize the overall utility of the network on a long-term scale, improve the long-term average revenue, and reduce the average cost of the system.

Keywords: Network slicing · Resource allocation · Dynamic

1 Introduction

In the mobile network, the service types of different users have different demands on the network. The introduction of mobile network slicing is to meet the diverse needs of vertical industry. The mobile network allows heterogeneous services to coexist in the same network architecture through network slicing. End-to-end network slicing includes core network (CN) slicing and radio access network (RAN) slicing, spanning the infrastructure of radio access network and core

X. Wang et al. (Eds.): AICON 2021, LNICST 396, pp. 251–267, 2021.
https://doi.org/10.1007/978-3-030-90196-7_22

network [1]. The process of slicing the network involves the allocation of multiple resources such as communication resource, computation resource, and cache resource on the CN side and the RAN side. Network slicing can be considered as a virtualized private network in the network. Through technologies such as software defined network (SDN) and network functions virtualization (NFV) [2], network functions are customized and tailored according to the needs of business scenarios, and network resources are reasonably allocated [3].

The infrastructure of end-to-end network slicing includes both CN and RAN. Therefore, it is an important research direction to consider the resources on the CN side and the RAN side when allocating resources for network slicing. In [4], To extend the coverage of NFV technology from the CN side to the field of radio access network, the radio virtualization network function (VNF) placement problem in the RAN was formalized as an integer linear programming problem, and a heuristic algorithm for VNF placement named radio network mapping was proposed to allow mobile virtual network operators to use customized resource allocation solutions to implement VNF placement on the RAN side. [5] proposed a communication and computation resource joint allocation algorithm in end-to-end network slicing for ultra reliable low-latency communication (URLLC), which can effectively reduce the end-to-end latency of network slicing, and guarantee the reliability requirements of network slicing. [6] proposed a radio resource allocation algorithm for Service Level Agreement (SLA) contract rate maximization, which can achieve a better SLA contract rate on the premise of ensuring isolation between slices, additionally increase the number of service users.

At present, most of the network slicing business requirements are dynamic, therefore the resource allocation process in network slicing will be affected by the randomness and time-varying nature of the actual environment [7]. However, most of the work still stays in the fixed environment to optimize the instantaneous network performance index. [8] set that the wireless channel is fixed. On the premise that the parameters of the radio channel are fixed, they proposed a cell planning scheme to maximize the resource utilization of the radio communication network. The proposed scheme optimized the resource allocation between network slices. From the perspective of information-centric networks and services, [9] studied the service function chain and optimization of IVCN on both the data plane and the control plane. In the fog-enabled heterogeneous RAN, they proposed a heuristic method ivcn-rano based on the ant colony optimization algorithm to solve the NP-hard problem, aiming to optimize the mapping of VNF and virtual content placement.

Dynamic slicing business scenarios often have a certain life cycle. In the existing researches, there are few research on dynamic resource allocation of network slicing that optimizes average performance indexes on a long-term scale for dynamic scenarios, and most of the existing researches on dynamic resource allocation of network slicing lack consideration of the overall state of the network, but consider the partial state of the network to optimize a single performance index. [1] proposed an upper-level priority algorithm with delay-limiting over-supply prevention to adjust capacity and traffic allocation to minimize the "over-supply ratio" while still meeting tenants' delay constraints and service level agreement. [10] designed a learning-based dynamic network slicing adjustment strategy, which can significantly reduce the overall expansion cost of network slicing while ensuring the quality of service. [11] proposed a dynamic communication resource sharing scheme for single-layer homogeneous C-RANs with multi-tenants, which considers the priority of tenants and maximizes the network utility. In the dynamic environment, the feasibility of solving optimization problems commonly used in static scenes is reduced, and new methods need to be explored.

In summary, in recent years, most of the work on slicing resource allocation only considers CN slicing or RAN slicing, and few studies consider the resource allocation of the entire end-to-end network slicing. And the process of network slicing deployment involves the joint allocation of multiple resources, so it is necessary to consider the joint allocation of communication and computation resource of end-to-end network slicing. In addition, the current work has less research on the dynamic allocation of network slicing resources. In response to the above problems, this paper takes into account the life cycle management of network slicing, studies the dynamic joint allocation of communication and computation resource based on the end-to-end network slicing architecture, aiming at the dynamic changes of network slicing data queues, radio channel status, and physical network topology. An end-to-end sliced dynamic resource allocation model is constructed, and a two-stage communication and computation resource joint allocation algorithm based on deep Q network (DQN) is proposed to maximize the overall utility of the network on a long time scale, to optimize the overall utility of the network, improve the long-term average revenue, and reduce the average cost of the system.

2   System Model

This paper proposes an end-to-end network slicing dynamic resource allocation scenario, as shown in Fig. 1. Based on the mobile network end-to-end network slicing scenario with dynamic service requests, for dynamic network slicing services with a certain life cycle, considering the dynamic joint allocation of communication and computation resource in the end-to-end network slicing, this paper studies the use of online resource management technology to maximize the overall network utility on a long-term scale. On the CN side, the underlying server of the infrastructure layer provides multiple types of network resources including computation resources and bandwidth resources. The virtualization layer virtualizes the network resources and provides various types of virtual network resources on the cloud server. According to the service requirements of network slicing, the CN side realizes the flexible allocation of physical node resources and link resources in discrete time slots according to the current system status and formulates the dynamic migration strategy for VNF, in which the computation resource is node CPU resource and the communication resource are link bandwidth resource between nodes. On the RAN side, the appropriate number of physical resource blocks (PRB) and computation resource are allocated to each network slice in discrete time slots according to the current system status. In the access network, the computation resource is related to the data processing capacity of each remote radio unit (RRU), and the communication resources are related to the PRB in each RRU.

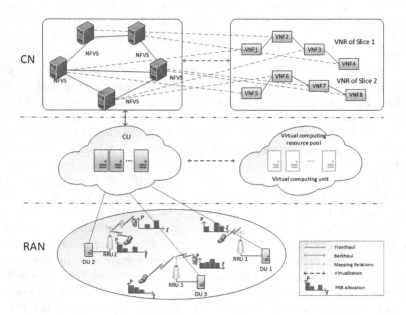

Fig. 1. End-to-end network slicing dynamic resource allocation scenario.

In this model, graph theory is used to describe the physical network and virtual network in the core network. The physical network can be expressed as an undirected weighted graph $G^P = \left(N^P, L^P, \eta_n^P, \eta_l^P\right)$, where N^P and L^P represent the set of physical nodes and the set of physical links between physical nodes respectively. In the core network, the set of general servers in the network is regarded as the set of physical nodes N^P, $N^P = \{1, 2, \cdots, N\}$. η_n^P represents the attribute set of physical nodes, such as CPU, memory, disk, etc. η_l^P represents the underlying link bandwidth. In the actual system, the specific resource requirements are usually related to the amount of data that the VNF needs to process.

Combine logical functions and generate virtual network topology according to service request. The virtual network request can be expressed as an undirected weighted graph $G^V = \left(N^V, L^V, \eta_n^V, \eta_l^V\right)$, where N^V represents the set of VNFs, that is, the set of virtual nodes; L^V represents the set of virtual links, η_n^V represents the attribute set of VNFs. The process of mapping VNF to the underlying network is expressed as $M : \{N^V \rightarrow N^P, L^V \rightarrow L^P\}$. The set of slices is $I = \{1, 2, \cdots, i\}$. The VNF function chain of the slice i is represented as $N^{Vi} = \{f_1^i, f_2^i, \cdots, f_K^i\}$.

In the computation resource pool on the access network side, each BBU provides the computation resource for RRU to process baseband data. The BBUs in the computation resource pool can share their own resources, and all computation resources are centralized to form a virtual computation resource pool through virtualization operation. In the access network, a time-varying random channel model is considered. This model assumes that there are multiple RRUs in a specific area. The total bandwidth of W Hz is divided into multiple physical resource blocks PRBs. The bandwidth of each PRB is w. These PRBs is shared by all RRUs. The entire network provides I slice service for U users in total, and the set of users is $\mathbf{U} = \{1, \cdots, U\}$. Each RRU can provide services for multiple types of slices. H is the set of limited channel states, $h_u^i(t) \in H = \{h_1, h_2, \cdots, h_H\}$ and $\sum_{m=1}^{H} P(h_m) = 1$, $h_{u,i}(t)$ is the channel gain when user u accesses slice i at time slot t, where $P(h_m)$ represents the probability that the channel state is h_m. When a user requests to access each slice, it is assumed that the channel state in each time slot is fixed, but the channel state between different time slots changes randomly, and the channel state among different time slots is independent of each other. $\overline{h^i}(t)$ represents the average channel gain when the user accesses slice i, and $\varepsilon^i(t)$ represents the spectral efficiency corresponding to time slot t.

In this paper, we construct the corresponding queue for data packets of each network slice service. We consider a discrete-time queuing system on the access network side. The length of each time slot is fixed, and multiple slices can be accessed in any time slot. $X_u^i(t)$ represents the number of data packets arriving in time slot t of the network slice i accessed by the user u, and the number of arriving data packets follows Gaussian distribution $E\{X_u^i(t)\} = \lambda_u^i$ and is independently and identically distributed among different time slots. The queue length of slice i at the beginning of time slot t is $Q^i(t)$, and $Q^i(t) = \sum_{u \in U} Q_u^i(t)$, where $Q_u^i(t)$ is the queue length of the slice i of the user u at time slot t. The dynamic update process of $Q^i(t)$ can be expressed as:

$$Q^i(t+1) = \max\left[Q^i(t) - D^i(t), 0\right] + X^i(t) \tag{1}$$

The number of data packets leaving the queue of slice i in time slot t is expressed as $D^i(t) = \varepsilon^i(t) \cdot w \cdot A^i(t) / S$, where $A^i(t)$ is the number of PRBs allocated to slice i by the network in time slot t, and S is the size of data packets in the slice queue. $X^i(t) = \sum_{u \in U} X_u^i(t)$ is the number of data packets arriving at slice i in time slot t. Let $Q(t) = \{Q^1(t), Q^2(t), \cdots, Q^I(t)\}$ represent the global queue status information of the system in time slot t, and $H(t) = \{\overline{h^1}(t), \overline{h^2}(t), \cdots, \overline{h^I}(t)\}$ represent the global channel status information in time slot t.

On the access network side, the set of computation resource is composed of multiple CPU cores, and the total number of CPU cores in the computation resource pool is Y. Each CPU core has the same data bandwidth processing capability, which is b Mbps. Let $\sigma^i(t)$ represent the computation resource allocation strategy in time slot t, and $\sigma^i(t)$ satisfies

$$\sigma^i(t) \geq 0, \sum_{i \in I} \sigma^i(t) \leq Y \tag{2}$$

Similarly, let $\omega^i(t)$ represent the PRB allocation strategy in time slot t, $\omega^i(t)$ satisfies

$$\omega^i(t) \geq 0, \sum_{i \in I} \omega^i(t) \leq Z \tag{3}$$

where Z is the total number of PRBs in the network.

The sum rate of all network slices of the entire network in time slot t can be expressed as

$$r(t) = \sum_{i \in I} r^i(t) = \sum_{i \in I} \varepsilon^i(t) \cdot w \cdot \omega^i(t) \tag{4}$$

On the core network side, define $\lambda_n(t) \in \{0,1\}$ to indicate the working status of the node, let $\lambda_n = 1$ indicate that node n is operating normally, otherwise the node fails. Define $l_{n,n'}(t) \in \{0,1\}$ to indicate the working status of the link between nodes n and n', let $l_{n,n'} = 1$ indicate that the link between node n and n' is operating normally, otherwise the link fails.

Define a linear relationship between the number of computation resources C_k^i required by VNF f_k^i and the required data processing rate R_k^i [12]. Let α_k be the correlation coefficient between the VNF computation resource requirement and the data processing rate, then the computation resource requirement of VNF f_k^i is expressed as

$$C_k^i = \alpha_k R_k^i \tag{5}$$

A binary node association factor $\beta_{k,n}^i \in \{0,1\}$ is defined to represent the mapping relationship between VNFs and physical nodes, if and only if the VNF f_k^i is needed in the VNR i, and the VNF f_k^i is mapped to the node n, $\beta_{k,n}^i = 1$. Assuming that there is a queuing process for the arriving data flow of each VNF mapped to the physical node, let $Q_{k,n}^i(t)$ represent the queue length of VNF f_k^i mapped to node n at the beginning of time slot t, and represent the number of data packets arriving at VNF f_k^i of slice i in time slot t. Similar to the access network side, the number of arriving data packets also follows Gaussian distribution $E\{X_u^i(t)\} = \lambda_u^i$ and is independently and identically distributed among different time slots. R_k^i is the data processing rate required by VNF f_k^i. The dynamic update process of VNF VNF f_k^i queue of node n can be expressed as

$$Q_{n,k}^i(t+1) = \max\left[Q_{n,k}^i(t) - R_k^i(t), 0\right] + X_k^i(t) \tag{6}$$

The data packet of VNF f_k^i which leave the f_k^i queue mapped to the node n is expressed as

$$L_{k,n}^i = \min\left[R_k^i, Q_{k,n}^i\right] \tag{7}$$

Let $B_{n,n'}$ denote the bandwidth consumption between physical nodes n and n', which can be expressed as

$$B_{n,n'} = \sum_{i \in I} \sum_{f_k^i, f_j^i \in N^{Vi}} \beta_{j,n}^i \beta_{k,n'}^i S \cdot L_{j,n}^i(f_j | f_k, i) \tag{8}$$

3   Problem Formulation

The optimization goal of this model is to maximize the overall average network utility on a long-term scale of end-to-end network slicing, maximize the average network revenue and minimize the average deployment cost while ensuring system transmission rate. The revenue comes from the service rate, and the expenditure comes from the VNF deployment cost, which can be expressed as

$$g_r^i = \overline{r}^i \delta_r \tag{9}$$

$$l_{CPU}^i = \sum_{f_k^i \in N^{Vi}} \sum_{n \in N^P} \beta_{k,n}^i \overline{C}_k^i \delta_n \tag{10}$$

$$l_B^i = \overline{B}_{n,n'}^i \delta_B \tag{11}$$

where δ_r, δ_n, δ_B respectively represent the unit price of the service rate, the unit price of the computation resource on the server node, and the unit price of the communication resource between the nodes.

The overall average network utility can be expressed as

$$\bar{u} = g_r - l_{CPU} - l_B \tag{12}$$

Therefore, the optimization goal of this paper can be expressed as

$$\max_{\sigma(t),\omega(t),\Psi(t),\beta(t)} \bar{u} \tag{13a}$$

$$\text{s.t. } \sigma^i(t) \geq 0, \sum_{i \in I} \sigma^i(t) \leq Y, \forall t \tag{13b}$$

$$\omega^i(t) \geq 0, \sum_{i \in I} \omega^i(t) \leq Z, \forall t \tag{13c}$$

$$\omega^i(t) r^i(t) \geq R_{rsv}^i, \forall i \in \mathbf{I}, \forall t \tag{13d}$$

$$\bar{C}_n^\pi(c) \leq C_n^{\max}, \forall n \in N^P \tag{13e}$$

$$\bar{B}_{n,n'}^\pi(c) \leq B_{n,n'}, \forall n, n' \in N^P \tag{13f}$$

$$\sum_{n \in N^P} \beta_{k,n}^i = \rho_k^i, \forall i \in \mathbf{I}, f_k^i \in N^{Vi} \tag{13g}$$

Constraint (13b) indicates that the allocation of computation resources shall not exceed the total computation resources. Constraint (13c) indicates that the total link bandwidth occupied by the data streams of each slice in the access network during transmission should not exceed the upper limit of the access network bandwidth. Constraint (13d) ensures that each slice is guaranteed a minimum data rate. Constraint (13e) indicates that the total computation resources required by the VNF mapped to the same node n cannot exceed the total computation resources of the node n; Constraint (13f) means that when VNF f_k^i is mapped to node n and VNF f_{k+1}^i is mapped to node n', the mapping from virtual link to physical link is realized, and the link bandwidth required by any virtual network function cannot exceed the maximum available bandwidth provided by any two nodes, where $B_{n,n'}$ is the upper limit of the maximum available bandwidth provided between any two physical nodes. Constraint (13g) indicates that for each slicing requirement, the VNF required by the slice should be mapped to the physical node, where ρ_k^i indicates whether slice i requires VNF f_k^i, if necessary, $\rho_k^i = 1$; otherwise, $\rho_k^i = 0$.

4   Joint Allocation of Two-Stage Communication and Computation Resource Based on DQN

In this paper, a two-stage DQN algorithm is used to jointly allocate dynamic communication and computation resource in end-to-end network slices. The optimization problem to be solved can be modeled as a constrained Markov decision process(CMDP) problem, which can be described by a four-tuple $\langle C, A, p_a\left(c'|c\right),\ R_a\left(c'|c\right)\rangle$, where C is a finite set of states of the system, and A is a finite set of actions that can be taken. $p_a\left(c'|c\right)$ is the probability of state c transitioning to c' after performing action a in state in current time slot t. $R_a\left(c'|c\right)$ is the reward function of state transfer to c' after system executes action a in state c, representing the instant cost/reward, which represents the learning goal.

4.1   DQN Training Algorithm

DQN algorithm takes state c as input and outputs the corresponding action after neural network analysis. The essence of the algorithm is to approximate the distribution of Q value by using neural network training function f_{ap}. Q value can be expressed as

$$\mathbf{Q}\left(c,a\right) \approx f_{ap}\left(c,a,\theta\right) \tag{14}$$

where θ represents the weight of the main network, $\mathbf{Q}\left(c,a\right) = [Q\left(c,a_1\right), Q\left(c,a_2\right), \cdots, Q\left(c,a_T\right)]$. The main network model used in this paper is CNN, and the network structure mainly includes an input layer, a convolutional layer, and a fully connected layer.

The target Q value y is expressed as

$$y = r\left(c,a\right) + \gamma\left[\max_{a'\in A} Q\left(c',a',\theta^-\right)\right] \tag{15}$$

where θ^- represents the weight of the target Q network. To fit complex environmental characteristics, it is necessary to repeatedly learn and train the weight function to improve the performance of network prediction. The training process of DQN algorithm is shown in Fig. 2. In this training model, the weight θ is optimized by minimizing the loss function between the main network and the target Q network. The loss function can be expressed as

$$L\left(\theta\right) = E\left[\left(y - Q\left(c,a,\theta\right)\right)^2\right] \tag{16}$$

After the main network of DQN algorithm undergoes the training process, the optimal allocation scheme of network slice resources can be obtained by using the trained main network. The global process of the two-stage learning algorithm proposed in this paper is: randomly generate a CPU resource and PRB allocation method $\sigma(t)$ and $\omega(t)$ that satisfy the constraints (13b)–(13d). Based on $\sigma(t)$ and $\omega(t)$, execute one-stage algorithm to get VNF migration decision $\Psi(t)$ and VNF resource allocation strategy $\beta(t)$ and update; based on $\Psi(t)$ and $\beta(t)$, the new CPU resource and PRB allocation method $\sigma(t)$ and $\omega(t)$ are obtained by executing the two-stage algorith. The final PRB and CPU resource allocation method, VNF migration decision and VNF resource allocation strategy are obtained.

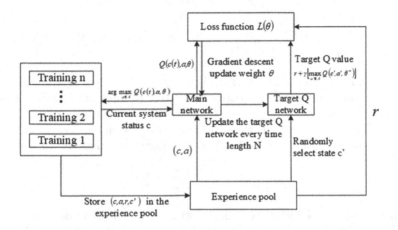

Fig. 2. DQN training model.

4.2   CN-Side Algorithm

The one-stage algorithm is a DQN-based CN-side communication and computation resource joint allocation algorithm. In the core network, the dynamic allocation of CPU resource on servers in the physical network, the dynamic allocation of link bandwidth resource between servers, and the migration strategy of VNF are described as a CMDP problem. A basic element is defined, which includes four tuples of system state, migration behavior, state transition probability and cost function. The state of the system in time slot t is defined as $c_t = \{Q(t), \lambda(t), l(t)\} \in C$, and the action in time slot t is defined as $a_t = \{\Psi(t), \beta(t)\} \in A$, where $\Psi(t)$ is the two-dimensional migration action vector of the VNF in time slot t. The decision is composed of $\phi_{f_k^i}(t)$ and $n_{f_k^i}(t)$, $\forall f_k^i \in N^{Vi}$, $i \in I$, $\phi_{f_k^i}(t) = 1$ means that VNF f_k^i of slice i is migrated in time slot t, otherwise $\phi_{f_k^i}(t) = 0$; $n_{f_k^i}(t)$ is the target node of VNF f_k^i migration; $\beta(t)$ is the set of mapping actions for each VNF in time slot t.

The process of mapping state space to action space is defined as $\pi : C \to A$, which is a stability strategy, that is, $a = \pi(c)$. According to strategy $\pi \in \Pi$, the expected cumulative CPU resource allocation in time slot t is as follows

$$
\begin{aligned}
\bar{C}^\pi(c) &= E^\pi \left\{ \sum_{t=0}^{\infty} \gamma_t C(c_t, a_t) | c_0 = c \right\} \\
&= E^\pi \left\{ \sum_{t=0}^{\infty} \gamma_t \sum_{f_k^i \in N^{Vi}} \sum_{n \in N^P} \beta_{k,n}^i(t) \alpha_k R_k^i | c_0 = c \right\}
\end{aligned}
\tag{17}
$$

The expected cumulative bandwidth resource allocation is as follows

$$
\begin{aligned}
\bar{B}_{n,n'}^\pi(c) &= E^\pi \left\{ \sum_{t=0}^{\infty} \gamma_t B_{n,n'}(c_t, a_t) | c_0 = c \right\} \\
&= E^\pi \left\{ \sum_{t=0}^{\infty} \gamma_t \sum_{i \in I} \sum_{f_k^i, f_j^i \in N^{Vi}} \beta_{j,n}^i \beta_{k,n'}^i S \cdot L_{j,n}^i(f_k | f_j, i) | c_0 = c \right\}
\end{aligned}
\tag{18}
$$

where $\gamma \in [0, 1)$ is a discount factor, indicating the degree of attenuation of the reward function value, which indicates the degree of influence of future rewards on the current behavior choice. The core network side optimization goal is to find the optimal VNF migration decision $\Psi(t)$ and VNF resource allocation strategy $\beta(t)$ to minimize deployment costs. The stochastic optimization model can be expressed as

$$
\min_{\Psi(t),\beta(t)} \bar{C}^\pi(c) + \sum_{n \in N^P} \bar{B}_{n,n'}^\pi(c)
\tag{19}
$$

Combined with the definition and description of the Markov decision problem above, the state, action, and reward of the one-stage algorithm are defined as follows:

State: $c_t = \{Q(t), \lambda(t), l(t)\} \in C$.

Action: A set of VNF migration and resource allocation actions that satisfy $[\Psi^*(t), \beta^*(t)] = \arg \min_{\Psi(t),\beta(t)} \bar{C}^\pi(c) + \sum_{n \in N^P} \bar{B}_{n,n'}^\pi(c)$.

Reward: We define the reward function as the respective utility of each slice. If the action selection does not satisfy the constraints (13b)-(13g), set the reward function to fixed –1.

$$
r^i(c, a) = \begin{cases} u^i, & C13a - C13f \\ -1, & otherwise \end{cases}
\tag{20}
$$

The one-stage algorithm is shown in Algorithm 1.

4.3 RAN-Side Algorithm

The two-stage algorithm is a DQN-based RAN-side communication and computation resource joint allocation algorithm. In the access network, the state of the system in time slot t is defined as $c_t = (Q(t), H(t)) \in C$, and the action in time slot t is defined as $a_t = (\sigma(t), \omega(t)) \in A$. The process of mapping state space to action space is defined as $\pi : C \to A$, which is a stability strategy, that

---

Algorithm 1. CN-side algorithm

Input:
  Physical network topology G^P, Virtual network topology G^V, PRB and CPU resource allocation method $\sigma(t), \omega(t)$;
1: for t=1, 2, ..., T do
2: Monitor the global status c_t of the core network side in current time slot t, including global queue status information $Q(t)$, global node status $\lambda(t)$, and global link status $l(t)$
3: if $\lambda_n(t) = 0$ or $l_{n,n'}(t) = 0$
4: Calculate the optimal VNF migration strategy $\Psi(t)$ and VNF communication and computation resource allocation strategy $a_t^* = \arg\min_{a \in A} Q(c_t, a, \theta)$ on the basis of migrating all $\forall f_k^i \in N^{Vi}$ satisfying $\beta_{k,n}^i = 1$ to other nodes
5: else
6: Directly calculate the optimal VNF migration strategy $\Psi(t)$ and VNF communication and computation resource allocation strategy $a_t^* = \arg\min_{a \in A} Q(c_t, a, \theta)$
7: Perform VNF migration based on the optimal action a_t^*, and allocate communication and computation resource
8: t=t+1
9: end for
Output:
  VNF migration strategy $\Psi(t)$ and VNF resource allocation strategy $\beta(t)$

---

is, $a = \pi(c)$. According to strategy $\pi \in \Pi$, the expected cumulative slice sum rate is

$$
\begin{aligned}
\bar{r}^\pi(c) &= E^\pi\left\{\sum_{t=0}^{\infty} \gamma_t r(c_t, a_t)|c_0 = c\right\} \\
&= E^\pi\left\{\sum_{t=0}^{\infty} \gamma_t \sum_{i \in I} \varepsilon^i(t) \cdot w \cdot \omega^i(t)|c_0 = c\right\}
\end{aligned} \tag{21}
$$

The objective of access network side optimization is to find the optimal allocation scheme of PRB and computation resources under the premise of satisfying the constraints of the minimum service rate of each network slice and the constraints of network bandwidth resource, so as to maximize the network revenue. The stochastic optimization model can be expressed as

$$
\max_{\sigma(t),\omega(t)} E^\pi\left\{\sum_{t=0}^{\infty} \gamma_t \sum_{i \in I} \varepsilon^i(t) \cdot w \cdot \omega^i(t)|c_0 = c\right\} \tag{22}
$$

The state, action, and reward of the two-stage algorithm are defined as follows:
  State: $c_t = (Q(t), H(t)) \in C$.
  Action: A set of PRB and computation resource allocation actions that satisfy $[\sigma^*(t), \omega^*(t)] = \arg\max_{\sigma(t),\omega(t)} \bar{r}^\pi(c)$.
  Reward: When the constraints (4-13b)-(4-13g) are satisfied, the reward function is defined as the sum of system utility obtained after the slices select their respective PRBs and computation resource, otherwise, it is defined as a negative feedback.

$$r\left(c,a\right) = \begin{cases} \sum\limits_{i\in I} u^i, C13a - C13f \\ -1, otherwise \end{cases} \tag{23}$$

The two-stage algorithm is shown in Algorithm 2. The core network-side VNF migration strategy and mapping method obtained by the one-stage algorithm are taken as the input of the two-stage algorithm to obtain the access network-side CPU resources and PRB allocation result. The entire algorithm will reach the end of the slice life cycle to obtain the final VNF migration strategy, VNF resource allocation strategy, PRB allocation strategy and CPU resource allocation method. The resource allocation process ends.

Algorithm 2. RAN-side algorithm

Input:
  VNF migration strategy $\Psi\left(t\right)$ and VNF resource allocation strategy $\beta\left(t\right)$;
1: for t=1, 2, ..., T do
2: Monitor the global status c_t of the access network side in the current time slot, including global queue status information $Q\left(t\right)$ and global channel status information $H\left(t\right)$
3: Calculate the optimal PRB and computation resource allocation actions $a_t^* = \arg\max\limits_{a\in A} Q\left(c_t, a, \theta\right)$
4: Adjusting the PRB and computation resource allocation of radio access network slices based on the optimal action a_t^*
5: t=t+1
6: end for
Output:
  PRB allocation strategy $\omega\left(t\right)$ and CPU resource allocation method $\sigma\left(t\right)$

---

5   Performance Evaluation

In the simulation, this paper assumes that the network scenario is a fully connected network, and the infrastructure has $N = 10$ general-purpose processors. Considering 3 types of network slices with different minimum rate requirements, 8 types of VNFs constitute the network function chain of the slices and the computation resource demand coefficient $\alpha_m = 0.1$. The service function chain of each slice includes multiple VNFs, and the number of VNFs follows the uniform distribution of 6 to 8. The arrival process of sliced data packets is independent and identically distributed Poisson distribution, and the node failure rate and link failure rate of the underlying network are uniformly distributed. The remaining simulation parameters are shown in Table 1.

The main network and the target Q network in the two-stage resource allocation algorithm based on DQN used in this paper are multi-layer convolutional CNN networks, including 3 layers of convolutional layers and 2 layers of fully connected layers. The parameters of the target Q network are updated every 200 iterations. Let the capacity of DQN experience playback pool in the training process be 10000, and the probability value of $\varepsilon-greedy$ strategy $\varepsilon = 0.7$.

Table 1. Simulation Parameters

Parameter	Value
Number of RRU CPU core Y	30
Number of PRB Z	50
System bandwidth W	10 MHz
Pathloss from RRU to user	$37.6 \log 10 \left(d\left[km \right] \right) + 128.1$ dB
Noise power spectral density	-174 dBm/Hz
Maximum RRU transmit power $P_{\max}$	39 dBm
Number of server nodes N	10
Number of VNF types	8
Minimum rate of slice i R_{rsv}^i	10 Mbps, 5 Mbps, 51 Mbps
Maximum queue length of each slice	20 packets
Data packet size S	4 kbit/packet
Time slot length	1 ms
Discount factor γ	0.9
Maximum number of iterations	2000
Learning rate	0.0001

To evaluate the feasibility of the model and the effectiveness of the algorithm, the overall network utility of the network slicing service, the average slicing rate, and the total cost of the network slicing system are used as performance evaluation indicators, and the performance of the algorithm proposed in this paper is compared with that of the proportional fair static sharing(PFSS) algorithm and the heuristic algorithm.

When the number of users is 30 and the unit price of the service rate is 7, the comparison results of network utility on the long-term scale obtained by different resource allocation algorithms are shown in Fig. 3. As the time series progresses, network utility tends to stabilize. Compared with the PFSS algorithm and heuristic algorithm, the algorithm proposed in this paper can obtain the maximum network utility.

Figure 4 shows the change in the average total slice rate of the three comparison algorithms as the number of users increases when the unit price of the service rate is 7. The simulation result shows that the average total slice rate corresponding to the three algorithms all increase with the increase of the number of users. When the number of users is less than 10, the heuristic algorithm can maintain the same total rate as the algorithm proposed in this paper; but as the number of users continues to increase, the rate of the heuristic algorithm gradually increases due to the limitation of the general service node resources. The two-stage dynamic resource allocation algorithm based on DQN proposed in this paper can guarantee the best system service rate.

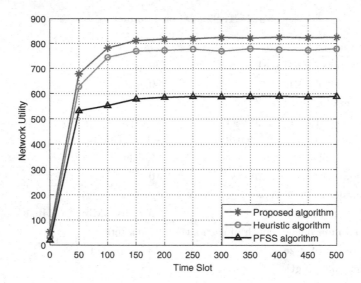

Fig. 3. Comparison of network utility of three algorithms.

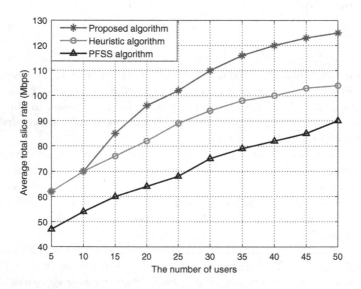

Fig. 4. Average total slice rate versus the number of users.

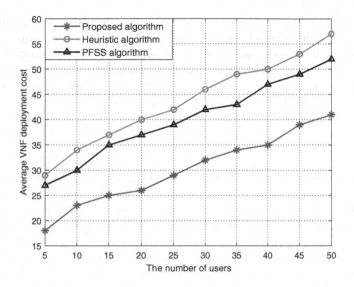

Fig. 5. Average VNF deployment cost versus the number of users.

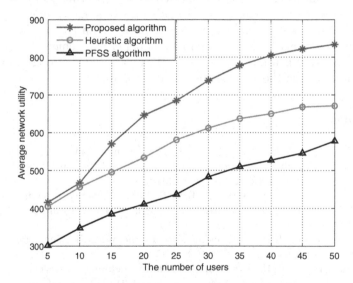

Fig. 6. Average network utility versus the number of users.

Figure 5 illustrates the change of the average slice VNF deployment cost with the increase in the number of users in the three comparison algorithms when the unit price of the service rate is 7. The simulation results show that the VNF deployment costs corresponding to the three algorithms all increase with the increase in the number of users. As can be seen from the figure, the algorithm proposed in this paper can achieve the lowest total system cost.

Figure 6 shows the change in the average network utility as the number of users increases when the service rate unit price is 7, and the number of users in each slice is as uniform as possible. The simulation results show that when the number of users increases, the average network utility increases. Compared with the PFSS algorithm and heuristic algorithm, the algorithm proposed in this paper can obtain the largest average network utility.

6   Conclusions

This paper proposes a joint allocation method of dynamic communication and computation resource in an end-to-end network slicing scenario, aiming at the dynamic changes of network slicing data queues, radio channel status, and physical network topology, constructs the end-to-end slicing dynamic resource allocation model. With the optimization goal of maximizing the overall utility of the network on a long-term scale, the dynamic joint allocation of communication and computation resources is performed on the network slicing. According to the service requirements of network slicing, the flexible allocation of communication and computation resources is realized in discrete time slots according to the current system state. This paper proposes a two-stage communication and computation resource joint allocation algorithm based on DQN. The simulation results show that the scheme proposed in this paper can achieve the purpose of optimizing the overall utility of the network, increasing the long-term average revenue, and reducing the average cost of the system.

References

1. Chien, H.T., Lin, Y.D., Lai, C.L., et al.: End-to-end slicing with optimized communication and computing resource allocation in multi-tenant 5G systems. IEEE Trans. Veh. Technol. **69**(2), 2079–2091 (2020)
2. Ordonez-Lucena, J., Ameigeiras, P., Lopez, D., et al.: Network slicing for 5G with SDN/NFV: concepts, architectures and challenges. IEEE Commun. Mag. **55**(5), 80–87 (2017)
3. Nakao, A., Du, P., Kiriha, Y., et al.: End-to-end network slicing for 5G mobile networks. J. Inf. Process. **25**, 153–163 (2017)
4. Riggio, R., Bradai, A., Harutyunyan, D., et al.: Scheduling wireless virtual networks functions. IEEE Trans. Netw. Serv. Manage. **13**(2), 240–252 (2016)
5. Tong, Z., Zhang, T., Zhu, Y., et al.: Communication and computation resource allocation for end-to-end slicing in mobile networks. In: IEEE/CIC International Conference on Communications in China (ICCC) 2020, China, pp. 1286–1291 (2020). https://doi.org/10.1109/ICCC49849.2020.9238794
6. Zhou, L., Zhang, T., Li, J., et al.: Radio resource allocation for RAN slicing in mobile networks. In: IEEE/CIC International Conference on Communications in China (ICCC) 2020, China, pp. 1280–1285 (2020). https://doi.org/10.1109/ICCC49849.2020.9238905
7. Qiang, Y., Zhuang, W., Shan, Z., et al.: Dynamic radio resource slicing for a two-tier heterogeneous wireless network. IEEE Trans. Veh. Technol. 1 (2018)

8. Florian, B., Ramos-Cantor, O.D., Steffen, H., et al.: Optimized cell planning for network slicing in heterogeneous wireless communication networks. IEEE Commun. Lett. **22**(8), 1676–1679 (2018)
9. Jin, H., Lu, H., Jin, Y., et al.: IVCN: information-centric network slicing optimization based on NFV in fog-enabled RAN. IEEE Access **7**, 69667–69686 (2019)
10. Xu, Q., Wang, J., Wu, K.: Learning-based dynamic resource provisioning for network slicing with ensured end-to-end performance bound. IEEE Trans. Netw. Sci. Eng. 28–41 (2018)
11. Zhang, J., Wu, M., Ma, R., et al.: Dynamic resource sharing scheme across network slicing for multi-tenant C-RANs. In: IEEE/CIC International Conference on Communications in China (ICCC Workshops) 2018, China, pp. 172–177 (2016). https://doi.org/10.1109/ICCChinaW.2018.8674479
12. Jian, Y., Zhang, S., Wu, X., et al.: Online learning-based server provisioning for electricity cost reduction in data center. IEEE Trans. Control Syst. Technol. **25**(3), 1044–1051 (2017)

Passive Target Detection Based on GLRT Using Multi-satellite Illumination

Huijie Zhu[1], Mingqian Liu[2(✉)], Ming Li[3], and Xiuhui Gao[4]

[1] Science and Technology on Communication Information Security Control Laboratory, The 36th Research Institute of China Electronics Technology Group Corporation, Jiaxing 314033, China
zhuhuijie@zju.edu.cn
[2] State Key Laboratory of Integrated Service Networks, Xidian University, Xi'an 710071, Shaanxi, China
mqliu@mail.xidian.edu.cn
[3] State 722 Factory, Guilin 541001, Guangxi, China
[4] State Key Laboratory of Integrated Service Networks, Xidian University, Xi'an 710071, Shaanxi, China

Abstract. This paper proposes a novel passive location parameter estimator using multiple satellites for moving aerial targets. Specifically, we consider target detection in the ground dual receiver system, which is divided into reference channel and monitoring channel. The reference channel receives the direct wave signals from multiple external emitters, and the monitoring channel receives the echo signals reflected by the target. We propose a target detection method based on a generalized likelihood ratio (GLRT). This detection algorithm is robust to the reference channel noise. Extensive simulations are conducted to evaluate the performance of the algorithm under various network settings.

Keywords: Generalized likelihood ratio test · Multi-satellite illumination · Passive detection · Target detection

1 Introduction

Passive detection systems utilize the reflected echo signals from a moving target generated by a non-cooperative radiation source and realize the target's passive detection [1–5]. As such, an external radiation source for obtaining the moving target detection has been extensively studied with its superiority on concealment and reliability [6].

This work was supported by the National Natural Science Foundation of China under Grant 62071364, in part by the Aeronautical Science Foundation of China under Grant 2020Z073081001, in part by the Fundamental Research Funds for the Central Universities under Grant JB210104, and in part by the 111 Project under Grant B08038.

The traditional method for passive detection is sensitive to the noise in the reference channel based on the reference channel's direct wave signal and the monitoring channel's echo signal [7–10]. Thus, the detection performance is readily affected by the noise of the reference channel [11,12]. At present, most works assume that the signal-to-noise ratio of the reference channel is high. On this basis, the echo signal is detected, which is inconsistent with the actual scene. The current works use the generalized likelihood ratio method to achieve the purpose of weak echo detection. However, these detection methods are related to the modeling and analysis in a single emitter scene. For effectively detecting the weak echo from multiple satellites in the multi-satellite joint scene, a multi-satellite collaborative target detection method based on the generalized likelihood ratio method is introduced as a more suitable alternative.

2   System Model

In the actual receiving scene, the ground receiving system consists of two antennas. One is called the monitoring channel antenna, and the other is the reference channel antenna. The reference antenna is placed in the satellite direction, and the monitoring antenna is an antenna with a wide beam pointing to the monitoring area. When the satellite emitter radiates signals, we expect to receive a direct wave signal and an echo signal reflected by the target. The time delay of the echo signal is τ, and the Doppler frequency shift is f_d. In this process, some clutter will inevitably be received. When there are multiple satellites as external radiation sources, the signal received by the monitoring channel is represented by $x(t)$, which can be given by

$$
\begin{aligned}
x(t) = &\sum_{\eta=1}^{M} a_\eta s_\eta (t - \tau_\eta) e^{j2\pi f_{d\eta} t} \\
&+ \sum_{\eta=1}^{M} \phi_{\eta,0} s_\eta(t) + \sum_{\eta=1}^{M} \sum_{k=1}^{N_c} \phi_{\eta,k}(t) s_\eta \left(t - \tau_{\eta,k}^{(c)} \right) \\
&+ \sum_{m=1}^{K} \gamma_m^{(t)} s_m \left(t - \tau_m^{(t)} \right) e^{j2\pi f_{dm}^{(t)} t} + n_s(t) \quad 0 < t < T,
\end{aligned}
\tag{1}
$$

where M is the number of satellite radiation sources; $f_{d\eta}$, τ_η and α_η are Doppler frequency shift, delay and amplitude of target echo respectively; $n_s(t)$ is Gaussian white noise; K is the number of jamming targets; $\beta_m^{(t)}$, $\tau_m^{(t)}$, $f_{dm}^{(t)}$ are amplitude, delay and Doppler frequency shift of the target echo; $\tau_{\eta,k}^{(c)}$ and $\phi_{\eta,k}(t)$ are the delay and amplitude of multipath signal respectively; T is the observation time; N_C is the number of multipath of a single satellite signal; the amplitude $\phi_{\eta,k}(t)$ of multipath is a random process with special power spectral density. In the signal model of this paper,we assume that the amplitude of multipath signal has special power spectral density,which can be expressed by multiple frequencies $f_i^{(c)}$, we can get the following results

$$
\phi_{\eta,k}(t) = \sum_{i=-Q}^{Q} \phi_{\eta,k,i} e^{j2\pi f_i^{(c)} t},
\tag{2}
$$

where $f_i(c) = (i - 1 - Q)\Delta f_c, i = 1, 2, \cdots, 2Q + 1$, and Q and Δf_c are two suitable parameters selected according to the actual scene. In this case, $\phi_{\eta,k,i}$ is the amplitude of the multipath signal at frequency $f_i^{(c)}$ and time delay $\tau_{\eta,k}^{(c)}$ at $k = 1, 2, \cdots, N_c$. In the actual scene, the reference signal in the reference channel may also be affected by multipath and target echo. Therefore, it will affect the performance of subsequent target detection. Therefore, before detecting the target in the monitoring channel, it is necessary to use some signal processing algorithms such as beamforming or channel equalization to suppress multipath and echo signals in the reference channel. The space-time constant modulus algorithm can recover the degradation of detection performance caused by the presence of echo and multipath signals in the reference channel. Therefore, after a proper signal processing algorithm and band-pass filter separation, the signal in the reference channel can be given by:

$$y_\eta(t) = b_\eta s_\eta(t) + n_\eta(t) \ 0 \le t < T\eta = 1, 2 \cdots, M, \tag{3}$$

where b_η is the amplitude of the direct wave signal received by the reference antenna; $n_\eta(t)$ is the sum of the noise of the reference channel receiver and the interference signal after signal processing. The signals $x(t)$ and $y_\eta(t)$ are sampled at time $t_n = {}^n\!/_{f_s} = nT_s, n = 1, 2, \cdots, N$. At the nth sampling interval, the sampling signals of the received signals in the monitoring channel and the reference channel are represented as $x(n)$ and $y_\eta(n)$, respectively, as follows

$$
\begin{aligned}
x[n] = &\sum_{\eta=1}^{M} a_\eta s_\eta[n - n_\eta] e^{j2\pi\Omega_n} + \sum_{\eta=1}^{M} \phi_{\eta,0} s_\eta[n] \\
&+ \sum_{\eta=1}^{M} \sum_{k=1}^{N_c} \sum_{i=-Q}^{Q} \phi_{\eta,k,i} s_\eta\left[n - n_{\eta,k}^{(c)}\right] e^{j2\pi\Omega_m^{(t)}} + n_s[n] \\
&+ \sum_{m=1}^{K} \gamma_m^{(t)} s_\eta\left[n - n_m^{(t)}\right] e^{j2\pi\Omega_m^{(t)}} \quad n = 1, 2, \cdots, N,
\end{aligned}
\tag{4}
$$

$$y_\eta(n) = b_\eta s_\eta(n) + n_\eta(n) \quad n = 1, 2, \cdots, N, \tag{5}$$

where $\Omega_\eta = 2\pi f_{d\eta} T_s$ and $\Omega_m^{(t)} = 2\pi f_{dm}^{(t)} T_s$ represent the normalized Doppler frequency of target echo and jamming target echo respectively. And $\tau_\eta = n_\eta T_s$, $\tau_m^{(t)} = n_m^{(t)} T_s$, $\tau_{\eta,k}^{(c)} = n_{\eta,k}^{(c)} T_s$, where n_η, $n_m^{(t)}$ and $n_{\eta,k}^{(c)}$ represent the echo signal of received signal in the monitoring channel, jamming target echo and multipath delay respectively. Substituting Eq. (5) into Eq. (4), the results can be given by

$$x(n) = \sum_{\eta=1}^{M} \frac{a_\eta}{b_\eta} y_\eta \left[n - n_\eta\right] e^{jn\Omega_\eta} + \sum_{\eta=1}^{M} \frac{\phi_{\eta,0}}{b_\eta} y_\eta[n]$$

$$+ \sum_{\eta=1}^{M} \sum_{k=1}^{N_c} \sum_{i=-Q}^{Q} \frac{\phi_{\eta,k,i}}{b_\eta} y_\eta \left[n - n_{\eta,k}^{(c)}\right] e^{j2\pi f_i^{(c)} T_s n}$$

$$+ \sum_{m=1}^{K} \frac{\gamma_m^{(t)}}{b_\eta} y_m \left[n - n_m^{(t)}\right] e^{jn\Omega_m^{(t)}} + n_s(n)$$

$$+ \sum_{\eta=1}^{M} \frac{a_\eta}{b_\eta} n_\eta \left[n - n_\eta\right] e^{jn\Omega_\eta} + \sum_{\eta=1}^{M} \frac{\phi_{\eta,0}}{b_\eta} n_\eta[n] \qquad (6)$$

$$+ \sum_{\eta=1}^{M} \sum_{k=1}^{N_c} \sum_{i=-Q}^{Q} \frac{\phi_{\eta,k,i}}{b_\eta} y_\eta \left[n - n_{\eta,k}^{(c)}\right] e^{j2\pi f_i^{(c)} T_s n}$$

$$+ \sum_{m=1}^{K} \frac{\gamma_m^{(t)}}{b_\eta} n_m \left[n - n_m^{(t)}\right] e^{jn\Omega_m^{(t)}},$$

By integrating the last four noise terms in Eq. (6) into $n_s[n]$, the above equation can be rewritten as follows

$$x(n) = \sum_{\eta=1}^{M} \alpha_\eta y_\eta[n - n_\eta]^{jn\Omega_\eta} + \sum_{\eta=1}^{M} c_{\eta,0} y_\eta[n]$$

$$+ \sum_{\eta=1}^{M} \sum_{k=1}^{N_c} \sum_{i=-Q}^{Q} c_{\eta,k,i} y_\eta \left[n - n_{\eta,k}^{(c)}\right] e^{j2\pi f_i^{(c)} T_s n} \qquad (7)$$

$$+ \sum_{m=1}^{K} \beta_m^{(t)} y_m \left[n - n_m^{(t)}\right] e^{jn\Omega_m^{(t)}} + n_s[n],$$

where $\alpha_\eta \triangleq \alpha_\eta/b_\eta$, $c_{\eta,0} \triangleq \alpha_\eta/b_\eta$, $c_{\eta,k,i} \triangleq \phi_{\eta,k,i}/b_\eta$, $\beta_m^{(t)} \triangleq \gamma_m^{(t)}/b_\eta$. By constructing the matrix Λ and matrix Γ as follows

$$\left[\Lambda^{(c)}\right]_{kj} = 2\pi f_k^{(c)} T_s \quad k = 1, 2, \cdots, 2Q+1, \mathrm{j} = 1, 2, \cdots, N_c, \qquad (8)$$

$$\left| D^{(c)} \right|_{kj} = n_j \quad k = 1, 2, \cdots, 2Q+1, \ j = 1, 2, \cdots, N_c, \qquad (9)$$

By defining vectors $\Omega \triangleq [0, vec(\Lambda)]^T$ and $n \triangleq [0, vec(D)]^T$, Eq. (6) can be given by

$$x[n] = \sum_{\eta=1}^{M} a_\eta y_\eta \left[n - n_\eta\right] e^{j2\pi\Omega_\eta} + \sum_{\eta=1}^{M} \phi_{\eta,0} y_\eta[n]$$

$$+ \sum_{\eta=1}^{M} \sum_{k=1}^{N_c} c_{\eta,k} y_\eta \left[n - n_{\eta,k}^{(c)}\right] e^{jn\Omega_{\eta,k}^{(c)}} + n_s[n] \qquad (10)$$

$$+ \sum_{m=1}^{K} \beta_m^{(t)} y_m \left[n - n_m^{(t)}\right] e^{j2\pi\Omega_m^{(t)}} \quad n = 1, 2, \cdots, N,$$

where $P = (2Q + 1)N_c + 1$; $\Omega_{\eta,k}^{(c)}$ and $n_{\eta,k}^{(c)}$ are the kth elements of $\Omega^{(c)}$ and $n^{(c)}$, respectively. As shown in the above formula, $\Omega_{\eta,k}^{(c)}$ and $n_{\eta,k}^{(c)}$ at $k = 2, 3, \cdots, P$ correspond to the Doppler frequency shift and time delay of multipath signal in the monitoring channel; c_1 at $k = 1$ corresponds to the amplitude of direct wave signal.

3   Multi-satellite Weak Target Echo Detection Based on GLRT

The general problem of detecting targets is characterized in that when there are K interfering target echoes, direct waves and multipaths, and the amplitude of the target echo signal α_η is unknown, the target is detected. The problem can be described by the following assumptions

$$H_0 : x(n) = \sum_{\eta=1}^{M} \sum_{k=1}^{P} c_{\eta,k} y_\eta \left[n - n_{\eta,k}^{(c)} \right] e^{jn\Omega_{\eta,k}^{(c)}}$$
$$+ \sum_{m=1}^{K} \beta_m^{(t)} y_m \left[n - n_m^{(t)} \right] e^{jn\Omega_m^{(t)}} + n_s[n],$$

(11)

$$H_1 : x(n) = \sum_{\eta=1}^{M} \alpha_\eta y_\eta [n - n_\eta] e^{jn\Omega_\eta}$$
$$+ \sum_{\eta=1}^{M} \sum_{k=1}^{P} c_{\eta,k} y_\eta \left[n - n_{\eta,k}^{(c)} \right] e^{jn\Omega_{\eta,k}^{(c)}}$$
$$+ \sum_{m=1}^{K} \beta_m^{(t)} y_m \left[n - n_m^{(t)} \right] e^{jn\Omega_m^{(t)}} + n_s[n],$$

(12)

where $n = 0, 1, \cdots, N - 1$, the first term is target echo, the second term is multipath and direct wave, the third term is interference echo, and the fourth term is Gaussian noise. M represents the number of satellites, P is the number of multipaths, $n_\eta, \Omega_\eta, \alpha_\eta$ are the time delay, Doppler shift, and amplitude of the echo signal respectively. When $k = 1$, $c_{\eta,k}$ is the amplitude of the direct wave. When $k = 2, 3, \cdots, P$, $\Omega_{\eta,k}^{(c)}, n_{\eta,k}^{(c)}, c_{\eta,k}$ are Doppler shift, time delay, amplitude of multipath signals respectively, K represents the number of interference targets, $\Omega_m^{(t)}, n_m^{(t)}, \beta_m^{(t)}$ respectively represent the Doppler shift, time delay, and amplitude of the echo signals of the interference target, n_s represents white Gaussian noise. To solve this detection problem, the assumptions are as following:

(1) When $m = 1, 2, \cdots, M$, the amplitude of the echo signals of the interference target $\beta_m^{(t)}$ is a certain unknown variable;
(2) The number of interference targets K is unknown, when $m = 1, 2, \cdots, K$, the time delay $n_m^{(t)}$ and Doppler shift $\Omega_m^{(t)}$ of each interference echo are known;

(3) When $\eta = 1, 2, \cdots, M$, $k = 2, \cdots, P$, the amplitude of the multipath signal $c_{\eta,k}$ is a certain unknown variable, and when $k = 1$, $c_{\eta,1}$ is the amplitude of the direct wave signal, which is a certain unknown variable;

(4) When $\eta = 1, 2, \cdots, M$, $k = 2, \cdots, P$, the time delay $n_{\eta,k}^{(c)}$ and the Doppler shift of the multipath signal are certain known variables;

(5) n_s represents Additive white Gaussian noise with unknown variance σ^2;

(6) The subsequent detection needs to construct the probability density function of the sampled signal $x = [x(0), x(2), \cdots x(N-1)]$ under two hypotheses.

According to formulas (11) and (12), the probability density function of $x[n]$ under the assumption H_0 can be given by

$$
\begin{aligned}
&p\left(x; \alpha_\eta, \sigma_2, c_{\eta,k}, \beta_m^{(t)}, H_0\right) \\
&= \frac{1}{(\pi\sigma^2)^N} \exp[-\frac{1}{\sigma^2} \sum_{n=0}^{N-1} |x[n] - \sum_{\eta=1}^{M} \sum_{k=1}^{P} c_{\eta,k} y_\eta \\
&\left[n - n_{\eta,k}^{(c)}\right] e^{jn\Omega_{\eta,k}^{(c)}} - \sum_{m=1}^{K} \beta_m^{(t)} y_m \left[n - n_m^{(t)}\right] e^{jn\Omega_m^{(t)}} |^2].
\end{aligned}
\tag{13}
$$

The probability density function of $x[n]$ under the assumption H_1 is

$$
\begin{aligned}
&p\left(x; \alpha_\eta, \sigma_2, c_{\eta,k}, \beta_m^{(t)}, H_1\right) \\
&= \frac{1}{(\pi\sigma^2)^N} \exp[-\frac{1}{\sigma^2} \sum_{n=0}^{N-1} |x[n] - \sum_{\eta=1}^{M} \alpha_\eta y_\eta [n - n_\eta] e^{jn\Omega_\eta} \\
&- \sum_{\eta=1}^{M} \sum_{k=1}^{P} c_{\eta,k} y_\eta \left[n - n_{\eta,k}^{(c)}\right] e^{jn\Omega_{\eta,k}^{(c)}} \\
&- \sum_{m=1}^{K} \beta_m^{(t)} y_m \left[n - n_m^{(t)}\right] e^{jn\Omega_m^{(t)}} |^2].
\end{aligned}
\tag{14}
$$

According to the Newman Pearson criterion, the optimal detection method for the hypothesis testing problems (11) and (12) is the likelihood ratio test, because the likelihood ratio test requires knowing the parameters, $\alpha = [\alpha_1, \alpha_2, \cdots, \alpha_M]^T$, $\hat{c} = \begin{bmatrix} \hat{c}_{1,1} & \cdots & \hat{c}_{M,1} \\ \vdots & \ddots & \vdots \\ \hat{c}_{1,P} & \cdots & \hat{c}_{M,P} \end{bmatrix}$, σ^2, $\beta = \left[\beta_1^{(t)}, \beta_2^{(t)}, \cdots, \beta_K^{(t)}\right]^T$, in actual situations, all parameters are unknown. One possible way to avoid this problem is to use GLRT, which is equivalent to replacing these unknown parameters with the maximum likelihood estimation of these parameters in the likelihood ratio test. In the following, the GLRT-based detector is derived in three cases: the noise variance σ^2 is known and there is no interference target, that is $K = 0$; the noise variance σ^2 is unknown and there is no interference target, that is $K = 0$; the noise variance σ^2 is unknown and there are interference targets, that is $K \neq 0$.

This part contains the derivation of GLRT when the noise variance σ^2 is known and there is no interference target. GLRT can be obtained by replacing the maximum likelihood estimation of unknown parameters under each assumption. GLRT can be written as

$$L_{GLR}(x) = \frac{\max_{\alpha,c} f(x; \alpha, c, H_1)}{\max_{\alpha,c} f(x; \alpha, c, H_0)} \overset{H_1}{\underset{H_0}{\gtrless}} \xi. \tag{15}$$

The selected threshold ξ should be determined according to the false alarm probability. In order to construct GLRT, first use MLE to estimate the unknown

parameter, the parameters $\hat{c}_1 = \begin{bmatrix} \hat{c}_{1,11} & \cdots & \hat{c}_{M,11} \\ \vdots & \ddots & \vdots \\ \hat{c}_{1,P1} & \cdots & \hat{c}_{M,P1} \end{bmatrix}$, $\alpha = [\alpha_1, \alpha_2, \cdots, \alpha_M]^T$ under

the assumption H_1 can be obtained by differentiating the unknown parameters $\hat{c}_1$ and α in Eq. (14) and setting the derivative equal to zero. That is to say, under the assumption H_1, $f(x; H_1)$ finds the partial derivative of α_η and $c_{\eta,k}$ respectively, then we can get

$$\sum_{n=0}^{N-1} x[n] y_r^*[n - n_r] e^{-jn\Omega_r}$$
$$= \sum_{\eta=1}^{M} \hat{\alpha}_\eta \sum_{n=0}^{N-1} y_\eta[n - n_\eta] y_r^*[n - n_r] e^{-jn(\Omega_r - \Omega_\eta)} \tag{16}$$
$$+ \sum_{\eta=1}^{M} \sum_{k=1}^{P} \hat{c}_{\eta,k1} \sum_{n=0}^{N-1} y_\eta\left[n - n_{\eta,k}^{(c)}\right] y_r^*[n - n_r] e^{-jn\left(\Omega_r - \Omega_{\eta,k}^{(c)}\right)},$$

$$\sum_{n=0}^{N-1} x[n] y_q^*\left[n - n_{q,s}^{(c)}\right] e^{-jn\Omega_{q,s}^{(c)}}$$
$$= \sum_{\eta=1}^{M} \hat{\alpha}_\eta \sum_{n=0}^{N-1} y_\eta[n - n_\eta] y_q^*\left[n - n_{q,s}^{(c)}\right] e^{-jn\left(\Omega_{q,s}^{(c)} - \Omega_\eta\right)} \tag{17}$$
$$+ \sum_{\eta=1}^{M} \sum_{k=1}^{P} \hat{c}_{\eta,k1} \sum_{n=0}^{N-1} y_\eta\left[n - n_{\eta,k}^{(c)}\right] y_q^*\left[n - n_{q,s}^{(c)}\right] e^{-jn\left(\Omega_{q,s}^{(c)} - \Omega_{\eta,k}^{(c)}\right)},$$

where $q, r = 1, 2, \cdots, M$, $s = 1, 2, \cdots, P$, the insertion symbol represents the estimated value of the unknown parameter, and the third parameter in $\hat{c}_{\eta,k1}$ represents the hypothesis H_1. In the same way, the unknown parameter $\hat{c}_0 = \begin{bmatrix} \hat{c}_{1,10} & \cdots & \hat{c}_{M,10} \\ \vdots & \ddots & \vdots \\ \hat{c}_{1,P0} & \cdots & \hat{c}_{M,P0} \end{bmatrix}$ under the assumption H_0 can be obtained by differentiating

the unknown parameter $\hat{c}_0$ in Eq. (13) and setting the derivative equal to zero. That is, under the assumption H_0, $f(x; H_0)$ finds the partial derivative of $c_{\eta,k}$ respectively, then we can get

$$\sum_{n=0}^{N-1} x[n] y_q^* \left[n - n_{q,s}^{(c)}\right] e^{-jn\Omega_{q,s}^{(c)}}$$

$$= \sum_{\eta=1}^{M} \sum_{k=1}^{P} \hat{c}_{\eta,k0} \sum_{n=0}^{N-1} y_\eta \left[n - n_{\eta,k}^{(c)}\right] y_q^* \left[n - n_{q,s}^{(c)}\right] e^{-jn\left(\Omega_{q,s}^{(c)} - \Omega_{\eta,k}^{(c)}\right)}.$$

(18)

Write (16) and (17) in matrix form

$$\begin{bmatrix} R_c & r_{sc} \\ r_{sc}^H & r_{ss} \end{bmatrix} \begin{bmatrix} \hat{c}_1 \\ \hat{\alpha} \end{bmatrix} = \begin{bmatrix} r_{xc} \\ r_{xs} \end{bmatrix},$$

(19)

where $\hat{c}_1 = \begin{bmatrix} \hat{c}_{1,11} & \cdots & \hat{c}_{M,11} \\ \vdots & \ddots & \vdots \\ \hat{c}_{1,P1} & \cdots & \hat{c}_{M,P1} \end{bmatrix}$, $\hat{\alpha} = \begin{bmatrix} \hat{\alpha}_1 \cdots \hat{\alpha}_M \end{bmatrix}^T$. $\hat{c}_1$ represents the amplitude of

the direct wave and multipath signal of each satellite under the assumption H_1, $\hat{c}_{M,P1}$ is the Pth multipath amplitude of the M-th satellite signal under the assumption H_0, and $p = 0$ represents the amplitude of the direct wave corresponding to the satellite. $\hat{\alpha}$ shows the amplitude of the echo signal of each satellite, α_M is the amplitude of the echo signal of the M-th satellite signal.

Under the assumption H_0, write (18) in matrix form

$$R_c \hat{c}_0 = r_{xc}.$$

(20)

In (20), $\hat{c}_0$ represents the maximum likelihood estimation of C under the hypothesis H_0, R_c represents the correlation of multipath signals, R_c is the matrix of $P * P$, and $[R_c]_{sk}$ is the element of R_c which can be expressed as

$$[R_c]_{sk} = \sum_{\eta=1}^{M} \sum_{q=1}^{M} \sum_{n=0}^{N-1} y_\eta \left[n - n_{\eta,k}^{(c)}\right] y_q^* \left[n - n_{q,s}^{(c)}\right] e^{-jn\left(\Omega_{q,s}^{(c)} - \Omega_{\eta,k}^{(c)}\right)},$$

(21)

where r_{ss} represents the auto-correlation between echoes, $[r_{ss}]$ is a matrix of $M * M$, $[r_{ss}]_{r\eta}$ represents the elements of r_{ss}, expressed as

$$[r_{ss}]_{r\eta} = \sum_{n=0}^{N-1} y_\eta \left[n - n_\eta\right] y_r^* \left[n - n_r\right] e^{-jn(\Omega_r - \Omega_\eta)},$$

(22)

where r_{sc} represents the correlation between multipath and echo, $[r_{sc}]$ is a matrix of $M * M$, $[r_{sc}]_{q\eta}$ represents the elements of r_{sc}, expressed as

$$[r_{sc}]_{q\eta} = \sum_{s=1}^{P} \sum_{n=0}^{N-1} y_\eta \left[n - n_\eta\right] y_q^* \left[n - n_{q,s}^{(c)}\right] e^{-jn\left(\Omega_{q,s}^{(c)} - \Omega_\eta\right)},$$

(23)

where r_{xc} indicates the correlation between the received signal, the direct wave and multipath signal at $\left(n_r^{(c)}, \Omega_r^{(c)}\right)$ in the monitoring channel. $[r_{sc}]$ is a matrix of $P * M$, which represents the elements of $[r_{xc}]_{qs}$, expressed as

$$[r_{xc}]_{qs} = \sum_{n=0}^{N-1} x[n] y_q^* \left[n - n_{q,s}^{(c)}\right] e^{-jn\Omega_{q,s}^{(c)}}, \tag{24}$$

where r_{xs} represents the cross-correlation of each target echo signal of the signal received by the monitoring channel at (n_r, Ω_r), $[r_{xs}]$ is the vector of $M * 1$, and $[r_{xs}]_r$ is the elements of r_{xs}, expressed as

$$[r_{xs}]_r = \sum_{n=0}^{N-1} x[n] y_r^* [n - n_r] e^{-jn\Omega_r}. \tag{25}$$

In order to obtain the maximum likelihood estimation of unknown parameters from (19), the inverse matrices of matrices $R_c, r_{sc}, r_{ss}, r_{xc}$ exist, and they are all positive semi-definite matrices, first calculate their inverse matrices, and then, unknown parameters under each assumption can be calculated

$$\begin{bmatrix} \hat{c}_1 \\ \hat{\alpha} \end{bmatrix} = \begin{bmatrix} R_c & r_{sc} \\ r_{sc}^H & r_{ss} \end{bmatrix}^{-1} \begin{bmatrix} r_{xc} \\ r_{xs} \end{bmatrix}, \tag{26}$$

$$\hat{c}_0 = R_c^{-1} r_{xc}. \tag{27}$$

In (26), we use the principle of inversion of the segmentation matrix, the maximum likelihood estimation of the unknown parameters under hypothesis H_1 is

$$\begin{bmatrix} R_c & r_{sc} \\ r_{sc}^H & r_{ss} \end{bmatrix}^{-1} = \begin{bmatrix} R_c^{-1} + R_c^{-1} r_{sc} g r_{sc}^H R_c^{-1} & -R_c^{-1} r_{sc} g \\ -g r_{sc}^H R_c^{-1} & g \end{bmatrix}, \tag{28}$$

where $g = \left(r_{ss} - r_{sc}^H R_c^{-1} r_{sc}\right)^{-1}$. From (27) and (28), we can get

$$\begin{bmatrix} \hat{c}_1 \\ \hat{\alpha} \end{bmatrix} = \begin{bmatrix} \hat{c}_0 + g R_c^{-1} r_{sc} r_{sc}^H \hat{c}_0 - g r_{xs} R_c^{-1} r_{sc} \\ -g r_{sc}^H \hat{c}_0 + g r_{xs}. \end{bmatrix}. \tag{29}$$

Substitute the maximum likelihood estimates of the unknown parameters under the two assumptions into the two probability density functions (13) and (14), construct the likelihood ratio, take the logarithm, and obtain the detection statistics after simplification

$$\ln L_{GLR} = \frac{r_{xc}^H \left(\hat{c}_1 - \hat{c}_0\right) + c_1^H \left(r_{xc} - R_c \hat{c}_1\right) + r_{ss} \hat{\alpha}}{\sigma^2} \underset{H_0}{\overset{H_1}{\gtrless}} \xi. \tag{30}$$

For (30), use (27) and (29) to further simplify, then we can get

$$
\frac{1}{\sigma^2} \frac{\left| r_{xs} - r_{sc}^H \hat{c}_0 \right|}{r_{ss} - r_{sc}^H R_c^{-1} r_{sc}} \underset{H_0}{\overset{H_1}{\gtrless}} \xi.
\tag{31}
$$

In order to obtain a more intuitive representation of the detection statistics, the detection statistics can be expressed as

$$
\frac{1}{\sigma^2} \frac{\sum_{q=1}^{M} \left| \sum_{n=0}^{N-1} \left(x[n] - \sum_{\eta=1}^{M} \sum_{k=1}^{P} \left[\hat{c}_0(:,\eta) \right]_k y\left[n - n_{\eta,k}^{(c)} \right] e^{-jn\Omega_k^{(c)}} \right) y_q^*[n - n_q] e^{-jn\Omega_q} \right|^2}{\left| r_{ss} - r_{sc}^H R_c^{-1} r_{sc} \right|} \underset{H_0}{\overset{H_1}{\gtrless}} \xi.
\tag{32}
$$

It can be seen from (32) that the numerator of the detection statistics represents the two-dimensional cross-correlation between the pure monitoring channel signal and the echo signal at $[n_q, \Omega_q]$.

4   Simulation Results and Discussion

In order to verify the performance of the algorithm, matlab is used for simulation. This article uses GPS, DVB-S, and inmarsat satellite signal models. The noise is Gaussian white noise. The definition of SNR can be expressed as

$$
SNR = 10 \lg(P_s / P_N),
\tag{33}
$$

where P_S and P_N are the power of the satellite signal and Gaussian white noise respectively. The intensity ratio SDR of direct wave and echo is defined as

$$
SDR = \frac{P_s}{P_D},
\tag{34}
$$

where P_D represents the power of a single direct wave, and P_S represents the power of a single echo. The evaluation standard of the detection of algorithm is the detection accuracy rate, which can be expressed by the following formula

$$
\delta_H = \frac{N_R}{N} \times 100\%,
\tag{35}
$$

where N_R and N are the number of correct detection and the total number of simulations respectively.

The direct wave and multipath in the monitoring channel are suppressed by the ECA method, and three satellite signals, i.e., GPS, DVB-S, Inmarsat, are used for simulation experiments. The carrier frequencies of the three signals are $f_G = 1.57\,\text{GHz}$, $f_D = 12.38\,\text{GHz}$ and $f_i = 4.2\,\text{GHz}$. Suppose the three echo signals' time delays are $1\,\mu\text{s}$, $2\,\mu\text{s}$, $3\,\mu\text{s}$ respectively, and the Doppler frequency shifts are $100\,\text{Hz}$, $150\,\text{Hz}$, $200\,\text{Hz}$ respectively. The strengths of the three direct waves of signals are $-130.1\,\text{dBw}$, $-111.83\,\text{dBw}$, $-120.61\,\text{dBw}$ in order.

The difference between the direct wave power and its corresponding echo power is 40 dB. The distances of the aircraft are 10 km, 15 km, 20 km and the speeds are 300 km/h (83 m/s), 350 km/h (97 m/s), 800 km/h (220 m/s), respectively. The number of sampling points is 10^5. We utilize Matlab for simulation and carry out 2000 Monte Carlos experiments.

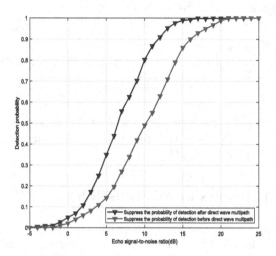

Fig. 1. Comparison of detection probability based on GLRT before and after direct wave and multipath are suppressed

To verify the influence of the direct wave and echo in the monitoring channel on the detection performance of GLRT, the simulation result is shown in Fig. 1. It can be seen from Fig. 1 that after suppressing the direct wave and multipath in the monitoring channel, the detection performance is improved. This is because when the direct wave and multipath are in the echo signal, the maximum likelihood estimation is used to estimate the amplitude of the direct wave and multipath. Although the maximum likelihood estimation is the best parameter estimation method, there will inevitably be errors. The existence of the direct wave and multipath itself is a substantial interference to the echo signal, so it will cause the echo signal's detection performance to decrease. After the direct wave and multipath of the monitoring channel are suppressed by the suppression method of the direct wave and multipath, the algorithm's performance will be improved to a certain extent.

To verify the influence of the number of satellite signals on the detection performance of GLRT, we compare the detection performance, using GPS, GPS+DVB-S, GPS+DVB-S +inmarsat satellite signals. It can be seen from Fig. 2 that under the same signal-to-noise ratio, as the number of satellite signals increases, the detection performance gradually decreases. This is because increasing the number of signals raises the direct ratio and multipath interference in the monitoring channel. As the multipath interference increases, mul-

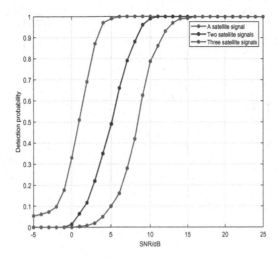

Fig. 2. Comparison of detection probability based on GLRT with different number of satelites

tiple echo signals affect each other, which affects the detection performance of echo signals. However, the joint detection of echo signals by multiple satellites will improve the detection results' reliability. This sacrifices a certain detection probability but improves detection reliability, which is of great significance in practical applications.

We evaluate the impacts of the distance between the target and the receiver and the speed of the target on the detection performance of GLRT. We conduct simulation experiments with three satellite signals, i.e., GPS, DVB-S, and Inmarsat, at different distances and speeds, and the simulation result is shown in Fig. 3. It can be seen from Fig. 3 that as the target speed increases, the detection performance of the echo signal gradually decreases. This is because when the target speed is different, the Doppler frequency shifts of the corresponding echo signals are becoming various. If the target's speed increases, one will affect the receiver's correct reception of the signal. The other will increase the corresponding Doppler shift, which will change the echo signal's detection. This indicates that the proposed method is suitable for detecting low-speed and low-altitude flying targets.

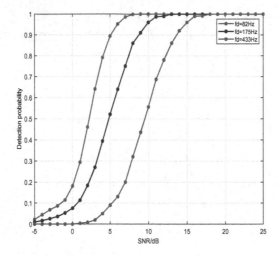

Fig. 3. Comparison of detection probability based on GLRT at different speeds

5   Conclusion

This paper developed a passive target detection method using multi-satellite illumination based on the generalized likelihood ratio. We derived the detector based on the generalized likelihood ratio. Furthermore, we established the adaptive detection threshold on this basis to complete the detection of the echo signal. Finally, various aspects that may affect the detection algorithm's performance were simulated respectively. The results indicate that the detection algorithm can be used to detect target using multi-satellite illumination.

References

1. Foged, L.J., Saporetti, M., Scialacqua, L.: Measurement and simulation comparison using measured source antenna representation of GNSS antenna on sentinel satellite. In: Proceedings of the 2017 IEEE International Symposium on Antennas and Propagation USNC/URSI National Radio Science Meeting, San Diego, CA, USA, 9–15 July 2017, pp. 1933–1934 (2017)
2. Powell, S.J., Akos, D.M.: GNSS reflectometry using the L5 and E5a signals for remote sensing applications. In: Proceedings of the 2013 US National Committee of URSI National Radio Science Meeting, Boulder, CO, USA, 9–12 January 2013, p. 1 (2013)
3. AlJewari, Y., Ahmad, R., AlRawi, A.: Impact of multipath interference and change of velocity on the reliability and precision of GPS. In: Proceedings of the 2014 2nd International Conference on Electronic Design, Penang, Malaysia, 19–21 August 2014, pp. 427–430 (2014)

4. Fernez-Prades, C., Arribas, J., Majoral, M., Ramos, A., Vil-Valls, J., Giordano, P.: A software-defined spaceborne GNSS receiver. In: Proceedings of the 2018 9th ESA Workshop on Satellite Navigation Technologies and European Workshop on GNSS Signals and Signal Processing, Noordwijk, The Netherlands, 5–7 December 2018, pp. 1–9 (2018)
5. Michael, E., Alexander, S., Fabienne, M.: Design and performance evaluation of a mature FM/DAB/DVB-T multi-illuminator passive radar system. IET Radar Sonar Navig. **8**, 114–122 (2014)
6. Liu, M., et al.: 2D DOA robust estimation of echo signals based on multiple satellites passive radar in the presence of alpha stable distribution noise. IEEE Access **7**, 2169–3536 (2019)
7. Gronowski, K., Samczynski, P., Stasiak, K., Kulpa, K.: First, results of air target detection using single channel passive radar utilizing GPS illumination. In: Proceedings of the 2019 IEEE Radar Conference, Boston, MA, USA, 22–26 April 2019, pp. 1–6 (2019)
8. Yan, X., Wang, S., Wang, K., Jiang, H.: Localization of near field cyclostationary source based on fourth-order cyclic cumulant. In: Proceedings of the 2008 9th International Conference on Signal Processing, Beijing, China, 26–29 October 2008, pp. 1629–1632 (2008)
9. Jun, H.: A proper integral representation of Marcum Q-Function. In: Proceedings of the 2014 XXXIth URSI General Assembly and Scientific Symposium, Beijing, China, 16–23 August 2014, pp. 1–3 (2014)
10. Liu, M., Zhang, J., Li, B.: Feasibility analysis of OFDM/OQAM signals as illuminator of opportunity for passive detection. In: Proceedings of the 2018 14th IEEE International Conference on Signal Processing, Beijing, China, 12–16 August 2018, pp. 1–4 (2018)
11. Wu, X., Gong, P., Zhou, J., Liu, Z.: The applied research on anti-multipath interference GPS signal based on narrow-related. In: Proceedings of the 2014 IEEE 5th International Conference on Software Engineering and Service Science, Beijing, China, 27–29 June 2014, pp. 771–774 (2014)
12. Niranjan, D., Ashwini, B.: Noise cancellation in musical signals using adaptive filtering algorithms. In: Proceedings of the 2017 International Conference on Innovative Mechanisms for Industry Applications, Bangalore, India, 21–23 February 2017, pp. 82–86 (2017)

Passive Target Detection Based on Rao Using Multi-satellite Illumination

Huijie Zhu[1], Mingqian Liu[2($\boxtimes$)], Ming Li[3], and Xiuhui Gao[2]

[1] Science and Technology on Communication Information Security Control Laboratory, The 36th Research Institute of China Electronics Technology Group Corporation, Jiaxing 314033, China
zhuhuijie@zju.edu.cn

[2] State Key Laboratory of Integrated Service Networks, Xidian University, Xi'an 710071, Shaanxi, China
mqliu@mail.xidian.edu.cn

[3] State 722 Factory, Guilin 541001, Guangxi, China

Abstract. In this paper, hypotheses of target detection features is proposed when constructing the signal model. Under this condition, the Rao detection method is extended to weak echo signal detection using multi-satellite illumination. Furthermore, a multi-satellite weak echo signal detection algorithm is proposed based on Rao detection. When the noise variance is unknown, the Rao detector is designed according to the existence of an interfering target. Moreover, the detector' detection thresholds are obtained given the false alarm probability, respectively. Finally, we evaluate the Rao detection performance in different situations with extensive simulations.

Keywords: Multi-satellite illumination · Passive detection · Rao detection · Target detection

1 Introduction

Target detection is significant in the ground dual receiver system. The system is divided into a reference channel and a monitoring channel. The reference channel receives the direct wave signals from multiple external emitters, while the monitoring channel receives the echo signals reflected by the target. The traditional passive detection method is susceptible to the noise in the reference channel based on the reference channel's direct wave signal and the monitoring channel's echo signal [4,5]. As such, the detection performance is easily affected by the noise of the reference channel [7–11]. At present, most of them assume that

This work was supported by the National Natural Science Foundation of China under Grant 62071364, in part by the Aeronautical Science Foundation of China under Grant 2020Z073081001, in part by the Fundamental Research Funds for the Central Universities under Grant JB210104, and in part by the 111 Project under Grant B08038.

the signal-to-noise ratio of the reference channel is high, and on this evidence, the echo signal is detected, which is inconsistent with the actual scene. The existing method of achieving weak echo detection is based on Rao detection. However, this detection method is in the single emitter scene modeling analysis.

To effectively detect the weak echo of multiple satellites, a multi-satellite joint target detection method based on the Rao detection method is proposed in this paper, which is not easily affected by the reference channel noise. Simulation results show that the detection method proposed in this paper is feasible and can detect weak echo signals.

2   System Model

In the actual receiving scene, the ground receiving system consists of two antennas. One is called the monitoring channel antenna, and the other is the reference channel antenna. The reference antenna is placed in the satellite direction, and the monitoring antenna is an antenna with a wide beam pointing to the monitoring area. When the satellite emitter radiates signals, we expect to receive a direct wave signal and an echo signal reflected by the target. The time delay of the echo signal is τ, and the Doppler frequency shift is f_d. In this process, some clutter will inevitably be received. If there are multiple satellites as external radiation sources, the signal received by the monitoring channel is represented by $x(t)$, which can be expressed as

$$
\begin{aligned}
x(t) = &\sum_{\eta=1}^{M} a_\eta s_\eta \left(t - \tau_\eta\right) e^{j2\pi f_{d\eta}t} \\
&+ \sum_{\eta=1}^{M} \phi_{\eta,0} s_\eta(t) + \sum_{\eta=1}^{M}\sum_{k=1}^{N_c} \phi_{\eta,k}(t) s_\eta \left(t - \tau_{\eta,k}^{(c)}\right) \\
&+ \sum_{m=1}^{K} \gamma_m^{(t)} s_m \left(t - \tau_m^{(t)}\right) e^{j2\pi f_{dm}^{(t)}t} + n_s(t),
\end{aligned}
\tag{1}
$$

where M is the number of satellite radiation sources; $f_{d\eta}$, τ_η and a_η are Doppler frequency shift, delay and amplitude of target echo respectively; $n_s(t)$ is Gaussian white noise; K is the number of jamming targets; $\beta_m^{(t)}$, $\tau_m^{(t)}$, $f_{dm}^{(t)}$ are amplitude, delay and Doppler frequency shift of the target echo; $\tau_{\eta,k}^{(c)}$ and $\phi_{\eta,k}(t)$ are the delay and amplitude of multipath signal respectively; T is the observation time; N_c is the number of multipath of a single satellite signal; the amplitude $\phi_{\eta,k}(t)$ of multipath is a random process with special power spectral density [1]. In the signal modelr, we assume that the amplitude of multipath signal has special power spectral density, which can be expressed by multiple frequencies $f_i^{(c)}$. We can obtain the following results

$$
\phi_{\eta,k}(t) = \sum_{i=-Q}^{Q} \phi_{\eta,k,i} e^{j2\pi f_i^{(c)}t},
\tag{2}
$$

where $f_i^{(c)} = (i-1-Q)\Delta f_c i = 1, 2, \cdots, 2Q+1$, and Q and Δf are two suitable parameters selected according to the actual scene. In this case, $\phi_{\eta,k,i}$ is the amplitude of the multipath signal at frequency $f_i^{(c)}$ and time delay $\tau_{\eta,k}^{(c)}$ at $K = 1, 2, \cdots, N_c$.

The reference channel's signal may also be affected by multipath and target echo in the actual scene. Therefore, it will affect the performance of subsequent target detection. Therefore, before detecting the target in the monitoring channel, it is necessary to use some signal processing algorithms such as beamforming or channel equalization to suppress multipath and echo signals in the reference channel. The space-time constant modulus algorithm [2] can recover the degradation of detection performance caused by the presence of echo and multipath signals in the reference channel. Therefore, after a proper signal processing algorithm and band-pass filter separation, the signal in the reference channel can be expressed as

$$y_\eta(t) = b_\eta s_\eta(t) + n_\eta(t) \quad 0 \le t < T \quad \eta = 1, 2, \cdots, M, \tag{3}$$

where b_η is the amplitude of the direct wave signal received by the reference antenna; $n_\eta(t)$ is the sum of the noise of the reference channel receiver and the interference signal after signal processing.

The signals $x(t)$ and $y_\eta(t)$ are sampled at time $t_n = nT_s, n = 1, 2, \cdots, N$. At the n-th sampling interval, the sampling signals of the received signals in the monitoring channel and the reference channel are represented as $x(t)$ and $y_\eta(t)$, respectively, as follows

$$x[n] = \sum_{\eta=1}^{M} a_\eta s_\eta [n - n_\eta] e^{j2\pi\Omega_n} + \sum_{\eta=1}^{M} \phi_{\eta,0} s_\eta[n]$$

$$+ \sum_{\eta=1}^{M} \sum_{k=1}^{N_c} \sum_{i=-Q}^{Q} \phi_{\eta,k,i} s_\eta \left[n - n_{\eta,k}^{(c)}\right] e^{j2\pi\Omega_m^{(t)}} \tag{4}$$

$$+ \sum_{m=1}^{K} \gamma_m^{(t)} s_\eta \left[n - n_m^{(t)}\right] e^{j2\pi\Omega_m^{(t)}} + n_s[n],$$

$$y_\eta(n) = b_\eta s_\eta(n) + n_\eta(n) \quad n = 1, 2, \cdots, N \tag{5}$$

where $\Omega_\eta = 2\pi f_{d\eta} T_s$ and $\Omega_m^{(t)} = 2\pi f_{dm}^{(t)} T_s$ represent the normalized Doppler frequency of target echo and jamming target echo respectively. And $\tau_\eta = n_\eta T_s$, $\tau_m^{(t)} = n_m^{(t)} T_s$, $\tau_{\eta,k}^{(c)} = n_{\eta,k}^{(c)} T_s$, where n_η, $n_m^{(t)}$ and $n_{\eta,k}^{(c)}$ represent the echo signal of received signal in the monitoring channel, jamming target echo and multipath delay respectively. Substituting Eq. (5) into Eq. (4), we can get the following results

$$x(n) = \sum_{\eta=1}^{M} \sum_{k=1}^{N_c} \sum_{i=-Q}^{Q} \frac{\phi_{\eta,k,i}}{b_\eta} y_\eta \left[n - n_{\eta,k}^{(c)} \right] e^{j2\pi f_i^{(c)} T_s n}$$

$$+ \sum_{\eta=1}^{M} \frac{a_\eta}{b_\eta} y_\eta \left[n - n_\eta \right] e^{jn\Omega_\eta} + \sum_{\eta=1}^{M} \frac{a_\eta}{b_\eta} n_\eta \left[n - n_\eta \right] e^{jn\Omega_\eta}$$

$$+ \sum_{m=1}^{K} \frac{\gamma_m^{(t)}}{b_\eta} y_m \left[n - n_m^{(t)} \right] e^{jn\Omega_m^{(t)}} + \sum_{\eta=1}^{M} \frac{\phi_{\eta,0}}{b_\eta} y_\eta[n] \tag{6}$$

$$+ \sum_{\eta=1}^{M} \sum_{k=1}^{N_c} \sum_{i=-Q}^{Q} \frac{\phi_{\eta,k,i}}{b_\eta} y_\eta \left[n - n_{\eta,k}^{(c)} \right] e^{j2\pi f_i^{(c)} T_s n} + n_s(n)$$

$$+ \sum_{m=1}^{K} \frac{\gamma_m^{(t)}}{b_\eta} n_m \left[n - n_m^{(t)} \right] e^{jn\Omega_m^{(t)}} + \sum_{\eta=1}^{M} \frac{\phi_{\eta,0}}{b_\eta} n_\eta[n].$$

By integrating the last four noise terms in Eq. (6) into $n_s[n]$, the above equation can be rewritten as follows

$$x(n) = \sum_{\eta=1}^{M} \alpha_\eta y_\eta \left[n - n_\eta \right] e^{jn\Omega_\eta} + \sum_{\eta=1}^{M} c_{\eta,0} y_\eta[n]$$

$$+ \sum_{\eta=1}^{M} \sum_{k=1}^{N_c} \sum_{i=-Q}^{Q} c_{\eta,k,i} y_\eta \left[n - n_{\eta,k}^{(c)} \right] e^{j2\pi t_i^{(c)} T_s n} \tag{7}$$

$$+ \sum_{m=1}^{K} \beta_m^{(t)} y_m \left[n - n_m^{(t)} \right] e^{jn\Omega_m^{(t)}} + n_s[n],$$

where $\alpha_\eta = \Delta a_\eta / b_\eta$, $c_{\eta,0} = \Delta \phi_{\eta,0} / b_\eta$, $c_{\eta,k,i} = \Delta \phi_{\eta,k,i} / b_\eta$, $\beta_m^{(t)} = \Delta \gamma_m^{(t)} / b_\eta$. By constructing the matrix Λ and matrix Γ as follows

$$[\Lambda^{(c)}]_{kj} = 2\pi f_k^{(c)} T_s, \tag{8}$$

$$[\Gamma^{(c)}]_{kj} = n_j, \tag{9}$$

where $k = 1, 2, \cdots, 2Q + 1; j = 1, 2, \cdots, N_c$.

By defining vectors $\Omega \triangleq [0, vec(\Lambda)]^T$ and $n \triangleq [0, vec(D)]^T$, Eq. (6) can be reexpressed as follows

$$x[n] = \sum_{\eta=1}^{M} a_\eta y_\eta \left[n - n_\eta \right] e^{j2\pi \Omega_\eta} + \sum_{\eta=1}^{M} \phi_{\eta,0} y_\eta[n]$$

$$+ \sum_{\eta=1}^{M} \sum_{k=1}^{N_c} c_{\eta,k} y_\eta \left[n - n_{\eta,k}^{(c)} \right] e^{jn\Omega_{n,k}^{(c)}} + n_s[n] \tag{10}$$

$$+ \sum_{m=1}^{K} \beta_m^{(t)} y_m \left[n - n_m^{(t)} \right] e^{j2\pi \Omega_m^{(t)}},$$

where $n = 1, 2, \cdots, N$; $P = (2Q + 1)N_c + 1$; $\Omega_{\eta,k}^{(c)}$ and $n_{\eta,k}^{(c)}$ are the k-th elements of $\Omega^{(c)}$ and $n^{(c)}$, respectively. As shown in the above formula, $\Omega_{\eta,k}^{(c)}$ and $n_{\eta,k}^{(c)}$ at $k = 2, 3, \cdots, P$ correspond to the Doppler frequency shift and time delay of multipath signal in the monitoring channel; c_1 at $k = 1$ corresponds to the amplitude of direct wave signal.

3   Multi Satellite Weak Echo Signal Detection Based on Rao Detection

The general problem of target detection is to detect the target when there are jamming target echo, direct wave and multipath with unknown amplitude a. The problem can be described by the following assumptions

$$
\begin{aligned}
H_0 : x(n) = &\sum_{\eta=1}^{M} \sum_{k=1}^{P} c_{\eta,k} y_\eta [n - n_{\eta,k}^{(c)}] e^{jn\Omega_{\eta,k}^{(c)}} \\
&+ \sum_{m=1}^{K} \beta_m^{(t)} y_m [n - n_m^{(t)}] e^{jn\Omega_m^{(t)}} + n_s[n],
\end{aligned}
\tag{11}
$$

$$
\begin{aligned}
H_1 : x(n) = &\sum_{\eta=1}^{M} \alpha_\eta y_\eta [n - n_\eta]^{jn\Omega_\eta} \\
&+ \sum_{\eta=1}^{M} \sum_{k=1}^{P} c_{\eta,k} y_\eta \left[n - n_{\eta,k}^{(c)}\right] e^{jn\Omega_{\eta,k}^{(c)}} \\
&+ \sum_{m=1}^{K} \beta_m^{(t)} y_m \left[n - n_m^{(t)}\right]^{jn\Omega_m^{(t)}} + n_s[n],
\end{aligned}
\tag{12}
$$

where $n = 0, 1, \cdots, N - 1$; the first item is target echo; the second item is multipath and direct wave; the third item is jamming echo; the fourth item is Gaussian noise; M is the number of satellites; P is the number of multipath paths; n_η, Ω_η, α_η are the delay, Doppler frequency shift and amplitude of echo signal; when $k = 1$, $c_{\eta,k}$ is the amplitude of direct wave; when $K = 2, 3, \cdots, P$, $\Omega_{\eta,k}^{(c)}$, $n_{\eta,k}^{(c)}$, $c_{\eta,k}$ are Doppler frequency shift, delay and amplitude of multipath signal; K is the number of jamming targets; $\Omega_m^{(t)}$, $n_m^{(t)}$, $\beta_m^{(t)}$ are Doppler frequency shift, delay and amplitude of jamming target echo signal; n_s is Gaussian white noise. To solve this problem, the following assumptions are made:

(1) When $m = 1, 2, \cdots, M$, the amplitude $\beta_m^{(t)}$ of jamming target echo signal is a certain unknown variable;

(2) The number of jamming targets K is unknown. When $m = 1, 2, \cdots, K$, the time delay $n_m^{(t)}$ and Doppler frequency shift $\Omega_m^{(t)}$ of each jamming echo are known;

(3) When $\eta = 1, 2, \cdots, M$ and $k = 2, \cdots, P$, the amplitude $c_{\eta,k}$ of multipath signal is an unknown variable. When $k = 1$, $c_{\eta,1}$ is the amplitude of the direct wave signal and is a certain unknown variable;

(4) When $\eta = 1, 2, \cdots, M$ and $k = 2, \cdots, P$, the delay $n_{\eta,k}^{(c)}$ and Doppler frequency shift $\Omega_{\eta,k}^{(c)}$ of multipath signal are known variables;

(5) n_s is additive white Gaussian noise with unknown variance σ^2;

(6) The subsequent detection needs to construct the probability density function of sampling signal $x = [x(0), x(1), \cdots, x(N-1)]$ under two assumptions.

Rao detection can be regarded as an approximate generalized likelihood ratio detection. Thus the two have comparable detection performance. Since Rao detection only needs to estimate unknown parameters under the hypothesis H_0 instead of estimating target signal parameters, the calculation amount and complexity can be effectively reduced. Therefore, Rao detection is relatively easy to implement and has good weak signal detection performance. The unknown parameters of the hypothesis H_0 can be estimated by the maximum likelihood estimation method. In the following, a detector based on Rao detection is deduced in two cases: the variance σ^2 of noise is unknown and there is no jamming target, i.e. $K = 0$; the variance σ^2 of noise is unknown and there are jamming targets, i.e. $K \neq 0$.

This part contains the derivation of Rao detection when the noise variance σ^2 is unknown, but there is no jamming target. Rao detection only needs to estimate unknown parameters under the hypothesis H_0, and the unknown parameters can be estimated with maximum likelihood. Rao detection can be expressed as [3]

$$
T(x)
$$

$$
= \left. \frac{\partial \ln p\big(\mathbf{x}; \alpha_\eta, \sigma^2, c_{\eta,k}, H_1\big)}{\partial \alpha_\eta} \right|_{\substack{\alpha_\eta = 0, \sigma^2 = \hat{\sigma}_0^2 \\ c_{\eta,k} = \hat{c}_{\eta,k0}}} \Big[\mathbf{I}^{-1}(\tilde{\theta}) \Big]_{\alpha_\eta \alpha_\eta \alpha_\eta} \mathop{\gtrless}_{H_0}^{H_1} \lambda, \tag{13}
$$

where λ is the detection threshold; $[\mathbf{I}(\theta)]$ is the Fisher information matrix; the unknown parameters under the hypothesis H_0 are expressed as vector form, i.e. $\theta = [a_\eta, c_{\eta,k}, \sigma^2]$, and $\tilde{\theta}$ is the maximum likelihood estimation of θ under the hypothesis H_0. Under the hypothesis H_0, $a_\eta = 0$, then $\tilde{\theta} = \Big[0, \hat{c}_{\eta,k0}, \hat{\sigma}_0^2\Big]$; $\hat{c}_{\eta,k0}$ and $\hat{\sigma}_0^2$ are the maximum likelihood estimates of $c_{\eta,k}$ and σ^2 under the hypothesis H_0. The probability density function under the hypothesis H_0 differentiates the unknown parameters $c_{\eta,k}$ and σ^2. Then set these two derivative values equal to zero. The maximum likelihood estimation of these two unknown parameters can be solved, consistent with the estimated value of $GLRT$ under the same situation.

Under the hypothesis H_1, the probability density of $x(n)$ can be expressed as

$$p\left(\mathbf{x}; \alpha_\eta, \sigma^2, c_{\eta,k}, H_1\right)$$

$$= \frac{1}{(\pi\sigma^2)^N} \exp\left[\left(-\frac{1}{\sigma^2} \sum_{n=0}^{N-1} \left|x[n] - \sum_{\eta=1}^{M} \alpha_\eta y_\eta\left[n - n_\eta\right] e^{jn\Omega_\eta}\right.\right.\right. \tag{14}$$

$$\left.\left.\left. - \sum_{\eta=1}^{M}\sum_{k=1}^{P} c_{\eta,k} y_\eta\left[n - n_{\eta,k}^{(c)}\right] e^{jn\Omega_{n,k}^{(c)}}\right|^2\right)\right].$$

After taking the logarithm of Eq. (14), differentiate a_η. Then, the maximum likelihood estimation of α_η, $c_{\eta,\kappa}$, σ^2 under the hypothesis H_0 is substituted into the formula. We can get the following results

$$\left.\frac{\partial \ln p\left(\mathbf{x}; \alpha_\eta, \sigma^2, c_{\eta,\kappa}, H_1\right)}{\partial a_\eta}\right|_{\substack{\alpha_\eta=0, \sigma^2=\hat{\sigma}_0^2 \\ c_{\eta,k}=\hat{c}_{\eta,k}}}$$

$$= \left(-\frac{2}{\hat{\sigma}_0^2} \sum_{n=0}^{N-1} \left|x[n] - \sum_{\eta=1}^{M} \alpha_\eta y_\eta[n - n_\eta] e^{jn\Omega_\eta}\right.\right. \tag{15}$$

$$\left.\left. - \sum_{\eta=1}^{M}\sum_{k=1}^{P} c_{\eta,k} y_\eta[n - n_{\eta,k}^{(c)}] e^{jn\Omega_{n,k}^{(c)}}\right| y_\xi^*[n - n_\xi] e^{-jn\Omega_\xi}\right),$$

where $\xi = 1, 2, \cdots, M$; $c(:,:)$ is the maximum likelihood estimation of the amplitude of all satellite direct wave multipath signals; $c(:, \eta)$ is the element of column η of $c(:,:)$, that is, the amplitude of the η-th satellite signal in terms of multipath signal and direct wave.

After the Fisher information matrix is expressed, the elements of the matrix except diagonal are all zero elements, so the Fisher information matrix can be simplified as

$$\mathbf{I}(\theta) = \begin{bmatrix} E\left[\frac{\partial^2 \ln p\left(\mathbf{x}; \alpha_\eta, \sigma^2, c_{\eta,k}, H_1\right)}{\partial \alpha_\eta \alpha_\eta}\right] & 0 & 0 \\ 0 & E\left[\frac{\partial^2 \ln p\left(\mathbf{x}; \alpha_\eta, \sigma^2, c_{\eta,k}, H_1\right)}{\partial \sigma^2 \sigma^2}\right] & 0 \\ 0 & 0 & E\left[\frac{\partial^2 \ln p\left(\mathbf{x}; \alpha_\eta, \sigma^2, c_{\eta,k}, H_1\right)}{\partial c_{\eta,k} c_{\eta,k}}\right] \end{bmatrix}. \tag{16}$$

The definition of each variable is as follows

$$\frac{\partial^2 \ln p\left(\mathbf{x}; \alpha_\eta, \sigma^2, c_{\eta,k}, H_1\right)}{\partial a_\eta a_\eta}$$

$$= \sum_{\eta=1}^{M}\sum_{n=0}^{N-1} y_\eta[n - n_\eta] y_\xi^*[n - n_\xi] e^{-jn(\Omega_\xi - \Omega_\eta)}, \tag{17}$$

$$\frac{\partial^2 \ln p(\mathbf{x}; \alpha_\eta, \sigma^2, c_{\eta,k}, H_1)}{\partial \sigma^2 \sigma^2} = \frac{N}{\sigma^4}, \tag{18}$$

$$\frac{\partial^2 \ln p\left(\mathbf{x}; \alpha_\eta, \sigma^2, c_{\eta,k}, H_1\right)}{\partial c_{\eta,k} c_{\eta,k}}$$

$$= \sum_{\eta=1}^{M} \sum_{k=1}^{P} \sum_{n=0}^{N-1} y_\eta \left[n - n_{\eta,k}^{(c)}\right] y_q^* \left[n - n_{q,s}^{(c)}\right] e^{-jn\left(\Omega_{q,s}^{(c)} - \Omega_{\eta,k}^{(c)}\right)}. \tag{19}$$

The Fisher information matrix is

$$\left[\mathbf{I}^{-1}(\tilde{\theta})\right]_{\alpha_\eta \alpha_\eta \alpha_\eta} = \left[\mathbf{I}_{\alpha_\eta \alpha_\eta}(\tilde{\theta}) - \mathbf{I}_{\alpha_\eta \sigma^2}(\tilde{\theta}) \mathbf{I}_{\sigma^2 \sigma^2}^{-1}(\tilde{\theta}) \mathbf{I}_{\sigma^2 \alpha_\eta}(\tilde{\theta})\right.$$

$$\left. -\mathbf{I}_{\alpha_\eta c_{\eta,k}}(\tilde{\theta}) \mathbf{I}_{c_{\eta,k} c_{\eta,k}}^{-1}(\tilde{\theta}) \mathbf{I}_{c_{\eta,k} \alpha_\eta}(\tilde{\theta})\right]^{-1}. \tag{20}$$

Since $\mathbf{I}_{\alpha_\eta \sigma^2}(\tilde{\theta}) = \mathbf{I}_{\alpha_\eta c_{\eta,k}}(\tilde{\theta}) = 0$, it can be reduced to

$$\left[\mathbf{I}^{-1}(\tilde{\theta})\right]_{\alpha_\eta \alpha_\eta \alpha_\eta}$$

$$= \left[\mathbf{I}_{\alpha_\eta \alpha_\eta \alpha_\eta}^{-1}(\tilde{\theta})\right]$$

$$= \frac{1}{\sum_{\eta=1}^{M} \sum_{n=0}^{N-1} y_\eta \left[n - n_\eta\right] y_\xi^* \left[n - n_\eta\right] e^{-jn(\Omega_\xi - \Omega_\eta)}}. \tag{21}$$

By substituting the above formula into $T(x)$, the detection statistics of Rao detection can be obtained as follows

$$T(x) = \frac{\frac{1}{N}\left(\|x\|^2 - \hat{c}_0^H \mathbf{R}_{ss} \hat{c}_0\right)}{\sum_{\eta=1}^{M} \sum_{n=0}^{N-1} y_\eta \left[n - n_\eta\right] y_\xi^* \left[n - n_\eta\right] e^{-jn(\Omega_\xi - \Omega_\eta)}}. \tag{22}$$

4 Simulation Results and Discussion

In order to verify the influence of direct wave and multipath on the detection performance based on Rao. Three satellite signals, GPS, DVB-S, and INMARSAT, are used for the simulation experiment. The carrier frequencies of the three signals are $f_G = 1.57\,\text{GHz}$, $f_D = 12.38\,\text{GHz}$ and $f_i = 4.2\,\text{GHz}$; The following assumptions are made: the time delay of the three echo signals is $1\,\mu\text{s}$, $2\,\mu\text{s}$ and $3\,\mu\text{s}$; the Doppler frequency shift of the three echo signals is $100\,\text{Hz}$, $200\,\text{Hz}$ and $300\,\text{Hz}$; the direct wave intensity of the three signals is $-130.1\,\text{dBw}$, $-111.83\,\text{dBw}$ and $-120.6\,\text{dBw}$; the power difference between the direct wave and its corresponding echo is $40\,\text{dB}$; the sampling points are 10^5. The simulation results are shown in Fig. 1.

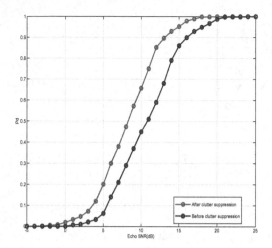

Fig. 1. Detection probability before and after suppressing direct wave and multipath

Figure 1 shows that the detection performance is improved by 4 dB after the direct wave and multipath are suppressed in the monitoring channel. This is because the amplitude of the direct wave and multipath must be estimated by maximum likelihood estimation when there are direct waves and multipath in the echo signal. Simultaneously, the existence of direct wave and multipath is a substantial interference to the target echo signal. The method of suppressing the direct wave and multipath can reduce their interference to the echo signal. However, the existence of the interference target echo still affects the detection of the echo signal.

In order to verify the influence of the number of satellite signals on the detection performance based on Rao. GPS, GPS + DVB-S, GPS + DVB-S + INMARSAT satellite signals are used for simulation experiments. The carrier frequencies of the three signals are $f_G = 1.57\,\text{GHz}$, $f_D = 12.38\,\text{GHz}$ and $f_i = 4.2\,\text{GHz}$; The following assumptions are made: the time delay of the three echo signals is $1\,\mu\text{s}$, $2\,\mu\text{s}$ and $3\,\mu\text{s}$; the Doppler frequency shift of the three echo signals is $100\,\text{Hz}$, $150\,\text{Hz}$ and $200\,\text{Hz}$; the direct wave intensity of the three signals is $-130.1\,\text{dBw}$, $-111.83\,\text{dBw}$ and $-120.6\,\text{dBw}$; the power difference between the direct wave and its corresponding echo is $40\,\text{dB}$; the sampling points are 10^5. The simulation results are shown in Fig. 2.

Figure 2 shows that the detection performance decreases with the increase of the number of signals at the same SNR. This is because with a rise in the number of satellite signals, the number of direct waves and multipath interference in the monitoring channel will also increase, which is equivalent to the increase of interference in the monitoring channel. In addition, multiple echo signals will affect each other, which will also affect the detection performance of echo signals. However, the joint detection of echoes by multiple satellites will improve the detection results' reliability, which is equivalent to improving the reliability of

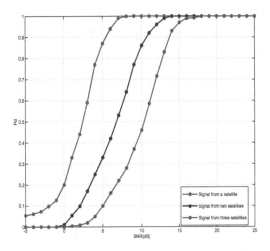

Fig. 2. Rao detection probability with different number of satellites

the detection results by reducing the detection performance, and it is of great significance in practical applications.

In order to verify the influence of the distance from the target to the receiver and the speed of the target on the RAO detection performance, three satellite signals, GPS, DVB-S, and INMARSAT, are used to simulate the performance of Rao detection. The following assumptions are made: the distances between the target and the receiver are 10 km, 15 km and 20 km, and the velocities are 300 km/h (83 m/s), 350 km/h (97 m/s) and 800 km/h (222 m/s) respectively; the carrier frequencies of the three signals are $f_G = 1.57$ GHz, $f_D = 12.38$ GHz and $f_i = 4.2$ GHz; the direct wave intensity of the three signals is -130.1 dBw, -111.83 dBw and -120.61 dBw; the power difference between the direct wave and its corresponding echo is 40 dB; the sampling points are 10^5. According to the relationship between time delay, distance, target velocity, and Doppler frequency shift [6], it can be obtained that the time delay is about 0.4 μs, 0.6 μs, and 0.8 μs, respectively. The simulation results are shown in Fig. 3.

Figure 3 shows that the detection performance of echo signals decreases with the increase of target velocity. This is because the Doppler frequency shift of each echo signal is different when the target velocity is different. The increase of target velocity will not only affect the receiver's reception, but also increase the corresponding Doppler frequency shift, which will affect the detection of echo signal. Therefore, this method is suitable for detecting low-speed flying targets.

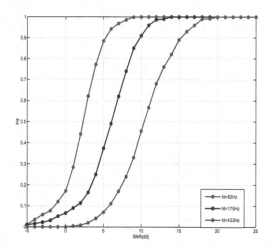

Fig. 3. Rao detection probability at different speeds

5   Conclusion

This paper theoretically deduces the detection method of multi-satellite weak target echo signal based on Rao detection. After the detection performance of the detector is analyzed theoretically, the adaptive detection threshold is set to complete the detection of the echo signal. Finally, the simulation of each aspect that may affect the detection algorithm's performance is carried out. The proposed method has low complexity and good detection performance, and it can detect target using multi-satellite illumination.

References

1. Hashim, I., Al-Hourani, A., Rowe, W., Scott, J.: Adaptive X-band satellite antenna for Internet-of-Things (IoT) over satellite applications. In: Proceedings of the 13th International Conference on Signal Processing and Communication Systems, Surfers Paradise, Australia, 16–18 December 2019, pp. 1–7 (2019)
2. Liu, M., et al.: 2D DOA robust estimation of echo signals based on multiple satellites passive radar in the presence of alpha stable distribution noise. IEEE Access **7**, 2169–3536 (2019)
3. Gronowski, K., Samczynski, P., Stasiak, K., Kulpa, K.: First, results of air target detection using single channel passive radar utilizing GPS illumination. In: Proceedings of the 2019 IEEE Radar Conference, Boston, MA, USA, 22–26 April 2019, pp. 1–6 (2019)
4. Yan, X., Wang, S., Wang, K., Jiang, H.: Localization of near field cyclostationary source based on fourth-order cyclic cumulant. In: Proceedings of the 2008 9th International Conference on Signal Processing, Beijing, China, 26–29 October 2008, pp. 1629–1632 (2008)
5. Jun, H.: A proper integral representation of Marcum Q-Function. In: Proceedings of the 2014 XXXIth URSI General Assembly and Scientific Symposium, Beijing, China, 16–23 August 2014, pp. 1–3 (2014)

6. Liu, M., Zhang, J., Li, B.: Feasibility analysis of OFDM/OQAM signals as illuminator of opportunity for passive detection. In: Proceedings of the 2018 14th IEEE International Conference on Signal Processing, Beijing, China, 12–16 August 2018, pp. 1–4 (2018)

7. Wu, X., Gong, P., Zhou, J., Liu, Z.: The applied research on anti-multipath interference GPS signal based on narrow-related. In: Proceedings of the 2014 IEEE 5th International Conference on Software Engineering and Service Science, Beijing, China, 27–29 June 2014, pp. 771–774 (2014)

8. Ilyushin, Y., Padokhin, A., Smolov, V.: Global navigational satellite system phase altimetry of the sea level: systematic bias effect caused by sea surface waves. In: Proceedings of the 2019 PhotonIcs and Electromagnetics Research Symposium-Spring (PIERS-Spring), Rome, Italy, 17–20 June 2019, pp. 1618–1627 (2019)

9. Ermolova, N., Tirkkonen, O.: Laplace transform of product of generalized Marcum Q, Bessel I, and power functions with applications. IEEE Trans. Sig. Process. **62**, 2938–2944 (2014)

10. Cardinali, R., Colone, F., Ferretti, C., Lombardo, P.: Comparison of clutter and multipath cancellation techniques for passive radar. In: Proceedings of the 2007 IEEE Radar Conference, Boston, MA, USA, 17–20 April 2007, pp. 469–474 (2007)

11. Zhang, Y., Xi, S.: Application of new LMS adaptive filtering algorithm with variable step size in adaptive echo cancellation. In: Proceedings of the 2017 IEEE 17th International Conference on Communication Technology, Chengdu, China, 27–30 October 2017, pp. 1715–1719 (2017)

Environment-Driven Modulation and Coding Schemes for Cognitive Multicarrier Communication Systems

Wei Yu[1], Di Lin[2(✉)], Qiudi Tang[2], Yuan Gao[3], and Jiang Cao[3]

[1] China Electronics Technology Group Corporation No. 10 Institute, Beijing, China
[2] University of Electronic Science and Technology of China, Sichuan, China
lindi@uestc.edu.cn
[3] Military Academy of Sciences, Beijing, China

Abstract. With the deterioration of the electromagnetic environment, it is difficult for a single wireless communication system to satisfy the quality of communication service requirements in congested frequency bands. An effective solution is to establish a unified communication platform, which can accordingly change its systematic parameters, such as modulation, coding, available spectrum resource, etc. In this paper, an environment-driven communication system is devised to realize intelligent communication with variant data transmission requirements and quality of services. Different modulation coding schemes (MCS) are integrated in the environment-driven communication system to deal with the time-varying spectrum constraint. Besides, based on information of channel condition, the environment-driven system can select a suitable MCS to achieve preferable systematic performance. Simulation results indicate that the devised environment-driven communication system has good performance in different conditions.

Keywords: Environment-driven · Modulation and coding scheme · Multicarrier systems · Cognitive radio · Spectrally modulated and spectrally encoded signals

1 Introduction

Spectrum crowding will grow continuously due to wireless applications and spectral limitations. Although spectrum is seriously scarce, it is more important to access it [1]. In order to use the unused spectrum more effectively in the dynamic environment, cognitive radio (CR) arises. CR accommodates to fast-changing environmental conditions and provides controlled intervention for existing users in the meantime [2]. Nevertheless, most of the research is limited to consider only a specific waveform, which is not applicable to a wide range of users [3]. So we provide an emerging adaptive communication transmission method based on intelligent decision-making.

In this paper, we consider the general analysis structure for spectrally modulated and spectrally encoded (SMSE) signals [4–6]. Some parameters (i.e., spectrum utility sequence, channel coding, data modulation, spread spectrum code) are utilized to

© ICST Institute for Computer Sciences, Social Informatics and Telecommunications Engineering 2021
Published by Springer Nature Switzerland AG 2021. All Rights Reserved
X. Wang et al. (Eds.): AICON 2021, LNICST 396, pp. 294–307, 2021.
https://doi.org/10.1007/978-3-030-90196-7_25

construct the framework. By changing these parameters, different communication systems can switch flexibly to achieve the purpose of matching user needs and reducing interference.

The communication technologies in SMSE framework include non-continuous orthogonal frequency division multiplexing (NC-OFDM), non-continuous multi-carrier code division multiple access (NC-MC-CDMA) and transform domain communication system (TDCS). Their brief description is as follows.

- OFDM is a multicarrier modulation technology, which can efficiently eliminate intersymbol interference by inserting cyclic prefix (CP) among symbols. By transmitting data in parallel on subcarriers, OFDM can achieve a higher data rate. However, in order to prevent mutual interference among subcarriers, it is required that the subcarriers are orthogonal to each other. Unfortunately, the orthogonality of OFDM subcarriers is easily destroyed by Doppler shift [7]. Therefore, OFDM is suitable for scenarios with low speed and high signal-to-noise ratio.
- MC-CDMA splits the original data stream into parallel data by modulating the signal on spread sequences. This modulation technique can effectively resist the codes interference (ISI) induced by multipath effect and possesses unique advantages in frequency diversity [8]. In this paper, Hadamard matrix is used to generate the spread spectrum sequence of MC-CDMA.
- As a typical spectrum sharing communication system, TDCS can actively avoid the spectrum interference or the occupied frequency band by sensing the spatial electromagnetic environment information in a certain frequency band. By dynamically changing the transmission frequency band according to the perception results, TDCS can well avoid the interference frequency band [9]. Due to its active anti-interference ability, TDCS supports low-data-rate communication in harsh environments [10].

Different combinations of parameters can form different modulation coding schemes. How to intelligently choose the modulation coding scheme in different scenarios is the key problem. In the process of formulating the adaptive modulation coding scheme, a corresponding table of channel conditions and modulation coding scheme is obtained through simulation [11–14]. In practical application, we not only need to select the optimal range of modulation coding schemes based on the estimation of channel transfer quality, but also consider the needs of users, such as communication rate, so a fuzzy decision is added to make the final decision.

The rest of this article is made up of the following organizations. Section 2 depicts the analysis structure of the adaptive transmission system and summarizes the channel models used in the simulation. In Sect. 3, the method of adaptive modulation is described in detail, and the frame diagram of the system is given. The simulation results and conclusions are addressed in Sect. 4 and the last part respectively.

2   Environment-Driven Communication System

The vectors are shown in bold capital letters below. The model defines the waveform design for the user's Kth data symbol. Time indexes of the discrete and continuous expressions are n and t, while the frequency indexes are m and f separately.

A. *Spectrum sensing*

Spectrum sensing module samples the electromagnetic spectrum environment over the system's operating bandwidth and estimates the spectral content. A thresholding process is applied to the spectral estimate, producing a magnitude vector involving ones and zeros [15]. In other words, if the power spectrum amplitude of the subcarrier exceeds the threshold value, the subcarrier is considered to have been occupied and marked as 0. Otherwise, the subcarrier is considered unoccupied and marked as 1 (as shown in Fig. 1 and Fig. 2). Let the resulting spectrum utility sequence be $\mathbf{a} = [a_0, a_1, \ldots, a_n, \ldots, a_{N_F-1}]$.

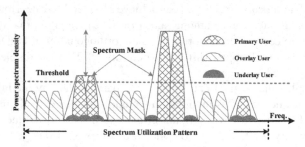

Fig. 1. Example of fully spectrum utilization pattern

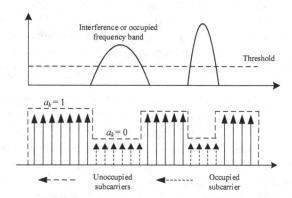

Fig. 2. Example of spectrum utilization vector

B. *Modulation and coding schemes in SMSE*

We choose the representation method of spectrum input and spectrum output framework (SMSE) in [1]. The spectrum is expressed as.

$$S_{SMSE} = \mathbf{A} \ \Theta \ \mathbf{F} \tag{1}$$

where e represents Hadamard product, that is, array multiplication by element. $\mathbf{A}$, Θ and $\mathbf{F}$ represent complex amplitude, phase, and frequency separately. In this paper, they are functions of four waveform design variables (data-in, encoding, frequency component availability and frequency component usage). Since we only discuss one-to-one transmission, $\mathbf{A}_k$, $\mathbf{\Theta}_k$ and $\mathbf{F}_k$ size $1 \times N_F$, every column for a different frequency component, a total of N_F frequency. The product of amplitude after spectrum operation is $A_{1m} \in \mathbf{A} = [A_{11}, A_{12}, .., A_{1N_F}]_{1 \times N_F}$. The phase sum of spectrum operation is $\Theta_{1m} \in \mathbf{\Theta} = [\Theta_{11}, \Theta_{12}, .., \Theta_{1N_F}]_{1 \times N_F}$. And the frequency on-off indicator is $F_{1m} \in \mathbf{F} = [F_{11}, F_{12}, .., F_{1N_F}]_{1 \times N_F}$.

When the frequency interval is set to $\Delta f = 1/T_{sym}$, subcarriers are orthogonal to each other within a symbol time, that is, spectrum components of each subchannel are zero at frequencies of other subcarriers. Thus the inter-channel interference is eliminated. The SMSE waveform expression is developed by using spectrum utility sequence (**a**), channel code (**u**), complex data modulation (**d**) and spread spectrum code (**c**) design variables. The mth frequency component of the kth data modulator $s_k[m]$ is expressed as

$$s_k[m] = a_m u_{m,l} c_m d_{m,k} e^{j(\theta_{cm} + \theta_{d_{m,k}})} \tag{2}$$

where $m \in \{0, 1, \ldots, N_F - 1\}$, a_m, $u_{m,l}$, c_m, $d_{m,k}$, θ_{cm} and $\theta_{d_{m,k}}$ are magnitude and phase of the design variables. Then we put these design variables together and get

$$A_{m,k} = u_{m,l} c_m d_{m,k}$$
$$\Theta_{m,k} = e^{j(\theta_{cm} + \theta_{d_{m,k}})}$$
$$F_m = a_m \tag{3}$$

The expression in (1) can be further modified to

$$s_k[m] = A_{m,k} \Theta_{m,k} F_m \tag{4}$$

The time-domain expression of SMSE symbols is produced by the application of IDFT operation to (4) and removing the imaginary part, written as

$$s_k[n]_{1 \times 1} = \text{Re}\{\frac{1}{N_F} \sum_{m=0}^{N_F-1} A_{m,k} \Theta_{m,k} F_m e^{j(2\pi f_m t_n)} \tag{5}$$

Since the spread spectrum code is not required, OFDM's expression can be obtained by removing the variable c_m:

$$s_k[m] = u_m d_{m,k} e^{j\theta_{d_{m,k}}} \tag{6}$$

For MC-CDMA and TDCS, although the spread spectrum code used is different, their expression forms are the same:

$$s_k[m] = a_m u_{m,l} c_m d_{m,k} e^{j(\theta_{cm} + \theta_{d_{m,k}})} \tag{7}$$

where $d_{m,k} e^{j\theta_{d_{m,k}}}$ represents data modulation. We set $d_{m,k} e^{j\theta_{d_{m,k}}} = \alpha_{m,k} + j\beta_{m,k}$. When the modulation mode is QPSK, $\alpha_{m,k}, \beta_{m,k} \in \{\pm 1\}$. When the modulation mode is 16QAM, $\alpha_{m,k}, \beta_{m,k} \in \{\pm 1, \pm 3\}$.

C. Determine adaptive modulation parameters

A table of channel conditions and modulation coding scheme (mainly the corresponding table of SNR and BER or SNR and system throughput) is needed. It's obtained through simulation and test of large data volume for a long time. In practical applications, according to the user's rate requirements, reliability requirements and channel estimation results, the adaptive modulation parameters (e.g., **u**, **c**, **d**) are obtained by using intelligent decision-making to select the optimal modulation coding scheme.

D. Channel models

In this paper, the channel conditions are simply divided into three disparate channel models: the additive Gaussian white noise (AWGN) channel, Rice multipath fading channel and Rayleigh multipath fading channel.

AWGN channel model indicates that the only impact of the channel on the transmission signal is the Gaussian white noise process. AWGN is the most commonly used channel model for communication system simulation, so we won't go into details here.

Rayleigh is a particular channel fading without major line-of-sight (LOS) component. There are serious fade-in and fade-out events that can cause an unexpected interruption of the communication chain due to the RSS drop. Under the circumstances, phase, angle of arrival and the received signal strength (RSS) change. As the traffic moves around, it occasionally fades away over time, which is rapid decay. Although there is no ISI, rapid fading is still disruptive because the gain for deep fading is low. Expression (8) characterizes the probability density function of the Rayleigh model.

$$p(r) = \begin{cases} \frac{r}{\sigma^2}\exp(-\frac{r}{2\sigma^2}), & (r \geq 0) \\ 0, & (r < 0) \end{cases} \tag{8}$$

where σ^2 is the mean power of the time signal. The square amplitude r^2 determines SNR value. The threshold R that cannot be exceeded is given a definition in [5].

$$P(R) = P(r \leq R) = \int_0^R p(r)dr = 1 - \exp(\frac{r}{2\sigma^2}) \tag{9}$$

Table 1 gives simulation parameters of Rayleigh channel.

Table 1. Parameters of Rayleigh channel

Properties	Parameters
Path delays (s)	[20, 30, 70, 90, 110, 190, 410] * (10^{-9})
Average path gains (dB)	[0, −1, −2, −3, −8, −17.2, −20.8]
Sample rate (s)	1e−8

With the existent of LOS component, the fading form turns to be Rice, because LOS component obscures others. Under Rice fading, the steady main LOS signal overlays with the random multipath components. Rice factor is K, the proportion of main LOS component to dispersion constituent part:

$$K(dB) = 10 \log(\frac{A^2}{2\sigma^2}) \tag{10}$$

Rician distribution is shown in (11), in which A is magnitude of main component. I_0 is the first kind of modified zeroth-order Bessel function. Along with the change of $A \to 0$ and $K \to -\infty$, Rician changes to Rayleigh.

$$p(r) = \begin{cases} \frac{r}{\sigma^2} \exp(-\frac{(r^2+A^2)}{2\sigma^2})I_0\frac{Ar}{\sigma^2}, & (r \geq 0) \\ 0, & (r < 0) \end{cases} \tag{11}$$

The simulation parameters of Rice channel are shown in Table 2.

Table 2. Parameters of Rice channel

Properties	Parameters
Path delays (s)	$[0, 30, 70, 90, 110, 190, 410]*(10^{-9})$
Average path gains (dB)	$[-1, -2, -3, -8, -17.2, -20.8]$
Sample rate (s)	1e−8

3 Adaptive Adjustment

A. Modulation of the transmitting signal

According to MCS, the corresponding bit allocation and modulation are performed on subcarriers. The detailed steps are described below (Fig. 3):

1) According to the adaptive modulation scheme, the corresponding convolutional code parameters are selected to encode binary data.
2) Data modulation, such as BPSK. Let the resulting digital information flow be $\mathbf{D} = [D_0, D_1, \ldots, D_n, \ldots, D_{N-1}]$.
3) Carry out corresponding sub-carrier data distribution.

   a) For NC-MC-CDMA, the frequency domain expression of the ith symbol is $\mathbf{S_i} = \lambda D_i \otimes \mathbf{P}_1$, among them, $\mathbf{P}_1 = [p_0, p_1, \ldots, p_n, \ldots, p_{N-1}]$ for the spread spectrum sequence, $\otimes$ for dot product, λ for the normalization factor. Data is placed on the subcarriers labeled 1 in turn, with the remaining subcarriers zeroed.
   b) For NC-OFDM, the frequency domain expression of data is $\mathbf{S} = \lambda \mathbf{D}$. The same as above, data is placed on the subcarriers labeled 1 in turn, with the remaining subcarriers zeroed.

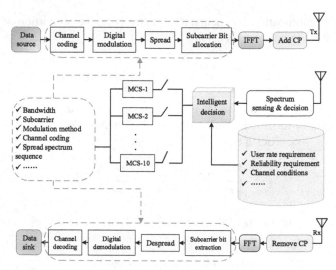

Fig. 3. Cognitive multicarrier communication system model

c) For TDCS, the detailed steps are as below: each user uses the pseudo-random sequence generator to generate the random bit sequence respectively, and then generates the corresponding pseudo-random sequence $\mathbf{P} = \{e^{jm_0}, e^{jm_1}, \ldots, e^{jm_n}, \ldots, e^{jm_{N-1}}\}$, according to the phase mapping diagram. m_n represents the phase of the nth element of the random phase sequence. The pseudo-random sequence for each user is separately multiplied by a utility sequence for each element to get the Fundamental Modulation Waveform (FMW). Its frequency domain expression is $\mathbf{B} = \lambda\mathbf{AP} = \lambda[A_0e^{jm_0}, A_1e^{jm_1}, \ldots, A_ne^{jm_n}, \ldots, A_{N-1}e^{jm_{N-1}}]$. In cyclic code shift keying (CCSK) module, $\log_2 N$ bits of data are taken every time to be converted into decimals, and the cyclic shift of $\mathbf{s}$ units of FMW is performed in time domain. For the ith symbol, the frequency-domain expression is $\mathbf{S_i} = [B_0e^{\frac{j2\pi d \cdot 0}{N}}, B_1e^{\frac{j2\pi d \cdot 1}{N}}, \ldots, B_ke^{\frac{j2\pi d \cdot k}{N}}, \ldots, B_{N-1}e^{\frac{j2\pi d \cdot (N-1)}{N}}]$.

4) Convert the above signal into a time-domain signal through IFFT module, and then add a cyclic prefix (CP) to each symbol.
5) Finally, send the signal through the transmission module.

B. Data processing at the receiving terminal

1) Receive the signal and complete the channel estimation, and remove the cyclic prefix of the acquired signal. Then obtain frequency-domain signal through the FFT module.
2) According to the electromagnetic characteristics of the external environment, spectrum characteristics of all regions are detected, and the spectrum perception results are compared with the pre-set threshold to generate the spectrum utility sequence.
3) Extract data of each corresponding position marked as 1 in spectrum utility sequence.

4) Perform adaptive demodulation. NC-MC-CDMA carries out related demodulation according to its spread spectrum code. NC-OFDM carries out digital demodulation directly. For TDCS, the specific steps are as follows: (i) Multiply the spectral utility sequence and the pseudo-random sequence of the user, and take the conjugate of the product. (ii) Multiply the data obtained in step 3. (iii) Carry out IFFT operation to extract the real part. (iv) Perform peak search, and output the peak position information as demodulation data.

5) Finally, the decimal demodulation data is converted into binary data, and the demodulation result is obtained.

4 Simulation Results

Considering transmission performance and anti-jamming capability, TDCS, NC-MC-CDMA, and NC-OFDM are chosen as the alternative data modulation systems. CCSK is selected as the digital modulation mode in TDCS. BPSK and 8PSK are selected as the digital modulation modes in NC-MC-CDMA and NC-OFDM. And the convolutional codes of 1/2 code rate and 2/3 code rate are selected as the channel encoding modes. Thus 10 fixed Modulation and Coding Schemes (MCS) are obtained, which are shown in Table 3.

Table 3. MCS parameters

Modulation and coding scheme	System	Modulation	Convolutional code
MCS-1	NC-MC-CDMA	BPSK	1/2
MCS-2	NC-MC-CDMA	BPSK	2/3
MCS-3	NC-MC-CDMA	8PSK	1/2
MCS-4	NC-MC-CDMA	8PSK	2/3
MCS-5	TDCS	CCSK	1/2
MCS-6	TDCS	CCSK	2/3
MCS-7	NC-OFDM	BPSK	1/2
MCS-8	NC-OFDM	BPSK	2/3
MCS-9	NC-OFDM	8PSK	1/2
MCS-10	NC-OFDM	8PSK	2/3

The simulation condition is 2048 subcarriers, in which the number of available subcarriers is 1024.

Adaptive modulation parameters are determined according to channel estimation and user requirements. Under different channel conditions, MCS performance will be different. Figure 4, Fig. 5, Fig. 6, Fig. 7, Fig. 8 and Fig. 9 show BER performance of each MCS under SNR and E_b/N_0 in AWGN channel, Rice fading channel and Rayleigh fading channel.

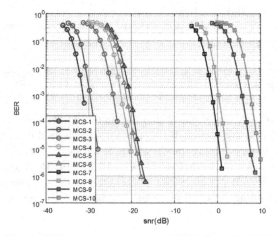

Fig. 4. BER performance under AWGN channel (SNR)

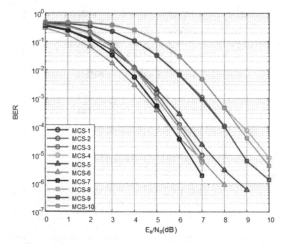

Fig. 5. BER performance under AWGN channel (E_b/N_0)

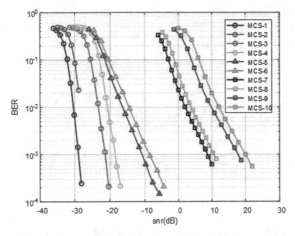

Fig. 6. BER performance under Rice channel (SNR)

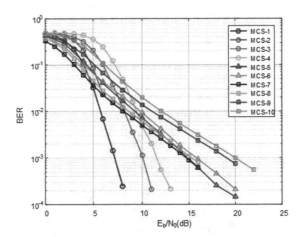

Fig. 7. BER performance under Rice channel (E_b/N_0)

Then, on the premise of achieving 10^{-3} BER, the minimum SNR or E_b/N_0 parameter model required for each MCS is obtained. AWGN channel is analyzed as a typical case. There are SNR and MCS mapping relation in Table 4 and E_b/N_0 and MCS mapping relation in Table 5.

Therefore, the MCS ladder diagram is obtained in Fig. 4 and Fig. 5.

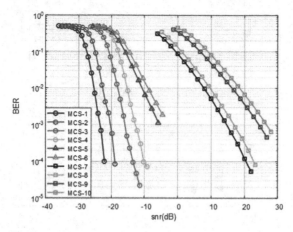

Fig. 8. BER performance under Rayleigh channel (SNR)

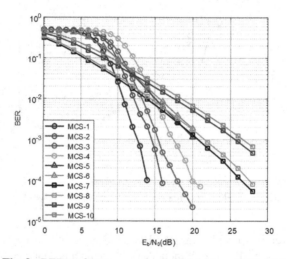

Fig. 9. BER performance under Rayleigh channel (E_b/N_0)

Table 4. SNR and MCS mapping relation

MCS type	SNR
1	[−31.4; −29.6] dB
2	[−29.6; −24.3] dB
3	[−24.3; −22.4] dB
4	[−22.4; −20.3] dB
5	[−20.3; −19.9] dB
6	[−19.9; −1.2] dB
7	[−1.2; 0.3] dB
8	[0.3; 5.8] dB
9	[5.8; 7.7] dB
10	[7.7; −] dB

Table 5. E_b/N_0 and MCS mapping relation

MCS type	E_b/N_0
5	[2.4; 2.8] dB
6	[2.8; 4.8] dB
1, 7	[4.8; 5.0] dB
2, 8	[5.0; 7.0] dB
3, 9	[7.0; 7.7] dB
4, 10	[7.7; −] dB

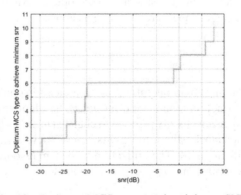

Fig. 10. Optimum MCS type to gain minimum SNR

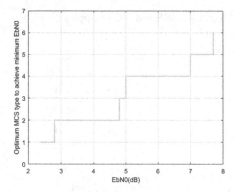

Fig. 11. Optimum MCS type to gain minimum E_b/N_0

In order to satisfy the requirement of BER and obtain a higher transmission rate, fuzzy factor can be used to further classify MCS. In Table 6, the greater the value of fuzzy factor is, the faster the data transfer rate is (Figs. 10 and 11).

Table 6. Fuzzy factor and MCS mapping relation

MCS type	Data transmission rate	Fuzzy factor
1, 2	Slow	1
3, 4, 5, 6	A bit slow	2
7, 8	Fast	3
9, 10	Very fast	4

Taking the above factors into consideration, the optimal MCS can be determined. The decision steps of other channels are the same as above.

5 Conclusion

For a complex and changing environment, the communication quality is unstable when adopting the traditional single communication system. The adaptive communication system proposed in this paper can flexibly respond to changes in environments, dynamically change MCS through channel estimation results, and achieve transmission rate maximization without sacrificing BER. The utilization of system resources can be improved and higher system throughput and capacity can be obtained.

References

1. Haykin, S.: Cognitive radio: brain-empowered wireless communications. IEEE J. Sel. Areas Commun. **23**(2), 201–220 (2005)

2. Chakravarthy, V.D., Shaw, A.K., Temple, M.A., Stephens, J.P.: Cognitive radio - an adaptive waveform with spectral sharing capability. In: IEEE Wireless Communications and Networking Conference, New Orleans, pp. 724–729 (2005)
3. Hong, S., Zhang, B., Yang, H.: Applying probability control to cognitive CDMA communication system for anti-interference. Electron. Lett. **49**(5), 370–372 (2013)
4. Roberts, M.L., Temple, M.A., Raines, R.A., Mills, R.F., Oxley, M.E.: Communication waveform design using an adaptive spectrally modulated, spectrally encoded (SMSE) framework. IEEE J. Sel. Top. Sig. Process. **1**(1), 03–213 (2007)
5. Chakravarthy, V., et al.: Novel overlay/underlay cognitive radio waveforms using SD-SMSE framework to enhance spectrum efficiency- part I: theoretical framework and analysis in AWGN channel. IEEE Trans. Commun. **57**(12), 3794–3804 (2009)
6. Chakravarthy, V., Li, X., Zhou, R., Wu, Z., Temple, M.: Novel overlay/underlay cognitive radio waveforms using SD-SMSE framework to enhance spectrum efficiency-part II: analysis in fading channels. IEEE Trans. Commun. **58**(6), 1868–1876 (2010)
7. Chakravarthy, V., Nunez, A.S., Stephens, J.P., Shaw, A.K., Temple, M.A.: TDCS, OFDM, and MC-CDMA: a brief tutorial. IEEE Commun. Mag. **43**(9), 11–16 (2005)
8. Cho, Y.S., Kim, J., Yang, W.Y., Kang, C.G.: MIMO-OFDM wireless communications with MATLAB®. IEEE (2010)
9. Hu, S., Bi, G., Guan, Y.L., Li, S.: Spectrally efficient transform domain communication system with quadrature cyclic code shift keying. IET Commun. **7**(4), 382–390 (2013)
10. Hu, S., Bi, G., Guan, Y.L., Li, S.: TDCS-based cognitive radio networks with multiuser interference avoidance. IEEE Trans. Commun. **61**(12), 4828–4835 (2013)
11. Chen, F.T., Tao, G.L.: A novel MCS selection criterion for supporting AMC in LTE system. In: 2010 International Conference on Computer Application and System Modeling (ICCASM 2010), Taiyuan, pp. 598–603 (2010)
12. Tang, C., Stolpman, V.J.: Multiple users adaptive modulation schemes for MC-CDMA. In: IEEE Global Telecommunications Conference, Dallas, pp. 3823–3827 (2004)
13. Ahlem, B.L., Dadi, M.B., Rhaimi, C.B.: Evaluation of BER of digital modulation schemes for AWGN and wireless fading channels. In: 2015 World Congress on Information Technology and Computer Applications (WCITCA), Hammamet, pp. 1–5 (2015)
14. Lye, S.C.K., Tan, S.E., Chin, Y.K., Chua, B.L., Teo, K.T.K.: Performance analysis of intelligent transport systems (ITS) with adaptive transmission scheme. In: 2012 Fourth International Conference on Computational Intelligence, Phuket, pp. 418–423 (2012)
15. Swackhammer, P.J., Temple, M.A., Raines, R.A.: Performance simulation of a transform domain communication system for multiple access applications. In: IEEE Military Communications, Atlantic City, NJ, USA, pp. 1055–1059 (1999)

Secure Communications for Dual-UAV-MEC Networks

Weidang Lu[1(✉)], Yu Ding[1], Yiming Du[2], Yuan Gao[3,4], Su Hu[5],
Shaochi Cheng[3], and Yang Guo[3]

[1] Zhejiang University of Technology, Hangzhou 310023, China
luweid@zjut.edu.cn
[2] University of Nottingham Ningbo China, Ningbo 315100, China
[3] Academy of Military Science of PLA, Beijing 100091, China
[4] Tsinghua University, Beijing 100084, China
[5] University of Electronic Science and Technology of China, Chengdu 610054, China

Abstract. With the on-demand deployment and high flexibility of the unmanned aerial vehicle (UAV), carrying mobile edge computing (MEC) systems can efficiently relieve the pressure of the explosive growth of data traffic. UAVs adopt line-of sight (LOS) transmission with broadcast characteristics, the information they transmit to ground users (GUs) are easy to be eavesdrop by malicious eavesdroppers. Therefore, secure communication is worth studying in UAV-MEC networks. In this paper, we propose a Dual-UAV-MEC system where GUs offload part of the tasks to UAV server carrying MEC for calculation in the presence of the eavesdropping of offloading information by UAV Eavesdropper, Jammer on the ground sends interference signals to reduce eavesdropping. We propose a secure communication scheme with time division multiple access (TDMA) to maximum the GUs minimum secure calculation capacity. Specifically, we optimize the UAV Servers trajectory and allocate wireless resources which include time allocation factor and local calculation. Numerical results show that the method we proposed efficiently increases the secure calculation capacity of the system.

Keywords: UAV · Secure communication · MEC · Secure calculation capacity · TDMA

1 Introduction

Mobile edge computing (MEC) makes plenty of contribution for 5G era, e.g., reducing communication service latency, which has been extensively studied [1–8]. [2] proposed a scheme of collaborative computation to effectively reduce data redundancy pressure. As the on-demand deployment and high flexibility of UAVs, they can assist the MEC system in the Internet of things to help GUs with offloading calculation, which cannot only expand the converage of the MEC service, but also save the laying cost. [3] pointed out that the innovative study

X. Wang et al. (Eds.): AICON 2021, LNICST 396, pp. 308–318, 2021.
https://doi.org/10.1007/978-3-030-90196-7_26

on interaction between UAV and MEC can improve the task computing efficiency and the wireless communication quality by signal blocking and shadow effect. [4] proposed a method with optimizing computation offloading and UAV trajectory to enhance the performance. UAV-MEC system can approach GUs to obtain efficient information transmission [5,6]. Physical layer security plays an indispensable role in the 5G era with the data's explosive growth [7,8].

In this paper, we propose a secure communication method for Dual-UAV-MEC networks based on TDMA to optimize UAVs' trajectory and wireless resources including time allocation and local calculation by combining block coordinate descent (BCD) and successive convex approximation (SCA) methods [9].

2 System Model and Problem Formulation

2.1 System Model

Figure 1 depicts a Dual-UAV-MEC secure communication system with two UAVs (UAV_S and UAV_E), K GUs and a ground jammer (GJ), where UAV_S assists GUs in completing the tasks for calculation, and UAV_E eavesdrops the offloading information by GUs to UAV_S as a mobile eavesdropper with given trajectory during the flight. In order to reduce the UAV_E eavesdropping, GJ sends interference signals. We assume that UAV_S has already known GJs interference signals, thus UAV_S is not disturbed by it. However, UAV_E knows nothing about it, thus the interference signals have noisy effects on UAV_E. UAVs, GUs and GJ are equipped with single antenna.

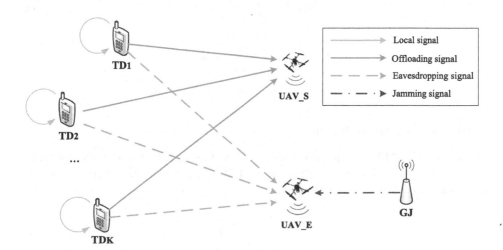

Fig. 1. Dual-UAV-MEC system model.

Denote $w_k = (x_k, y_k, 0), w_j = (x_j, y_j, 0)$ as the coordinates of the k-th GU and GJ, respectively. Define T as the UAV flight period, which is divided into N equal time slots, $\delta_t = N/T$, and UAV_$i(i \in \{S, E\})$'s location is denoted by $q_i(n) = (x_i[n], y_i[n], H_i), n \in \{1, 2, ..., N\}$, where H_i represents UAV_i's flight altitude. Define q_s^I, q_s^F and $V_s^{\max}$ as the start position, the end position and the maximum flight speed of UAV_S, respectively. Then, we have

$$q_s[1] = q_s^I \tag{1a}$$

$$q_s[N] = q_s^F \tag{1b}$$

$$||q_s[n+1] - q_s[n]|| \leq V_s^{\max} \delta_t, \forall n = 1, 2, ..., N-1 \tag{1c}$$

Denote $d_{\min}$ as the minimum anti-collision distance between UAV_S and UAV_E, which needs to satisfy

$$||q_s[n] - q_e[n]||^2 \geq d_{\min}^2, \forall n \in \{1, 2..., N\} \tag{2}$$

The distance between UAV_S and GU$_k$, $k \in \{1, 2, ..., K\}$, UAV_E and GJ, UAV_E and GU$_k$ in the time slot n are $d_{k,s}[n] = \sqrt{H_s^2 + ||q_s[n] - w_k||^2}, \forall k, n$ and $d_{j,e}[n] = \sqrt{H_e^2 + ||q_e[n] - w_j||^2}, \forall n$, respectively. We consider the channels between UAVs and GUs are modeled as LOS channels. The channel coefficient between GU$_k$ and UAV_S, GJ and UAV_E, GU$_k$ and UAV_E are expressed as

$$h_{k,s}[n] = \sqrt{\frac{\beta_0}{d_{k,s}^2[n]}}, \forall k, n \tag{3}$$

$$h_{j,e}[n] = \sqrt{\frac{\beta_0}{d_{j,e}^2[n]}}, \forall n \tag{4}$$

$$h_{k,e}[n] = \sqrt{\frac{\beta_0}{d_{k,e}^2[n]}}, \forall k, n \tag{5}$$

where β_0 represents the channel power gain at unit distance.

2.2 Problem Formulation

We utilize a TDMA scheme for GUs task offloading, in which we divide one time slot n into K sub-slots with $\tau_k[n]\delta_t, k \in \{1, 2, ...K\}$, where $\tau_k[n]$ represents the time allocation factor, which is given by

$$\sum_{k=1}^{K} \tau_k[n] \leq 1, \forall n \tag{6a}$$

$$0 \leq \tau_k[n] \leq 1, \forall k, n \tag{6b}$$

Communication Model

Since UAV_S has known GJs interference signals, UAV_S is not disturbed by it. Define $p_k[n]$ as the transmit power of GU_k, thus the signal-to-interference and noise ratio (SINR) of UAV_S in the time slot n is expressed as

$$r_{k,s}[n] = \frac{|h_{k,s}[n]|^2 p_k[n]}{\delta_s^2}, \forall k, n \tag{7}$$

While UAV_E knows nothing about the presence of GJ, UAV_E cannot determine who sent the received signals. Thus, the SINR of UAV_E is given by

$$r_{k,e}[n] = \frac{|h_{k,e}[n]|^2 p_k[n]}{|h_{j,e}[n]|^2 P_j + \delta_e^2}, \forall k, n \tag{8}$$

where P_j denotes the given transmit power of GJ, δ_s^2 and δ_e^2 denote the noise power of UAV_S and UAV_E, respectively. Thus, the task offloading rate from GU_k to UAV_S and the task eavesdropping rate from GU_k to UAV_E are given by

$$R_{k,s}[n] = \tau_k[n]\log_2\left(1 + \frac{|h_{k,s}[n]|^2 p_k[n]}{\delta_s^2}\right), \forall k, n \tag{9}$$

$$R_{k,e}[n] = \tau_k[n]\log_2\left(1 + \frac{|h_{k,e}[n]|^2 p_k[n]}{|h_{j,e}[n]|^2 P_j + \delta_e^2}\right), \forall k, n \tag{10}$$

As a result, the secrecy offloading rate from GU_k to UAV_S with UAV_E participation is formulated as

$$R_{k,\text{sec}}[n] = (R_{k,s}[n] - R_{k,e}[n])^+, \forall k, n \tag{11}$$

Computing Model

The tasks of GUs can be completed by local calculation and offloading to UAV_S for calculation. Let c_k and c_s describe the CPU cycles for GU_k and UAV_S computing one bit of task respectively. Let $F_k^{\max}$ and $F_s^{\max}$ represent GU_k and UAV_Ss maximum CPU frequency. Define B as the bandwidth. Both of the local calculation bits $l_{loc,k}[n]$ of GU_k and the secure calculation bits of UAV_S cannot exceed their respective maximum calculation capability, which meet the constraints as

$$c_k l_{loc,k}[n] \leq F_k^{\max}\delta_t, \forall k, n \tag{12}$$

$$B\delta_t c_s R_{k,\text{sec}}[n] \leq \tau_k[n]\delta_t F_s^{\max}, \forall k, n \tag{13}$$

The total calculation of GU_k consists of the local calculation and offloading calculation. Since GU_k have a secure task requirements Q_m to calculate, it needs to satisfy the following minimum secure calculation constraints

$$l_{loc,k}[n] + B\tau_k[n]\delta_t R_{k,\text{sec}}[n] \geq Q_m, \forall k, n \tag{14}$$

The energy consumption calculated locally by GU_k is expressed as

$$E_{loc,k}[n] = \frac{k_k (c_k l_{loc,k}[n])^3}{\delta_t^2}, \forall k, n \tag{15}$$

where k_k denotes the effective capacitance of GU_k.

The energy consumption calculated by offloading to UAV_S is $\tau_k[n]\delta_t p_k[n]$. Define P_{ave}^k as GU_k's average power budget, the GU_k energy constraint over T is limited as

$$\sum_{n=1}^{N} \left(\tau_k[n]\delta_t p_k[n] + \frac{k_k(c_k l_{loc,k}[n])^3}{\delta_t^2} \right) \leq P_{ave}^k T, \forall k, n \tag{16}$$

Problem Formulation

In order to ensure GUs fairness and enhance the Dual-UAV-MEC systems secure calculation capacity, define GU_k average secure calculation bits as the objective,

$$\overline{R}_{k,\text{sec}} = \frac{1}{T} \left(\sum_{n=1}^{N} l_{loc,k}[n] + B\delta_t \sum_{n=1}^{N} \tau_k[n]R_{k,\text{sec}}[n] \right), \forall k, n \tag{17}$$

Under the constraints of the maximum flight speed of UAVs, anti-collision between UAV_S and UAV_E, GU_k average power budget, GUs and UAV_S calculating capability and GU_k secure task calculation requirements, we optimize the time allocation factor $\tau_k[n]$, the local calculation $l_{loc,k}[n]$ and the trajectory of UAV_S $q_s[n]$ to maximize the minimum GU_k average secure calculation capacity, as follows,

$$(P1): \max_{\{\tau_k[n], l_{loc,k}[n], q_s[n]\}} \min_{\forall k} \overline{R}_{k,\text{sec}} \tag{18}$$

$$s.t.(1), (2), (6), (12), (13), (14), (16)$$

The problem (P1) is hard to solve as the non-convexity of (2), (13) and (14).

3   Problem Solution

We introduce $\{t, t_{1,k}[n], t_{2,k}[n]\}$ as auxiliary variables to convexify the problem (P1), which can be solved by optimizing $S = \{\tau_k[n], l_{loc,k}[n], q_s[n], t, t_{1,k}[n], t_{2,k}[n]\}$, which is rewritten as

$$(P2): \max_{S} t \tag{19a}$$

$$s.t.(1), (2), (6), (12), (16)$$

$$t \leq \frac{1}{T} \left(\sum_{n=1}^{N} l_{loc,k}[n] + B\delta_t \sum_{n=1}^{N} (t_{1,k}[n] - t_{2,k}[n]) \right), \forall k, n \tag{19b}$$

$$t_{1,k}[n] \leq \tau_k[n]\log_2 \left(1 + \frac{|h_{k,s}[n]|^2 p_k[n]}{\delta_s^2} \right), \forall k, n \tag{19c}$$

$$\tau_k[n]\log_2 \left(1 + \frac{|h_{k,e}[n]|^2 p_k[n]}{|h_{j,e}[n]|^2 P_j + \delta_e^2} \right) \leq t_{2,k}[n], \forall k, n \tag{19d}$$

$$c_s B (t_{1,k}[n] - t_{2,k}[n]) \leq \tau_k[n]F_s^{\max}, \forall k, n \tag{19e}$$

$$l_{loc,k}[n] + B\delta_t (t_{1,k}[n] - t_{2,k}[n]) \geq Q_m, \forall k, n \tag{19f}$$

The lower bound of the objective function $\overline{R}_{k,\text{sec}}$ is represented by t. $t_{1,k}[n]$ and $t_{2,k}[n]$ are expressed as the lower bound of $R_{k,s}[n]$ and the upper bound of $R_{k,e}[n]$, respectively. Then the secrecy offloading rate $R_{k,sec}[n]$ is represented as $(t_{1,k}[n] - t_{2,k}[n])$. We can omit $(\cdot)^+$ because it is guaranteed that the objective is non-negative, $p_k[n]$ is given which is non-negative, and at least $l_{loc,k}[n]$ can be set to 0. The problem (P1) is equivalently formulated as (19).

Since constraints (2), (19c) and (19d) is non-convex, we utilize BCD and SCA algorithms to solve problem (P2) in two steps, i.e., step 1, with given UAV_S trajectory to optimize time allocation factor and local calculation, and step 2, with given time allocation factor and local calculation to optimize UAV_S trajectory.

3.1 Step 1: Time Allocation and Local Calculation Allocation

For any given trajectory of UAV_S, the problem (P2) is rewritten as

$$(P3.1): \max_{\{\tau_k[n], l_{loc,k}[n], t_{1,k}[n], t_{2,k}[n]\}} t \qquad (20)$$
$$s.t.(6), (12), (16), (19b) - (19f)$$

Note that the optimization problem (P3.1) is typically convex as the constraints of (P3.1) are linear, which can be effectively solved by utilizing standard optimization software e.g., CVX [10].

3.2 Step 2: Trajectory Optimization

For any given trajectory of time allocation factor and local calculation, the problem (P2) is rewritten as

$$(P3.2): \max_{\{q_s[n], t_{1,k}[n], t_{2,k}[n]\}} t \qquad (21)$$
$$s.t.(1), (2), (19b) - (19f)$$

Since (P3.2) is a non-convex problem as the non-convexity of the constraints (2) and (19c), we apply SCA to solve (P3.2). (P3.2) is an approximately convex in r-th iteration. Then, we update the trajectory of UAV_S iteratively to obtain $q_s[n]$.

Constraint (2) can be transformed as the following expression in terms of UAV_S flight trajectory in the r-th iteration, $\{q_s^r[n]\}$, by first-order Taylor expansion, given by

$$||q_s^r[n] - q_e[n]||^2 + 2||q_s^r[n] - q_e[n]||\,||q_s[n] - q_s^r[n]|| \geq d_{\min}^2, \forall n \in \{1, 2..., N\} \quad (22)$$

According to (19c), similarly we have

$$t_{1,k}[n] \leq A_{1,k}[n] - A_{2,k}[n], \forall k, n \qquad (23)$$

where $A_{1,k}[n] - A_{2,k}[n]$ represent the lower-bounded of the right term in (19c) approximately. $A_{1,k}[n]$ and $A_{2,k}[n]$ are as follows, respectively,

$$A_{1,k}[n] = \log_2 \left(\left(||q_s^r[n] - w_k||^2 \right) \delta_s^2 + H_s^2 + \beta_0 p_k[n] \right)$$

$$+ \frac{2}{\ln 2} \frac{\left(||q_s^r[n] - w_k|| \right) \delta_s^2 \left(q_s[n] - q_s^r[n] \right)}{\left(\delta_s^2 \left(||q_s^r[n] - w_k||^2 + H_s^2 \right) + \beta_0 p_k[n] \right)}, \forall k, n$$

(24)

$$A_{2,k}[n] = \log_2 \left(\left(||q_s^r[n] - w_k||^2 \right) \delta_s^2 + H_s^2 \right)$$

$$+ \frac{2}{\ln 2} \frac{\left(||q_s^r[n] - w_k|| \right) \delta_s^2 \left(q_s[n] - q_s^r[n] \right)}{\delta_s^2 \left(||q_s^r[n] - w_k||^2 + H_s^2 \right)}, \forall k, n$$

(25)

Problem (P3.2) can be optimized by solving

$$(\text{P3.3}): \max_{\{q_s[n]\}, \{t_{1,k}[n], t_{2,k}[n]\}} t$$

$$s.t.(1), (19b), (19d), (19e), (19f), (22), (23)$$

(26)

Note that (P3.3) is convex, which can be solved by using standard optimization software effectively.

As a result, we can optimize the problem (P1) by solving (P3.1) and (P3.3) alternatively in the case of updating all optimizing variables, which is concluded in Algorithm 1.

Algorithm 1. Proposed algorithm based on BCD to optimize (P1)

1: **Initialize** Given $\tau_k^r[n], q_s^r[n], l_{loc,k}^r[n], r = 0$ and $\theta, \theta > 0$.
2: **Repeat**
3:     Given $q_s^r[n]$, and obtain the time allocation factor $\tau_k[n]$ and local calculation $l_{loc,k}[n]$ to solve (P3.1).
4:     Update $\tau_k^r[n] = \tau_k[n], l_{loc,k}^r[n] = l_{loc,k}[n]$.
5:     Given $\tau_k^r[n]$ and $l_{loc,k}^r[n]$, and obtain UAV_S trajectory optimization $q_s[n]$.
6:     Update $q_s^r[n] = q_s[n]$.
7:     Update $r = r + 1$.
8: **Until** Objective increase is less than θ or r is equal to r_{max}.
9: **Output** $\tau_k[n], l_{loc,k}[n], q_s[n], t, t_{1,k}[n]$ and $t_{2,k}[n]$.

---

4   Simulation Results

In this section, we present simulation results of the optimization objective by our proposed algorithm. In the Dual-UAV-MEC system, GJ is set at $[0, 0, 0]^T$, and 5 GUs are randomly fixed in a $400 \times 400 \, \text{m}^2$ area. UAV_E flies at a constant speed from $[200, -10, 100]^T$ to $[-200, 50, 100]^T$ with given trajectory, and UAV_S flies from $[-200, -10, 100]^T$ to $[200, -10, 100]^T$. UAV_i's maximum flight speed is 50 m/s. UAV_S and UAV_E anti-collision minimum distance is 1 m.

Figure 2 shows the convergence of our proposed algorithm with different T and p_k. We can find from Fig. 2 that the algorithm we proposed is converged and the secure calculation capacity of the system is better with larger T and P_k.

Figure 3 shows the UAV_S and UAV_E trajectory after optimization when $T = 20$ s. In Fig. 3, UAV_E files with a constant speed to eavesdrop GUs offloading information, and we can find that UAV_S flies as close to GUs as possible to get better channel condition to obtain GUs offloading information.

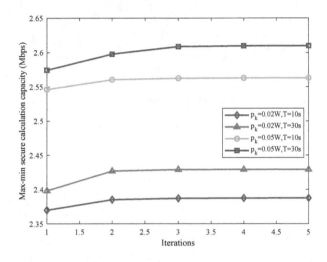

Fig. 2. Convergence.

Figure 4 shows the objective, max-min secure calculation capacity, versus T with different GUs' transmit power p_k. In Fig. 4, we find that the secure performance becomes better with the increase of T. This is because that UAV_S has more chance and time to get closer to GUs to improve get more GUs offloading information when T increases. And when p_k is larger, the more energy GUs could get, thus GUs is able to send more information offloading and the objective is larger.

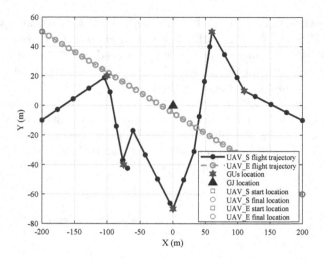

Fig. 3. The optimization trajectory of UAV_S and UAV_E.

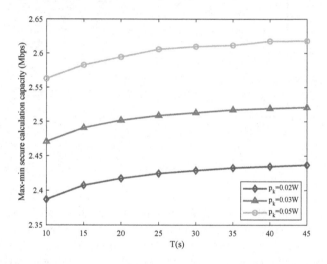

Fig. 4. The objective comparison versus T.

Figure 5 depicts the objective changes in case of time and local calculation allocation without trajectory optimization, trajectory optimization without time and local calculation allocation and joint optimization we proposed. It is clear to find that joint optimization scheme outperforms the other schemes, which proves greatly the significant effect of the algorithm we proposed.

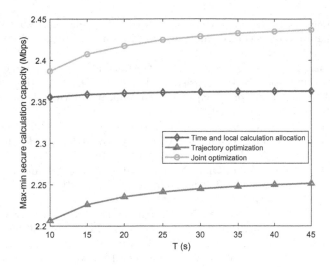

Fig. 5. The objective versus T.

5   Conclusion

This paper investigated the secure calculation capacity of the Dual-UAV-MEC system, in which multiple GUs offload partial tasks to UAV_S for calculation with the presence of UAV_E eavesdropping. In order to enhance the security communication performance, we set GJ to send interference information to disturb UAV_E. To maximize the minimum objective, the secure calculation capacity, we optimize time allocation factor, local calculation and the trajectory of UAV_S with the constraints of UAVs maximum flight speed, the anti-collision between UAV_S and UAV_E, GU_k average power budget, GUs and UAV_S calculating capability and GU_k secure task calculation requirements. We proposed the efficient algorithm to solve the optimization problem by combining BCD and SCA methods. Simulation results show that the algorithm can enhance the security communication performance of the system effectively.

Acknowledgment. This work was supported by China National Science Foundation under Grand No. 61871348.

References

1. Lee, S., Lee, S., Shin, M.-K.: Low cost MEC server placement and association in 5G networks. In: 2019 International Conference on Information and Communication Technology Convergence (ICTC), Jeju, Korea (South), pp. 879–882 (2019)
2. Nguyen, T.D.T., Nguyen, V., Pham, V.-N., Huynh, L.N.T., Hossain, M.D., Huh, E.-N.: Modeling data redundancy and cost-aware task allocation in MEC-enabled Internet-of-vehicles applications. IEEE Internet Things J. **8**(3), 1687–1701 (2021)

3. Yu, Z., Gong, Y., Gong, S., Guo, Y.: Joint task offloading and resource allocation in UAV-enabled mobile edge computing. IEEE Internet Things J. **7**(4), 3147–3159 (2020)
4. Guo, F., Zhang, H., Ji, H., Li, X., Leung, V.C.M.: Joint trajectory and computation offloading optimization for UAV-assisted MEC with NOMA. In: IEEE INFOCOM 2019 - IEEE Conference on Computer Communications Workshops (INFOCOM WKSHPS), Paris, France (2019)
5. Du, Y., Yang, K., Wang, K., Zhang, G., Zhao, Y., Chen, D.: Joint resources and workflow scheduling in UAV-enabled wirelessly-powered MEC for IoT systems. IEEE Trans. Veh. Technol. **68**(10), 10187–10200 (2019)
6. Zhou, F., Wu, Y., Hu, R.Q., Qian, Y.: Computation rate maximization in UAV-enabled wireless-powered mobile-edge computing systems. IEEE J. Sel. Areas Communi. **36**(9), 1927–1941 (2018)
7. Lu, W., Wu, W., Qian, L., Wu, Y., Yu, N., Huang, L.: Optimal power allocation for secure non-orthogonal multiple access transmission. In: 2020 IEEE 92nd Vehicular Technology Conference (VTC2020-Fall), Victoria, BC, Canada (2020)
8. Zhao, N., et al.: Security enhancement for NOMA-UAV networks. IEEE Trans. Veh. Technol. **69**(4), 3994–4005 (2020)
9. Marks, B., Wright, G.P.: A general inner approximation algorithm for nonconvex mathematical programs. Oper. Res. **26**(4), 681–683 (1978)
10. Boyd, S., Vandenberghe, L.: Convex Optimization. Cambridge University Press, Cambridge (2004)

An Improved MAX-Log MPA Multiuser Detection Algorithm in SCMA System

Guanghua Zhang[1(⊠)], Zongyuan Fan[1], Zonglin Gu[1], Lin Zhang[1], Xiaoxin Wang[1], and Weidang Lu[2]

[1] Northeast Petroleum University, Daqing 163318, China
dqzgh@nepu.edu.cn
[2] Zhejiang University of Technology, Hangzhou 310014, China

Abstract. Sparse code multiple access (SCMA) technology is a new type of Non-Orthogonal Multiple Access (NOMA) technology for next-generation mobile communications. Aiming at the poor bit error rate (BER) performance of Max-Log messaging scheme (MPA) based on log domain in SCMA technology. In this paper, the user node message and the resource node message are updated simultaneously, the threshold value is set and the stability judgment of the user node is increased, and the above two methods are combined. Three improved multi-node detection algorithms, namely, S-Max-Log-MPA, T-Max-Log-MPA, and S-T-Max-Log-MPA, are proposed. Through simulation, the BER performance of these three algorithms is obtained and their performance characteristics are compared and summarized.

Keywords: SCMA · Node message · MPA · BER

1 Introduction

The new generation of mobile communication technology is 5G communication technology. Its core technologies mainly include Carrier aggregation, dense networks, D2D, non-orthogonal multiple access, simultaneous same-frequency full-duplex and new network architectures, etc. [1, 2]. Compared with 4G mobile communication, the technology further improves throughput, delay, connection number and energy consumption in terms of traffic density and connection density, which largely makes up for the deficiency of 4G technology [3, 4]. Sparse Code Multiple Access (SCMA) is a new type of non-orthogonal multiple access technology that has emerged from the expansion and promotion of Low Density Spreading (LDS) technology. It is one of the new multiple access technologies selected by the next generation mobile communication technology [5, 6]. The SCMA system combines modulation and spread spectrum, and the information of data acquisition node is mapped to n-dimensional complex digital word to realize system overload transmission, which can well meet the requirements of 5g high data rate, improving system capacity, increase coverage area, increase hot spot high capacity and reduce delay [7, 8]. In SCMA system, multiple node detection (MND) is used at the

X. Wang et al. (Eds.): AICON 2021, LNICST 396, pp. 319–328, 2021.
https://doi.org/10.1007/978-3-030-90196-7_27

receiver, and message passing algorithm (MPA) is used to process codebook in multi node detection [9, 10], but the algorithm has high complexity and poor bit error rate. Therefore, multi node detection algorithm has become one of the important research contents of SCMA system performance [11, 12].

When 5G high-speed information is transmitted and processed, the accuracy of data transmission is also an extremely important indicator. The author uses the serial-based MAX-Log-MPA Multi-node detection algorithm (referred to as S-Max-log-MPA), Threshold-based MAX-Log-MPA Multi-node Passing Algorithm (referred to as T-Max-log-MPA) and Max-log-MPA Multi-node Passing Algorithm based on Serial and Threshold (referred to as ST-Max-log-MPA) these three improved multi-node detection algorithms the analysis and comparison are carried out, and the characteristics of the three multi-node detection algorithms are compared and analyzed [13–15].

2 SCMA Data Transmission System Model

In the SCMA transmission system, taking the number of K data processing systems and J data collection nodes as an example, when the data collection point transmits data to the data processing system for processing, the data overload rate is $\lambda = J/K$. The data collected at the data collection point $j(1, 2, \cdots, J)$ is $u_j(u_1, u_2, \cdots, u_J)$, which is pre-encoded through FEC encoding to obtain a binary bit data. The binary bit data stream is directly mapped to the K-dimensional data processing system through the SCMA encoder to obtain the K-dimensional code word $x_j(x_1, x_2, \cdots, x_J)$. The encoder is a mapping that maps $\log_2 M$ bits of data $b_j(b_1, b_2, \cdots, b_J)$ collected at the data collection point j to the K-dimensional code x_j corresponding to the codebook u_j of the data collection point j.

Therefore, the codebook mapping process of the SCMA system can be expressed as:

$$f : B^{\log_2 M} \rightarrow \chi \tag{1}$$

Among them, the M is the codebook size, The size of M depends on the number of non-zeros in the binary data stream, and χ is the data codebook of the data collection point. The process of SCMA encoder mapping binary bit data stream into sparse codeword can be defined as:

$$x_j = f(b_j) \tag{2}$$

Among them, x_j is the K-dimensional codeword obtained by SCMA encoder mapping, and b_j is the binary bit data stream obtained by FEC encoding preprocessing.

This article uses the 4-dimensional codebook published by Huawei, that is, there are 6 data collection points and 4 data processing systems. The corresponding factor diagram is:

$$F_{4\times6} = \begin{bmatrix} 0 & 1 & 1 & 0 & 1 & 0 \\ 1 & 0 & 1 & 0 & 0 & 1 \\ 0 & 1 & 0 & 1 & 0 & 1 \\ 1 & 0 & 0 & 1 & 1 & 0 \end{bmatrix} \tag{3}$$

Among them, 0 denotes the data collection point does not transmit data, 1 represents the data collection point transmits data, and $F_{4 \times 6}$ denotes the data processing system.

The data collection point processes the data through FEC encoding and SCMA encoder, then sends it to the channel, and sends it to the data processing system after processing with additive white Gaussian noise. Define the signal received during K-dimensional data processing as $y_j = [y_1, y_2, \cdots, y_K]^T$, then:

$$y = \sum_{j=1}^{J} diag(h_j)x_j + n \tag{4}$$

Among the $h_j(h_1, h_2, \cdots, h_J)$ is the channel attenuation factor vector, In addition, adding a variance of $n(n(0 \sim N_o^2))$ to the system, additive white noise $n_j = [n_1, n_2 \cdots, n_K]^T$, and $diag()$ is the diagonal operation of the matrix.

3   Max-log-MPA Multi-node Detection Algorithm

The Message Passing Algorithm based on Maximum logarithm (Max-log-MPA) is a classic multi-user detection scheme in the SCMA system. It uses the maximum logarithm operation to calculate the exponent in the original message passing algorithm. Operation and product operations are transformed into sum-product operations, and the data collection points and data processing system messages are updated through factor graphs, thereby reducing the complexity of the algorithm in the SCMA system and improving the BER of the SCMA system. Therefore, the Max-log-MPA message passing algorithm update process mainly includes the following three processes:

Step 1: Conditionally initialize the probability of all codewords based on the Max-log-MPA message passing logarithm:

$$I_{c_k \to u_j}^0(x_j) = \frac{1}{M}(j = 1, 2, \cdots, J) \tag{5}$$

Among them, c_k denotes the $k(k = 1, 2, ..., K)$ data server, u_j denotes the j data collection node, and $I_{c_k \to u_j}^0(x_j)$ denotes the message that the data server transmits to the data collection node during the first iteration.

Step 2: Updating process of function nodes and variable nodes of Max-log-MPA message passing algorithm:

$$I_{c_k \to u_j}^t(x_j) = \max_{i=1,2,\cdots,N} \left\{ -\frac{1}{2d^2} \left\| y_k - \sum_{v \in x_k} h_{k,v} x_{k,v} \right\|^2 + \prod_{m \in x_k/j} I_{c_m \to u_k}^t(x_j) \right.$$
$$\left. + \prod_{m \in x_k/j} I_{c_m \to u_k}^{t-1}(x_j) \right\} \tag{6}$$

Among them, $I_{c_k \to u_j}^t(x_j)$ denotes the message transmitted by the data server to the data collection node, ξ_k/j denotes the collection of all data collection nodes except the j-th collection node and the k-th data point connected to the data server, $\sim \{x_j\}$ denotes the Marginal probability of x_j, $h_{v,k}$ denotes the channel gain of the v-th data collection node on the k-th data server, $x_{k,v}$ denotes the codeword of the k-th data server on the v-th data collection node, the ξ_k denotes the position set of the non-zero codeword in the kth row in the factor graph.

Step 3: Based on the Max-log-MPA message passing scheme, after reaching the set Maximum times of calculations, it will be judged:

$$Q(x_{j,m}) = ap_v(x_{j,m}) \times \prod_{m \in \xi_k/j} I_{c_m \to u_k}(x_j) \tag{7}$$

Among them, $Q(x_{j,m})$ denotes the probability of transmitting the code word $x_{j,m}$ on the j-th data collection node, and $ap_v(x_{j,m})$ denotes the prior probability of the j-th data collection node.

In the formula, The $Q(x_{j,m})$ denotes the probability of transmitting the codeword on the data collection node $x_{j,m}$, and The $ap_v(x_{j,m})$ denotes the prior probability of the j-th data collection node.

The data collection node uses the log-likelihood ratio (LLR) to make a decision:

$$LLR_{j,x} = \log\left(\frac{P(b_i = 0)}{P(b_i = 1)}\right) = \log\left(\frac{\sum_{m:b_{m,i}=0} Q(x_{j,m})}{\sum_{m:b_{m,i}=1} Q(x_{j,m})}\right) \tag{8}$$

Among them, $b_i = 0$ denotes the probability that the data collection node v_i can be successfully parsed, $b_i = 1$ denotes the v_i decoding failure of the data collection node, and $LLR_{j,x}$ denotes the log-likelihood ratio.

4   S-Max-log-MPA Multi-node Detection Algorithm

The original message passing algorithm updates the messages of the data collection point and the data processing system through the factor graph, which is one of the main data analysis methods of SCMA. In the original message passing algorithm, the data collection point and the processing system are respectively regarded as: variable node (VN) and function node (FN). When analyzing the time data, first update the message of the function node, then update the information of the variable node, and finally make a decision when the number of calculation times reaches the preset Maximum times.

In the S-Max-log-MAP multi-node detection algorithm, each iteration transmits the updated information from the previous node to the next node, and the previous node and the next node update the functional nodes at the same time. In the specific calculation, the information of the function node and the variable node is updated at the same time.

Therefore, In the specific calculation, the information of the function node and the variable node is iterated at the same time:

$$I_{c_k \to u_j}^t(x_j) = 2 \times \max_{\sim x_j} \left\{ -\frac{1}{2\delta^2} \left\| y_k - \sum_{v \in \xi_k} h_{k,v} x_{k,v} \right\|^2 + \prod_{m \in \xi_k/j} I_{c_m \to u_k}^t(x_j) \right.$$

$$\left. + \prod_{m \in \xi_k/j} I_{c_m \to u_k}^{t-1}(x_j) \right\} \quad (9)$$

Among them, $I_{c_k \to u_j}^t(x_j)$ denotes the message transmitted by the data server to the data collection node, ξ_k/j denotes the set of data collection nodes in the data collection node except the j-th collection node and the k-th data server connected, $\sim \{x_j\}$ denotes the Marginal probability of x_j, and, $h_{k,v}$ denotes the channel gain of the v-th data collection node on the k-th data server, $x_{v,k}$ denotes the codeword of the k-th data server on the v-th data collection node, and ξ_k denotes the position set of the non-zero elements in the k-th row of the factor graph.

The decision process of the S-Max-log-MPA message passing algorithm becomes:

First estimate the probability of the code word combination on the k-th data collection node: $Q^t(x_j)$

$$Q^t(x_j) = \exp\left(-\frac{1}{N_{0,k}} \left\| y_k - \sum_{v \in \xi_k} h_{k,v} x_{k,v} \right\|^2 \right) \quad (10)$$

Among them, $t(t = 1, 2, ..., T_{max})$ denotes the number of iterations, $N_{0,k}$ represents the noise power on the data server k,

Then estimate the probability $Q(x_{j,m})$ of transmitting the codeword $x_{j,m}$ on the j-th data collection node:

$$Q(x_{j,m}) = ap_v(x_{j,m}) \times \prod_{m \in \xi_k/j} I_{c_m \to u_k}(x_j) \quad (11)$$

Where $ap_v(x_{j,m})$ denotes the prior probability of the j-th data collection node.

Finally, the data collection node uses the log-likelihood ratio (LLR) to make a decision.

5 T-Max-log-MPA Multi Node Detection Algorithm

T-Max-log-MPA multi-node detection algorithm updates the information of function nodes and variable nodes at the same time, adds the necessary conditions for the certainty of data collection point information, and then judges the threshold conditions. Pre decoding can only be performed if the threshold conditions are met.

Using the Jacobi formula:

$$\log\left(\sum_{i=1}^{N} \exp(f_i)\right) \approx \max_{i=1,2,\cdots,N} \{f_1, f_2, \cdots, f_N\} \quad (12)$$

The message update of the T-Max-log-MPA multi-node detection algorithm can be modified to:

$$I_{c_k \to u_j}^t(x_j) = \max_{i=1,2,\cdots,N} \left\{ -\frac{1}{2\delta^2} \left\| y_k - \sum_{v \in \xi_k} h_{k,v} x_{k,v} \right\| + \sum_{v \in \xi_k} I_{u_j \to c_k}^{t-1}(x_j) \right\} \qquad (13)$$

After the Maximum times of iterations, the codeword output probability is:

$$Q(x_j) = \sum_{v \in \varepsilon_j} I_{c_k \to u_j}^{t\max}(x_j) \qquad (14)$$

Among them, ξ_j denotes the position set of the non-zero elements in the j-th column of the factor graph.

6   S-T-Max-log-MPA Multi-node Detection Algorithm

The S-T-Max-log-MPA multi-node detection algorithm is a synthesis of the ideas of the first two algorithms. First, it judges the reliability of the codeword, and then judges the log-likelihood of the data server. The two judgment results will be combined as the decisive index for the final decision of the data collection node.

Since the S-T-Max-log-MPA multi-node detection algorithm must first determine the reliability of the codeword of the data collection node, the message update process can be modified as follows:

$$I_{c_k \to u_j}^t(x_j) = 2 \times \frac{1}{\sqrt{2\pi}\delta} \times \max_{\sim x_j} \left\{ -\frac{1}{2\delta^2} \left\| y_k - \sum_{v \in \xi_k} h_{k,v} x_{k,v} \right\|^2 \right.$$
$$\left. + \prod_{m \in \xi_k / j} I_{c_m \to u_k}^t(x_j) + \prod_{m \in \xi_k / j} I_{c_m \to u_k}^{t-1}(x_j) \right\} \qquad (15)$$

7   Simulation Analysis

In order to verify the accuracy of the three improved message passing algorithms, the BER performance can be analyzed separately. Because the codebook of this article uses Huawei's 6 × 4 codebook, this article selects the three cases where the maximum number of iterations is 2, 3, and 5, and analyzes the bit error rates of the three algorithms respectively.

Figure 1 shows the BER of the three improved algorithms when the maximum times of iterations is 2. It can be seen from the figure that the average BER performance of the three improved message passing schemes is better than the high threshold in the case of a low threshold. When the Eb/No/dB = 0, the BER of S-Max-log-MPA multi-node detection algorithm is 0.19, while T-Max-log-MPA multi-node detection algorithm and ST-Max-Log-MPA multi-node detection scheme The BER under the three threshold

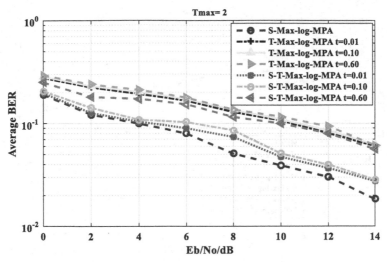

Fig. 1. Bit error ratio comparison of three algorithms when $T_{max} = 2$

conditions of 0.01, 0.10 and 0.60 are respectively: 0.2733, 0.2848, 0.2927 and 0.197, 0.206, 0.2503. When Eb/No/dB = 14, the BER of S-Max-log-MPA multi-node detection scheme is 0.01833, while T-Max-log-MPA multi-node detection scheme and ST-Max-log-MPA multi-node detection scheme The BER are: 0.062, 0.04383, 0.0615 and 0.0275, 0.0285, 0.056. Although it can be seen from the figure that the BER performance of T-Max-Log-MPA multi node detection scheme and S-T-Max-Log-MPA multi node detection scheme is worse than that of S-Max-Log-MPA multi node detection scheme. The BER performance of the first two scheme under low threshold is better than that of S-Max-Log-MPA multi node detection scheme.

Figure 2 shows the BER of the three improved algorithms when the maximum times of iterations is 3. It can be concluded from the figure that the BER of T-MaX-Log-MPA multi node detection scheme and S-T-Max-log-MPA multi node detection scheme is better at low threshold. In addition, it can be seen that the bit error rate performance of S-T-Max-log-MPA multi node detection scheme will be better with the increase of iteration times. When Eb/No/dB = 0, the BER of S-Max-log-MPA multi-node detection scheme is 0.1562, while T-Max-log-MPA multi-node detection scheme and ST-Max-log-MPA multi-node detection scheme. The BER under three threshold conditions of 0.01, 0.10 and 0.60 are respectively: 0.2372, 0.2585, 0.2768 and 0.1715, 0.1912, 0.2455. When Eb/No/dB = 14, the bit error rate of S-Max-Log-MPA multi-node detection scheme is 0.0075, while T-Max-log-MPA multi-node detection scheme and ST-Max-log-MPA multi-node detection scheme the BER are: 0.0395, 0.04383, 0.04467 and 0.0155, 0.0175, 0.05333. Compared with Fig. 1, the BER performance of the three denotes is improving with the increase of the maximum number of iterations. At the same time, the bit error rate performance of T-Max-log-MPA multi node detection algorithm and S-T-Max-log-MPA multi node detection algorithm is also improving at low threshold.

When the maximum number of iterations is 5, the BER performance of the three denotes can be obtained from Fig. 3. It can be seen that with the increase of threshold and

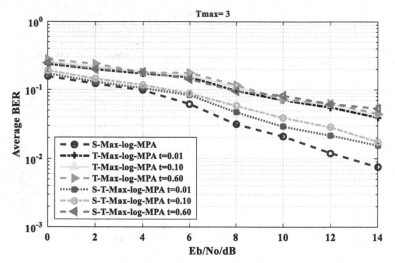

Fig. 2. Bit error ratio comparison of three algorithms when $T_{max} = 3$

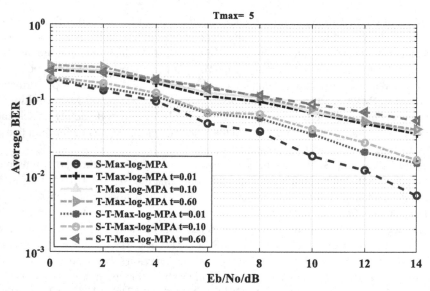

Fig. 3. Bit error ratio comparison of three algorithms when $T_{max} = 5$

the maximum number of iterations, the bit error rate performance of s-t-max-log-mpa multi node detection algorithm is much higher than that of the other two denotes. When Eb/No/dB $= 0$, the bit error rate of S-Max-log-MPA multi-node detection algorithm is 0.1813, while T-Max-log-MPA multi-node detection algorithm and ST-Max-log-MPA multi-node detection algorithm The bit error rates under three threshold conditions of 0.01, 0.10 and 0.60 are respectively: 0.2507, 0.262, 0.286 and 0.1878, 0.1957, 0.241.

When Eb/No/dB $= 14$, the bit error rate of S-Max-log-MPA multi-node detection algorithm is 0.0055, while T-Max-log-MPA multi-node detection algorithm and ST-Max-log-MPA multi-node detection algorithm The bit error rates are: 0.036, 0.03817, 0.04067 and 0.01483, 0.01617, 0.05333. Compared with the numerical analysis of the bit error rate performance of the previous two figures, it can be seen that the overall bit error rate performance of the three denotes is improving as the maximum number of iterations increases. And the error rates of the three denotes are also approaching as the number of iterations increases.

8 Conclusion

From the above research and simulation, it can be summed up that the average BER of S-Max-log-MPA multi node detection algorithm is the smallest, and the average bit error rate of T-Max-log-MPA multi node detection algorithm and S-T-Max-log-MPA multi node detection algorithm increases with the increase of threshold. However, in some communication environments requiring threshold restrictions, T-Max-log-MPA multi node detection algorithm and S-T-Max-log-MPA multi node detection algorithm are more suitable for these scenarios. In the low threshold scenario, S-T-Max-log-MPA multi node detection algorithm is better than T-Max-log-MPA multi node detection algorithm, but in the high threshold communication environment, T-Max-log-MPA multi node detection algorithm is more suitable. In other application scenarios, S-Max-log-MPA multi node detection algorithm is better than the other two algorithms.

References

1. Kaur, A., Kaushik, S., Bajpai, R., Gupta, N.: Performance analysis of millimeter-wave based device-to-device communications system. In: International Conference on Telecommunications (2020)
2. Tehrani, M.N., Uysal, M., Yanikomeroglu, H.: Device-to-device communication in 5G cellular networks: challenges, solutions, and future directions. IEEE Commun. Mag. **52**(5), 86–92 (2014)
3. Yang, N., Wang, L., Geraci, G., et al.: Safeguarding 5G wireless communication networks using physical layer security. IEEE Commun. Mag. **53**(4), 20–27 (2015)
4. Liu, X., Jia, M., Zhang, X., et al.: A novel multichannel Internet of Things based on dynamic spectrum sharing in 5G communication. IEEE Internet Things J. **6**(4), 5962–5970 (2019)
5. Joint channel estimation and multi-user detection for MC-CDMA system using genetic algorithm and simulated annealing. In: 2010 IEEE International Conference on Systems Man and Cybernetics (2010)
6. Feng, L., He, X., Sun, L.: A new method of joint channel estimation and multiuser detection based on adaptive matching pursuit algorithm in NOMA system. J. Sig. Process. **36**(7), 1136–1143 (2020). (in Chinese)
7. Zhang, S., et al.: A capacity-based codebook design method for sparse code multiple access systems. In: International Conference on Wireless Communications and Signal Processing (2016)
8. Ma, X., Yang, L., Lin, X.: Codebook assignment optimization in sparse code multiple access system. J. Sig. Process. **34**(2), 148–154 (2018). (in Chinese)

9. Lei, L., Chen, Y., Guo, W., et al.: Prototype for 5G new air interface technology SCMA and performance evaluation. China Commun. **12**(Supplement), 1–10 (2015)
10. Zhang, J., Lei, L., Sun, Y., et al.: PoC of SCMA-based uplink grant-free transmission in UCNC for 5G. IEEE J. Sel. Areas Commun. **35**(6), 66–78 (2017)
11. Moltafet, M., Parsaeefard, S., Javan, M.R., et al.: Radio resource allocation in MISO-SCMA assisted C-RAN in 5G networks. IEEE Trans. Veh. Technol. **68**(6), 132–145 (2019)
12. Chen, Y., Bayesteh, A., Wu, Y., et al.: SCMA: a promising non-orthogonal multiple access technology for 5G networks. In: 2016 IEEE 84th Vehicular Technology Conference (VTC-Fall), Montreal, QC, Canada (2016). https://doi.org/10.1109/VTCFall.2016.7881213
13. Zhang, G., Gu, Z., Zhao, Q., Ren, J., Lu, W.: A threshold-based max-log-MPA low complexity multiuser detection algorithm. Sensors **20**(7), 1–13 (2020). https://doi.org/10.3390/s20041016
14. Zhang, G., Gu, Z., Zhao, Q., Ren, J., Han, S., Lu, W.: A multi-node detection algorithm based on serial and threshold in Intelligent Sensor Networks. Sensors **20**(4), 1016–1028 (2020). https://doi.org/10.3390/s20071960
15. Zhang, G., Gu, Z., Lu, W., Han, S.: A Max-log-MPA multiuser detection algorithm based on serial in SCMA system. In: CSPS 2020 (2020)

Artificial Intelligence in Electromagnetic
Signal Processing

An Adaptive Slice Type Decision Algorithm for HEVC Based on Local Luminance Histogram

Pengyu Liu[1,2,3]([✉]), Yue Zhang[1,2,3], Shanji Chen[4], Kun Duan[1,2,3], Xuan Sun[1,2,3], and Tenghe Cui[1,2,3]

[1] Faculty of Information Technology, Beijing University of Technology, Beijing 100124, China
liupengyu@bjut.edu.cn
[2] Advanced Information Network Beijing Laboratory, Beijing 100124, China
[3] Computational Intelligence and Intelligent Systems Beijing Key Laboratory, Beijing 100124, China
[4] School of Physics and Electronic Information Engineering, Qinghai Nationalities University, Xining 810007, China

Abstract. Video frame type decision is one of the key factors affecting coding efficiency. Based on the framework of High Efficiency Video Coding (HEVC), an adaptive frame type decision algorithm based on local luminance histogram is proposed in this paper. Firstly, the local luminance histogram was calculated at the coding tree unit (CTU) level, and the difference of local luminance histogram between two frames was used to characterize the degree of inter-frame content variation. Secondly, scene-change frame is determined by comparing the degree of inter-frame content variation in the scene-change detection window, and it is defined as I frame. Finally, the Mini-GOP size is adaptively determined according to the correlation between the degree of inter-frame content variation and Mini-GOP size. GPB frame and B frame are adaptively determined for the video sequences with I frame defined. The experimental results show that, compared with the relevant algorithms in x265, the proposed algorithm can achieve efficient adaptive decision of video frame type under the premise of reducing the algorithm complexity by nearly 5%, and effectively improve the efficiency of video coding.

Keywords: High Efficiency Video Coding (HEVC) · Local luminance histogram · Scene-change detection · Slice type decision

1 Introduction

With the continuous development of multimedia technology, videos with high definition (HD), high frame rate (HFR) and multi-view point have resulted in an explosion of actual data thus presenting more formidable challenges to video coding. Compared with Advanced Video Coding (AVC), High Efficiency Video Coding (HEVC) which was published by the Joint Collaborative Team on Video Coding (JCT-VC) in 2013 has achieved

X. Wang et al. (Eds.): AICON 2021, LNICST 396, pp. 331–345, 2021.
https://doi.org/10.1007/978-3-030-90196-7_28

higher compression performance [1–3]. However, the introduction of new technologies such as partitioning structure, quad-tree coding structure for coding unit (CU) and mode decision makes the coding complexity increase significantly [3, 4]. The encoding time of HEVC is higher than H.264/AVC by 253% on average, making it impractical for implementation in multimedia applications. The open source encoder x265 based on HEVC standard is an efficient video encoder for practical industrial scenarios, which significantly reduces the encoding complexity by utilizing many accelerating methods [5].

According to the definition of the slice type of each frame in the video sequence by HEVC, frames can be divided into Intra frame (I frame), Predictive frame (P frame), Bi-directional interpolated prediction frame (B frame) and Generalized P and B frame (GPB frame). Noticeably, GPB frame that references its previous two frames replaces P frame in the low delay mode. I frame is usually determined according to the results of scene-change in the video sequence and the interval of I frame required by the business scene in encoders. And the rest of the frames in the video sequence should be decided into GPB frame or B frame. Under the premise of controllable encoding complexity, the efficient decision of slice type of video sequence can effectively improve the coding efficiency.

The variation of inter-frame scene-change changes dramatically. If the previous frame is used as the reference frame, the quality of the encoded video will inevitably decline seriously. There are three kinds of scene-change detection methods, mainly based on Motion Estimate (ME), the Rate-Distortion Cost (RD Cost) or the luminance histogram [7–13]. For the scene-change detection algorithm based on ME, Shu et al. [7] proposed a scene-change detection algorithm based on block matching, which calculated the Motion Vector Difference (MVD) between the current and the previous frame to judge whether there is a scene-change frame. Ding et al. [8] substituted the Sum of Absolute Difference (SAD) and the Sum of Absolute Transformed Difference (SATD) for the Sum of Absolute Difference (SAD) to obtain more accurate Motion Vector (MV). In addition, Lee et al. [9] proposed a scene-change detection algorithm based on optical flow field, which also relies on the calculation of MV. However, the performance of the above algorithm depends too much on the accuracy of the MV obtained by MV, which is affected by many coding parameters, resulting in limited efficiency of the scene-change detection algorithm based on motion search. Calculating the intra-frame and inter-frame RD Cost of each frame of the video sequence to decide the scene-change frame in x265 delivers excellent performance with high coding complexity. In [10], Kim et al. proposed to compare the global luminance histogram differences between the current frame and the previous one. In [11, 12], scene-change frames were judged by calculating two-dimensional histogram to extract the shape of histogram. Although significantly reduced the coding complexity, the above methods based on the global luminance histogram cannot take the changes in frames into consideration bringing about low detection accuracy and making it difficult to set the threshold.

There are mainly two kinds of methods for deciding GPB frames and B frames. The fixed GPB frame and B frame decision methods used a configurable single frame structure to determine the frame type of the entire video sequence [6, 13]. These methods are simple and suitable for most video sequences, but they cannot further improve the compression performance according to the temporal characteristics of each video sequence. The other is the adaptive GPB frame and B frame decision methods [14, 15]. Compared with the fixed methods, these methods can adaptively adjust the size of Mini Group of Picture (Mini-GOP) according to the temporal characteristics, so as to achieve higher coding efficiency. At present, fast adaptive method and method based on Viterbi have been integrated in x265. The former compared the RD Costs of different sizes of Mini-GOP to accomplish the frame type decision, and the latter completes the frame type decision through iteration based on Viterbi algorithm. Compared with the former, the algorithm based on Viterbi significantly improves the encoding efficiency, but also increases the computational complexity. Therefore, reducing the algorithm complexity under the premise of high compression efficiency is urgent to be solved.

Inspired by the low computational complexity of luminance histogram and the strong correlation of video sequences, we propose the adaptive slice type decision algorithm based on local luminance histogram. Through analyzing the degree of inter-frame content variation, our method can improve the efficiency of video coding while reducing the algorithm complexity.

2   Adaptive Frame Type Decision Algorithm

Figure 1 shows the flow of adaptive frame type decision algorithm based on local luminance histogram proposed in this paper.

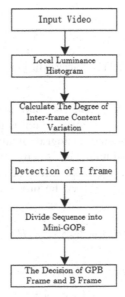

Fig. 1. The flow chart of adaptive frame type decision algorithm based on local luminance histogram

2.1   The Motion of Local Luminance Histogram

Images in the video sequence are composed of luminance component Y and chromaticity component U and V. The core of the methods based on luminance histogram is that the luminance histogram reflects the frequency of each luminance level in the image, and different frames have different luminance histogram. We can decide the type of video frames according to the luminance histogram differences.

Figure 2 shows the comparison of global luminance histogram of the scene-change in Wolf Warrior 2 [16]. We can find that the difference of the two global luminance histograms is negligible.

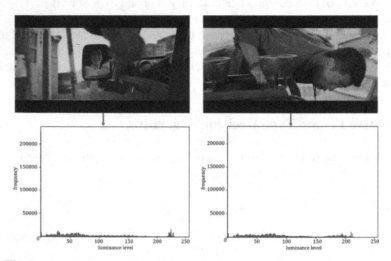

Fig. 2. The comparison of global luminance histogram of scene-change frames

Since the luminance histogram is a statistical variable, it cannot reflect the spatial information of a frame, and the spatial information is the key factor to determine the content. We propose the local luminance histogram in this paper to make up for the lack of spatial information in the global luminance histogram. This paper takes CTU as the basic unit to divide each frame of the video into blocks and obtain the corresponding local luminance histogram. Figure 3 shows the process to obtain the local luminance histogram of a frame,

$$H_n = \left\{ H_{n,0,0}, H_{n,0,1}, ..., H_{n,i,j}, ... \right\}$$

$$H_{n,i,j} = \{l_0, l_1, ..., l_{255}\} \tag{1}$$

where H_n refers to the collection of local luminance histograms for all CTUs in nth frame, $H_{n,i,j}$ denotes the local luminance histogram of CTU in row i, column j in nth frame, l_k represents the frequency of the kth luminance value.

Fig. 3. Obtain local luminance histogram of each frame

Figure 4 shows the local luminance histogram of CTU at the same position in the two frames before and after the scene change in Wolf Warrior 2. Compared with the global luminance histogram, there are great differences in the brightness distribution of the local luminance histogram.

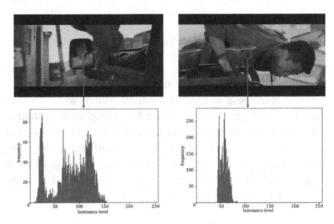

Fig. 4. The comparison of local luminance histogram of scene-change frames

We selected Kimono and three dynamic video sequences from the Internet, including Wolf Warrior 2, A Little Red Flower, Report on COVID-19 Prevention and Control in Beijing, to analyze global luminance histogram differences D_{hist} and the sum of local luminance histogram differences $D_{\text{local\_hist}}$ in Table 1. We can see that $D_{\text{local\_hist}}$ is always larger than D_{hist} and the difference between D_{hist} and $D_{\text{local\_hist}}$ is large, which better reflects the spatial characteristics of videos. The difference between D_{hist} and $D_{\text{local\_hist}}$ is calculated as follows,

$$P_D = \frac{D_{\text{local\_hist}} - D_{\text{hist}}}{D_{\text{hist}}} \times 100\% \tag{2}$$

Table 1. The comparison of global luminance histogram differences and the sum of local luminance histogram differences

Sequences	Total frames	Scene change numbers	$P_D < 0$	$0 < P_D \leq 1\%$	$1\% < P_D < 100\%$	$P_D \geq 100\%$
Kimono1	240	1	0	0	1	0
A Little Red Flower	4089	92	0	5	40	47
Wolf Warrior 2	4423	185	0	0	95	90
Report on COVID-19 Prevention and Control in Beijing	2659	42	0	0	19	23

2.2 The Degree of Inter-frame Content Variation Between Frames

By analyzing the content characteristics of videos, it can be seen that when there is not scene change, the contents of two frames in the same scene are basically the same, and the difference of local brightness histogram is small. When scene change occurs, the contents of the two frames differ greatly, and the local brightness histogram difference between the two frames is significantly larger than that between the two frames without scene change. We determine the current CTU as a content change block by comparing the local luminance histogram difference of CTU at the same position between two frames and the size of the set threshold in this paper. The local luminance histogram difference of CTU can be calculated as follows,

$$\text{diff}_{i,j} = \sum_{k=0}^{255} |H_{\text{cur},i,j}[k] - H_{\text{ref},i,j}[k]| \tag{3}$$

where $\text{diff}_{i,j}$ is the local luminance histogram difference of CTU between the current frame and the reference one at row i, column j. $H_{\text{cur},i,j}[k]$ and $H_{\text{ref},i,j}[k]$ represent the local luminance histogram of CTU at row i, column j in the current frame and the reference one, respectively.

In order to avoid the influence of noises and false detections on scene-change block, this paper defines the current CTU as a scene-change block by detecting whether there are a certain number of content-changing blocks in neighboring CTUs, and calculates the degree of inter-frame content variation of the current frame based on the scene-change blocks. We use content-changing flag $F_{i,j}$ to indicate whether the block is a content-changing block. When $F_{i,j}$ is equal to one, the block is a content-changing block, otherwise it is not a content-changing block. Figure 5 shows how the four zones around CTU are currently divided.

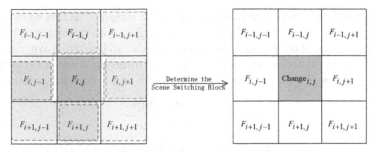

Fig. 5. Division of the area around the current block

$$\text{Change}_{i,j} = \begin{cases} 1, \ (F_{i,j-1} + F_{i-1,j-1} + F_{i-1,j}) > 1 \ or \ (F_{i-1,j} + F_{i-1,j+1} + F_{i,j+1}) > 1 \\ \quad or \ (F_{i,j+1} + F_{i+1,j+1} + F_{i+1,j}) > 1 \ or \ (F_{i+1,j} + F_{i+1,j-1} + F_{i,j-1}) > 1 \\ 0, \ otherwise \end{cases} \quad (4)$$

$$\text{inter\_diff} = \sum_i \sum_j \text{Change}_{i,j} \quad (5)$$

2.3 The Decision of I Frame

In order to further improve the accuracy of our method, this paper uses the scene-change detection window as the basic unit to traverse the entire video sequence to detect I frame. We set the size of the detection window and the step as 5 according to our experience. Figure 6 shows how the detection window moves and the detection process.

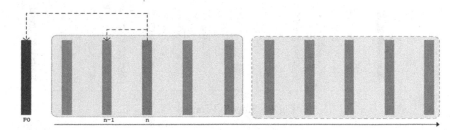

Fig. 6. The movement of the detection window and the detection process

We set the second frame of the video sequence (POC = 1) as the start of the detection window, and five frames in the detection window are detected successively from left to right. In each detection, the previous frame N − 1 of the current frame N and P0 outside the detection window are taken as the reference frames. We calculate the degree of inter-frame content variation inter_diff_{n-1} and inter_diff_{P0} respectively, and decide whether the current frame is a keyframe according to the threshold. We set key_frame as the flag of the keyframe.

After five frames in the detection window are detected successively, there are three possible scenarios for the number of keyframes $n_{\text{key\_frame}}$. When $n_{\text{key\_frame}}$ equals to

0, it means that there is no scene-change frame in the current detection window. When n_{key_frame} equals to 1, this frame is I frame. When n_{key_frame} is greater than 1, we should calculate the average of the degree of content variation of all keyframes avg_diff according to the formula (6) and select the first frame that meets the formula (7) as the final scene-change frame. Figure 7 shows how to select the final scene-change frame.

$$avg\_diff = \frac{\sum inter\_diff_{P0}}{n_{key\_frame}} \tag{6}$$

$$change\_frame_n = \begin{cases} 1, & key\_frame = 1 \text{ and } inter\_diff_{n-1} > 1.1 \times avg\_diff \\ 0, & otherwise \end{cases} \tag{7}$$

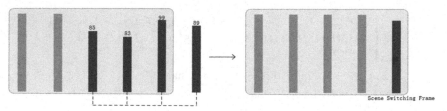

Fig. 7. The rectification of keyframes

In addition, considering the problem that frequently inserting I frames will result in a sharp increase in bit rate, this paper introduces *Flag* between Windows to smooth the density of I frames. Figure 8 shows the process of smoothing I frames.

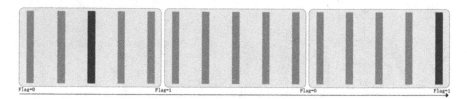

Fig. 8. Smooth I frames

Step 1: Initialize *Flag* (*Flag* = 0) and find I frame in the detection window.
Step 2: If I frame is detected and *Flag* = 0, the Flag will be changed to 1 (*Flag* = 1). Otherwise, the detected I frame is cleared and perform the next detection.
Step 3: The *Flag* will be reset when the I frame is no longer detected in the detection window.

2.4 The Decision of GPB Frame and B Frame

By analyzing the motion characteristics of the video sequence, it can be seen that the content of the video sequence with violent motion varies greatly in two successive frames, while the content of the video sequence with gentle motion is almost the same in two successive frames. If the same Mini-GOP size is used for videos with different motion characteristics, the differences in coding efficiency of two videos will be inevitably large.

On the basis of Formula 2, we use Formula 8 to calculate the overall difference of the current frame and the previous one.

$$\text{frame\_diff}_{n,n-1} = \sum_i \sum_j \sum_{k=0}^{255} |H_{n,i,j}[k] - H_{n-1,i,j}[k]| \tag{8}$$

The Mini-GOP size obtained by the adaptive frame type decision algorithm based on Viterbi thought in x265 is the Mini-GOP ground truth. Figure 9 shows the correlation between the Mini-GOP ground truth and $\text{frame\_diff}_{n,n-1}$. It's obvious that when $\text{frame\_diff}_{n,n-1}$ is greater than 3000, the ground truth concentrates on 1 and 2, and the corresponding GPB frame interval is 0 and 1. And when $\text{frame\_diff}_{n,n-1}$ is less than 1500, the ground truth concentrates on 4 and 5, and the corresponding GPB frame interval is 3 and 4. The correlation between the ground truth and $\text{frame\_diff}_{n,n-1}$ in the video sequence is fully explained.

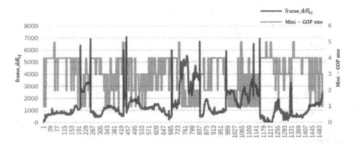

Fig. 9. The correlation between the Mini-GOP ground truth and $\text{frame\_diff}_{n,n-1}$

Firstly, our method decides the Mini-GOP size according to Algorithm 1. Traversing the video whose frame I has been determined for the first time, the video is divided into several Mini-GOPs according to the Mini-GOP size. Last frames in each Mini-GOP are set as GPB frame, and the others are set as B frame. In addition, I frame in the video sequence includes Clean Random Access (CRA) frame and Instantaneous Decoding Refresh (IDR) frame. If I frame is CRA, it will be processed as the end frame of the previous Mini-GOP according to the operation logic of GPB frame (without changing the frame type). And the first frame after CRA is the start of a new Mini-GOP. If I frame is IDR, it will be processed according to the logic at the end of the video sequence. The previous frame will be set as GPB frame and be regarded as the end frame of the previous Mini-GOP. IDR will be regarded as an independent Mini-GOP, and the first subsequent frame will be regarded as the start of a new Mini-GOP.

Alogrithm 1
Input: *diff_i[n], Max_Size, Thr0, Thr1, Thr2, Thr3*

Input: $diff_i[n]$, Max_Size, Thr0, Thr1, Thr2, Thr3
Output: Mini_GOP_Size
1: $j=0$, flag0=false, flag1=false, flag2=false
2: **while** $(j<Max\_size-1)$ **do**
3:    **if** $diff_i[j]>Thr2$ **then**
4:        flag2=flag1=flag0=true
5:    **else if** $diff_i[j]>Thr1$ **then**
6:        flag1=flag0=true
7:    **else if** $diff_i[j]>Thr0$ **then**
8:        flag0=ture
9:    **end if**
10:    **if** $(diff_i[j]>Thr3)$ **then**
11:        Mini_GOP_Size=$j+1$
12:        **goto 25**
13:    **else if** $(j>1$ **and** $(diff_i[j]>Thr2$ **or** flag2$))$ **then**
14:        Mini_GOP_Size=$j+1$
15:        **goto 25**
16:    **else if** $(j>2$ **and** $(diff_i[j]>Thr1$ **or** flag1$))$ **then**
17:        Mini_GOP_Size=$j+1$
18:        **goto 25**
19:    **else if** $(j>3$ **and** $(diff_i[j]>Thr0$ **or** flag0$))$ **then**
20:        Mini_GOP_Size=$j+1$
21:        **goto 25**
22:    **end if**
23:    $j++$
24: **end while**
25: Mini_GOP_Size=$j+1$
26: **return**

Secondly, the video is traversed for the second time, and the number of layers of coding structure L is determined according to Table 2. When L equals to 1, the display order is the coding order. When L is greater than 1, the video is determined according to the Formula 9 to realize the rearrangement from display order to encoding order.

Table 2. The relationship between Mini-GOP size and the number of layers of coding structure

Mini-GOP size	The number of layers L
1	1
2	2
3–5	3
6–8	4

$$L = 2 \quad M[n], M[1] - M[n-1]$$

$$L = 3 \quad M[n], M[\frac{n}{2}], M[1] - M[\frac{n}{2} - 1], M[\frac{n}{2} + 1] - M[n-1]$$

$$L = 4 \quad M[n], M[\frac{n}{2}], M[\frac{n}{4}], M[1] - M[\frac{n}{4} - 1], M[\frac{n}{4} + 1] - M[\frac{n}{2} - 1],$$

$$M[\frac{3n}{4}], M[\frac{n}{2} + 1], M[\frac{3n}{4} - 1], M[\frac{3n}{4} + 1], M[n-1] \tag{9}$$

3 Experimental Results

In order to verify the performance of the proposed method, we compared our method with the relevant algorithms in x265 and conducted the experiments on x265 3.0 with AMD Ryzen 7 4800H with Radeon Graphics whose main frequency is 2.90 GHz and the memory is 16.0 GB. The software is Microsoft Visual Studio 2019 experimental platform.

3.1 Performance of Scene-Change Detection Method Comparison

In this subsection, correctly detected scene-change TP and wrongly detected scene-change FP were used to measure the detection accuracy. At the same time, we use the structural similarity Index Measure (SSIM) and the peak signal-to-noise ratio (PSNR) to measure the objective compression performance. And running time was used to measure the coding complexity. During the experiment, we selected 8 video sequences with different scenes switching situations, including Traffic (2560 × 1600), Kimono (1920 × 1080), FourPeople (1280 × 720), BQMall (832 × 480), RaceHorses (416 × 240), A Little Red Flower (1920 × 1056), Wolf Warrior 2 (1280 × 720), Report on COVID-19 Prevention and Control in Beijing (832 × 468). Notably, Traffic, Kimono, FourPeople, BQMall and RaceHorses are involved in JCT-VC test set, and A Little Red Flower, Wolf Warrior 2 and Report on COVID-19 Prevention and Control in Beijing are selected from the Internet [16–18]. From Table 3 to Table 5, we can find that our scene-change detection method greatly reduces the complexity of the algorithm and improves the coding performance (Table 4).

3.2 Performance of GPB Frame and B Frame Decision Method Comparison

In this subsection, we selected the coding performance and time of the fixed frame type decision algorithm with x265 as the anchor. In order to compare our algorithm with the fast frame type decision algorithm based on inter-frame rate distortion cost and the adaptive frame type decision algorithm based on Virerbi thought in x265. The encoding complexity can be investigated as follows,

$$\Delta T = \frac{T_A - T_F}{T_F} \times 100\% \tag{10}$$

Table 3. Performance of the proposed scene-change detection method with x265 in terms of the detection accuracy

Sequences	Scene cut numbers	x265			Proposed		
		Detection numbers	TP	FP	Detection numbers	TP	FP
Traffic	0	0	0	0	0	0	0
Kimono	1	1	1	0	1	1	0
FourPeople	0	0	0	0	0	0	0
BQMall	0	0	0	0	0	0	0
RaceHorses	0	0	0	0	0	0	0
A Little Red Flower	92	66	59	7	75	75	0
Wolf Warrior 2	185	160	154	6	125	121	4
Report on COVID-19 Prevention and Control in Beijing	42	18	16	2	35	35	0

Table 4. Performance of the proposed scene-change detection method with x265 in terms of the objective compression performance

Sequences	Resolution	BDBR-PSNR	BDBR-SSIM
Traffic	2560 × 1600	−4.79%	−3.98%
Kimono	1920 × 1080	−2.17%	−1.57%
FourPeople	1280 × 720	−1.70%	−1.14%
BQMall	832 × 480	−7.95%	−4.05%
RaceHorses	416 × 240	−1.29%	−1.67%
A Little Red Flower	1920 × 1056	−0.41%	−1.45%
Wolf Warrior 2	1280 × 720	−1.76%	−1.77%
Report on COVID-19 Prevention and Control in Beijing	832 × 468	−1.04%	−0.94%

where T_F represents the encoding time of the fixed frame type decision algorithm with x265, T_A represents the encoding time of the fast frame type decision algorithm based on inter-frame rate distortion cost, the adaptive frame type decision algorithm based on Virerbi thought in x265 or our algorithm.

During the experiment, we selected tested test sequences in the A, B, C, D, E, F classes, including Traffic, PeopleOnStreet, Cactus, Kimono, BasketballDrill, PartyScene, BasketballPass, RaceHorses, FourPeople, vidyo4, SlideShow and SlideEditing.

Table 5. Performance of the proposed scene-change detection method with x265 in terms of the coding complexity

Sequences	Resolution	x265	Proposed
Traffic	2560 × 1600	46071.3	34.13
Kimono1	1920 × 1080	24382.7	10.41
FourPeople	1280 × 720	9684.6	7.34
BQMall	832 × 480	3333.9	2.46
RaceHorses	416 × 240	1249.8	0.92

Table 6 reports that compared with the fast decision algorithm in X265, our algorithm is significantly superior in both compression efficiency and coding complexity. And compared with the adaptive frame type decision algorithm based on Viterbi in x265, our algorithm has a slight lead in compression efficiency and saves more than 5% coding time on average. In addition, considering different motion characteristics of video sequences, the compression performance of our method is significantly reduced for video sequences with obvious lens occlusion or irregular motion (such as rotation and scaling), including Cactus, Basketballpass and PartyScene. However, it has a good compression performance for gently moving or still video sequences, including Kimono, Fourpeople, SlideEditing, etc.

Through the experimental results, our method improves the compression efficiency for most videos with encoding time reducing (Table 7).

Table 6. Performance of the proposed GPB frame and B frame decision with x265 in terms of compression efficiency

Class	Sequences	Proposed		x265 fast method		x265 Viterbi method	
		BDBR-PSNR (%)	BDBR-SSIM (%)	BDBR-PSNR (%)	BDBR-SSIM (%)	BDBR-PSNR (%)	BDBR-SSIM (%)
Class A	Traffic	0.5	0.1	2.6	7.8	−1.2	−0.2
	PeopleOnStreet	−1.1	−0.8	0.1	2.6	−2.3	−0.7
Class B	Cactus	3.9	2.7	5.7	8.2	−0.6	1.1
	Kimono	−1.4	−2.2	−1.2	0.4	−2.4	−2.2
Class C	BasketballDrill	−1.3	2.4	4.2	6.7	0.1	0.8
	PartyScene	2.1	5.5	8.2	9.8	−1.3	1.2
Class D	BasketballPass	1.7	0.4	1.0	2.1	−2.1	−0.4
	RaceHorses	−1.7	−1.2	−0.2	2.6	−1.1	0.0
Class E	FourPeople	−3.8	−4.7	3.7	4.5	1.5	1.6
	vidyo4	−1.4	0.8	1.6	0.2	3.2	2.4
Class F	SlideShow	−9.8	−5.9	−0.9	4.9	−10.4	−4.5
	SlideEditing	−10.6	−6.4	−0.7	−0.3	−7.4	−8.1
Average		−1.91	−0.78	2.01	4.13	−2.00	−0.75

Table 7. Performance of the proposed GPB frame and B frame decision with x265 in terms of coding complexity

Class	Sequences	Proposed	x265 fast method	x265 Viterbi method
		ΔT (%)	ΔT (%)	ΔT (%)
Class A	Traffic	−1.1	1.6	2.5
	PeopleOnStreet	−0.5	0.5	3.2
Class B	Cactus	0.6	2.7	6.4
	Kimono	−1.6	1.6	2.4
Class C	BasketballDrill	0.8	2.4	7.6
	PartyScene	1.4	6.4	4.7
Class D	BasketballPass	−0.8	4.7	4.2
	RaceHorses	−1.4	4.3	9.5
Class E	FourPeople	−0.2	2.0	2.8
	vidyo4	−0.6	3.4	2.0
Class F	SlideShow	−0.1	3.8	5.2
	SlideEditing	−1.7	2.5	8.6
Average		−0.43	2.99	4.93

4 Conclusion

In order to improve the efficiency of HEVC and reduce the complexity, this paper takes CTU as the basic unit to partition each frame of the video sequence and obtain local luminance histogram, and proposes an adaptive frame type decision algorithm based on local luminance histogram. Firstly, the degree of inter-frame content variation is calculated according to the difference of local luminance histogram. Secondly, the scene-change detection window is used to traverse the whole video sequence, and the scene-change frame is determined by comparing the degree of inter-frame content variation. Finally, the Mini-GOP size is adaptively determined through the degree of inter-frame content variation, and the types of frames in the whole video are determined. The experimental results show that the proposed method can effectively improve the coding efficiency while reducing the computational complexity by nearly 5% compared with the relevant algorithm in x265, and realize the efficient adaptive decision of video frame type with strong robustness.

Acknowledgement. This work was supported in part by the National Key Research and Development Program of China under Grant No. 2018YFF01010100, the Beijing Natural Science Foundation under Grant No.4212001 and the Basic Research Program of Qinghai Province under Grant No. 2021-ZJ-704.

References

1. ITU–T, and ISO/IEC JCT–VC: High efficiency video coding [S]. ITU–T Rec. H.265 and ISO/IEC 23008-2 (HEVC), April 2013
2. BITMOVIN Inc.: Video developer report (2019). https://go.bitmovin.com/
3. Sullivan, G.J., Ohm, J.-R., Han, W.-J., Wiegand, T.: Overview of the high efficiency video coding (HEVC) standard. IEEE Trans. Circ. Syst. Video Technol. **22**(12), 1649–1668 (2012)
4. Correa, G., Assuncao, P., Agostini, L., et al.: Performance and computational complexity assessment of high–efficiency video encoders. IEEE Trans. Circ. Syst. Video Technol. **22**(12), 1899–1909 (2012)
5. Bossen, F., Bross, B., Suhring, K., et al.: HEVC complexity and implementation analysis. IEEE Trans. Circ. Syst. Video Technol. **22**(12), 1685–1696 (2012)
6. MulticoreWare Inc.: x265 HEVC Encoder/H.265 Video Codec. http://www.x265.org/
7. Shu, H., Chau, L.P.: A new scene change feature for video transcoding. In: International Symposium on Circuits and Systems (ISCAS 2005), Kobe, Japan, 23–26 May 2005. DBLP (2005)
8. Ding, J.R., Yang, J.F.: Adaptive group-of-pictures and scene change detection methods based on existing H.264 advanced video coding information. IET Image Process. **2**(2), 85–94 (2008)
9. Lee, J., Kim, S.J., Lee, C.S.: Effective scene change detection by using statistical analysis of optical flows. Appl. Math. Inf. Sci. **6**(1), 177–183 (2012)
10. Kim, J.R., Suh, S., Sull, S.: Fast scene change detection for personal video recorder. IEEE Trans. Consum. Electron. **49**(3), 683–688 (2003)
11. Kang, S.J.: Positional analysis-based scene-change detection algorithm. In: 2015 IEEE International Conference on Consumer Electronics, Taiwan, China, pp. 11–12 (2015)
12. Cho, S.I., Kang, S.J.: Histogram shape-based scene-change detection algorithm. IEEE Access **7**, 27662–27667 (2019)
13. VideoLAN ORG x264 The best H.264/AVC encoder. https://www.videolan.org/developers/x264.html
14. Liu, Z., Wang, L., Li, X., et al.: Optimize x265 rate control: an exploration of lookahead in frame bit allocation and slice type decision. IEEE Trans. Image Process. **28**(5), 2558–2573 (2018)
15. Forney, G.D.: The viterbi algorithm. Proc. IEEE **61**(3), 268–278 (1973)
16. "Wolf Warriors 2" clip: Leng Feng and Rachel compete with mercenaries. https://www.mgtv.com/l/100009562/4052086.html?lastp=so_result
17. "A Little Red Flower" clip: "Trilogy of Life" directed by Han Yan. https://www.mgtv.com/b/348435/10455525.html?fpa=se&lastp=so_result
18. Report on COVID-19 prevention and control in Beijing. https://www.mgtv.com/b/340731/10748501.html?fpa=se&lastp=so_result
19. Bjontegaard, G.: Calculation of average PSNR differences between RD-curves. In: 13th Video Coding Experts Group Meeting, Austin, TX, USA, pp. 290–291 (2001)

Research on Sound Source Recognition Algorithm of Pickup Array Based on Adaptive Background Noise Removal

Chengyu Hou, Liu Can, and Di Chen[✉]

Harbin Institute of Technology, Harbin, China
dchen@hit.edu.cn

Abstract. Nowadays, the pickup array is used in a large number of occasions, such as human voice recognition, audio conference, video conference and sound source localization. The research of sound source recognition algorithm based on pickup array has broad application prospects in the military field. The sound source recognition technology at this stage is implemented by a relatively fixed pickup array. However, due to the high requirements for the number of array elements, it faces severe environmental noise interference. Therefore, the sound source signal needs to be pre-processed before being formally processed. This paper discusses the sound source recognition algorithm based on the pickup array, which reduces the influence of environmental noise interference by preprocessing the sound source signal; realizes the target sound source recognition through feature extraction and the establishment of a recognition model. This article starts with the study of the preprocessing method of the sound source signal of the L-shaped pickup array node, and discusses an LMS noise cancellation model based on an improved variable step size. At the same time, this article identifies the target sound source signal and uses the MFCC feature extraction method. On the basis, the MFCC feature extraction method for high frequency suppression is given, and then the sound source recognition algorithm based on GMM-UBM is introduced.

Keywords: L-shaped pickup array · Noise cancellation · Sound source identification

1 Introduction

Since the array signal processing technology was successfully introduced into the field of speech signal processing by Professor Silverman and others, the use of pickup arrays in speech signal processing has become a new research hotspot [1]. Nowadays, pickup arrays are used in many occasions, such as human voice recognition, video conferencing, sound source localization, etc. [2–4]. However, the sound source identification research based on the pickup array is rarely seen in the military field due to its low anti-interference ability and complex terrain environment. However, due to the relatively long sound wave wavelength, its unique diffraction characteristics and low-cost low-power consumption. The pickup makes a very high economic benefit [3].

© ICST Institute for Computer Sciences, Social Informatics and Telecommunications Engineering 2021
Published by Springer Nature Switzerland AG 2021. All Rights Reserved
X. Wang et al. (Eds.): AICON 2021, LNICST 396, pp. 346–361, 2021.
https://doi.org/10.1007/978-3-030-90196-7_29

At this stage, the sound source identification is realized by a relatively fixed pickup array. However, due to the high requirement on the number of array elements, it faces severe environmental noise interference [4–7]. Therefore, the sound source signal needs to be preprocessed first. At the same time, due to the sound signal It is a wideband signal, and the phase difference output after it is received is not only related to the direction, but also related to the signal frequency, which increases the amount of calculation for the sound source recognition algorithm.

The main research content of this paper is the sound source recognition algorithm based on the L-shaped pickup array, which reduces the influence of environmental noise interference by preprocessing the sound source signal; realizes the target sound source recognition through feature extraction and establishment of a recognition model [8–10].

2 Adaptive Variable Step Size NLMS Algorithm

2.1 Analysis of L-Shaped Pickup Array Structure

Figure 1 shows the signal model of the L-shaped pickup array. Since the pickup array needs to be a two-dimensional or three-dimensional structure, the algorithm of the latter is more complicated and costly. Therefore, the design of the pickup array structure in this paper is L-shaped.

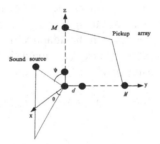

Fig. 1. Signal model of L-shaped pickup array

The sound sources used in this paper are tank sound, truck sound and infantry walking sound. The noise of the three sound sources is between 10 Hz and 850 Hz. Therefore, the half-wavelength theory can be used to obtain the expression of the distance d of the pickup array:

$$d \leq \frac{1}{2}\lambda = \frac{1}{2} \times \frac{c}{f} = \frac{340 \text{ m/s}}{2 \times 850 \text{ Hz}} \approx 0.20 \text{ m} \tag{1}$$

In formula (1), d is the element spacing between two adjacent elements in the L-shaped array, c represents the propagation speed of sound in the air (under a standard atmospheric pressure, the speed is 340 m/s), and λ is the wavelength of the sound wave, f is the sound source frequency.

From formula (1), it can be seen that if the array element spacing $d \leq 0.2$, the aperture of the array is no longer limited by the half-wavelength theory, so in this article d = 0.20 m; Considering the computational complexity and cost issues, choose to install 3 pickup elements in the horizontal and vertical directions, that is, the horizontal and vertical directions share one element at the junction. Considering that environmental noise will affect the reception of the target signal by the pickup array in the actual situation, the next section will discuss the preprocessing process of the sound source signal received by the pickup array, and uses the method of noise cancellation to restore the sound spectrum structure of the sound source.

2.2 Nodal Sound Source Signal Preprocessing

2.2.1 Analysis of Adaptive Noise Cancellation System

The adaptive noise cancellation system of the pickup element is shown in Fig. 2. In order to obtain the environmental background noise, this article uses two types of high and low sensitivity pickups. The high-sensitivity pickup mainly collects the mixed signal of the sound source and the noise, namely: $x_i(t) = s(t) + n_i(t)$ A low-sensitivity pickup is placed on the top of the pickup array to collect background noise $n_0(t)$ that is not related to the sound source signal $s(t)$ but related to $n_i(t)$ in the experimental environment. After the background noise $n_0(t)$ passes through the adaptive filter, a noise estimation signal $\hat{n}_i(t)$ can be obtained, which is subtracted from the main signal $\hat{n}_i(t)$ can get the required sound source signal after denoising, namely:

$$y_i(k) = x_i(t) - \hat{n}_i(t) = s(t) + n_i(t) - \hat{n}_i(t) \tag{2}$$

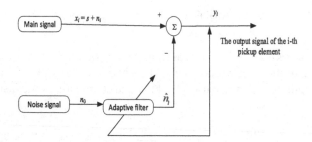

Fig. 2. Adaptive noise cancellation system

Figure 3 is a schematic diagram of the adaptive noise cancellation algorithm. The pollution signal is $x_i(k)$ in Fig. 2, namely:

$$x_i(k) = s(k) + n_i(k) \tag{3}$$

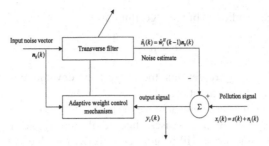

Fig. 3. Adaptive noise cancellation algorithm

In Eq. (3), i represents the i-th high-sensitivity pickup, and $n_0(k)$ is the noise vector collected by the low-sensitivity pickup. A noise estimate $\hat{n}_i(k)$ can be obtained through the transversal filter in the figure, namely:

$$\hat{n}_i(k) = \hat{w}_i^H(k-1)n_0(k) \tag{4}$$

The $\hat{w}_i(k-1)$ in Eq. (4) represents the least mean square estimation of the weight vector of the transversal filter in the system at $k-1$.

From Eq. (3), the output signal $y_i(k)$ can be:

$$y_i(k) = s(k) + n_i(k) - \hat{n}_i(k) \tag{5}$$

Then its mean square value is:

$$E[y_i^2(k)] = E[s^2(k)] + E[(n_i(k) - \hat{n}_i(k))^2] + 2E[s(k)(n_i(k) - \hat{n}_i(k))] \tag{6}$$

It can be obtained by the irrelevant nature of the signal and noise:

$$E[y_i^2(k)] = E[s^2(k)] + E[(n_i(k) - \hat{n}_i(k))^2] \tag{7}$$

It can be seen that in the case of the minimum mean square of the transversal filter, $\hat{n}_i(k)$ and $n_0(k)$ are the closest, then the output signal $y_i(k)$ and the target sound source signal $s(k)$ are also the closest at this time, and the original signal can be restored to the maximum extent.

2.2.2 Adaptive Noise Cancellation Algorithm

The most classic type of adaptive noise cancellation algorithms is the LMS algorithm, namely:

$$e(k) = d(k) - \hat{w}^H(k-1)x(k) \tag{8}$$

$$\hat{w}(k) = \hat{w}(k-1) + \mu x(k)e^*(k) \tag{9}$$

In formula (9), μ is the step factor, which is a fixed value, and corresponds to the above:

$$d(k) = s(k), \hat{w}(k) = \hat{w}_i(k), u(k) = x_i(k) \tag{10}$$

The convergence conditions of the algorithm are:

$$0 < \mu < \frac{2}{\lambda_{max}} \tag{11}$$

In formula (11), λ_{max} represents the largest eigenvalue corresponding to the autocorrelation matrix of the input signal $\mu(k)$.

LMS adaptive calculation cannot achieve the best compromise between convergence rate and steady-state error. As μ increases, the rate of convergence is greater, but at the same time the steady-state error will be greater. In order to solve this contradiction, the step factor μ can be adjusted with the iteration process.

The normalized least mean square (NLMS) adaptive algorithm is proposed on this basis, and its convergence result has nothing to do with the strength of the input signal, so its step adjustment function is as follows:

$$\mu(k) = \frac{\tilde{\mu}}{\delta + \|u(k)\|^2} \tag{12}$$

In formula (12), $\tilde{\mu}$ is an adaptive constant; δ is a small constant greater than 0, which is used to solve the calculation problem with a denominator of 0.

The NLMS algorithm can be regarded as a variable step size algorithm. Its convergence rate is faster than that of the LMS algorithm, but it cannot effectively solve its contradiction with steady-state errors.

Another idea that can effectively solve this problem is to use a larger step size to increase the convergence rate at the beginning of the algorithm iteration, and use a smaller step size when the iteration is about to complete to reduce the steady-state error. The change of $u(k)$ is related to the error signal $e(k)$. Professor Qun Niu developed a variable step size LMS algorithm in 2018, and the $u(k)$ is:

$$\mu(k) = \beta[1 - \exp(-\alpha|e^2(k)e(k-1)|)] \tag{13}$$

In formula (13), both α and β are constants.

The form of formula (13) is relatively simple, and the step length changes slowly when the error approaches 0, which optimizes the convergence characteristics, but does not describe the physical meaning of the exponential term. The adaptive step size NLMS algorithm proposed in this paper takes into account the interference of colored noise and uses the third-order correlation of the error signal $e(k)$ to adjust the step size, which can effectively improve the contradiction between the convergence speed and the steady-state error. Long and unaffected by system noise, its $u(k)$ is:

$$\mu(k) = \beta[1 - \exp(-\alpha|e(k)e(k-1)e(k-2)|)] \tag{14}$$

In formula (14), $a > 0$, the function is to control the step change trend of the adaptive algorithm in the iterative process, $0 < \beta < 2/\lambda_{max}$, is a constant used to control the step change interval. When a is constant, the initial step size and convergence rate increase with the increase of β, but the steady-state error will also increase; when β is constant, the change of step size tends to be flat with the increase of a, and the rate will decrease during the convergence process. Increase, but the steady-state error also increases. Therefore, the algorithm in this paper can choose a smaller a value and a larger β value, which can effectively improve the convergence rate and steady-state error.

2.2.3 Experimental Results and Analysis

Based on the content of the previous section, this section compares the three algorithms of LMS, NLMS and the algorithm in this paper, and analyzes the recovery and convergence performance of the signal added with white noise/color noise. Table 1 below is the white noise condition experimental simulation parameters.

Table 1. Simulation experiment parameters of various adaptive algorithms under white/color noise conditions

Algorithm	SNR	Filter order	Fixed step μ	Adaptive constan $\tilde{\mu}$	Constant α	Constant β
LMS	15 dB	10	0.005	—	—	—
NLMS	15 dB	10	—	0.05	—	—
Algorithm	15 dB	10	—	—	1000	0.08

The experimental results are shown in the figure below:

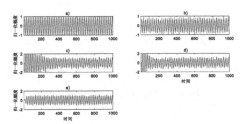

Fig. 4. Time-domain types of algorithms under white noise under white noise conditions

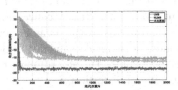

Fig. 5. The learning curve of the three types of algorithms under white noise conditions

Figure 4 is a comparison diagram of the time-domain signals output by the three types of algorithms under white noise conditions, where a) is the original signal sin(0.1πt + 10), b) is the signal with white noise, and c) is the LMS cancellation After the output signal, d) is the output signal after NLMS cancellation, e) is the output signal after cancellation by the algorithm in this paper. It can be seen from the figure that the noise-added signal has some residual noise after passing through the LMS algorithm and the

NLMS algorithm. The algorithm in this paper has a significantly better effect of filtering noise.

Figure 5 is the learning curve of the three types of algorithms under white noise conditions. The number of sampling points is 2000, and the simulation iterations are 150 times. From the figure, it can be seen that the LMS algorithm completes convergence after about 800 iterations, while the NLMS algorithm is 300 times. The algorithm used in this article Convergence is reached after only 50 iterations. At the same time, it can be seen from the figure that the steady-state error after convergence is the last one. It can be seen that the algorithm in this paper has a faster convergence rate compared with the two algorithms of LMS and NLMS. As well as lower steady-state error, it can deal with the contradiction between convergence rate and steady-state error very effectively.

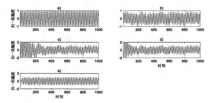

Fig. 6. Three types of algorithms output time-domain signals under colored noise conditions

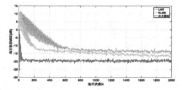

Fig. 7. The learning curve of the three types of algorithms under the color noise condition

Figure 6 is a comparison diagram of the time-domain signal output by the three types of algorithms under the color noise condition, where a) is the original signal sin $(0.1\pi t + 10)$, b) is the signal with white noise, and c) is the LMS cancellation After the output signal, d) is the output signal after NLMS cancellation, e) is the output signal after cancellation by the algorithm in this paper. It can be seen from the figure that the color-added noise signal has more noise residue and distortion after passing through the LMS algorithm and the NLMS algorithm. The algorithm in this paper has a significantly better effect of filtering noise without distortion.

Figure 7 is the learning curve of the three types of algorithms under the color noise condition. The number of sampling points is 2000, and the simulation iteration is 150 times. It can be seen from the figure that the LMS algorithm has completed convergence after about 800 iterations, while the NLMS algorithm is 400 times. The algorithm used in this article Convergence is reached after only 60 iterations; at the same time, it can be seen from the figure that the steady-state error after convergence is the last one. It can be seen that the algorithm in this paper has a faster convergence rate compared with LMS and NLMS As well as lower steady-state error, it can deal with the contradiction between convergence rate and steady-state error very effectively.

In order to verify the effect of this algorithm in practical applications, a section of tank traveling sound is used as an experiment. Considering the serious influence of colored noise on the spectrum structure of the sound source in the actual environment, the additional frequencies of the original sound source are 1000 Hz, 1500 Hz, 2000 Hz and The sound of 2500 Hz is used to simulate the interference of colored noise. The specific experimental parameters are as follows (Table 2).

Table 2. Experimental parameters of adaptive noise reduction spectrum of actual tank sound source

Filter order	Sampling frequency	Step change trend control constant α	Step change interval control constant β
100	48 kHz	1	0.01

The experimental results are as follows:

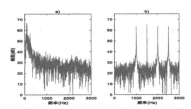

Fig. 8. a) Comparison of the original sound spectrum and b) the colored interference sound spectrum of the low-sensitivity channel.

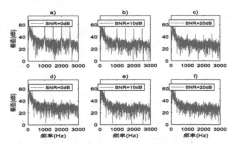

Fig. 9. Comparison of adaptive noise vs. anechoic spectrum under different SNR conditions of high-sensitivity channels

Figure 8 shows the original sound spectrum a) of the tank moving sound source, and the color noise interference sound spectrum obtained by the low-sensitivity pickups in the array b), while Fig. 9 shows the noise-containing spectrum obtained by the high-sensitivity channel and preprocessed Sound spectrum comparison, where a), b), and c) are the colored noise spectrum under different signal-to-noise ratio conditions, and d), e), and f) are the corresponding adaptive noise cancellation spectra. From the above results, it can be seen that the algorithm in this paper can effectively filter the interference of colored noise, and at the same time SNR will affect its removal effect. There is some noise interference under the condition of 0 dB, and the effect of 10 dB and 20 dB is better.

3   Sound Source Recognition Algorithm Based on L-Shaped Pickup Array

3.1   MFCC Feature Extraction Method for High Frequency Suppression

The most commonly used feature extraction method for the target sound source is the MFCC feature extraction method, which is to obtain the characteristic parameters of the target sound source by simulating the non-linear mapping characteristics of the human ear when receiving sound. From the previous analysis, it can be seen that the spectral characteristics of the target sound source are concentrated in the low-frequency region, so the target sound source needs to be subjected to low-pass filtering before feature extraction to suppress high-frequency noise. The specific process is as follows.

Fig. 10. MFCC feature extraction flowchart

Figure 10 shows the MFCC feature extraction process. The target sound source signal is first passed through a low-pass filter to suppress the high frequency part, and then the signal is processed by FFT after framing and windowing, so as to change the signal spectrum into a linear spectrum, and then use mei After the Mf filter is processed by the logarithmic transformation, the logarithmic nonlinear spectrum after dynamic range compression can be obtained, where the mel frequency is $f_{mel} = 2595 \ \log_{10}(1+f/700)$, and the mel frequency filtering is achieved by Mf triangular bandpass filters. The sound source is converted from a linear frequency spectrum to a mel frequency spectrum. The transfer function is as follows:

$$H_i(k) = \begin{cases} 0 & (k < f(i-1)) \\ \frac{k-f(i-1)}{f(i)-f(i-1)} & (f(i-1) \le k \le f(i)) \\ \frac{f(i+1)-k}{f(i+1)-f(i)} & (f(i) \le k \le f(i+1)) \\ 0 & (k > f(i+1)) \end{cases} \tag{15}$$

Finally, perform discrete cosine transform on it, namely:

$$o(l) = \sum_{i=1}^{M_f} S(i)cos\left(\frac{l\pi(i+1/2)}{M_f}\right) \quad 1 \le l \le D/2 \tag{16}$$

$S(i)$ in Eq. (16) is the logarithmic spectrum obtained by the i-th triangular filter, and $o(l)$ is the l-dimensional static characteristic of the obtained target sound source. Then, the difference operation with an interval of 2 can be performed on different frames to obtain the dynamic characteristics. The combination of the two forms a D-dimensional MFCC feature vector, which is the MFCC feature parameter of the target sound source signal.

3.2 GMM-UBM Sound Source Recognition Algorithm

GMM model is mainly used to recognize the speaker's voice. Its advantage is that it does not need to care about the semantic and contextual connection during training and pattern matching, so it is suitable for sound source recognition. The disadvantage is that its parameter scale and characterization ability are not coordinated. When the decomposed Gaussian component is relatively small, the accuracy of the characteristic model obtained is low. Therefore, it needs to be improved. GMM-UBM algorithm is improved on this basis, and its target sound source identification process is shown in the figure below (Fig. 11).

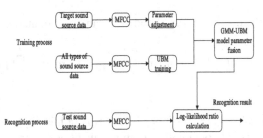

Fig. 11. Sound source recognition process of GMM-UBM model

First, a large number of sound source data need to be UBM training to obtain its model parameter h_{UBM} Then, based on the maximum posterior probability adaptive principle, the model parameter H is obtained by fine-tuning the data obtained from a small amount of target sound $h_{t\,arg\,et}$ and the two model parameters were fused to obtain the parameter h of GMM-UBM $h_{fus,s}$. When identifying the target sound source, it is necessary to first extract the features of the identified sound source data, then calculate the posterior probability of UBM and GMM-UBM model, and then calculate the logarithmic likelihood ratio of the two models respectively for scoring and identification.

3.2.1 GMM Model

Suppose that the sound source feature vector of the t-th frame of the target sound source signal obtained after MFCC feature extraction is $o_t = [o_t(1), o_t(2)...o_t(D)]$, and the likelihood function of its GMM model is fitted with G Gaussian components as follows:

$$p(o_t|h) = \sum_{i=1}^{G} \omega_i p_i(o_t) \tag{17}$$

$$p_i(o_t) = \frac{1}{(2\pi)^{D/2}|\Sigma_i|^{1/2}} \exp\left[-\frac{1}{2}(o_t - \mu_i)(\Sigma_i)^{-1}(o_t - \mu_i)'\right] \tag{18}$$

$$\sum_{i=1}^{G} \omega_i = 1 \tag{19}$$

In formula (17), $p(o_t|h)$ is the Gaussian mixture function of ot; h is the parameter set of the GMM model; $p_i(o_t)$ is the distribution function of the i-th Gaussian component, and ω_i is the corresponding weight. In Eq. (18), μ_i is the mean vector of the Gaussian component distribution function, and Σ_i is the corresponding covariance matrix (usually an DxD dimensional diagonal matrix).

The principle of GMM training is: Given a training sample, use the Expectation Maximum (EM) method to obtain the maximum likelihood estimation of h. The likelihood of the model parameter set h of the T-frame sound training sample is calculated as follows:

$$L(h|O) = P(O|h) = \prod_{t=1}^{T} p(o_t|h) \tag{20}$$

From Eq. (20), the maximum likelihood of h can be estimated as follows:

$$\hat{h} = \arg\max_{\hat{h}} L(h|O) = \arg\max_{\hat{h}} P(O|h) = \arg\max_{\hat{h}} \prod_{t=1}^{T} p(o_t|h) \tag{21}$$

When the initial value $h_0 = \{(\omega_i^{(0)}, \mu_i^{(0)}, \Sigma_i^{(0)})\}$ A of h is given, the EM method can be used to loop iteratively to obtain its maximum likelihood estimation solution.

3.2.2 UBM Model

Affected by the number of Gaussian components, the recognition performance of the GMM model is also related to it. The greater the number of Gaussian components, the better the recognition effect. However, with the increase of Gaussian components, the corresponding target sound source data required increases, which leads to the increase of model parameters that need to be estimated, and the amount of calculation is huge. Based on this, a UBM training algorithm is proposed. The principle of the UBM algorithm is to use the EM algorithm to train all types of sound source samples to obtain a GMM model that is not related to the sound source type. This model is the feature model $h_{UBM} = \{(\omega_{UBM,i}, \mu_{UBM,i}, \Sigma_{UBM,i})\}$ common to all types of sound sources. After obtaining the required GMM model, based on the shared feature model, only a few target sound sources can be adapted to the model parameters based on the maximum posterior probability criterion. The process includes parameter fine-tuning and parameter fusion based on UBM.

If the characteristic sample of the sound source to be identified is $O_{t\,arg\,et} = \{O_{t\,arg\,et,1}, O_{t\,arg\,et,2}\cdots, O_{t\,arg\,et,T}\}$, the posterior probability of the j Gaussian components of the parameter adjustment model is as follows:

$$Pr(j|o_{target,t}, h_{UBM}) = \frac{\omega_{UBM,j} p_j(o_{target,t}, \mu_{UBM,j}, \Sigma_{UBM,j})}{\sum_{i=1}^{G} \omega_{UBM,i} p_i(o_{target,t}, \mu_{UBM,i}, \Sigma_{UBM,i})} \tag{22}$$

The weights are as follows:

$$\omega_{target,j} = \frac{\sum_{t=1}^{T} Pr(j|o_{target,t}, h_{UBM})}{T} \tag{23}$$

The mean vector is as follows:

$$\mu_{target,j} = \frac{\sum_{t=1}^{T} Pr(j|o_{target,t}, h_{UBM})o_{target,t}}{\sum_{t=1}^{T} Pr(j|o_{target,t}, h_{UBM})} \tag{24}$$

The covariance matrix is as follows:

$$\Sigma_{target,j} = \frac{\sum_{t=1}^{T} Pr(j|o_{target,t}, h_{UBM})(o_{target,t} - \mu_{target,j})'(o_{target,t} - \mu_{target,j})}{\sum_{t=1}^{T} Pr(j|o_{target,t}, h_{UBM})} \tag{25}$$

After the above calculation is completed, the UBM parameter set and the fine-tuned parameter set are combined to obtain the GMM-UBM model $h_{fus} = \{(\omega_{fus,i}, \mu_{fus,i}, \Sigma_{fus,i})\}$ of the target sound source to be identified, where

$$\omega_{fus,j} = \alpha_j^{\omega}\omega_{target,j} + \left(1 - \alpha_j^{\omega}\right)\omega_{UBM,j} \tag{26}$$

$$\mu_{fus,j} = \alpha_j^{\mu}\mu_{target,j} + \left(1 - \alpha_j^{\mu}\right)\mu_{UBM,j} \tag{27}$$

$$\Sigma_{fus,j} = \alpha_j^{Sigma}\Sigma_{target,j} + \left(1 - \alpha_j^{Sigma}\right)\left(Sigma_{UBM,j} + mu_{target,j}^2\right) - mu_{fus,j}^2 \tag{28}$$

$$\alpha_j^{\rho} = \left\{\alpha_j^{\omega}, \alpha_j^{\mu}, \alpha_j^{\Sigma}\right\} = \frac{\sum_{t=1}^{T} Pr(j|o_{target,t}, h_{UBM})}{\sum_{t=1}^{T} Pr(j|o_{target,t}, h_{UBM}) + \tau^{\rho}}, \rho \in \{\omega, \mu, \Sigma\} \tag{29}$$

3.2.3 Voice Scoring Recognition

After training all the sound source data to obtain the GMM parameters, the sound source identification can be performed. You only need to calculate the likelihood function corresponding to the h_{target} G of the target sound source, and then traverse the maximum posterior probability to obtain the estimation of the maximum posterior probability. The recognition results are as follows:

$$\hat{s} = \arg \max_{1 \le s \le S} p(O|h_{fus,s}) = \arg \max_{1 \le s \le S} \sum_{t=1}^{T} \log p(o_t|h_{fus,s}) \tag{30}$$

In Eq. (30), $\hat{s}$ represents the recognition result of the sound source to be identified, and $h_{fus,s}$ is the GMM-UBM model parameter of the s-th sound source.

If there is only one type of sound source to be identified and the accuracy requirements are low, only this type of sound can be trained.Then calculate its log likelihood:

$$\Lambda(O) = \frac{1}{T} \sum_{t=1}^{T} \log p\left(o_t | h_{fus,s}\right) - \log p(o_t | h_{UBM}) \tag{31}$$

In formula (31), h_{fus} is the GMM-UBM model parameter of the target sound source signal; h_{UBM} is the UBM model parameter of all types of sound. You can also reduce the amount of calculation by setting the decision threshold.

The larger $\Lambda(O)$ is, the greater the similarity of features between the sound source to be identified and the target sound source is, and the smaller the $\Lambda(O)$, the higher the similarity between the sound source to be identified and E that is not related to the target sound source.

3.3 Experimental Results and Analysis

First do MFCC feature extraction, and the simulation parameters are set as follows (Table 3):

Table 3. MFCC feature extraction experimental parameters

Sampling frequency	Feature dimension	Filter order	Framing number	Oneframe duration	Frame shift ratio	FFT	Cut-off frequency
48 kHz	24	24	100	20 ms	1/4	2048	2000 Hz

The experimental results are as follows (Fig. 12):

As shown in Fig. 13, it is a normalized feature map of MFCC feature extraction for three sound sources of military truck sound, marching sound and tank sound. It can be seen that if high frequency suppression is not done, the MFCC static characteristics of various sound sources The difference in the first three dimensions is very small, and the distinction of dynamic features is not good. After high-frequency suppression, the static features of the target sound source are very different, and it clearly reflects the difference between different frames. Therefore, it is necessary to perform high frequency suppression before performing MFCC feature extraction.

Then the target sound source is identified. The following table shows the experimental parameters of feature extraction of the GMM-UBM algorithm and the experimental parameters of its training and recognition process (Table 4).

The experimental results are as follows:

As shown in Fig. 14 above, the false alarm rate is 1.099%. Figure 14 is the scoring result of the normalized fusion of the two tank sounds of m109 and Leopard by the GMM-UBM algorithm, where m109 is the 11th type of sound source, and leopard is the 10th type. From the above figure, we can see that the algorithm is for non-targets. The score of the sound source category is lower, which means that when the normalized threshold is the same, the false alarm rate is smaller, that is, the algorithm has fewer incorrectly associated nodes.

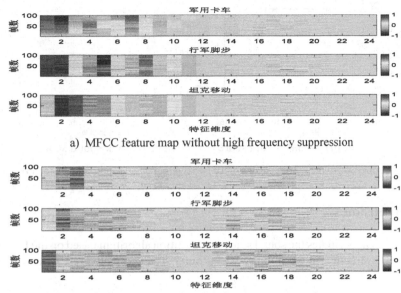

a) MFCC feature map without high frequency suppression

b) MFCC feature map for high frequency suppression

Fig. 12. Comparison of MFCC features without high frequency suppression and high frequency suppression

Table 4. GMM-UBM feature extraction experimental parameters

Sampling frequency	Feature dimension	Filter order	Framing number	One frame duration	Frame shift ratio	FFT	Cut-off frequency
4819.98 kHz	24	24	550	24 ms	1/4	4096	2000 Hz

Table 5. GMM-UBM training and recognition experiment parameters

Experimental model	Number of test samples	Number of training samples	Gaussian component number	Number of samples per type	Model correlation factor
GMM-UBM	14	14	128	15	10

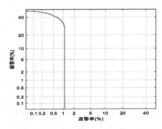

Fig. 13. GMM-UBM warning error curve

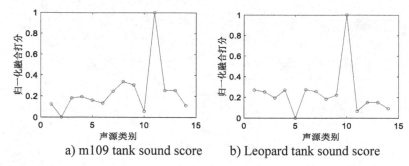

a) m109 tank sound score   b) Leopard tank sound score

Fig. 14. Comparison of the scoring results of the two types of target sound sources by GMM-UBM

4   Conclusion

This paper mainly studies the sound source recognition algorithm based on the L-shaped pickup array structure in the military background. The completed research work is as follows:

(1)   The structure of the L-shaped pickup array is analyzed, and the signal preprocessing algorithm of the array node is studied. Based on the LMS adaptive noise cancellation technology, the variable step LMS algorithm that can change the sound spectrum structure of the signal is discussed. It was verified by simulation.

(2)   Identify the target sound source to determine the target type. The high-frequency suppression MFCC feature extraction algorithm that can improve the sound spectrum structure of the sound source and the sound source recognition algorithm based on GMM-UBM are studied, and the simulation analysis is carried out. It is proved that the MFCC feature extraction method with high frequency suppression can better distinguish the target sound source, and the GMM-UBM recognition algorithm has a lower score for the non-target sound source category, and its false alarm rate is lower, that is, this algorithm There are fewer nodes that are incorrectly associated.

Acknowledgments. This work was supported by the Natural Science Foundation of Heilongjiang Province [LH2019F017].

References

1. Qin, Y.: Research on Sound Source Localization Technology Based on Microphone Array. Beijing University of Posts and Telecommunications, pp. 1–2 (2019)
2. Deng, Y., Li, J., Zhang, F., Luo, D., Zhu, C., Feng, Z.: Research on improved MUSIC algorithm based on far-field sound source localization. Appl. Electron. Technol. **44**(12), 69–72 (2018)
3. Li, H., Zhou, Y., Liu, H.: Microphone array noise elimination method using phase time-frequency masking. Sig. Process. **34**(12), 1490–1498 (2018)

4. Laufer-Goldshtein, B., Talmon, R., Gannot, S.: Semi-supervised source localization on multiple manifolds with distributed microphones. IEEE Trans. Audio Speech Lang. Process. 25(3), 1477–1491 (2017)
5. Zhao, C.: Research on adaptive noise canceller. signal processing expert com-mittee of China high-tech industrialization research association. In: Proceedings of the Sixth National Conference on Signal and Intelligent Information Processing and Application. Sig-nal Processing of China High-tech Industrialization Research Association Expert Committee: China High-Tech Industrialization Research Association, pp. 366–368 (2012)
6. Sun, H., Teutsch, H., Mabande, E., et al.: Robust localization of multiple sources in rever-berant environments using EB-ESPRIT with spherical microphone arrays. In: 2011 IEEE International Conference on Acoustics, Speech and Signal Processing. Prague, Czech Republic, pp. 117–120 (2011)
7. Li, Y.: Discussion on mel cepstrum MFCC algorithm in speech signal feature extraction. J. Adv. Correspondence Educ. (Nat. Sci. Ed.), 25(04), 78–80 (2012)
8. Shao, H.J., Zhang, X.P., Wang, Z.: Novel closed-form auxiliary variables based algorithms for sensor node localization using AOA. In: 2014 IEEE International Conference on Acoustics, Speech and Signal Processing (ICASSP). IEEE, pp. 1414–1418 (2014)
9. Zong, J., Cui, X.X., Yang, H., et al.: Algorithm and accuracy analysis of weighted maximum likelihood estimation in multi-station DF crossing localization. In: 4th International Conference on Computer, Mechatronics, Control and Electronic Engineering. Atlantis Press (2015)
10. Jingfan, Q., Jingzheng, O.: A novel variable step size LMS adaptive filtering algorithm based on sigmoid function. J. Data Acquisition Process. vol. 3 (1997)

A New Direct Radio Frequency Generation Technology for Downlink Navigation Signals

Zhimei Yang$^{(\boxtimes)}$, Lingling Chen, Hao Tang, and Lixin Zhang

Xi'an Institute of Space Radio Technology, Xi'an 710100, China

Abstract. In order to effectively solve the influence of satellite navigation signal generation equipment on the fixed ambiguity, the Beidou high-precision signal radio frequency direct generation technology is studied, which can effectively separate the initial phase of the carrier phase and the hardware delay in the channel, and reduce the carrier phase fractional deviation caused by the spaceborne device to reduce the ambiguity. The influence of the fixed degree can effectively solve the consistency of the pseudo code and the carrier, so that the phase of the carrier and the pseudo code is fixed, and the phase relationship will not change with the passage of time, so as to realize the consistency of the navigation signal and ensure the generation of the signal carrier. The stability of the initial phase of the phase reduces the influence on the estimation of the fractional fluctuation of the carrier phase, thereby improving positioning accuracy.

Keywords: Direct radio frequency generation · Carrier phase · Carrier pseudo code consistency

1 Introduction

At present, Beidou-3, GPS III, and Galileo satellites all adopt the intermediate frequency navigation signal generation scheme [1], that is, the baseband signal is directly modulated with the intermediate frequency carrier in the digital domain after being generated, and then sent to the DAC, and then modulated on the carrier to generate the radio frequency signal. However, because the generation path of the carrier and the baseband signal is not completely consistent, due to temperature changes or device aging, the phase of the carrier and the pseudo code cannot be guaranteed to be consistent, resulting in a decimal deviation of the carrier phase at the satellite, and fluctuations with temperature and aging. In order to effectively solve the influence of satellite navigation signal generating equipment on the fixed ambiguity, the primary principle of satellite navigation signal generation is that the phases of the three elements of the carrier, ranging code, and telegram in the navigation signal are strictly consistent, and do not change over time, at least to ensure that it is stable, Predictable.

To this end, this paper proposes a new radio frequency signal direct generation technology, which uses the digital domain to directly generate radio frequency navigation signals, effectively separating the initial phase of the carrier phase and the hardware

X. Wang et al. (Eds.): AICON 2021, LNICST 396, pp. 362–371, 2021.
https://doi.org/10.1007/978-3-030-90196-7_30

delay in the channel, and reducing the carrier phase fractional deviation caused by the spaceborne device to fix the ambiguity. The influence of, can effectively solve the consistency of pseudo code and carrier.

2 Signal Generation Design

Different from the previous intermediate frequency signal generation technology, the digital radio frequency signal generation is to generate the baseband signal and the carrier signal separately and then perform quadrature modulation in the digital domain, and then generate the radio frequency navigation signal through digital-to-analog conversion. The principle block diagram is shown as in Fig. 1.

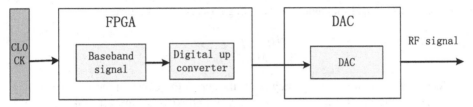

Fig. 1. Direct digital radio frequency modulation.

The direct generation of radio frequency signals is based on the principle of high Nyquist zone signal generation [2]. The principle of high Nyquist zone signal generation is that the sample-and-hold circuit converts the digital signal into a continuous analog signal when the signal is converted by the DAC. The sampling frequency fs is attenuation of the Sinc function at the zero point. As a result, multiple Nyquist zones are formed. These Nyquist zones are divided by fs/2 and have a mirror image relationship with respect to fs/2. Using the image signal in the high Nyquist region as an effective signal for work can make the sampling rate lower, and perform digital processing in the digital domain with a lower clock frequency.

The radio frequency navigation signal needs to generate baseband elements and carrier elements at the same time. The two main principles of the direct radio frequency signal generation scheme are: firstly, ensure the integer characteristics of the generated elements, that is, the clock of the generated elements is an integer or fractional relationship; secondly, the elements are deterministic Relationship. Analyzing each frequency signal, the minimum constant envelope baseband signal generation frequency is shown in Table 1, and its least common multiple is 859.32 MHz, that is, all baseband information can be accurately generated under 859.32 MHz. Considering the baseband signal, the sampling frequency should be able to ensure the accurate generation of messages, sub-codes, codes, and sub-carriers.

It can be seen from the above analysis that using the same clock, it is impossible to generate the elements of the three frequency points in integers. Therefore, consider using clock generation for each of the three frequency points, and then use a synchronization design to ensure synchronization. The signal center frequency and bandwidth have been fixed. The Mix mode of the radio frequency DAC device is used to ensure

Table 1. Carrier frequency factor.

Signal	Center frequency/MHz	Factor
B1	1575.42	$154 \times 10.23 = 2 \times 7 \times 11 \times 10.23$
B2	1191.795	$233 \times 5 \times 1.023$
B3	1268.52	$124 \times 10.23 = 4 \times 31 \times 10.23$

the maximum output power [3, 4] (DAC Mix mode). At this time, the signal generation clock (sampling frequency) needs to be equivalent to the signal center frequency, and the sampling frequency is about 900 ~ Between 1800 MHz.

The baseband signal and the radio frequency carrier signal need to be accurately generated at the same time under the sampling clock, which requires:

$$\begin{cases} N(f_S - f_{RF}) = f_S \\ Mf_{BS} = f_S \end{cases} \tag{1}$$

where f_S is the sampling frequency, f_{RF} is the center frequency of the radio frequency carrier, f_{BS} is the baseband signal frequency, N and M is an integer. Take B2 as an example:

B2 IF frequency $f_{BS} = 86.955$ MHz, RF frequency $f_{RF} = 1191.795$ MHz, sampling frequency $f_S = 1104.84$ MHz, because $1104.84/86.955 = 12.7$, the IF carrier generated by the signal cannot be divided evenly. Therefore, the design plan will adopt a double conversion design:

$$\begin{cases} N(f_S - f_{RF}) = f_S \\ Mf_{BS} = f_S \end{cases} \text{Becomes} \begin{cases} f_1 + f_2 = f_S - f_{RF} \\ Pf_1 = f_S \\ Qf_2 = f_S \\ Mf_{BS} = f_S \end{cases} \tag{2}$$

where P and Q can be exchanged. Therefore, the sampling rate that can be selected is shown in Table 2:

Table 2. B2 signal sampling rate analysis.

M	P	Q	Remarks
9	12	216	$92.07 - 5.115 = 86.955$
9	24	27	$46.035 + 40.92 = 86.955$

Here are two options (the two options have the same hardware, only the design parameters are changed):

(1) Configuration scheme one.
     86.955 = 46.035 + 40.92 MHz, for 46.035 MHz, 24 points per cycle; for 40.92 MHz, 27 points per cycle.
(2) Configuration scheme two.
     86.955 = 92.07–5.115 MHz, for 92.07 MHz, 12 points per cycle; for 5.115 MHz, 216 points per cycle.

The performance of the two designs is similar. Because 92.07 MHz is a multiple of 5.115 MHz in the second configuration, all elements of the carrier can be generated at the 1104.84 MHz sampling frequency, so the design is simpler, so when $M = 9$, $P = 12$, $Q = 216$ When, it is the preferred solution.

3   Test Verification

A test platform was set up as shown in Fig. 2. The digital radio frequency signal generation unit sends out three radio frequency signals. In order to prevent spectrum aliasing, it needs to pass through the filter before entering the signal acquisition equipment; to ensure the sampling accuracy, the signal acquisition equipment and the signal generation unit are of the same source.

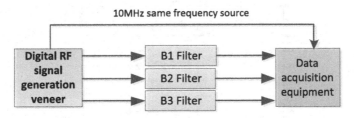

Fig. 2. Block diagram of test equipment connection.

This section takes the B2a signal as an example for simulation verification. The B2a signal [5] is QPSK modulation, the code rate is 10.23 Mbps, and the carrier frequency is 1176.45 MHz. In order to measure the main performance indicators of the direct radio frequency signal, the signal quality is examined from the three aspects of frequency domain, correlation domain and time domain. The specific index requirements [6] and simulation results are shown in Table 3, and the simulation diagrams are shown in Fig. 3 and Fig. 4.

Through simulation verification, it can be seen that the direct radio frequency signal is evaluated in the frequency domain, correlation domain, and time domain, and the results all meet the indicators, and the signal quality is very good.

Table 3. Signal quality index requirements and simulation results.

Category	Name	Index requirements	Results
Frequency domain characteristics	Synthetic power spectrum deviation	≤0.5 dB	0.153
Related domain characteristics	Related losses	≤0.5 dB	0.03
	S-curve zero crossing deviation	≤0.5 ns	0.0336
Time domain waveform	Baseband signal waveform distortion	≤5 ns	0.031

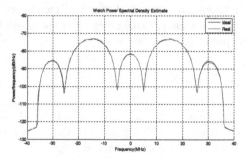

Fig. 3. Power spectrum

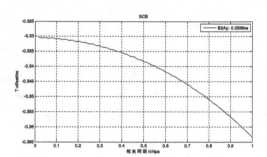

Fig. 4. S Curve zero crossing deviation.

In order to verify the superiority of the signal directly generated by the radio frequency in the phase relationship of the carrier pseudo-code, the two methods of long-term evaluation after a single power-on and multiple power-on and power-off methods were used to test and verify. Data collection is divided into the following two situations: (1) Long-term power-on operation of the navigation signal generation unit, data collection every other day, each collection is 3 s, a total of 6 sets of data are collected to verify the carrier pseudocode phase relationship Stability and predictability; (2) The navigation signal generating unit is powered on and off for 6 times, and each time is collected for 3 s, a total of 6 sets of data are collected to verify the carrier pseudocode phase relationship under different power on and off conditions Consistency.

The software receiver is used to separately capture and track each signal of the collected data [7], and obtain the pseudorange measurement value and carrier phase measurement value of each signal component. Assuming that within the 1 ms time period, the receiver has been locked to the carrier without loss of lock and cycle of the carrier. Therefore, the value of the round ambiguity N in the measured value of the carrier phase remains unchanged at each time. The pseudorange and carrier phase of two adjacent epochs are subtracted separately, then the pseudorange change $\Delta\rho_k$ and the carrier change $\lambda \cdot \Delta\phi_k$ in units of distance should theoretically be equal. Ideally, the difference between the pseudorange change $\Delta\rho_k$ and the integrated distance $\lambda \cdot \Delta\phi_k$ indirectly reflects the phase difference between the code phase and the carrier phase when the transmitted signal is generated.

According to the above software receiver method for analysis, Fig. 5 shows the software receiver acquisition and tracking process:

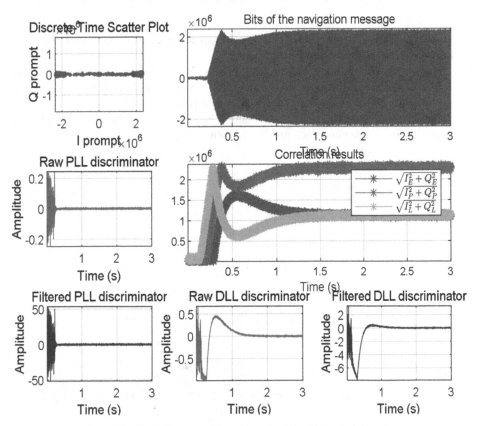

Fig. 5. Software receiver to capture tracking results.

It can be seen from Fig. 5 that the software receiver has entered stable tracking after 1 s, so the last second of stable data in the 3 s data is analyzed according to the above method. The simulation result of the carrier pseudo-code coherence is shown in Fig. 6.

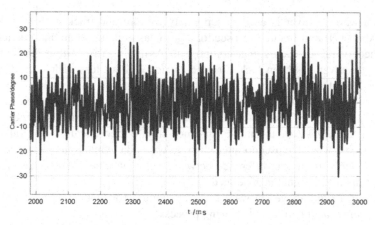

Fig. 6. Direct RF signal carrier pseudo-code coherence (the last second of the 3-s data).

(1) Stability analysis of the phase relationship of the pseudo-code download wave during long-term power-on and stable state.
The 6 groups of data collected in the first case were captured and tracked with the software receiver, and the last second data after the tracking was stabilized was analyzed according to the above method, and averaged every 100 ms. For intuitive reflection, the 6 groups were simulated The result combination is displayed on a simulation graph, and the carrier pseudo-code coherence result is shown in Fig. 7.

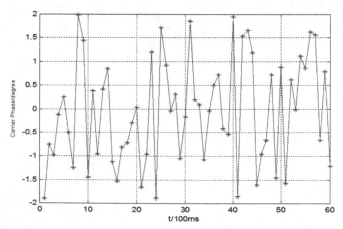

Fig. 7. Carrier pseudo-code coherence of 6 groups of 3S data of direct radio frequency signal.

From the analysis of Fig. 7, it can be seen that the long-term (6 days) carrier pseudo-code phase difference of the direct radio frequency signal after a single power-on is very stable, stable around 0°, and the fluctuation does not exceed 2°. The carrier pseudo-code phase relationship has good long-term stability.

(2) Analysis of the consistency of the phase relationship of the pseudo-codes in the state download waves of multiple power on and off.

In order to compare with the direct RF signal in the second case, the IF upconversion data of the traditional scheme was collected at the same time, as shown in Fig. 8, the data was collected from the triplexer outlet, and the IF signal generation unit was powered off respectively. A total of 6 sets of data are collected for 3 s each time.

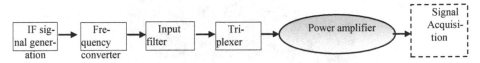

Fig. 8. Block diagram of IF up-conversion data acquisition.

The first group of 3 s signals in the collected direct RF signal and IF up-conversion signal are analyzed according to the above method respectively, and the simulation results of the carrier pseudo-code coherence are obtained as shown in Fig. 9.

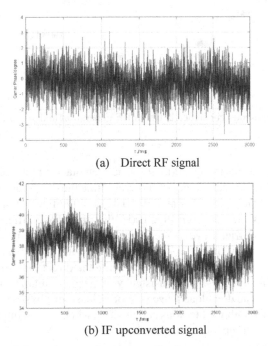

(a) Direct RF signal

(b) IF upconverted signal

Fig. 9. Comparison of the coherence between radio frequency generation and intermediate frequency up-conversion carrier pseudo-code.

Each time the machine is turned on and off, a set of 3 s data is collected and analyzed according to the above method. 6 sets of direct radio frequency data analysis results and 6 sets of intermediate frequency up-conversion data analysis results can be obtained. In order to directly reflect the difference from the figure, 6 sets of the analysis result combination is displayed on a graph, as shown in Fig. 10.

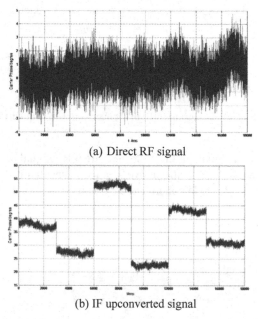

(a) Direct RF signal

(b) IF upconverted signal

Fig. 10. Carrier pseudo-code coherence between RF generation and IF up-conversion 6 groups of 3 s data.

By analyzing the results in Fig. 10(a), it can be seen that the phase difference between the pseudo code and the carrier is very stable every time the direct radio frequency signal is turned on and off, and it is stable at about 0.4°, and the fluctuation does not exceed 2°. However, it is easy to see from Fig. 10(b) that the phase difference between the pseudo code and the carrier wave of the intermediate frequency up-conversion signal is not a stable value every time it is switched on and off, and fluctuates greatly, with the fluctuation range reaching tens of degrees, while the direct radio frequency signal is switched on and off many times. The consistency of the phase relationship of the pseudo-code of the machine state download wave is good. The semi-physical simulation results are in good agreement with the previous conclusions when discussing the advantages of direct RF signals over IF upconverted signals.

4   Conclusions

In order to solve the influence of the satellite navigation signal generation equipment on the ambiguity fixation in the fixed ambiguity factor, this paper proposes a new radio frequency direct generation technology, and takes B2 as an example to verify it through experiments. The direct radio frequency signal is from the frequency domain and the correlation domain. It is evaluated in terms of time domain and other aspects, and the results all meet the indicators, and the signal quality is very good; the direct RF signal has passed the long-term copy machine assessment, and the carrier pseudo-code phase relationship has good long-term stability; the direct RF signal has a pseudo-code when the machine is switched on and off many times. The phase difference with the carrier is very stable, and the phase relationship of the carrier pseudo code has good consistency. The new radio frequency generation method can make the phase of the carrier and the pseudo code fixed, and the phase relationship will not change with the passage of time, ensuring the stability of the initial phase of the generated signal carrier, reducing the influence on the estimation of the carrier phase decimal fluctuation, thereby improving positioning accuracy.

References

1. Xie, J.: Satellite Navigation System and Technology. Beijing Institute of Technology Press, Beijing (2018)
2. Pany, T., Eissfeller, B.: Code and phase tracking of generic PRN signals with sub-Nyquist sample rates. Navig. Wiley Online Libr. **51**(2), 143–159 (2004)
3. Gutierrez-Aitken, A., Matsui, J., Kaneshiro, E.N., et al.: Ultrahigh-speed direct digital synthesizer using InP DHBT technology. IEEE J. Solid-State Circ. IEEE **37**(9), 1115–1119 (2002)
4. Li, X.P., Wang Z.G., Zhang, Y., et al.: 12-bit 2.6 GS/s RF DAC based on return-to-zero technology. J. China Univ. Posts Telecommun. **26**(4), 36–42 (2019)
5. Yuan, L.F., Guo, C.J., Zhan, H.Y.: A new signal modulation for compass B2 band. Sci. Technol. Eng. **14**(19), 243–247 (2013)
6. Ouyang, X.F.: Evaluation Technology and Analysis of BDS Signal Quality. National University of Defense Technology, Changsha (2013)
7. Xie, G.: Principles of GPS and Receiver Design [M]. Publishing House of Electronics Industry, Beijing (2009)

A Clutter Samples Increase Jamming Method to Airborne STAP

Ming Li[1], Mingqian Liu[2(✉)], and Shouzhong Zhu[3]

[1] State 722 Factory, Guilin 541001, Guangxi, China
[2] State Key Laboratory of Integrated Service Networks, Xidian University,
Xi'an 710071, Shaanxi, China
mqliu@mail.xidian.edu.cn
[3] Hunan Positive Ship Technology Co., Ltd., Changsha 410075, Hunan, China

Abstract. Proposed a clutter samples increase non-homogeneous jamming method to airborne space-time adaptive processing. The method uses digital radio frequency storage as a realization method. First, the number of interference samples is obtained by estimating the radar range resolution and the target radar interference distance, and then modulate jamming information with non-homogeneous clutter background environment parameters on the radar clutter echo, include signal amplitude, interference phase and Doppler frequency. Lastly, with the Clutter echo in protected areas for the pollution of the co-variance matrix by STAP, the method can reduce the STAP processing target detection ability. The validity is verified by the simulated processing results of a real airborne radar data.

Keywords: Non-homogeneous clutter · Space-time adaptive processing · Digital radio frequency memory · Airborne radar

1 Introduction

Airborne early warning radars widely use space-time adaptive processing (STAP) to locate accurate target information in a complex clutter background [1]. The technology not only eliminates clutter and interference, but also improves the ability of early warning radar to detect targets in complex backgrounds through adaptive filtering in the space and time domain. Since the 1990s, one began to propose a series of STAP algorithms for dimensionality reduction [2–4]. However, the algorithms are all in the case of sub-optimal adaptive performance, reducing the amount of calculation and sample requirements by reducing the

This work was supported by the National Natural Science Foundation of China under Grant 62071364, in part by the Aeronautical Science Foundation of China under Grant 2020Z073081001, in part by the Fundamental Research Funds for the Central Universities under Grant JB210104, and in part by the 111 Project under Grant B08038.

X. Wang et al. (Eds.): AICON 2021, LNICST 396, pp. 372–381, 2021.
https://doi.org/10.1007/978-3-030-90196-7_31

degree of adaptive freedom, so as to solve the real-time work problem of STAP in engineering.

One of the core contents of STAP is how to achieve the problem of quasi-optimal interference filtering in a non-uniform environment. Non-uniform environments include non-uniform power, interference targets, and isolated interference. The clutter samples of different distance gates have different statistical characteristics. If the range gate samples do not contain part or all of the clutter information in the sample to be detected, adaptive processing will not be able to effectively suppress the clutter in the sample to be detected, resulting in an increase in the false alarm rate and a decrease in detection performance. In order to obtain independent and identically distributed (IID) samples, SATP usually screens the collected samples through a non-homogeneous detector (NHD), and detects and eliminates the samples in the training samples that do not meet the clutter distribution conditions of the samples to be filtered.

For the SATP of non-uniform detection to obtain sufficient IID samples, a STAP method to enhance the non-uniform characteristics of echo samples is proposed. Firstly, the method estimates the radar range resolution and interference distance data to obtain the number of interference samples through digital radio frequency storage [5,6], and then obtains the interference density of complex background clutter through the number of interference samples to achieve accurate generation of complex background template interference. After that, The interference signal is calculated, which is based on the target scattering modulation matrix and the radar range resolution, and forwards it to the interference radar. Finally, the preset non-uniform clutter environmental parameters are superimposed on the early warning radar echo, Comprehensive interference modulation is performed on the amplitude, phase and Doppler frequency of the signal re-transmitted to realize the pollution of the STAP processing covariance matrix by the interference echo in the protection area, thereby reducing the STAP target detection capability. Based on the actual processing results of an early warning radar data, the effectiveness of the method in this paper is verified [7].

2   The Principles of Space-Time Adaptive Processing

Due to the movement characteristics of airborne radar, its Doppler frequency of ground clutter varies from different directions. The radar will seriously broaden the Doppler frequency of the moving target according to the Doppler frequency of the ground clutter received by its antenna pattern. From the perspective of the Doppler domain, the moving target and the clutter are aliased together, and the traditional one-dimensional time-domain Doppler filter processing method of separating the moving target and the stationary ground clutter will no longer be effective. The space-time coupling characteristic that the Doppler spectrum of the clutter will change with the spatial direction of the scattered clutter is a basic characteristic of the moving platform radar. According to the Doppler (time domain) and the direction of arrival (space domain), the method to distinguish moving targets and stationary ground clutter is space-time signal processing. In addition to the uncertainties of the environment and the system, adaptive space-time adaptive processing (STAP) is usually used in practice.

The airborne radar causes the space and time domain of the echo signal to be coupled due to the movement of the platform. Assuming that the radar antenna has a uniform linear array structure (it can also be an equivalent linear array structure of a surface array synthesized by microwaves), the number of array elements is N, for the lth range gate, the number of pulses in a coherent processing interval (CPI) is K, the received space-time data X is a matrix of $N \times K$, the echo of the nth element under the kth pulse is represented by $x_{n,k}$ in the matrix, and the matrix can be expressed as follows.

$$
\mathbf{X} = \begin{bmatrix} x_{1,1} & x_{1,2} & \cdots & x_{1,K} \\ x_{2,1} & x_{2,2} & \cdots & x_{2,K} \\ \vdots & \vdots & \ddots & \vdots \\ x_{N,1} & x_{N,2} & \cdots & x_{N,K} \end{bmatrix} \tag{1}
$$

According to the same matrix structure, the target signal S can also be expressed as a one-dimensional matrix of $N \times K$, which is composed of a spatial steering vector and a time-domain steering vector. The two vectors are as follows:

$$
\mathbf{S}_S(\psi_{S0}) = [1, \exp(j\phi_S(\psi_{S0})), \cdots, \exp(j(N-1)\phi_S(\psi_{S0}))]^{\mathrm{T}} \tag{2}
$$

$$
\mathbf{S}_T(f_{d0}) = [1, \exp(j\phi_T(f_{d0})), \cdots, \exp(j(K-1)\phi_T(f_{d0}))]^{\mathrm{T}} \tag{3}
$$

Here, $\varphi_S(\psi_{S0}) = \frac{2\pi d}{\lambda} \cos\theta_0 \cos\varphi_0$ represents spatial steering vector, where d is the element spacing, λ and θ_0 is the wavelength and the azimuth angle of the target respectively. Similarly, $\varphi_T(f_{d0}) = \frac{2\pi f_{d0}}{f_r}$ is the time-domain steering vector, where f_{d0} and f_r is the Doppler frequency of the target and the pulse repetition frequency. Here are examples of the front view array, the target signal S is expressed as follows.

$$
\mathbf{S} = \mathbf{S}_S(\psi_{S0}) \otimes \mathbf{S}_T^{\mathrm{T}}(f_{d0}) \tag{4}
$$

Space-time processing is the weighted summation of the $N \times K$ dimensional matrix X, and the detection output of the target direction and Doppler. The process can be illustrated in Fig. 1.

The premise of dimensionality reduction STAP is that the degree of freedom of clutter should be less than NK, which provides a theoretical basis for dimensionality reduction processing. The dimensionality reduction STAP technology is divided into two types: adaptive dimensionality reduction structure and fixed dimensionality reduction structure. The processing structure of the former is variable, while the latter is fixed. Either fixed dimensionality reduction or adaptive dimensionality reduction can be considered to obtain an N-dimensional dimensionality reduction matrix, where N and K are the dimensions of the space-time signal before and after the dimensionality reduction, respectively. Of course,

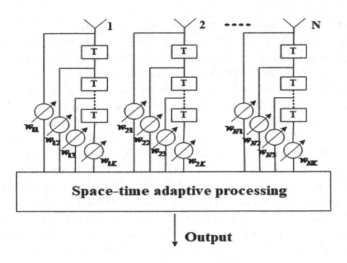

Fig. 1. Block diagram of space-time adaptive processing principle.

this is a dimensionality reduction only when the situation of $Q < NK$ is true. The difference is that the acquisition of the former has nothing to do with the data than the latter. The following relationship exists between the data vector before and after the dimensionality reduction and the signal steering vector.

$$\begin{cases} \mathbf{x}_r = T^H \mathbf{x} \\ \mathbf{s}_r = T^H \mathbf{s} \end{cases} \tag{5}$$

The clutter co-variance matrix after dimensionality reduction is as follows:

$$\mathbf{R}_{\mathbf{X}_r} = E\left[\mathbf{x}_r \mathbf{x}_r^H\right] = T^H \mathbf{R}_{\mathbf{X}} T \tag{6}$$

STAP for dimensionality reduction is equivalent to solving the following optimization problem:

$$\begin{cases} \min_{\mathbf{W}_r} \mathbf{W}_r^H \mathbf{R}_{\mathbf{X}_r} \mathbf{W}_r \\ s.t. \mathbf{W}_r^H \mathbf{s}_r = 1 \end{cases} \tag{7}$$

The optimal weight vector is obtained as follows:

$$\mathbf{W}_r = \mu_r \mathbf{R}_{\mathbf{X}_r}^{-1} \mathbf{s}_r \tag{8}$$

Where $\mathbf{R}_X = E[xx^H]$ is the co-variance matrix of space-time sampled data, which is obtained by estimation. Therefore, the clutter co-variance matrix of STAP can be obtained through distance sample statistics. The prerequisite for the optimal performance of STAP is that there are sufficient clutter samples that meet the independent and identical distribution condition, so that the clutter co-variance matrix can be estimated according to $\hat{\mathbf{R}}_x = \frac{1}{L} \sum_{l=1}^{L} \mathbf{x}_l \mathbf{x}_l^H$. Literature

[8] discussed the convergence characteristics of statistical STAP in the Gaussian independent identically distributed sample environment, and pointed out that when the number of independent identically distributed training samples is more than twice the dimension of the processor, it can ensure that the output signal-to-noise ratio loss does not exceed 3 dB compared with ideal optimal processing.

It is well known that the basic problem of setting one is to correctly estimate the true unknown interference co-variance matrix and to calculate an excellent adaptive weight vector when designing the STAP system. In a non-uniform environment, choosing appropriate training samples is an important way to correctly estimate the interference co-variance matrix. The STAP including sample rejection is as follows: select A training samples along the distance dimension, process these training samples with an NHD (Non-Homomorphic Detector), and pick out B uniform training samples (i.e. does not include interfering targets) to estimate the co-variance matrix according to the NHD processing results. The basis for this is that NHD is a statistic that can reflect changes in the statistical characteristics of the sample. According to whether there are interfering samples, the different output results of NHD are used to achieve the effect of eliminating samples containing interfering targets. Training the STAP processor with the remaining samples will not cause performance loss due to interference with the target.

The generalized inner product is defined as following:

$$\eta(\mathbf{X}_l, \hat{\mathbf{R}}_{L+O}) = \mathbf{X}_l^H \hat{\mathbf{R}}_{L+O}^{-1} \mathbf{X}_l \tag{9}$$

Where $\hat{\mathbf{R}}_{L+O}$ is the co-variance matrix estimated with $L + O$ candidate reference samples. The generalized inner product is a typical non-uniform detector, which represents the remaining energy after whitening and suppressing the clutter in the vector $\mathbf{X}_l$. Generally, if the structure of the co-variance matrix of $\mathbf{X}_l$ is the same or similar to that of $\hat{\mathbf{R}}_{L+O}$, it is uniform and should be retained; otherwise, it should be eliminated. The expected value of the GIP test statistic under a uniform sample is expressed as follows:

$$E[\eta(\mathbf{X}_1, \hat{\mathbf{R}}_{L+O})] \approx trace(\hat{\mathbf{R}}_{L+O}^{-1} \hat{\mathbf{R}}_{L+O}) = M \tag{10}$$

Let M denote the dimension of the processor and $trace$ represents the trace calculation of the matrix. In the case of non-uniform samples, there are the following equations.

$$E[\eta(\mathbf{X}_1, \hat{\mathbf{R}}_{L+O})] = trace(\hat{\mathbf{R}}_{L+O}^{-1} \Delta\hat{\mathbf{R}}) + M \tag{11}$$

It can be seen that the GIP test statistics under non-uniform samples will deviate from the output under uniform samples. Therefore, the non-uniformity can be detected based on the degree of deviation of the GIP test statistic from the expected value, that is, the non-uniformity can be detected based on the degree of deviation of $\eta(\mathbf{X}_1, \hat{\mathbf{R}}_{L+O})$ from M.

$$\eta(\mathbf{X}_l, \hat{\mathbf{R}}_{L+O}) = \mathbf{X}_l^H \hat{\mathbf{R}}_{L+O}^{-1} \mathbf{X}_l \tag{12}$$

3   Implementation of Non-uniform STAP Radar Interference

For generalized inner product sample extraction, if the conventional isolated strong interference method is used, the statistical characteristics of the range gate echo where the jammer is located will be different from the samples within other distances around it. The GIP test statistic under non-uniform samples will deviate from the output under uniform samples, and thus will be eliminated and cannot achieve effective interference.

The jammer uses a higher power method to interfere, and the corresponding STAP samples will be eliminated. Therefore, the interference signal power needs to be equivalent to the actual background echo. According to the characteristics of actual radar processing, an interference modulation parameter library with a complex city as the background is constructed. The specific interference realization process is as follows:

(1) According to the echo parameters received by the jammer, estimate the distance range that needs to be interfered and calculate the required distance towing delay.

$$\tau = \frac{R_{\max} - R_{\min}}{c} \tag{13}$$

Where c is the speed of light, $R_{\max}$ and $R_{\min}$ represent the longest and shortest jamming range respectively.

(2) Then refer to the reconnaissance receiver to obtain the radar signal parameters to estimate the radar range resolution $\rho = \frac{c}{2B}$,where B is the bandwidth of the radar signal. And calculate the number of samples that need interference as follows:

$$N = \text{int}\left(\frac{R_{\max} - R_{\min}}{\rho}\right) \tag{14}$$

(3) Take complex background templates to extract radar echo parameters such as urban areas, and generate interference scene modulation parameters to construct target scattering modulation matrix S_J according to the number of range gates.

$$S_{J(K \times N)} = \begin{cases} A_1 e^{j\phi_1} e^{jf_1}, A_2 e^{j\phi_2} e^{jf_1}, ..., A_{N-1} e^{j\phi_{N-1}} e^{jf_1} & A_N e^{j\phi_N} e^{jf_1} \\ A_1 e^{j\phi_1} e^{jf_2}, A_2 e^{j\phi_2} e^{jf_2}, ..., A_{N-1} e^{j\phi_{N-1}} e^{jf_2} & A_N e^{j\phi_N} e^{jf_2} \\ ... & ... \\ A_1 e^{j\phi_1} e^{jf_{K-1}}, A_2 e^{j\phi_2} e^{jf_{K-1}}, ..., A_{N-1} e^{j\phi_{N-1}} e^{jf_{K-1}} & A_N e^{j\phi_N} e^{jf_{K-1}} \\ A_1 e^{j\phi_1} e^{jf_K}, A_2 e^{j\phi_2} e^{jf_K}, ..., A_{N-1} e^{j\phi_{N-1}} e^{jf_K} & A_N e^{j\phi_N} e^{jf_K} \end{cases} \tag{15}$$

(4) The constant K can be set with reference to the number of radar pulses acquired by the electronic reconnaissance aircraft. Among them, A_N is the amplitude corresponding to the Nth distance unit, $e^{j\phi_N}$ is the phase, and e^{jf_K} is the Doppler modulation amount.

(5) Two-dimensional modulation of the amplitude and frequency of the echo received by the jammer to produce an interference signal based on a complex background is as follows.The entire interference process is shown in Fig. 2.

$$S_{\mathrm{J}}(n,t) = \sum_{n=1}^{N} \sum_{k=1}^{K} S_{J(n,\mathrm{k})} S_t(n, t - \frac{n\rho}{c}) \tag{16}$$

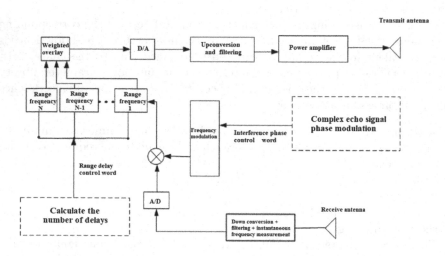

Fig. 2. Block diagram of space-time processing interference.

4   Simulation Results

Take the airborne early warning MCARM radar measured data (without considering the distance ambiguity) to verify the performance of the jamming method in this paper. The height of the early warning carrier is 3073 m, the speed of the carrier is 100 m/s, the operating frequency is about 1.2 GHz, the distance gate is 630, and the number of antennas is 11. Intercept the data from 200 to 630 range gates. Figure 3 shows the echo power brightness map of the fifth spatial channel after MTD processing.

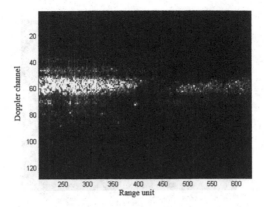

Fig. 3. Single-channel MTD processed image.

Take the interference 150 to 300 range gate as the complex interference background, because this piece of data belongs to the urban background, it can be seen that the main clutter area occupies nearly 20 Doppler channels and the echo is strong. The 450–600 range gate is used as the processing target to verify the interference effect of this method, and 3DT-STAP is used for clutter suppression.

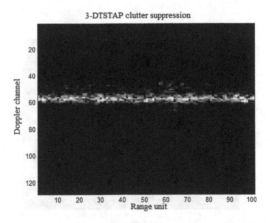

Fig. 4. 3DT-STAP space-time adaptive processing results.

It can be seen from Fig. 4 that after 3DT-STAP space-time adaptive processing, the ground clutter can be significantly suppressed, while the Doppler channel of the main clutter is significantly narrowed. This verifies the effectiveness of space-time adaptive processing. The method in this paper modulates the urban clutter with complex background to the relatively uniform range gate echo, which produces interference effects on the original IID samples, thereby reducing the clutter suppression and moving target detection capabilities of STAP.

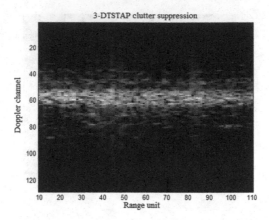

Fig. 5. Channel MTD image with increased interference.

Figure 5 is a single-channel range Doppler image after adding non-uniform echoes. It is obvious that the modulated clutter still has certain distribution characteristics. 3DT-STAP can no longer achieve better clutter suppression, especially after the contamination of non-uniform samples Compared with the processing result without sample contamination, the main clutter area is obviously widened.

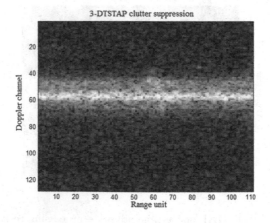

Fig. 6. 3DT-STAP with increased interference.

It is obvious from Fig. 6 that the use of complex echoes to forward interference samples destroys the independent and identical distribution characteristics of the original better sample distribution, resulting in a significant decrease in clutter suppression. At the same time, the target detection ability of the Doppler channel outside the main clutter is also reduced, which effectively suppresses the clutter suppression ability of STAP.

5   Conclusion

Aiming at the typical processing process of STAP's non-uniform sample detection to obtain sufficient IID samples, this paper proposes a STAP interference method that enhances the non-uniform characteristics of echo samples. This method obtains the number of interference samples by estimating the radar range resolution and target radar interference distance. Then the interference density of the complex background clutter can be effectively obtained through the number of interference samples, and the accurate generation of the interference of the complex background template can be realized. By superimposing the preset non-uniform clutter environmental parameters on the early warning radar echo, comprehensive interference modulation is performed on the amplitude, phase and Doppler frequency of the forwarded signal to achieve the pollution of the STAP co-variance matrix. Enhance the non-uniformity of the echo, thereby reducing the ability of STAP to process target detection. The processing results based on the actual data of a certain early warning radar verify that improving the non-uniformity of the echo can reduce the target detection performance of SATP.

References

1. Shen, J.Q., Jiang, D.X.: Intermittent sampling and forwarding jamming of early warning radar STAP. Ship Electr. Warf. **40**(3), 21–25 (2017)
2. Bao, Z., Liao, G.S.: Temporal-spatial two-dimensional adaptive filtering of phased array airborne radar clutter suppression. Chin. J. Electr. **9**, 1–7 (1993)
3. Zhou, Y., Wang, X.G., Duan, R.: An improved JDL-STAP algorithm for airborne early warning radar. Chin. J. Radio Sci. **25**(6), 1052–1057 (2010)
4. Peckham, C.D., Haimovich, A.M., Ayoub, T.F., Goldstein, J.S., Reed, I.S.: Reduced-rank STAP performance analysis. IEEE Trans. AES **36**(2), 664–676 (2000)
5. Wu, C., Yan, Z.Y., Xu, L., et al.: Accurate self-defense jamming technology of phased array radar. Modern Radar **41**(1), 80–83, 87 (2019)
6. Zhang, J.Z., Wen, S.L., Gao, H.W., et al.: A new type of jamming technology and implementation based on intermittent sampling. Modern Radar **40**(11), 81–85 (2018)
7. Ouyang, Z.H., Shen, Y., Li, X.H.: Mono-pulse radar track deception jamming technology based on jamming the main lobe of the crew network. Syst. Eng. Electr. **40**(1), 80–85 (2018)
8. Reed, I.S., Mallett, J.D., Brennan, L.E.: Rapid convergence rate in adaptive arrays. IEEE Trans. Aerospace Electr. Syst. **10**(6), 853–863 (1974)

A Space-Time Jointing Moving Target Detection Method for FMCW Radar

Ming Li[1], Mingqian Liu[2(✉)], and Shouzhong Zhu[3]

[1] State 722 Factory, Guilin 541001, Guangxi, China
[2] State Key Laboratory of Integrated Service Networks, Xidian University, Xi'an 710071, Shaanxi, China
mqliu@mail.xidian.edu.cn
[3] Hunan Positive Ship Technology Co., Ltd., Changsha 410075, Hunan, China

Abstract. Point to the problem of small target detection in single channel linear frequency modulation continuous wave (FMCW) radar, this paper proposed a Space-time jointing moving target detection method, the method combined single channel in the process of the radar scanning form different continues pulse interval (CPI) for ground clutter cancellation and target detection, by using adaptive target detection processing, this method can improve the ability of the ground clutter suppression, and increase the performance of ground moving target detection. The simulation result based on the real radar data shows validly of the method.

Keywords: Frequency modulation continuous wave · Ground clutter suppression · Adaptive target detection · Airborne radar · Digital radio frequency memory

1 Introduction

The relevant information of the ground target can be provided by the portable ground reconnaissance radar adopting the linear frequency modulation continuous wave (LFMCW) [1]. With the development of radar electronic technology, the Armies of various countries are paying more and more attention to portable ground reconnaissance radar equipment, and this type of radar will become more popular in infantry equipment. At the same time, LFMCW radar as a ground surveillance radar has broad application prospects, especially for small detection. Usually ground radar receives target echo data, uses MTD processing, and then removes the Doppler channel where ground clutter is located. Because the beam has a certain width, the target will have a certain scanning time in the beam,

---

This work was supported by the National Natural Science Foundation of China under Grant 62071364, in part by the Aeronautical Science Foundation of China under Grant 2020Z073081001, in part by the Fundamental Research Funds for the Central Universities under Grant JB210104, and in part by the 111 Project under Grant B08038.

X. Wang et al. (Eds.): AICON 2021, LNICST 396, pp. 382–392, 2021.
https://doi.org/10.1007/978-3-030-90196-7_32

which corresponds to multiple coherent processing pulse groups for mechanical scanning radar. The current project is mainly to perform MTD processing on the coherent signal in each CPI [2,3], and then perform target judgment on multiple pulse groups according to certain criteria. For ground targets, since the scattering characteristics of ground clutter in the beam are basically the same, the conventional directly MTD processing has insufficient suppression of ground clutter, and the detection ability of some low-speed small targets is insufficient, such as pedestrians and small drone [4,5].

Space-time adaptive signal processing (STAP) was firstly proposed in the study of airborne early warning radar clutter suppression [6,7]. Combined with the characteristics of space-time two-dimensional adaptive signal processing, a long coherent processing time was divided into several A short period of time to deal with. In a short time, the DOA and Doppler frequency are unchanged, and the adaptive weight is estimated to suppress clutter with the radar echo data in a short time. Aiming at the problem of small slow target detection for LFMCW radar, this paper proposes A Space-time Jointing Moving Target Detection Method, which combines different coherent pulse groups in the radar scanning process for ground clutter cancellation and target detection and uses multiple coherent pulse processing interval data are used for adaptive target detection processing. The method improves the performance of single-channel MTD target detection and processes the actual single-channel LFMCW radar data. The actual radar data processing results show that the method can effectively improve the effectiveness of the single-channel LFMCW radar's detection ability for low-speed and small targets.

2   Radar Echo Signal Model

The principle of de-chirp pulse compression processing is to use the same FM slope signal as the transmitted signal as a reference signal, and after mixing with the echo signal, the time difference between the two is converted to a difference frequency. After the analog-digital converter (ADC) and discrete Fourier transform (DFT) processing, the distance information of the target can be obtained, and the detection of the moving target can be completed. The principle of LFMCW radar is shown in Fig. 1.

Assume that the radar emits a frequency-modulated continuous wave signal as follows:

$$s(t) = rect(\frac{t}{T}) \exp[j2\pi(f_0 t + \frac{1}{2}kt^2)] \tag{1}$$

In the above formula, f_0 and B is the signal center frequency and the signal bandwidth, T and $k = B/T$ represent the signal pulse repetition period and the signal chirp slope respectively. The following discussion ignores the signal amplitude and envelope information, and only considers the phase change. The echo received by the radar can be expressed as follows:

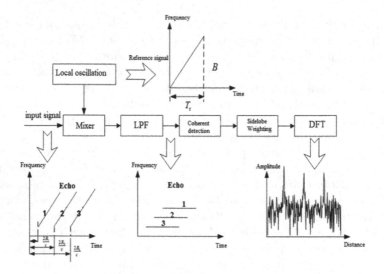

Fig. 1. The diagram of LFMCW radar schematic.

$$s_r(t) = rect(\frac{t - \tau_r}{T}) \exp[j2\pi(f_0(t - \tau_r) + \frac{1}{2}k(t - \tau_r)^2)] \qquad (2)$$

Here, $\tau_r = 2(R_0 - vt)/c$ represents the target transmission delay, where R_0 is the initial radial distance between the target and the radar, c and v is the speed of light and the target's radial velocity relative to the radar, respectively. The reference signal with the same frequency modulation slope as the transmitted signal is expressed as:

$$s_{ref}(t) = rect(\frac{t - \tau_{ref}}{T_{ref}}) \cdot \exp[j2\pi(f_0(t - \tau_{ref}) + \frac{1}{2}k(t - \tau_{ref})^2)] \qquad (3)$$

Where $\tau_{ref} = 2R_{ref}/c$ is the delay of the reference signal relative to the transmitted signal, R_{ref} and T_{ref} is the reference distance and the pulse width of the reference signal. It is worth noting that T_{ref} is usually slightly larger to T ensure that all echoes can be mixed with the reference signal. The output signal is made up of $s_r(t)$ and $s^*_{ref}(t)$, the details are as follows:

$$
\begin{aligned}
s_0(t) &= s_r(t) \cdot s^*_{ref}(t) \\
&= rect(\frac{t - \tau_r}{T}) \cdot rect(\frac{t - \tau_{ref}}{T_{ref}}) \cdot \exp\left\{ j\left[2\pi f_0(\tau_{ref} - \tau_r) + 2\pi kt(\tau_{ref} - \tau_r) + \pi k(\tau_r^2 - \tau_{ref}^2)\right]\right\} \\
&= rect(\frac{t - \tau_r}{T_{ref} \cap T}) \cdot \exp[j(2\pi f_b t + \varphi)]
\end{aligned}
$$
$$\qquad (4)$$

Where $\varphi = 2\pi f_0(\tau_{ref} - \tau_r) + \pi k(\tau_r^2 - \tau_{ref}^2)$ and $f_b = k(\tau_{ref} - \tau_r)$. From the above derivation, it can be seen that after the signal is dechirp, a single-frequency signal with a constant frequency is output, and the frequency value of the output signal is proportional to the difference between the delay of the reference signal and the delay of the echo signal.

The relative distance between the target and the reference position, defined as

$$\Delta R = \frac{1}{2}c(\tau_r - \tau_{ref}) = -\frac{1}{2} \cdot \frac{cf_b}{k} \tag{5}$$

The actual distance between the target and the radar transmitter, defined as

$$R_0 = \frac{1}{2}c\tau_r = R_{ref} + \Delta R = R_{ref} - \frac{1}{2} \cdot \frac{cf_b}{k} \tag{6}$$

3   Detection of Moving Target

Usually the LFMCW of the radar is transformed by DFT to produce a one-dimensional range profile, a frequency-domain range profile, and then perform MTD processing on the echoes of each group of CPI and the same range unit to obtain Doppler velocity information. Finally, two-dimensional CFAR is used for target detection. The detailed detection process is as follows.

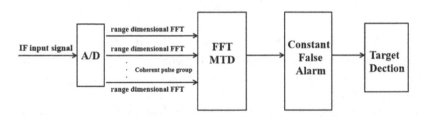

Fig. 2. The conventional LFMCW radar signal processing.

The current project mainly performs MTD processing on the coherent signals in each CPI, and then performs target determination on multiple pulse groups according to certain criteria. For example, if multiple CPIs meet the discovery target of 0.8 or more, it is considered that there is a target. In practice, since the statistical characteristics of ground clutter in a beam are basically similar in the mechanical scanning process, it is considered that the idea of using space-time adaptive processing can be adopted to combine multiple CPIs to achieve detection enhancement of slow ground targets.

It is proposed to use Doppler channels in different CPIs to perform adaptive processing technology for clutter suppression. First, the MTD results of each CPI are combined, and then the output of three Doppler channels is processed adaptively, thus Ground clutter is filtered out.

Figure 3 shows the processing structure for filtering clutter with dimensionality reduction. After the Doppler is localized by the weighted DFT, the output data of three adjacent channels are sent to the adaptive processing for processing.

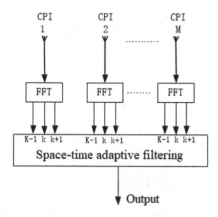

Fig. 3. Structure of 3DT-SAP dimensionality reduction.

The processor can describe digital optimization problems as:

$$\begin{cases} \min W^H R W \\ s.t. W^H S = 1 \end{cases} \tag{7}$$

$R = E\left[XX^H\right]$ and $S = S_s \otimes S_t$ denote as the co-variance matrix and the two-dimensional steering vector respectively, where $S_s = [1, 0 \ldots 0]^T$ and $S_t = \left[1, e^{j\omega_t} \ldots e^{j(N-1)\omega_t}\right]^T$. And ω_t Indicates the phase of each Doppler multichannel processed by MTD.

Finally,the optimized weight vector can be solved by the above formula.

$$W_{opt} = \mu R^{-1} S \tag{8}$$

Where μ is a constant. It can be seen that the expression is composed of the clutter covariance inverse matrix and the target vector. The first part is equivalent to whitening the clutter, and the latter part is equivalent to the target signal Perform matched filtering, so this is actually a generalized Wiener optimized matched filter.

The whole radar signal processing block diagram based on joint multi-CPI target detection is shown in Fig. 4.

Compared with the traditional method, the multi-frame processing results are jointly processed to realize the detection of slow targets on the ground, which can be applied to the existing single-channel LFMCW radar. The detailed implementation steps of the algorithm in this paper are as follows:

1) The received intermediate frequency data is calculated by the distance dimension FFT, and then FFT transformation is performed on the K coherent signals of each CPI according to the coherence.

2) Filter the results of N MTD processing in the beam scanning process and rearrange the data, where N is the number of coherent processing in the beam, and the first Doppler channel is selected as the main channel.

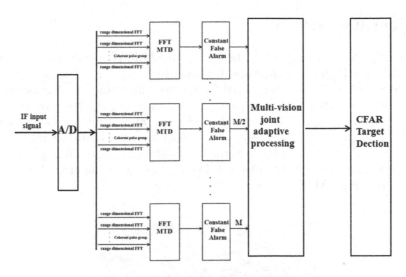

Fig. 4. Diagram of Jointed process.

3) The co-variance matrix formed by the received data. At the same time, define as a two-dimensional steering vector.

$$R = E\left[XX^H\right] \tag{9}$$

$$S = S_s \otimes S_t \tag{10}$$

$$S_s = [1, 0 \ldots 0]^T \tag{11}$$

$$S_t = \left[1, e^{j\omega_t} \ldots e^{j(N-1)\omega_t}\right]^T \tag{12}$$

4) The optimized weight vector can be rewritten as the above formula.

$$W_{opt} = \mu R^{-1} S \tag{13}$$

$$\mu = {}^1\!/_{S^H R^{-1} S} \tag{14}$$

5) The first Doppler channel composed of each joint channel is subjected to clutter suppression processing according to the adaptive weight vector W.

$$Y_k = W^H{}_{opt} X \tag{15}$$

6) Screen the second Doppler channel, repeat steps 3–5 to achieve clutter suppression for all Doppler channels
7) The result of moving target detection is formed by using CFAR to detect the target from the suppressed range Doppler image of each channel.

4   Simulation Results

According to the measured echo data of the real LFMCW ground reconnaissance radar, the overall shape of the radar is shown in Fig. 5. The radar is a ground-mounted radar, which is mainly used for the reconnaissance of slow targets on the ground. It works in the X frequency band, with a range detection accuracy of 10 m, and a sweep period of 1000 Hz. The cumulative number of sweeps for a single MTD process is 64, There are 8 CPIs for each scan target in the main lobe beam. Take a section of measured data with a distance ranging from 3000 m to 6000 m for analysis. The distance Doppler image of the ground echo after a traditional single MTD is shown in Fig. 6.

Fig. 5. LFMCW radar physical object.

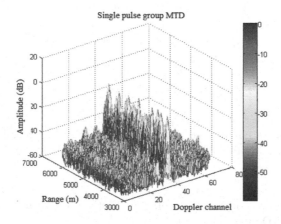

Fig. 6. Three-dimensional Range-Dopple image of echo.

In actual radar detection, if a target is detected more than 5 times in 8 CPIs, it is considered that the target exists. After adopting multi-CPI adaptive cancellation of text, it can effectively realize the detection and enhancement of the original ground clutter and the ground slow and small targets. Figure 7 is the three-dimensional range Doppler image after the 8-detection joint adaptive processing. It can be seen that after the joint processing, the ground clutter can be effectively suppressed, and the ground target can be better detected at the same time.

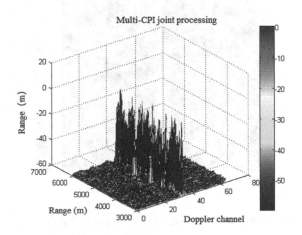

Fig. 7. Range-Dopple image of joint-cancellation.

Figures 8 and 9 are Range-Dopple images used for CFAR detection. It can be seen that the method can effectively suppress ground clutter and noise, especially

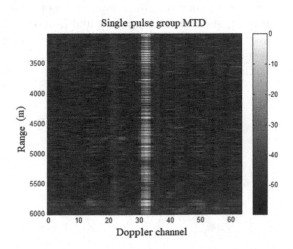

Fig. 8. Range-Dopple image of single-channel.

the detection ability of slow targets on the ground can be greatly improved. Currently, mechanical scanning radars urgently need to improve the detection ability of targets when detecting slow targets on the ground and at low altitudes. Through this solution, the detection performance of slow small targets can be quickly improved without modifying the existing radars.

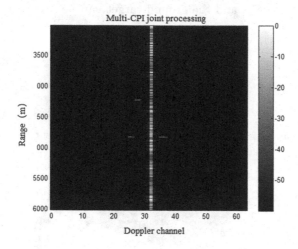

Fig. 9. Range-Dopple image of Joint-channel.

The main clutter suppression and target detection capabilities are significantly improved through the joint processing. Figures 10 and 11 are the comparison of the Doppler channel clutter suppression capabilities after the original single-channel MTD processing and the combined processing. Obviously, when the joint processing is not performed, the radar does not have the detection capability for low-speed targets near the main lobe and cannot effectively achieve target detection. However, the clutter of the entire Doppler channel is reduced by nearly 16 dB on average through the joint processing, so that the slow target that was originally annihilated in the ground clutter can be effectively detected.

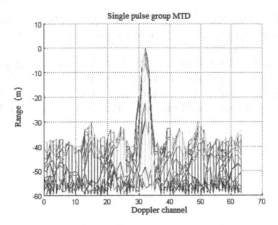

Fig. 10. Single-channel MTD target amplitude comparison.

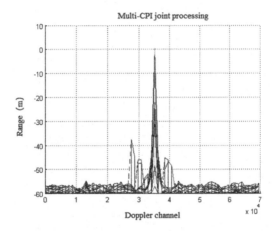

Fig. 11. Comparison of target range for joint processing.

References

1. Liu, G.S., Sun, G.M., Gu, H., et al.: Continuous wave radar and its signal processing technology. Modern Radar **17**(6), 20–36 (1995)
2. Gu, D.M.: Continuous wave radar signal recognition and parameter extraction technology research. Master's thesis, Nanjing University of Information Technology, pp. 44–46 (2009)
3. Dai, L., Gao, M.G.: Application of uniform DFT filter bank in radar jamming system. J. Syst. Eng. Electron. **17**(3), 527–530 (2006)
4. Gürbüz, S.Z., Melvin, W.L., Williams, D.B.: Detection and identification of human targets in radar data. In: Signal Processing, Sensor Fusion, and Target Recognition XVI, vol. 6567 (2007)

5. Zhou, Y.S.: Research on human body detection and feature extraction algorithms based on micro-Doppler. Master's degree thesis of University of Electronic Science and Technology of China (2010)
6. Shen, J.Q., Jiang, D.X.: Intermittent sampling and forwarding jamming of early warning radar STAP. Ship Electron. Warfare 40(3), 21–25 (2017)
7. Zhou, Y., Wang, X.G., Duan, R.: An improved JDL-STAP algorithm for airborne early warning radar. Chinese J. Radio Sci. 25(6), 1052–1057 (2010)

Calculation of Pulse Fuze Signal's Ambiguity Function and Study of Its Parameters Extraction Based on DSP

Wu Wei$^{(\boxtimes)}$, Zhu Huijie, and Bu Zirong

China Electronics Technology Group the 36th Research Institution, Key Laboratory, JiaXing 314001, Zhejiang, China

Abstract. This paper proposes a method of LFM pulse fuze signal's parameter extraction based on ambiguity function and implementation by DSP. Firstly, two-dimensional autocorrelation is done for the received signal, namely calculating the signal's ambiguity function, then according to the characteristic of fuze signal, the characteristic parameters is extracted on ambiguity function. The whole system is based on TMS320C6416 chip produced by TI company. The simulation result shows that the frequency modulation characteristic of signal can be detected effectively and parameters can be estimated accurately, the method which needs no prior information has good anti-noise ability. The test result verifies that the system competed has high reliability and real-time property.

Keywords: Fuze · LFM pulse train signal · Ambiguity function · Digital signal process

1 Introduction

The chirp fuze is to determine the distance between the source and the target by measuring the delay time between the transmitted signal and the target echo signal, due to it can solve the contradiction between the range resolution and the transmitted average power, and it retains the pulse signal high-range resolution and has been widely used in modern radio fuzes [1–3]. Many scholars at home and abroad have done a lot of work [4, 5]. Literature [4] proposes an algorithm for phase domain parameter estimation, but it needs to estimate the carrier frequency of the signal first, transform the intermediate frequency signal into a baseband signal, and then extract the parameters. The algorithm is more complicated. Literature [5] gives the theory and simulation analysis of LFM continuous wave signal modulation parameter extraction based on ambiguity function, but it does not analyze the chirp signal, nor does it analyze the feasibility of this method in practical applications. In recent years, electronic products have developed by leaps and bounds. TI's high-performance fixed-point DSP-TMS320C6416 [6, 7] has strong data processing capabilities and high computing speeds, which can meet the requirements of real-time processing of large amounts of data. This paper studies the problem of LFM burst fuze signal parameter extraction. Starting from the correlation domain, the extraction

© ICST Institute for Computer Sciences, Social Informatics and Telecommunications Engineering 2021
Published by Springer Nature Switzerland AG 2021. All Rights Reserved
X. Wang et al. (Eds.): AICON 2021, LNICST 396, pp. 393–401, 2021.
https://doi.org/10.1007/978-3-030-90196-7_33

algorithm of its characteristic parameters is proposed based on the fuzzy map of the LFM burst signal, and the feasibility of its practical application is verified by implementing it on a high-speed DSP.

2 Principle of Pulse Fuze

The principle block diagram of the chirp pulse fuze is shown in Fig. 1 [8, 9]. The pulse generator forms narrow pulses to pulse modulate the chirp signal to generate the chirp pulse train signal, which is amplified by the radio frequency amplifier and radiated by the transmitting antenna. The echo signal is mixed with the local reference signal after being low-noise amplifier. The latter signal is processed by the signal processor to extract the time delay and Doppler information of the echo signal. Due to the special working environment of the fuze, its operating distance is relatively short, and the processing and warning time is short, which requires the signal processing equipment to have high calculation speed and strong processing capability.

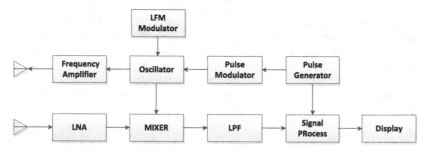

Fig. 1. Block diagram of LFM pulse train fuze system

3 Chirp Burst Signal and Its Ambiguity Function

3.1 Chirp Pulse Train Signal

The expression of the chirp burst signal is:

$$s(t) = \frac{A}{\sqrt{N}} \sum_{n=0}^{N-1} v(t - nT_r) \tag{1}$$

$v(t) = e^{j2\pi(f_0 + \frac{1}{2}kt)t}$ $t \leq t_p$, A is the amplitude of the transmitted signal, N is the number of sub-pulses, f_0 is carrier frequency of the signal, ΔF is modulation bandwidth, t_p is modulation period (Sub-pulse width), T_r is sub-pulse repetition period, k is the modulation slope of the signal, $k = \Delta F / t_p$。Observation formula (1) shows that the feature parameters of being extracted are ΔF, t_p, T_r and k。

3.2 Ambiguity Function of Chirp Burst Signal

In the theory of fuze signal analysis, ambiguity function is an important tool for analyzing and comparing the "optimization" degree of signal processing system. The definition of the fuzzy function is as follows [9]:

$$\chi(\tau, \xi) = \int_{-\infty}^{+\infty} u(t)u^*(t + \tau)e^{j2\pi\xi t}dt \tag{2}$$

According to the derivation [9], The ambiguity function of the chirp signal is:

$$\chi(\tau, \xi) = \frac{1}{N} \sum_{p=-(N-1)}^{N-1} \chi_1(\tau - pT_r, \xi)\left[e^{j\pi\xi(N-1-p)T_r} \cdot \frac{\sin \pi\xi(N - |p|)T_r}{\sin \pi\xi T_r}\right] \tag{3}$$

$$|\chi_1(\tau - pT_r, \xi)| = \begin{cases} \left|\dfrac{\sin\left[\pi\left(\xi - k|\tau - |p|T_r|\right)\left(t_p - |\tau - |p|T_r|\right)\right]}{\pi\left(\xi - k|\tau - |p|T_r|\right)}\right| & |\tau - |p|T_r| < t_p \\ 0 & \text{其他} \end{cases} \tag{4}$$

It can be seen that the ambiguity function of the chirp burst signal is composed of a series of different values p of the chirp sub-pulse ambiguity function $|\chi_1(\tau - pT_r, \xi)|$ on the delay axis τ, which is weighted by a factor $\frac{\sin \pi\xi(N-|p|)T_r}{N \sin \pi\xi T_r}$.

4   Algorithm for Extracting Characteristic Parameters of Chirp Burst Fuze Signal

After obtaining the ambiguity function for the intercepted LFM burst fuze signal, the characteristic parameters of the LFM burst fuze signal are extracted according to the result of the ambiguity function. For the convenience of discussion, first record the calculated ambiguity function data as $\tau_{1 \times i}$ (time delay matrix), corresponding to the τ axes in the 3D fuzzy graph; $\xi_{1 \times j}$ (frequency offset matrix), corresponding to the ξ axes in the 3D fuzzy graph; $\chi_{i \times j}$ (fuzzy function matrix) Corresponding to the vertical axis in the 3D blur graph, that is, the blur function value at position (τ_i, ξ_j) is $\chi_{i \times j}$. It can be seen from the analysis that the contour map of the ambiguity function of the LFM pulse train signal with N repetition periods is composed of $(2N - 1)$ parallel lines, and the distance between any two adjacent parallel lines with the same frequency offset corresponding to the delay axis is Pulse repetition period T_r; half of the difference between the maximum frequency shift ξ_{max} and the minimum frequency shift ξ_{min} in the contour map is the modulation bandwidth ΔF; half of the delay axis distance corresponding to ξ_{max} and ξ_{min} is the modulation period (sub-pulse width) t_p. Therefore, the extraction steps of the characteristic parameters of the LFM burst signal are as follows:

(1) Extraction of pulse repetition period T_r.

Step1: For each frequency offset ξ_n, Obtain the respective delay vectors corresponding to the peaks of the slice of $\chi_{i \times n}$, denoted as $\{\tau_1, \tau_2, \tau_3, \cdots\}$;

Step2: Calculate the difference between adjacent delays and get the interval vector of adjacent delays $\Delta\tau = \{\Delta\tau_1, \Delta\tau_2, \Delta\tau_3 \cdots\}, (\Delta\tau_i = |\tau_{i+1} - \tau_i|)$。

Step3: Searched delay interval vector $\Delta\tau$, Calculate the average value $\Delta\tau_{mean}$ of $\Delta\tau_i$, you can estimate that the pulse repetition period T_r is $\hat{T}_r = \Delta\tau_{mean}$.

(2) Extraction of modulation bandwidth ΔF and modulation period t_p.

Step1: Search the frequency shift axis in the 2D ambiguity graph to find ξ_{max} and ξ_{min} and their corresponding delays τ_{max} and τ_{min}.

Step2: Calculate their difference $\Delta\xi = \xi_{max} - \xi_{min}, \Delta\tau = \tau_{max} - \tau_{min}$. From the above analysis, it can be estimated that the modulation bandwidth ΔF of the signal is $\Delta\hat{F} = \Delta\xi/2$, and the modulation period t_p is $\hat{t}_p = \Delta\tau/2$.

(3) Extraction of FM slope k.

According to the modulation period t_p and modulation bandwidth ΔF extracted above, the frequency modulation slope k can be directly estimated as $\hat{k} = \Delta\hat{F}/\hat{t}_p$. Since both $\Delta\hat{F}$ and $\hat{t}_p$ are estimated by the algorithm, it is inevitable that they are not accurate enough. If the modulation slope $\hat{k}$ is directly estimated from the above formula, it may be even more inaccurate. Here, you can directly search for the point on the oblique knife edge in the fuzzy picture of the LFM pulse train signal, and use the least square method to directly estimate the modulation slope $\hat{k}$.

5   Realization of Ambiguity Function of LFM Burst Fuze Signal Based on DSP

As shown in Fig. 2, the system hardware uses the TMS320C6416 DSP chip produced by TI as the digital signal processor. The system uses the Virtex-II Pro FPGA produced by Xilinx to generate two orthogonal chirp train signals, then pack the data, and transmit the data to the DSP through the EMIFA bus for signal processing. Due to the large amount of data that needs to be processed, an off-chip SDRAM needs to be used as a cache.

5.1   The Performance Characteristics of TMS320C6416 DSP

TMS320C6416 DSP is a high-performance fixed-point DSP launched by TI. Its clock frequency is up to, the highest processing capacity is, and 8 instructions can be executed per clock cycle. It uses the unique VelociTI structure of TI, which is a CPU with an

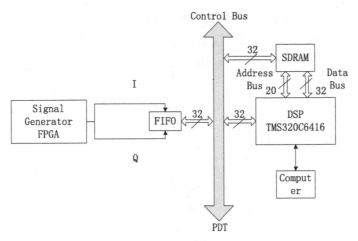

Fig. 2. Hardware structure of the system

improved Harvard structure and super long instruction word. This structure makes it exceed the performance of traditional superscalar CPUs. It contains 64 Kb on-chip data memory, which can be configured as a program memory in cache mode. In addition, the uniformly addressed 2 GB off-chip address space provides effective support for all memory types, with non-sticky memory interfaces and various DRAM refresh logic. This system uses two SDRAMs with a total capacity of 64 MB.

5.2 Procedure Flow

The flow chart of the realization of the LFM burst ambiguity function is shown in Fig. 3. In the calculation process, each frequency shift needs to be cross-correlated once, and the amount of calculation data is very large. TMS320C6416 provides 8 arithmetic units that can be operated at the same time, which can complete the multiplication of two 32-bit numbers at the same time, which is of great significance for a large number of butterfly operations in FFT/IFFT in this system. In this system, FFT/IFFT uses TI library functions DSP_fft32 × 32 and DSP_ifft32 × 32. When the library function is used, 1101196 clock cycles are required for each 1024-point cross-correlation operation [10]. This article intends to perform 100 cross-correlation to obtain the ambiguity function. Since the DSP clock frequency can be reached 600 MHz, the ambiguity function is completed. The calculation only needs 0.183 s, and the real-time performance is high. With the rapid development of electronic devices and continuous optimization of software algorithms, real-time performance will be further improved.

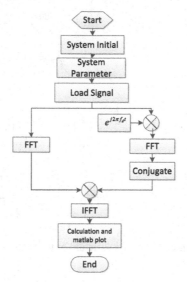

Fig. 3. Flow chart of the realization of LFM pulse train ambiguity function

6   Experimental Result

6.1   Chirp Signal Generation

Generate the target echo signal of the LFM burst fuze through FPGA simulation, set the signal carrier frequency (ie intermediate frequency) $f_0 = 5.5\,MHz$, modulation bandwidth $\Delta F = 1\,MHz$, modulation period $t_p = 10\,\mu s$, Pulse repetition period $T_r = 100\,\mu s$, pulse repetition period $N = 4$, the number of sub-pulses for signal processing E, The signal is shown in Fig. 4.

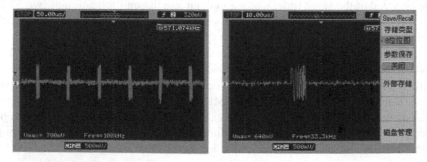

Fig. 4. The diagram of the LFM pulse train signal designed

6.2 Implementation of Ambiguity Function of Linear Frequency Modulation Burst Signal on DSP

The LFM pulse train signal generated above is transmitted to the DSP through the PDT transmission mode. After the DSP receives the signal, it calculates the ambiguity function of the signal. The result of the calculation is shown in Fig. 5, which is a fuzzy map without adding noise.

According to Sect. 3, by searching for the maximum frequency shift ξ_{max} and minimum frequency shift ξ_{min} in the 2-D ambiguity graph and their corresponding time delays τ_{max} and τ_{min}, half of the frequency shift difference is the modulation bandwidth $\Delta F = 1\,MHz$ of the signal, corresponding to Half of the delay difference is the modulation period $t_p = 10\,\mu s$ of the signal. Search for the delay vector corresponding to the peak of each frequency shift slice, find the delay interval of adjacent delays and take the average value to obtain the pulse repetition period $T_r = 100\,\mu s$.

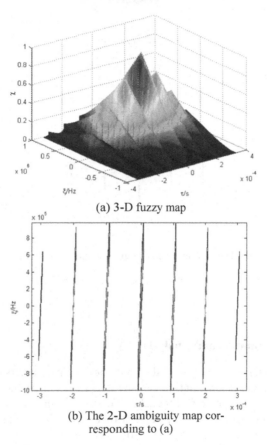

(a) 3-D fuzzy map

(b) The 2-D ambiguity map corresponding to (a)

Fig. 5. Ambiguity graph of LFM pulse train signal calculated by DSP ($N = 4$)

When the signal-to-noise ratio is $SNR = 0\,dB$, the ambiguity function diagram of the signal is shown in Fig. 6. It can be seen from the figure that when the signal-to-noise ratio is $SNR = 0\,dB$, its modulation parameters can still be extracted very accurately.

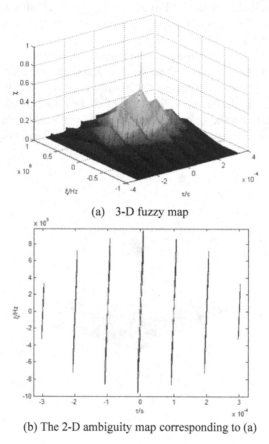

(a)   3-D fuzzy map

(b) The 2-D ambiguity map corresponding to (a)

Fig. 6. Ambiguity graph of LFM pulse train signal calculated by DSP when $SNR = 0\,$dB

6.3 Parameter Estimation and Analysis

According to the method of identifying the characteristic parameters of the LFM burst signal introduced above, that the anti-noise performance of using the fuzzy function to extract the modulation parameters of the LFM burst fuze signal is very good. Because the cross-correlation function of the LFM burst fuze signal is concentrated at a specific frequency shift, and the Gaussian white noise does not have this rule, its ambiguity function is "pushpin", and it cannot effectively interfere with the characteristic parameters of the LFM burst fuze signal. Extraction. In addition, the anti-noise performance can be enhanced by appropriately increasing the amplitude of the LFM burst signal.

7   Conclusion

This paper describes an algorithm for realizing the ambiguity function of LFM burst fuze signal based on high-speed fixed-point DSP, and extracts the modulation parameters of the signal according to the ambiguity function theory. This method first performs a two-dimensional autocorrelation transformation on the intercepted or received LFM burst fuze signal, that is, calculates the ambiguity function of the signal, and then combines the characteristics of the LFM burst signal itself to extract the modulation period, modulation bandwidth, and pulse in the correlation domain. Modulation parameters such as repetition period. The experimental results show that the method has high parameter estimation accuracy and strong anti-noise performance without any prior information.

Due to the excellent performance of TMS320C6416 DSP in real-time signal processing with large data volume, the method of extracting characteristic parameters by fuzzy function can be realized. The experimental results show that the system has high reliability and real-time performance, which has certain reference value for the design of fuze jammers.

1. References

1. Stove, A.G.: Liner FMCW radar technique. IEEE Proceed.-F, **139**(5), 343–350 (1992)
2. Geroleo, F.G., Brandt-Pearce, M.: Detection and estimation of muti-pulse LFMCW radar signals. In: Radar Conference. DC, USA, pp. 1009–1013 (2010)
3. Wu, F., Han, Z., He, Q.: Simulation testing of LFM compression performances based on identification. In: 2010 International Conference on Intelligent System Design and Engineering Application. Changsha, China, pp. 383–386 (2010)
4. Sheng, J., Wang, F., Deng, Z., et al.: A fast and high-precision parameter estimation algorithm for LFM signal phase domain. Syst. Eng. Electron. Technol. **33** (2), 264–267 (2011)
5. Liu, J., Zhao, H., Zhou, X., et al.: Radio fuze signal parameter extraction based on fuzzy function. J. Detect. Control, **31**(5), 42–47 (2009)
6. Texas Instruments Corporation: TMS320C64X DSP Library Programmer's Reference. Texas Instruments Corporation, California, USA (2003)
7. Texas Instruments Corporation: TMS320C6000 Chip Support Library API Reference Guide. Texas Instruments Corporation, California, USA (2004)
8. Govoni, M.A., Li, H.: Complex, aperiodic random signal modulation on pulse LFM chirp radar waveform. Orlando, USA: Radar Sensor Technology XIV (2010). 76690s1–11
9. Xingang, Z., Zhao, H., Gao, Z.: Analysis of multi-period ambiguity function of LFMCW radar signal restudy. J. Nanjing Univ. Sci. Tech. (Nat. Sci. Ed.) **34**(5), 624–627 (2010)
10. Zhao, Y., Pan, D., Song, Y.: Research on real-time performance of acousti localization intelligent fuze based on DSP. J. Projectiles Rockets Rockets Guid. **30**(2), 133–140 (2010)

Distributed Jamming Method for STAP Radar Based on Algorithm of Improved MOEA/D-PBI

Wenbo Yang🆔, Gaogao Liu$^{(\boxtimes)}$, Dongjie Huang🆔, and Minhua Zheng

Xidian University, Xi'an, China
hywbwyang@163.com, ggliu@xidian.edu.cn, 546669844@qq.com,
906383787@qq.com

Abstract. In modern warfare, the role of airborne early warning aircraft is becoming more and more significant. The airborne early warning radar can accurately detect moving targets in a chaotic environment. Its suppression of strong clutter and jamming by radar is mainly through space-time adaptive processing (STAP) technology to achieve. The STAP algorithm uses the two domains of time and space to perform two-dimensional joint processing on the echo data, adaptively forming a notch that matches the clutter and jamming, and its excellent jamming suppression capability increases the difficulty of radar countermeasures. In this case, it is very necessary to conduct a comprehensive jamming study about the technology. At present, relevant jamming methods at home and abroad are still in the preliminary research stage. In this paper, we take genetic algorithm as an example, and a new distributed jamming method for STAP radar based on improved penalty-based boundary intersection decomposition multiobjective evolutionary algorithm (MOEA/D-PBI) is introduced in the many-to-many confrontation. Through simulation experiments, the optimized distributed jamming scheme is compared with the distributed jamming scheme before optimization, verifying the feasibility of the method proposed in this paper, which simplifies the problem of jamming resource allocation and realizes a fast search for the optimal allocation strategy, and complete real-time jamming decision-making on the battlefield.

Keywords: Improved penalty-based boundary intersection · Distributed jamming · Genetic algorithm

1 Introduction

Compared with the simpler clutter suppression process of ground-based radars, the signal detection environment faced by airborne radars is more complicated. The radar's suppression of strong clutter and jamming is mainly achieved through space-time adaptive processing (STAP) technology [1]. STAP radar has strong adaptability and can deal with strong clutter and conventional jamming effectively. It can be seen that the STAP radar with superior clutter suppression performance makes it difficult for the interfering side to implement countermeasures [2]. At present, the field of STAP radar jamming is in its infancy. Current jamming research on the STAP algorithm only focuses on designing

X. Wang et al. (Eds.): AICON 2021, LNICST 396, pp. 402–414, 2021.
https://doi.org/10.1007/978-3-030-90196-7_34

effective jamming patterns, thereby destroying the independent and identical distribution conditions of the training samples in the STAP algorithm [1]. Therefore, the jamming research on the signal of STAP radar is an effective means to suppress the performance of STAP radar, and it is of great significance to cover the jammer's target.

The traditional jamming method against STAP radar is single-point source main lobe jamming [3]. In the long-distance support sidelobe jamming, because the number of jammers is small and the target is far away, it will be suppressed by the space-time two-dimensional processing, and will not bring a certain threat to the target detection [2]. At the same time, radar jamming resource allocation scenarios are often for jammers against a single radar. When the number of radars increases, considering that a single jammer will be affected by various factors such as jamming pattern, jamming power and frequency band, the effectiveness of jamming is difficult to guarantee [4].

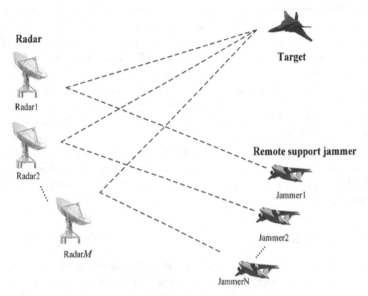

Fig. 1. Many-to-many jamming situation.

In addition, due to the many-to-many jamming situation (Fig. 1), the research on the countermeasures between the radar network platform and the cooperative jamming system becomes more and more important. How to reasonably allocate the jamming resources under the existing multiple jammers to obtain a more accurate jamming decision, which has a strong guide for the action direction of the interferer [4]. Since the radar countermeasures process is affected by many factors such as environment and man-made factors, different strategies will have different jamming effects. If rely on traditional experience to make decisions, it will be biased.

To overcome above drawbacks, a distributed jamming method for STAP radar based on improved penalty-based boundary intersection decomposition multiobjective evolutionary algorithm (MOEA/D-PBI) is proposed in this paper to effectively allocate jamming resources, thereby realizing effective jamming to STAP radars. This method takes into consideration the landscape of each subproblem and adaptively adjust each subproblem's penalty value during the search. Our experimental study validate the effectiveness of the proposed method. The rest of this paper is organized as follows. Section 2 presents traditional work and illustrates the improved PBI approach. The proposed distributed jamming method is described in Sect. 3. Experimental studies are presented in Sect. 4. Finally, Sect. 5 concludes this paper.

2 MOEA/D-PBI Algorithm

2.1 MOEA/D Algorithm

Multiobjective evolutionary algorithm based on decomposition (MOEA/D) used in this paper needs to decompose the MOP under consideration [5, 6]. MOEA/D employs a set of predefined weight vectors that uniformly partition the entire objective space to specify a number of search directions, and defines a single-objective problem or a multiobjective subproblem by decomposition approaches for each search direction. For each search direction, MOEA/D also specifies T closest neighbours before-hand, which helps to efficiently solve the associated single-objective problem in a collaborative manner [7]. During the course of search, mating selection and replacement are considered among solutions associated with the T neighbouring search directions. MOEA/D is a steady-state algorithm and up-dates solutions one by one, so it approximates the true Pareto-optimal front (POF) quickly [8].

The algorithm framework of distributed jamming method based on improved MOEA/D-PBI is proposed in Sect. 2.3. Any decomposition approaches can serve this purpose. In this paper, we only study the following decomposition approach in our experimental studies.

2.2 Traditional PBI Review

Decomposition approaches play a key role in converting a multiobjective optimization problem (MOP) into a number of scalar optimizations subproblems in decomposition-based multiobjective evolutionary algorithms (MOEAs). Several recent MOP decomposition methods such as Normal-Boundary Intersection Method [9] and Normalized Normal Constraint Method [10] can be classified as the boundary intersection (BI) approaches. They were designed for a continuous MOP. Under some regularity conditions, the Pareto front (PF) of a continuous MOP is part of the most top right boundary of its attainable objective set. Geometrically, these BI approaches aim to find intersection points of the most top boundary and a set of lines. If these lines are evenly distributed in a sense, one can expect that the resultant intersection points provide a good approximation to the whole PF. These approaches are able to deal with nonconcave PFs.

The traditional PBI approach has its advantages in obtaining a good distribution of solutions in the objective space [7] and handling many objective problems, but its performance is very sensitive to the setting of the penalty factor [8]. The specific decomposition method based on traditional PBI is as follows.

$$\text{minimize}\left\{ g^{pbi}\left(x|\lambda, z^*\right) = d_1 + \theta d_2 \right\}, x \in \Theta \tag{1}$$

Where, minimize$\{\cdot\}$ is minimum operation and x is variable to be optimized. As shown in Fig. 2, d_1 is the distance between z^* and y, d_2 is the distance between $F(x)$ and L. $z^* = \left(z_1^*, z_2^*, \cdots, z_i^* \cdots, z_N^*\right)^T$ is the reference point. λ is a weight vector. Θ is decision space. $\theta > 0$ is preset penalty parameter.

According to the following formula (2), calculate d_1

$$d_1 = \frac{\|(F(x) - z^*)^T \lambda\|}{\|\lambda\|} \tag{2}$$

According to the following formula (3), calculate d_2

$$d_2 = \|F(x) - \left(z^* + d_1 \frac{\lambda}{\|\lambda\|}\right)\| \tag{3}$$

A brief illustration of the traditional PBI approach is shown in Fig. 2. It is easy to see that θ takes the responsibility for balancing convergence (measured by d_1) and diversity (measured by d_2). By minimizing g^{pbi}, the PBI approach drives the solution toward the obtained idea point z^* and stresses the closeness of the solution to the predefined search direction. If possible, the traditional PBI approach will try to locate a solution on the intersection of each search direction and the true POF when a set of uniformly-distributed search directions are given.

However, one has to set the value of the penalty factor. It is well-known that a too large or too small penalty factor θ will worsen the performance of a penalty method. These disadvantages limit the wide application of the algorithm.

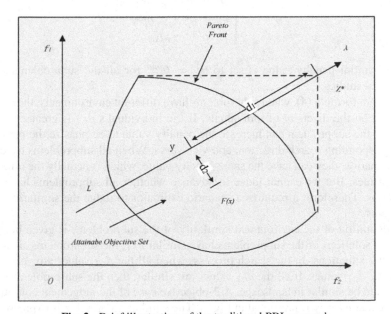

Fig. 2. Brief illustration of the traditional PBI approach.

In this paper, our main purpose is to study the efficiency and feasibility of the algorithm framework. Therefore, we only use the following improved decomposition approach in the experimental studies.

2.3 Improved PBI Introduction

According to formula (1), in order to overcome the sensitivity caused by θ. Consider adjusting the penalty value θ_i of the ith subproblem in each generation of search and optimization [11, 12].

$$\theta_i^{t+1} = \begin{cases} min_{1 \leq j \leq N} \left\{\theta_j^t\right\}, & \text{if similar environments,} \\ \theta_i^t + \Delta\theta_i, & \text{otherwise.} \end{cases} \tag{4}$$

Where θ_i^t is the θ_i at generation t, and $\Delta\theta_i$ is calculated by:

$$\Delta\theta_i = sgn(\alpha - 1) \cdot \alpha \cdot \theta_i^{min} \tag{5}$$

Where $\alpha = \frac{d_{i,2}}{\overline{d_2}}$ in which $\overline{d_2}$ is the average of all $d_{i,2}$ values. $sgn(\cdot)$ is the sign function, and θ_i^{min} is the minimum allowable value of θ_i. Correspondingly, θ_i^{max} is the maximum allowable value of θ_i.

Then, θ_i^{t+1} obtained from formula (4) should be repaired to keep its value in the range $\left[\theta_i^{min}, \theta_i^{max}\right]$, which can be achieved by:

$$\theta_i^{t+1} = \begin{cases} \theta_i^{min}, & \theta_i^{t+1} < \theta_i^{min} \\ \theta_i^{max}, & \theta_i^{t+1} > \theta_i^{max} \\ \theta_i^{t+1}, & else \end{cases} \tag{6}$$

Where the initial penalty value is set to $\theta_i^1 = \theta_i^{min}$ for all the subproblems in our experimental studies.

Seen from formula (4), when subproblems have different environments, their penalties depend on the diversity of individuals. If the individual's $d_{i,2}$ is greater than the average $\overline{d_2}$, the subproblem can increase the penalty value to emphasize the proximity to the corresponding search direction, and vice versa. When all subproblems have very similar scenarios, they can have the same penalty value, which is actually the minimum of all θ_i^t values. But we cannot judge in advance whether all subproblems have similar scenarios. Therefore, it requires a scenario estimator to judge the similarity of the subproblems.

The definition of the environment similarity of the subproblems is given below: If the optimal solutions of the subproblems have similar $d_{i,1}$, the subproblems are said to have similar situations. In the search process, when all the $d_{i,2}$ values are very small, consider the $d_{i,1}$ values. If all the $d_{i,1}$ values are similar, then the sub-problems can be considered to be similar in landscape. A 2-objective case of the judgement condition of environment similarity is presented in Fig. 3. The similarity condition is expressed as:

$$\overline{d_2} < \delta \wedge d_{max,1} < \sqrt{M} \cdot d_{min,1} \tag{7}$$

Where δ is a very small non-negative threshold value. For simplicity, δ is set to 10^{-3}, indicating all $d_{i,2}$ values are very small and good population diversity has been achieved. $d_{min,1}$ and $d_{max,1}$ are the minimum and maximum value of $d_{i,1}$, respectively, and M is the number of objectives.

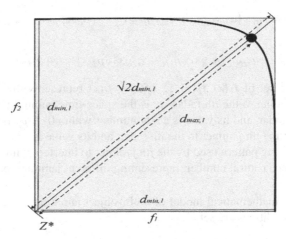

Fig. 3. An illustration of the condition of environment similarity in the 2 objectives case.

3 Distributed Jamming Method

In this paper, we propose a new distributed jamming method based on improved PBI decomposition approach.

- **Step 0: Initialization:**

- First of all, to determine the threat level $\omega_{r1}, \omega_{r2}, ..., \omega_{ri}, ..., \omega_{rN}$ of each radar, the reconnaissance equipment must master the parameter information of the N intercepted radars set $R = [R_1, R_2, ..., R_i, ..., R_N]$. Among them, the key parameters include, but are not limited to the signal bandwidth $B_1, B_2, ..., B_i, ..., B_N$ of each radar pulse signal, the carrier frequency $f_{c1}, f_{c2}, ..., f_{ci}, ..., f_{cN}$ of each radar pulse signal, the transmission power $P_{r1}, P_{r2}, ..., P_{ri}, ..., P_{rN}$ of each radar pulse signal, etc. N represents the number of radars, and the value is a positive integer; R_i represents the ith radar, i is the radar index, and it's value is a positive integer; ω_{ri} represents the threat level of the ith radar, and the value is a real number within 0–1; B_i represents the bandwidth of the ith radar, and the value is a positive integer; f_{ci} represents the carrier frequency of the ith radar, and the value is positive integer; P_{ri} represents the transmit power of the ith radar;
- Consider setting up M jammers $J = [J_1, J_2, ..., J_j, ..., J_M]$, where J_j means the j th jammer, M is the number of jammers, $M > 0$;
- A mathematical model of multiobjective jamming resource scheduling considering decision variables such as jamming pattern and jamming power. The objective function is shown in the following formula (8).

$$F(x): \begin{cases} f_1(x) = \omega_{r1} \cdot (a_{11}s_{11}p_{11} + a_{21}s_{21}p_{21} + \cdots + a_{M1}s_{M1}p_{M1}) \\ f_2(x) = \omega_{r2} \cdot (a_{12}s_{12}p_{12} + a_{22}s_{22}p_{22} + \cdots + a_{M2}s_{M2}p_{M2}) \\ \qquad\qquad\vdots \\ f_i(x) = \omega_{ri} \cdot (a_{1i}s_{1i}p_{1i} + a_{2i}s_{2i}p_{2i} + \cdots + a_{ji}s_{ji}p_{ji} \cdots + a_{Mi}s_{Mi}p_{Mi}) \\ \qquad\qquad\vdots \\ f_N(x) = \omega_{rN} \cdot (a_{1N}s_{1N}p_{1N} + a_{2N}s_{2N}p_{2N} + \cdots + a_{MN}s_{MN}p_{MN}) \end{cases} \tag{8}$$

Where $F(x)$ is the set of $f_1(x), f_2(x), \ldots, f_N(x)$, $f_i(x)$ represents the jamming target function corresponding to the ith radar. a_{ji} is the space-time jamming factor of the jth jammer to the ith radar, and its value is a real number within 0–1. p_{ji} is the normalized jamming power of the jth jammer to the ith radar, and its value is a real number within 0–1. s_{ji} is the jamming pattern used by the jth jammer to interfere with the ith radar. Its value is a continuous natural number, representing different jamming patterns;

- Considering the mathematical model of multi-object jamming resource scheduling, the constraint conditions are set as.

$$\begin{cases} \sum_{i=1}^{N} p_{ji} = 1, j = 1, 2, \cdots, M \\ s_{1i} = s_{2i} = \cdots = s_{ji} = \cdots = s_{Mi} \end{cases} \tag{9}$$

Where $\sum_{i=1}^{N} p_{ji} = 1$ indicates that the sum of the normalized jamming power of a jammer is 1. $s_{1i} = s_{2i} = \cdots = s_{ji} = \cdots = s_{Mi}$ means that the jamming patterns used by the jammers are all the same jamming pattern when jamming the same radar;

- **Step 1: Reproduction and Update:**

- Before starting the optimization, first set the population optimal solution set EP as an empty set ϕ. Then set a set of ideal points $z = (z_1, z_2, \ldots, z_i, \ldots, z_N)$, z_i denotes the ith ideal point. Randomly initialize all ideal point values according to constraint conditions, and define a set of weight vectors $\lambda^1, \ldots, \lambda^k, \ldots \lambda^K$. Where, λ^k represents the kth weight vector, K is the population size;
- Euclidean distance is used to calculate the T neighboring vectors that are closest to each weight vector. Calculate the Euclidean distance between the adjacent weights, and the T vectors closest to the weight vector λ^k are the adjacent vectors of the weight vector λ^k. Where the adjacent vectors index set is denoted as $B(k) = (k_1, \ldots, k_T)$, $\lambda^{k_1}, \lambda^{k_2}, \ldots, \lambda^{k_T}$ is the T adjacent vectors of λ^k;
- Generate the initial population weight vector set $P = \{x^1, \ldots, x^k, \ldots x^K\}$, $x \in \Theta$. Sample from the decision space Θ uniformly and randomly. Where, x^k represents the kth weight vector of the population, and the initial k value is set to 1;

- Select two indexes m, n arbitrarily from the set $B(k) = (k_1, \ldots, k_T)$ of adjacent vector indexes, and implement the crossover operation based on the standard genetic algorithm on x^m and x^n to obtain a new individual y;
- Perform mutation operation based on standard genetic algorithm on the new individual y to get the mutated individual y';
- Update the ideal point: if $z_w < f_w\left(y'\right)$, $w = 1, \ldots, N$, then $z_w = f_w\left(y'\right)$;
- Update the adjacent solution: If y' is better than x^w which is any one of $B(k)$ (measured by the fitness of the kth subproblem), then x^w is replaced by y'. That is, for $w \in B(k)$, if $g^{pbi}\left(y'|\lambda^w, z\right) \le g^{pbi}(x^w|\lambda^w, z)$, then $x^w = y', z_w = f_w\left(y'\right)$. Where, g^{pbi} represents the decomposition operation based on improved penalty boundary intersection;
- Judge $F\left(x^k\right), k = 1, \ldots, K$ whether it is dominated by $F\left(y'\right)$: if dominated, $F\left(x^k\right)$ will be removed from the population optimal solution set EP. For $\forall i = 1, \cdots, N$, if there is no dominance, $F\left(y'\right)$ will be added to the population optimal solution set EP, and the value of k increased by one.

- **Step 2: Stopping Criteria:**

- Repeat the last five steps of **Step 1** until $k = K$, the population optimal solution set EP after evolution is obtained, and the population optimal solution set EP contains the jamming style decision result $s_1^{opt}, s_2^{opt}, \ldots, s_i^{opt}, \ldots, s_N^{opt}$ and the jamming power decision result $p_{ji}^{opt}, j = 1, \ldots, M, i = 1, \ldots, N$. Where, s_i^{opt} represents the jamming pattern adopted to interfere with the ith radar, and p_{ji}^{opt} represents the jamming power applied by the jth jammer to the ith radar.

- **Step 3: Output:**

- According to the optimal distributed jamming method obtained in **Step 2**, consider that each jammer J_j in the set $J = \left[J_1, J_2, \ldots, J_j, \ldots, J_M\right]$ adopts an jamming pattern s_i^{opt} to transmit jamming signals to the ith radar for the jamming power p_{ji}^{opt}, and finally complete the distributed jamming to the other radar network.

4 Simulated Experiments

4.1 Experimental Settings

The space confrontation scene is shown in Fig. 1. In order to validate the effectiveness of the proposed approach, the simulation condition is set as the total number of radars to 3, the distributed jamming network contains 8 jammers, the number of neighbors of the multi-target evolutionary algorithm decomposed by PBI is 200, the crossover probability is 0.5, the mutation probability is 0.5, and the crossover operator used in this paper is simulate binary crossover (SBX), its crossover mutation parameter is 1. The mutation operator parameter is 1, the external population output threshold is 200, and the maximum number of iterations is 200. The bandwidth of the STAP radar is 20 MHz, the carrier frequency is 1.5 GHz, the number of array elements is 12, and the number of pulses is 24.

The settings of above simulation condition are summarized as follows (Table 1).

Table 1. Experimental simulation parameters configuration

Parameters style	Configuration information
Number of radars	3
Number of jammers	8
Number of neighbors	200
Crossover probability	0.5
Mutation probability	0.5
SBX crossover mutation	1
Mutation operator	1
External population output	200
Maximum number of iterations	200
Bandwidth of the STAP radar	20 MHz
carrier frequency	1.5 GHz
Number of array elements	12
Number of pulses	24

In the case of jamming from the mth jammer to the nth radar, we define the jamming power allocation matrix P_{JR}. As shown in formula (10), the jamming power allocation matrix represents the power allocated when the mth jammer interferes with the nth radar.

$$
P_{JR} = \begin{bmatrix} p_{11} & p_{12} & \cdots & p_{1N} \\ p_{21} & p_{22} & \cdots & p_{2N} \\ \cdots & \cdots & p_{mn} & \cdots \\ p_{M1} & p_{M2} & \cdots & p_{MN} \end{bmatrix}
\tag{10}
$$

In addition, conditional constraints on the jammer include the same jammer can only interfere with up to 3 radars at the same time; the sum of the normalized power of the jammer is 1. And conditional constraints on radars include each radar is jammed by at least one jammer; when jamming the same radar, the jammers use the same jamming pattern.

4.2 Experimental Results

Now use the above experimental parameters to optimize the multiobjective problem. The decision optimization result is the normalized power allocation scheme of the jammer in the many-to-many confrontation.

Table 2 shows the normalized power allocation scheme of jammers obtained by optimization. Where taking the first line as an example, it represents that the normalized power allocated by jammer 1 to radar 1, radar 2, and radar 3 are 0.23, 0.05, and 0.72, respectively. In order to observe the tendency of jamming power resource allocation more intuitively, the statistical results shown in the table are drawn into power distribution diagram, as shown in Fig. 4. Since the solution obtained by the multiobjective optimization algorithm is a non-dominated solution, the optimization result is not unique.

Table 2. Power distribution

	Radar 1	Radar 2	Radar 3
Jammer 1	0.23	0.05	0.72
Jammer 2	0.15	0.26	0.59
Jammer 3	0.34	0.14	0.52
Jammer 4	0.38	0.02	0.60
Jammer 5	0.13	0.23	0.64
Jammer 6	0.20	0.09	0.71
Jammer 7	0.49	0.11	0.41
Jammer 8	0.05	0.32	0.63

It can be seen from Fig. 4 and Table 2 that most jammers allocate most of the power to radar 3, which is consistent with the degree of jamming power set in the scene. Since radar 1 and radar 2 have similar threat levels, there is a situation of competing for the remaining jamming resources, which is also consistent with the actual setting. It shows that the allocation scheme of jamming resources obtained from optimization is reasonable to a certain extent.

After verifying the rationality of the multi-objective optimization scheme, the effectiveness of the obtained jamming resource allocation scheme will be verified. The jamming power is allocated as Table 2, and the rest of the simulation parameters remain unchanged as above.

Under above simulation conditions, comparing jamming signals not optimized by improved MOEA/D-PBI, and jamming signals obtained by the present invention to interfere with STAP radar. The output improvement factor statistical graphs are shown in Fig. 5, Fig. 6 and Fig. 7, respectively.

From the comparison graphs of the improvement factors of three radars, it can be seen that the radar 3 with the highest jamming threat level obtains the most jamming resources, and the notch in the improvement factor is enlarged, and the decline is the most obvious. It proves that the optimized jamming decision-making program by the improved MOEA/D-PBI algorithm is more flexible and can be adjusted strategically and adaptively according to the threat level of the battlefield target. Meanwhile, the improvement factors of radar 2 and radar 1 have the second highest jamming threat level, and have also been reduced to varying extent.

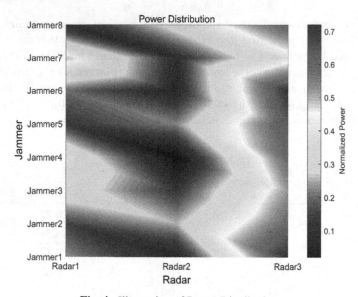

Fig. 4. Illustration of Power Distribution.

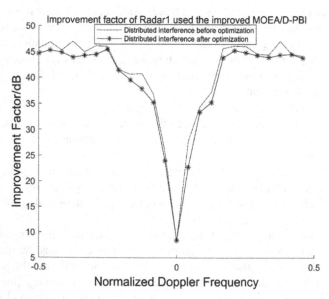

Fig. 5. Improvement factor of Radar 1 with the improved MOEA/D-PBI.

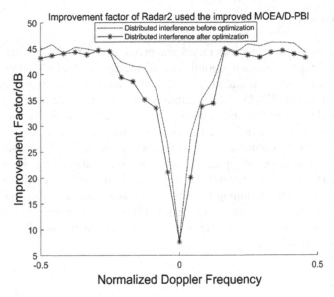

Fig. 6. Improvement factor of Radar 2 with the improved MOEA/D-PBI.

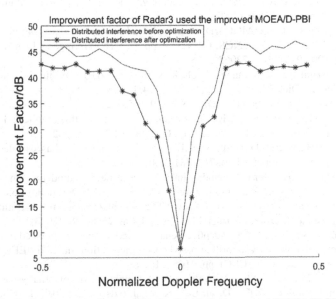

Fig. 7. Improvement factor of Radar 3 with the improved MOEA/D-PBI.

5 Conclusions

Due to competition among various radars and preemptive jamming resources, it is difficult to find a unique solution to optimize the jamming effects of all radars at the same time. Based on the above situation, a new distributed jamming optimization scheme based on improved MOEA/D-PBI algorithm is proposed to solve multiobjective function values in this paper, and the optimal solution set can achieve the balance among the objective functions. It can be seen from the simulation results that the optimization scheme obtained by the optimization algorithm is reasonable, and the power of the jammer can be distributed more obliquely according to the actual radar threat level, which is consistent with the actual environment settings. Finally, through simulation experiments, the optimized distributed jamming scheme is compared with the distributed jamming scheme before optimization, verifying the feasibility of the distributed jamming optimization scheme proposed in this paper, which can effectively interfere with radar in multiobjective situation.

References

1. Guerci, J.R.: Space-time Adaptive Processing for Radar. Boston: Artech House, pp. 23–38 (2003)
2. Melvin, W.L.: A STAP overview. IEEE AES Mag. **19**(1), 19–35 (2004)
3. Klemm, R.: Principles of Space-time Adaptive Processing: Inst Elect Eng, pp. 22–39. London, U.K (2002)
4. Commander, C.W., Pardalos, P.M., Ryabchenko, V.: The wireless network jamming problem. J. Comb. Optim. **4**, 481–498 (2007)
5. Chen, J., Zhang, Q., Li, G.: MOEA/D for multiple multi-objective optimization. In: Ishibuchi, H., et al. (eds.) EMO 2021. LNCS, vol. 12654, pp. 152–163. Springer, Cham (2021). https://doi.org/10.1007/978-3-030-72062-9_13
6. Sato, H.: Adaptive update range of solutions in MOEA/D for multi and many-objective optimization. In: Dick, G., et al. (eds.) SEAL 2014. LNCS, vol. 8886, pp. 274–286. Springer, Cham (2014). https://doi.org/10.1007/978-3-319-13563-2_24
7. Li, H., Zhang, Q.: Multiobjective optimization problems with complicated pareto sets, MOEA/D and NSGA-II. IEEE Trans. Evol. Comput. **12**(2), 284–302 (2009)
8. Zhang, Q., Li, H.: MOEA/D: a multiobjective evolutionary algorithm based on decomposition. IEEE Trans. Evol. Comput. **11**(6), 712–731 (2007)
9. Das, I., Dennis, J.E.: Normal-bounday intersection: a new method for generating Pareto optimal points in multicriteria optimization problems. SIAM J. Optim. **8**(3), 631–657 (1998)
10. Messac, A., Ismail-Yahaya, A., Mattson, C.: The normalized normal constraint method for generating the Pareto frontier. Struct. Multidisc. Optim, **25**, 86–98 (2003)
11. Guo, J., Yang, S., Jiang, S.: An adaptive penalty-based boundary intersection approach for multiobjective evolutionary algorithm based on decomposition. In: 2016 IEEE Congress on Evolutionary Computation (CEC), pp. 2145–2152 (2016)
12. Li, H., Sun, J., Zhang, Q., Shui, Y.: Adjustment of weight vectors of penalty-based boundary intersection method in MOEA/D. In: Deb, K., et al. (eds.) EMO 2019. LNCS, vol. 11411, pp. 91–100. Springer, Cham (2019). https://doi.org/10.1007/978-3-030-12598-1_8

Research on GPU Parallel Acceleration of Efficient Coherent Integration Processor for Passive Radar

Zirong Bu[1,2], Lijun Wang[1,2], and Huijie Zhu[1,2(✉)]

[1] Science and Technology on Communication Information Security Control Laboratory, Jiaxing 314033, China
[2] No. 36 Research Institute of China Electronics Technology Group Corporation, Jiaxing 314033, China

Abstract. The traditional algorithm of cross-ambiguity function requires a large amount of computation and storage capacity, which brings difficulties to real-time processing. In addition, the long-integration time will cause range migration problems, resulting in a decrease in the SNR, and reducing the weak target detection ability of the system. Based on the characteristics of the passive radar, this paper adopts the method of combining segmental frequency domain pulse compression and Keystone transform to correct the range migration in the target detection, which improves the detection ability of weak targets. However, due to the relatively large amount of data and computation of the algorithm, this paper takes the advantages of graphics processing unit (GPU) with large data throughput and strong floating-point computing capabilities to propose an efficient coherent integration method which is suitable for GPU parallel processing.

Keywords: Passive radar · Range migration · Graphics processing unit (GPU)

1 Introduction

Passive radar exploits the opportunity signal in the environment for target detection, which has the advantages of high concealment, low power consumption, high concealment, and strong anti-interference ability [1]. The core problem of passive radar is to detect weak targets in strong interference. Usually, the direct wave and clutter signals received by the radar are much stronger than the target echo. After the direct wave and clutter are suppressed, the time delay-Doppler two-dimensional correlation (ambiguity function) still needs to be calculated to obtain accumulated benefits. However, the traditional algorithm of cross-ambiguity function requires a large amount of computation and storage capacity, which brings difficulties to real-time processing. In addition, the long-integration time will cause range migration problems, resulting in a decrease in the SNR, and reducing the weak target detection ability of the system. this paper proposes an efficient integration integration method which is suitable for GPU parallel processing.

X. Wang et al. (Eds.): AICON 2021, LNICST 396, pp. 415–422, 2021.
https://doi.org/10.1007/978-3-030-90196-7_35

In recent years, with the development of large-scale integrated circuit technology, the performance of the GPU has increased day by day, which provides a new solution for real-time signal processing of passive radar. Compared with traditional solutions such as LPGA, DSP and so on. GPU has the advantages of low cost, simple structure and easy development. A large number of research at home and abroad have confirmed the feasibility of real-time processing of passive radar signal using high-performance CPUs and GPUs. The coherent integration algorithms are more suitable for GPU implementation because GPU can be calculated in parallel, and has the advantages of sufficient storage space, large data throughput, and strong floating-point operating capabilities.

2 Efficient Coherent Integration Processor with Range Migration Compensation

2.1 Segmented Frequency Domain Pulse Compression (FDPC) of Passive Radar

Due to the long-integration time, the calculation amount of direct coherent integration is very huge, the segmented FDPC method can greatly reduce the computational complexity [4]. The signal is divided into segments of equivalent pulses, which can be understood as analog active radar pulse processing, and the continuous signal is divided into the form of fast-slow time. The segmentation method of the reference signal and the echo signal is shown in Fig. 1. Determine the slow time segment number M according to the maximum radial velocity of the target, so as to avoid the phenomenon of spanning the distance gate caused by the target movement during the integration time. The length of the reference signal within the segment is N, and the length of the echo signal within the segment is $N_t = N + N_d$, and N_d is determined by the maximum delay of system detection. Among them, the segmentation of the reference signal adopts the method of zero-filling at the end of the non-overlapping segment, and the echo signal adopts the method of overlapping segmentation.

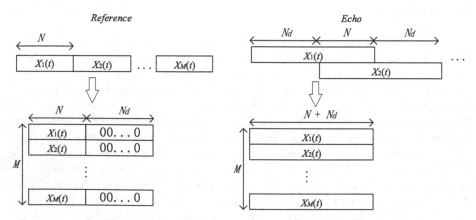

Fig. 1. Segmentation of reference signal and echo signal

Combining the above motion model and the continuous signal segmentation method, the fast-slow time form of the target echo baseband signal is expressed as:

$$s_e(t_n, t_m) = Au(t_n - \tau_0 - a_\tau t_m)e^{-j2\pi f_c \tau_0}e^{-j2\pi f_c a_\tau t_m} \tag{1}$$

Among them, $u(t)$ is the transmitting baseband signal, f_c is the carrier frequency, t_n means fast time, t_m means slow time, Then the reference signal and the echo signal are respectively Fourier transformed along the fast time dimension and then conjugate multiplied to obtain the frequency domain pulse compression result:

$$\begin{aligned} S(f, t_m) &= S_e(f, t_m)U * (f, t_m) \\ &= A|U(f)|^2 e^{-j2\pi(f_c+f)\tau_0}e^{-j2\pi(f_c+f)a_\tau t_m} \end{aligned} \tag{2}$$

$U(f)$ means the Fourier transform of the transmitted baseband signal $u(t)$, $S_e(f, t_m)$ means that the echo signal has a fast edge The Fourier transform of the time dimension, $U^*(f, t_m)$ represents the conjugate of $u(t)$ along the fast-time Fourier change. It can be seen from the above formula that in the second exponential term, the distance Doppler frequency and slow time are coupled, so that the echo signal cannot be effectively accumulated along the same distance unit, and distance migration occurs.

In order to correct the change of Doppler frequency shift with frequency f, the envelope can be corrected by applying the keystone transform to the slow time scale transformation. Let t_n denote the new slow time

$$t_n = \frac{(f_c + f)t_m}{f_c} \tag{3}$$

Equation (2) can be expressed as

$$S(f, t_m) = A|U(f)|^2 e^{-j2\pi(f_c+f)\tau_0}e^{-j2\pi f_c a_\tau t_n} \tag{4}$$

At this time, the coupling between the range Doppler frequency and the slow time in the second exponential phase is eliminated, and the movement of the unit across the range is corrected. The result of the Keystone transform is transformed into the fast time-slow time domain by inverse Fourier transform in the fast time dimension to obtain

$$\begin{aligned} \tilde{s}(t_f, t_m) &= A'\tilde{u}(t_f - \tau_0)e^{-j2\pi f_c a_\tau t_m} \\ A' &= Ae^{-j2\pi f_c \tau_0} \end{aligned} \tag{5}$$

Then perform Fourier transform in the slow time dimension to realize the coherent integration of the signal to obtain the range-Doppler two-dimensional matrix $\chi(t_f, f_m)$, we can obtain target delay and Doppler information at the same time。

2.2 Filtering and Decimation in Slow Time Dimension

In the actual external source radar system, the actual Doppler frequency range of the target to be observed is smaller than the actual sampling rate of the slow time dimension, and the whole spectrum of the signal obtained by directly performing the FFT on the slow time dimension, resulting in calculations redundancy. Therefore, we can decimate the slow time dimension by D times, because the frequency domain resolution of the radar is only related to the integration time. Therefore, the sampling rate of the slow time dimension can be reduced while the Doppler resolution is unchanged, and the distance migration compensation can be performed on the narrow frequency domain, which can effectively reduce the amount of calculation.

The FIR anti-aliasing filter is used for decimation. Suppose the FIR filter order is P, the filter coefficient is h(n), and the decimation factor is D. The pulse compression signal before filtering is $S(f, t_m)$, and its slow time dimension discretization form is $S(f, n)$, Then the signal after FIR filtering is expressed as

$$S_{fir}(f, n) = \sum_{k=0}^{P-1} S(n - k, f)h(k) \tag{6}$$

The signal after D times decimation is:

$$S_D(f, n_D) = Sfir(f, n_D D + P - 1) \tag{7}$$

Among them, n_D represents the sampling point of the slow time dimension after D times downsampling.

2.3   Range Migration Compensation Algorithm Based on Keystone Transform

Keystone Transformation Implementation Use Chirp-Z Transformation
Chirp-Z transform (CZT) can essentially be regarded as an improvement of the DFT + IFFT method. Through CZT, circular convolution can be used to replace linear convolution for calculation, which can reduce the amount of calculation. The Keystone transform based on CZT is expressed as

$$S_{er}(l, \frac{k}{\alpha}) = CZT[S_{er}(l, m)] \tag{8}$$

$$S_{er}(l, m') = \frac{1}{M|\alpha|} IFFT\left[S_{er}(l, \frac{k}{\alpha})\right] \tag{9}$$

3   Implementation of GPU Parallel Acceleration of Efficient Coherent Integration Algorithm

The GPU parallel acceleration implementation process of the efficient coherent integration algorithm is shown in Fig. 2.

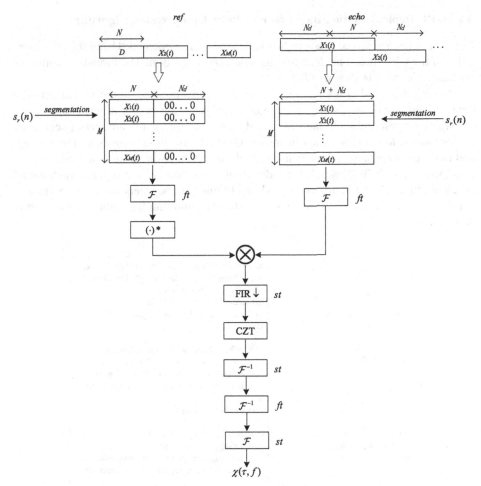

Fig. 2. The GPU parallel acceleration implementation process of the efficient coherent integration algorithm

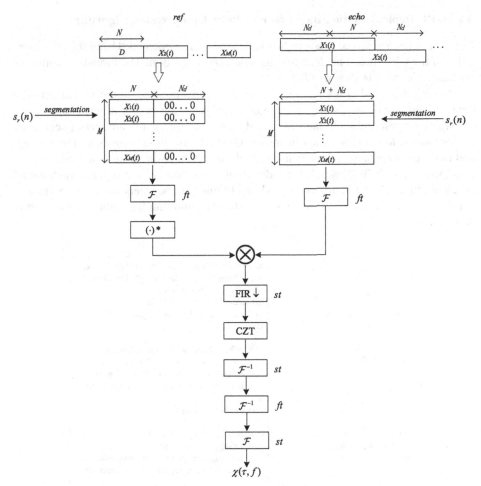

Fig. 3. The thread allocation of the kernel function

3.1 GPU Implementation Based on Fast Pulse Compression Algorithm

First, the reference signal needs to be overlapped and segmented. Using the characteristics of the GPU, it can be done through one kernel function. The thread allocation of the kernel function is shown in Fig. 3.

Among them, Nd is the fast time dimension corresponding to the maximum time delay of the signal, and Npseg is the number of sampling points of each segment of the signal, corresponding to the fast time dimension. Nseg is the number of segments, corresponding to the slow time dimension. GPU adopts two-dimensional thread block and two-dimensional thread indexing method, so that the x-direction index range of the allocated threads is 0~ Npseg-1, the y-direction index range is 0~Nseg, and each thread is related to $S_r(n)$ and $S_e(n)$ correspond one to one. The segment matrix of $S_r(n)$ and $S_e(n)$ can be calculated by the index value. The algorithm implementation flow chart is shown in Fig. 4.

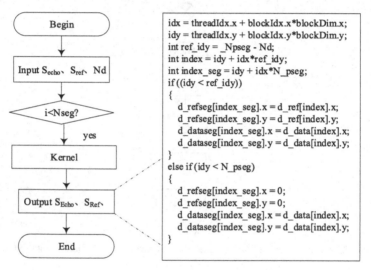

Fig. 4. Flow chart of the algorithm implementation

Then the segmented signals S_{Echo} and S_{Ref} are pulse compressed. The FFT part uses the FFT function in the cuFFT library to realize the parallel calculation of fast-time dimension FFT, and finally realizes the conjugate multiplication through the kernel function to complete the segmented pulse compression.

3.2 GPU Implementation of Decimation and CZT Transformation Based on Low-Pass Filter

Filtering and decimation aim to decimate the slow-time dimension of the pulse-compressed signal through FIR filtering, and then perform CZT transformation on the slow-time dimension. Because in CZT transformation, the slow-time dimension needs to use a large number of rotation factors. When implemented in a GPU, the filter coefficients and CZT rotation factors can be stored in the GPU memory in advance to increase the computational efficiency. Similarly, the complex multiplication part is realized by the kernel function, and the final FFT and IFFT are realized by the cuFFT library.

4 Performance Valuation

The Parameters of signal used in the experiment is shown in the Table 1.

Table 1. Parameters of signal used in the experiment.

Carrier number	Carrier frequency	Bandwidth	Sample rate
1	910 MHz	7.56 MHz	10.08 MHz

The CPU software environment of the experiment is MATLAB R2019a, and the GPU software environment is visual studio 2015. The CPU and GPU model parameters and data processing parameters used in the experiment are listed in Table 2 and Table 3.

Table 2. CPU and GPU model parameters used in the experiment.

Parameters model	Number of cores	Clock frequency	RAM
Core(TM) i7-9700K	8	3.60 GHz	16 GB
GeForce RTX 2070	2304	1.62 GHz	8 GB

Table 3. Data processing parameters used in the experiment

Sample rate	Slow time dimension	Fast time dimension	Decimation	Delay
10.08 MHz	100	10000	2 s	14

The slow time dimension is designed to be 100 and the fast time dimension is 10000 according to the actual target motion. The GPU acceleration is implemented according to the method described above, and the GPU time-consuming analysis is shown in the following Fig. 5.

Through the processing of multiple pieces of data, the average time of the efficient coherent integration algorithm implemented on the CPU and GPU is 1.83 s and 0.013 s, respectively.

Name	Invocations	Avg. Duration	Regs	Static SMem	Avg. Dynamic SMem
void dpRadix0243C::kernel1Mem<unsigned int, double, fftDirection_t=-1, unsigned int=8, unsigned int=2, CO...	2	2.98004 ms	88	15552	0
void dpRadix0125C::kernel3Mem<unsigned int, double, fftDirection_t=-1, unsigned int=8, unsigned int=2, CO...	3	1.72873 ms	62	8000	0
void dpRadix0081B::kernel1Mem<unsigned int, double, fftDirection_t=-1, unsigned int=8, unsigned int=2, CO...	1	1.0731 ms	94	5184	0
void dpRadix0025B::kernel1Mem<unsigned int, double, fftDirection_t=-1, unsigned int=32, unsigned int=3, C...	7	1.04865 ms	64	6400	0
_nv_static_41__28_bluestein_compute_75_cpp1_ii_d293d249_Z14bluestein_initId7ComplexIdEiEvT1_S2_S2_T_S3_...	4	939.55 μs	44	0	0
void dpRadix0025B::kernel1MemBluestein<unsigned int, double, fftDirection_t=1, unsigned int=32, unsigned i...	2	919.903 μs	80	6400	0
void dpRadix0025B::kernel1MemBluestein<unsigned int, double, fftDirection_t=-1, unsigned int=32, unsigned ...	2	864.208 μs	64	6400	0
void dpRadix0008A::kernel1Mem<unsigned int, double, fftDirection_t=-1, unsigned int=128, unsigned int=4, C...	3	848.315 μs	72	0	0
void dpRadix0025B::kernel1Mem<unsigned int, double, fftDirection_t=1, unsigned int=32, unsigned int=3, CO...	2	809.073 μs	64	6400	0
void regular_fft<unsigned int=7, unsigned int=16, padding_t=1, twiddle_t=0, loadstore_modi...	3	528.715 μs	80	0	6272
void regular_fft<unsigned int=128, unsigned int=8, unsigned int=16, padding_t=1, twiddle_t=0, loadstore_mo...	2	426.248 μs	62	0	16384
void dpRadix0032B::kernel3MemBluestein<unsigned int, double, fftDirection_t=1, unsigned int=32, unsigned i...	2	392.873 μs	74	8448	0
void dpRadix0032B::kernel3Mem<unsigned int, double, fftDirection_t=-1, unsigned int=32, unsigned ...	2	338.074 μs	80	8448	0
fft_shift(double2*, int, int, int)	1	248.219 μs	18	0	0
KT_segment(double2*, double2*, int, int, int, double2*, double2*)	1	231.388 μs	18	0	0
data_filter_mulFFT(double2*, int, double2*, int)	1	179.613 μs	18	0	0
fft_shift_fy(double2*, int, int, int)	1	154.269 μs	16	0	0
conj_Complex_mul(double2*, int, double2*, int, int)	3	118.973 μs	18	0	0
void scal_kernel_val<double2, double>(cublasScalParamsVal<double2, double>)	1	103.87 μs	16	0	0
void regular_fft<unsigned int=3, unsigned int=3, unsigned int=256, padding_t=1, twiddle_t=0, loadstore_modi...	3	98.793 μs	40	0	0
norm_decimate(double2*, int, int, int, int, double2*)	1	97.79 μs	16	0	0
Complex_mul_fy(double2*, int, double2*, int, int, double2*)	1	76.927 μs	18	0	0
void dpRadix0032B::kernel1MemBluestein<unsigned int, double, fftDirection_t=1, unsigned int=32, unsigned i...	2	16.992 μs	85	8192	0
void dpRadix0032B::kernel1MemBluestein<unsigned int, double, fftDirection_t=-1, unsigned int=32, unsigned ...	2	13.983 μs	82	8192	0
void dpRadix0032B::kernel1Mem<unsigned int, double, fftDirection_t=-1, unsigned int=32, unsigned int=4, C...	1	12.8 μs	80	8192	0
void dpRadix0032B::kernel3Mem<unsigned int, double, fftDirection_t=-1, unsigned int=32, unsigned int=4, C...	1	8.256 μs	80	8448	0

Fig. 5. GPU time-consuming analysis

5   Conclusion

Aiming at the poor real-time performance of traditional mutual ambiguity algorithm and long-term integration of distance migration, this paper studies the method of combining segmental frequency domain pulse compression and Keystone transform, and proposes an efficient coherent integration algorithm suitable for GPU parallel processing. By filtering and decimating the slow time, the calculation amount is further reduced, and the distance migration is corrected, which improves the detection ability of weak targets. The effectiveness of the method is verified by the measured data.

References

1. Zeng, Y., Zhang, R., Lim, T.J.: Wireless communications with unmanned aerial vehicles: opportunities and challenges. IEEE Commun. Mag. **54**(5), 36–42 (2016)
2. Das, S.R., Beldingroyer, E.M., Perkins, C.E.: Ad hoc On-Demand Distance Vector (AODV) Routing. RFC Editor (2003)
3. Moqimi, E., Najafi, A., Aajami, M.: An enhanced dynamic source routing algorithm for the mobile ad-hoc network using reinforcement learning under the COVID-19 conditions. J. Comput. Sci. 1477–1490 (2020)
4. Bhuvaneswari, R., Ramachandran, R.: Denial of service attack solution in OLSR based manet by varying number of fictitious nodes. Clust. Comput. **22**(5), 12689–12699 (2018). https://doi.org/10.1007/s10586-018-1723-0
5. Surhone, L.M., Tennoe, M.T., Henssonow, S.F.: Temporally-Ordered Routing Algorithm. Mobile Ad Hoc Networks (2010)
6. Usman, M., Oberafo, E.E., Abubakar, M.A., et al.: Review of interior gateway routing protocols. IEEE ICECCO, pp. 1–5 (2019)

Research on Optimization of Radome Based on Phased Array Radar-Seeker

Huang Feng-Sheng[⊠], Chen Ming, and Wang Kai

38th Research Institute, China Electronic Technology Corporation, Hefei 230031, China

Abstract. As protection of radar-seeker, the shape and material of the radome may have great influence on the radar antenna beam. In this paper, we provided the modeling and simulation of antenna and radome and analyzed the influence of antenna beam with radome. With the method of intrinsic extraction adopted, we the optimization of the antenna beam with radome by adjusting the phase compensation realized value of phased array element, and the simulation is provided.

Keywords: Compensation · Phased array · Radar-seeker · Radome

1 Introduction

With the rapid development of modern military technology, precision-guided weapons have become an effective means of implementing precision strikes. Radar-seeking missiles, as an important branch of precision-guided weapons, occupy an important position in the missile weapon family. Radome is a common device to protect the radar antenna of the seeker, which is located in the head of the missile to avoid the radar antenna being damaged by the harsh external environment. In general, it is both an integral part of the missile body and the radar guidance system [1–10].

After the radome is installed on the missile head, the radome shape, processing accuracy and material consistency will definitely have certain effects on the electrical performance of the radar antenna: the radome wall will cause attenuation to the electromagnetic wave from the antenna, resulting in transmission loss, reflection and refraction to the electromagnetic wave. Thus it has caused the deterioration of the antenna sub-flap; phase insertion and refraction to the electromagnetic wave causing the beam pointing offset. The final cause of the radar wave through the radome when the distortion of radiation pattern of the antenna, including attenuation loss, sub-flap elevation, zero depth drop and pointing offset and other effects. For the seeking missiles, the main characterization is the deterioration of the aiming error and aiming error slope.

2 Current Situation and Problems

At present, through the analysis of the radome characteristics and the working principle of the seeker, two types of methods are usually used to compensate the radome error: One is

X. Wang et al. (Eds.): AICON 2021, LNICST 396, pp. 423–432, 2021.
https://doi.org/10.1007/978-3-030-90196-7_36

the "grinding" method, i.e., the compensation method through mechanical processing, i.e., through the small amount of grinding of the radome inner surface local area, to adjust and improve the performance of the radome error slope purpose [1]. The other is the mathematical compensation method [2], i.e., a filter analysis loop or DSP is used in the missile control loop to achieve compensation of the radome error, and a digital compensation circuit is introduced in the seeker to compensate for the targeting line error component. The mechanism of the first compensation method is to reduce the impact on the radar antenna performance index by correcting the radome characteristics. However, the method is limited by the processing and manufacturing accuracy. While for non-axisymmetric shape radome, it is difficult to achieve. In addition, the mechanism of the second compensation method is to compensate the antenna aiming error from the angle measurement result. On the whole, the above two methods are mainly for the seeking seeker, from the aiming error and error slope angle for compensation. In fact, they do not solve the problems of loss, pointing deviation, deformation and reflection caused by the antenna beam through the radome, and can only compensate the angle measurement results. What's more, they cannot compensate the influence of the radome on the radar antenna radiation pattern characteristics (attenuation, sub-flap, zero depth, pointing).

For phased array seeker, the phased array antenna with radomeis should be regarded as a whole, and the radiation characteristics of each channel of the antenna's antenna unit are adjusted by simulation calculation [3]. So it can realize the optimization of antenna radiation pattern compensation after adding the radome. The basic principle of this method is to calculate the antenna unit amplitude phase change before and after radomeing through modeling and simulation, and to achieve the optimal compensation of antenna radiation pattern by compensating the amplitude phase change of each unit. In this work, the compensation algorithm based on eigen-solution extraction is used to calculate the correction code of phased array antenna unit with cover, and the modeling simulation is carried out to verify the effectiveness of the method [10–14].

3   Simulation Results and Discussion

3.1   Antenna Simulation

First, a phased array antenna with a center frequency of 20 GHz is designed, as shown in Fig. 1. The antenna array is placed on top of a metal backplane with a spacing of 7 mm.

3.2   Radome Simulation

The radome is modeled, for the sake of simplification, the processing error and material consistency of the cowl have been ignored here, only the structural shape and the material of different parts are considered. A conical radome with a height of 1 m and a base radius of 0.25 m is designed here, and the cone top angle is 23.8°, as shown in Fig. 3 below. The radomecone top is spherical structure, while the spherical surface is tangent to the cone surface. And the design of the radome has been taken into account the different head cone, sidewall wall thickness and incidence angle, taking into account the electrical

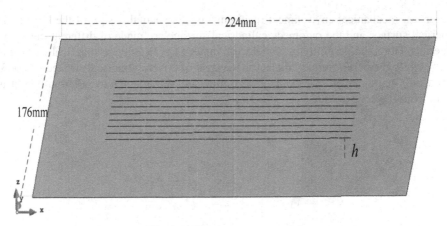

Fig. 1. 2D antenna array model.

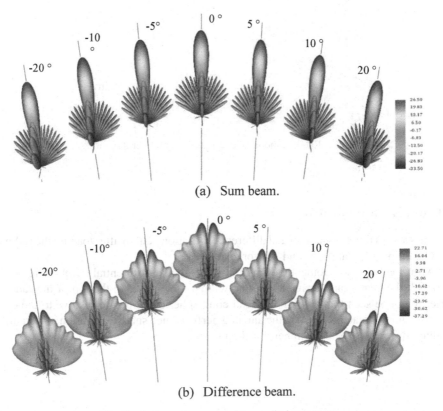

(a) Sum beam.

(b) Difference beam.

Fig. 2. Antenna beam scanning radiation pattern.

properties, mechanical environment requirements. The actual design of the head cone spherical surface and the radomecy cylindrical surface are made of different dielectric materials. Here, the permittivity of dielectric material of head cone spherical surface is 0.005, while the permittivity of dielectric material of cover cylindrical surface is 0.003. Meawhile, the thickness of radome is 12.6 mm, and the antenna installation height is 0.2 m from the cone bottom.

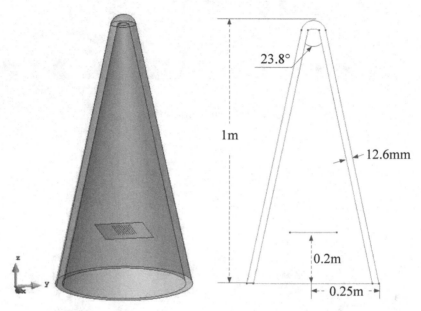

Fig. 3. Radome model and structure parameter diagram.

3.3 Radiation Simulation

Figure 4 shows the antenna sum and difference radiation pattern after loading the radome with beam pointing at 0°, 5° and 20° for example.

After loading the radome, the gain of both beam and differential beam are reduced, in which the beam gain decreases more obviously the closer to the top of the radome cone. It can be seen that the radome head cone spherical structure relative to the cone structure has a greater impact on the antenna performance such as radiation pattern loss, subflap, differential beam symmetry and aiming.

(a) 0° scan, sum and difference beam

(b) 5°scan, sum and difference beam

(c) 20°scan, sum and difference beam

Fig. 4. Radiation pattern of loaded radome at typical angle.

4 Compensation Algorithm Based on Eigen Solution Extraction

The integrated simulation calculation of antenna and radome has been a difficult problem in computational electromagnetics because of its large electrical size and complex structure. Due to the limitation of computational resources, it is difficult to perform accurate calculation by full-wave method in engineering at present. Generally speaking, it is mainly obtained by some approximate methods.

The method of moments (MoM) is a numerical method to transform the integral equation into a linear matrix equation, and the right side of the equation of the matrix equation is the excitation term. When using the MoM to calculate the array antenna, the matrix equation can be written in the following form.

$$
\begin{bmatrix}
Z_{11} & Z_{12} & \cdots & Z_{1n} \\
Z_{21} & Z_{22} & \cdots & Z_{2n} \\
\vdots & \vdots & \ddots & \vdots \\
Z_{n1} & Z_{n2} & \cdots & Z_{nn}
\end{bmatrix} \cdot [I] =
\begin{bmatrix}
V_1 \\
V_2 \\
\vdots \\
V_n
\end{bmatrix}
\tag{1}
$$

Where the right side of the equation for each unit antenna corresponding to the excitation vector, the matrix equation of the excitation term V_i that is the ith unit of the feed. Calculate the radiation problem under a certain feed state, just give all the unit feed values in turn, and then solve the current coefficient I in Eq. (1) can quickly obtain the radiation characteristics of the antenna. Since the matrix equation is linear, it is also possible to split the excitation vector on the right side into the form of n-units superposition.

$$
\begin{bmatrix}
Z_{11} & Z_{12} & \cdots & Z_{1n} \\
Z_{21} & Z_{22} & \cdots & Z_{2n} \\
\vdots & \vdots & \ddots & \vdots \\
Z_{n1} & Z_{n2} & \cdots & Z_{nn}
\end{bmatrix} \cdot ([I_1] + [I_2] + \cdots + [I_n]) =
\left(
\begin{bmatrix}
V_1 \\
0 \\
\vdots \\
0
\end{bmatrix} +
\begin{bmatrix}
0 \\
V_2 \\
\vdots \\
0
\end{bmatrix} + \cdots +
\begin{bmatrix}
0 \\
0 \\
\vdots \\
V_n
\end{bmatrix}
\right)
\tag{2}
$$

In Eq. (2), the current coefficient I_i corresponding to the i-th cell feed V_i (it is important to note that the current is not only distributed on the feed cell, but on the whole array). Then the matrix equation can be written for any cell individually excited in the following form.

$$
\begin{bmatrix}
Z_{11} & Z_{12} & \cdots & Z_{1n} \\
Z_{21} & Z_{22} & \cdots & Z_{2n} \\
\vdots & \vdots & \ddots & \vdots \\
Z_{n1} & Z_{n2} & \cdots & Z_{nn}
\end{bmatrix} \cdot [I_i] =
\begin{bmatrix}
0 \\
V_i \\
\vdots \\
0
\end{bmatrix}
\tag{3}
$$

In Eq. (3), under the condition of $V_i = 1$, solving the matrix equation yields the eigen-solution $\tilde{I}_i$ when the ith cell in the array is fed individually.

$$
\left[\tilde{I}_i\right] =
\begin{bmatrix}
Z_{11} & Z_{12} & \cdots & Z_{1n} \\
Z_{21} & Z_{22} & \cdots & Z_{2n} \\
\vdots & \vdots & \ddots & \vdots \\
Z_{n1} & Z_{n2} & \cdots & Z_{nn}
\end{bmatrix}^{-1}
\cdot
\begin{bmatrix}
0 \\
1 \\
\vdots \\
0
\end{bmatrix}
\tag{4}
$$

It can be seen that the meaning of the array antenna eigensolution is the solution of each cell antenna individually feeding the unit amplitude voltage state. Since the matrix equation of the method of moments is linear, the solution of the method of moments under any excitation form can be obtained by the weighted linear combination of the eigensolutions as long as the eigensolutions of each cell are obtained. Equation (4) shows that the impedance matrix is invariant during the solution of the eigenvalue solution because the structure is not changed. This means that the inverse matrix of the impedance matrix needs to be solved only once. Therefore, the way of calculating the eigen-solution does not increase the computational effort significantly. For any feeder combination $(V_1, V_2, \cdots, V_n)$, the corresponding method-of-momentum solution is

$$
I = \sum_{i=1}^{n} V_i \left[\tilde{I}_i\right]
\tag{5}
$$

The extraction of the eigensolution brings great convenience to the calculation of multi-beam antennas such as phased arrays and array feed optimization, which greatly reduces the computation time. When the radiation characteristics of the array antenna need to be optimized by adjusting the feed, the optimization algorithm only needs to update the feed amplitude and phase $(V_1, V_2, \cdots, V_n)$ to quickly combine the excitation response with feed form, and then obtain the radiation characteristics of the antenna with feed.

5 Radome Compensation Simulation

By modeling the antenna and the radome and using the compensation algorithm based on the eigen-solution extraction, the amplitude phase correction code values of each unit under different angles after the radome addition can be calculated. According to the simulation calculation results, the amplitude phase of each unit of phased array antenna is corrected, which can realize the optimal compensation of antenna radiation patern after radomeing.

Based on the above antenna simulation results, typical $0°$, $5°$ and $20°$ angles are selected to simulate the optimized radomeed radiation patern. The typical angles such as overhead cone are selected for the azimuthal tangent of the directional diagram without radome, with radome, and after optimization as follows.

From the above simulation results, it can be seen that with beam scanning angles of $0°$, $5°$ and $20°$, for example.

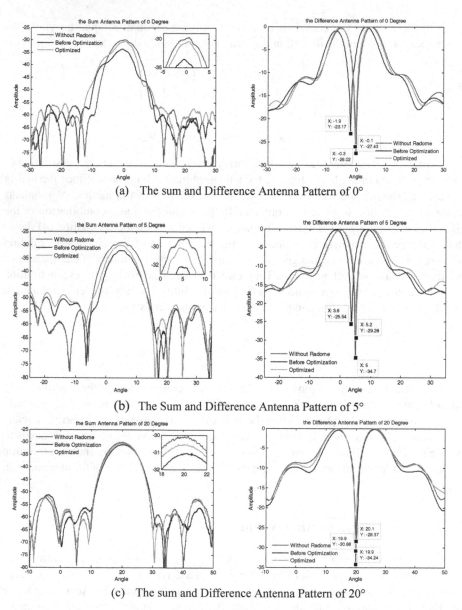

(a)   The sum and Difference Antenna Pattern of 0°

(b)   The Sum and Difference Antenna Pattern of 5°

(c)   The sum and Difference Antenna Pattern of 20°

Fig. 5. Radiation pattern of loaded radome at typical angle (compensation simulation).

After radomeing and beam gain decreased by 3.8 dB, 2.9 dB and 1 dB respectively, and the symmetry of the two main flaps of the differential beam became worse. Between 0° and 5°, the aiming line deviation is 1.5°. This is due to 0° and 5° over the top spherical part of the head cone after radomeing, due to the large difference between the cone top structure and the side wall, which has a large impact on the radiation patern loss and pointing, zero depth, etc. Then, the 20° pointing beam main flap range is not over the head cone part of the radome, and the radome side structure is uniformly symmetrical, so the impact is smaller.

After optimized compensation, the loss of 0°, 5°, 20° is 0.8 dB, 0.9 dB, 0.6 dB. Between 0° and 5°, the deviation of aiming line is optimized from 1.5° to 0.3° before compensation. After compensation, the directional loss, pointing, zero depth and other indexes of antenna are significantly optimized.

6   Conclusion

The introduction of the radome will bring about the deterioration of radar seeker antenna loss, pointing, aiming line error and other indexes, and there are certain limitations of the conventional structural modelling and mathematical compensation methods. In this paper, a compensation method is proposed to obtain the amplitude and phase correction values of the channel unit of the phased array seeker based on the simulation solution of the radome, which reduces the influence of the radome on the antenna performance of the seeker and ensures the working performance of the seeker under the condition of adding the radome, and the effectiveness of the method is verified by simulation.

References

1. Priyanka, B.M., Mathur, P., Singh, H., Nair, R.U.: EM analysis of planar phased array-radome system for ground-based FCR applications. In: 2018 IEEE Indian Conference on Antennas and Propogation (InCAP), Hyderabad, India, pp. 1–2 (2018)
2. Lin, S., Lin, D., Wang, W.: A novel online estimation and compensation method for strapdown phased array seeker disturbance rejection effect using extended state kalman filter. IEEE Access 7, 172330–172340 (2019)
3. Bui, V.P., Zhao, J., Oo, Z.Z., Sun, M., Png, C.E.: Enhanced beam scanning angle using radome design for phased array antennas. In: 2019 IEEE Asia-Pacific Microwave Conference (APMC), Singapore, pp. 1592–1594 (2019)
4. Wang, H., Zhao, Y., Huang, K., Liu, T., Gao, P.: Design of a high-performance radome for satellite communication phased array antennas. In: 2018 International Applied Computational Electromagnetics Society Symposium - China (ACES), Beijing, China, pp. 1–2 (2018)
5. Fang, C.: The calculation of quantum radar scattering characteristic for the 3d circular cone target. In: 2018 IEEE Int. Symp. Electromagn. Compat. 2018 IEEE Asia-Pacific Symp. Electromagn. Compat., pp. 248–250 (2018)
6. Fang, C.: The simulation of quantum radar scattering for 3D cylindrical targets. In: 2018 IEEE International Conference on Calculational Electromagnetics (ICCEM), Chengdu, pp. 1–3 (2018)
7. Fang, C.H.: The simulation and analysis of quantum radar cross section for 3D convex targets. IEEE Photonics J. 10(1), 1–8 (2018)

8. Brandsema, M.J., Narayanan, R.M., Lanzagorta, M.: Theoretical and computational analysis of the quantum radar cross section for simple geometrical targets. Quantum Inf. Process. **16**(1), 1–27 (2016). https://doi.org/10.1007/s11128-016-1494-6

9. Fang, C.H., et al.: The calculation and analysis of the bistatic quantum radar cross section for the typical 2D plate. IEEE Photonics J. **10**(2), 1–14 (2018)

10. Fang, C., Han, K.: Analytical formulation for the quantum radar scattering of the rectangular plate. In: 2019 IEEE 2nd International Conference on Electronic Information and Communication Technology (ICEICT), pp. 677–681 (2019)

11. Fang, C., Shi, X.: The analysis of quantum radar scattering for the typical pyramid structure. In: 2019 IEEE International Applied Computational Electromagnetics Society Symposium in China (ACES-China) (2019)

12. Fang, C.: The analysis of mainlobeslumping quantum effect of the cube in the scattering characteristics of quantum radar. IEEE Access **7**, 141055–141061 (2019)

13. Fang, C.: The closed-form expressions for the bistatic quantum radar cross section of the typical simple plates. IEEE Sensors J. **20**(5), 2348–2355 (2020)

14. Fang, C.H., et al.: An improved physical optics method for the computation of radar cross section of electrically large objects. In: 2008 IEEE Int. Symp. Electromagn. Compat. 2008 IEEE Asia-Pacific Symp. Electromagn. Compat., pp. 722–725 (2008)

A Survey of Few-Shot Learning for Radio Frequency Fingerprint Identification

Hao Li[1], Yu Tang[1(✉)], Di Lin[1], Yuan Gao[2], and Jiang Cao[2]

[1] University of Electronic Science and Technology of China, Chengdu, Sichuan, China
yutang@uestc.edu.cn
[2] Military Academy of Sciences, Beijing, China

Abstract. With the development of the Internet of Things technology, the radio frequency (RF) fingerprint identification technology of wireless communication equipment has also risen, providing new ideas for network security and RF perception systems. The existing RF fingerprint identification technology is mainly based on traditional machine learning or deep learning. In the face of small sample data or data imbalance, the classification effect is not satisfactory. Therefore, in this paper, we propose the use of Few-Shot Learning (FSL) to solve the problem of radio frequency fingerprint small sample recognition. We review the current RF fingerprint identification technology and FSL methods. What's more, we analyze some available methods from two aspects. (i) From the perspective of data, the samples of RF signal training data set can be expanded manually or by using transformation function, can also be generated by generative model; (ii) From the perspective of algorithms, prior knowledge can be used to train the new model through fine-tuning, metric, and meta-learning. Finally, we look forward to the challenges and opportunities that the RF fingerprint identification technology may face from theory and application.

Keywords: Radio frequency fingerprint · Few-shot learning · Meta-learning

1 Introduction

In recent years, with the rapid development of the Internet of Things and artificial intelligence technology, wireless communication devices have played an irreplaceable role in the civilian and military fields, and how to ensure the security of wireless communication devices in the network is particularly important. Compared with wired network, wireless network is more vulnerable to attack, because traditional methods to ensure wireless network security are usually based on cryptographic mechanisms and security protocols, and wireless communication devices exposed to the network still have security risks. Therefore, people urgently need a new type of security mechanism to effectively identify authorized users and unauthorized users to reduce potential threats in the network.

Different wireless communication devices emit different signals due to hardware differences. The hardware feature extracted by analyzing the small difference of the

X. Wang et al. (Eds.): AICON 2021, LNICST 396, pp. 433–443, 2021.
https://doi.org/10.1007/978-3-030-90196-7_37

radio frequency (RF) signal is called the Radio Frequency Fingerprint [1] of the device, and the method of using RF fingerprint to identify different wireless communication devices is called RF fingerprint identification.

At present, the existing RF fingerprint identification technology mainly adopts traditional machine learning or deep learning to train a large number of signal data sets of a group of wireless communication devices. After extracting signal features as RF fingerprint, these methods construct a classifier based on the training model and training parameters to confirm the identity of the wireless communication device. However, in some cases, we can't obtain a large number of I/Q signal samples, but a small amount of data can be collected. The signal of these communication equipment, such as shortwave communication equipment for long-distance communication or short-range tactical communication, medium-wave communication equipment for emergency communications, with relatively concealed environment is weak and has long transmission period, which is not easy for the receiver to collect. It cannot obtain a large amount of data, resulting in the signal sample data imbalance. In the case of small data sets, traditional machine learning and deep learning approaches for data-intensive applications are no longer applicable because too few training sets are prone to reduce the accuracy of the algorithm and overfitting.

Recently, a machine learning method, few-shot learning (FSL) is proposed. Using prior knowledge, FSL can quickly generalize to new tasks that contain only a small number of samples with supervised information. Therefore, it can be considered to combine FSL with RF fingerprint, in order to solve the small sample problem of RF fingerprint.

The contributions of this survey are as follows:

- We discuss how to perform RF fingerprint identification through FSL in the case of insufficient or unbalanced data sources to help confirm the identity of wireless communication devices.
- According to the existing FSL methods, two types of RF fingerprint small sample identification methods are proposed: On the one hand, from the perspective of data, the data volume of RF signal is expanded by means of manual or Generative Adversarial Network (GAN). On the other hand, from the perspective of algorithm, the prior knowledge is used to fine-tune the existing RF fingerprint training model parameters.
- We look forward to the development trends and application prospects of RF fingerprint small sample identification technology.

The remainder of this survey is organized as follows. Section 2 provides overview for RF fingerprint identification and FSL. Section 3 is for methods that augment data to deal with RF fingerprint small sample identification problem. Section 4 is for methods that optimize the algorithm to solve RF fingerprint small sample identification problem. Finally, the survey closes with conclusion in Sect. 5 And we propose future directions for RF fingerprint small sample identification in terms of theories and applications.

2 Overview

At present, RF fingerprint technology is becoming more and more developed. And FSL has also been paid attention to and applied in the field of image and text recognition. This section mainly reviews the research status of RF fingerprint identification technology based on traditional machine learning in recent years, and introduces FSL.

2.1 RF Fingerprint Identification Technology

As shown in Fig. 1, RF fingerprint identification usually includes three stages: signal collection, pretreatment and RF fingerprint extraction. According to the requirements of RF fingerprint, the identification system needs to carry out several preprocessing processes for the collected signals, such as phase compensation, energy normalization and discarded unqualified signal. The fingerprint extraction mainly includes training and classification stage. In the training stage, the host receiver receives the signal from the device for sampling, and then extracts the features to generate the RF fingerprint. In the classification stage, after receiving signals from the devices to be identified, the receiver will classify the devices according to the similarity of these features by comparing the characteristics of each type.

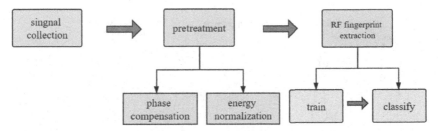

Fig. 1. RF fingerprint identification process.

Traditional Machine Learning for RF Fingerprint Identification. The traditional machine learning can identify the transmitter by extracting the signal features and comparing fingerprint database. In [2], a novel approach has been proposed to use a digital noise radar (DNR) to actively interrogate microwave devices and classify defective units by using radio frequency distinct native attribute (RF-DNA) fingerprinting and various classifier algorithms, such as multiple discriminant analysis/maximum likelihood (MDA/ML) and generalised relevance learning vector quantisation-improved (GRLVQI) classifiers. In [3] , the feasibility of RF-DNA extraction from different devices is successfully proved by using MDA/ML classifier, and one-to-many device classification and one-to-one device ID verification are performed by using Gabor-based method. It is proved that using dimensionality reduction analysis can reduce the number of required fingerprint features while maintaining consistent discrimination performance. In [4], the RF fingerprinting is proposed by extracting the parameter characteristics such as information dimension, constellation feature and phase noise spectrum in the transmitted information when it is applied to the universal software radio peripheral (USRP) software defined radio (SDR) platform. In proposed methods, the traditional support vector machine (SVM) classifier, the machine-based integrated classifier bagged tree and the adaptive weighting algorithm weighted k-nearest neighbor (KNN) achieved good classification performance under different signal-to-noise ratios (SNR).

Deep Learning for RF Fingerprint Identification. Deep learning relies on large amounts of data to train the models that can recognize existing RF fingerprint without the need to extract data features in advance, as shown in Fig. 2. In [5], a long short-term memory (LSTM) based recurrent neural network is proposed and used for automatically identifying hardware-specific features and classifying transmitters. In [6], By combining the software defined radio (SDR) sensing capability with the convolutional neural network (CNN) morphing on the basis of AlexNet, a specific radio frequency can be uniquely identified between similar devices. The main advantage of this approach is that the CNN learning framework operates on the raw I/Q sample. In [7], data diversity in the training set is key to extracting broadly-applicable features and achieving high accuracy with incremental models. The implementation of the above methods is based on a large amount of data in a specific environment but is not applicable to small sample data sets. Therefore, we need find new method to solve this problem.

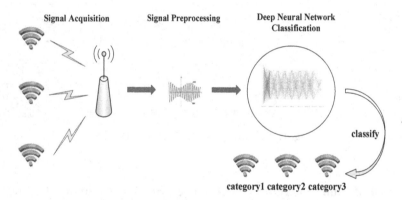

Fig. 2. Deep learning based RF fingerprint identification framework.

2.2 Few-Shot Learning

Few-Shot Learning (FSL) is a machine learning method proposed in recent years to solve the problem of small amount of data and data imbalance. It makes use of prior knowledge to quickly generalize to a new task containing only a small number of samples with supervised information, so as to help relieve the burden of collecting large-scale supervised data. Transfer Learning [8] and Meta-Learning [9] methods transfer prior knowledge from source task to small sample task, which is widely used in FSL. In [10], Yaqing Wang et al. point out that the core issue of FSL supervised learning problem is the unreliable empirical risk minimizer. According to the utilization of prior knowledge, FLS methods can be divided into three categories: data, model and algorithm. From the perspective of data, signal samples with less data can be expanded, such as transforming samples based on training data, transforming samples based on weakly labeled or unlabeled data, transforming samples based on similar data sets, etc. From the perspective of model, multi-task learning, embedded learning, learning based on external storage and generative modeling can be carried out. From the perspective of algorithm, the existing training model parameters can be fine-tuned and the optimizer can be learned.

Therefore, FSL provides a new idea for solving the imbalance problem of small sample identification data of RF fingerprint and improving the generalization ability of the model. This paper will demonstrate the feasibility of FSL in RF fingerprint identification technology from two aspects of augmenting data and optimizing algorithm.

3 Data Augmentation

When the amount of collected RF signal data is insufficient, the RF signal data set can be augmented in different ways to obtain enough samples, and then the machine learning or deep learning algorithm mentioned in Sect. 2 can be used for RF fingerprint identification. Table 1 shows the classification of methods used to enrich RF signal samples.

Table 1. Data augmentation methods for RF sample. The transformer t takes input (x, y) and returns generated sample (x', y') to augment the few-shot RF sample data.

Method	Input (x, y)	Transformer t	Output (x', y')
Augmenting samples from RF training data sets	Raw data (x, y)	Artificial augmentation or a transformation function	$(t(x), y)$
Generating samples by generative model	Fabricating data (x, y)	A generator to generate new data sets	$(t(x), t(y))$

3.1 Augmenting Samples from RF Training Data Set

The strategy expands the data set by transforming each RF signal sample into several changing samples with transformation. We can do manual amplification, for example by using MATLAB and other tools for signal simulation to get more data. Besides, after the signal is transformed in the time-frequency domain to get the spectrum image, the data is expanded by flipping, translation, scaling, rotation and other methods. However, it requires expensive labor cost and depends heavily on the knowledge of communication domain.

An earlier FSL learned a set of geometric transformations, which is applied to each sample, from similar classes by iteratively aligning each sample with other samples. Similarly, in [11], a single transformation function is learned to transfer the variation between sample pairs learned from other categories to the sample pair. Therefore, we can consider constructing a transformation function that automatically expands the data set based on the existing RF signals to form a large data set that can then be learned by standard machine learning methods, as shown in Fig. 3.

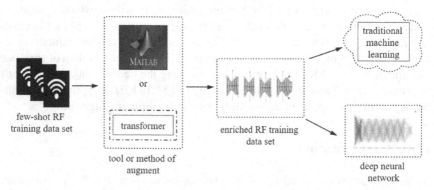

Fig. 3. Data augmentation methods for few-shot RF training data set.

3.2 Generating Samples by Generative Model

The strategy expends the data set via generative model. In essence, the generative model is a kind of maximum likelihood estimation, which is used to generate the model of the specified distribution data. The distribution generated by the generator we have now can be assumed to be $P_G(x; \theta)$, and this is a distribution controlled by θ, where θ is the parameter of the distribution. Suppose we take some data out of the real distribution, $\{x_1, x_2..., x_m\}$, and then we want to compute a likelihood $P_G(x_i; \theta)$, as shown in Formula (1).

$$L = \prod_{i=1}^{m} P_G(x_i; \theta) \tag{1}$$

In order to maximize this likelihood, we need to find a θ^*.

$$\theta^* = \underset{\theta}{argmax} \prod_{i=1}^{m} P_G(x_i; \theta) \tag{2}$$

Therefore, a generative adversarial network (GAN) [12] is designed to generate indistinguishable synthetic samples. GAN has two networks, one generator that is responsible for fabricating data and one discriminator that is responsible for judging the authenticity of data. The best generation effect is achieved by two networks against each other. In order to augment data, we can use the existing few-shot RF samples to establish the generation model via GAN.

In Fig. 4, the generator can fabricate fake RF samples based on noise samples, and use these fake samples to deceive the discriminator. The discriminator is responsible for identifying whether this is a real or fake sample and will give a score. When the score

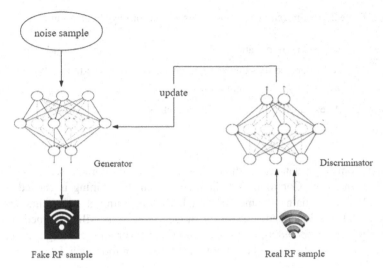

Fig. 4. A GAN model for generating RF samples.

value is high, it indicates that the discriminator can effectively distinguish between true and false samples, but the effect of the generator is not good, so the parameters of the generator needs to be adjusted. However, generative modeling methods have high inference cost, and are more difficult to derive than deterministic models.

3.3 Summary

The choice of which method to expand data depends on the application scenario. When there are only a small number of RF signal samples, the method of augmentation can be manually generated or transformed function. When there are a small number of target RF signal samples and other data sets similar to the sample, GAN can be used for data augmentation. Then standard machine learning methods are used for RF fingerprint identification. However, it is only suit for specific data with specific rules, but not easy to use on other data sets. Therefore, in the case of not changing the existing RF samples, we can also consider from the perspective of model algorithm.

4   Optimization of Algorithm

Due to the limitation of data, the problem of small sample identification of RF fingerprint can also be solved from the perspective of algorithm. No matter what model, it needs the support of data to carry on the training. We can use the prior knowledge to adjust and optimize the existing model parameters and apply it to the small sample data set of RF signals. This section presents several learning methods, as shown in Table 2.

4.1   Finetune

This method has been widely used in Transfer Learning. A certain amount of annotated data is obtained and then fine-tuned based on a pre-trained model. This pre-trained model

Table 2. Optimization methods of Algorithm for few-shot RF samples.

Method	Supervised information	Prior knowledge
Finetune	A few labeled RF samples for target class	Pre-trained basic model
Metric	A few labeled RF samples for each class	Embedding learned model
Meta-learning	A few labeled RF samples for each class of the target task	Meta learner

is obtained from large datasets with rich tags, such as the Oracle RF Fingerprinting Dataset, known as the Common Data Domain. Then the training is carried out on a small sample data domain of some RF signal. During training, the parameters of the pre-trained model will be fixed and specific model parameters will be trained. There are many training tricks, including how to set the fixed layer and learning rate, etc. This method can be relatively fast and does not have to rely on too much data.

4.2 Metric

The method is to model the distance distribution between samples, so that the samples the same kind are close, and the samples of different kinds are far away. By learning an end-to-end nearest neighbor classifier, it benefits from the advantages of both parameters and no parameters, in order that it cannot only learn new samples quickly, but also have good generalization for known samples. Siamese Networks [13] judges whether they belong to the same class through the distance of sample pairs. Then the features extracted from the network are reused for One/Few-Shot Learning. In Prototypical Network [14], each category has a prototype representation whose archetype is the mean value of the support set in the embedding space. The classification problem then becomes a problem of the nearest neighbor in the embedding space. Matching Networks [15] builds different encoders for the support set and the batch set. The output of the final classifier is the weighted sum of predicted values between support set and query set, which can generate labels for unknown categories under the premise of not changing the network model. Therefore, the above three network models can be considered to apply to the identification of few-shot RF fingerprint.

4.3 Meta-learning

Meta-Learning acquires meta-knowledge through meta-training on known tasks, which helps model to learn quickly on new tasks with a good ability of model generalization. In Fig. 5, meta-learning task is divided into training and testing in two stages.

As for parameter θ in the Fig. 5, At the t th iteration, $\theta_t = \theta_{t-1} + \Delta\theta_{t-1}$, where $\Delta\theta_{t-1}$ is the update. For the popular stochastic gradient descent (SGD), θ is updated as

$$\theta_t = \theta_{t-1} - \alpha_t \nabla_{\theta_{t-1}} \ell(h(x_t; \theta_{t-1}), y_t), \tag{3}$$

where αt is the step size. With θ initialized at θ_0, θ_t can be written as

$$\theta_t = \theta_0 + \sum_{i=1}^{t} \Delta\theta_{t-1}. \tag{4}$$

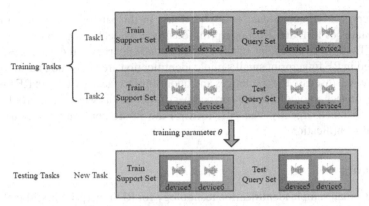

Fig. 5. The two stage of meta-learning task. In the first stage, training a large number of tasks to get a training parameter θ. In the second stage, in the face of a new category of tasks, there is no need to change the existing model to classify by updating parameter θ.

MAML [16] is an example of an approach that learns from prior knowledge and provides a good initialization parameter. The MAML algorithm is independent on model, which means it can be applied to any model, with the only requirement being that the model is trained using gradient descent. The idea is to learn an initialization parameter that can achieve good results with only a few steps of gradient descent using a small number of samples when a new task is encountered. In [17], A Meta Learner model based on LSTM is proposed for learning optimization of algorithm, which is used to train another learner neural network classifier in the case of small samples. The model learns a general initialization for the learner network, the classifier network, which can help the learner network to converge quickly during training. Similarly, the above two Meta-Learning methods can be adjusted and then applied to the identification of few-shot RF fingerprint.

4.4 Summary

The fine-tune method can help identify few-shot RF fingerprint via the existing pre-trained model parameters, but this strategy may sacrifice precision for speed. Metric method can be used to train a network model by calculating the spacing of few-shot RF samples without existing parameter, which has good generalization for known samples. Meta-Learning method mainly obtains a learner through multi-task training, which can use fewer RF samples to learn to identify new RF fingerprint. All of these methods can be used as solutions for small sample identification of RF fingerprint.

5 Conclusion and Future Work

RF fingerprint identification technology is a non-cryptographic security authentication technology. It can be identified by using the hardware difference of the device, which effectively solves the security hidden danger and controls the power consumption. The combination of small sample learning can help reduce the burden of collecting large scale supervised RF signal data in applications. In this survey, we review the recent research status of FSL and RF fingerprint identification technology based on machine learning. Then, from the point of view of data and algorithm, the FSL methods that can be used in RF fingerprint small sample identification are analyzed and summarized. Finally, we will discuss the challenges and opportunities faced by FSL in RF fingerprint identification technology from the perspective of theories as well as the problems to be solved and studied urgently, and puts forward the future application scenarios of RF fingerprint identification.

5.1 Theories

At present, small sample identification technology for RF fingerprint is still in the exploration and research stage. Traditional machine learning methods are only aimed at the processing of massive data, while FSL is only studied in the field of image and text. Therefore, we can try to use the methods mentioned in Sect. 3 and Sect. 4 to construct the RF fingerprint small sample identification model from two perspectives of data or algorithm. It can solve the overfitting problem and improve the generalization ability of the existing model with few-shot RF sample or imbalance of data.

5.2 Applications

RF fingerprint technology as a kind of high reliability of wireless access technology, does not need to send additional access authentication information. Under the background of a variety of applications have some practical.

The small sample identification technology of RF fingerprint can be applied to the wireless Internet of Vehicles under the background of 5G. The use of radio frequency fingerprints to replace traditional license plate vehicle identity authentication methods not only saves the cost of redundant information transmission, but also has the advantages of non-tampering, uniqueness, and security. Using the RF fingerprint of the terminal device as the authentication information of the access network can effectively solve the problem of access power consumption. Using RF fingerprints as an indicator of security authentication can effectively solve the multi-port security access problem under the 5G background. In the future, RF fingerprint identification technology will enter people's lives and improve people's quality of life.

Acknowledgement. Partially Funded by Science and Technology Program of Sichuan Province (2021YFG0330), partially funded by Grant SCITLAB-0001 of Intelligent Terminal Key Laboratory of SiChuan Province, and partially Funded by Fundamental Research Funds for the Central Universities (ZYGX2019J076)).

References

1. Polak, A.C., Goeckel, D.L.: Identification of wireless devices of users who actively fake their RF fingerprints with artificial data distortion. IEEE Trans. Wireless Commun. **14**(11), 5889–5899 (2015)

2. Lukacs, M., Collins, P.: Classification performance using 'RF-DNA' fingerprinting of ultra-wideband noise waveforms. Electron. Lett. **51**(10), 787–789 (2015)
3. Reising, D.R., Temple, M.A., Jackson, J.A.: Authorized and rogue device discrimination using dimensionally reduced RF-DNA fingerprints. IEEE Trans. Inf. Forensics Secur. **10**(6), 1180–1192 (2015)
4. Hu, S., Lin, D.: Machine learning for RF fingerprinting extraction and identification of soft defined radio devices. Lecture Notes in Electrical Engineering 572, 189–204 (2020)
5. Wu, Q., Feres, C., Kuzmenko, D.: Deep learning based RF fingerprinting for device identification and wireless security. Electron. Lett. **54**(24), 1405–1407 (2018)
6. Riyaz, S., Sankhe, K., Ioannidis, S.: Deep learning convolutional neural networks for radio identification. IEEE Commun. Mag. **56**(9), 146–152 (2018)
7. Youssef, K., Bouchard, L.S., Haigh, K.Z.: Machine learning approach to RF transmitter identification. IEEE J. Radio Freq. Identification **2**(4), 197–205 (2018)
8. Wu, L., Wang, Y., Yin, H.: Few-shot deep adversarial learning for video-based person re-identification. IEEE Trans. Image Process. **29**, 1233–1245 (2020)
9. Santoro, A., Sergey, B.: Meta-Learning with memory-augmented neural networks. In: International Conference on Machine Learning, ICML 4, pp. 2740–2751 (2016)
10. Wang, Y., Yao, Q., Kwok, J.T.: Generalizing from a few examples: a survey on Few-shot Learning. ACM Comput. Surv. **53**(3), 1–34 (2020)
11. Hariharan, B.: Low-shot visual recognition by shrinking and hallucinating features. Proc. IEEE Int. Conf. Comput. Vis. **10**, 3037–3046 (2017)
12. Goodfellow, I.J., Pouget-Abadie, J., Mirza, M.: Generative adversarial networks. Adv. Neural. Inf. Process. Syst. **3**, 2672–2680 (2014)
13. Koch, G., Zemel, R., Salakhutdinov, R.: Siamese neural networks for one-shot image recognition. ICML Deep Learning Workshop 2 (2015)
14. Snell, J., Swersky, K., Zemel, R.S.: Prototypical networks for few-shot learning. In: Advances in Neural Information Processing Systems, vol. 6 (2017)
15. Oriol, V., Blundell, C., Lillicrap, T.: Matching networks for one shot learning. In: Advances in Neural Information Processing Systems, vol. 12, pp. 3630–3638 (2016)
16. Finn, C., Abbeel, P., Levine, S.: Model-agnostic meta-learning for fast adaptation of deep networks. In: International Conference on Machine Learning, vol. 3, pp. 1126–1135 (2017)
17. Ravi, S., Larochelle, H.: Optimization as a model for few-shot learning. In: International Conference on Learning Representations (2017)

An Anomaly Detection Method Based on GCN and Correlation of High Dimensional Sensor Data in Power Grid System

Liu Weiwei[1]([✉]), Lei Shuya[1], Zheng Xiaokun[1], Li Han[1], Wang Xinyu[1], Liang Xiao[1], and Xu Houdong[2]

[1] Artificial Intelligence On Electric Power System State Grid Corporation Joint Laboratory (GEIRI), Global Energy Interconnection Research Institute Co. Ltd., Beijing 102209, China
[2] State Grid, Sichuan Electric Power Company, Chengdu 610041, China

Abstract. Monitoring data or sensor data could reflect the working situation of power grid system at a fine-grained level. Specifically, when an anomaly event happened, some variations will appear and propagate between these interrelated sensor data. However, their latent relationship are complex and difficult to capture. To address this challenge, we propose a data-driven anomaly detection method, which performs real-time correlation analysis of sensor data and implements anomaly detection at runtime. Firstly, the method adopts the correlation coefficient calculation methods to obtain the time-varying correlation between sensed data. Additionally, graph is applied to represent the relationship between them. The edges of the graph are labeled with the degree of correlation and the nodes are marked with some statistical characteristics of the original sensor data. Moreover, an anomaly detection algorithm based on graph convolution network is implemented. The effectiveness of this approach is verified based on real power grid datasets.

Keywords: Anomaly detection · Time-series data · GCN · Correlation analysis

1 Introduction

In recent years, an increasing number of sensors has been deployed in the physical world. Due to the collaboration of large autonomous and heterogeneous sensors, new challenges for developing IoT applications have emerged. Consequently, IoT data and their analysis are becoming a hot topic because they can provide a consistent way to access sensor data from different stakeholders [1–4].

One of the most important purpose of analysis of sensor data is to detect potential anomalies in them. Hawkins [5] defines anomalies as those data that are distinctive in a data set, raising the suspicion that they do not arise from random deviations, but from completely different mechanisms. Anomaly detection is the process of discovering anomaly data in data resources based on various data processing models and techniques. Traditional anomaly detection mostly targets outliers, based on statistics, distance, density, and clustering. However, these methods usually consider sensor data in isolation and ignore correlations between sensors.

© ICST Institute for Computer Sciences, Social Informatics and Telecommunications Engineering 2021
Published by Springer Nature Switzerland AG 2021. All Rights Reserved
X. Wang et al. (Eds.): AICON 2021, LNICST 396, pp. 444–454, 2021.
https://doi.org/10.1007/978-3-030-90196-7_38

In real scenarios, there is a certain connection among the data of sensors. One sensor data may be normal on its own, but may be anomalous when considered together with other sensor data [6]. In addition, if more relevant sensors are considered together, it is possible to detect anomalies earlier and avoid future serious damage. However, due to the complex and diverse correlation existing in the large number of sensors, and the correlations between sensors vary with the situation, it is difficult to handle this situation.

Hence, a correlation-based sensor data anomaly detection method is proposed to address the above issues, which can carry out anomaly detection at runtime based on real-time sensor data correlation analysis.

The main contributions of this manuscript study are listed below.

- We try to capture the correlation of multiple monitoring data and represent it as graph data which will benefit anomaly detection in the power grid system.
- We use GCN to learn the correlation graph data which will detect the changes in the correlation data. The principle behind this method is the assumption that multiple monitoring data will impact others in a certain time.
- Experiments on power quality datasets demonstrate that the proposed method outperforms several anomaly detection methods.

2 Related Work

Anomaly detection methods [7–9] for outlier points can be broadly classified into four categories, which are statistical-based, distance-based, density-based, and clustering-based. With the continuous development of anomaly detection techniques, anomaly detection has started to focus more attention not only on outliers but also on the massive amount of temporal data [10–17]. Therefore, some research focus on the area of temporal data anomaly detection. The anomaly detection of time series data usually performs related anomaly detection by using the time characteristics of the data which is analyzing the data pattern in a specific time period.

There are three main cases of anomalies in temporal data, the first is contextual anomalies, which are point anomalies in temporal data, and the contextual anomalies must be in the context of the sequence data. The second type is a subsequence anomaly whose subsequence pattern is very different from the pattern of the overall sequence. The third type is the anomalous sequence that is different from the base sequence. Such anomalies are determined by giving a base sequence, and by comparing the test sequence with the base sequence to determine whether the test sequence is anomalous or not.

Recently, some research on anomaly detection of time series data has been done. Fei Huan et al. [18] used a sliding window model to detect and verify anomalous data but it requires a priori knowledge of the data and has poor applicability.

Wang Lei et al. [19] used the support vector regression estimation model, which takes into account the characteristics of the smoothness of the regression curve to achieve the separation of anomaly data and improves the accuracy of the power station performance. However it has poor applicability when targeting subseries.

Chen et al. [20] used network density and decay factor for anomaly detection with high accuracy and low time overhead to satisfy real-time. However, many parameters need to be set.

A Hadoop-based time-series anomaly detection method was proposed by Zhang et al. [21]. To address the problem of high computational complexity of the traditional DTW algorithm, the constraint calculation method of intelligent matching of salient features is introduced, which effectively reduces the time complexity and space complexity of the algorithm while ensuring a high detection accuracy through local restrictions on non-linear paths. However, the Hadoop platform has high latency and the actual operability is yet to be tested.

Cai et al. [22] proposed a new anomaly detection algorithm for time series data by constructing a distributed recursive computation strategy as well as a k-nearest neighbor selection strategy. Yan et al. [23] used a probability density function instead of the Euclidean distance to determine the similarity of two sequences, but this algorithm does not have a suitable method to determine the size of the detection window and has certain data requirements. Xu Junmei et al. [24] set up a constant deviation function to find the minimum value as a way to set the check threshold and use the Kmeans++ algorithm to cluster the data to obtain the set of anomaly detection objects, which effectively improves the real-time anomaly detection.

However, it is necessary to adjust the number of clusters in advance, otherwise the difference between anomalies and normal points may be small.

Qiu Yuan et al. [25] proposed a streaming data anomaly detection method based on long short-term memory (LSTM) network and sliding window. Firstly, data prediction by LSTM to find the predicted difference, and then the distribution of the difference sequence is modeled within the sliding window to dynamically assign a more appropriate anomaly score for each data to improve the accuracy of streaming data anomaly detection. However, it also requires a priori knowledge of the data, which is less applicable, and at the same time, there is often relatively large noise in the sequence. Liu Fenglin et al. [26] proposed a DBSCAN-based threshold selection algorithm for timing data anomaly detection, and did experimental validation based on Yahoo's EGADS framework for secondary development, with good results and practical engineering value. However, the characteristics of periodicity and seasonality are not fully considered in the modeling of time-series data, and the algorithm has a large time window for detecting anomalies, which needs to be improved in the time-series prediction and error metric models.

Li Rui et al. [27] proposed a time-series based anomaly detection method, which firstly models the user behavior to predict the development trend, and then performs anomaly detection based on the actual behavior, which can effectively detect user's violation and network attack, but the limited extracted feature values cannot completely demonstrate the user behavior, and the seasonal ARIMA model cannot fully match all user traffic.

Although many works have been proposed, there are various challenges in anomaly detection of time-series data, such as the length of the anomalous subsequence is difficult to determine effectively. Moreover, the anomaly does not appear in training set, and there is often relatively large noise in the time series, i.e., the distance between the anomaly and the normal point is small or even difficult to distinguish. In addition, anomaly detection methods for temporal data usually utilize only the sensed data itself and the static relationships between sensed data, and do not fully utilize the time-varying correlations between sensors. As a result, we propose a correlation-based anomaly detection method for sensor data that can dynamically discover the relationships between data at runtime and find data anomalies based on them.

3 Methodology

Our method try to capture the correlation of time-series data and its latent relationships. These correlations between time-series data could be represented as graph data. Moreover, we train GCN (graph convolution neural network) to classify the new high dimensional data. More details are shown in Fig. 1. As shown in Fig. 1, the left part is the training process. We calculate the CC (correlation coefficient) and feature of these sensor data to build graph data. The GCN based model is trained as classification model which is applied to detect possible anomaly in un-labeled sensor data.

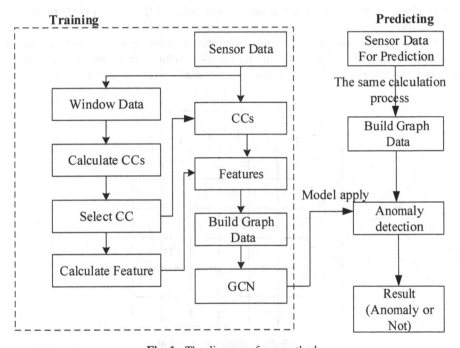

Fig. 1. The diagram of our method.

3.1 Calculation of Correlation Coefficient

The sensor is often in the form of time-series data, and we can use a fixed time window to calculate the CCs (Correlation Coefficient) for each pair of them. Figure 2 shows an example of the process of calculation of CC between different monitoring points. Each monitoring point owns multiple sensor data, we calculate the data correlation coefficient between each pair of sensor data. One example is shown in Fig. 2.

Function of Correlation Coefficient

TimeStamp	Mornitoring point1			Mornitoring point1				CC of MP1,MP2
	Sensor 1	Sensor 2	......	Sensor 1	Sensor 2	......	......	......
11:10 AM	0.7439	56.359		0.6501	59.307			0.39
11:11 AM	0.7438	53.474		0.6505	59.861			0.45
11:12 AM	0.6826	51.629		0.6499	56.359			-
11:13 AM	0.6586	44.368		0.6442	51.245			0.47
11:14 AM	0.6567	45.203		0.5181	50.687			-
...	...	...		...	...			...

Fig. 2. Calculation of correlation coefficient (time series)

According to the characteristics of specific time-series data, different correlation evaluation methods can be applied to represent the extent of interrelation of them. As shown in Fig. 2, some widely used methods, such as MIC [9] and dCor [11] are utilized in our method.

We calculate the correlation between the features according to different correlation calculation methods to obtain different time series correlation matrices, and then merge the correlation matrices into a three-dimensional matrix array, as shown in Fig. 3.

feature	f1	f2	f3	f4	f5
f1	1.0	-0.07	-0.02	0.79	0.78
f2		1.0	0.35	-0.05	-0.06
f3			1.0	-0.03	-0.04
f4				1.0	0.97
f5					1.0

Fig. 3. Three-dimensional matrix array

The different correlation calculation methods are as follows. Firs is the Euclidean distance and is shown in Eq. 1.

$$\sqrt{\sum_{i=1}^{n} (x_i - y_i)^2} \tag{1}$$

The formula of calculating the Chebyshev distance is expressed in Eq. 2.

$$\lim_{p \to \infty} \left(\sum_{i=1}^{n} |x_i - y_i|^p \right)^{1/p} = \max|x_i - y_i| \qquad (2)$$

The formula of calculating Cosine Similarity is illustrated in Eq. 3.

$$\cos(\theta) = \frac{\sum_{k=1}^{n} x_{1k} x_{2k}}{\sqrt{\sum_{k=1}^{n} x_{1k}^2} \sqrt{\sum_{k=1}^{n} x_{2k}^2}} \qquad (3)$$

The formula of calculating Pearson Correlation Coefficient is shown in Eq. 4.

$$\rho_{X,Y} = \frac{\sum XY - \frac{\sum X \sum Y}{N}}{\sqrt{\left(\sum X^2 - \frac{(\sum X)^2}{N} \right) \left(\sum Y^2 - \frac{(\sum Y)^2}{N} \right)}} \qquad (4)$$

3.2 Feature Selection

Obviously, as the number of sensors increases, the number of CCs will also in-crease. When time series data are multi-dimensional data, correlation calculations will become very complicated. Many anomaly detection algorithms are difficult to solve high-dimensional data anomaly detection well. Existing work [8] proposed a latent corre-lation vector, which composes all CCs into a vector. Considering that not all sensors have a correlation relationship, the CC between two uncorrelated sensors has no effec-tive value. Therefore, based on this consideration, we designed a correlation selection function, which is used to select CCs according to the relationship between the two data relevant strength and stability.

$$x^2 = \sum \frac{(A - E)^2}{E} \qquad (5)$$

3.3 GCN Anomaly Detection Model

Graph Convolutional Neural Network (GCN) can learn the correlation between nodes effectively and be successfully applied to analyze social network.

We take advantage of GCN's in extracting correlation features between nodes and apply it to the power indicator correlation graph $G = (V,E)$ for anomaly detection. Among them, V represents a power feature, and E represents the relationship between power indicators. Assuming that the number of vertices of the index feature correlation graph is N and the number of edges is M, then the graph can be represented by an adjacency matrix A of size N × N. The attribute of the vertex is the feature vector of each indicator, and the attribute of the edge is the correlation between the two indicators, which is calculated by the correlation calculation methods introduced in the previous section.

Our goal is to establish a correlation relationship between various power indicators within a period of time, so as to detect anomaly event when it occurs or will occur in the power network. Firstly, a correlation coefficient-based graph data are prepared based on different data source. What is more, some certain anomaly and non-anomaly graph data are labeled to construct a supervised dataset. In addition, we trained GCN to find the relationship between the power indicators which can classify and detect anomaly event in these time series data. The process is shown in Fig. 4, which shows the graph data constructing process. There are many power indicators, such as voltage, current, harmonics, etc.

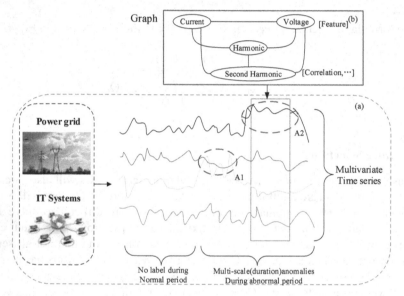

Fig. 4. Unsupervised anomaly detection and diagnosis in multivariate time series data.

4   Experiments

4.1   Dataset

The datasets used in our experiments are the real sensor data and artificial maintenance records from power quality data of charging posts in a region. Dozens of power quality data measurement points for the number of charging posts have been deployed in the region. Each measurement point consists of 4 attributes, including harmonic current content, total voltage harmonic distortion rate, fundamental current content, and flicker composition. Each measurement point generated a set of values per 30 s. We choose three datasets to verify the effectiveness of our data-driven anomaly detection method, and construct the experimental data set by adjusting the time period. The detail information of the datasets is shown in Table 1.

Table 1. Detail information of datasets in our experiments

Datasets	Time period	Number of measuring points	Time window
DS1	2015–04-29 00:00:00 to 23:59:59	5	1 h
DS2	2015–09-20 00:00:00 to 23:59:59	7	30 min
DS3	2015–11-15 00:00:00 to 23:59:59	6	2 h

4.2 Data Preprocessing

Standardization requires calculating the mean and standard deviation of features. The formula is as follows:

$$x' = \frac{x - \overline{X}}{S} \tag{6}$$

For feature encoding of time series data, the core is to set a threshold. The value greater than the threshold is assigned to 1, and the value less than or equal to the threshold is assigned to 0. The formula is as follows:

$$x' = \begin{cases} 1, x > threshold \\ 0, x \leq threshold \end{cases} \tag{7}$$

The missing values of time series data are calculated by linear regression. Based on the current data set, the regression equation is established. For the objects with null values, the known attribute values are substituted for the equation to estimate the unknown attribute values, then the estimated values are used to fill lost value.

4.3 Experiment Setup

Our experiment is conducted in a desktop computer with configuration as follows: CentOS 7.7, four Intel Core i7–8750, 8.00 GB RAM, 200 GB hard disk and GTX2080Ti GPU. All the algorithms mentioned above are implemented in Python and Pytorch 1.6.

The model settings for GCN is as follows. The node feature matrix $X \in \mathbb{R}^{N \times d}$ is constructed with $d = 4$ corresponding to the minimum and maximum latitude and longitude extents of the zone corresponding to the node. The encoder uses $L = 2$ layers of GCN to learn the node-level embedding. The model is trained for 200 epochs with a batch size of 30. In training set, 10% is kept out as validation set for early stopping.

4.4 Result and Analysis

Baselines. We compare our method with two commonly used anomaly detection methods.

- SVM. The baseline method uses One-Class SVM model (OC-SVM), it applies the SVM to learn a model to determine whether the new data belongs to a specific class (whether it is normal data), if it does not belong to this class, then it is anomaly.

- CNN. The baseline method uses CNN to detect anomalies in time series data. The convolutional neural network has four layers. Each input channel shares the same convolutional layer. The essence of the MaxPool layer is to take the largest element operation of the vector for each channel to adapt to different lengths of time series data.
- GCN_Corr. This is our method. We capture the correlation of time-series data and their latent relationships. We train GCN to classify the new high dimensional data based on these correlations between time-series data.

Table 2. The AUC score for anomaly detection in different datasets.

Method dataset	SVM	CNN	GCN_Corr
DS1	0.352	0.561	0.712
DS2	0.290	0.623	0.689
DS3	0.411	0.518	0.774

The performance of different methods for anomaly detection is reported in Table 2, we can see that GCN_Corr constantly outperforms the other methods in different datasets.

Compared with SVM and CNN, our approachpay attention to the correlation of each time series data. By modeling the varying relationship of each time series data, we can better mine the relationship between the abnormality and the change trend of each time series data, and then use the graph convolutional neural network to detect the time series anomalies.

5 Conclusion

The correlation between sensor data is dynamic and time dependent. According to the correlation between sensor data, more related sensors are able to be detected, and the effectiveness of anomaly detection for these sensor data can be promoted. In this paper, we propose a data-driven anomaly detection method for handling sensor data. The proposed method builds graph data based on correlation analysis, and then uses graph convolution to capture changes of sensor data, which can analyze changes of dynamic sensor data in the IoT environment. Our method performs anomaly detection of multidimensional sensors and obtain higher accuracy. We apply our method to the anomaly detection of the power quality data in power grid system, and verify that our anomaly detection method can detect anomalies with high precision and recall through a series of experiments.

Acknowledgement. This work is supported by the science and technology project of State Grid Corporation of China: "Research on data governance and knowledge mining technology of power IOT based on Artificial Intelligence" (Grand No.5700-202058184A-0-0-00).

References

1. Han, Y.B., Liu, C., Su, S., et al.: A decentralized and service-based approach to proactively correlating stream data. In: International Conference on Internet of Things, pp. 93–100 (2016)
2. Chu, V.W., Wong, R.K., Liu, W., et al.: Traffic analysis as a service via a unified model. In: IEEE International Conference on Services Computing, pp. 195–202. IEEE (2014)
3. Zhang, J., Radia, N., Li, Z., et al.: An infrastructure supporting considerate sensor service provisioning. In: The 6th IEEE International Conference on Service Oriented Computing and Applications (SOCA), pp. 69–76. IEEE (2013)
4. Guilly, T.L., Olsen, P., Ravn, A.P., et al.: HomePort: middleware for heterogeneous home automation networks. In: IEEE International Conference on Pervasive Computing and Communications Workshops, pp. 627–633. IEEE (2013)
5. Atkinson, A.C., Hawkins, D.M., et al.: Identification of outliers. Biometrics 37(4), 860 (1981)
6. Budgaga, W., Malensek, M., Pallickara, S.L., et al.: A framework for scalable real-time anomaly detection over voluminous, geospatial data streams. In: Concurrency & Computation Practice & Experience, pp. 1–24 (2017)
7. Kieu, T., Yang, B., Jensen, C.S., et al.: Outlier detection for multidimensional time series using deep neural networks. In: 2018 19th IEEE International Conference on Mobile Data Management (MDM), pp. 125–134 (2018)
8. Subramaniam, S., Palpanas, T., Papadopoulos, D.: Online outlier detection in sensor data using non-parametric models. In: 32nd International Conference on Very Large Data Bases, pp. 187–198 (2006)
9. Nguyen, H.T., Thai, N.H.: Temporal and spatial outlier detection in wireless sensor networks. ETRI J. 41(8), 437–451 (2019)
10. Huang, H.: Data anomaly detection method of sensor nodes in Internet of Things. Computer Simul. 05, 167–170 (2012)
11. Qi, Z., Yupeng, H., Cun, J.: Edge computing application: real-time anomaly detection algorithm for sensing data. J. Comput. Res. Dev. 55(3), 524–536 (2018)
12. Xie, M., Hu, J., Guo, S.: Distributed segment-based anomaly detection with kullback–leibler divergence in wireless sensor networks. IEEE Trans. Inf. Forensics Secur. 12(1), 101–110 (2017)
13. Tian, L., Zhang, D.: An anomaly detection method of sensor data based on information entropy. Comput. Eng. Softw. 39(09), 77–81 (2018)
14. Grabaskas, N., Si, D.: Anomaly detection from kepler satellite time-series data. In: International Conference on Machine Learning & Data Mining in Pattern Recognition, pp. 220–232 (2017)
15. Khatkhate, A., Ray, A., Keller, E., et al.: Symbolic time-series analysis for anomaly detection in mechanical systems. IEEE/ASME Trans. Mechatron. 11(4), 439–447 (2006)
16. Laptev, N., Amizadeh, S., Flint, I., et al.: Generic and scalable framework for automated time-series anomaly detection. In: 21th ACM SIGKDD International Conference on Knowledge Discovery and Data Mining, pp. 1939–1947 (2015)
17. Burgess, M.: Two dimensional time-series for anomaly detection and regulation in adaptive systems. In: 13th IFIP/IEEE International Workshop on Distributed Systems: Operations and Management, pp. 169–180 (2002)
18. Fei, H., Xiao, F., Li, G., et al.: An anomaly detection method of wireless sensor network based on multi-modals data stream. Chin. J. Comput. 40(8), 1829–1842 (2017)
19. Wang, L., Zhang, R., Sheng, W., et al.: Regression forecast and abnormal data detection based on support vector regression. Proc. CSEE 08, 94–98 (2009)
20. Chen, Y.: Density-based clustering for real-time stream data. In: ACM International Conference on Knowledge Discovery & Data Mining, pp. 133–142 (2007)

21. Zhang, J., Li, B., Liu, X., et al.: Abnormal time series detection in wireless sensor network based on hadoop. Chin. J. Sens. Actuators **12**, 1659–1665 (2014)
22. Cai, L., Thornhill, N., Kuenzel, S., et al.: Real-time detection of power system disturbances based on k-nearest neighbor analysis. IEEE Access **5**, 5631–5639 (2017)
23. Yan, Q.Y., Xia, S.X., Feng, K.W., et al.: Probabilistic distance based abnormal pattern detection in uncertain series data. Knowl.-Based Syst. **36**, 182–190 (2012)
24. Xu, J.M.: Anomaly detection of mobile network interaction behavior based on Internet of Things. J. Eastern Liaoning Univ. (Nat. Sci. Ed.) **28**(01), 34–38 (2021)
25. Qiu, Y., Chang, X., et al.: Stream data anomaly detection method based on long short-term memory network and sliding window. J. Comput. Appl. **40**(05), 1335–1339 (2020)
26. Liu, F.: Research on threshold selection algorithm of time series data anomaly detection based on DBSCAN. Modern Comp. **04**, 3–6 (2020)
27. Li, R., Jia, Y., Jiao, Z., et al.: Network behavior anomaly detection based on time series. Commun. Technol. **53**(10), 2550–2554 (2020)

Continuous IFF Response Signal Recognition Technology Based on Capsule Network

Yifan Jiang[1], Zhutian Yang[1(✉)], Chao Bo[2], and Dongjia Zhang[3]

[1] School of Electronic and Information Engineering, Harbin Institute of Technology,
Harbin, China
yangzhutian@hit.edu.cn
[2] Nanjing Institute of Electronic Equipment, Nanjing, China
[3] China Aerospace Science and Industry Corporation Limited, Beijing, China

Abstract. Identification of friend or foe (IFF) system has become an indispensable part in modern war. In order to meet the needs of air target situation control in rapid response operations, it is urgent to find an intelligent IFF signal recognition method. Aiming at the problems of low recognition accuracy and high false alarm rate of continuous IFF signal of single channel multiple air maneuvering targets in low SNR environment, a signal pattern recognition method of continuous IFF signal based on capsule network and attention mechanism in complex environment is proposed by improving signal data set and capsule network model structure. Using the good generalization ability and strong feature interpretation ability of attention mechanism provided by capsule network, the improved method has a certain degree of improvement in the pattern recognition ability of simulated complex signals compared with traditional frame detection method and multilayer convolutional neural network. At the same time, the false alarm rate and the missed alarm rate are significantly improved, which can meet the actual detection requirements.

Keywords: Identification of friend or foe (IFF) · DM-CapsNet · Attention mechanism · Co-frequency interference

1 Introduction

With the development of the times, the demand for rapid response combat air mobile target situation control is increasing, the electromagnetic environment has become more and more complex, and multiple modulation, coding methods, and encryption protocols have begun to be applied to the identification friend or foe system.

There are some common algorithms for IFF signal recognition. As far as multi-channel array received signals are concerned, the ICA algorithm [1] proposed by P·Comon and the Fast-ICA algorithm [2] proposed by Hyvarinen can be applied to the separation of IFF signals. However, the high-order statistics

© ICST Institute for Computer Sciences, Social Informatics and Telecommunications Engineering 2021
Published by Springer Nature Switzerland AG 2021. All Rights Reserved
X. Wang et al. (Eds.): AICON 2021, LNICST 396, pp. 455–468, 2021.
https://doi.org/10.1007/978-3-030-90196-7_39

of IFF signals have been proved to be pseudo-Gaussian, so any signal classification and recognition algorithm based on kurtosis is not robust. At present, the projection algorithm (PA) proposed by Petrochilos [3] is more effective. This algorithm can realize effective signal recognition in the case of different mode signals. However, when the signal is polluted by noise, the sorting effect of the algorithm is poor, and the amplitude of the sorted signal is quite different from the original signal, which is easy to cause decoding errors.

As far as the single channel received signal is concerned, because each mode response signal is on the same carrier frequency, it can only use the pulse frame information for detection, and the feature is relatively single, so there are few recognition algorithms related to machine learning. At present, sliding window method is commonly used [4]. After combining correlation detection and pulse PRI sequence analysis, this method also has the ability to detect the response signals of new mode signals such as Mode S and Mode 5. However, this method only uses frame information in real-time signal detection, because the signal amplitude changes too much, there will be false alarm and missing alarm. At the same time, because of the need to detect multiple modes of the framework, and mode 5 synchronization pulse also need to carry out MSK demodulation and correlation detection, it takes too long.

On the other hand, through the actual test, it is found that although the traditional convolutional neural network and the general capsule network have good detection performance in the verification set, they also have a high false alarm rate in the continuous signal detection, causing serious interference to the whole recognition system. In order to solve the above problems, this paper proposes a common channel automatic pattern recognition method (DM-CapsNet) based on capsule network. This method directly processes the intermediate frequency signal, uses supervised learning method, and directly takes the simulated low signal-to-noise ratio mode signals as the training set. When verifying the measured signals, the classification results are obtained by threshold determination.

2   Problem Statement

2.1   IFF Signal Model

The Mark X mode response signal includes 16 information codes, and the sequence of the signals is F1, C1, A1, C2, A2, C4, A4, X, B1, D1, B2, D2, B4, D4 and F2 in the order of time, where the last one is SPI pulse. The format of the response signal is shown in Fig. 1. Each code has two states, that is, with pulse or without pulse, with pulse as '1' state and without pulse as '0' state. F1 and F2 are called frame pulses with a time interval of 20.3 us ± 0.1 us. They are the flag pulses of the response signal, which are always in the '1' state, and X is the spare bit, which is always in the '0' state. SPI is a special location identification code, which will not be used in general. The time interval between the pulse at each code point and the front edge of the F1 pulse is an integer multiple of 1.45 us. The SPI pulse is at 4.35 us after the F2 pulse with an allowable tolerance of ±0.1 us, and the width of each pulse is 0.45 us.

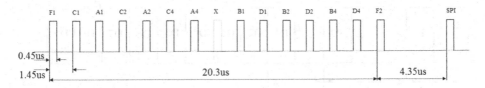

Fig. 1. Mark X series reply pulse.

Mark XII system is the second generation of IFF enemy identification systems, which adds a secure mode (Mode 4) on the original basis, and its response signal format is shown in Fig. 2. The mode signal is a response pulse group composed of three pulse widths of 0.45 us ± 0.1 us, and the pulse interval is 1.75 us ± 0.1 us. The responder starts to respond after receiving the query pulse P4 and fixing the delay 202 us. The response pulse group starts at the delay $t_x = (202 + 4N)$ us (N = 0,1,2...15).

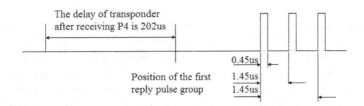

Fig. 2. Mode 4 response signal.

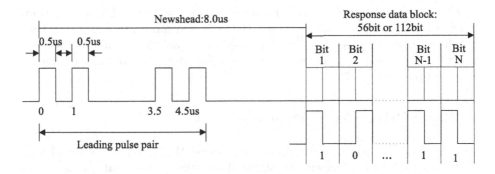

Fig. 3. Mode S response signal.

The inquiry signal of Mode S is added with the address of the inquiry plane [5], which can be used for roll call inquiry. The signal format of Mode S downlink response data link is shown in Fig. 3.

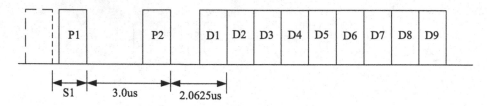

Fig. 4. Mode 5 level 1 signal diagram.

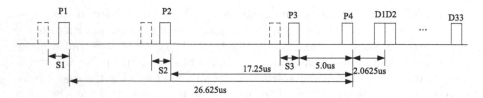

Fig. 5. Mode 5 level 2 signal diagram.

The mode signal consists of four leading pulses and response data pulse blocks. The pulse width of the leading pulse is 0.5 us, and pulse amplitude modulation is adopted. At the same time the duration of the response data pulse group is 56 us or 112 us (containing 56 or 112 bit data pulse), which uses binary pulse position modulation, pulse occurs in the first half segment represents '1', a pulse occurs in the second half for '0', and the last 24 bits are the combined parity and address field. The interval between the first preamble pulse and the following three preamble pulses of the Mode S response is 1 us, 3.5 us, and 4.5 us, respectively.

The waveform of level 1 reply signal of mode5 is shown in Fig. 4. It is composed of two synchronous header pulses (P1, P2) and nine data pulses (D1–D9), and the modulation mode is MSK. The response signal format of level 2 type is shown in Fig. 5. Due to space limitation, more information about mode 5 can be found in literatures [6, 7].

3   Basic Principle of Algorithm

According to the characteristics of the measured IFF signal, it is found that the amplitude of the received IFF signal fluctuates greatly and the signal-to-noise ratio is low. Because the frequency band of IFF system is 1030 MHz and 1090 MHz, it is not easy to be interfered by other types of radar signals, so the noise is basically composed of Gaussian noise and system noise. Combined with the actual situation, this paper assumes that the system only contains Gaussian white noise, the intermediate frequency of the signal is 70 MHz, the sampling rate is 240 MHz, and the SNR of the simulation data set is between −10 dB and 0 dB. Considering the length of the synchronous pulse group and the actual length of the received signal, it is found that the length of the network input signal is about 30 us, which can ensure the recognition of all mode signals. Therefore, this paper sets the length of the data set as 8000 points.

Single signal is used as sample in training set and verification set. In order to meet the needs of real-time test, a long-time complex signal sample needs to be designed. This part will be explained in detail in the algorithm section. When simulating the actual test environment, only using these five mode signals as the training set and simple capsule network structure is not enough to meet the actual needs, so we need to improve the existing samples.

3.1 Dual Task Capsule Network Structure of Attention Mechanism (DM-CapsNet)

Assuming that the neural network can only intercept longer signals for classification and recognition, the input of the network at this time is 35 us, and it happens that there is a shorter mode signal (such as Mode 4, about 4 us) followed by a longer one. Mode signal (such as Mode S, at least 64 us), because the Mode S signal with more features accounts for too much of the input of the entire network, the first signal is directly ignored because of too few features, leading to missed alarms. On the other hand, when the network input is too short, it is impossible to extract all the characteristic information of the long signal. In order to avoid these situations, this paper designs a new dual-task constrained capsule neural network (DM-CapsNet).

Overall Framework

In this part, we will describe how DM-CapsNet identifies different patterns of continuous IFF signals.

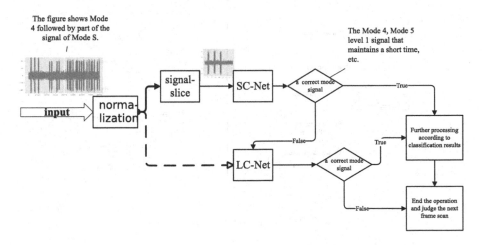

Fig. 6. Overall framework of the system.

The overall approach of the method is shown in Fig. 6. Starting from any position of IFF signal, we first intercept a longer signal, then intercept a shorter signal from the starting position of the longer signal, and finally use the signal characteristics of the intercepted short signal to dynamically normalize the amplitude of the input signal. Then, this short signal is applied to the attention capsule neural network of the simplified parameters of the short signal (SC-Net) for the first classification, and if the short characteristic signal is detected, the detection result is used for further processing.

When it is detected that the signal does not belong to short feature signal, the normalized input will be reclassified using a complete long capsule network (LC-net) suitable for long signal. When it is detected that the signal belongs to long feature signal, it will use the detection results and use different signal processing methods for further interpretation and other operations. Finally, the signal recognition process of this frame ends, and the scanning frame moves forward to continue the process.

Network Model

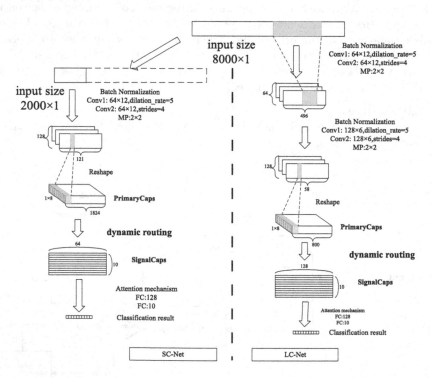

Fig. 7. DM-CapsNet network model.

The overall network structure model is shown in Fig. 7. The feature extraction network is divided into two parts: long signal (LC-Net) and short signal (SC-Net). The reason why it is not set as a convolutional network with shared weights, so as to improve the speed of training and the generalization ability of the network, is because the short signal itself can extract fewer features, if the same convolutional layer is used as the long signal Compared with the convolutional layer that uses non-weight sharing but fewer network parameters, although this can extract more detailed feature maps, the amount of calculation required for the convolution operation is larger, so the convolution with shared weights is used The network to extract features here does more harm than good. At the same time, because relatively short signals require higher accuracy of the extracted features when recognizing, the capsule input layer of SC-Net has more capsule neurons than the input layer of LC-Net.

Dynamic Routing Algorithm

Each capsule neuron is actually a set of directional scalar neurons, and its output is a multidimensional vector, so it can be used to represent some attribute information of entities [8–10]. Capsule neural network is divided into 4 steps, namely matrix transformation, input weighting, weighted summation and nonlinear transformation. The process is formulated as:

$$\hat{u}_{ji} = W_{ij}u_i \tag{1}$$

The first step is as shown in Eq. (1). The purpose of this step is to transform the spatial relationship between the low-level features and the high-level features and other important relationships through the matrix.

$$c_{ij} = \frac{\exp(b_{ij})}{\sum_k (b_{ij})} \tag{2}$$

$$s_j = \sum_i c_{ij}\hat{u}_{j|i} \tag{3}$$

c_{ij} in Eq. (2) is calculated by the softmax function, which is the coupling coefficient determined by the dynamic routing process. And the input weight of the second step and the weighted sum of the third step are realized by Eq. (3).

$$v_j = \frac{||s_j||^2}{1 + ||s_j||^2} \frac{s_j}{||s_j||} \tag{4}$$

The fourth step is to perform a nonlinear transformation on A to obtain B. The activation function used is shown in the formula EC. The first part of the formula is to compress, and the second part is to unitize the output vector. Through the above steps, the length of the output vector is between 0 and 1, so as to determine the probability of having a certain feature.

3.2   Attention Mechanism

In the above network model, the convolutional layer is responsible for feature extraction of the signal, and the capsule layer is responsible for compressing the extracted features into multiple vectorized capsule neurons through the mapping relationship between the underlying features and the high-level features.

According to the processing method described in the literature [8], the extracted neurons directly obtain the probabilities of different categories through multiple fully connected layers. It is obvious that because different capsule neurons may contain different attribute characteristics of the signal, not all capsule neurons are helpful for the final classification and recognition, so a method is needed to weight different capsule neurons.

Because some words have a decisive influence on sentence semantics, and the concept of time step is consistent with that of capsule neuron, we can introduce the idea of attention mechanism into the field of signal processing based on capsule network, that is, to pay attention to the output of capsule neuron we are interested in.

The use of the attention mechanism in the capsule network is divided into 3 steps, as follows:

1) Denote the last capsule hidden states as $[h_1, ..., h_N]$, multiply it with each of the remaining capsule neurons, that is, the hidden states, to obtain the current capsule neuron's attention scores, denoted as $e^1 = \left[s_1^T h_1, ..., s_1^T h_N \right]$, finally use softmax to convert the scores into an attention distribution with a probability sum of 1. The formula is $\alpha^1 = softmax\left(e^1\right)$.
2) Use the probability distribution obtained in step 1 to sum all hidden states to get the attention output. The formula is $\alpha_1 = \sum \alpha_i^1 h_i$. Finally, the residual connection of the attention output and the last capsule will give $[\alpha_1; s_1]$.
3) Use the fully connected layer to merge again and output it as the attention module.

3.3   Enhanced Dataset

According to the previous introduction, there are only 5 types of IFF response signals, namely Mark X series, Mode 4, Mode S, Mode 5 level 1 and level 2. At the same time, because these signals are in the same channel and frequency, it is easy to cause false alarms when scanning similar features in real-time detection, and general data enhancement methods such as short-time Fourier transform STFT and discrete wavelet transform commonly used in speech signals DWT and Wigner-Ville distribution (WVD) are of little use here, so we can only consider the data enhancement method of negative sample enhancement from the data set itself.

Because the IFF signal has both long and short, and the length of the data set is fixed, when constructing the negative sample data set, the starting position of the different modes of signals is shielded into negative samples according to the length percentage of 20–80%, and the proportion of positive and negative samples should be in the range of 0.5 and 2.0. By adopting this method of generating negative samples with varying length ratios, the number of negative samples can be adjusted adaptively, and the ratio of positive and negative samples can be adjusted within an appropriate range. Finally, the new data set consists of the original data set and the supplementary negative sample data set, which contains 10 different types of samples.

3.4 Training Parameters and Similarity Calculation

The deep learning model in this paper uses a common index to evaluate and predict the signal recognition, that is, the mean square error (MSE) based on L2 loss, which can be expressed as:

$$MSE = \frac{1}{n} \sum_{i=1}^{N} (\hat{y}_i - y_i)^2. \tag{5}$$

where $\hat{y}_i$ is the prediction result of sample i, and y_i is the ground truth of the corresponding response signal mode.

The reason why MSE is used here is that it is easy to calculate, and the gradient of loss increases with the increase of loss, while the gradient decreases when the loss approaches zero, which makes the result of MSE model more accurate at the end of training.

The network is trained by proper training samples, which can effectively classify the continuous overlapped signals of the same channel. The output of DM-CapsNet is a 10-dimensional vector. $f(x)$ is a threshold decision function, expressed as:

$$f(x) = \begin{cases} 1 \; if \; x \in [T, 1] \\ 0 \; if \; x \in [0, T) \end{cases} \tag{6}$$

where T is the threshold set manually.

4 Experimental Results and Discussion

4.1 Experimental Conditions and a Simulation Data Set for Testing

All experiments in this chapter are based on a 16 GB RAM workstation, equipped with 3700X CPU and NVIDIA GeForce GTX 2080Ti GPU. And we use the Keras framework with Tensorflow as the back-end for network construction and performance optimization experiments.

When using other methods to compare with the method proposed in this paper, the test data set used is different from the data set with negative sample data enhancement used in the training process. The samples of test data set usually contain multiple signals of different modes, and the amplitude and position are floating in a certain range. The data set used for training can ensure that the input of each signal has a corresponding pattern, which is very simple to recognize, while the data set used for testing can only scan the entire sample point by point or pulse. At this time, the network input signal will have different types of defects, as shown in Fig. 8(a), (b); or the input contains multiple mode signals, as shown in Fig. 8(c); or the signal amplitude may be missed due to too low signal amplitude, as shown in Fig. 8(d). It can be seen that the identification of the actual test signal is very difficult.

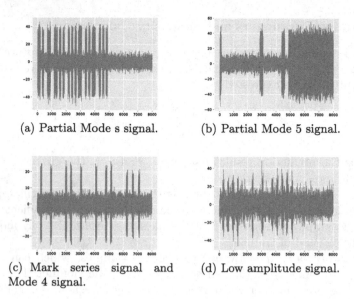

(a) Partial Mode s signal.   (b) Partial Mode 5 signal.

(c) Mark series signal and   (d) Low amplitude signal.
Mode 4 signal.

Fig. 8. Possible wrong input test samples.

The related parameters of the simulated test data set are shown in the table below Table 1. Each sample contains 3–8 IFF signals with random mode type. The position of each IFF signal in the sample is random, and the amplitude fluctuates within a certain range. Because the duration of the IFF signal of different modes is different, and the system only collects the signal part when the signal is actually received, there is no guarantee that each sample has the same length. Therefore, the signal length should be dynamically adjusted according to the mode type and the number of signals contained in each sample, so the signal length of the data set is not fixed. A sample in the test data set is shown in Fig. 9.

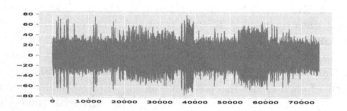

Fig. 9. Sample in test set.

This sample contains a total of 7 signals, starting from the starting point on the left, there are one Mark X series IFF signal, two Mode 4 IFF signals, one Mode S IFF signal, one Mode 5 level1 IFF signal, one Mode 5 level2 IFF signal, and one Mark X series IFF signal.

Table 1. Parameters of test data set.

Signal parameter	Specific values
Number of signal types	5
Center frequency	70 MHz
Sampling rate	240 MHz
Amplitude range of each IFF signal	25–60
SNR of a sample	−9 dB to 9 dB
Points of each sample	⩾50000
Number of signals per sample	3–8
Sample size	10000

4.2 Experimental Result

In the process of continuous detection of IFF signal, we need to pay attention to the changes of accuracy, instantaneous false alarm rate and missing alarm rate under different SNR. The global false alarm rate is 10^{-4} order of magnitude in most cases because of more non signal detection, which has no practical reference significance. The instantaneous false alarm rate only compares the detection performance of the method at the pulse position, and the instantaneous false alarm rate can make the comparison of results more intuitive. If there is no special explanation in this paper, the false alarm rate refers to the instantaneous false alarm rate.

Compare the loading and testing time of DM-CapsNet, multilayer convolutional neural network (CNN) and traditional detection method sliding window method (SW), as shown in Table 2. Although the sliding window method (SW) does not use the machine learning method, it needs multi-step correlation calculation because of the introduction of mode 5 signal. At the same time, compared with the neural network method, the sliding window method can only use CPU operation, and can not use GPU acceleration technology. It can be seen that the test time of the improved sliding window method is close to that of the multilayer convolution network. Because DM-CapsNet contains LC-Net and SC-Net, the time of DM-CapsNet is twice as long as the former two, but it also shows that the network has the possibility of further improvement.

The accuracy can intuitively understand the classification effect of the network on the test data set or continuous signal, and the recognition result is shown in Fig. 10. It can be seen that because the training data set uses low SNR signals as training samples, the recognition effect of neural network method is much

Table 2. Related parameters of the test data set.

	SW	CNN	DM-CapsNet
Load	–	0.82 s	1.35 s
Test	1481 s	1739 s	3517 s

better than sliding window method for low SNR test data set. However, with the improvement of SNR, the recognition accuracy of neural network method decreases, and the recognition accuracy of sliding window method increases gradually because of the higher requirement of SNR. At the same time, DM-CapsNet has the best recognition accuracy in the range of −9 and 9 dB.

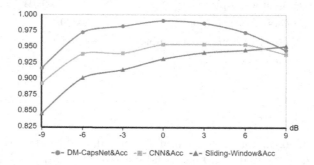

Fig. 10. Accuracy comparison results.

By comparing the results of false alarm rate and missing alarm rate of the three methods in Fig. 11, it can be seen that the false alarm rate of the multi-layer convolution neural network is high, and it can be found that the network has weak comprehensive ability to the characteristics of the signal by synthesizing the recognition accuracy of the method. Although the false alarm rate is low, the false alarm rate is relatively high. On the whole, false alarm rate and missed alarm rate are positively correlated with SNR, which shows that the method is most sensitive to the signal-to-noise ratio and has poor robustness. The average false alarm rate of the proposed dual task attention capsule neural network is less than 15%, and the false alarm rate is the lowest in the range of −9 dB to 9 dB. At the same time, the false alarm rate is less than 5% when it is more than 3 dB. To sum up, the overall recognition effect of the network is the best.

It can be seen from the analysis of the experimental results that: 1) Because the threshold value of sliding window method is fixed, when the signal amplitude is low and the signal-to-noise ratio is low, the situation of missing detection and wrong detection will occur, and the signals must be all in the frame before the method can be detected; 2) Although the multilayer convolution neural network also uses one-dimensional convolution layer to extract the signal features,

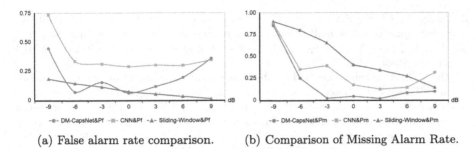

(a) False alarm rate comparison.   (b) Comparison of Missing Alarm Rate.

Fig. 11. Compare results

because the feature processing ability is not enough, each time in the pulse detection will output a large detection probability, so the false alarm rate will be very high, and when the signal amplitude is too low, it can not be detected, so the detection ability has defects; 3) The method proposed in this paper can use convolution neural network to extract features, and then use capsule network and attention mechanism to further strengthen and weight the features, so that the method always has good recognition effect when the SNR is within a certain range.

5 Conclusion

In this paper, a recognition and classification method of continuous IFF signal based on attention mechanism and capsule neural network is proposed. The capsule network is creatively applied to the advanced feature extraction of IFF signal, and the effect is much better than that of traditional convolution neural network, The network structure of dual task output can deal with the error recognition caused by multiple signals input at the same time, and further improve the recognition performance. At the same time, negative samples are added to the signal training set to enhance the data, which makes the recognition ability of the network better, and the false alarm rate in the test samples decreases significantly, which is of great help to the recognition of continuous signals. Finally, through continuous IFF analog signal experiment, the test results show that DM-CapsNet has good and stable performance in the test set. In the future, we can try to optimize the network model parameters or new routing algorithm to improve the classification and recognition effect.

References

1. Comon, P.: Independent component analysis, a new concept? Signal Process. **36**(3), 287–314 (1994)
2. Hyvarinen, A.: Fast and robust fixed-point algorithms for independent component analysis. IEEE Trans. Neural Networks **10**(3), 626–634 (1999)

3. Tang, B., Cheng, S.Y., Zhang, H.: Separation of Garbled secondary surveillance radar signal based on multichannel array processing. Telecommun. Eng. **54** (2014)
4. Qian, T., Mao, Y.L., Rong, Z.: A study on the analysis and identification of IFF signals. Radar ECM (2008)
5. Zhao, B.: Research on method of interrogator code assignment of mode S secondary surveillance radar based on distance matrix. Radio Eng. (2017)
6. Duan, H., Cheng, Y., Seen, B., He, K., Bai, G.: LFM interference cancellation algorithm based on MDPT-WC for mark XIIA mode 5. In: 2020 IEEE 20th International Conference on Communication Technology (ICCT), pp. 246–252 (2020). https://doi.org/10.1109/ICCT50939.2020.9295892
7. Min, L.: A sorting method of mark XIIA mode 5 signals. Telecommun. Eng. (2019)
8. Sabour, S., Frosst, N., Hinton, G.E.: Dynamic routing between capsules (2017)
9. Hinton, G.E., Sabour, S., Frosst, N.: Matrix capsules with EM routing (2018)
10. Ma, X., Zhong, H., Li, Y., et al.: Forecasting transportation network speed using deep capsule networks with nested LSTM models. IEEE Trans. Intell. Transp. Syst. **PP**(99), 1–12 (2020)
11. Pang, T., Li, Y., Niu, Y., et al.: Periodic pulsed jamming detection method and its performance in wireless communication. J. Terahertz Sci. Electron. Inf. Technol. (2019)
12. Ke, W., Hao, C.: Research on radar main lobe false target jamming feature extraction based on time-frequency domain and fluctuation characteristics. J. Phys. Conf. Ser. **1871**(1) (2021)
13. Rosario, D., Martins, V., Mauricio, B., Edson, B.: Efficiency and scalability of multi-lane capsule networks (MLCN). J. Parallel Distrib. Comput. (2021)

Interference Analysis of Anti Micro and Small Unmanned Aircraft Systems and Code Division Multiple Access Systems at Frequency Band 835–845 MHz

Junfang Li[1], Changqing Zhang[2(✉)], Jie Liu[3], Yangmei Zhang[1], Kun Liu[1], and Fei Song[1]

[1] School of Electronic Engineering, Xi'an Aeronautical University, Xi'an 710077, China
lijf@aliyun.com, 201707019@xaau.edu.cn
[2] College of Information Engineering,
Xinyang Agriculture and Forestry University, Xinyang 464000, Henan, China
[3] Xi'an Branch, China Academy of Space Technology, Xi'an 710100, China

Abstract. An anti micro and small unmanned aircraft system (AmsUAS) is a radio technology used for civil micro and small unmanned aircraft systems (msUASs) control. Along with blocking the communication link of the msUAS, the AmsUAS also interferes with other radio communication systems such as civil aviation and mobile communication systems. In this study, an analysis method based on the interference-to-noise ratio (INR) criterion is proposed and interference analysis is performed on AmsUAS and code division multiple access (CDMA) systems. First, to control msUASs, it is necessary to calculate the minimum transmit power of the AmsUAS in the corresponding frequency band according to the uplink and the radio wave propagation distance of the msUAS. Second, to avoid harmful interference to other radio systems (such as CDMA), the frequency and distance separation between the AmsUAS and CDMA radio systems should be calculated according to factors such as application scenarios, radio wave propagation distance, and working frequency band. Finally, a simulation analysis provides the transmit power, off-axis angle, frequency separation, and distance separation of the AmsUAS and CDMA systems in different environments.

Keywords: Anti micro and small unmanned aircraft system · Code division multiple access · Interference analysis · Interference-to-noise ratio criterion

1 Introduction

With the development of civil unmanned aircraft systems, micro and small unmanned aircraft systems (msUASs) have been widely used in various fields [1–3]. With their low cost, low volume, and light weight, msUASs can perform remote operations conveniently, acquire high-resolution images, access hard-to-reach areas, and obtain flexible response to complex geographical environments. Owing to such advantages, msUASs

X. Wang et al. (Eds.): AICON 2021, LNICST 396, pp. 469–482, 2021.
https://doi.org/10.1007/978-3-030-90196-7_40

are widely used in aviation filming [4], infrastructure detection monitoring [5], accident scene investigation [6], disaster assessment, and other fields [7].

However, with the increase in the number of msUASs held by general public, the problem of disorderly flight is becoming increasingly serious, and the corresponding flight safety problem of civil msUASs is gaining prominence [2]. Incidents of msUAS flight affecting the take-off and landing safety of civil aviation aircraft and threatening the security of important areas and facilities occur from time to time. To reduce the existing or potential security problems of civil msUASs to other facilities and areas, the control technology of msUASs has emerged and has been widely used [8].

An anti micro and small Unmanned Aircraft System (AmsUAS) is a radio technology for civilian msUAS control [9], which is closely related to the msUAS radio communication system. The common AmsUAS [10] is mainly the radio-based msUAS control technology, which achieves control by blocking the communication link of the msUAS, thus hindering its normal operation and forcing landing. According to the Report ITU-R M.2171 [11], the communication links of civil msUASs generally include the uplink remote control link, downlink information transmission link, telemetry link, and satellite links such as GPS, Beidou, and GLONASS used for navigation. Therefore, in general, the AmsUAS aims to block one or more of the above communication links to divert or force the landing of civil msUASs to realize the control of civil msUASs.

However, in the process of controlling the radio links of msUASs, high-power signal suppression is usually adopted, which causes interference not only to the communication link of msUASs but also to other radio systems that use the same frequency band or adjacent frequency band, such as the GPS altitude measuring equipment on aircraft, GPS positioning equipment of mobile communication base stations, and the uplink and downlink of mobile communication systems. The civil GPS signal is the spread spectrum signal with a frequency of 1575 MHz, a bandwidth of 2.046 MHz, and a spread spectrum gain of 43 dB [12]. The high spread spectrum gain of the GPS signal results in poor performance of some frequency band interference of the AmsUAS. Therefore, the AmsUAS will normally control the uplink remote control link and downlink information transmission link of msUASs.

In general, the msUAS is easier for controllers to find than the UA control station (UACS), and the radio transmission conditions between the controller and the msUAS are better. Therefore, it is easier to control the msUAS by suppressing its uplink. According to the report ITU-R M.2237 [13] and the frequency division of ITU region 3, as well as the frequency usage of the existing civil msUASs, the operating frequency of the uplink remote link of msUASs is 840.5–845.0 MHz. In the process of controlling this link, harmful interference will be generated to the code division multiple access (CDMA) mobile communication system in adjacent frequency bands.

Therefore, this paper aims to conduct interference analysis and determine the minimum frequency and distance intervals required for both AmsUAS and CDMA systems to coexist. Thus, the study aims to prevent the high-power repressive interference generated by the AmsUAS from affecting the uplink of CDMA.

The rest of this paper is organized as follows. The system model is presented in Sect. 2, and the proposed interference analysis of AmsUAS and CDMA system is presented in Sect. 3. Section 4 presents numerical examples to verify the derived result. Finally in Sect. 5 we conclude the main results of this paper.

2   System Model

We consider the interference between the AmsUAS and CDMA system as shown in Fig. 1, where the AmsUAS operates in the adjacent frequency band of CDMA. The msUAS comprises a msUA and a UACS, which is a type of remote control equipment and usually fixed on the ground or handheld. The CDMA system is equipped with a base station and mobile terminals. The AmsUAS controls the msUAS by high-power noise interference on the uplink remote control link. In Fig. 1, Line 1 is the control link of the AmsUAS to the msUAS, Line 2 is the interference link of the AmsUAS to the uplink of the CDMA system, and Line 3 and Line 4 are the communication links of the msUAS and CDMA systems, respectively.

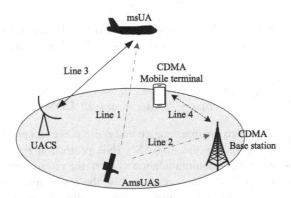

Fig. 1. System model

3   Interference Analysis of AmsUAS and CDMA System

Wireless interference always exists in the radio system [14–15]. The power of the interference signal is closely related to the distance between the transmitter and the receiver. As the distance increases, the interference signal decreases. Whether one radio system is harmful to another is assessed by interference analysis, which is usually based on a simple relationship [16–17]. A jamming signal with power within the allowable range of the receiver will generally not cause harmful interference to the receiver [12]. In this paper, interference analysis of a wireless communication system is performed based on the interference-to-noise ratio (INR) criterion to determine the ranges of frequency and distance separation for the two systems to coexist in time, frequency, and space domains [18].

3.1 Interference-To-Noise Ratio Criterion

Due to msUASs generally use frequency hopping and spread spectrum technology, and frequency hopping parameters can be self-adaptive, they have a certain ability of anti-jamming. In general, the controller does not know any other parameters other than the frequency band of the msUASs, so a high-power noise can only be used for full frequency band coverage.

When the AmsUAS controls the uplink of the msUASs, the power of the noise must be increased such that it exceeds the INR protection requirements of the msUASs, thereby allowing it to block the control of the UACS over the msUASs. According to report ITU-R M.2119 [19], the long-term protection requirement for an msUAS is −3 dB and the short-term protection requirement is 0 dB. To avoid harmful interference to the CDMA system of an adjacent channel, the power of the interference signal received by the CDMA base station must meet the INR protection requirements of normal communication. The INR protection requirement for the CDMA base station is $\eta_{CDMA} < -7\text{dB}$. INR is defined as

$$\text{INR} = \frac{I}{N},\tag{1}$$

where I and N denote the interference and noise power in W, respectively. The units of power can be converted into dB as $INR(\text{dB}) = I - N$. The INR criterion can be defined as

$$\text{INR} = \begin{cases} I_{msUAS} - N_{msUAS} \geq \eta_{msUAS} & \text{msUAS} \\ I_{CDMA} - N_{CDMA} < \eta_{CDMA} & \text{CDMA} \end{cases},\tag{2}$$

where I_{msUAS} and N_{msUAS} are the interference and noise power received by the msUAS receiver, respectively. η_{msUAS} is the msUAS's INR protection requirement. For the AmsUAS to block the msUAS communication system, the requirement $INR \geq \eta_{\text{msUAS}}$ must be met. I_{CDMA} and N_{CDMA} are, respectively, the interference and noise power received by the CDMA system. To ensure the normal quality of service, the requirement $INR < \eta_{\text{CDMA}}$ must be met.

3.2 Calculation of Interference Power

In case of either the msUA or CDMA base station, the received interference power is a function of the gain and path loss. The interference power received by the jammed radio receiver is expressed by

$$I = P_t + G_t - L_t + G_r - L_r - L_p(d) - FDR(\Delta f).\tag{3}$$

Here, P_t is the transmit power of the interference source (dBm); G_t and G_r are the antenna gain of the transmitter and the receiver, respectively; L_t and L_r are the feeder loss of the AmsUAS and CDMA, respectively; and $L_p(d)$ is the transmission path loss for a separation distance d between the interferer and receiver (dB). $FDR(\Delta f)$ is a frequency-dependent rejection of a certain frequency separation Δf (dB), which is a measure of the rejection produced by the receiver selectivity curve on an unwanted transmitter emission spectra, defined as

$$FDR(\Delta f) = -10\log \frac{\int\limits_{-\infty}^{+\infty} P(f)|H(f+\Delta f)|^2 df}{\int\limits_{-\infty}^{+\infty} P(f)df} \quad \text{dB.} \qquad (4)$$

Here, $P(f)$ is the power spectral density of the interfering signal equivalent intermediate frequency (IF); $H(f)$ is the frequency response of the receiver; Δf is the frequency separation between jammed receivers and interfering transmitters, defined as $\Delta f = f_t - f_r$, where f_t is the interferer-tuned frequency and f_r is the receiver-tuned frequency. In particular, $\Delta f = 0$ indicates co-channel interference.

As can be seen from (4), the interference signal power is $P_t = \int_{-\infty}^{+\infty} P(f)df$, $|H(f+\Delta f)|^2$ reflects the characteristics of the receiver spectrum mask, and $FDR(\Delta f) \geq 0$.

It is evident from (4) that $FDR(\Delta f)$ is strongly dependent on the extent of overlapping between the receiver passband and the power spectrum of the interfering signal. As Δf increases, the extent of overlapping diminishes, thus resulting in lower interference power, and, equivalently, higher $FDR(\Delta f)$.

Considering the effect of the off-axis angle on the antenna gain, the off-axis angle of the transmitting antenna is defined as θ_1 and that of the receiving antenna is defined as θ_2. Then the interference power is

$$I = P_t + G_t(\theta_1) - L_t + G_r(\theta_2) - L_r - L_p(d) - FDR(\Delta f), \qquad (5)$$

where, $G_t(\theta_1)$ is the antenna gain of the AmsUAS in the direction of the receiver when the off-axis angle is θ_1 (dBi); $G_r(\theta_2)$ is the antenna gain of the jammed receiver (e.g., msUAS) in the direction of interference when the off-axis angle is θ_2 (dBi).

According to the calculation method of a 100 MHz–70 GHz antenna radiation pattern given in ITU-R F.699–7 and ITU-R F.1245–1 recommendations, D is the diameter or length of the antenna and λ is the wavelength, G_{max} is the maximum gain for the antenna and G_1 is the first side lobe gain, and θ_{3dB} is a 3 dB beam width. Then, the antenna gain $G_\Lambda(\theta_i)(\Lambda = t,r; i = 1, 2, 3)$ corresponding to different off-axis angles θ_i is given as follows.

When $D/\lambda > 100$,

$$G_\Lambda(\theta_i) = \begin{cases} G_{max} - 2.5 \times 10^{-3}(D\theta_i/\lambda)^2, & 0° < \theta_i < \varphi_m \\ G_1, & \varphi_m \leq \theta_i < \max(\varphi_m, \varphi_r) \\ 29 - 25\log\theta_i, & \max(\varphi_m, \varphi_r) \leq \theta_i < 48° \\ -13, & 48° \leq \theta_i \leq 180° \end{cases} \qquad (6)$$

where $G_{max} = 20\log(D/\lambda) + 7.7$, $\varphi_m = (20D\sqrt{G_{max} - G_1})/\lambda$, $G_1 = 2 + 15\log(D/\lambda)$ and $\varphi_r = 12.02(D/\lambda)^{-0.6}$.

When $D/\lambda \leq 100$,

$$G_\Lambda(\theta_i) = \begin{cases} G_{max} - 2.5 \times 10^{-3}(D\theta_i/\lambda), & 0° < \theta_i < \varphi_m \\ 39 - 5\log(D/\lambda) - 25\log\theta_i, & \varphi_m \leq \theta_i < 48° \\ -3 - 5\log(D/\lambda), & 48° \leq \theta_i \leq 180° \end{cases} \quad (7)$$

3.3 Calculation of Path Loss

A spatial factor is used in the computation of distance-related signal attenuation; it is closely related to the radio propagation model adopted in this study and the statistical distribution of the interfering signal at the front end of the interfered receiver [22].

Path loss is calculated by radio propagation models. In this study, a radio propagation model is selected according to the system configuration, system bandwidth, operating frequency band, and geographical environment surrounding the service area [23].

Considering that the AmsUAS generally uses high-power signal suppression, in order to minimize its effect on other surrounding radio services, directional antenna is used for jamming the msUAS. To attain the minimum interference power of the AmsUAS, the free-space radio propagation model is used to calculate the path loss by the following formula:

$$L_p(d) = 32.4 + 20\log d + 20\log f. \quad (8)$$

In the interference analysis of the AmsUAS and CDMA systems, path loss calculation methods of urban, suburban, or open scenarios in the Okumura–Hata model are adopted according to different application scenarios. The formulas of path loss in the three scenarios are as follows.

Radio propagation model in the urban scenario:

$$L_p(d) = 49.55 + 26.16\lg f - 13.82\lg h_1 - \alpha(h_2) + (44.9 - 6.55\lg h_1)\lg d, \quad (9)$$

Where f is the operating frequency; h_1 is the effective height of the base station antenna (m); h_2 is the effective height of the mobile station antenna (m); and $\alpha(h_2)$ is the height factor of the mobile station antenna (dB), and when $f > 400$ MHz, it is defined as

$$\alpha(h_2) = 3.2[\log(11.75h_2)]^2 - 4.97 \ (f > 400\,\text{MHz}). \quad (10)$$

Radio propagation model in the suburban scenario:

$$L_p(d) = 69.55 + 26.16\log f - 13.82\log h_1 - \alpha(h_2) + (44.9 - 6.55\log h_1)\log d. \quad (11)$$

For the suburbs scenario, $\alpha(h_2)$ is defined as

$$\alpha(h_2) = 2[\log(f/28)]^2 + 5.4. \quad (12)$$

Radio propagation model in the open scenario:

$$L_p(d) = 28.6 + 26.16\log f - 13.82\log H_b$$
$$+[44.9 - 6.55\log(H_b)]\log d - 4.78(\log f)^2 + 18.33\log f, \quad (13)$$

where H_b is the base station height.

3.4 Calculation of Minimum Interference Power

The transmit power of the AmsUAS is closely related to the transmit power, bandwidth, antenna gain, and anti-interference threshold of the receiver of the msUA. In practice, the maximum power received by the receiver is

$$P_{r\_max} = \max\{P_t + G_t(\theta_1) - L_t + G_r(\theta_2) - L_r - L_p(d_1)\}, \tag{14}$$

where P_{r_max} is the maximum power received by the msUA and d_1 is the propagation distance between the UACS and msUA.

To realize the effective interference of the AmsUAS to the msUAS uplink, the following inequation must be satisfied:

$$P_{t\_AmsUAS} + G_t(\theta_1) - L_t + G_r(\theta_2) - L_r - L_p(d_2) - Th_{msUAS} \geq P_{r\_max}, \tag{15}$$

where P_{t_AmsUAS} is the transmit power of the AmsUAS, Th_{msUAS} is the anti-jamming threshold of the msUA, d_2 is the propagation distance between the AmsUAS and msUA. In general, d_2 is greater than d_1.

Suppose the UACS and AmsUAS have the same $G_t(\theta_1)$ and L_t, then for a given d_2, the interference power must satisfy

$$P_{t\_AmsUAS} \geq P_{r\_max} - G_t(\theta_1) + L_t - G_r(\theta_2) + L_r + L_p(d_2) + Th_{msUAS}. \tag{16}$$

3.5 Interference Analysis

With the high-power noise emitted by the AmsUAS, not only does the bottom noise in the surrounding airspace greatly increase but the main and side lobes of the antenna also cause interference to other nearby radio services, thus seriously affecting their normal operation.

The interference power received by the disturbed receiver is closely related to the operating frequency of the transmitted signal, the transmit power, and the distance between the transmitter and the receiver [25]. According to the INR criterion, measures that should be taken to avoid harmful interference include increasing the frequency separation, reducing the transmit power, increasing off-axis angles, or increasing the distance between transmitters and disturbed receivers [26, 27].

According to (2) and (5), when the AmsUAS generates interference, the receiver of adjacent frequency bands can only work normally when the following equation is satisfied.

$$I - N = P_{t\_AmsUAS} + G_t(\theta_1) - L_t + G_r(\theta_3) - L_r - L_p(d_3) - FDR(\Delta f) - N_{CDMA} < \eta_{CDMA} \tag{17}$$

Where, d_3 is the propagation distance between AmsUAS and CDMA. $G_r(\theta_3)$ is the antenna gain of the jammed receiver (e.g. CDMA) in the direction of interference when the off-axis angle is θ_3. N_{CDMA} is mainly generated by the thermal motion of charged particles, and its power is.

$$N_{CDMA} = -174 + 10\log B + NF \ dBm, \tag{18}$$

where B is the medium frequency bandwidth (Hz) and NF denotes the noise figure (dB).

In case when the radio wave propagation distance d_3 is given, the relationship between the transmit power of the AmsUAS and frequency separation can be obtained as follows.

$$P_{t\_AmsUAS} < \eta_{CDMA} - G_t(\theta_1) + L_t - G_r(\theta_3) + L_r + L_p(d_3) + FDR(\Delta f) + N_{CDMA} \tag{19}$$

Then, the maximum transmitting power is $P_{t\_max} = \max\{P_{t\_AmsUAS}\}$. As can be seen from (14), $P_{t\_AmsUAS} \in [P_{t\_min}, P_{t\_max}]$.

In case P_{t_AmsUAS} is given, according to (17), the frequency and distance separation between the AmsUAS and CDMA systems can be obtained as follows.

$$20\log(d_3) \geq P_{t\_AmsUAS} + G_t(\theta_1) - L_t + G_r(\theta_3) - L_r$$
$$-FDR(\Delta f) - N_{CDMA} - 32.4 - 20\log f - \eta_{CDMA} \tag{20}$$

4   Numeric Simulation and Discussion

In this section, we present the simulation results to verify the proposed interference analysis method. The simulation scenario includes an msUA, a UACS, an AmsUAS, and a CDMA base station. DQPSK modulated signals are transmitted by the msUAS. The flight altitude of the msUAS is less than 1000 m, and the simulation parameters of the msUAS are shown in Table 1.

Table 1. Simulation parameters of msUAS.

	Bandwidth (MHz)	Transmit power (dBm)	Antenna gain (dBi)	Antenna height (m)	Feeder loss (dB)	NF (dB)	INR Requirements (dB)
Transmitter	50	33	20	1.5	2	5	/
Receiver	50	/	3	<1000	1	5	−3

To determine the maximum power received by the msUAS, as the propagation model of the msUAS, the free space model is used to calculate the path loss. Figure 2 shows the signal power received by the msUA at different propagation distances and receiving off-axis angles.

When $\theta_2 = 0°$, there is no off-axis angle between the receiving antenna and the main beam direction of the UACS. $\theta_2 \neq 0°$ indicates that the receiving antenna deviates from the main beam direction at θ_2. When $\theta_2 = 0°$, the power of the received signal is maximum; the larger the off-axis angle, the smaller the received signal power. For a given transmit power, the greater the transmission distance, the smaller the received signal power.

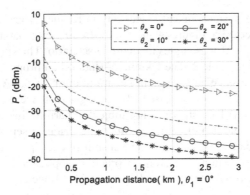

Fig. 2. Power of the received signal corresponding to different propagation distances, where $\theta_1 = 0^\circ$.

Figure 3 shows comparison of the minimum interference power of the AmsUAS for different propagation distances and off-axis angle θ_1. To block the uplink communication system of the msUAS, the minimum noise interference signal power transmitted by the AmsUAS should be greater than or equal to the sum of the maximum received signal power and the anti-interference threshold of the msUAS. In general, when the main beam direction of the AmsUAS is directly opposite to the msUA, i.e., $\theta_1 = 0^\circ$, the transmitted power is the least. However, to avoid interference with other radio communication systems in the same direction, the main beam direction can be deviated from the msUA, i.e., $\theta_1 \neq 0^\circ$. A short communication link between the AmsUAS and msUA ensures less interference power, and thus a low possibility of interfering with other radio services. Considering the effect of path loss, the minimum interference power obtained by the free space radio propagation model is the least. With other radio propagation models, the minimum interference power will be larger.

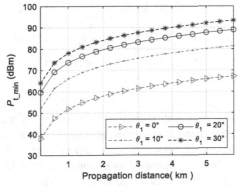

Fig. 3. Minimum interference power of the AmsUAS corresponding to different propagation distances.

A high-power noise-jamming signal transmitted by the AmsUAS will interfere with radio equipment located within a certain distance. To avoid harmful interference, the

AmsUAS and CDMA systems need to meet certain frequency and distance separation as mentioned in Subsect. 3.5. Figures 4 and 5 show frequency separation versus distance separation for different off-axis angles in an urban scenario. The simulation parameters of CDMA are shown in Table 2. The Okumura–Hata urban propagation model is used to calculate the path loss. When the main beam direction of the AmsUAS is directed toward the CDMA base station, i.e., $\theta_3 = 0°$, a larger distance separation is required to ensure that the CDMA base station is not subject to harmful interference. Increasing the off-axis angle θ_3 can also effectively reduce the distance separation. Comparison of Figs. 4 and 5 indicates that reducing the transmit power P_{t_min} can also effectively reduce the distance separation. Therefore, in practical applications, the transmit power of the AmsUAS and off-axis angle should be reasonably selected.

Table 2. Simulation parameters of CDMA.

	Bandwidth (MHz)	Antenna gain (dBi)	Antenna height (m)	Feeder loss (dB)	NF (dB)	INR requirements (dB)
Base station	1.25	15	30	2	5	−7

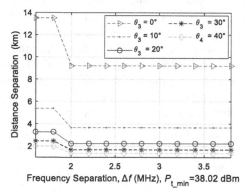

Fig. 4. Frequency separation with respect to distance separation under different off-axis angles in an urban scenario with $P_{t\_min} = 38.02$ dBm.

According to the radio propagation theory, path loss is an important factor in the analysis of interference between different wireless communication systems. Figures 6 and 7 show frequency separation versus distance separation in suburban and open scenarios, respectively. Path loss is calculated using the Okumura–Hata suburban and the open environment propagation models, respectively. The figures indicate that the path loss of a suburban scenario is greater than that of an open scenario. Therefore, under the condition of the same frequency separation, the distance separation of an open scenario is greater than that of a suburban scenario. Therefore, in an open scenario, the power of the interference signal should be carefully selected to avoid harmful interference to other radio systems.

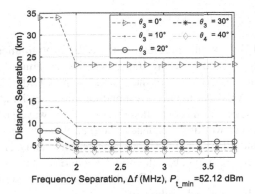

Fig. 5. Frequency separation with respect to distance separation under different off-axis angles in an urban scenario with $P_{t\_min} = 52.12$ dBm.

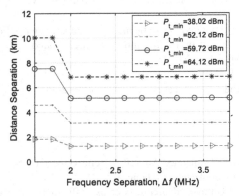

Fig. 6. Frequency separation with respect to distance separation under different P_{t_min} in a suburban scenario

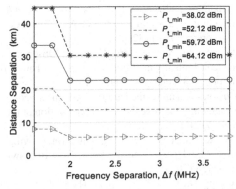

Fig. 7. Frequency separation with respect to distance separation under different P_{t_min} in an open scenario

5 Conclusions

In practice, the AmsUAS not only interferes with msUAS communication links but also can cause harmful interference to civil aviation and mobile communication systems. This study analyzed the radio interference of the AmsUAS and CDMA. First, the minimum transmit power of the AmsUAS in the corresponding frequency band was calculated on the basis of the parameters of the controlled msUA and the wave propagation distance. Second, according to the working frequency band, application scenario, and distance between AmsUAS and CDMA base stations, interference analysis was performed on the basis of the INR criterion to obtain the frequency and distance separation that must be satisfied for both systems to coexist. Finally, the simulation verified the feasibility and effectiveness of the proposed method.

Author Contributions. J. Li conceived and designed the experiments; C. Zhang and J. Liu performed the experiments; J. Li,Y. Zhang and K. Liu analyzed the data; J. Li, K. Liu and F. Song wrote the paper. All authors have read and agreed to the published version of the manuscript.

Funding. This work was supported in part by the Aeronautical Science Foundation under Grant No. 2019ZH0T7001 and in part by the Scientific Research Foundation of Xi'an Aeronautical University under Grant No. 2019KY0207.

Conflicts of Interest. The authors declare no conflict of interest.

References

1. Papa, U.: Introduction to Unmanned Aircraft Systems (UAS). Embedded Platforms for UAS Landing Path and Obstacle Detection, January 2018
2. Lieb, T.J., Volkert, A.: Unmanned aircraft systems traffic management: a comparison on the FAA UTM and the European CORUS ConOps based on U-space. In: 39th Digital Avionics Systems Conference (DASC), San Antonio, TX, USA, pp.1–6 (2020)
3. Karaca, Y., Cicek, M., et al.: The potential use of unmanned aircraft systems (drones) in mountain search and rescue operations. Am. J. Emergency Med. **36**(4), 583–588 (2018)
4. Grubinger, S., et al.: Modeling realized gains in Douglas-fir (Pseudotsuga menziesii) using laser scanning data from unmanned aircraft systems (UAS). Forest Ecol. Manage. **473** (2020). https://doi.org/10.1016/j.foreco.2020.118284
5. Adkins, K., Wambolt, P., Sescu, A., Swinford, C., et al.: Observational practices for urban microclimates using meteorologically instrumented unmanned aircraft systems. Atmosphere (11) (2020). https://doi.org/10.3390/atmos11091008
6. Gaston, M.D., et al.: Customizing unmanned aircraft systems to reduce forest inventory costs: can oblique images substantially improve the 3D reconstruction of the canopy? Int. J. Remote Sens. **41**(9), 3480–3510 (2020)
7. Cunningham, M., et al.: Aeromagnetic surveying with a rotary-wing unmanned aircraft system: a case study from a zinc deposit in Nash Creek, New Brunswick, Canada. Pure Appl. Geophys. **175**(9), 3145–3158 (2018)
8. Jie, L., Chaofeng, L., Cheng, D., Tong, F., Nimin, Z., Hang, Z.: Necessity analysis and scheme of constructing ultra-low-altitude defense system in megacities. IEEE Aerosp. Electron. Syst. Mag. **36**(1), 14–21 (2021)

9. Xufang, S., Chaoqun, Y., Weige, X., Liang, C., Shi, Z., Chen, J.: Anti-drone system with multiple surveillance technologies: architecture implementation and challenges. IEEE Commun. Mag. **56**(4), 68–74 (2018)
10. Daojing, H., et al.: A friendly and low-cost technique for capturing non-cooperative civilian unmanned aerial vehicles. IEEE Network **33**(2), 146–151 (2019)
11. International Telecommunication Union Radiocommunication Study Group. Characteristics of unmanned aircraft systems and spectrum requirements to support their safe operation in non-segregated airspace (Report ITU-R M.2171). International Telecommunication Union Publications 2009 (2009)
12. Oh, M., Kim, Y.H.: Statistical approach to spectrogram analysis for radio-frequency interference detection and mitigation in an l-band microwave radiometer. Sensors **19**, 306 (2019). https://doi.org/10.3390/s19020306
13. International Telecommunication Union Radiocommunication Study Group. Compatibility study to support the line-of-sight control and non-payload communications link(s) for unmanned aircraft systems proposed in the frequency band 5 030–5 091 MHz (Report ITU-R M.2237). International Telecommunication Union Publications 2011
14. Biswas, S., Singh, K., Taghizadeh, O., Ratnarajah, T.: Coexistence of MIMO radar and FD MIMO cellular systems with QoS considerations. IEEE Trans. Wireless Commun. **17**(11), 7281–7294 (2018)
15. Chen, H., Hua, J., Li, F., Chen, F., Wang, D.: Interference analysis in the asynchronous f-OFDM systems. IEEE Trans. Commun. **67**(5), 3580–3596 (2019). https://doi.org/10.1109/TCOMM.2019.2898867
16. Biswas, S., Singh, K., Taghizadeh, O., Ratnarajah, T.: Design and analysis of FD MIMO cellular systems in coexistence with MIMO radar. IEEE Trans. Wireless Commun. **19**(7), 4727–4743 (2020)
17. Prasan, S., Sudhir, P., Shih-Lin, W.: A reliable data transmission model for IEEE 802.15.4e enabled wireless sensor network under WiFi interference. Sensors **17**(6), 1320 (2017). https://doi.org/10.3390/s17061320
18. International Telecommunication Union Radiocommunication Study Group. Recommendation ITU-R SM.337–6 Frequency and distance separations. International Telecommunication Union Publications 2008
19. International Telecommunication Union Radiocommunication Study Group. Sharing between aeronautical mobile telemetry systems for flight testing and other systems operating in the 4400–4940 and 5925–6700 MHz bands (Report ITU-R M.2119). International Telecommunication Union Publications 2007
20. International Telecommunication Union Radiocommunication Study Group. Reference radiation patterns for fixed wireless system antennas for use in coordination studies and interference assessment in the frequency range from 100 MHz to 86 GHz. International Telecommunication Union Publications 2018
21. International Telecommunication Union Radiocommunication Study Group. Mathematical model of average and related radiation patterns for line-of-sight point-to-point radio-relay system antennas for use in certain coordination studies and interference assessment in the frequency range from 1 GHz to about 70 GHz, Recommendation ITU-R F.1245–1. International Telecommunication Union Publications 2000
22. International Telecommunication Union Radiocommunication Study Group. Propagation curves for aeronautical mobile and radionavigation services using the VHF, UHF and SHF bands (ITU-R P.528–2). International Telecommunication Union Publications 1986
23. Raymond, S., Abubakari, A., Jo, H.-S.: Coexistence of power-controlled cellular networks with rotating radar. IEEE J. Sel. Areas Commun. **34**(10), 2605–2616 (2016)
24. Andersen, J.B., Rappaport, T.S., Yoshida, S.: Propagation measurements and models for wireless communications channels. IEEE Commun. Mag. **33**(1), 42–49 (1995)

25. Khawar, A., Abdelhadi, A., Clancy, T.C.: Coexistence analysis between radar and cellular system in LoS channel. IEEE Antennas Wireless Propag. Lett. **15**, 972–975 (2016)
26. Yusra, B., Rather, G.M., Begh, G.R.: SINR analysis and interference management of macrocell cellular networks in dense urban environments. Wireless Personal Commun. **111**(9), 1645–1665 (2020)
27. Polak, L., Milos, J.: Performance analysis of LoRa in the 2.4 GHz ISM band: coexistence issues with Wi-Fi. Telecommun. Syst. Model. Anal. Des. Manage. **74**(3), 299–309 (2020)

Research on Far Field Calculation of Antenna with Conductor Interference

Wei Wang[(✉)], Li Wang, and Boni Liu

Xi'an Aeronautical University, Xi'an 710077, Shaanxi, China

Abstract. In a two-dimensional space, the conductor outline is approximated by a triangular column, and an array antenna is simulated with a set of infinitely long line current sources. The calculation is carried out using the methods of moments (MoM) and the finite element method (FEM) respectively, to analyze the influence on the radiation field of the array antenna in the presence of a conductor nose cone. Experimental results show that, as the rotation angle of the antenna array changes, conductor shielding has a significant impact on the far field strength and deviation angle, especially the nose cone size has a significant effect on the antenna radiation field.

Keywords: Conductor nose cone · Array antenna · Radiation field

1 Introduction

For good penetration of electromagnetic waves, generally radome are made of dielectric materials. But when it is necessary to resist the impact of raindrops and the heating of air friction, the top of the radome is installed with a rain erosion head [1] or an anti-ablation head [2] made of conductive material. And sometimes it is necessary to install a pitot tube for speed measurement. These conductor nose cones are located near the antenna, and people have to consider their influence when analyzing the wave transmission characteristics of the radome. Zhang used a hybrid physical optics-moment method to analyze the transmission characteristics of an airborne radome with a metal pitot tube [3]. Meng proposed to analyze and calculate by the hybrid finite element-physical optics method, and calculated the influence of the airborne radome with a metal cap on the millimeter wave antenna pattern [4]. Rao uses 3D EM simulations to analyze the insertion loss and bore-sight error of the quartz ceramic missile radome with metal tip [5]. Wang analyzed the wave-transmitting characteristics of the radome with anti-ablation head using geometric optics method [2]. The literature [6, 7] analyzes the transmission loss of a radome with complex structures such as conductors. These literatures regard the near-field conductor as a part of the radome design, and pay more attention to the design of the dielectric radome, but lack the targeted analysis of the influence of the shape and size characteristics of the near-field conductor on the antenna radiation. In order to provide reference for the design of rain erosion head and anti-ablation head, this paper uses the method of moments (MoM) and the finite element

X. Wang et al. (Eds.): AICON 2021, LNICST 396, pp. 483–490, 2021.
https://doi.org/10.1007/978-3-030-90196-7_41

method (FEM) to perform numerical simulations to analyze the influence of the shape and electrical size of the conductor nose cone on the far-field radiation of the array antenna.

2   Mathematical Model

The nose cone is usually in the shape of a conical rotating body, which is mathematically modeled by a two-dimensional infinite triangular column; for an array antenna that rotates mechanically with its own center as the axis, mathematical simulation is performed with a set of equally spaced infinite current sources, the mathematical calculation model is shown in Fig. 1.

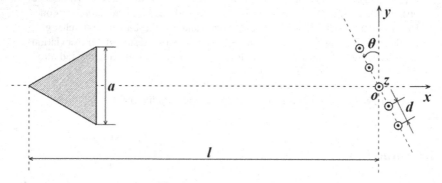

Fig. 1. Calculation model.

Among them, a represents the cross-sectional side length of the conductor triangular column, l represents the distance between the conductor and the antenna array, the coordinate origin o is the center of the array antenna, d is the antenna element spacing, and θ corresponds to the rotation angle of the antenna.

The research goal of this paper is to solve the electric field of distant points distributed on the arc centered on the origin, and analyze the influence of the far field in the relevant radiation direction. Since the target cylinder and the line current as the excitation source are parallel to the z coordinate axis, the electric field generated by each line current can be expressed as [6],

$$E_z^{inc}\left(\vec{\rho}\right) = -I_z\frac{\omega\mu_0}{4}H_0^{(2)}\left(k_0\left|\vec{\rho}-\vec{\rho}'\right|\right) \tag{1}$$

When using the method of moments to solve, the electric field integral equation of the research target is [7],

$$\frac{\omega\mu_0}{4}\oint_c J_z\left(\vec{\rho}'\right)H_0^{(2)}\left(k_0\left|\vec{\rho}-\vec{\rho}'\right|\right)dl' = E_z^{inc}\left(\vec{\rho}\right) \tag{2}$$

Select the pulse basis function, solve the integral equation by the point matching method [8], obtain the current distribution on the conductor surface, and then calculate the far field [9],

$$E_z^{sca}\left(\vec{\rho}\right) = -\frac{\omega\mu_0}{4}\sum_{n=1}^{N} J_n\left(\vec{\rho}'\right)\int_{C_n} H_0^{(2)}\left(k_0\left|\vec{\rho}-\vec{\rho}'\right|\right)dl' \qquad (3)$$

When the finite element method [10] is used to solve the problem, the problem can be expressed by Helmholtz equation as,

$$\frac{\partial}{\partial x}\left(\frac{1}{\mu_r}\frac{\partial E_z}{\partial x}\right) + \frac{\partial}{\partial y}\left(\frac{1}{\mu_r}\frac{\partial E_z}{\partial y}\right) + k_0^2\varepsilon_r E_z = 0 \qquad (4)$$

Combining the second-order absorbing boundary conditions, using the Ritz method to discretize the corresponding variational formula, the near-field distribution around the conductor is solved, and the far-field expression is:

$$E\left(\vec{\rho}\right) = \oint_\Gamma \left[E\left(\vec{\rho}'\right)\frac{\partial G_0\left(\vec{\rho},\vec{\rho}'\right)}{\partial n'} - G_0\left(\vec{\rho},\vec{\rho}'\right)\frac{\partial E\left(\vec{\rho}'\right)}{\partial n'}\right]d\Gamma' \qquad (5)$$

Where,

$$G_0\left(\vec{\rho},\vec{\rho}'\right) = \frac{1}{4j}H_0^{(2)}\left(k_0\left|\vec{\rho}-\vec{\rho}'\right|\right) \qquad (6)$$

3 Experimental Results and Analysis

During the experiments, set the triangular column side length a to 2 λ, the conductor-array distance l to 30 λ, the antenna array element spacing d to 0.5 λ, and the antenna array rotation angle θ to be within the range of 0 to 30°. The far filed is 530 λ away from the center of the antenna array.

When the array width is 10 λ, that is, when 21-unit line current sources are included, the far-field distribution calculated by MoM and FEM are shown in Fig. 2. Due to the need to observe the peak direction angle offset the irradiation direction angle, the electric field amplitude curve in Fig. 2 has been shifted moderately, so that $\varphi = 180°$ always indicates the direction of the array antenna. It can be seen from the figure that, the calculation results of the two methods are consistent, and both show the changing law of the far field distribution under different rotation angles.

When the conductor is directly in front of the array, the shielding effect is most significant. With the increase of the rotation angle, the field distribution gradually approaches the situation without shielding. At a certain rotation angle, the presence of conductor shielding even increases the peak value of the electric field amplitude.

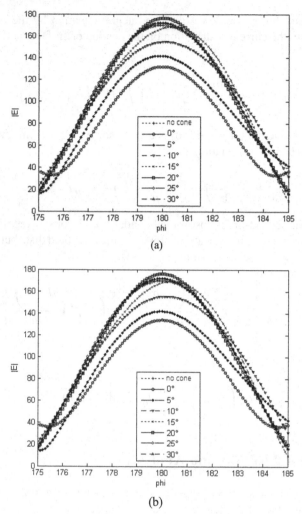

Fig. 2. The distribution of the antenna's far field varies with the rotation angle of the array. (a) MoM; (b) FEM.

When the array width is 10 λ and 15 λ, the offset results of the electric field peak value to the incident direction are shown in Fig. 3 and Fig. 4. It can be found from the figures that, when the array width is small, the influence of conductor shielding on the peak direction and amplitude is more obvious. In both array widths, the peak value is enlarged, which occurs when the rotation is 20° and 25°, respectively. When the maximum peak occurs, the peak direction is always close to the actual array direction.

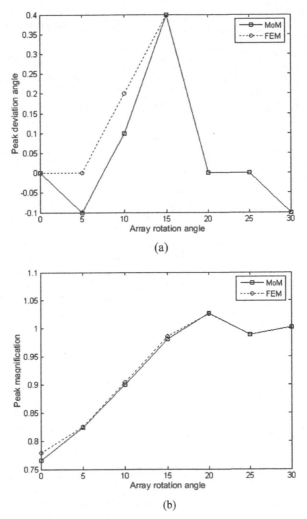

Fig. 3. Variation of far-field peak value with rotation angle, 21-element array. (a) Angle offset; (b) Amplitude change.

Replace the right straight line boundary of the triangular column conductor section in Fig. 1 with an arc boundary. The radius of the arc is 2λ. The center of the arc on the left side of the boundary represents the convex bottom of the nose cone, and the right side means the bottom is concave. The MoM is used to calculate the far-field distribution to analyze the influence of the bottom shape of the nose cone on the array radiation. During the calculation process, the array is not rotated, and the width is 10λ. The calculation result is shown in Fig. 5. It can be seen from Fig. 5 that, the shape of the bottom of the nose cone has little effect on the far-field distribution, indicating that the shape of the bottom of the nose cone is not the decisive factor on affecting the antenna radiation effect.

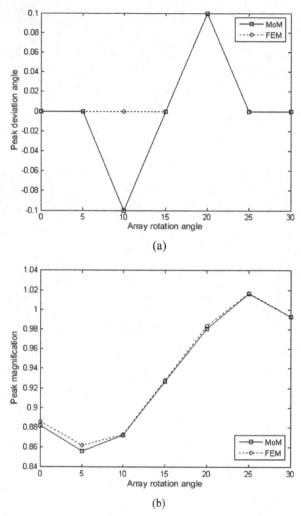

Fig. 4. Variation of far-field peak value with rotation angle, 31-element array. (a) Angle offset; (b) Amplitude change.

Set the side length a of the conductor cross-section in Fig. 1 to be in the range of 0.1λ–5λ, use an unrotated array with a width of 10λ to illuminate, and use the MoM to calculate the far-field distribution to investigate the influence of the size of the conductor target on the antenna radiation. The far-field distribution is shown in Fig. 6. The results in the figure show that the larger the nose cone size, the more significant the occlusion effect.

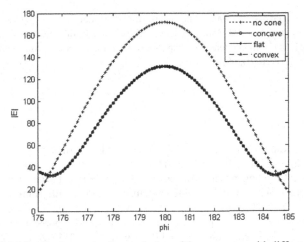

Fig. 5. The far-field distribution under the occlusion of the nose cone with different bottom shapes.

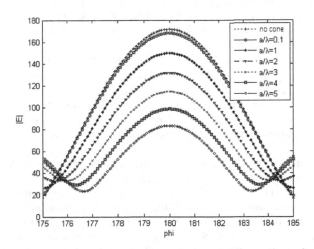

Fig. 6. The far-field distribution under the occlusion of different sizes of nose cones.

4 Conclusion

In this paper, the influence of the shielding of the conductor target in the near area of the antenna on the radiation characteristics of the antenna is studied. The MoM and the FEM methods are used to calculate the change law of the far field under different array widths. The experimental results show that, as the rotation angle of the antenna array changes, the conductor shielding has a significant impact on the far field strength and deviation angle, and even the radiation field strength is amplified. At the same time, the shape change of the conductor bottom has no obvious effect on the antenna radiation field, while the nose cone size has a significant effect on the antenna radiation field.

Acknowledgments. This work was supported by the National Natural Science Foundation of China under grant number 61901350, Aeronautical Science Foundation of China under grant number 2019ZH0T7001, and Science Research Foundation of Xi'an Aeronautical University under grant number 2019KY0208.

References

1. Crone, G.A.E., Rudge, A.W., Taylor, G.N.: Design and performance of airborne radomes: a review. IEEE Proc. **128**(7), 451–464 (1981)
2. Wang, C., et al.: Coupling model and electronic compensation of antenna-radome system for hypersonic vehicle with effect of high-temperature ablation. IEEE Trans. Antennas Propag. **68**(3), 2340–2355 (2020)
3. Qiang, Z.: Analysis of effects of pitot-tube on performance of airborne nose radome. In: 2009 3rd European Conference on Antennas and Propagation, pp. 3718–3719 (2009)
4. Meng, H., Dou, W.: Hybrid IPO-BI-FEM for the analysis of 2D large radome with complex structure. Microw. Opt. Technol. Lett. **51**(5), 1348–1353 (2009)
5. Rao, G.V.R.K., Mukherjee, J., Bhatta, R.K., Jahgirdar, D.R.: Design and development of tapered ceramic radome with metal tip. In: 2019 IEEE Indian Conference on Antennas and Propogation (InCAP), pp. 1–4 (2019)
6. Whalen, E., Gampala, G., Hunter, K., Mishra, S., Reddy, C.J.: Aircraft radome characterization via multiphysics simulation. In: 2018 AMTA Proceedings, Williamsburg, VA, pp. 1–4 (2018)
7. Sukharevsky, O.I., Vasilets, V.A., Nechitaylo, S.V., Ryapolov, I.E.: The radiation characteristics of antenna systems with a cone-sphere radome. In: 2017 IEEE First Ukraine Conference on Electrical and Computer Engineering (UKRCON), Kiev, pp. 106–109 (2017)
8. Balanis, C.A.: Advanced Engineering Electromagnetics. John Wiley & Sons, New York (1989)
9. Lu, C.C.: Calculation and Measurement of Electromagnetic Scattering. Beijing University of Aeronautics and Astronautics Press, Beijing (2006)
10. Zhang, L., Shi, X., Lu, Z.Y., Tong, M.S.: On the difference between the Nyström method and point-matching method. In: 2020 IEEE International Symposium on Antennas and Propagation and North American Radio Science Meeting, pp. 2037–2038 (2020)
11. Sukharevsky, O.I., Vasilets, V.A.: Scattering of MiG-29 antenna with dielectric radome. In: 2013 IX Internatioal Conference on Antenna Theory and Techniques, Odessa (2013)
12. Jin, J.M.: The Finite Element Method in Electromagnetics, 3rd edn. John Wiley & Sons, New York (2014)

Artificial Intelligence Application in Wireless Caching and Computing

Artificial Neural Network Assisted Mitigation of Cross-modulation Distortion in Microwave Photonics Link

Yihui Yin[1], Wanli Yang[1(✉)], Xu Yang[2], Yong Qin[1], and Hongtao Zhu[1]

[1] The 34th Research Institute of China Electronics Technology Group Corporation, Guilin 541004, China

[2] The 54th Research Institute of China Electronics Technology Group Corporation, Shijiazhuang 050081, China

Abstract. A multi-carrier down-conversion microwave photonics link (MDC-MWPL) is designed to deliver the broadband radio frequency (RF) signals with multiple frequency and down-conversion the RF signal to intermediate frequency (IF) signal, contributing to the wide bandwidth, low loss, strong immunity to electromagnetic interference property of microwave photonics link. However, the link performance is often degraded by the cross-modulation distortion (XMD). So, a kind of artificial neural network genetic algorithm (ANN-GA) distortion compensation technique is proposed to mitigate the XMD of the MDC-MWPL. The trained artificial neural network fits the input-to-output mapping of the link and predicts the link output. Taking the predicted output as the individual fitness value of the genetic algorithm, the optimal compensation factor γ is found. Taking advantage of the γ, the XMD is mitigated by extracted and reconstructed compensation signal, with a suppression ratio of -65 dB. Different from the traditional digital distortion compensation method, the proposed technique can realize distortion compensation for any kinds of links, which is not limited to a fixed microwave photonics link and its mathematical model, improving the intelligence and flexibility of microwave photonic link linearization design.

Keywords: Microwave photonics · Cross modulation distortion · Artificial neural network · Genetic algorithm

1 Introduction

As the RF bandwidth of communication and radar applications continues to grow, the transmission, processing, and reception of the ultra-broadband, multi-carrier RF signal are difficult to conducted by traditional electrical technology. The rapid development of photonic technology has made people realize that photonic technology will become a prospective analogue signal processing platform. Combining the microwave and photonics, contributing to its wide bandwidth, low loss, strong immunity to electromagnetic interference property, the microwave photonics technology addresses the

© ICST Institute for Computer Sciences, Social Informatics and Telecommunications Engineering 2021
Published by Springer Nature Switzerland AG 2021. All Rights Reserved
X. Wang et al. (Eds.): AICON 2021, LNICST 396, pp. 493–503, 2021.
https://doi.org/10.1007/978-3-030-90196-7_42

processing capabilities of the complex RF signals in conventional microwave systems. In recent years, significant progress has been made in the design of single carrier or multiple carrier RF Over Fiber link (ROF) and down-conversion microwave photonics link. To obtain the high sensitivity, large dynamic range link property, many kinds of linear techniques are proposed. Linearity in RF photonic links is frequently limited by the modulator response. In a conventional narrow-band link where the third-order inter modulation distortion (IMD3) dominates, the linearization has been demonstrated by several designs, such as cascaded or parallel electro-optic modulators [1, 2], in which, an MZM operating at the opposite slopes of the transfer functions, or a pair of parallel MZMs operating at opposite slopes of the transfer functions. In addition, electronic pre-distortion [3, 4], feed-forward compensation [5, 6], and post digital signal compensation [7, 8] are also important means. However, in a channelized RF photonic link, where the input RF signal is broadband with multiple frequency components, the link linearity is not only distorted by IMD3, but also impacted by cross-modulation distortion (XMD). In [9], the XMD is suppressed by pre-distortion. In [10], the XMD is mitigated through post-digital-distortion compensation. For the digital distortion compensation, the most of XMD suppression methods are based on the small signal model, which are failed when the modulation depth is deep.

Artificial intelligence microwave photonics technique is an emerging direction in microwave photonics. The Artificial Neural Networks (ANNS) originated in 1943, and has developed for more than half a century. The ANNS has made tremendous progress contributing to the ability of self-study, associate storage, high-speed search for the best solutions, and drawing arbitrarily complex nonlinear relationships. In recent years, the ANN has been applied in the field of optoelectronics to enhance the system performance [11–13]. A microwave photonics link is mathematically viewed as a nonlinear function with specifying the input output variables. Thus, by training the ANNS with input and output data of the microwave photonics link, the ANNS enables the fitting of the input-to-output nonlinear mapping of the microwave photonics link. Then, the trained ANNS can predict the output of the microwave photonics link with the given input.

Taking advantage of the traditional digital distortion compensation method, based on the artificial neural network genetic algorithm (ANN-GA), a kind of ANN-GA based distortion compensation technique is proposed for multi-carrier down-conversion microwave photonics link (MDC-MWPL). The link structure consists of a laser, modulators, a photodiode (PD), an analog digital converter (ADC) module, a digital signal process (DSP) module, and a ANN-GA module. In the ADC and DSP modules, compensation signal is extracted and reconstructed using the compensation factor γ. The γ is given by the ANN-GA module. In the ANN-GA module, the artificial neural networks learn and predict the input-to-output mapping of the link, and give a predicted output value as the fitness value of the genetic algorithm. Based on the fitness value, the genetic algorithm found the optimal compensation factor γ. Thus, extracted compensation signal is multiplied by the appropriate compensation factor γ, and fed back to the link to eliminate the XMD with a suppression ratio great than -65 dB.

2   Principle of the ANN-GA Distortion Compensation Technique

2.1   Principle of XMD Compensation for MDC-MWPL

The MDC-MWPL structure, shown in the Fig. 1(a), consists of a laser, two modulators (one for the modulation of broadband multi-carrier signals and the other for down-conversion the target carriers), a photoelectric detector, the ADC module, the DSP module, and the ANN-GA module. The broadband multi-radio carrier RF signals are modulated on the optical carrier in the modulator 1. The polarization controller is used to adjust the polarization state of the output optical carrier, keeping the polarization state of the light carrier into the modulator 1 to be consistent with the modulator spindle. The modulated output light signal is then modulated by a local oscillator (LO) signal in the modulator 2 operating at the orthogonal bias point to down-convert the RF signal to the IF signal. The IF signal is recovered by low-speed PD. The recovered signal is sampled by the ADC module and converted to digital signal. Within the digital domain, by using a narrow band digital filter, the signal is further divided into two sections, denoted by signal 1 (S_1) and 2 (S_2), respectively, and the two signals are used to construct a compensation signal to suppress the XMD. The DSP process is shown in Fig. 1(b).

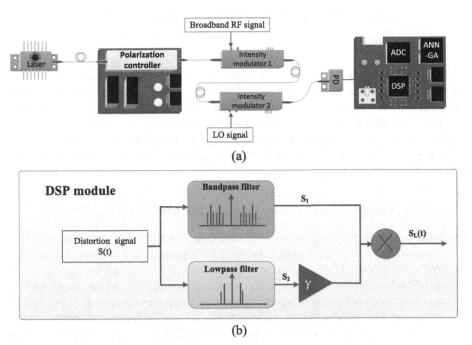

Fig. 1. (a) The multi-carrier down-conversion microwave photonics link, (b) the diagram of the DSP process for reconstructing the compensation signal.

To explain the XMD compensation mechanism, the compensation process is expressed by the mathematical form. Mathematically, the modulated broadband multi-carrier RF signal, denoted as $x(t)$, can be written as Eq. (1), which is expressed as a center frequency of ω_n with amplitude of $A_n(t)$ and the phase of $\phi_n(t)$.

$$x(t) = \sum_n A_n(t) \cos(\omega_n t + \phi_n(t)) \tag{1}$$

For an intensity modulation with direct detection link, nonlinear distortion information is represented by a transfer function that expanded in terms of the Tyler functions.

$$P(t) = a_0 + a_1 x(t) + a_2 [x(t)]^2 + a_3 [x(t)]^3 + ... \tag{2}$$

To convenient to extract the nonlinear signal for compensation, the expression of the recovered electrical signals after the PD is obtained by using the Eq. (2) with the Eq. (1), in which S_1 is the nonlinear distortion related to XMD, and S2 is the distortion term related to XMD and IMD3.

$$S(t) = S_1 + S_2 A_n(t) \cos(\omega_n t + \phi_n(t)) \tag{3}$$

The nonlinear signal for compensation is obtained as following:

$$S_c(t) = S_1 * S_2^\gamma \tag{4}$$

In Eq. (4), the compensation factor γ is introduced to eliminate the XMD. By obtaining the appropriate compensation factor γ, constructing the $S_c(t)$ to feedback to the link, the XMD will be mitigated. Instead of calculating the compensation factor γ by mathematical small signal model of the link, the γ is obtained by the ANN-GA. The ANN is trained to predict the input-to-output mapping of the link, and give a predicted output value as the fitness value. Based on the fitness value, the genetic algorithm found the optimal compensation factor γ.

2.2 Seeking Compensation Factor γ Based on the ANN-GA

The process of seeking compensation factor γ based on the ANN-GA is divided into two steps, as shown in Fig. 2. Step 1: training back propagation (BP) neural network and predict the output of the link, and Step 2: seeking the γ value and the corresponding minimal XMD suppression ratio value by genetic algorithm. We do not need to derive the exact function relationship of input-output of the microwave photon link, but instead of training the BP neural network with a certain amount of input and output data of the link. Then, the trained BP neural network can predict the output of the microwave photon link according to the fitted input-to-output mapping. Use the predicted results as individual fitness values of the genetic algorithm. With the selection, the crossover and the mutation operations, the global optimal value of the XMD suppression ratio and the corresponding γ are found.

Obviously, the compensation factor γ is one of the key factor that determines the suppression ratio. In addition, another impotent impact factor is the modulator bias point. So, the compensation factor and the modulator bias point are identified as the two input variables for the link, and the XMD suppression ratio as the output. The predicted output accuracy of the neural network is key to the ability of the genetic algorithm to find the optimal XMD suppression ratio, the corresponding compensation factors and the modulator bias point. The learning capabilities of the BP neural network is closely related to its structure. Because, the memory capacity of the network, the speed of training, and the amount of response depend on the structure, which corresponds to the number of hidden layers and nodes. According to the Kolmogorov theory, a continuous function $F(x)$ in the closed intervals, can be precisely implemented with a three-layer neural network. Where the number of nodes in the input layer is M, the number of nodes in the hidden layer is $K = 2M + 1$, and the number of nodes in the output layer is N. Here we select the compensation factor and the modulator bias point as the input (M = 2, K = 5), and the XMD suppression ratio as the output (N = 1). The neural network structure is '2-5-1' type, as shown in Fig. 3.

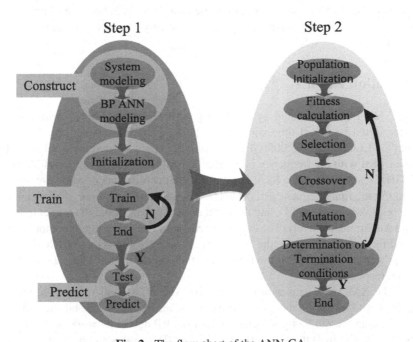

Fig. 2. The flow chart of the ANN-GA

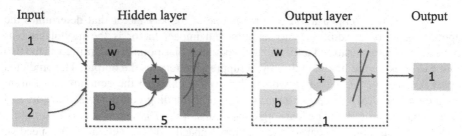

Fig. 3. The structure of the neural network

Basic operations of the genetic algorithm include the selection, the crossover, and the mutation. In the selection, the individuals which are more suited to the environment are selected to multiply the next generation from a group. The amount of reproduction is determined according to the individual's fitness to the environment. The individual fitness value comes from the predicted value of the BP neural network. And the smaller the fitness value, the better the individual. The individual in the genetic algorithm is encoded as a real number, and the length of the individual is 2, because of only 2 input parameters for the optimization function. The probability of crossover and mutation are set as needed.

3 Simulation Results

The MDC-MWPL is simulated by MATLAB with the model shown as in Fig. 1(a). the carrier signal is a dual tone signal with the frequency interval of 5 MHz, at the frequency of 15 GHz and 15.005 GHz, respectively. The selected crosstalk signal is a dual tone signal with the frequency interval of 1.5 MHz, at the frequency of 3 GHz and 3.0015 GHz, respectively. The local oscillator signal is introduced to down-convert the carrier to the medium frequency of 80 MHz. The switching voltage of modulator, the effective responsivity of the PD, and the input optical power of the PD are set to 6 V, 0.9 A/W, and 5 dBm, respectively. The output spectrum of the link without compensation is shown in Fig. 4. As we can see, the IF signals are seriously interfered by XMD signals with the power of −63 dBm, at the frequency of 73.5 MHz, 76.5 MHz, 78.5 MHz and 81.5 HMz, respectively.

Then, the XMD compensation based on the ANN-GA is also simulated using the MATLAB. A total of 2500 sets of input and output data of the link are taken, from which 2250 sets of data are randomly selected to train the BP neural network, and 250 sets of data are used to test the fitting performance of the BP neural network. The comparison results of BP neural network prediction output and expected output are shown in the Fig. 5(a). then the error percentage of prediction κ is calculated by:

$$\kappa = (XMD_{pre} - XMD_{exp})/XMD_{exp} \tag{5}$$

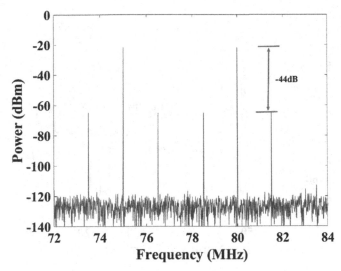

Fig. 4. The output spectrum of the link without compensation

XMD$_{pre}$ and XMD$_{exp}$ are prediction and expectation value of the XMD suppression ratio, respectively. From the error percentage of the prediction results, the ANN can accurately predict the output of the link. So, the predicted output can be approximately regarded as the actual output of the link.

After the BP neural work training, the genetic algorithm is used to find the compensation factor γ and the minimum value of the XMD suppression ratio. The iteration number, the population size, the crossover and the mutation probability are set to 100, 20, 0.4 and 0.2, respectively. The evolution curve of the optimal individual fitness value in the optimization process is shown in the Fig. 6(a). From the evolution curve, the fitness value of the optimal individual and the corresponding optimal individual are −65 and [0.15, 2.6], respectively. When the phase bias point and the compensation factor are 0.15rad and 2.6, respectively, the corresponding XMD suppression ratio is −65 dB. As shown in Fig. 6(b), after compensation, the power of XMD is reduced from −63 dBm to −86 dBm, which exhibits the excellent XMD mitigation performance of the proposed technique.

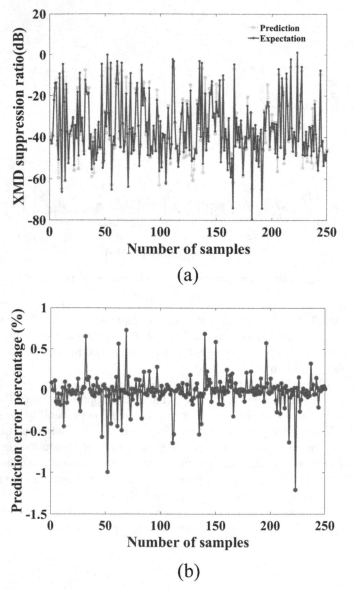

(a)

(b)

Fig. 5. The prediction of the trained ANN versus the number of samples, (a) the comparison of prediction and expectation values of XMD suppression ratio (link output), (b) the error percentage of prediction.

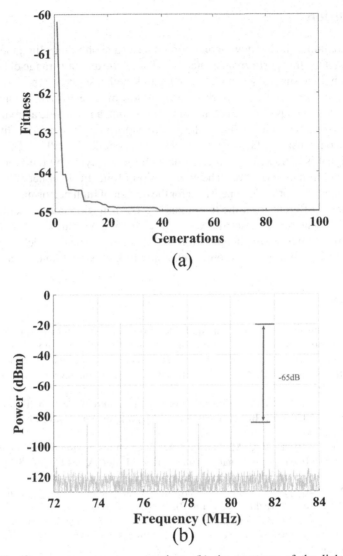

Fig. 6. (a) The fitness curve versus generations, (b) the spectrum of the link after XMD compensation by using the ANN-GA.

4 Conclusion

In broadband, multi-carrier, down-conversion microwave photonics link, the XMD will seriously affect the link performance, such as reducing the dynamic range of the link. The proposed technique suppresses the XMD of the link with a suppression ratio of −65 dB, based on the artificial neural network genetic algorithm. The artificial neural networks learn and predict the input-to-output mapping of the link, and provide a predicted output value as the individual fitness value of the genetic algorithm. Based on the fitness value, the optimal compensation factor γ is found by the genetic algorithm. Then, the compensation signal is extracted, and reconstructed by multiplying by the γ, and fed back to the link to eliminate the XMD. The combination of the artificial neural network and microwave photonics provides a new idea for the design of high performance microwave photonics link. Different from the traditional digital distortion compensation, the proposed technique can realize distortion compensation for any kinds of links, which is not limited to a fixed microwave photonics link and its mathematical model, improving the intelligence and flexibility of microwave photonic link linearization design.

References

1. Skeie, H., Johnson, R.V.: Linearization of electro-optic modulators by a cascade coupling of phase modulating electrodes. In: Proceedings of the SPIE, vol. 1583, pp. 153–164 (1991)
2. Brooks, J.L., Maurer, G.S., Becker, R.A.: Implementation and evaluation of a dual parallel linearization system for AM-SCM video transmission. J. Lightwave Technol. **11**(1), 34–41 (1993)
3. Magoon, V., Jalali, B.: Electronic linearization and bias control for externally modulated fiber optic link. In: 2020 IEEE International Topical Meeting on Microwave Photonics, pp. 145–147. IEEE (2000)
4. Childs, R.B., O'Byrne, V.A.: Multichannel AM video transmission using a high-power Nd: YAG laser and linearized external modulator. IEEE J. Sel. Areas Comm. **8**(7), 1369–1376 (1990)
5. Haas, B.M., Murphy, T.E.: A simple, linearized, phase-modulated analog optical transmission system. IEEE Photon. Technol. Lett. **19**(10), 729–731 (2007)
6. Masella, B., Hraimel, B., Zhang, X.: Enhanced spurious-free dynamic range using mixed polarization in optical single sideband mach-zehnder modulator. J. Lightwave Technol. **27**(15), 3034–3041 (2009)
7. Lv, Q., Xu, K., Dai, Y., Li, Y., Wu, J., Lin, J.: I/Q intensity-demodulation analog photonic link based on polarization modulator. Opt. Lett. **36**(23), 4602–4604 (2011)
8. Clark, T.R., Dennis, M.L.: Coherent opticalphase modulation link. IEEE Photon. Technol. Lett. **19**(16), 1206–1208 (2007)
9. Agarwal, A., Banwell, T., Toliver, P., Woodward, T.K.: Predistortion compensation of nonlinearities in channelized RF photonic links using a dual-port optical modulator. IEEE Photon. Technol. Lett. **23**(1), 24–26 (2011)
10. Banwell, T., Agarwal, A., Toliver, P., Woodward, T.K.: Compensation of cross-gain modulation in filtered multi-channel optical signal processing applications. In: 2010 Optical Fiber Communication Conference, pp. OWW5. IEEE (2010)
11. Zou, X., Xu, S., Li, S., Chen, J., Zou, W.: Optimization of the brillouin instantaneous frequency measurement using convolutional neural networks. Opt. Lett. **44**(23), 5723–5726 (2019)

12. Ye, H., Li, G.Y., Juang, B.H.: Power of deep learning for channel estimation and signal detection in OFDM. IEEE Wirel. Commun. Lett. **7**(1), 114–117 (2018)
13. Khan, F.N., Fan, Q., Lu, C., Lau, A.P.T.: An optical communication's perspective on machine learning and its applications. J. Lightwave Technol. **37**(2), 493–516 (2019)

Analysis of Optimal Gain of MPSK Signal Based on BSR

ZhiChong Shen[✉], JinQuan Ma, Di Yang, and XiaoLong Shen

Information System Engineering College, Information Engineering University, ZhengZhou, China

Abstract. Bistable Stochastic Resonance (BSR) system is a nonlinear system. When the noise variance of the noisy periodic signal has a certain relationship with the signal, after the noisy signal passes through the system, the noise energy can be partially converted to the signal energy, thus providing a means of signal enhancement. Later, with the introduction of the Aperiodic Stochastic Resonance (ASR) system theory, the stochastic resonance theory can be applied to the field of communication. At present, the most application of stochastic resonance in communication is in binary modulation signal area. This paper will be discussing the enhanced effect of stochastic resonance on the multi-ary phase modulation signal, deriving the expression of the MPSK signal power after resonance, and proving that the signal power spectral density after stochastic resonance has no effect on phase. Defining the signal-to-noise ratio's gain and amplitude's gain, and giving the range of the gain and the maximum value of the gain that stochastic resonance can improve the signal-to-noise ratio when the signal amplitude and signal carrier frequency are determined.

Keywords: Stochastic resonance · Signal processing · Bistable system

1 Introduction

As one of the commonly used digital modulation signals, the phase modulation signal has always been widely concerned in the communication field. In recent years, attention to detecting PSK signals has begun to enter the field of low signal-to-noise ratio. As a method of using noise energy to achieve signal enhancement, stochastic resonance has naturally attracted widespread attention [1,2]. In 2014, Liu Jin studied the enhancement effect of stochastic resonance on the BPAM signal and gave the corresponding enhancement model [3]. In the same year, Liu Jin again extended the enhancement model to FSK signals [4], and again in 2015 to MPAM signals [5]. In 2018, Zhang Zheng proposed a PSK signal symbol rate estimation method based on stochastic resonance [6]. The following year, Zhang Zheng introduced an artificial fish swarm algorithm to realize the application of stochastic resonance in the detection of a variety of digital modulation signals [7]. In the same year, Linlin Liang et al. studied the

X. Wang et al. (Eds.): AICON 2021, LNICST 396, pp. 504–514, 2021.
https://doi.org/10.1007/978-3-030-90196-7_43

application of stochastic resonance in 4PAM signal detection [8]. However, for MPSK signals, the discussion of stochastic resonance is mainly concentrated in the field of computer algorithms, and there are still few discussions on theoretical models.

In order to explore the common points of different types of PSK signals after stochastic resonance, this paper takes the signal power as the starting point, and through derivation, gives the expression of the power spectral density of the MPSK signal after the stochastic resonance of the bistable system, and proves the PSK signal The phase change of ϕ will not affect the power spectral density, thus simplifying the influence of stochastic resonance on the signal. Then, define the signal-to-noise ratio gain and give its expression, calculate the range of the signal-to-noise ratio when stochastic resonance obtains the gain, and prove that there is a maximum gain, which provides an idea for processing unknown low-signal-to-noise ratio signals.

2   MPSK Parameter Calculation Based on Bistable System

2.1   Power Spectral Density

Suppose the model of the signal is $s(t) = Ag_t(t)\cos(2\pi f_c t + 2\pi(m-1)/M)$, where A is the signal amplitude, $g_t(t)$ is the signal pulse shape, f_c is the signal carrier frequency, $2\pi(m-1)/M$ is the M phases of the signal. The probability that the output signal of the bistable system will transition to the steady-state point of the signal at time t is respectively $m_{\pm}(t)$. and the probability within the two potential wells satisfies

$$m_+(t) = 1 - m_-(t) = \int_{x_0}^{+\infty} p(x)dx \tag{1}$$

Considering the driving force of the periodic signal, due to the periodic driving of the periodic signal, the transfer rate $R_{\pm}(t)$ of the bistable system output signal between the discrete steady states of the two potential wells is also periodic in time, and satisfies The relationship is as follows:

$$\frac{dm_+(t)}{dt} = -\frac{dm_-(t)}{dt} = R_-(t) - [R_+(t) + R_-(t)]m_+(t) \tag{2}$$

The solution to linear first-order differential equation (2) is given by:

$$\begin{cases} m_+(t) = g^{-1}(t)m_+(t_0)g(t_0) + g^{-1}(t)\int_{t_0}^{t} R_-(\tau)g(\tau)d\tau \\ g(t) = e^{\int_{t_0}^{t} [R_+(\tau)+R_-(\tau)]d\tau} \end{cases} \tag{3}$$

Assume that $R_{\pm}(t) = f(\lambda \pm \varphi_0 \cos(\omega_c t + 2\pi(m-1)/M))$ Where f is an exponential function, λ, φ_0 are dimensionless constants, $\omega_c = 2\pi/T = 2\pi f_c$, $M = 2^k$,

$k \in N^+$, $m = \{1, 2, \cdots, M\}$. Although $\varphi_0 \cos(\omega_c t + 2\pi(m-1)/M)$ have discontinuous points in $(-\infty, \infty)$, it is a continuous function in one period. So we can use Taylor expansion for $R_\pm(t)$ in one period, then we have

$$R_\pm(t) = \frac{1}{2}(\alpha_0 \mp \alpha_1\varphi_0 \cos(\omega_c t + \theta) + \alpha_1\varphi_0^2\cos^2(\omega_c t + \theta) \mp \cdots) \tag{4}$$

$$R_+(t) + R_-(t) = \alpha_0 + \alpha_1\varphi_0^2\cos^2(\omega_c t + \theta) + \cdots) \tag{5}$$

where $\frac{1}{2}\alpha_0 = f(\lambda)$, $\frac{1}{2}\alpha_n = \frac{(-1)^n}{n!}\left(\frac{d}{d\varphi}\right)^n f(\lambda)$. Substituting Eqs. (4) and (5) into Eq. (3), the asymptotic analytical solution of the probability $m_+(t)$ that the output signal of the system is in the steady-state position of the potential well is obtained:

$$m_+(t|x_0, t_0) = \frac{1}{2}e^{-\alpha_0(t-t_0)}\left(2\delta_{x_0c} - 1 - \frac{\alpha_1\varphi_0 \cos(\omega_c t + \theta - \phi)}{\sqrt{\alpha_0^2 + \omega_c^2}}\right)$$
$$+\frac{1}{2}\left(1 + \frac{\alpha_1\varphi_0 \cos(\omega_c t + \theta - \phi)}{\sqrt{\alpha_0^2 + \omega_c^2}}\right) \tag{6}$$

where $\phi = \arctan\frac{\omega_c}{\alpha_0}$, $\delta_{x_0c} = \begin{cases} 1, c = +\sqrt{a/b} \\ 0, c = -\sqrt{a/b} \end{cases}$.

According to Eq. (6), it can be calculated:

$$\langle x(t)x(t+\tau)\rangle = c^2 e^{-\alpha_0|\tau|}\left(1 - \frac{\alpha_1^2\varphi_0^2\cos^2(\omega_c t + \theta - \phi)}{\alpha_0^2 + \omega_c^2}\right)$$
$$+\frac{c^2\alpha_1^2\varphi_0^2\{\cos(\omega_c\tau) + \cos^2[\omega_c(2t + 2\theta + \tau) + 2\phi]\}}{2(\alpha_0^2 + \omega_c^2)} \tag{7}$$

Further calculations to get the average autocorrelation:

$$\langle\langle x(t)x(t+\tau)\rangle\rangle_t$$
$$= \frac{\omega_c}{2\pi}\int_0^{\frac{2\pi}{\omega_c}}\left[\begin{array}{c} c^2 e^{-\alpha_0|\tau|}\left(1 - \frac{\alpha_1^2\varphi_0^2\cos^2(\omega_c t + \theta - \phi)}{\alpha_0^2 + \omega_c^2}\right) \\ +\frac{c^2\alpha_1^2\varphi_0^2\{\cos(\omega_c\tau) + \cos^2[\omega_c(2t + 2\theta + \tau) + 2\phi]\}}{2(\alpha_0^2 + \omega_c^2)}\end{array}\right]dt \tag{8}$$
$$= \frac{\omega_c}{2\pi}\int_0^{\frac{2\pi}{\omega_c}}[f_1(t) + f_2(t) + f_3(t)]dt$$

where

$$f_1(t) = c^2 e^{-\alpha_0|\tau|} + \frac{c^2\alpha_1^2\varphi_0^2 \cos(\omega_c\tau)}{2(\alpha_0^2 + \omega_c^2)} \tag{9}$$

$$f_2(t) = \frac{c^2 e^{-\alpha_0|\tau|}\alpha_1^2\varphi_0^2\cos^2(\omega_c t + \theta - \phi)}{\alpha_0^2 + \omega_c^2} \tag{10}$$

$$f_3(t) = \frac{c^2\alpha_1^2\varphi_0^2\cos^2[\omega_c(2t + 2\theta + \tau) + 2\phi]}{2(\alpha_0^2 + \omega_c^2)} \tag{11}$$

Because of

$$\frac{\omega_c}{2\pi}\int_0^{\frac{2\pi}{\omega_c}} f_2(t)dt$$
$$= \frac{\omega_c}{2\pi}\int_0^{\frac{2\pi}{\omega_c}} \frac{c^2 e^{-\alpha_0|\tau|}\alpha_1^2\varphi_0^2\cos^2(\omega_c t + \theta - \phi)}{\alpha_0^2 + \omega_c^2} dt$$
$$= -\frac{\omega_c c^2 e^{-\alpha_0|\tau|}\alpha_1^2\varphi_0^2}{2\pi(\alpha_0^2 + \omega_c^2)}\left(\frac{t + \theta - \phi}{2} + \frac{\sin[2(\omega_c t + \theta - \phi)]}{4\omega_c}\right)\Big|_0^{\frac{2\pi}{\omega_c}} \tag{12}$$
$$= -\frac{c^2 e^{-\alpha_0|\tau|}\alpha_1^2\varphi_0^2}{2(\alpha_0^2 + \omega_c^2)}$$

$$\frac{\omega_c}{2\pi} \int_0^{\frac{2\pi}{\omega_c}} f_3(t) dt$$

$$= \frac{\omega_c}{2\pi} \int_0^{\frac{2\pi}{\omega_c}} \frac{c^2 \alpha_1^2 \varphi_0^2 \cos^2[\omega_c(2t+2\theta+\tau)+2\phi]}{2(\alpha_0^2+\omega_c^2)} dt \qquad (13)$$

$$= \frac{c^2 \alpha_1^2 \varphi_0^2 \cos[\omega_c(2t+2\theta+\tau)+2\phi]}{8\pi(\alpha_0^2+\omega_c^2)} \Big|_0^{\frac{2\pi}{\omega_c}} = 0$$

so

$$\langle\langle x(t)x(t+\tau)\rangle\rangle_t$$
$$= \frac{\omega_c}{2\pi} \int_0^{\frac{2\pi}{\omega_c}} [f_1(t) + f_2(t) + f_3(t)] dt \qquad (14)$$
$$= c^2 e^{-\alpha_0|\tau|} \left(1 - \frac{\alpha_1^2 \varphi_0^2}{2(\alpha_0^2+\omega_c^2)}\right) + \frac{c^2 \alpha_1^2 \varphi_0^2 \cos(\omega_c \tau)}{2(\alpha_0^2+\omega_c^2)}$$

From Eq. (14), we can get the bilateral power spectral density of the output signal:

$$\langle S(\omega)\rangle_t = \int_{-\infty}^{+\infty} \langle\langle x(t)x(t+\tau)\rangle\rangle_t e^{-j\omega\tau} d\tau$$
$$= \left(1 - \frac{\alpha_1^2 \varphi_0^2}{2(\alpha_0^2+\omega_c^2)}\right) \left(\frac{2c^2\alpha_0}{\alpha_0^2+\omega^2}\right) + \frac{\pi c^2 \alpha_1^2 \varphi_0^2}{2(\alpha_0^2+\omega_c^2)}[\delta(\omega-\omega_c)+\delta(\omega+\omega_c)] \qquad (15)$$

Then the unilateral power spectral density is:

$$S(\omega) = \left(1 - \frac{\alpha_1^2 \varphi_0^2}{2(\alpha_0^2 + \omega_c^2)}\right) \left(\frac{4c^2\alpha_0}{\alpha_0^2+\omega^2}\right) + \frac{\pi c^2 \alpha_1^2 \varphi_0^2}{\alpha_0^2+\omega_c^2}\delta(\omega-\omega_c) \qquad (16)$$

Where the signal component is $S_s(\omega) = \frac{\pi c^2 \alpha_1^2 \varphi_0^2}{\alpha_0^2+\omega_c^2}\delta(\omega-\omega_c)$, the noise component is $S_n(\omega) = \left(1 - \frac{\alpha_1^2 \varphi_0^2}{2(\alpha_0^2+\omega_c^2)}\right) \left(\frac{4c^2\alpha_0}{\alpha_0^2+\omega^2}\right)$.

It can be seen from Eq. (6) and (16) that the change of the phase component θ in $R_\pm(t)$ has no effect on the power spectral density $S(\omega)$, so the expressions for any θ and $S(\omega)$ remain unchanged, means that for any MPSK signal, the signal power spectrum expression is unique.

2.2 Gain of Signal-to-Noise Ratio

The bistable system model can be expressed as $\frac{dx}{dt} = ax + bx^3 + A\cos(\omega_c t + \theta) + \sqrt{D}n(t)$, where $n(t)$ is AWGN and satisfied $\langle n(t)\rangle = 0$, $\langle n(t)n(t+\tau)\rangle = \delta(\tau)$, D is the variance. According to the literature [1], Eq. (10) can be calculated as:

$$S(\omega) = \left(1 - \frac{\frac{4a^3 A^2}{b\pi^2 D^2}e^{-\frac{a^2}{bD}}}{\frac{2a^2}{\pi^2}e^{-\frac{a^2}{bD}}+\omega_c^2}\right) \left(\frac{\frac{4\sqrt{2}a^2}{b\pi}e^{-\frac{a^2}{2bD}}}{\frac{2a^2}{\pi^2}e^{-\frac{a^2}{bD}}+\omega^2}\right) + \left(\frac{\frac{8a^4 A^2}{b^2\pi D^2}e^{-\frac{a^2}{bD}}}{\frac{2a^2}{\pi^2}e^{-\frac{a^2}{bD}}+\omega_c^2}\right)\delta(\omega-\omega_c) \qquad (17)$$

Where

$$S_s(\omega) = \left(\frac{\frac{8a^4 A^2}{b^2\pi D^2}e^{-\frac{a^2}{bD}}}{\frac{2a^2}{\pi^2}e^{-\frac{a^2}{bD}}+\omega_c^2}\right)\delta(\omega-\omega_c) \qquad (18)$$

and

$$S_n(\omega) = \left(1 - \frac{\frac{4a^3 A^2}{b\pi^2 D^2}e^{-\frac{a^2}{bD}}}{\frac{2a^2}{\pi^2}e^{-\frac{a^2}{bD}}+\omega_c^2}\right) \left(\frac{\frac{4\sqrt{2}a^2}{b\pi}e^{-\frac{a^2}{2bD}}}{\frac{2a^2}{\pi^2}e^{-\frac{a^2}{bD}}+\omega^2}\right) \qquad (19)$$

Obviously $S_s(\omega) > 0$ and $S_n(\omega) > 0$, so $1 - \dfrac{\frac{4a^3A^2}{b\pi^2D^2}e^{-\frac{a^2}{bD}}}{\frac{2a^2}{\pi^2}e^{-\frac{a^2}{bD}}+\omega_c^2} > 0$, substitute $\omega_c = 2\pi f_c$ to get:

$$f_c > \frac{a}{\sqrt{2\pi^2}}e^{-\frac{a^2}{2bD}}\sqrt{\frac{2aA^2}{bD^2}-1} \tag{20}$$

Therefore, when the signal carrier frequency f_c meets the conditions described in Eq. (20), the input signal can trigger stochastic resonance.

According to Eq. (17), the average power of the signal after system enhancement can be obtained as:

$$P_{S_s(\omega),out} = \frac{1}{2\pi}\int_0^{+\infty} S_s(\omega)d\omega = \frac{\frac{4a^4A^2}{b^2\pi^2D^2}e^{-\frac{a^2}{bD}}}{\frac{2a^2}{\pi^2}e^{-\frac{a^2}{bD}}+\omega_c^2} \tag{21}$$

$$P_{S_n(\omega),out} = \frac{1}{2\pi}\int_0^{+\infty} S_\xi(\omega)d\omega = \frac{a}{b} - \frac{\frac{4a^4A^2}{b^2\pi^2D^2}e^{-\frac{a^2}{bD}}}{\frac{2a^2}{\pi^2}e^{-\frac{a^2}{bD}}+\omega_c^2} \tag{22}$$

Then the output signal-to-noise ratio is:

$$SNR_{out} = 10\lg\frac{P_{S_s(\omega),out}}{P_{S_\xi(\omega),out}} = 10\lg\frac{\frac{4a^3A^2}{b\pi^2D^2}e^{-\frac{a^2}{bD}}}{\frac{2a^2}{\pi^2}e^{-\frac{a^2}{bD}}\left(1-\frac{2aA^2}{bD^2}\right)+\omega_c^2} \tag{23}$$

Define the signal-to-noise ratio gain $Gain = SNR_{out} - SNR_{in}$, from the MPSK signal model we know that the input signal-to-noise ratio is $SNR_{in} = 10\lg\frac{A^2}{2D}$, then we have

$$Gain = 10\lg\frac{\frac{8a^3}{b\pi^2D}e^{-\frac{a^2}{bD}}}{\frac{2a^2}{\pi^2}e^{-\frac{a^2}{bD}}\left(1-\frac{2aA^2}{bD^2}\right)+\omega_c^2} = 10\lg G \tag{24}$$

When $G > 1$, we have

$$\frac{2a^2}{b\pi^2}(4aD - bD^2 + 2aA^2) - \omega_c^2D^2e^{\frac{a^2}{bD}} = G_1 - G_2 > 0 \tag{25}$$

Notice that $\frac{\partial G_2}{\partial D} = \omega_c^2(2D - \frac{a^2}{b})e^{\frac{a^2}{bD}}$, when $\frac{\partial G_2}{\partial D} = 0$ we have $D = \frac{a^2}{2b}$, then $G_{2\min} = \frac{a^4\omega_c^2e^2}{4b^2}$.

When $D > \frac{a^2}{2b}$, expand $\omega_c^2D^2e^{\frac{a^2}{bD}}$ to $\omega_c^2D^2(1 + \frac{a^2}{bD} + \frac{a^4}{2b^2D^2})$, the formula (25) is transformed into

$$\frac{2a^2}{b\pi^2}(4aD - bD^2 + 2aA^2) - \omega_c^2D^2(1 + \frac{a^2}{bD} + \frac{a^4}{2b^2D^2}) > 0 \tag{26}$$

then

$$D < \frac{\frac{8a^3}{b} - \frac{a^2\pi^2\omega_c^2}{b} + \pi^2\sqrt{\left(\frac{8a^3}{b\pi^2} - \frac{a^2\omega_c^2}{b}\right)^2 + 4\left(\frac{2a^2}{\pi^2} + \omega_c^2\right)\left(\frac{4a^3A^2}{b\pi^2} - \frac{1}{2}a^4b^2\omega_c^2\right)}}{2\left(2a^2 + \pi^2\omega_c^2\right)} = D_{\max}$$

(27)

When $0 < D < \frac{a^2}{2b}$, multiply both sides of formula (25) by D^2 and expand $\omega_c^2 D^2 e^{\frac{a^2}{bD}}$ to $\omega_c^2 D^2 (1 + \frac{a^2}{bD} + \frac{a^4}{2b^2D^2} + \frac{a^6}{6b^3D^3} + \frac{a^8}{24b^4D^4})$, the formula (25) is transformed into

$$\frac{2a^2}{b\pi^2}D^2(4aD - bD^2 + 2aA^2) - \omega_c^2 D^4(1 + \frac{a^2}{bD} + \frac{a^4}{2b^2D^2} + \frac{a^6}{6b^3D^3} + \frac{a^8}{24b^4D^4}) > 0 \quad (28)$$

then $D_{\min}$ can be calculated.

Finally we get the variance range when stochastic resonance has positive gain, and the signal-to-noise ratio range of the input signal is

$$10\lg\frac{A^2}{2D_{\max}} < SNR_{in} < 10\lg\frac{A^2}{2D_{\min}} \quad (29)$$

When the signal-to-noise ratio of the input signal is within the range described in formula (29), stochastic resonance can achieve the effect of enhancing the signal.

3   Simulations

3.1   Amplitude Enhancement Effect

First, we observe the signal waveform when the signal-to-noise ratio is different when the amplitude and carrier frequency of the input signal are constant. Verify that when the signal amplitude and signal carrier frequency are determined, when the signal-to-noise ratio is within a given range, stochastic resonance can produce an amplitude enhancement effect.

Take the QPSK signal as an example, set the bistable parameters as $a = 1$, $b = 1$, and the signal amplitude $A = 0.5$. Then, when the signal-to-noise ratio gain is greater than 1, the noise variance can be solved by Eqs. (27) and (28) and the range is $0.1543 < D < 2.9022$, so the input signal SNR range is -13.6582 dB $< SNR_{in} < -0.9146$ dB. Set the signal-to-noise ratio $SNR_{in} = -5$ dB, and the noise variance is 0.3953, which meets the requirements. Set the signal carrier frequency $f_c = 0.0318$ Hz, then $f_c > 0.03$ Hz conforms to the range described in formula (20). Number of symbols $N = 5$, symbol rate $R_s = 0.01$ bps.

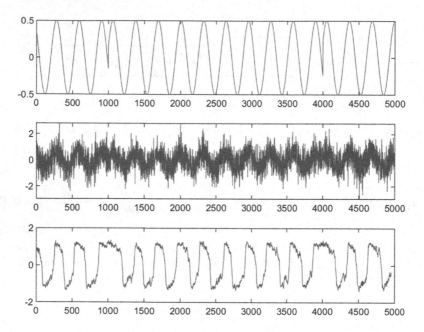

Fig. 1. QPSK signal waveform before and after stochastic resonance

As shown in Fig. 1, the first column of Fig. 1 is the noise-free QPSK signal waveform, the second column is the noise-added QPSK signal waveform, and the third column is the QPSK signal waveform after resonance.

According to formula (18), we can assume that the unilateral power spectral density of a certain signal $s_h(t)$ is equal to formula (18), then

$$s_h(t) = \frac{\frac{2\sqrt{2}a^2 A}{b\pi D}e^{-\frac{a^2}{2bD}}}{\sqrt{\frac{2a^2}{\pi^2}e^{-\frac{a^2}{bD}} + \omega_c^2}} \cos(\omega_c t + \theta) \tag{30}$$

can be obtained, and the amplitude gain is defined as

$$G_{Amplitude} = \frac{A_{s_h}}{A_{s_s}} = \frac{\frac{2\sqrt{2}a^2}{b\pi D}e^{-\frac{a^2}{2bD}}}{\sqrt{\frac{2a^2}{\pi^2}e^{-\frac{a^2}{bD}} + \omega_c^2}} \tag{31}$$

according to the aforementioned QPSK signal parameters, we can calculate $G_{Amplitude} = 2.2828$, which is consistent with the experimental results. It shows that after stochastic resonance, noise energy is successfully converted into signal energy, which shows the effectiveness of stochastic resonance.

Similarly, for 8PSK signals, set the signal-to-noise ratio $SNR_{in} = -5\,\text{dB}$ and the signal carrier frequency $f_c = 0.0318\,\text{Hz}$. Number of symbols $N = 10$, symbol rate $R_s = 0.01\,\text{bps}$ (Fig. 2).

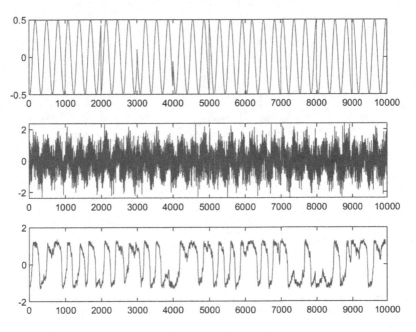

Fig. 2. 8PSK signal waveform before and after stochastic resonance

It can be seen that after stochastic resonance, for QPSK and 8PSK signals, the noise energy is successfully transferred to the signal energy, which illustrates the effectiveness of stochastic resonance for MPSK signals.

3.2 Signal-to-Noise Ratio Gain Gurve

Now we examine the signal-to-noise ratio and signal-to-noise ratio gain of the output signal when the signal-to-noise ratio of the input signal changes.

Take the QPSK signal as an example, set the variance D from 0.1 to 1.3, the signal carrier frequency $f_c = 0.04\,\text{Hz}$, and the other parameters remain unchanged.

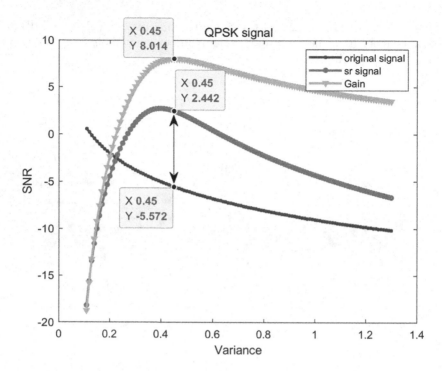

Fig. 3. Input, output signal-to-noise ratio and gain curve of QPSK signal

It can be seen from Fig. 3 that when the variance $D = 0.45$, the difference of the signal-to-noise ratio before and after the signal resonance is the largest, which is 8.0140 dB. System parameters, signal amplitude and carrier frequency, signal-to-noise ratio gain have maximum values.

For different PSK signals, observe the changes in the signal-to-noise ratio before and after the signal resonance when the variance changes. Set the BPSK, QPSK, and 8PSK signals with the same signal parameters. The parameters are: the number of symbols $N = 500$, the signal amplitude $A = 0.5$, the carrier frequency $f_c = 0.04$ Hz, and the symbol rate $R_s = 0.01$ bps. Set the input signal-to-noise ratio SNR_{in} to increase from -12 dB to 0 dB, perform 500 Monte Carlo experiments and take the average value of the signal-to-noise ratio gain. The experimental results are as Fig. 4 follows.

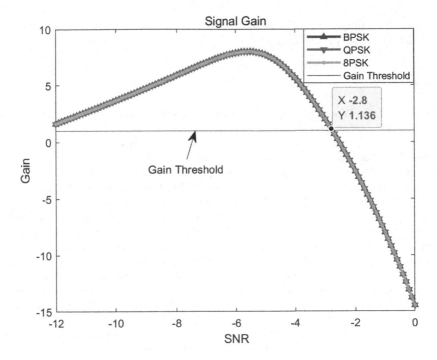

Fig. 4. BPSK, QPSK, 8PSK signal-to-noise ratio gain curve

As shown in Fig. 4, the purple solid line is the gain threshold $G = 1$. When $G > 1$, $SNR_{out} - SNR_{in} > 0$, that is, the output signal-to-noise ratio is higher than the input signal-to-noise ratio. At this time, resonance can enhance the effect. When $SNR_{in} > -2.7\,\mathrm{dB}$, the gain $G > 1$, and the noise variance $D \approx 0.2$, which means that when the variance $D > 0.2$, stochastic resonance can enhance the effect, and when the signal amplitude is the same as the signal carrier frequency, the gain of different MPSK signals is the same. It shows that the enhancement effect of stochastic resonance has nothing to do with the change of signal phase.

4   Conclusions

Based on the adiabatic approximation theory, starting from the expression of the bistable system, this paper proves through calculation that the signal phase change will not affect the signal power spectral density of the noisy signal after stochastic resonance. It shows that the MPSK signal has the stochastic resonance of the bistable system. Uniform power spectrum density, and the correctness of the conclusion is verified by simulation experiment. When the signal amplitude and carrier frequency are determined, within a certain range, stochastic resonance can enhance MPSK, and there is a maximum gain related to the amplitude and the carrier frequency. It provides a new idea for the application of stochastic resonance in signal processing.

References

1. Mcnamara, B., Wiesenfeld, K.: Theory of stochastic resonance. Phys. Rev. A Gen. Phys. **39**(9), 4854–4869 (1989)
2. Collins, J.J.: Aperiodic stochastic resonance in excitable systems. Phys. Rev. E Stat. Phys. Plasmas Fluids Rel. Interdisc. Top. **52**(4), R3321 (1995)
3. Liu, J., Li, Z., Guan, L., Pan, L.: A novel parameter-tuned stochastic resonator for binary PAM signal processing at low SNR. IEEE Commun. Lett. **18**(3), 427–430 (2014). https://doi.org/10.1109/LCOMM.2014.011214.132465
4. Liu, J., Li, Z., Gao, R., Bo, J., Guan, L.: A Novel detector based on parameter-induced bistable stochastic resonance for FSK signal processing at low SNR. In: 2014 IEEE International Conference on Computer and Information Technology, Xi'an, China, pp. 832–836 (2014). https://doi.org/10.1109/CIT.2014.127
5. Liu, J., Li, Z., Gao, R., Bai, J., Liang, L.: Multi-ary pulse amplitude modulated signal processing using bistable stochastic resonance. In: 2015 International Conference on Noise and Fluctuations (ICNF), Xi'an, China, pp. 1–4 (2015). https://doi.org/10.1109/ICNF.2015.7288557
6. Zhang, Z., Ma, J., et al.: A PSK signal symbol rate estimation algorithm based on the combination of stochastic resonance and wavelet transform. IOP Conf. Ser. Mater. Sci. Eng. **449** (2018)
7. Zhang, Z., Ma, J.: Adaptive parameter-tuning stochastic resonance based on SVD and its application in weak IF digital signal enhancement. J. Adv. Signal Process. **2019**(1) (2019)
8. Liang, L., Zhang, N., Huang, H., Li, Z.: Bistable stochastic resonance enhanced 4-ary PAM signal detection under low SNR. China Commun. **16**(4), 196–207 (2019). https://doi.org/10.12676/j.cc.2019.04.015

Energy-Efficient Partial Offloading with Transmission Power Control in Mobile-Edge Computing

Meng Wang[1], Shuo Shi[1,2,3(✉)], Jian He[1], Cong Zhou[1], and Zhong Zheng[1,3]

[1] School of Electronic and Information Engineering, Harbin Institute of Technology, Harbin 150001, Heilongjiang, China
crcss@hit.edu.cn
[2] Network Communication Research Centre, Peng Cheng Laboratory, Shenzhen 518052, Guangdong, China
[3] International Innovation Institute of HIT in Huizhou, Huizhou 516000, Guangdong, China

Abstract. Mobile-Edge Computing (MEC) is a promising paradigm which enables mobile devices (MDs) to offload the computation-sensitive tasks (e.g., Augmented Reality) to the MEC server in close proximity to MDs to obtain low execution latency and energy consumption. Different from traditional partial offloading scheme, in this paper, we study the partial offloading in MEC. Consider single user scenario and Rayleigh fading channel, we first formulate the energy-efficient partial offloading problem as a non-convex problem. To solve the problem optimally, we reformulate the problem into two subproblems and use block coordinate descent method to solve the problem separately. For each subproblem, we give the proof of its feasibility. Simulation results show that the proposed method consumes less energy compared with two benchmark algorithms.

Keywords: Mobile-edge computing · Partial computation offloading · Convex optimization · Transmission power control

1 Introduction

Mobile devices (MDs) has been gaining enormous attention since 4G era. With the continuous development of information and communication technology (ICT), more and more new mobile applications with high requirement on quality of experience (QoE) are envisioned to be integrated into smart MDs [1]. However, those novel applications including augmented reality (AR), virtual reality (VR) are typically resource-hungry, requiring huge computation capacity [2]. Although the processing power of MDs has been greatly improved in recent years, due to the physical size limit, MDs are still lack of computation resource and battery life. The contradiction between resource-sensitive services and resource-constrained MDs poses a great challenge for future ICT system.

© ICST Institute for Computer Sciences, Social Informatics and Telecommunications Engineering 2021
Published by Springer Nature Switzerland AG 2021. All Rights Reserved
X. Wang et al. (Eds.): AICON 2021, LNICST 396, pp. 515–525, 2021.
https://doi.org/10.1007/978-3-030-90196-7_44

One promising approach to address such a challenge is mobile cloud computing, where MDs offload their resource-hungry tasks to the remote cloud center (e.g., Amazon EC2, Windows Azure) with rich computation resource through wireless access to reduce the energy consumption of MDs [3]. However, MDs may experience a long latency to finish the task since the cloud servers are typically far away from MDs and the backhaul network is congested. High task processing latency will hurt the QoE severely, since people are sensitive to delay and jitter. To address this issue, mobile-edge computing (MEC) as a new paradigm has been proposed in recent years [4]. The key idea for MEC is to set powerful servers in close proximity to MDs (e.g. wireless access point, base stations), so that MDs can offload the tasks with fast connection and low latency.

Many existing works have been focused on the computation offloading issue in MEC. [5] proposes a distributed energy-efficient computation offloading scheme based on game theory and shows the convergence and effectiveness. [6] formulates the multi-user computation offloading problem as a mixed integer nonlinear problem and prove its NP-hard property, and solves the problem suboptimally through reinforcement learning approach. [7] studies the energy-optimal mobile-cloud computing under stochastic wireless channel, which shows the impact of wireless channel in computation offloading. [8] studies the joint task offloading and resource allocation for multi-server MEC networks and decomposes the MINLP problem into two subproblems. [9] studies the energy-latency trade-off for energy-aware offloading in MEC networks, where communication and computation resource allocation are jointly optimized under the limited energy and latency constraints. Although the existing works are insightful, they mainly focused on binary computation offloading, namely each task is either offloaded to the MEC server or executed locally. However, for some typical tasks, e.g., virus scan and image compression, a task can be partitioned into several subtasks so that a MD can offload part of the task to MEC server and process the rest of the task locally. Moreover, the performance of computation offloading is affected significantly by wireless channel state, so it is important to analyze the computation offloading issue under realistic channel state. Toward this end, [12] studies the energy-efficient partial computation offloading and resource allocation issue under IoT scenario. The problem is formulated as an non-convex optimization problem solved by block coordinate descent and successive convex optimization method. [13] studies the online partial offloading method in multi-user MEC networks by leveraging Deep Deterministic Policy Gradient (DDPG) framework. [14] studies the stochastic partial computation offloading problem where the stability issue is considered. The authors use lyapunov optimization method to convert the complex global optimization problem into a single time slot decision problem. However, the algorithm proposed in [12] is with high complexity so that it cannot adapt to the real-time MEC. Moreover, [13] faces the challenge of convergence, and DDPG needs a lot of pre-training. [14] gives a $[O(1/V), O(V)]$ tradeoff between stability and effectiveness, however it does not consider the realistic wireless channel model.

Different from existing works, in this paper, we focus on the jointly optimizing the partial offloading ratio and the transmission power of the MD. Specifically, the optimization objective is the total energy consumption in a time period under the task process latency constraint. In the single-user scenario with Rayleigh fading channel, we first formulate the energy-efficient partial offloading problem as a non-convex problem. By using block coordinate descent method, we reformulate the problem into two subproblems and solve the problem separately with low complexity. Our contributions can be summarized as follows:

1) Different from previous work, we study the partial offloading method under rayleigh fading channel through monte carlo method, and the transmission power control issue is jointly considered.

2) We formulate the energy-efficient partial offloading problem as a non-convex problem and decompose the problem into two subproblems. Instead of using traditional block coordinate descent method, we analyze the monotonicity property of each subproblem and solve them with low-complexity.

3) Simulation results show that our proposed partial offloading method consumes less energy compared with three benchmark algorithms.

The rest of this paper is organized as follows: Sect. 2 gives the system model and problem formulation. In Sect. 3, we propose our energy-efficient partial offloading method to solve the non-convex optimization problem. Finally, simulation and results are given in Sect. 4 and 5, respectively.

2   System Model and Problem Formulation

2.1   Network Model

Figure 1 gives the network model. Specifically, we consider a single MD either offloading the tasks to a single MEC server located in an e-NodeB or execute the task locally. Different from previous works in binary offloading, partial offloading in this paper allows a single task being partitioned (e.g., virus scan, video compression) so that it can be executed simultaneously both in MEC server and local processor (i.e., CPU). We consider a discrete time period $\mathcal{T} = \{1, 2, 3, ..., T\}$, in each time slot $t \in \mathcal{T}$ a task $A(X, L)$ needs to be executed, where X denotes the size, L denotes the maximum tolerant delay of the task, respectively. According to [10], each bit of the task need to consume α CPU circles. $\lambda(t) \in [0, 1]$ represents the offloading ratio to the MEC server in time slot t.

2.2   Communication Model

In each time slot, the MD offloads the task through wireless channel. For convenience, we consider the channel coherence time is larger than a single time slot, namely the channel fading is constant in each time slot but varies among different time slots. Considering the white noise power density is N_0, the uplink transmission rate in time slot t is given by:

$$r(t) = B\log_2(1 + \frac{P_t|h(t)|^2}{N_0 B}),\tag{1}$$

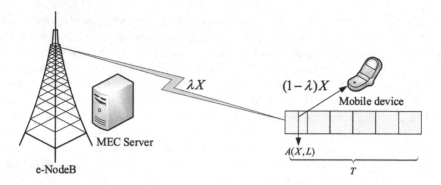

Fig. 1. Single-user partial offloading in mobile-edge computing

where B denotes the bandwidth allocated to the MD, P_t is the transmission power, $h(t)$ is a random variable which represents the channel fading coefficient. In this paper, we assume the probabilistic density function (PDF) of $h(t)$ is given as:

$$p(h(t) = r) = \frac{r}{\sigma^2}\exp(-\frac{r^2}{2\sigma^2}), 0 < r < \infty, \tag{2}$$

where σ^2 is the average receive power. According to the probabilistic theory, the PDF of $|h(t)|^2$ is given as:

$$p(|h(t)|^2 = r) = \frac{1}{2\sigma^2}\exp(-\frac{r}{2\sigma^2}), 0 < r < \infty. \tag{3}$$

In this paper, we assume the base station have perfect channel state information (CSI) of the uplink channel. The uplink transmission time can thus be modelled as:

$$T_U(t) = \frac{\lambda(t)X}{r(t)}. \tag{4}$$

The transmission energy in each time slot is given as:

$$E_U(t) = P_t T_U(t). \tag{5}$$

According [5], we do not take the downlink transmission into consideration, since after processing in MEC server the size of the task and the downlink transmission time is negligible.

2.3   Computation Model

According to [7], we model the computation energy consumption of CPU as

$$P = \theta f^3, \tag{6}$$

where θ and k are the coefficient and computation speed of the CPU, respectively. Since f denotes CPU cycles per second, the energy consumption per cycle can be expressed as θf^2. Thus, the computation energy consumption in MD can be expressed as

$$E_l(t) = \alpha(1 - \lambda(t))X\theta f^2. \tag{7}$$

In this paper, we focus on the energy consumption in MD, thus the energy consumption in MEC server is not considered. Furthermore, the execution delay is given as

$$T_l(t) = \frac{(1 - \lambda(t))X\alpha}{f} \tag{8}$$

2.4   Problem Formulation

Based on the model, the total energy consumption in a single time slot is given as

$$E_{total}(t) = E_U(t) + E_l(t) \tag{9}$$

The total execution latency in time slot t is given as

$$T_{total}(t) = \max(T_U(t), T_l(t)) \tag{10}$$

Therefore, the energy-efficient partial computation offloading problem can be formulated as

$$(\mathbf{P1}) \quad \min_{\lambda, P} \sum_{t=1}^{T} \alpha(1 - \lambda(t))X\theta f^2) + \frac{P(t)\lambda(t)X}{B\log_2(1 + \frac{P(t)|h(t)|^2}{N_0 B})}$$

$$s.t. \quad C1 : 0 \leq \lambda(t) \leq 1$$
$$C2 : 0 \leq P(t) \leq P_{\max}$$
$$C3 : T_{total}(t) < L$$

The objective is to minimize the total energy consumption of the MD in a time period T. C1 gives the range of λ, C2 constrains the transmission energy, C3 guarantees the task should be finished under the maximum tolerant delay constraint.

3   Proposed Energy-Efficient Partial Offloading Method

Note that in P1, λ and P are coupled in both objective function and C3, therefore P1 is not a standard convex optimization problem. To obtain the optimal solution, we first reformulate the problem as:

$$(\mathbf{P2}) \quad \min_{\lambda, P} \alpha(1 - \lambda)X\theta f^2 + \frac{P\lambda X}{B\log_2(1 + \frac{P|h|^2}{N_0 B})}$$

$$s.t. \quad C1 : 0 \leq \lambda \leq 1$$
$$C2 : 0 \leq P \leq P_{\max}$$
$$C3 : T_{total} < L$$

Since in each time slot t MU needs to execute one independent task, in order to minimize the total energy consumption in time period T, we just need to minimize the energy consumption in every single time slot t, which reduces the number of optimization variables significantly. However, P2 is still non-trivial to solve due to the couple of λ and P and the non-convex optimization objective and constraint.

Lemma 1: It is always true that

$$\inf_{x,y} f(x,y) = \inf_{x} \tilde{f}(x)$$

where $\tilde{f}(x) = \inf\limits_{y} f(x,y)$

[11] gives the complete proof, we do not expand in this paper due to the page limit. Lemma 1 allows us to solve P2 through minimizing λ and P sequentially.

We first consider P as a constant and try to find λ^*. The problem can then be formulated as:

$$\textbf{(P3)} \quad \min_{\lambda} \alpha(1-\lambda)X\theta f^2 + \frac{P\lambda X}{B\log_2(1 + \frac{P|h|^2}{N_0 B})},$$

$$s.t. \qquad C1 : 0 \le \lambda \le 1$$

$$C2 : \max\{\frac{\lambda X}{r}, \frac{(1-\lambda)X\alpha}{f}\} < L$$

where $r = B\log_2(1 + \frac{P|h|^2}{N_0 B})$ is the uplink transmission rate in time slot t. It can be observed that P3 is a linear programming problem with respect to λ, thus it can be solved through convex optimization.

Theorem 1. *The optimal value of λ in each time slot is:*

$$\lambda^* = \begin{cases} \min\left\{\frac{1-Lf}{X\alpha}, 0\right\}, r < \frac{P}{\alpha\theta f^2} \\ \forall \lambda \in [0,1], r = \frac{P}{\alpha\theta f^2} \\ \max\left\{\frac{Lr}{X}, 1\right\}, r > \frac{P}{\alpha\theta f^2} \end{cases}$$

Proof. We rewrite the objective function as $f(\lambda) = \lambda(\frac{PX}{r} - \alpha X\theta f^2) + \alpha X\theta f^2$. Since $f(\lambda)$ is a linear function of λ. The minimum value of $f(\lambda)$ is determined by the sign of $f(r) = \frac{PX}{r} - \alpha X\theta f^2$. If $f(r) > 0$, to obtain the minimum $f(\lambda)$, $\lambda^* = \min\{\lambda | \lambda \in dom\}$. Relatively, If $f(r) < 0$, to obtain the minimum $f(\lambda)$, $\lambda^* = \max\{\lambda | \lambda \in dom\}$. For the special case when $f(r) = 0$, $\lambda = \forall \lambda \in [0,1]$ since the objective value is not related with λ. Furthermore, C2 should be satisfied. $\lambda_0 = \frac{1}{1+\frac{\alpha r}{f}}$ denotes the case when $\frac{\lambda X}{r} = \frac{(1-\lambda)X\alpha}{f}$. If $\lambda > \lambda_0$, we have $\lambda_0 < \lambda < \frac{Lr}{X}$. If $\lambda < \lambda_0$, we have $\frac{1-Lf}{X\alpha} < \lambda < \lambda_0$. Taking intersection with C2, we finally finish the proof.

By using λ^* obtained from P3, we now consider the P as optimization variable and try to find P^*. The problem can then be formulated as

$$(\textbf{P4}) \quad \min_{P} \alpha(1-\lambda)X\theta f^2 + \frac{P\lambda X}{B\log_2(1+\frac{P|h|^2}{N_0 B})}$$

$$s.t. \quad C1: 0 \le P \le P_{\max}$$

$$C2: \max\left\{\frac{\lambda X}{B\log_2(1+\frac{P|h|^2}{N_0 B})}, \frac{(1-\lambda)X\alpha}{f}\right\} < L$$

Theorem 2. $f(P) = \frac{\lambda X P}{B\log_2(1+\frac{P|h|^2}{N_0 B})}$ *is monotonically increasing with respect to variable P.*

Proof. Let $\Delta P \to 0$, we define function $g(P) = f(P+\Delta P) - f(P)$. By substituting $f(P)$, $g(P)$ can be expressed as: $g(P) = \frac{abP[\log_2(1+aP)-\log_2(1+aP+a\Delta P)]+ab\Delta P\log_2(1+aP)}{a^2\log_2(1+aP+\Delta P)\log_2(1+aP)}$. Since the denominator is always positive, we observe the numerator $h(P) = P[\log_2(1+aP)-\log_2(1+aP+a\Delta P)] + \Delta P\log_2(1+aP)$. Divide both sides of the equation by the term $P\log_2(1+aP)$: $\frac{h(P)}{P\log_2(1+ap)} = 1 - \log_2(a\Delta P) + \frac{\Delta P}{P} > 1 - \log_2(a\Delta P)$. Since, $\Delta P \to 0$, thus $1 - \log_2(a\Delta P) > 0$, which indicates $h(P) > 0$, i.e., $g(P) > 0$. Since $f(P+\Delta P) - f(P) > 0$, we finish the proof.

Theorem 2 gives the fact that the optimization objective value is monotonically increasing with respect to P, thus the minimum value can be obtained according to the lower bound of the domain. Since λ is constant in C2 and $\frac{\lambda X}{B\log_2(1+\frac{P|h|^2}{N_0 B})}$ is monotonically decreasing with respect to P. Define $P_0 = \frac{N_0 B}{|h|^2}\left[2^{\frac{\lambda f}{(1-\lambda)B\alpha}} - 1\right]$ which satisfies $\frac{\lambda X}{B\log_2(1+\frac{P_0|h|^2}{N_0 B})} = \frac{(1-\lambda)X\alpha}{f}$. Therefore, when $P_{max} > P > P_0$, $\frac{(1-\lambda)X\alpha}{f} < L$ must hold, this gives the feasible set of L, namely $L > \frac{X\alpha}{f}$, and $P^* = P_0$. When $P < P_0$, $\frac{\lambda X}{B\log_2(1+\frac{P|h|^2}{N_0 B})} < L$, which gives $P > \frac{N_0 B}{|h|^2}\left(2^{\frac{\lambda X}{LB}} - 1\right)$. Thus, when $0 < P < P_0$, $P^* = \frac{N_0 B}{|h|^2}\left(2^{\frac{\lambda X}{LB}} - 1\right)$. Finally, we solve P4 with $P^* = \min\left\{\frac{N_0 B}{|h|^2}\left(2^{\frac{\lambda X}{LB}} - 1\right), P_0\right\}$.

Algorithm 1 gives the detailed procedure of the proposed algorithm. For each task i, we do a total of $\mathcal{M}$ monte carlo simulations to illustrate the statistic property of rayleigh fading. We first give the input parameters according to [5–10]. For each task i, we first take λ as variable and give an initial value P_0 to find the optimum λ^* according to Theorem 1. Then we take P as variable and let $\lambda = \lambda^*$, and find the optimum P^* through Theorem 2. The average energy consumption is the mean value of $f_j(\lambda^*, P^*)$.

Algorithm 1. Proposed energy-efficient partial offloading method

1: Initialize input parameters B, N_0, θ, f, α, X, L, M
2: **for** task i in $\mathcal{N}$ **do**
3:    **for** j in $\mathcal{M}$ **do**
4:       Obtain the channel coefficient $h(t)$ through channel state information
5:       Take λ as variable, let $P = P_0$
6:       Find λ^* through linear programming method according to Theorem 1
7:       Take P as variable, let $\lambda = \lambda^*$
8:       Calculate $P^* = \min\left\{\frac{N_0 B}{|h|^2}\left(2^{\frac{\lambda X}{LB}} - 1\right), P_0\right\}$.
9:       Find the optimum value of the objective function $f_j(\lambda^*, P^*)$ in j-th simulation
10:    **end for**
11:    Find the average energy consumption of task i under rayleigh fading channel.
12: **end for**
13: Calculate total energy consumption $E_{total} = \sum\limits_{i=1}^{N} f_i(\lambda^*, P^*)$

4   Simulation Results

4.1   Parameters Settings

The main parameters are listed in Table 1. Specifically, we consider a time period T consists of 100 time slots. The bandwidth and the white noise density is set as 10 MHz and 10^{-9} W/Hz, respectively. The size and maximum tolerant delay of each task are assumed to be equal in this paper, with specific value 2000 Kb and 0.1 s, respectively. The computation capacity of MD is set as 1 GHz and the maximum transmission power of MD is 0.2 W. According to [10], α is set as 40, θ is set as 10^{-26}. The simulation environment is Windows 10 under Python 3.7.

Table 1. Parameters settings

Parameters	Values
Bandwidth B	$2 * 10^6$
Noise power density N_0	10^{-9}
Data input size X	500–2000 KB
Maximum tolerant delay L_{max}	0.1 s
Maximum CPU frequency of mobile devices f_{max}	1 GHz
Maximum transmission power P_t	0.2 W
Computation factor α	40
Average receive power σ^2	0.1 W
Computation energy coefficient θ	10^{-26}

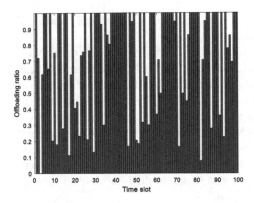

Fig. 2. Offloading ratio with respect to each executed task

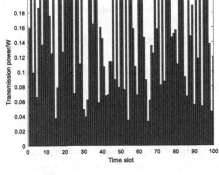

Fig. 3. Transmission power with respect to each executed task

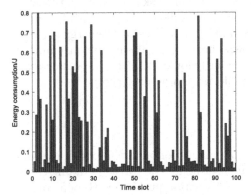

Fig. 4. Total energy consumption versus each task

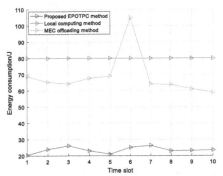

Fig. 5. Performance comparison with benchmark algorithms

4.2 Performance Analysis

Figure 2 gives the offloading ratio versus each executed task. Note that, the offloading ratio varies with each time slot. However, the tasks in this paper all have the same property, which indicates that the channel state has significant influence on the offloading ratio. When the channel fading is severe, MDs tend to offload a small part of taks to MEC server to obtain a better performance. When the channel state is ideal, MDs tend to offload the whole task to the MEC server, since the transmission energy and latency are relatively low.

Figure 3 gives the transmission power with respect to each executed task, the maximum transmission power of each MD is 0.2 W. Figure 3 shows that instead of transmitting message with maximum power, the transmission power can change adaptively under the latency constraints, which can reduce the energy consumption of MDs significantly. Furthermore, this result also shows the impact of wireless channel in MEC, namely when the channel fading is severe, the MD needs to use higher transmission energy to guarantee the transmission rate so that the transmission delay can be reduced.

Figure 4 gives the total energy consumption with respect to each task. Note that, the energy consumption of each task varies significantly. The reason is that local execution consumes more energy than offloading to MEC server, however, when the channel state is poor, offloading the task to MEC server can not satisfy the latency constraint. Therefore, Fig. 4 gives the insight that, when the channel state is ideal, offloading the task to MEC server can guarantee the latency constraint, resulting in a low energy consumption. When the channle fading is severe, offloading to MEC still consume less energy than local offloading, however, due to the latency constraint, part of the task should be executed locally, which results in a higher energy consumption.

Figure 5 gives the performance comparison of the proposed EPOTPC method with two benchmark algorithms in terms of energy consumption through monte-carlo simulation. Local computing represents that all tasks are executed locally, and MEC offloading represents that all tasks are offloaded to the MEC server if the transmission time is above the maximum tolerant delay, a energy punishment factor will be added. It can be shown that, the total energy consumption of the proposed EPOTPC method is significantly lower than the two benchmark algorithms, which shows the effectiveness of our proposed method.

5   Conclusion

In this paper, we study the energy-efficient partial computation offloading and transmission power control of single mobile user under the Rayleigh fading channel. We first formulate the problem as an optimization problem with non-convex optimization objective and constraints. To solve the problem, we first reformulate the problem and analyze the property of each subproblem using block coordinate descent method to optimize each variable separately. Simulation results show that the proposed method has a better performance compared with two benchmark algorithms in terms of total energy consumption. As for future work, studying the joint optimization of computation and communication resource allocation and partial offloading in multi-user scenario will be challenging and interesting which is our future work direction.

References

1. Shi, W., Cao, J., Zhang, Q., Li, Y., Xu, L.: Edge computing: vision and challenges. IEEE Internet Things J. **3**(5), 637–646 (2016)
2. Mach, P., Becvar, Z.: Mobile edge computing: a survey on architecture and computation offloading. IEEE Commun. Surv. Tutor. **19**(3), 1628–1656 (2017, thirdquarter)
3. Mao, Y., You, C., Zhang, J., Huang, K., Letaief, K.B.: A survey on mobile edge computing: the communication perspective. IEEE Commun. Surv. Tutor. **19**(4), 2322–2358 (2017, Fourthquarter)

4. Dinh, T.Q., Tang, J., La, Q.D., Quek, T.Q.S.: Offloading in mobile edge computing: task allocation and computational frequency scaling. IEEE Trans. Commun. **65**(8), 3571–3584 (2017)
5. Chen, X., Jiao, L., Li, W., Fu, X.: Efficient multi-user computation offloading for mobile-edge cloud computing. IEEE/ACM Trans. Netw. **24**(5), 2795–2808 (2016)
6. Wang, M., Shi, S., Gu, S., et al.: Q-learning based computation offloading for multi-UAV-enabled cloud-edge computing networks. IET Commun. **14**(15), 2481–2490 (2020)
7. Zhang, W., Wen, Y., Guan, K., Kilper, D., Luo, H., Wu, D.O.: Energy-optimal mobile cloud computing under stochastic wireless channel. IEEE Trans. Wireless Commun. **12**(9), 4569–4581 (2013)
8. Tran, T.X., Pompili, D.: Joint task offloading and resource allocation for multi-server mobile-edge computing networks. IEEE Trans. Veh. Technol. **68**(1), 856–868 (2019)
9. Zhang, J., et al.: Energy-latency tradeoff for energy-aware offloading in mobile edge computing networks. IEEE Internet Things J. **5**(4), 2633–2645 (2018)
10. Wang, Y., Sheng, M., Wang, X., Wang, L., Li, J.: Mobile-edge computing: partial computation offloading using dynamic voltage scaling. IEEE Trans. Commun. **64**(10), 4268–4282 (2016)
11. Boyd, S., Vandenberghe, L.: Convex Optimization. Cambridge Univ. Press, Cambridge (2004)
12. Mao, Y., Zhang, J., Song, S.H., Letaief, K.B.: Stochastic joint radio and computational resource management for multi-user mobile-edge computing systems. IEEE Trans. Wireless Commun. **16**(9), 5994–6009 (2017)
13. Guo, K., Gao, R., Xia, W., Quek, T.Q.S.: Online learning based computation offloading in MEC systems with communication and computation dynamics. IEEE Trans. Commun. **69**(2), 1147–1162 (2021)
14. Xie, R., Tang, Q., Liang, C., Yu, F.R., Huang, T.: Dynamic computation offloading in IoT fog systems with imperfect channel-state information: a POMDP approach. IEEE Internet Things J. **8**(1), 345–356 (2021)

A Tree-Based Approach for Building Efficient Task-Oriented Dialogue Systems

Tao Gan$^{(\boxtimes)}$, Chunang Li, Yuhui Xi, and Yanmin He

School of Information and Software Engineering, University of Electronic
Science and Technology of China, Chengdu 610054, China
gantao@uestc.edu.cn

Abstract. Task-oriented dialogue systems have attracted increasing attention. The traditional rule-based approaches suffer from limited generalization ability as well as the high cost of system deployment, whereas the data-driven deep learning approaches are data-hungry and the domain-specific data is insufficient for full training their models. In this paper, we present a hybrid method which combines the strengths of both rule-based and data-driven approaches. We first establish intent-slot trees from the standard multi-turn dialogue corpus in specific domain. During the dialogue, the power of deep language understanding model is exploited to enhance the generalization ability of the system and the multi-turn dialogue proceeds following the path of the intent-slot tree established. Experimental results show that the proposed approach achieves superior performance over deep learning ones which demonstrates its effectiveness in building task-oriented dialogue systems under a limited amount of training data.

Keywords: Task-oriented · Rule-based · Data-driven · Intent-slot tree

1 Introduction

In recent years, the task-oriented dialogue system has attracted more and more attention in both academic and industrial communities. A task-oriented dialogue system aims to help the user to accomplish certain tasks, such as restaurant reservation, flight booking or business consultation, etc. Unlike the non-task-oriented dialogue system which is in open-domain setting, the task-oriented one is more targeting at handling problems in specific domains.

The typical task-oriented dialogue systems often implement a complicated pipeline architecture, consisting of natural language understanding (NLU), dialogue management (DM) and natural language generation (NLG) [1]. The function of NLU is to transform the user's input into the form that the computer can understand using grammatical and semantic analysis. It usually has two main tasks: intent detection and semantic slot filling. The DM takes the output of NLU as well as dialogue context information to determine the corresponding actions to be taken by the system. A typical DM component includes two stages: dialogue state tracking and policy learning. In the last module NLG, the

X. Wang et al. (Eds.): AICON 2021, LNICST 396, pp. 526–536, 2021.
https://doi.org/10.1007/978-3-030-90196-7_45

system's responses are converted into appropriate statements in natural language that users can understand.

Different implementations of the above modules result in different dialogue systems. Approaches for developing dialogue systems are typically categorized into rule-based and data-driven. Traditional systems are based on rules [2]. In such systems, a set of domain-dependent rules are predefined and user utterances are matched against the rules during the dialogue. Typical approaches to dialogue management are based on finite state models, where user utterances trigger transitions between the dialogue states, and these states determine the system's response [3, 4]. The main advantage of rule-based systems is that they do not need training data and so that they have no cold-start problem. Yet such systems have a disadvantage of limited generalization ability. When the user utterances do not match the established rules well, the dialogue performance will noticeably decline. Moreover, the use of hand-crafted rules for the state and action space representations makes it expensive and time-consuming to deploy a real dialogue system [1]. In contrast, data-driven approaches rely on training the dialogue system using training data. For example, in dialogue state tracking, the generative model is built to learn the relevant joint probability density distribution from the training data and calculate the conditional probability distribution of all dialogue states [5, 6]. Furthermore, to model the dialogue state more accurately, the discriminative model which treats dialogue state tracking as a classification task is proposed [7]. In addition, with the advance of end-to-end neural generative models in recent years, many attempts have been made to construct end-to-end trainable frameworks for dialogue systems and promising results have been shown [8]. However, most data-driven approaches are data-hungry, requiring a large amount of data to fully train the model [9]. This poses a big problem to the application in task-oriented dialogue systems, where the domain-specific data are often hard to collect and expensive to annotate.

The goal of this work is to develop efficient task-oriented dialogue systems under a limited amount of training data. To this end, we propose a hybrid approach which leverages the benefits from both rule-based and data-driven approaches. We first establish intent-slot trees from the standard multi-turn dialogue corpus in specific domain. The intent-slot tree then servers as rules for subsequent dialogue. During the dialogue, the power of deep language understanding model is exploited to enhance the generalization ability of the system and the multi-turn dialogue proceeds following the path of the intent-slot tree established. Our main contributions are as follows:

1. We define an intent-slot tree structure to implicitly specify rules for the dialogue system at low cost.
2. Based on the intent-slot tree defined, we present a rule-based and data-driven hybrid approach for building efficient task-oriented dialogue systems where the domain-specific data is insufficient for full training deep learning models.

2 Methodology

As mentioned above, in task-oriented dialogue circumstance, both the rule-based and the data-driven approaches have their own advantages and disadvantages. We attempt to take the benefits from the both approaches. Our main idea is to integrate domain-specific rules into the dialogue system in a simple and effective way. To do so, we propose the intent-slot tree model to represent and organize the rules, based on which the dialogue system is built.

2.1 Overview

The proposed dialogue system consists of three principle components: mode selection, single-turn dialogue and multi-turn dialogue. In mode selection, the mode of single-turn dialogue or multi-turn dialogue is chosen based on a joint intent-slot model. In single-turn dialogue, a two-stage text matching algorithm is used. The matching algorithm combines relevance matching and semantic matching for retrieving proper answers to simple questions or greetings, where the semantic matching is based on semantic matching model. While in multi-turn dialogue, the user will be guided in completing his or her tasks following intent-slot trees previously constructed. The system structure is illustrated in Fig. 1. In the following sections, we first introduce the proposed intent-slot tree model and then present the above principle components in detail.

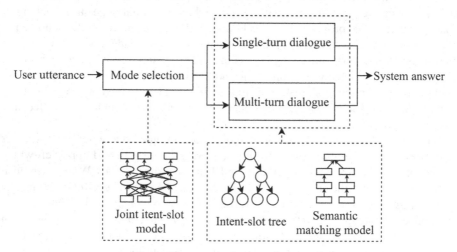

Fig. 1. The proposed system framework.

2.2 Intent-Slot Tree

Before getting into the details of the proposed intent-slot tree, we first introduce the corpus we used.

Dialogue Corpus. The corpus contains multiple standard multi-turn dialogues between the users and the robot. One dialogue represents one typical interaction scene that the robot helps the user in completing one specific task. for notation convenience, the content of the dialogue is logically represented in a tree structure (hereinafter referred to as dialogue tree $\overline{T}$). Suppose the level number of the tree starts from 1, i.e., level 1 is the first level, so the largest level number of $\overline{T}$ is even. The nodes in odd levels of the tree store user sentences, and each one of which has only one child node. The nodes in even levels store the robot sentences, and each of which has one or more child nodes. Figure 2 gives an example of dialogue tree that represents one typical interaction between the use and the robot in bank business consultation.

Intent-Slot Tree Construction. For one input dialogue tree $\overline{T}$, we target to construct a corresponding intent-slot tree T. the construction procedure consists of the following steps:

Intent Labeling. Assign a user's intent u for the input dialogue tree $\overline{T}$. Take the dialogue tree depicted in Fig. 2 for example, the intent u assigned is "consult + deduction + fail".

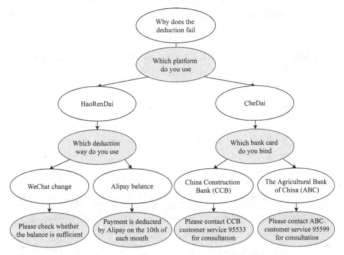

Fig. 2. An example of the multi-turn dialogue tree. White and gray nodes represent user and robot parts, respectively.

Root Node Creation. 1) Create a pair (u, a), where a is the sentence contained in the child of root of $\overline{T}$. 2) Create a tree node n with pair (u, a) as its content, and add the node n to empty T as its root.

Other Nodes Creation. For each node in odd level of $\overline{T}$ do: 1) Extract one slot value s manually for the sentence contained in current node. 2) Create a pair (s, a'), where a' is the sentence contained in the child of current node. 3) Create a tree node n' with pair (s, a') as Its content, and add the node n' to T as the child of the node that corresponds to the grandparent of current node in $\overline{T}$.

Figure 3 shows an example of an intent-slot tree created from the dialogue tree in Fig. 2.

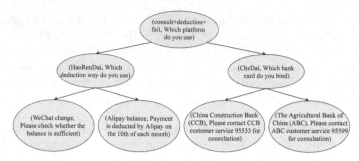

Fig. 3. Example of an intent-slot tree created from the dialogue tree in Fig. 2.

2.3 Mode Selection

As the first step of our method, we use a joint intent-slot model to extract intent from the user input utterance. Based on the result of intent extraction, the mode of the following dialogue is determined.

Joint Intent-Slot Model. We use BERT-based intent-slot joint recognition model [10]. Figure 4 Illustrates a high-level view of the model.

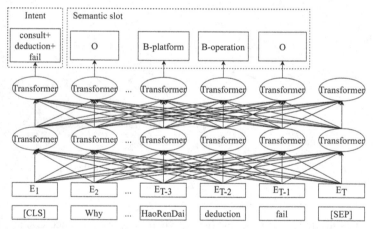

Fig. 4. A high-level view of BERT-based intent-slot joint recognition model. The input sentence is "Why does HaoRenDai deduction fail".

BERT [11] can be easily extended to a joint intent classification and slot filling model. A special classification embedding ([CLS]) is inserted as the first token and a special token ([SEP]) is added as the final token. Given an input token sequence $x = (x_1, \ldots, x_T)$, the output of BERT is $H = (h_1, \ldots, h_T)$.

Based on the hidden state of the first special token ([CLS]), denoted h_1, the intent is predicted as:

$$y^i = softmax\left(W^i h_1 + b^i\right) \tag{1}$$

For slot filling, this model feed the final hidden states of other tokens $h_2, \ldots, h_T$ into a softmax layer to classify over the slot filling labels, the formula is expressed as.

$$y_t^s = softmax(W^s h_t + b^s), t \in 2 \ldots T \tag{2}$$

where h_t is the hidden state corresponding to the first sub-token of word x_t.

To jointly model intent classification and slot filling, the objective is formulated as:

$$p(y^i, y^s|x) = p(y^i|x) \prod_{n=1}^{N} p(y_n^s|x) \tag{3}$$

The learning objective is to maximize the conditional probability $p(y^i, y^s|x)$. The model is fine-tuned end-to-end via minimizing the cross-entropy loss.

Dialogue Mode Selection. For a user input utterance, we try to extract the main intent u using the joint intent-slot model previously trained. If the intent is extracted successfully, the multi-turn dialogue mode is chosen and the intent-slot tree whose intent matches u is selected as the matching tree T_M for the following multi-turn dialogue. Otherwise, the single-turn dialogue mode will be selected for completing the dialogue task.

2.4   Single-Turn Dialogue

In real task-oriented dialogue, users often have simple questions which are frequently asked in specific domain or even they just give greetings. In that case, the system may just give the answer directly. We design a framework specific for such single-turn dialogue situations.

Firstly, we collect the frequently asked questions and their standard answers. We organize them as questions and answer (QA) pairs in database. Then, during the dialogue, the system retrieves the question in database that matches the user utterance best and returns its answer to the user. Thus, the key task here is to develop an accurate and efficient way to perform the match task. Toward this end, we propose a two-stage matching framework for retrieving the matched question in database. In the first stage, a group of relevant questions are retrieved through relevance matching. In the second stage, the similarity between the retrieved questions and the user utterance are computed using similarity matching technique. Finally, the overall score of each retrieved question is computed by combining the scores obtained in two stages and the question with highest score is selected as the question of best match. The framework of the single-turn dialogue is shown in Fig. 5.

In the first stage, we use the BM25 [12] to perform the relevance matching. BM25 is a ranking function to estimate the relevance of documents to given search query. BM25 is a bag-of-words retrieval function that ranks a set of documents based on the query terms appearing in each document.

In the second stage, we build the Sentence-BERT (SBERT) [13] semantic matching model to perform the similarity matching. SBERT uses a Siamese network structure based on BERT which calculates the fixed sized sentence embeddings. At inference,

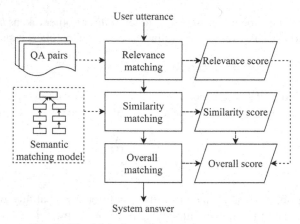

Fig. 5. The basic flow of the single-turn dialogue.

SBERT computes the similarity score of two sentences by calculating the cosine similarity of their embeddings. In training the SBERT model, we use the corresponding pre-trained model for initialization and fine-tune the parameters on a few domain-specific data.

In the overall matching, we integrate the literal relevance and the semantic similarity. Suppose the relevance score is S_1 and the similarity score is S_2, then the overall score S_3 is calculated by the following formula:

$$S_3 = \alpha \cdot S_1 + (1 - \alpha) \cdot S_2 \tag{4}$$

with α the adjustment factor which is derived from experiments.

2.5 Multi-turn Dialogue

In contrast to most data-driven approaches, our policy for multi-turn dialogue does not heavily rely on the model trained by the data. Instead, the dialogue proceeds following the path of the intent-slot tree established from the standard corpus. The whole procedure consists of following two steps: start point location and tree matching dialogue.

Start Point Location. In the previous mode selection step, we have obtained the matching tree T_M which matches the intent extracted from the user utterance. Besides intent, one or more slot values may also be extracted. We define a set SV to contain all these slot values. The values in SV may happen to be equal to the ones in the child nodes of the root of T_M. In this case, it is inappropriate to start the dialogue from the root of T_M, since the user will have unpleasant feelings when being asked the questions whose answers have been previously given. So once the matching tree has been selected, it is better to find its node that is most appropriate for starting the multi-turn dialogue. We achieve this by executing the following matching procedure.

Suppose the matching tree has M leaves, then from root to leaf there are M different paths. For each of these M paths, starting from its second node, we try to find a consecutive node list in which the slot value of each node matches one of element of SV. Here, we utilize the semantic matching technique described in the previous section to measure the matching degree. Then we compare the lengths of lists of all paths and select the one that has the longest length. The elements which match the nodes of the selected list are removed from SV. Finally, the procedure returns the last node of the selected list. This node severs as the start node of the following dialogue.

Tree Matching Dialogue. From the start point, the dialogue runs iteratively following one path of the T_M. In each iteration, each child of the current node is matched against all elements of SV. Again, we utilize the semantic matching technique to measure the matching degree. If there is a successful match, we remove the corresponding element from SV and the current iteration ends by setting the corresponding child node as the working node for next iteration. Otherwise, the robot sentence contained in the current node is read and replied to the user. After the user gives a response, the slot values are then extracted from the response and the one with the highest prediction confidence is selected. Then we match each child of the current node against the selected slot value semantically. If there is a successful match, we set the corresponding child node as the working node for next iteration. Otherwise, the following re-matching procedure is launched for the first time and out-of-domain process is executed for the other time. The dialogue continues until the leaf of the tree is reached.

Re-matching Strategy. Like other pipeline-based systems, our dialogue system faces the problem of error propagation. If the NLU module does not correctly extract the semantic slots from the user utterance in multi-turn dialogue, the above tree matching will fail, leading to the failure of the dialogue. To circumvent this problem, we propose the following strategy. For Each node of the intent-slot tree, we maintain a weighting parameter w and initialize it to 0. The weight w is increased by 1 once the corresponding node has been visited. For the case that none of the children of the current node can match the user slot value, a single-choice question is raised by the system. The options of the question come from slot values of the children with m highest weights. Based on the new reply given by the user, the tree matching dialogue will continue as usual.

3   Experiments

We extracted 1283 multi-turn dialogue corpus and 2000 frequently asked simple questions from dialogue records in bank business consultation. From the corpus, we labeled 45 intents and 13 slots, and for each intent, we built an intent-slot tree.

3.1   Baselines for Comparison

We use the open-source toolkit, ConvLab-2 [14], to build two dialogue systems as baselines. The first system, named Baseline (Rule), is mainly based on rules and the second one, named Baseline (Learning), employs deep learning method for dialogue state tracking. Table 1 shows the components modules of baseline systems and ours in detail.

Table 1. The composition of each module of baselines and our system.

	NLU	DM	NLG
Baseline (Rule)	Joint Intent-slot	RuleDST + Rule Policy	TemplateNLG
Baseline (Learning)	-	TRADE + Rule Policy	TemplateNLG
Our system	Joint Intent-slot	Intent-slot tree	-

We use a set of rule-based models in ConvLab-2 in this experiment. Specifically, the RuleDST model and the Rule Policy model are chosen for DM, and the TemplateNLG model is deployed for NLG. For the Baseline (Learning) system, we deploy the TRADE (Transferable Dialogue State Generator) [15] model for dialogue state tracking, in which an end-to-end deep learning method is used to directly generate dialogue states from user utterances. For the Baseline (Rule) and our system, we implement the joint intent-slot model introduced in Sect. 2.3 for NLU.

3.2 Results and Analysis

Model Performance. We evaluate the performance of the entire dialogue system on task finish rate T which is defined as follows:

$$T = \frac{M_f}{M_t} \tag{5}$$

where M_f is the number of multi-turn dialogues that successfully completed the task, and M_t is the total number of multi-turn dialogues.

Table 2. Performance comparison between baselines and our system.

	NLU Accuracy (%)	DM Accuracy (%)	System Task finish rate (%)
Baseline (Rule)	85.43	77.52	69.14
Baseline (Learning)	-	68.62	60.75
Our system	85.43	82.19	76.21

Table 2 shows the performance comparison of baselines and our system. As can be seen from the table, our system shows the best performance among the three systems. Compared with baseline (Rule), our system achieves accuracy gain of 4.67% for DM module and 7.07% improvement on the task finish rate. Compared with baseline (Learning), our system achieves gains of 13.57% and 15.46% for DM accuracy and task finish rate, respectively. The inefficiency of baseline (Learning) system is due to the fact that there is no sufficient labeled training data to fully train the model.

Table 3. Performance comparison between the system with and without re-matching strategy. Sys-with represents the system with re-matching strategy, Sys-without represents the system without it. Avg. turns represents the average number of turns of all test dialogues.

	Task finish rate	Avg. turns
Sys-without	67.41	3.3
Sys-with	76.21	4.5

Re-matching Strategy. To demonstrate the effectiveness of re-matching strategy, we compare the performance between our system and the one without re-matching strategy. The results are shown in Table 3.

The task finish rate of the system with re-matching strategy is significantly higher than that without it. We notice that the average number of turns of our system with re-matching strategy is larger than that without it. This is because that during re-matching process, the system raises single-choice questions to the user, leading to the increase of the number of dialogues turns. Whereas in case of the system without re-matching strategy, the system just launches the out-of-domain process which directly ends the whole dialogue.

4 Conclusion

This paper presents a practical way to develop task-oriented dialogue systems under a limited amount of training data. The proposed approach leverages the benefits from both rule-based and data-driven approaches. The intent-slot tree is built to implicitly specify rules for the dialogue system at low cost. Meanwhile, the power of deep language understanding model is used to enhance the generalization ability. Future work is expected to extend this method to deal with more complex tasks, such as cross-domain dialogue applications.

References

1. Chen, H., Liu, X., Yin, D., et al.: A survey on dialogue systems: recent advances and new frontiers. ACM SIGKDD Explor. Newsl. **19**(2), 25–35 (2017)
2. Nakano, M., Miyazaki, N., Yasuda, N., et al.: Wit: a toolkit for building robust and real-time spoken dialogu systems. In: 1st SIGdial Workshop on Discourse and Dialogue, pp. 150–159 (2000)
3. Goddeau, D., Meng, H., Polifroni, J., et al.: A form-based dialogue manager for spoken language applications. In: IEEE Processing, vol. 2, pp. 701–704 (1996)
4. Zue, V., Seneff, S., Glass, J.R., et al.: JUPITER: a telephone-based conversational interface for weather information. IEEE Trans. Speech Audio Process. **8**(1), 85–96 (2000)
5. Thomson, B., Young, S.: Bayesian update of dialogue state: a POMDP framework for spoken dialogue systems. Comput. Speech Lang. **24**(4), 562–588 (2010)

6. Young, S., Gašić, M., Keizer, S., et al.: The hidden information state model: a practical framework for POMDP-based spoken dialogue management. Comput. Speech Lang. **24**(2), 150–174 (2010)
7. Williams, J.D., Raux, A., Henderson, M.: The dialog state tracking challenge series: a review. Dialogue Discourse **7**(3), 4–33 (2016)
8. Zhao, T., Eskenazi, M.: Towards end-to-end learning for dialog state tracking and management using deep reinforcement learning. In: Proceedings of the SIGDIAL 2016 Conference, pp. 1–10. Association for Computational Linguistics, Los Angeles (2016)
9. Zhang, Z., Takanobu, R., Zhu, Q., Huang, M., Zhu, X.: Recent advances and challenges in task-oriented dialog systems. Sci. China Technol. Sci. **63**(10), 2011–2027 (2020). https://doi.org/10.1007/s11431-020-1692-3
10. Chen, Q., Zhuo, Z., Wang, W.: BERT for joint intent classification and slot filling. ArXiv preprint arXiv:1902.10909 (2019)
11. Devlin, J., Chang, M.W., Lee, K., et al.: BERT: pre-training of deep bidirectional transformers for language understanding. In: Proceedings of the 2019 Conference of the North American Chapter of the Association for Computational Linguistics, pp. 4171–4186. Association for Computational Linguistics, Minneapolis, Minnesota (2019)
12. Robertson, S., Hugo, Z.: The probabilistic relevance framework: BM25 and beyond. Now Publishers Inc. (2009)
13. Reimers, N., Gurevych, I.: Sentence-bert: Sentence embeddings using siamese bert-networks. ArXiv preprint arXiv:1908.10084 (2019)
14. Zhu, Q., Zhang, Z., Fang, Y., et al.: Convlab-2: An open-source toolkit for building, evaluating, and diagnosing dialogue systems. ArXiv preprint arXiv:2002.04793 (2020)
15. Wu, C.S., Madotto, A., Hosseini-Asl, E., et al.: Transferable multi-domain state generator for task-oriented dialogue systems. In: Proceedings of the 57th Annual Meeting of the Association for Computational Linguistics, pp. 808–819. Association for Computational Linguistics, Florence, Italy (2019)

Service Migration Based on Replaying

Hexin Zheng[1]([✉]), Di Lin[1], Yu Tang[1], Yuan Gao[2], and Jiang Cao[2]

[1] School of Information and Software Engineering, University of Electronic Science and Technology of China, Chengdu 610054, China
201822090541@std.uestc.edu.cn, lindi@uestc.edu.cn
[2] Military Academy of Sciences, Beijing, China

Abstract. With the rapid development of the Internet, more and more data are transmitted on the Internet, and the demand for computing power of end users is also increasing. At the same time, the response delay of the service is becoming more and more sensitive. The traditional data center faces This situation has become increasingly inadequate. Mobile Edge Computing (MEC) has hope to solve this problem. By deploying computing resources to the edge of the network, MEC shortens the distance from users geographically, can handle user requests nearby, improves the speed of service impact, and avoids long network transmissions. A key issue of MEC is to ensure that users always provide services through the geographically closest edge node to ensure service quality. This paper proposes a new idea to migrate user services, by reducing the amount of data transmission in the process of service migration, so as to complete the service migration as quickly as possible.

Keywords: MEC · Service migration · Iterative migration

1 Introduction

With the advent of the "Internet of Everything" era and the popularization of smartphones, the number of various Internet of Things devices and smart terminals has begun to explode, which has also resulted in a substantial increase in network traffic. This makes it increasingly difficult for traditional centralized data centers to meet the network delay requirements of delay-sensitive applications. The proposal of Mobile Edge Computation (MEC) makes it possible to solve this problem [4].

The main idea of MEC is to decentralize computation resources and storage capabilities to the edge of the network to shorten the distance from users geographically. When the terminal sends a request, the request will not go through the long transmission network to reach the data center and then be processed, but locally, directly processed and returned by the MEC server deployed at the edge of the network. Since the request is responded locally, the transmission delay will be greatly reduced, thereby improving the user experience. In addition, data is not transmitted to the cloud data center via the Internet, which also improves data security to a certain extent and reduces the risk of data leakage.

The incoming problem is that because the MEC server is deployed at the edge of the network and its coverage is relatively small, ordinary user movement may cause the terminal device to move from the coverage of one edge node to the coverage of another edge node. In order to ensure the quality of service, the user's service at the previous edge node also needs to follow the user's movement. In addition, in the MEC environment, the network environment between the edge node and the edge node is very complicated, and there may be multiple network topologies and communication systems [22], which makes the bandwidth between nodes extremely limited, which brings a lot of challenges to the rapid realization of service migration.

This paper mainly discusses how to achieve faster user service migration under different bandwidth conditions (Fig. 1).

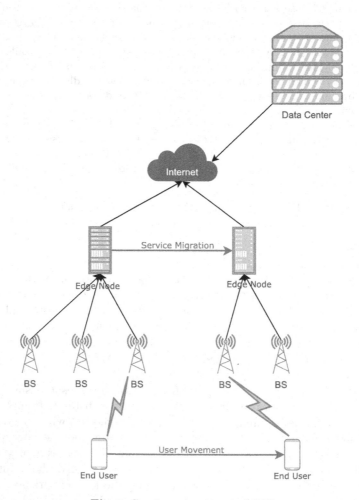

Fig. 1. Service migration in MEC

2   Related Work

Before this thesis, there have been a lot of related researches on user service migration, and the research focus is mainly on the following aspects:

Part of the main research is when and where to migrate. Research in this area mainly uses tools such as Markov Decision Process (MDP) and Reinforcement Learning (RL).

The author of [21] based on MDP, a one-dimensional MDP model based on distance is first proposed. When the user moves under one-dimensional conditions, the moving range is relatively limited and the solution space is relatively small, so it is easier to find the optimal under this condition solution. Subsequently, the author extended the one-dimensional MDP model to the two-dimensional MDP model. In a two-dimensional environment, the user's moving direction is almost infinite, so the author refers to the idea of a cellular network and divides the space into several adjacent regular hexagons. Modeling is then used to simulate the user's movement in space. When solving, the complexity of the direct search algorithm is too high, so heuristic algorithm is used to find the suboptimal solution. [9,10,17,19,20,23] also use MDP in their work about MEC.

Gao in [5] through modeling, abstracts the MEC network model into a graph, each node in the graph represents an edge node, and a node can be connected to multiple nodes. The edges between nodes represent the network between edge nodes. Under the model with several assumptions, the problem can be transformed into a problem that can be processed by reinforcement learning, and then solved by means of reinforcement learning and deep reinforcement learning. Reinforcement learning is also used in the work of others to study service migration strategies in the MEC environment such as [17,18,24,25].

The other part focuses on how to migrate from one edge node to another node faster. Research in this area mainly proposes various solutions to achieve faster service migration. At present, the measurement indicators of the service migration plan are mainly the time required for the entire service migration and the time of the service interruption during the service migration process.

Puliafito mentioned an iterative-based service migration method in [14] (we call it iterative migration). Under the condition of continuous service provision, the data that needs to be transmitted is transmitted to the destination node; when iterating to the threshold, the service is interrupted, and then the remaining data and unsynchronized data are transmitted to the destination node; finally, the service is restored on the destination node to realize the migration. This method shortens the service interruption time caused by service migration through iteration, but this method requires repeated iterations, resulting in a large amount of data transmission, thereby making the entire service migration time-consuming. Kaneda et al. [7] searches the application-level delay in MEC environment by using iterative migration; Kondo in [8] designs a platform which brings cooperative processing between an edge server and a mobile device based on iterative migration. [1,2] also used iterative migration in their work.

Machen proposes a service migration scheme based on layered thinking in [11]. When the traditional solution is used for service migration, related programs will package and transmit many low-level files including the system kernel, resulting in a large number of low-level public files that need to be transmitted. This solution divides the user's services on the virtual machine into three layers: GuestOS, Application, and Instance. When performing service migration, first determine whether the destination node has the same GuestOS as the source node. If they are not the same, the destination node loads the relevant GuestOS. If the same, continue to determine whether there is the binary code of the current service and the dependent files required for service operation in the GuestOS under the destination node. If it does not exist, download the relevant files of the service from the relevant server according to the configuration, and finally transfer the user's service instance. The layered-based service migration idea can greatly reduce the amount of data transmission compared with the traditional solution. Many service migration solutions are based on this idea. The same layering idea is also used in [6,12]'s work

In addition, there are some applied research based on service migration. [16] uses service migration as a tool to maximize the throughput of the regional MEC environment through wireless transmission power control and service migration. The specific idea is that when there is a load imbalance between edge nodes in the area, wireless transmission power control is used to adjust the number of access users of each base station in the area. When the user's access base station changes, service migration is triggered to make the load of edge nodes in this area is balanced, thereby improving the throughput of edge nodes in the whole area.

3   Methodology

In the view of the current migration methods that generally need to transmit a large amount of data, this paper proposes a migration method based on replay (we call it replay migration). This kind of thinking is used in many applications. For example, the database engine InnoDB of MySQL comes with a redo log module, and HBase also uses the Write Ahead Log (WAL) mechanism.

In the current mainstream iterative migration method, when the service migration is triggered, a pre-dump operation will be performed. The file generated by this operation only saves part of the process information and these files cannot be used to restore the service(the file generated by the subsequent dump operation is required to restore the service); then the file generated by the pre-dump operation is transferred to the destination node; after several iterations, the dump operation is performed and the service is suspended, and then the file generated by the dump operation Transmit to the destination node and restore service. Algorithm 1 shows the entire process of iterative migration.

In the replay migration, when the service migration is triggered, it will go through the following stages (assuming the migration from node A to node B):

Algorithm 1: Iterative Migration

    `// number of iterations can be used instead`
    Input: dirt data rate threshold *threshold*
1 First pre-dump;
    `// ddr means dirt data rate`
2 Calculation *ddr* ;
3 **while** *ddr > threshold* **do**
4 | Pre-dump ;
5 | Transmit data ;
6 | Update *ddr* ;
7 **end**
8 Dump ;
9 Transmit data ;
10 Restore service at destination node ;
11 Terminate source service ;
12 Start to provide service ;

---

1. Node A generates a snapshot file of the corresponding service, and at the same time redirects the input data of the client to node B; at this time, the client can still provide services
2. When there is data coming in from the client, node B caches the received data and forwards a copy to node A at the same time. When node A returns the calculation result, node B also caches and forwards it to the client; at the same time, node A starts to transmit the generated service snapshot file to node B through the network;
3. After the node snapshot file transfer is completed, node B restore the service according to the snapshot file, and synchronizes the service status according to the cached input data; the service on node A temporarily maintains the status; node B stops receiving data from the client at this time to temporarily stop providing services;
4. When the service synchronization on node B is completed, node A terminates the service; node B stops the forwarding of input data, and starts to provide services to the client;

The whole process of replay migration is shown in Algorithm 2. Figure 2 shows the procedure of replay migration.

Replay migration greatly reduces the amount of data that needs to be transferred by transferring data from the client instead of transferring the memory pages of the service. Due to the small network bandwidth and poor network environment in the MEC environment, reducing the amount of data transmission can effectively speed up the service migration process.

Algorithm 2: Replay Migration

1 Dump service ;
2 Cache input data ;
3 Transmit data ;
4 Restore service at destination node ;
5 Suspend source service ;
6 Replay cached data ;
7 Terminate source service ;
8 Start to provide service ;

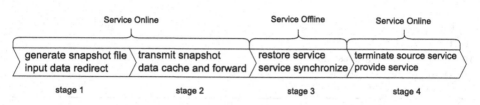

Fig. 2. Replay migration stages

4 Implementation

In the process of method realization, this thesis designed experimental schemes of iterative migration and replay migration respectively, and recorded experiment data for comparison.

In the experiment, we use TensorFlow as the back-end Keras implementation of the YOLOv3 algorithm [15], use the open source image data set Pascal VOC Dataset [13] as the input data, and use the model to identify the pictures in the VOC data set to simulate a service. The two nodes are simulated separately by two computers with the same hardware and in the same LAN environment. The maximum bandwidth between two computers in a local area network is about 580 Mbps. Between the two computers, Wondershaper is used to limit the bandwidth between the two machines. Use iPerf to test the bandwidth between the two machines to ensure that it is within the range we set, file transfer is done by using rsync. The realization of the migration method is mainly realized through CRIU (Checkpoint/Restore In Userspace) [3].

In the experiment, first use Wondershaper to limit the bandwidth between the two computers, and then use iPerf to test and record the available bandwidth between the two computers. Subsequently, CRIU and rsync were used to implement iterative migration and replay migration respectively. After each migration, the relevant logs were analyzed to obtain experimental data.

When implementing iterative migration, we first use CRIU's pre-dump function several times. This operation only dumps part of the information about the process and does this by freezing the task in the shortest possible time. The image file generated by the pre-dump cannot and should not be used for restoration. After each pre-dump is completed, use rsync to transfer the generated image file. After the transfer is completed, the next pre-dump operation can be performed. After reaching the preset threshold, perform a dump operation and use rsync to transfer related files. After the transmission is completed, use CRIU to restore the service at the destination node. At this point, an iterative migration is completed.

Since CRIU does not have relevant functions to support the completion of replay migration, so replay migration needs to be completed by using some basic functions of CRIU and combining some code changes. When implementing replay migration, first use CRIU's dump operation to generate a snapshot file of the entire service, and keep the service running, at the same time, the operating system sends control information to destination node to start the preset program at the destination node (the program is used to forward and cache related data) and change the destination of input data to destination node; then start to use rsync to transfer the generated snapshot file; when the snapshot file transfer is completed, the operating system will send control information to stop accepting input data and restore the service at the destination node, and then start to calculate the cached data; when the execution of the cached data is completed, it means that the service status has been synchronized and destination node can start to provide service.

In the experiment, by performing iterative migration and replay migration under different bandwidths, the experiment under each condition was repeated three times, and then the average value of the obtained data was calculated as the experimental data. The obtained experimental data are as follows.

From Fig. 3, we can see that when the available bandwidth is reduced to a certain extent, whether it is replay migration or iterative migration, the time required for migration will increase significantly. In comparison, under any bandwidth conditions, the entire service migration time for replay migration is less than 50% of the iterative migration, which fully reflects the advantages of the replay migration method, which is to transmit the input data of the client instead of the memory of the service Pages are used to reduce the time consuming in the transmission process, which in turn consumes the computing performance of the node to ensure that the service can achieve synchronization.

It can be found from Fig. 4 that similar to the migration time, when the bandwidth drops to a certain level, the service interruption time starts to increase significantly. By comparison, the service interruption time of replay migration is much shorter than iterative migration. From the view of migration methods, the service interruption time of iterative migration is mainly concentrated in the last dump operation and the time consumption of subsequent file transfer and service restore, while the service interruption time of recurring migration is concentrated in service restore and replaying cached data. During the migration process, the replay migration only transmits the service snapshot file when the migration is triggered, and because the client's data input has a certain time interval, it can quickly synchronize the service status after the transmission is completed; for the iterative migration, as a result of providing services in the migration's iterative phase, the data in the memory is constantly changing due

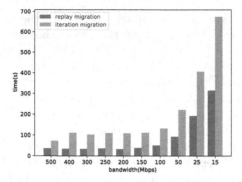

Fig. 3. Total migration time

to processing input data. It is easy to cause the data transmitted in the last iteration to have changed during the next iteration. Due to the existence of this phenomenon, as a result, the file size generated during the last dump operation will increase to a certain extent, resulting in a longer service interruption time for iterative migration.

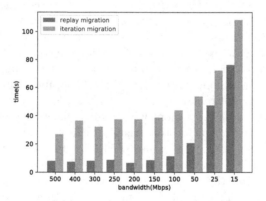

Fig. 4. Interruption time

It can be seen from Fig. 5 that file transfer is the most time-consuming part in iterative migration or replay migration. For replay migration, when the bandwidth is reduced, the time it takes to replay the file will increase. The main reason is that the time required to transfer the file increases, which increases the cached data, which in turn requires more time to replay the file. For iterative migration, there are two main reasons why CRIU takes more time than replay migration. On the one hand, CRIU needs to track memory changes, and on the other hand, it reads and processes more files to ensure that the recovered data is up to date when restoring services.

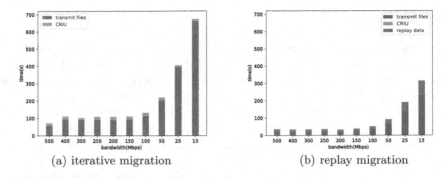

(a) iterative migration   (b) replay migration

Fig. 5. Proportion of operation time of service migration

Here we need to introduce a concept called Service Jitter. Service Jitter refers to the fact that the terminal can access the service but cannot access the service through the nearest edge node, which leads to a decrease of the Quality of Service (QoS). Figure 6 shows the ratio of the service interruption duration and service jitter duration of iterative migration and replay migration to the overall service migration duration under different bandwidth conditions. For iterative migration, as the bandwidth continues to decrease, the proportion of service interruption time is generally decreasing. The main reason is that iterative migration requires a large number of files to be transferred under a lower bandwidth, which greatly increases the overall service migration time. Correspondingly, the time proportion of service jitter increases as the bandwidth decreases. For replay migration, the percentage of service interruption time is generally stable and has not changed much with the decrease in bandwidth. In addition, in the case of high bandwidth, the proportion of service interruption time is also lower than iterative migration.

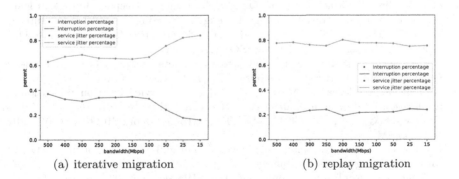

(a) iterative migration   (b) replay migration

Fig. 6. Service jitter time and service interruption time

5   Conclusion

In this paper, we first discussed the advantages and some existing problems. Then we introduced the two main research directions in the field of service migration, and introduced in detail the current mainstream iterative migration related content. Then we proposed a recurrence-based migration method, which reduces the amount of data transmission by transmitting user input data instead of memory page files, thereby reducing the time of service migration in a network environment with a small bandwidth. From the experimental results, the replay migration can complete the service migration in a shorter time under suitable broadband conditions, and there is no obvious gap between the service interruption time and the iterative migration.

Acknowledgment. This work is partially funded by Science and Technology Program of Sichuan Province (021YFG0330), partially funded by Grant SCITLAB-0001 of Intelligent Terminal Key Laboratory of SiChuan Province, and partially funded by Fundamental Research Funds for the Central Universities (ZYGX2019J076).

References

1. Addad, R.A., Cadette Dutra, D.L., Bagaa, M., Taleb, T., Flinck, H.: Towards a fast service migration in 5g. In: 2018 IEEE Conference on Standards for Communications and Networking (CSCN), pp. 1–6, October 2018. https://doi.org/10.1109/CSCN.2018.8581836, iM
2. Avramidis, I., Mackay, M., Tso, F.P., Fukai, T., Shinagawa, T.: Live migration on arm-based micro-datacentres. In: 2018 15th IEEE Annual Consumer Communications Networking Conference (CCNC), pp. 1–6, January 2018. https://doi.org/10.1109/CCNC.2018.8319241, iM
3. CRIU. https://criu.org/. Accessed 20 July 2020
4. ETSI: Industry specification group (ISG) on multi-access edge computing (MEC). https://www.etsi.org/committee/mec. Accessed 20 July 2020
5. Gao, Z., Jiao, Q., Xiao, K., Wang, Q., Mo, Z., Yang, Y.: Deep reinforcement learning based service migration strategy for edge computing. In: 2019 IEEE International Conference on Service-Oriented System Engineering (SOSE), pp. 116–1165, April 2019. https://doi.org/10.1109/SOSE.2019.00025, rL
6. Ha, K., et al.: Adaptive VM handoff across cloudlets. School of Computer Science Carnegie Mellon University, Pittsburgh, PA 15213 (2015). Layered
7. Kaneda, J., Arakawa, S., Murata, M.: Effects of service function relocation on application-level delay in multi-access edge computing. In: 2018 IEEE 5G World Forum (5GWF), pp. 399–404, July 2018. https://doi.org/10.1109/5GWF.2018.8517045, iM
8. Kondo, T., Isawaki, K., Maeda, K.: Development and evaluation of the MEC platform supporting the edge instance mobility. In: 2018 IEEE 42nd Annual Computer Software and Applications Conference (COMPSAC), vol. 02, pp. 193–198, July 2018. https://doi.org/10.1109/COMPSAC.2018.10228, iM
9. Ksentini, A., Taleb, T., Chen, M.: A Markov decision process-based service migration procedure for follow me cloud. In: 2014 IEEE International Conference on Communications (ICC), pp. 1350–1354, June 2014. https://doi.org/10.1109/ICC.2014.6883509, mDP

10. Lee, J., Kim, J., Tae, Y., Pack, S.: QoS-aware service migration in edge cloud networks. In: 2018 IEEE International Conference on Consumer Electronics - Asia (ICCE-Asia), pp. 206–212, June 2018. https://doi.org/10.1109/ICCE-ASIA.2018. 8552103, mDP

11. Machen, A., Wang, S., Leung, K.K., Ko, B.J., Salonidis, T.: Live service migration in mobile edge clouds. IEEE Wirel. Commun. **25**(1), 140–147 (2018). https://doi. org/10.1109/MWC.2017.1700011

12. Machen, A., Wang, S., Leung, K.K., Ko, B.J., Salonidis, T.: Migrating running applications across mobile edge clouds: poster. In: Proceedings of the 22nd Annual International Conference on Mobile Computing and Networking, MobiCom 2016, pp. 435–436. Association for Computing Machinery, New York (2016). https://doi. org/10.1145/2973750.2985265. https://doi.org/10.1145/2973750.2985265, layered

13. PASCAL VOC TEAM: The pascal VOC project. http://host.robots.ox.ac.uk/ pascal/VOC/. Accessed 20 July 2020

14. Puliafito, C., Vallati, C., Mingozzi, E., Merlino, G., Longo, F., Puliafito, A.: Container migration in the fog: a performance evaluation. Sensors **19**, 1488 (2019). https://doi.org/10.3390/s19071488

15. qqwweee. https://github.com/qqwweee/keras-yolo3. Accessed 20 July 2020

16. Rodrigues, T.G., Suto, K., Nishiyama, H., Kato, N., Temma, K.: Cloudlets activation scheme for scalable mobile edge computing with transmission power control and virtual machine migration. IEEE Trans. Comput. **67**(9), 1287–1300 (2018). https://doi.org/10.1109/TC.2018.2818144

17. Tang, Z., Zhou, X., Zhang, F., Jia, W., Zhao, W.: Migration modeling and learning algorithms for containers in fog computing. IEEE Trans. Serv. Comput. **12**(5), 712–725 (2019). https://doi.org/10.1109/TSC.2018.2827070, mDP & RL

18. Vita, F.D., Bruneo, D., Puliafito, A., Nardini, G., Virdis, A., Stea, G.: A deep reinforcement learning approach for data migration in multi-access edge computing. In: 2018 ITU Kaleidoscope: Machine Learning for a 5G Future (ITU K), pp. 1–8, November 2018. https://doi.org/10.23919/ITU-WT.2018.8597889, rL

19. Wang, S., Urgaonkar, R., He, T., Zafer, M., Chan, K., Leung, K.K.: Mobility-induced service migration in mobile micro-clouds. In: 2014 IEEE Military Communications Conference, pp. 835–840, October 2014. https://doi.org/10.1109/ MILCOM.2014.145, mDP

20. Wang, S., Urgaonkar, R., Zafer, M., He, T., Chan, K., Leung, K.K.: Dynamic service migration in mobile edge-clouds. In: 2015 IFIP Networking Conference (IFIP Networking), pp. 1–9, May 2015. https://doi.org/10.1109/IFIPNetworking. 2015.7145316, mDP

21. Wang, S., Urgaonkar, R., Zafer, M., He, T., Chan, K., Leung, K.K.: Dynamic service migration in mobile edge computing based on Markov decision process. IEEE/ACM Trans. Networking **27**(3), 1272–1288 (2019). https://doi.org/10.1109/ TNET.2019.2916577, mDP

22. Wang, S., Xu, J., Zhang, N., Liu, Y.: A survey on service migration in mobile edge computing. IEEE Access **6**, 23511–23528 (2018). https://doi.org/10.1109/ ACCESS.2018.2828102

23. Wang, W., Ge, S., Zhou, X.: Location-privacy-aware service migration in mobile edge computing. In: 2020 IEEE Wireless Communications and Networking Conference (WCNC), pp. 1–6, May 2020. https://doi.org/10.1109/WCNC45663.2020. 9120551, mDP

24. Yuan, Q., Li, J., Zhou, H., Lin, T., Luo, G., Shen, X.: A joint service migration and mobility optimization approach for vehicular edge computing. IEEE Trans. Veh. Technol. 1 (2020). https://doi.org/10.1109/TVT.2020.2999617, rL
25. Zhang, M., Huang, H., Rui, L., Hui, G., Wang, Y., Qiu, X.: A service migration method based on dynamic awareness in mobile edge computing. In: NOMS 2020–2020 IEEE/IFIP Network Operations and Management Symposium, pp. 1–7, April 2020. https://doi.org/10.1109/NOMS47738.2020.9110389, rL

Task Offloading and Resource Allocation in an Unfair Environment in Mobile Edge Computing

Yiping Li[1]([✉]), Yu Tang[1], Di Lin[1], Yuan Gao[2], and Jiang Cao[2]

[1] School of Information and Software Engineering, University of Eletronic Science and Technology of China, Chengdu 610054, China
201852090716@std.uestc.edu.cn, yutang@uestc.edu.cn
[2] Military Academy of Sciences, Beijing, China

Abstract. This paper studies the problem of offloading and resource allocation of user tasks when the user group's tasks are divided into primary tasks and secondary tasks in Mobile Edge Computing (MEC) networks. In order to ensure that the computing of primary user tasks is not disturbed. This paper proposes a parameter called calculating interference ratio (CIR), and uses CIR to limit the resources allocated by the server to secondary user tasks. In addition, the problem of offloading and resource allocation is transformed into a mixed integer programming problem (MIP). Then, we use parallel DNN networks to generate offloading and caching decisions, and transform the MIP problem into a resource allocation problem. We verify the effectiveness of CIR in dealing with the resource allocation problem in such special scenarios through simulation.

Keywords: MEC · Computing offloading · Resource allocation

1 Introduction

In recent years, many emerging applications like AR and VR have appeared, and the mobile data traffic generated by these emerging applications is increasing day by day. However, due to the limited computing capabilities of existing mobile devices, computing tasks that are computationally expensive and time-sensitive are not suitable for processing on mobile devices. Therefore, MEC, which migrates computing and storage resources to the edge of the network, is considered to be a promising technology to support the next generation of the Internet [1].

With the development of mobile networks and mobile devices, the number of mobile Internet users has exploded, which has also led to the scarcity of mobile user spectrum [2]. In order to solve the problem of scarcity of spectrum resources, researchers have proposed cognitive radio (CR) technology. CR technology is

© ICST Institute for Computer Sciences, Social Informatics and Telecommunications Engineering 2021
Published by Springer Nature Switzerland AG 2021. All Rights Reserved
X. Wang et al. (Eds.): AICON 2021, LNICST 396, pp. 549–560, 2021.
https://doi.org/10.1007/978-3-030-90196-7_47

considered to be an important role in realizing 5G dynamic spectrum access [3]. In the CR network, the primary user (PU) as a licensed user has the absolute right to access its spectrum band, while the unlicensed secondary user (SU) can access these frequency bands under the license of the PU [4].

But compared with scarce spectrum resources, although the computing resources of edge servers are not scarce, they are still insufficient compared with cloud data centers. Facing the contradiction between the limited computing resources on edge servers and the explosive growth of mobile Internet users. The edge server obviously lacks a user task classification system to ensure the resource allocation and calculation of PU tasks.

This paper studies the method of unfair resource allocation in MEC network. The characteristics of this paper are as follows:

1. The user tasks are divided into two levels: PU tasks and SU tasks. We consider the problem of computing resource allocation in MEC networks under unfair environments. By referring to the concepts of interference temperature threshold and signal-to-noise ratio in communication, the parameter of calculating interference ratio is defined. The CIR can limit the total computing resources of the edge server that can be allocated to the SU tasks in the current environment, so that the calculation of the SU tasks will not interfere with the calculation of the PU tasks. In an unfair scenario, CIR can effectively limit the occupation of server resources by SU tasks.

2. We considered the caching function. Zipf distribution is used to evaluate the popularity of content and rank the popularity of task content as the basis for caching decision.

The rest of this article is organized as follows. The Sect. 2 summarizes the past work. The Sect. 3 introduces the system model. The Sect. 4 formulates the problem. The numerical results are given in Sect. 5. Finally, the conclusion is given in Sect. 6.

2   Related Work

At present, there have been many results on the resource allocation problem of MEC, but most of these results are based on fair resource allocation. Literature [2] introduces the Nash bargaining scheme, and takes the maximum delay required by the user as the criterion for determining its transmission priority. Literature [5] proposed a power control scheme based on latent game theory and a calculation resource allocation scheme based on linear programming. Literature [6] divides the entire solution process into two parts. First, the optimal unloading decision is obtained through the neural network, so that the target problem is transformed into a convex problem, and then various optimization tools can be used to solve the bandwidth allocation problem.The literature [7–9] considered the problem of energy harvesting when solving the problem of resource allocation. The energy harvested on the mobile edge cloud and the energy consumed by task offloading have reached a good balance. Literature [10] models a series of decision-making problems of terminal equipment as Markov decision-making processes, and uses an offloading algorithm based on ϵ greedy Q-learning to solve them. Literature [11] is based on the characteristics of AR mobile applications, using the cooperative characteristics of tracker, mapper and object recognizer components to reduce mobile energy consumption and offload delay. Literature [12] created an optimization problem with a combination of minimizing energy costs and packet congestion. By establishing a priority queue and adopting a probability enhancement scheme, it effectively controlled the congestion of MEC by packets of different priorities. Although the literature [12] considered the priority of the task, it still did not consider the problem of unfair computing resource allocation on the edge server. Literature [13] uses the alternate direction multiplier method to optimize the offloading decision and wireless transmission and computing resource allocation of each cognitive base station in the CR scenario. However, although it considers authorized users and unauthorized users, It does not highlight user unfairness in computing resource allocation.

Therefore, in the scenario of dividing user groups into PUs and SUs, how to ensure the calculation of PU tasks while ensuring as much as possible the server resource allocation for SU tasks is an urgent need solved problem.

3   System Model

3.1   Network Model

We consider an MEC network, which consists of an edge server, a wireless access point (AP) and N user equipments. N users generate N tasks to be processed at each moment. Let $N = 1, 2, ..., N$. According to the importance of the task, the tasks of the user equipment are divided into two types: Primary Tasks and Secondary Tasks.

In our system model, the AP and the edge server are wired via optical fiber, and the transmission delay between the two parties can be ignored. Each user device (UD) has primary or secondary tasks that need to be processed locally or offloaded to the edge server. Without loss of generality, we assume that there are N user devices that will generate tasks that need to be processed at the same time, and the tasks are independent of each other, and assume that the tasks will end after the current time ends. c_n represents the amount of calculation required by user n at the current moment, B_n represents the amount of task data, UD n can determine whether to offload its task to the edge server, and the offload decision is represented by the binary variable a_n, where $a_n = \{0, 1\}$. Specifically, when $a_n = 0$, it means that user n decides to perform computing tasks locally, and $a_n = 1$ means that user n decides to offload tasks to the edge server for processing.

After the user submits the task to the edge server, the edge server will decide whether to cache the calculation results of the task. The cache decision is represented by the binary variable x_n, where $x_n = \{0, 1\}$. Specifically, $x_n = 0$ indicates that the calculation result of user n will not be cached by the edge server, and

$x_n = 1$ indicates that the edge server decides to cache the calculation result of user n.

Table 1. Related variable table

Variable	Meaning
r_n	Transmission rate
c_n	The amount of calculation required by the task
B_n	Task data size
$B_n^{\cdot}$	Data size of the task after calculation
F	Total edge server computing resources
N_0	Noise power, $N_0 = -174$ dBm
p_n	User transmission power
P_f	Zip distribution function
ζ_n	Unit price to improve user n's performance
α_n	Unit price of user ji's data transmission
β_n	Unit price of using licensed spectrum
γ_n	The cost saved per bps of data
ψ_n	Cache unit price to be paid

3.2 MEC Offloading Model

Assuming that each computing task can be described as $T_n = \{B_n, B_n^{\cdot}, c_n, p_f, tag\}$. For the task T_n, first of all, we need to calculate the time cost that the user needs to complete the task calculation on the local device [2]:

$$t_n^{local} = \frac{c_n}{f_{user}} \qquad (1)$$

Among them, f_{user} is the computing capacity of the user device. Then we need to calculate the time cost of offloading the task T_n to the edge cloud server for processing. d_n is the proportion of computing resources allocated by the server to the task of user n, where $d_n \in [0,1]$. Then we can get the calculation execution time of the task T_n at the MEC server [2]:

$$t_n^{off} = \frac{c_n}{d_n F}, \forall n \in N, d_n \in [0,1] \qquad (2)$$

We express the improved performance after uninstallation as $\frac{t^{local}}{t_n^{off}}$, then the calculated revenue of user n can be expressed as [13]:

$$U_e = a_n * \zeta_n \frac{t_n^{local}}{t_n^{off}} = a_n * \zeta_n \frac{d_n F}{f_{user}} \qquad (3)$$

3.3   Transmission Model

When the user equipment n decides to offload the task to the edge server for calculation, the user equipment n transmits its task to the AP through the wireless channel. Then the AP forwards the task to the edge server, and the edge server will process the task. Finally, the processing result is sent back to the user device. Because the data size of the processing result is usually very small, we ignore the downlink delay [13]. Let b_n represent the proportion of transmission resources allocated to user n, where W represents the spectrum bandwidth of the AP, and $b_n \in [0, 1]$. Let h_n represent the channel gain between user n and AP, assuming that this channel has reciprocity.

$$\sum_{n=1}^{N} a_n b_n \leq 1, \forall n \in N, N = PT \cup ST \tag{4}$$

The spectrum rate between user equipment n and BS is [14]:

$$r_n = b_n W \log_2(1 + \frac{p_n |h_n|^2}{N_0}), \forall n \in N, N = PT \cup ST \tag{5}$$

Therefore, the revenue transmitted by the user can be expressed as [14]:

$$U_t = a_n(\alpha_n r_n - \beta_n b_n), \forall n \in N, N = PT \cup ST \tag{6}$$

3.4   Cache Model

The MEC server can decide whether to cache the results according to the popularity distribution of the content of each task. We assume that the cache resources of MEC server are sufficient.

For each time frame, it is assumed that there are F different popular content distributed in the network. We use the vector $P = [P_1, P_2, ..., P_F]$ to represent the popularity of task content. That is, the probability that each user independently requests each content f is P_f, and the content popularity p is represented by the Zipf distribution [14]:

$$P_f = \frac{\frac{1}{f^\epsilon}}{\sum_{f=1}^{F} \frac{1}{f^\epsilon}} \tag{7}$$

Among them, ϵ represents the popularity and popularity of the content. The higher the value of ϵ, the higher the possibility that it may be used. Its typical value is 0.5 to 1.5. After the task T_n with content f offloads to the MEC server, if the server finds a cache record with content f, the server can directly return the result. The gain brought by the calculation result of the cache content f can be expressed as [14]:

$$g_n = \frac{P_{T_n} B_n}{t_n^{back}} \tag{8}$$

The cache price of low-popular content should be set to a higher value, so that the less popular content may not be cached in the MEC server. We assume that the price is known, the system's cache revenue can be expressed as [14]:

$$U_c = a_n x_n (\gamma_n g_n - \psi_{B_n} B_n) \tag{9}$$

4   MEC Resource Allocation with CIR

4.1   Calculation Interference Ratio

CR was born before edge computing. There are many ideas in CR's division of user groups and the utilization and allocation of spectrum resources. In the CR network, the user group is divided into authorized PU and unauthorized SU. The interference power of SU to PU must be subject to certain constraints. This constraint is called the interference temperature threshold. The interference temperature threshold is determined by the worst signal-to-noise ratio that the PU can withstand. In the CR network, the PU as an authorized user has the absolute right to access its frequency band [15], while the SU must meet the interference temperature threshold constraint when accessing the spectrum, which is extremely restrictive. Greatly guarantees the use of frequency spectrum by major users. In order to apply the idea of CR to the resource allocation of edge servers, we consider an unfair user task scenario. We divide the tasks of the user group into PT and ST.

According to circuit theory, the CPU power is mainly determined by the dynamic power. The dynamic power is derived from the switching activity of the logic gates inside the CPU and is proportional to the $v_{cir}^2 f_c$ in the CMOS circuit, where v_{cir} is the circuit voltage and f_c is the CPU cycle frequency [16]. In addition, when running at low voltage, the CPU cycle frequency is approximately linear with the chip voltage [16]. Therefore, the power on the CPU is:

$$P = \kappa_c f_c^3 \tag{10}$$

κ_c is the chip architecture constant, $\kappa_c = 10^{-27}$. If the server is regarded as an M-core CPU, the power on the server can be expressed as [16]:

$$P = \sum_{m=1}^{M} \kappa_m f_m^3, \forall m \in M \tag{11}$$

The interference temperature threshold in CR is mainly determined by the worst signal-to-noise ratio that the PU can work normally. With reference to the concept of signal-to-noise ratio, we can define the CIR. Since there is no noise interference on the server, the calculation interference of the PU tasks are composed of the CPU power occupied by the SU tasks. We define F_P/F_S as CIR, where f_p is the computing resource required by the PU task, and f_s is the computing resource required by the SU task. Obviously, when $\frac{F_P}{F_S}$ is 0, the task of the PU will not get any resource allocation.

$$\frac{F_P}{F_S} = \frac{f_P}{f_S} \tag{12}$$

4.2 Problem Formulation

N_P represents the primary user task group, N_S represents the SU task group, and n represents the total task group, where $N_P \cup N_S = N, n_P \in N_P, n_S \in N_S$. The total revenue of the system can be divided into two parts: the revenue of the PU tasks and the revenue of the SU tasks. Among them, the revenue of the PU/SU tasks are composed of transmission revenue, calculation revenue and cache revenue respectively. U. Mathematically, in order to maximize the total revenue of the system, the problem can be formulated as:

$$OP1: \max_{\{a_n, b_n, x_n, d_n\}} \sum_{n_P=1}^{N_P} U_{n_P}^P + \sum_{n_S=1}^{N_S} U_{n_S}^S$$

$$C1: 0 \leq d_n, b_n \leq 1$$

$$C2: \sum_{n=1}^{N} a_n b_n, \sum_{n=1}^{N} a_n d_n \leq 1 \tag{13}$$

$$C3: \sum_{n_P=1}^{N_P} a_{n_P} d_{n_P} \geq \frac{F_P}{F_S} \sum_{n_S=1}^{N_S} a_{n_S} d_{n_S}$$

Among them, $\sum_{n_P=1}^{n_P} U_{n_P}^P$ is the total revenue of the primary user tasks. $\sum_{n_S=1}^{n_S} U_{n_S}^S$ is the total revenue of the SU task. C1 represent the value ranges of d_n and b_n. C2 indicate that the allocated resources for tasks participating in offloading calculations shall not exceed the total resources for transmission and calculation. C3 is the CIR constraint, which is used to limit the total resources allocated to the SU task group. F_P/F_S is a constant for CIR. Among them, $\forall n = \{n_P, n_S\}, \forall n_P \in N_P, \forall n_S \in N_S, N_P \cup N_S = N$.

4.3 Solve

Obviously, the problem to be optimized in the previous section is a discrete and non-convex NP-hard problem. Therefore, it is challenging to find the global optimal solution. In order to make the solution more convenient, we choose the algorithm of literature [6] to solve the Problem. The unfair MEC offloading and resource allocation (UMORA) pseudo code is as follows Algorithm 1. We can use task content popularity and task data size as input items, parallel neural networks are used for offloading decisions and caching decisions. So far, we have obtained feasible offloading decisions and caching decisions. Since the solution of integer variables is solved by the neural network, the original problem is transformed into a simple resource allocation problem. For this new problem, mathematical methods can be used to optimize the solution. This paper selects the simplex method to solve the next step, and the optimal term obtained is the solution of the current iteration number. Then, the environment variables and decisions are stored in a limited memory pool. The data in the memory pool will be continuously updated over time. Each training of each neural network will randomly extract a batch of data samples from the memory pool, and use the gradient descent algorithm to minimize crossover Entropy loss function, and then optimize the parameters of each neural network.

Algorithm 1. UMORA pseudo code

Input: P_f, c_n, B_n
Output: a_n, x_n, d_n, b_n
 1: **for** $t = 0$ to T **do**
 2:     K neural network generation offloading decision list and cache decision list;
 3:     Let total revenue of the system $U_{Opt} = 0, index = 0$;
 4:     **for** $k = 0$ to K **do**
 5:         Substitute $a_n[k]$ and $x_n[k]$ into OP1;
 6:         solving $OP2[k]$ and get the maximum benefit U_k;
 7:         **if** $U_{Opt} < max(U_{Opt}, U_k)$ **then**
 8:             $U_opt = max(U_opt, U_k)$
 9:             $index = k$
10:         **end if**
11:     **end for**
12:     Get the optimal solution outOpt at the current moment and Store the input items and decisions into the memory pool;
13:     Extract data from the memory pool to train DNNs.
14: **end for**

$$OP2: \max_{\{b_n, d_n\}} U$$
$$C1 \sim C3 \tag{14}$$

5   Performance Evaluation

In this section, we show the results of MEC resource allocation with CIR. In real life, multi-core parallel computing can be performed to solve the optimal offloading decision and cache decision. But in order to facilitate the realization, we adopted a serial method to optimize the solution during the simulation.

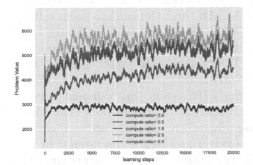

Fig. 1. System benefits under different calculation ratios

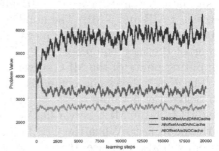

Fig. 2. System benefits of not caching and DNN caching when all users are offloaded to MEC

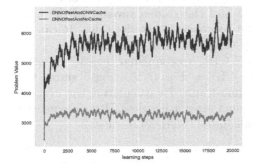

Fig. 3. System benefits under different CIR

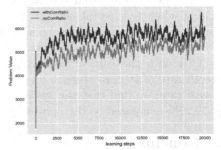

Fig. 4. System benefits of no caching and DNN caching when using DNN to offload

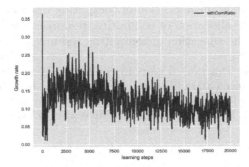

Fig. 5. The growth rate of system revenue after using CIR parameter

With reference to the 3GPP protocol [17] and other open source data, the input data size is bet1ween 0 MB and 30 MB, and the calculation result is between 1 MB and 3 MB. The number of CPU revolutions required by the task is between 100 mega and 1000 mega. The bandwidth is 10 MHz. The computing power of the user equipment is 2 GHz. The transmission power is 2 W. The computing power of the MEC server is 10 GHz.

The Fig. 1 shows the comparison of the CIR results with different values. We tested the 5 values of $\frac{F_P}{F_S} = [0, 0.5, 1.5, 2.5, 5.0]$. It can be seen that when the CIR is 0, the MEC server has no computing resources that can be allocated to the main user. When the CIR becomes larger and larger, the revenue of the system will also increase. However, due to the limitation of the total computing resources of the MEC server, the system revenue will not increase all the time. Therefore, we choose the calculated interference ratio to be 2.5.

The cache model of our MEC server caches the task results after computing. We assumed that the storage resources are extremely large. The Fig. 2 shows the comparison between the system revenue of the cache and the system revenue of the non-caching when the tasks are all offloaded. The Fig. 3 shows the comparison between the system revenue of the cache and the system revenue of the non-caching when the neural network is used to generate the decisions. It can be found that the result with cache is better than the result without cache.

Regarding the practical effectiveness of CIR, we compared the case of using the CIR with the case of not using the CIR as Fig. 4. The Fig. 5 shows the growth rate of system revenue for each time frame. By calculating the average growth rate, we find that the system revenue after using the CIR has increased by 12.27% compared to the non-using calculated interference ratio.

6   Conclusion

In this work, we considered the MEC resource allocation problem in an unfair scenario. We designed the CIR to limit the total amount of computing resource allocation that can be allocated to SU task groups. In addition, we also used a parallel neural network to generate offloading decision and cache decision variables to simplify the original problem. The simulation results show that the CIR can indeed play a role in the allocation of computing resources in unfair scenarios, ensuring that the allocation of computing resources for primary user tasks is not interfered by the allocation of computing resources for SUs.

Acknowledgements. This work is partially funded by Science and Technology Program of Sichuan Province (2021YFG0330), partially funded by Grant SCITLAB-0001 of Intelligent Terminal Key Laboratory of SiChuan Province, and partially Funded by Fundamental Research Funds for the Central Universities (ZYGX2019J076).

References

1. ETSI: MEC in 5G networks. Write Paper, European Telecommunications Standards Institute (ETSI) (2018). https://www.etsi.org/images/files/ETSIWhitePapers/etsi_wp28_mec_in_5G_FINAL.pdf

2. Zhu, Z., et al.: Fair resource allocation for system throughput maximization in mobile edge computing. IEEE Access **6**, 5332–5340 (2018). https://doi.org/10. 1109/ACCESS.2018.2790963
3. Zhao, Z., Peng, M., Ding, Z., Wang, W., Poor, H.V.: Cluster content caching: an energy-efficient approach to improve quality of service in cloud radio access networks. IEEE J. Sel. Areas Commun. **34**(5), 1207–1221 (2016). https://doi.org/ 10.1109/JSAC.2016.2545384
4. Jaya, T., Raaja, V.K., Sharanya, C., Rajendran, V.: An efficient power allocation and joint optimal sensing of spectrum in CDMA-based cognitive radio networks. In: 2017 International Conference on Communication and Signal Processing (ICCSP), pp. 1769–1773 (2017). https://doi.org/10.1109/ICCSP.2017.8286697
5. Liu, H., et al.: Computing resource allocation of mobile edge computing networks based on potential game theory. In: 2018 IEEE 4th International Conference on Computer and Communications (ICCC), pp. 693–699 (2018). https://doi.org/10. 1109/CompComm.2018.8780576
6. Huang, L., Feng, X., Feng, A., Huang, Y., Qian, L.P.: Distributed deep learning-based offloading for mobile edge computing networks. Mobile Networks Appl. 1–8 (2018). https://doi.org/10.1007/s11036-018-1177-x
7. Huang, L., Bi, S., Zhang, Y.J.A.: Deep reinforcement learning for online computation offloading in wireless powered mobile-edge computing networks. IEEE Trans. Mobile Comput. **19**(11), 2581–2593 (2020). https://doi.org/10.1109/TMC.2019. 2928811
8. Ji, L., Guo, S.: Energy-efficient cooperative resource allocation in wireless powered mobile edge computing. IEEE Internet Things J. **6**(3), 4744–4754 (2019). https:// doi.org/10.1109/JIOT.2018.2880812
9. Chen, W., Wang, D., Li, K.: Multi-user multi-task computation offloading in green mobile edge cloud computing. IEEE Trans. Serv. Comput. **12**(5), 726–738 (2019). https://doi.org/10.1109/TSC.2018.2826544
10. Liu, X., Yu, J., Wang, J., Gao, Y.: Resource allocation with edge computing in IoT networks via machine learning. IEEE Internet Things J. **7**(4), 3415–3426 (2020). https://doi.org/10.1109/JIOT.2020.2970110
11. Al-Shuwaili, A., Simeone, O.: Energy-efficient resource allocation for mobile edge computing-based augmented reality applications. IEEE Wirel. Commun. Lett. **6**(3), 398–401 (2017). https://doi.org/10.1109/LWC.2017.2696539
12. Yang, Y., Ma, Y., Xiang, W., Gu, X., Zhao, H.: Joint optimization of energy consumption and packet scheduling for mobile edge computing in cyber-physical networks. IEEE Access **6**, 15576–15586 (2018). https://doi.org/10.1109/ACCESS. 2018.2810115
13. Jia, F., Zhang, H., Ji, H., Li, X.: Distributed resource allocation and computation offloading scheme for cognitive mobile edge computing networks with NOMA. In: 2018 IEEE/CIC International Conference on Communications in China (ICCC), pp. 553–557 (2018). https://doi.org/10.1109/ICCChina.2018.8641192
14. Zhou, Y., Yu, F.R., Chen, J., Kuo, Y.: Resource allocation for information-centric virtualized heterogeneous networks with in-network caching and mobile edge computing. IEEE Trans. Vehicular Technol. **66**(12), 11339–11351 (2017). https://doi. org/10.1109/TVT.2017.2737028
15. Hoang, A.T., Liang, Y., Wong, D.T.C., Zhang, R., Zeng, Y.: Opportunistic spectrum access for energy-constrained cognitive radios. In: VTC Spring 2008 - IEEE Vehicular Technology Conference, pp. 1559–1563 (2008). https://doi.org/10.1109/ VETECS.2008.363

16. Mao, Y., Zhang, J., Song, S.H., Letaief, K.B.: Stochastic joint radio and computational resource management for multi-user mobile-edge computing systems. IEEE Trans. Wirel. Commun. **16**(9), 5994–6009 (2017). https://doi.org/10.1109/TWC.2017.2717986
17. 3GPP: NR; User Equipment (UE) radio transmission and reception. White Paper 38.101, 3rd Generation Partnership Project (3GPP) (2017). https://portal.3gpp.org/desktopmodules/Specifications/SpecificationDetails.aspx?specificationId=3201, version 0.0.1

The Computation of Quantum Radar Cross Section for the Regular Five-Pointed Star

Chonghua Fang[1(✉)], Liang Hua[2], Shi Xinyang[3], Yang Xu[4], and Xianliang Zeng[1]

[1] China Ship Development and Design Centre and Science and Technology on Electromagnetic Compatibility Laboratory, Wuhan 430000, Hubei, China
[2] Institute of Technology Zhejiang Business College, Hangzhou 310053, Zhejiang, China
[3] Wuhan Maritime Communication Research Institute, Wuhan 430000, Hubei, China
[4] Hubei Medical Devices Quality Supervision and Test Institute, Wuhan 430000, Hubei, China

Abstract. The quantum radar cross section is a kind of measure of the "quantum stealth performance" of the targets of interest. Obviously, it is extraordinary essential for the design and development of stealth weapon systems and platforms. In this paper, we have shown the simulation of quantum radar cross section (QRCS) and classical radar cross section (CRCS) for the regular five-pointed star. Based on quantum electrodynamics and interferometric considerations, we demonstrated the side-lobe quantum effect between QRCS and CRCS.

Keywords: Computation · Quantum radar cross section · Regular five-pointed star

1 Introduction

Quantum radar means is a speculative exploratory technology based on quantum dynamics which is the quantum version of classical dynamics. The QRCS could be a measure of the amount of returns from the given object illuminated with a handful of photons [1, 2]. Furthermore, due to the huge potentiality in term of different mechanism and counter-stealth, it has obtained extensive concern in the academy [3–14]. What's more, a prototype of quantum radar has been built in Austria in 2019 [15].

Nevertheless, this state-of-the-art technology is still stay in initial stage. Objectively, there are a lot of issues need to dispose, such as the target properties of all kinds of typical targets. Therefore, the computation of QRCS of the typical targets of interest, such as the regular five-pointed star, are worth demonstrating. In this work, we presented the interest curves of QRCS and the CRCS for the typical regular five-pointed star which is never published before.

2 Typical Scenario and Algorithm

Figure 1 shows the monostatic incident scenario of quantum radar that detects a regular five-pointed star.

X. Wang et al. (Eds.): AICON 2021, LNICST 396, pp. 561–565, 2021.
https://doi.org/10.1007/978-3-030-90196-7_48

In general, if we assume we could ignore both the diffraction and absorption contribution, the simplified expression of QRCS for the case of single-photon incidence is given by [16–25]. More arguments specification may be seen in [16].

$$
\sigma_Q = \frac{4\pi A_\perp(\theta_i, \Phi_i)\left|\sum_{n=1}^{N} e^{i(\vec{k_i} - \vec{k_s})\bullet\vec{x_n}}\right|^2}{\int_0^{2\pi}\int_0^{\pi/2}\left|\sum_{n=1}^{N} e^{i(\vec{k_i} - \vec{k_s})\bullet\vec{x_n}}\right|^2 \sin\theta_s d\theta_s d\Phi_s} \tag{1}
$$

Based on this formula, we used the novel algorithm to calculate the QRCS the cases with single photon incidence by ourselves [26–34].

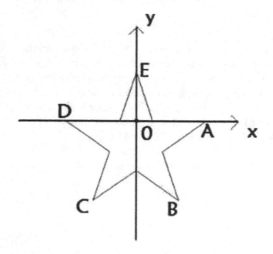

A $(a+a*sin18°, 0)$
B $(acos36°, -acos36°*cot18°+acos18°)$
C $(-acos36°, -acos36°*cot18°+acos18°)$
D $(-a-a*sin18°, 0)$
E $(0, acos18°)$

Fig. 1. The geometry of the regular five-pointed star with a = 0.7265 m so that the distance between the barycenter and any convex vertex is 1 m.

3   Simulation Results and Discussion

From Fig. 2, from the green arrows, we can also observe the entirely different quantum effect of the sidelobe enhancement. Maybe we explain that means QRCS are larger than CRCS. Please note that the curves of CRCS are from the typical physical optics approximate method from FEKO software [35] (Fig. 3).

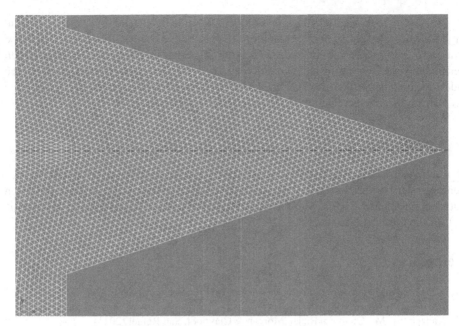

Fig. 2. Mesh of a regular five-pointed star.

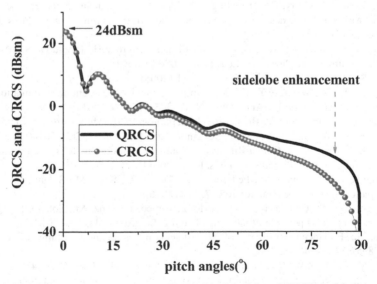

Fig. 3. Similarities and differences of the QRCS (black solid) and CRCS (red balls) curves for the regular five-pointed star with the single photon. (Color figure online)

According to the analytical expression of peak value in QRCS curve for the 2D plate in [1], $\sigma_{QMax\_rec} = 4\pi A^2/\lambda^2$, A denotes the area of the regular five-pointed star, the peaks at $\theta = 0°$ must be about 24 dBsm that QRCS values precisely are. They have been verified the precision of the technique in part. Then, for the regular five-pointed star, the side-lobe quantum effect from each side face may be superposed and almost reach the great difference in some angular range, such as 70°–90° nearby.

4 Conclusion

In this paper, a new calculated curve of QRCS for the regular five-pointed star was demonstrated. We also observed the similar side-lobe quantum effect in the comparison between QRCS and CRCS. More delicate work on the case of verifiable experiment is left for the recent future study.

References

1. Lanzagorta, M.: Quantum radar cross section. In: Proceedings of SPIE, vol. 7727, p. 77270K (2010)
2. Lanzagorta, M.: Quantum Radar. Morgan & Claypool, San Rafael (2011)
3. Lopaeva, E.D., Ruo Berchera, I., Olivares, S., Brida, G., Degiovanni, I.P., Genovese, M.: A detailed description of the experimental realization of a quantum illumination protocol. Phys. Scr. **T160**, 014026 (2014)
4. Lopaeva, E.D., Berchera, I.R., Degiovanni, I.P., Olivares, S., Brida, G., Genovese, M.: Experimental realisation of quantum illumination. Phys. Rev. Lett. **110**, 1–6 (2013)
5. Jiang, K., Lee, H., Gerry, C.C., Dowling, J.P.: Super-resolving quantum radar: coherent-state sources with homodyne detection suffice to beat the diffraction limit. J. Appl. Phys. **114**(19), 193102 (2013)
6. Barzanjeh, S., Guha, S., Weedbrook, C., Vitali, D., Shapiro, J.H., Pirandola, S.: Microwave quantum illumination. Phys. Rev. Lett. **114**(8), 080503 (2015)
7. Lloyd, S.: Quantum illumination. Science 1–11 (2008)
8. Xiong, B., Li, X., Wang, X.Y., Zhou, L.: Improve microwave quantum illumination via an optical parametric amplifier. Ann. Phys. (N. Y.) **385**, 757–768 (2017)
9. Nakamura, Y., Yamamoto, T.: Breakthroughs in photonics 2012: breakthroughs in microwave quantum photonics in superconducting circuits. IEEE Photonics J. **5**(2), 701406 (2013)
10. Sanz, M., Las Heras, U., García-Ripoll, J.J., Solano, E., Di Candia, R.: Quantum estimation methods for quantum illumination. Phys. Rev. Lett. **118**(7), 1–5 (2017)
11. Las Heras, U., Di Candia, R., Fedorov, K.G., Deppe, F., Sanz, M., Solano, E.: Quantum illumination unveils cloaking. Sci. Rep. **7**, 1–8 (2016)
12. Las Heras, U., Di Candia, R., Fedorov, K.G., Deppe, F., Sanz, M., Solano, E.: Quantum illumination reveals phase-shift inducing cloaking. Sci. Rep. **7**(1), 1–7 (2017)
13. Lloyd, S.: Enhanced sensitivity of photodetection via quantum illumination. Science **321**(5895), 1463–1465 (2008)
14. Malik, M., Boyd, R.W.: Quantum Imaging Technologies. vol. 37, no. 5 (2014)
15. Barzanjeh, S., et al.: Experimental microwave quantum illumination. Quantum Phys. 1–10 (2019)
16. Brandsema, M.J.: Formulation and Analysis of the Quantum Radar Cross Section. Ph.D. dissertation, Department of Electrical Engineering, The Pennsylvania State University, ProQuest Dissertations Publishing, PA (2017)

17. Liu, K., Xiao, H., Fan, H., Fu, Q.: Analysis of quantum radar cross section and its influence on target detection performance. IEEE Photonics Technol. Lett. **26**(11), 1146–1149 (2014)
18. Liu, K., Fan, X.H., Fu, H.: Analysis and simulation of quantum radar cross section. Chin. Phys. Lett. **31**(3), 034202–034223 (2014)
19. Kun, C., Shuxin, C., Dewei, W., Xi, W., Mi, S.: Analysis of quantum radar cross section of curved surface target. Acta Optica Sinica. **36**(12), 1227002-1-9 (2016)
20. Lin, Y., Guo, L., Cai, K.: An efficient algorithm for the calculation of quantum radar cross section of flat objects. In: Progress in Electromagnetics Research Symposium Proceedings, no. 3, pp. 39–43 (2014)
21. Liu, K., Jiang, Y., Li, X., Cheng, Y., Qin, Y.: New results about quantum scattering characteristics of typical targets. In: International Geoscience and Remote Sensing Symposium, vol. 2016–Novem, pp. 2669–2671 (2016)
22. Lanzagorta, M., Venegas-Andraca, S.: Algorithmic analysis of quantum radar cross sections. In: Proceedings of SPIE, p. 946112 (2015)
23. Brandsema, M.J., Narayanan, R.M., Lanzagorta, M.: Cross section equivalence between photons and non-relativistic massive particles for targets with complex geometries. In: Progress in Electromagnetics Research M, vol. 54, pp. 37–46 (2017)
24. Brandsema, M.J., Narayanan, R.M., Lanzagorta, M.: Electric and magnetic target polarization in quantum radar. In: Proceedings of SPIE, vol. 10188, p. 101880C (2017)
25. Xu, S.-L., Hu, T.-H., Zhao, N.-X., Wang, Y.-Y., Li, L., Guo, L.-R.: Impact of metal target's atom lattice structure on its quantum radar cross-section. Acta Phys. Sinica **64**(15), 1–6 (2015)
26. Fang, C.: The calculation of quantum radar scattering characteristic for the 3D circular cone target. In: 2018 IEEE International Symposium on Electromagnetic Compatibility and 2018 IEEE Asia-Pacific Symposium on Electromagnetic Compatibility, pp. 248–250 (2018)
27. Fang, C.: The simulation of quantum radar scattering for 3D cylindrical targets. In: 2018 IEEE International Conference on Calculational Electromagnetics (ICCEM), Chengdu, pp. 1–3 (2018)
28. Fang, C.H.: The simulation and analysis of quantum radar cross section for 3D convex targets. IEEE Photonics J. **10**(1), 1–8 (2018)
29. Brandsema, M.J., Narayanan, R.M., Lanzagorta, M.: Theoretical and computational analysis of the quantum radar cross section for simple geometrical targets. Quantum Inf. Process. **16**(1), 1–27 (2016). https://doi.org/10.1007/s11128-016-1494-6
30. Fang, C.H., et al.: The calculation and analysis of the bistatic quantum radar cross section for the typical 2D plate. IEEE Photonics J. **10**(2), 1–14 (2018)
31. Fang, C., Han, K.: Analytical formulation for the quantum radar scattering of the rectangular plate. In: 2019 IEEE 2nd International Conference on Electronic Information and Communication Technology (ICEICT), pp. 677–681 (2019)
32. Fang, C., Shi, X.: The analysis of quantum radar scattering for the typical pyramid structure. In: 2019 IEEE International Applied Computational Electromagnetics Society Symposium in China (ACES-China), to be published.
33. Fang, C.: The analysis of mainlobeslumping quantum effect of the cube in the scattering characteristics of quantum radar. IEEE Access **7**, 141055–141061 (2019)
34. Fang, C.: The closed-form expressions for the bistatic quantum radar cross section of the typical simple plates. IEEE Sens. J. **20**(5), 2348–2355 (2020)
35. Fang, C.H., et al.: An improved physical optics method for the computation of radar cross section of electrically large objects. In: 2008 Asia-Pacific Symposium on Electromagnetic Compatibility and 19th International Zurich Symposium on Electromagnetic Compatibility, pp. 722–725 (2008)

Design of On-Orbit Monitoring System for GNSS Signal Quality Based on Intelligent Processing

Qibing Xu[✉], Zhimei Yang, and Lixin Zhang

Xi'an Institute of Space Radio Technology, Xi'an 710100, China

Abstract. Global Navigation Satellite System (GNSS) signal is the medium that provides users with navigation, positioning and timing. The signal quality determines the user's service level and accuracy. GNSS signal quality includes signal continuity and accuracy. Satellite in-orbit service requires timely ground monitoring. There are more and more satellites, and ordinary monitoring methods cannot meet the real-time monitoring. It is necessary to adopt intelligent monitoring methods to realize autonomous on-orbit monitoring. This article introduces a GNSS signal on-orbit intelligent monitoring system, including the composition of the system, intelligent monitoring process, monitorable indicators and monitoring methods. This solution has been applied to current monitoring stations, which greatly simplifies the complexity of monitoring. To improve the efficiency of monitoring.

Keywords: GNSS signal · Quality monitoring · Intelligent processing

1 Introduction

Satellite navigation system is an important space infrastructure, which has brought huge social and economic benefits to mankind. At the same time, it has become an important strategic resource related to national security in the military field. Because of its potential great value, major countries and major groups are competing to develop their own global navigation satellite systems. The Beidou satellite navigation system is an independently developed and independently operated global satellite navigation system that China is implementing. It is compatible with the United States' GPS and Russian satellite navigation systems [1]. GLONASS and the EU's GALILEO system are compatible with the shared global satellite navigation system, and are called the world's four largest satellite navigation systems. In order to provide high-precision navigation and positioning services, navigation satellites must provide continuous, high-precision, and high-integrity signals.

After the satellite is launched, it is necessary to monitor the status of the satellite through the ground monitoring system and carry out the evaluation of the satellite status [2]. The existing ground monitoring system uses monitoring receivers [3]. The monitoring receivers can only monitor the signal continuity, and only provide general and

© ICST Institute for Computer Sciences, Social Informatics and Telecommunications Engineering 2021
Published by Springer Nature Switzerland AG 2021. All Rights Reserved
X. Wang et al. (Eds.): AICON 2021, LNICST 396, pp. 566–578, 2021.
https://doi.org/10.1007/978-3-030-90196-7_49

conventional observation information, and cannot monitor the changes in signal quality indicators. Secondly, due to its hardware resources The monitoring receiver cannot monitor and evaluate all the signals of all visible satellites in the current visible field of view in real time, especially the signal quality cannot be monitored with higher performance. The German Aerospace Research Institute used a 30-m large antenna Monitoring the Galileo satellite system has the disadvantage of not having strong monitoring timeliness, and flexibility also has major difficulties in monitoring flexibility and use [4].

2   GNSS Signal Quality Index System

The measurement of GNSS signal quality is mainly carried out through related methods. At present, navigation signal quality evaluation is widely studied. Scholars have proposed a lot of signal quality evaluation methods, which are more mainstream and widely recognized evaluation indicators, mainly from frequency domain characteristics, time Domain characteristics, correlation domain characteristics, and modulation characteristics are used to evaluate signal quality.

2.1   Frequency Domain Characteristics

The frequency domain characteristic mainly analyzes the power spectrum of the downlink signal, and monitors the change of the transmission power at the same time, which is a basic indicator of signal quality evaluation. The German Aerospace Research Institute used a large 30-m antenna to monitor the Galileo GIOVE-B test satellite in the E1 frequency band with a significant asymmetry of at least 1 dB in the power spectrum [5, 6] (Fig. 1).

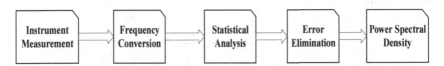

Fig. 1. Signal frequency domain monitoring data analysis process.

Signal power spectrum monitoring mainly uses large-scale monitoring antennas or directly monitors satellite signals during production. Regardless of the monitoring method, the general monitoring process is to collect the radio frequency signal by the instrument, then down-convert the signal, analyze the signal for a period of time, and eliminate the interference and error terms, and finally get the power spectral density of the corresponding signal, the signal. In order to prevent the interference of other signals, when analyzing the power spectral density, a sharp cut filter can be used to analyze only the signal in the main lobe, while increasing the averaging time of the signal to ensure stability.

2.2 Time Domain Characteristics

The signal time domain characteristic mainly analyzes the waveform distortion and constellation diagram of the baseband signal. The baseband signal waveform distortion mainly analyzes the distortion of the baseband signal waveform. First, the collected data is preprocessed, and the baseband waveform "0" and "1" duty ratios are analyzed, and then the time length corresponding to each positive and negative chip of the signal in the code period is counted. And make the difference with the ideal chip length to obtain the time difference series of the "1" and "0" chips and the ideal chip, and finally calculate the standard deviation and mean value of the two time series respectively [2, 5].

At present, there is no effective constellation diagram evaluation method for the more complicated modulation type navigation signals. For example, the eye diagrams commonly used in communication are not suitable for navigation signals. However, the analysis of the constellation diagram can provide an intuitive impression for the evaluation of the signal quality. If the distortion is serious, the corresponding constellation diagram and the constellation diagram of the ideal signal will be obviously inconsistent. It should be noted that when comparing the real signal with the ideal signal, it is necessary to ensure that the effective bandwidth of the two is the same.

2.3 Related Domain Characteristics

After the navigation downlink signal is distorted, the correlation function is distorted, causing pseudorange measurement errors. The correlation function is used to analyze the influence of the transmission channel on the navigation downlink signal ranging performance. First, the software receiver is used to carry out carrier stripping and Doppler removal on the navigation satellite signal to obtain the signal ranging code, and calculate the normalized cross-correlation with the local reference code, which is defined as the following formula:

$$CCF(\tau) = \frac{\int_0^{T_p} S_{\mathrm{Pr}\,o}(t) S_{\mathrm{Ref}}^*(t - \tau) dt}{\sqrt{\left(\int_0^{T_p} |S_{\mathrm{Pr}\,o}(t)|^2\right)\left(\int_0^{T_p} |S_{\mathrm{Ref}}^*(t)|^2\right)}} \tag{1}$$

In the above formula, $S_{\mathrm{Pr}\,o}(t)$ represents the ranging code of the actual satellite signal, the reference signal $S_{\mathrm{Ref}}(t)$ represents the ideal signal copy code generated by the local receiver, the symbol $*$ represents the conjugate operation, and the integration time T_p is a main code period of the reference signal. Use the correlation loss of the actually measured correlation curve, the receiver code loop phase detection curve deviation (S-curve Bias, SCB), and the S-curve slope deviation to evaluate the distortion of the correlation peak [1, 7].

a) **Related Loss** [2, 7].

The correlation loss is the difference between the actual received signal power of the signal and the ideal signal power. The expression for solving the correlation loss is:

$$P = \max_{over\ all\ \varepsilon} (20 \log_{10}(|CCF(\varepsilon)|))$$
$$PCL[dB] = P_{ideal} - P_{real} \tag{2}$$

Where P is the signal power, P_{ideal} is the ideal signal power, P_{real} is the actual received signal power, and PCL is the relative loss.

b) S-curve Bias (SCB).

The zero-crossing point of the ideal S curve should be located at the position where the phase of the phase discrimination curve does not deviate. In fact, due to the influence of channel transmission distortion, the code loop phase discrimination curve is often locked at the position where the phase is deviated [4]. Taking the incoherent lead minus lag phase detector as an example, set the lead minus lag distance of the correlator as, then the S curve can be expressed as:

$$S(s_{out}, s_{in,k}, \varepsilon) = [CF(s_{out}, s_{in,k}, \varepsilon + \delta/2)^2 - CF(s_{out}, s_{in,k}, \varepsilon - \delta/2)^2] \qquad (3)$$

In the above formula, CF represents the related function:

$$CF(\tau) = \int_0^{T_p} S(t)S^*(t - \tau)dt \qquad (4)$$

Locking point deviation satisfies

$$SCurve(\varepsilon_{bias}(\delta), \delta) = 0 \qquad (5)$$

The lock-in point deviation satisfies that when there is more than one zero-crossing point (such as BOC modulation signal), the zero-crossing point closest to the maximum relevant power should be selected. S-curve deviation is defined as:

$$SCB = \max_{overall\ \delta} (\varepsilon_{bias}(\delta)) - \min_{overall\ \delta} (\varepsilon_{bias}(\delta)) \qquad (6)$$

The δ value range is $[0, \delta_{max}]$, and the δ_{max} values are as follows:

$$\delta_{max}[chips] = \begin{cases} \dfrac{1.5}{4\frac{m}{n} - 1} BOC(m, n) \\ 1.5\ BPSK - n \end{cases} \qquad (7)$$

From (6) and (7), the variation curve of the lock point deviation $\varepsilon_{bias}(\delta)$ with the distance δ can be obtained.

2.4 Modulation Characteristics

The modulation characteristics of the signal mainly analyze the effective power ratio deviation of the signal components and the carrier phase deviation between the signal components. The calculation process of the effective power ratio deviation of the signal components is as follows: First, the collected signal is filtered and demodulated to obtain the baseband signal. Then use Eq. (8) to calculate the correlation function between the local code generator and the received baseband signal, and calculate the power value of the signal. The power ratio of each signal component is:

$$E(j) = (\frac{1}{N} \sum_{i=1}^{N} \sqrt{(P_{Ii}^2 + P_{Qi}^2)})^2 \qquad (8)$$

The statistical number of power ratios can be selected as the number of code cycles for a period of time, expressed as a percentage of the total power of a single signal. Calculate the carrier phase deviation between signal components based on the tracked data. Use the signal components after stable tracking to recover the complete carrier phase, compare the phase difference of each signal component with the relative phase value of the ideal signal component, and count the data for a period of time. The carrier phase deviation is the carrier between the signals. The maximum value of the absolute value of the relative phase error [7].

3   GNSS Signal Quality Index System

Satellite operation after launching requires continuous ground monitoring to ensure the quality and level of signal service. The ground monitoring system generally consists of an antenna unit, radio frequency channel unit, baseband processing unit, time-frequency reference unit, acquisition/playback storage unit, and integrated The control processing software unit is constituted together. As shown in Fig. 2.

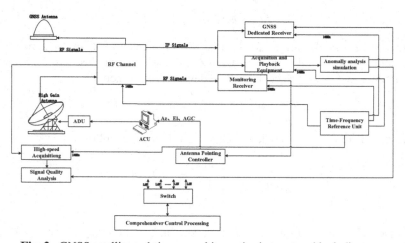

Fig. 2. GNSS satellite real-time on-orbit monitoring system block diagram.

The composition of signal quality analysis based on intelligent processing is shown in the Fig. 3 below.

GNSS satellite in-orbit intelligent signal quality monitoring composition block diagram. The omnidirectional antenna completes the reception of all GNSS signals, and the receiver realizes the reception and processing of the signals to analyze the continuous performance of the signal, ranging performance and other indicators, and judge the availability of the signal, The stability of the phase center of the antenna directly determines the accuracy level of the signal evaluation. This system uses the GNSS-750 four-system GNSS choke antenna in the design, and supports GPS, GLONASS, Galileo and Beidou. GNSS-750 has strong multi-system signal receiving ability and is suitable

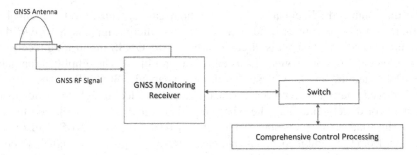

Fig. 3. Block diagram of GNSS satellite intelligent signal quality monitoring.

for application fields such as the construction of ground reference stations and geological monitoring.

High-gain antennas are used to monitor and process the signal quality of a single satellite. Since signal quality monitoring and analysis require relatively high signal carrier noise, high-gain antennas must be used to achieve this. The use of GNSS high-gain antennas can be very good Realize the evaluation of the signal quality, the monitoring receiver completes the calculation of the position information through the position information of a currently selected tracked satellite, and then converts the calculation of the pointing control system into the driving command of the ACU to complete the high-gain antenna The alignment and tracking action of the currently selected satellite.

3.1 Radio Frequency Channel Unit

The function of the radio frequency channel unit is to complete the processing of amplification, filtering, frequency conversion and power division of the signals output by the two antenna feed elements, so that the output signal frequency and power can be adapted to the input range of the back-end baseband processing unit. Figure 4 shows the principle block diagram of the radio frequency channel unit.

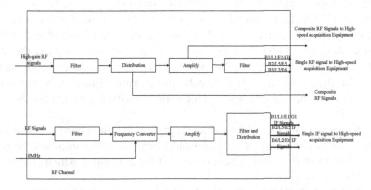

Fig. 4. Block diagram of the realization of the RF channel unit.

For the combined RF signal output by the high-gain antenna, the RF channel unit first filters it to suppress out-of-band interference. The filtered signal is then divided into two channels, and one channel is directly output to the GNSS monitoring receiver for receiving processing. One signal also needs to be amplified. The amplification gain is about 70 dB, and the amplified signal level range is about −30–0 dBm. The amplified signal is directly output as a combination and can be provided to high-speed acquisition equipment for direct sampling. The other amplified signal is then subjected to band-pass filtering, and three independent RF signals of B1/L1/E1, B2/E5/L5, B3/E6/L2 are filtered out from the combined signal, and the purpose is to purify the signal. To ensure the quality of signal acquisition, the branched radio frequency signal is still provided to the high-speed acquisition and storage device for subsequent processing. For the combined RF signal output by the omnidirectional antenna, it is also filtered to suppress out-of-band interference. The filtered signal needs to be down-converted. The converted signal is amplified (amplification gain is about 90 dB). The amplified 3 channels of IF signals are further processed by power division filtering. Each frequency signal is divided into 13 channels, of which 12 channels are provided to the BD dedicated receiver for baseband processing, and the other channel is output to the IF acquisition and playback storage device for completion. Continuous real-time collection of records.

3.2 GNSS Monitoring Receiver

As a high-precision measurement device, the monitoring receiver simultaneously observes the Beidou satellite signal in the field of view to obtain precise pseudorange, carrier phase, navigation message and other information, for the system satellite-ground time synchronization, precise orbit determination, and ionospheric propagation Delay correction and integrity monitoring provide observation data. Its key design indicators such as pseudorange measurement accuracy and carrier measurement accuracy are better than or equivalent to the current international advanced measurement receivers. In order to ensure stable operation in the increasingly complex electromagnetic environment in the future and ensure receiving performance, interference monitoring and suppression are A necessary function for monitoring receivers.

Through the GNSS receiver, the uninterrupted monitoring of the full system signals of 12 visible satellites can be completed in parallel in real time. On the basis of completing the monitoring of conventional observations, the expansion and improvement of monitoring items can be realized, especially the correct channel coding of the downlink signal. Performance verification and the analysis and processing functions of the original message, and at the same time, the automatic monitoring capability is improved from the software level, so that the efficiency of the entire monitoring system has been greatly improved.

The GNSS receiver includes 12 baseband signal processing boards, as well as a high-performance workstation. One of the baseband boards jointly completes the reception and processing of the full system signal of a single GNSS satellite, which can be regarded as a single-satellite receiver.

The basic block diagram of the baseband processing board is shown in Fig. 4. The baseband processing board includes a receive channel and a transmit channel. The receive channel includes 6 ADCs (ADS5402), and the transmit channel includes 4 DACs

(AD9736). It uses an external clock source and trigger signal., The receiving channel and the sending channel each correspond to a set of FPGA (XC5VLX330) and DSP (TMS32C6713B) devices, and both FPGA and DSP chip have expanded high-speed memory. A piece of TMS320C6455 processor implements CPCI bus and gigabit network interface, the EMIFA interface of TMS320C6455 is connected to two pieces of FPGA, and a piece of CPLD device is designed to control the hardware logic on the board. TMS320C6455 is designed with FLASH devices outside the chip for curing procedures. There are 10 pairs of bidirectional LVDS channels designed between the two FPGAs to facilitate data transmission between each other. Both FPGAs are designed with 10 pairs of bidirectional LVDS channels connected to the CPCI J3 and J5 connectors respectively for high-speed data between boards. transmission. Each FPGA is designed with one UART connected to the CPCI J3 connector, and each FPGA is designed with 32 single-ended signals connected to the CPCI J4 connector (Fig. 5).

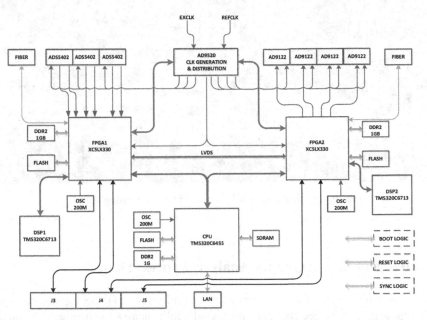

Fig. 5. Block diagram of the realization of the baseband signal processing boards.

The CPCI hardware board is shown in the figure. The two TMS320C6713Bs communicate through the McBSP interface. The EMIF and HPI interfaces of the two TMS320C6713Bs are connected to the corresponding FPGA. The HPI interface is mainly used to implement the host loading of the TMS320C6713B program. The programs of the two TMS32C6713B are solidified on the FLASH device on the board, and are automatically loaded when the board is powered on. The baseband processing board is integrated in a standard 4U-8 slot CPCI chassis for use, which facilitates the maintenance and upgrade of the equipment. A group of FPGAs and DSPs corresponding to the receiving channel on the board complete the baseband receiving and processing of the entire navigation signal, and a group of FPGAs and DSPs corresponding to the transmitting channel complete the generation of zero-value baseband signals. The C6455 on the board is responsible for completing the communication and control between the entire baseband board and the external network port.

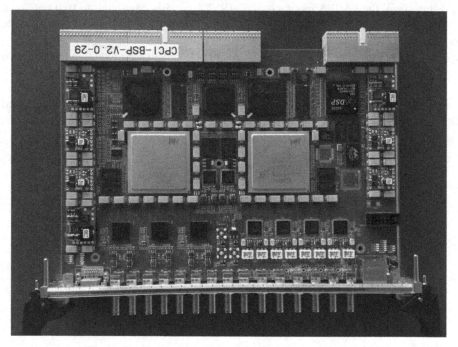

Fig. 6. Physical image of baseband signal processing board.

4   Intelligent Signal Quality Analysis Process Design

In addition to monitoring receivers for on-orbit monitoring of GNSS signals, the signal quality indicators described above require signal quality analysis software. The function of the signal quality analysis module is relatively independent, and the core is to realize the high-precision analysis and evaluation of data under the condition of high sampling rate through the idea of software receiver. Due to the huge amount of data and the complex processing algorithm, the quality analysis is realized by non-real-time post-processing, as a functional module of the comprehensive control software to realize the corresponding functions.

Figure 6 shows a block diagram of the software processing flow of the signal quality analysis module. First, the working mode is completed through the top layer, and the simulation analysis frequency point, sampling rate, simulation time and other working parameters are set. The signal quality analysis module will control the signal according to the given conditions. The way to read in. After the signal is captured, it enters the tracking loop. Through closed-loop analysis, the precise pseudo-code phase, carrier phase, data path integral value and other intermediate parameters of each signal component are obtained. Then, the system will use the code phase and carrier phase after stable tracking to correct the signal, and calculate its power spectrum, EVM index, constellation diagram, IQ orthogonality, and amplitude imbalance. Finally, all the intermediate parameters are processed, the pseudo-code mutual difference of each signal component, the phase deviation of the signal component and other indicators are calculated, and all the results are drawn and displayed.

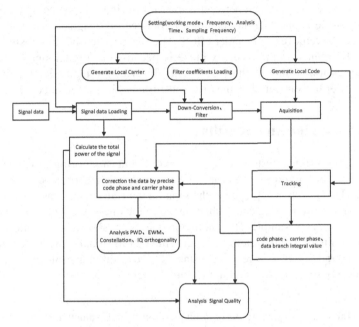

Fig. 7. Intelligent processing flow for signal quality analysis

Navigation signal quality parameters are divided into two categories. The first category is typical communication system parameters, including power spectral density, constellation diagrams, and eye diagrams; the second category is closely related to navigation, including code power, autocorrelation function shape, and correlation Loss, S-curve offset, multi-channel pseudo code consistency, pseudo code and data delay consistency, amplitude/phase frequency transfer characteristics, etc.

The signal quality parameter needs to process baseband signal samples up to tens of seconds to obtain the instantaneous transmission distortion characteristic of the navigation signal.

The power spectrum analysis usually uses the Welch periodogram method. The Welch periodogram method uses an improved average periodogram method to estimate the power spectrum of a random signal. It uses signal segment overlap, windowing, FFT and other techniques to calculate the power spectrum. The Welch method can improve the smoothness of the spectrum estimation curve and increase the resolution of the spectrum estimation. Comparing the measured power spectrum of the signal with the ideal power spectrum can check the power spectrum characteristics of the signal.

In the process of data analysis, use eye diagrams to observe the effects of inter-symbol crosstalk and noise. After filtering, demodulating, and Doppler frequency shift removal on the collected original data, the initial phase is used as the starting point, and the time-domain waveform diagram Repeatedly draw multiple chip data in.

The constellation diagram is used to analyze the characteristics of the signal modulation domain and calculate the signal quadrature modulation parameters. The constellation diagram is a diagram that represents the digital signal in the complex plane and visually shows the signal and the relationship between the signals. The constellation diagram needs to remove the Doppler effect. The reason why the digital signal can be represented by points on the complex plane is because the digital signal itself has a complex expression. Although the signal generally needs to be modulated to a higher frequency carrier for transmission, the final detection is still carried out on the baseband.

5 Test and Verification Results

This on-orbit monitoring system realizes the intelligent monitoring of GNSS satellite on-orbit signals, and improves the efficiency and real-time performance of monitoring processing. This system is deployed at the monitoring station, and has completed multiple GNSS signal monitoring and evaluation. Take the one-star evaluation result of the Compass system as an example. The evaluation results are shown in the following table. Through the evaluation, this system can realize the GNSS signal Flexible and intelligent monitoring, all indicators truly reflect the status of the satellite in orbit, and the statistics of the monitoring results are shown in the Table 1 below.

Table 1. Compass signals on-orbit monitoring and evaluation results.

Signal	Corrlation loss	S-curve bias	Time-domain bias
B1Cp	−0.102	0.111	0.803
B1Cd	−0.137	0.092	0.837
B1I	0.368	0.004	−0.115
B2ad	0.197	0.123	0.065
B2ap	0.190	0.125	0.002
B2b_I	0.161	0.051	−0.029
B2b_Q	0.176	0.051	−0.012
B3I	0.035	0.015	−0.115

In addition to the above relevant domain indicators, the system has qualitatively analyzed the time domain waveforms, constellation diagrams and eye diagrams. Figure 7 is the power spectral density, and Fig. 8 is the difference between the analyzed actual time domain waveform and the theoretical time domain waveform. Figure 9 shows the eye diagrams of various different signals. The entire analysis and processing process is automated (Fig. 10).

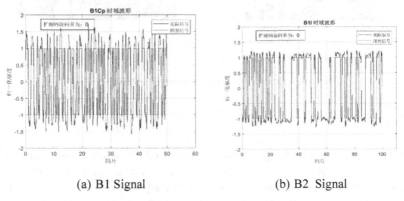

(a) B1 Signal   (b) B2 Signal

Fig. 8. Power spectral density of GNSS signal

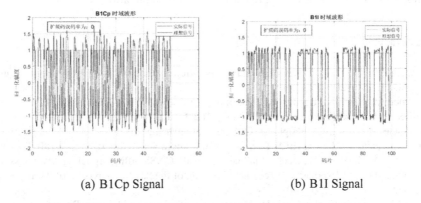

(a) B1Cp Signal   (b) B1I Signal

Fig. 9. Time-domain waveform monitoring results of some signals

Judging from the test results, this system has well realized the on-orbit signal quality monitoring and analysis, and can meet the system requirements in terms of monitoring efficiency and monitoring performance.

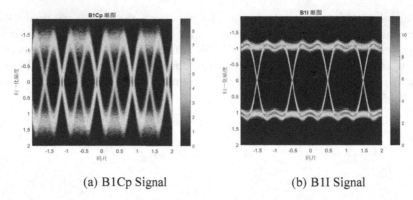

(a) B1Cp Signal   (b) B1I Signal

Fig. 10. Partial signal eye diagram monitoring results

6 Conclusion

This paper introduces the design of an intelligent-based on-orbit monitoring system for GNSS signal quality. It gives a detailed introduction to the intelligent workflow, processing methods, system composition and other aspects of the system. Through on-orbit monitoring and analysis, this system can be very good. The improved monitoring efficiency provides a reference and reference for the monitoring of the performance of multiple GNSS systems, and has greater engineering application value.

References

1. Yang, Z., Xu, Q., Han, H.: Research on Pre-distortion Method of Navigation Satellite Launch Channel, CSNC (2016)
2. Soellner, M., Kohl, R., Luetke, W.: The impact of linear and non-linear signal distortions on Galileo code tracking accuracy. Pac. J. Math. **162**(1), 27–44 (2002)
3. Li, X., Ge, M., Lu, C., et al.: High-rate GPS seismology using real-time precise point positioning with ambiguity resolution. IEEE Trans. Geosci. Remote Sens. **52**(10), 6165–6180 (2014)
4. Soellner, M., Kurzhals, C., Hechenblaikner, G., et al.: GNSS offline signal quality assessment. In: Proceedings of International Technical Meeting of the Satellite Division of the Institute of Navigation, pp. 909–920 (2008)
5. Betz, J.W., Corporation T M: Effect of linear time-invariant distortions on RNSS code tracking accuracy. In: Proceedings of International Technical Meeting of the Satellite Division of the Institute of Navigation, pp. 1636–1647 (2002)
6. Falcone, M., Lugert, M., Malik, M., et al.: GIOVE-a in orbit testing results. In: Proceedings of International Technical Meeting of the Satellite Division of the Institute of Navigation (2006)
7. Felhauer, T.: On the impact of RF front-end group delay variations on GLONASS pseudorange accuracy. In: Proceedings of International Technical Meeting of the Satellite Division of the Institute of Navigation, pp. 1527–1532 (1997)

Dynamic Data Storage and Management Strategies for Distributed File System

Feng Liu[1](✉), Di Lin[1], Yao Qin[1], Yuan Gao[2], and Jiang Cao[2]

[1] University of Electronic Science and Technology of China, Chengdu, Sichuan, China
201921090328@std.uestc.edu.cn, lindi@uestc.edu.cn
[2] Military Academy of Sciences, Beijing, China

Abstract. HDFS has a very wide range of applications in the field of big data, but HDFS was designed for a homogeneous environment at the beginning. HDFS adopts a static replica management strategy, the storage location and number of file replicas will not change after determination. This strategy will low overall system performance. In this paper, we propose optimized replica management strategy, abbreviated as ORMP to fix this problem. ORMP is based on file heat value and LSTM. File heat value is proposed to evaluate the activity of files. LSTM is used to predict the access times of files. Based on LSTM, the file heat value can be updated regularly, so we can dynamically change the storage location and number of replicas. Experiments show that ORMP is 22.08% faster in reading speed compared with the default replicas management strategy.

Keywords: HDFS · File heat value · ORMP · LSTM

1 Introduction

Hadoop Distributed File System (HDFS [1]) is a widely used distributed file storage system. HDFS has the ability to store ultra-large-scale data [2]. The use of multiple replica technology and erasure coding technology makes the system highly fault-tolerant. HDFS allows clusters to be built in a number of inexpensive general-purpose computer devices, and performs well in homogeneous computer clusters with similar node performance [3].

With the development of storage technology, solid state drive (SSD) with high read-write performance has been widely used in various applications. Compared with traditional mechanical hard disk drive (HDD), SSD has absolute performance advantages. However, the price of solid state disk is very expensive, so HDD is still the mainstream storage medium in HDFS system. SSD is mainly used to improve the performance of the system [4]. This kind of HDFS cluster using HHD, SSD and other storage media is called heterogeneous HDFS cluster [5].

HDFS adopts multi replica technology to ensure the reliability of data and fault tolerance of cluster. The replica placement, replica management strategy and replica retrieval algorithm are a series of strategies related to multi replica

X. Wang et al. (Eds.): AICON 2021, LNICST 396, pp. 579–592, 2021.
https://doi.org/10.1007/978-3-030-90196-7_50

mechanism [6], because HDFS is mainly based on homogeneous cluster environment. The default replicas management strategy is not suitable for the heterogeneous cluster environment mentioned above. The storage location of replicas will not change after the first placement. Those files placed in low-performance storage devices may be read frequently. However, HDFS is unable to automatically adjust the storage location of those file to other nodes with better performance. The storage resources in heterogeneous HDFS system are not effectively utilized.

The contribution of this paper is as follows.

- We proposed a new strategy based on LSTM to calculate HDFS file heat values.
- We proposed a heterogeneous replicas management strategy based on file heat value. The number and storage position of replicas can change with the heat value dramatically.

2   Related Works

The topic of optimization of replica strategies and algorithms in heterogeneous HDFS environment is one of the significant research directions, and many optimization schemes have been proposed in the related literature.

Literature [7] proposes a heterogeneous perception layered storage scheme based on heterogeneous HDFS cluster named hatS. hatS is a multi-tier storage system that integrates heterogeneous storage technologies into the Hadoop ecosystem. It can actively recognize various hardware devices with different storage performance in the cluster, and create diverse hierarchical structures according to the I/O performance of the storage devices. The three-layer structure mentioned in the paper includes a fast layer, an intermediate layer, as well as a slow layer.

With respect to the replica placement strategy, a hybrid awareness strategy that comprehensively considers layer awareness and network awareness. Compared with the default strategy, a layer awareness technology is proposed to improve the utilization of storage devices by reasonably using different storage devices, while retaining the network-aware technology to ensure data fault tolerance and security. With respect to the replica selection strategy, by considering both the performance of the layer where the replica is located and the distance of network topology, different weights are assigned to different replicas of the same file, and then the weighted random function is further used to access the replica, thereby mitigating the overload problem of the nodes with good performance. Results show that by directing 64% of I/O access to the SSD layer, in terms of Hadoop job execution speed, hatS is 32.6% faster than native HDFS.

Literature [8] presents a hybrid design (Triple-H) that can minimize the I/O bottlenecks in HDFS and ensure efficient utilization of the heterogeneous storage devices (e.g. RAM, SSD, and HDD) available on HPC clusters. This paper also propose an effective data placement policies to speed up Triple-H. Our design integrated with parallel file system (e.g. Lustre) can lead to significant storage space savings and guarantee fault-tolerance. Performance evaluations show that

Triple-H can improve the write and read throughputs of HDFS by up to 7× and 2×, respectively. The execution times of data generation benchmarks are reduced by up to 3×. Triple-H also improves the execution time of the Sort benchmark by up to 40%. Over default HDFS and 54% over Lustre. The alignment phase of the Cloudburst application is accelerated by 19%. Triple-H also benefits the performance of SequenceCount and Grep in PUMA over both default HDFS and Lustre.

Literature [9] optimizes the data placement strategy on heterogeneous HDFS nodes by considering the disk space difference of each node. Literature [10] proposes a new replica placement strategy, which considers the disk utilization and the real-time status of each node when selecting the node to place the replica, so as to balance the workload of the node.

Literature [11] proposes a variable number of replica placement strategy, which highlights node performance, data access frequency and storage capacity. Literature [12] proposes a load balancing algorithm to balance the read and write load of heterogeneous nodes. Literature [13] proposes a serpentine data placement mechanism, which divides different nodes into multiple virtual storage layers, and uses the hot and cold proportional replication strategy to determine the replication factor of each file block. Literature [14] summarizes the relationships between files by analyzing file upload requests, and then allocates the high correlated files to the initial position of nodes, thereby improving the efficiency of data access.

3   Proposed Method

In this section, we propose the concept of file heat value. File heat value is composed of two parts: subjective heat value and objective heat value. The subjective heat value can be calculated by the initial storage policy specified by user. The Objective heat value is based on the LSTM. And then we use the file heat value to optimize the replica management strategy of HDFS.

3.1   File Heat Value

File heat value is used to evaluate the activity of files. The more times a file is read, the higher the value is. By considering the user's expectation of the files' popularity and the real-time access characteristics, a hybrid calculation method based on subjective and objective heat is proposed to calculate the real-time popularity of files.

Subjective Temperature, abbreviated as St: indicates the initial heat value of a file, $St \in [0, 100]$. The subjective heat value depends on the user's estimation on file for a period of time after the file is created, this value will not change over time. $St(f)$ represents the subjective heat value of file f.

The calculation formula of $Temperature_0(f)$ is described as follows:

$$St(f) = \frac{max[Heat(policy_0)] + min[Heat(policy_0)]}{2} \tag{1}$$

$policy_0$ is the initial storage policy of file specified by user. So St is actually determined by user when uploading the file. The relationship between file heat value and storage policy is shown in Table 1.

Table 1. Relationship between file heat value and storage policy

Strategy name	Storage strategy	Explanation	Heat range
Hottest	RAM_DISK:1 SSD:3	One replica puted in RAM_DISK, other three puted in SSD	[80.100]
Hot	SSD:3	All three replicas puted in SSD	[60.80)
Warm	RAM_DISK:1 SSD:2	One replica puted in RAM_DISK, other two puted in SSD	[40.60)
Cold	DISK:3	All three replicas puted in DISK	[20.40)
Coldest	DISK:1	ALL one replica puted in DISK	[0.20)

Objective Temperature, abbreviated as Ot: indicates the predicted heat of a file obtained by prediction algorithm in a period of time, $Ot \in [0, 100]$. In order to calculate the objective popularity, we use LSTM to predict the number of times a file is read. $O_t(f, T_c)$ indicates the objective heat value of the file in the time period T_c.

After the LSTM model is trained, it can predict the read number of file in the next time interval through the access of file in the first n time intervals, as shown in the formula:

$$\hat{c}(f, T_c) = LSTM \{c(f, T_{c-n}), c(f, T_{c-n+1}), \cdots, c(f, T_{c-2}), c(f, T_{c-1}))\} \quad (2)$$

$\hat{c}(f, T_c)$ represents the predicted access times obtained by LSTM. $c(f, T_i)$ represents the access times of files in the period of T_i. $LSTM$ represents the prediction process using LSTM model. We can calculate the access prediction values of all files in the T_C time period, and then calculate the average of the access prediction values in the T_C time period system. The formula is described as follows:

$$\overline{\hat{C}(f^*, Tc)} = \frac{\sum_n^{i=0} \hat{c}(f, T_c)}{n} \quad (3)$$

n in this formula is the number of files in system. Now we can calculate the Objective heat value of each file: Ot. Ot reflects the access level of files in the whole system, the formula is described as follows:

$$Ot(f, T_c) = \frac{\hat{c}(f, T_c)}{\hat{C}(f^*, Tc)} * 50 \quad (4)$$

50 is the middle of the file heat value. The final formula to calculate real-time heat of file is described as:

$$Temperature(f, T_c) = \lambda * St(f) + (1 - \lambda) * Ot(f, T_c) \quad (5)$$

λ is a attenuation factor, which indicates the degree of attenuation of the influence of subjective heat on real-time heat. It will gradually decrease from 1 to 0 over time. This means subjective heat has a certain timeliness.

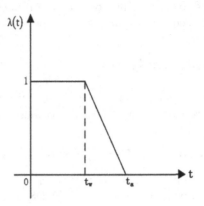

Fig. 1. The decrease process of λ

The heat values of files are re-calculated at every fixed time interval. This time interval is called as the update cycle of temperature, abbreviated as Tc_{temp}. If the update cycle is too long, the heat value cannot be updated in time, resulting in the resources in the system cannot be fully utilized; if the update cycle is too short, the update process will costs lots of system resources. We set Tc_{temp} to 8.

In order to provide sufficient data support for the subsequent optimization work, the new storage strategy and the duration of the storage strategy will be saved in the metadata of the file. New fields are shown in Table 2.

Table 2. New field added in the metadata of HDFS file

Field name	Description
StoragePolicy	The storage policy after updated
Duration	The duration of current storage policy, the unit of this field is Tc, when policy is updated, this field is setted to zero
UpdateTime	The update time of policy

3.2   Optimization of Replica Placement and Management Strategy

In this section, we will use the file heat value to optimize the replica placement and management strategy of HDFS. In our Strategy, When users need to store files to HDFS, they must specify an initial storage policy ($policy_0$), this parameter decides the number of replica and the position of replica shown in

Table 1. Then we use $policy_0$ to calculate the initial heat value of files as shown in Formula 1.

After files are stored in HDFS. The heat value of files will constantly changes with time. So we use LSTM to predict their future heat value. And we will use the predicted heat value to change the position and replica number of files. This strategy is called Optimized replica management policy, abbreviated as ORMP.

4   Experiment and Analysis

This chapter will design experiments based on cloudsim [15] simulation tool to verify the actual optimization effect of ORMP strategy proposed in Sect. 3.

4.1   Simulation Environment Configuration

This experiment simulation uses a tool of CloudSim, which is an open source cloud computing framework developed by CLOUDS Lab at University of Melbourne. CloudSim has built-in rich modeling and simulation functions, covering almost all cloud computing scenarios. It supports modeling and simulation of large cloud data centers, federal cloud modeling and simulation, as well as virtual server modeling. In this paper, we run the relevant simulation program on a single physical host, and the detailed information of software and hardware configuration is shown in Table 3.

Table 3. Hardware and software configuration of experimental environment

Hardware&Software	Configuration
CPU	Intel(R)Core(TM)i7-8700k@3.70 GHz
Memory	LPX DDR4 16G
Hard disk	Intel 660P SSD 215G
Operating system	Windows 10
Compiling environment	JDK 1, 8.0_172
Development tool	Intellig IDEA 2019.1.1

In this experiment, a host node is configured as a NameNode in CloudSim, and 24 host nodes are used as DataNodes, from DN1 to DN18 respectively. They are scattered on three racks (Rack1, Rack2, Rack3). Specifically, the DataNodes of DN_1-DN_6 are located on Rack1, the DataNodes of DN_7-DN_{12} are located on Rack2, and the DataNodes of $DN_{13}-DN_{18}$ are located on Rack3. The detailed information on the configuration of each host node is shown in Table 4.

This experiment need to simulate the reading and writing of data from various storage media, so the respective I/O speeds are set according to the performance of various storage media in the real environment as follows. The reading

Table 4. Detailed configuration parameters of each node

Node number	CPU	Memory (GB)	Hard disk (GB)
1, 2, 7, 8, 13, 14	3200/16	8192	SSD1024
3, 4, 9, 10, 15, 16	2400/12	4096	SSD512
5, 6, 11, 12, 17, 18	2000/8	4096	HDD1024

and writing speed of the solid state hard disk are set to 400 MB/s, the reading speed and writing speed of the mechanical hard disk are set to 150 MB/s, as well as the reading speed and writing speed of the memory are set to 8 GB/s. In addition, in reference with the parameters in the actual cluster, the network card bandwidth of each host is set to 1000 MB/s, the maximum transmission bandwidth in the same rack is set to 1200 MB/s, and the maximum transmission bandwidth between racks is set to 600 MB/s.

4.2   Experiment on Replica Management Strategy

The purpose of this experiment is to verify the effect of optimized replica management policy (ORMP) on dynamically adjusting the location and number of replicas in heterogeneous HDFS cluster environment. This experiment can be divided into two parts in structure: the first part verifies the feasibility and actual effect of LSTM network predicting the access times of files in HDFS. The second part verifies the optimization effect of ORMP strategy based on LSTM prediction results compared with DRMP strategy.

Prediction of File Heat Value Based on LSTM. We take 180 day file access records in heterogeneous HDFS cluster environment as data set. The original data includes 4269 file access records.

Through data cleaning, 50 files are selected, which have been in HDFS for 180 days. Through data preprocessing, the access records of each file are divided into 8-h intervals to get the total access times of each interval. Finally, we get 27000 pieces of data from 50 files in 180 days. The structure of LSTM cell is shown in Fig. 2.

The structure of the neural network consists of an input layer, a hidden layer and an output layer. The number of neurons in the hidden layer is 200. After the input value enters the input layer, it is connected to a fully connected layer through LSTM. In the fully connected layer, an output value is obtained through linear operation, which is the predicted value. In order to enhance the nonlinearity of the neural network model, the activation function is relu and the loss function is MSE. In order to solve the problem of large swing amplitude and accelerate the convergence speed of the function, $RMSprop$ [16] algorithm is selected as the optimization method of the model.

In this experiment, the access data of each file is divided according to the ratio of 7:3, with the first 70% of the data (from May 1, 2019 to September 4,

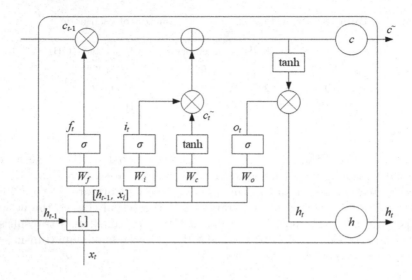

Fig. 2. The structure of LSTM cell

2019) as the training set, and the last 30% of the data (from September 5, 2019 to October 28, 2019) as the test set. The step size of training is 8, that is, the real value of file access times in the past 8 time periods is used to predict the file access times in the next time period in the future. After 100 epoch iterations, the loss function converges and a LSTM neural network model is obtained.

After this model is trained, we randomly select the last 30% data of the file to test the network model. The test results are shown in Fig. 3. The MSE of the prediction results is 73.014.

As shown in the figure, the overall trend of the data can be obtained through the prediction. The short-term prediction effect in most areas is better, but in some areas with abrupt changes in quantity, the prediction deviation is larger, especially the fit of the valley bottom is not ideal.

The root cause of inaccurate prediction in some regions is that the amount of data in the training set is still too small. In general, LSTM can be used to predict the file access, which can basically meet the needs of calculating the real-time heat value in the optimized replica management strategy.

Optimization Effect of ORMP. The ORMP policy dynamically manages the replica based on the prediction of file access. We will analyze the impact of replica management strategy on the read performance by reading files from HDFS. Before the experiment, 200 files are written to HDFS. Each file is 1 GB and divided into 16 file blocks. Since it is impossible to simulate users' subjective judgment on files, the initial heterogeneous storage policy of files is set to warm, one copy stored in SSD, the other two copies stored in HDD.

Select files A, B and C with different activity from the cluster as the research object. We will track six heat value update cycles Tc_{temp}, which are recorded

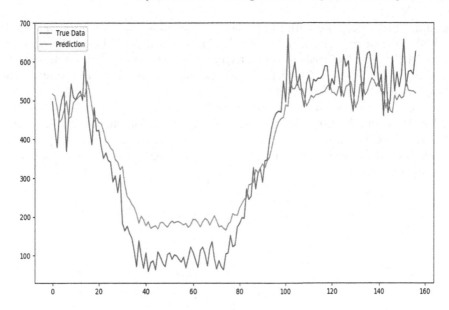

Fig. 3. Comparison between predicted value and real value

as $T_1 - T_6$. Because it is difficult to simulate the user's subjective judgment of file access characteristics, in order to eliminate the influence of subjective heat on the experimental results, the six Tc_{temp} selected in this experiment are later than the subjective heat active period τ_a of each file.

Table 5, 6, 7 and 8 shows the predicted and real file access values of files A, B and B in T_1–T_6 cycle, as well as the average of the predicted file access values in the whole system.

Table 5. Predicted and real file access values of files

Time period	Predicted num			Real num			Error			Average predicted num
	A	B	C	A	B	C	A	B	C	
T1	730	202	22	758	210	15	28	8	−7	170.62
T2	759	199	11	761	181	9	2	−18	−2	154
T3	786	157	5	799	352	4	13	195	−1	202.86
T4	840	310	8	857	574	0	17	264	−8	157.4
T5	897	869	3	872	947	5	−25	78	2	199.06
T6	909	968	7	928	941	0	19	−27	−7	272.76

During T_1–T_6, the real value of access times of file A fluctuates slightly, but it has always been at a high level; the real value of access times of file B fluctuates greatly in the observation period, the overall trend is gradually increasing; the real value of access times of file C has always remained at a very low level. At the same time, it can be found that the error between the predicted value and the real value of files A and C is very small, which means the predicted value can reflect the real change of file activity; while the predicted value and the real value of file B are different in some time periods, but it can still reflect the change trend to a certain extent.

Figure 4, 5 and 6 show the adjustment of the location and number of replicas of files A, B and C after $ORMP$ strategy optimization during T_1–T_6, which are marked on the horizontal axis; the three pictures also show the location and number of replicas of files under $ORMP$ strategy, which are marked with $Default$ on the horizontal axis.

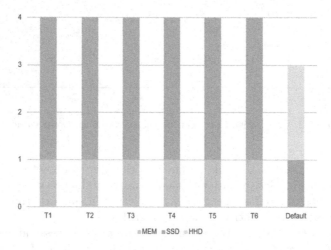

Fig. 4. Replica change trends of file A

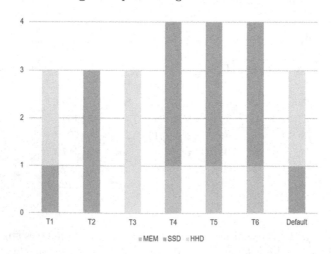

Fig. 5. Replica change trends of file B

Under the ORMP strategy, the access times of file A are always very high, and all of them are always in the hottest policy, that is, three copies are placed in SSD and one copy is placed in memory.

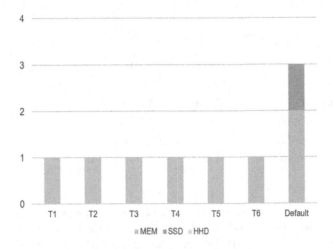

Fig. 6. Replica change trends of file C

The access times of file B are unstable, and the storage policies are warm, hot, cold and hottest in turn, which are consistent with the trend of the real access times of file B.

The access times of file C are close to zero 0, so file C is the coldest storage strategy, only one copy placed in the HDD. Table show the experiment results of three files under two different replica management strategies from T_1 to T_6.

Table 6 shows the experimental results of continuously reading file A based on DRMP strategy and ORMP strategy in T_1–T_6. It can be found that the number of times to read the replica in SSD using ORMP is significantly higher than that using DRMP policy. We can read replicas in memory when using ORMP strategy. Therefore, the cumulative read time of ORMP strategy is much lower than that of DRMP strategy. The average single read time of ORMP is 27.78% less than that of DRMP strategy.

Table 6. Experiment results of file A

	DRMP	ORMP	Optimization degree
Total read num	4975	4975	
Read SSD	26556	70354	
Read memory	0	9246	
Read time (s)	57692.738	41665.563	
Average read time (s)	11.597	8.375	29.78%

Table 7 shows the experimental results of file B. The experimental results of file B are similar to file A. The ORMP strategy performs better in hit SSD and hit memory. The average single read time when using the ORMP strategy is 14.11% less than that of DRMP strategy.

Table 7. Experiment results of file B

	DRMP	ORMP	Optimization degree
Total read num	3205	3205	
Read SSD	17084	39971	
Read memory	0	3697	
Read time (s)	37184.847	31937.356	
Average read time (s)	11.602	9.9065	14.11%

Table 8 shows the experimental results of file C. The reading times of file C is much lower than file A and file B. We can see that the efficiency of reading file is higher than that of ORMP when using DRMP strategy. This is due to the fact that the real-time heat value of file C is low and will not be accessed frequently according to the ORMP policy, so the replicas of file C is placed in the HDD with relatively poor reading performance. So the reading time using the DRMP policy is much lower than that of ORMP policy.

Table 8. Experiment results of file C

	DRMP	ORMP	Optimization degree
Total read num	33	33	
Read SSD	177	0	
Read memory	0	0	
Read time (s)	379.328	617.520	
Average read time (s)	11.495	18.713	−62.07%

In order to analyze the impact of ORMP strategy on the whole file system, we comprehensively analyze the experimental results of files A, B and C, as shown in Table 9.

Table 9. Comprehensive experiment results of all three files

	DRMP	ORMP	Optimization degree
Total read num	8213	8213	
Read SSD	43827	110925	
Read memory	0	12943	
Read time (s)	95256.913	74220.439	
Average read time (s)	11.598	9.037	22.08%

Compared with DRMP, ORMP is 22.08% faster in reading speed. The strategy proposed in this paper obtains the real-time heat value of the file by predicting the number of file accesses, and then dynamically adjusts the location and number of replicas, finally reducing the unit reading time of the data. The strategy proposed in this paper can reduce the number of copies of inactive data and reduce the storage cost of the system.

5 Conclusion

In this paper, we proposed the concept of file heat value and its calculation method. Then the LSTM algorithm is used to predict the access number files in the future. Based on these predicted visits, the storage strategy of the file is updated, and the storage location and the number of copies of the file are dynamically adjusted. Experimental results show that compared with the default storage strategy of HDFS, the proposed strategy can improve the reading speed of the system.

Acknowledgments. Partially Funded by Science and Technology Program of Sichuan Province (2021YFG0330), partially funded by Grant SCITLAB-0001 of Intelligent Terminal Key Laboratory of SiChuan Province, and partially Funded by Fundamental Research Funds for the Central Universities (ZYGX2019J076).

References

1. White, T.: Hadoop: The Definitive Guide (2009)
2. Shvachko, K., Kuang, H., Radia, S., Chansler, R.: The hadoop distributed file system. In: 2010 IEEE 26th Symposium on Mass Storage Systems and Technologies (MSST), pp. 1–10 (2010)
3. Shafer, J., Rixner, S., Cox, A.L.: The hadoop distributed filesystem: balancing portability and performance. In: 2010 IEEE International Symposium on Performance Analysis of Systems and Software (ISPASS), pp. 122–133 (2010)
4. Park, N., Lee, B., Kim, K.T., Youn, H.Y.: Cold data eviction using node congestion probability for HDFS based on hybrid SSD. In: 2015 IEEE/ACIS 16th International Conference on Software Engineering, Artificial Intelligence, Networking and Parallel/Distributed Computing (SNPD), pp. 1–6 (2015)

5. Yingxun, F., Shilin, W., Li, M.: A data distribution method under a heterogeneous HDFS cluster (2018)
6. Bui, D.M., Hussain, S., Huh, E.N., Lee, S.: Adaptive replication management in HDFS based on supervised learning. IEEE Trans. Knowl. Data Eng. **28**(6), 1369–1382 (2016)
7. Krish, K.R., Anwar, A., Butt, A.R.: hats: a heterogeneity-aware tiered storage for hadoop. In: 2014 14th IEEE/ACM International Symposium on Cluster, Cloud and Grid Computing (CCGrid), pp. 502–511 (2014)
8. Islam, N.S., Lu, X., Wasi-ur-Rahman, M., Shankar, D., Panda, D.K.: Triple-h: a hybrid approach to accelerate HDFS on HPC clusters with heterogeneous storage architecture. In: 2015 15th IEEE/ACM International Symposium on Cluster, Cloud and Grid Computing, pp. 101–110 (2015)
9. Zhao, W., Meng, L., Sun, J., Ding, Y., Zhao, H., Wang, L.: An improved data placement strategy in a heterogeneous hadoop cluster. Open Cybern. Systemics J. **9**(1), 8 (2015)
10. Xu, X., Yang, C., Shao, J.: Data replica placement mechanism for open heterogeneous storage systems. Procedia Comput. Sci. **109**, 18–25 (2017)
11. Ye, X., Huang, M., Zhu, D., Xu, P.: A novel blocks placement strategy for hadoop. In: 2012 IEEE/ACIS 11th International Conference on Computer and Information Science, pp. 3–7 (2012)
12. Liu, Y., Li, M., Alham, N.K., Hammoud, S., Ponraj, M.: Load balancing in mapreduce environments for data intensive applications. In: 2011 Eighth International Conference on Fuzzy Systems and Knowledge Discovery (FSKD), vol. 4, pp. 2675–2678 (2011)
13. Xiong, R., Luo, J., Dong, F.: SLDP: a novel data placement strategy for large-scale heterogeneous hadoop cluster. In: 2014 Second International Conference on Advanced Cloud and Big Data, pp. 9–17 (2014)
14. Shaochun, W., Xiang, S., Liang, C., Ling, Y., Bowen, Y.: A replica pre-placement strategy based on correlation analysis in cloud environment. In: 1st International Workshop on Cloud Computing and Information Security, pp. 541–544 (2013)
15. Calheiros, R.N., Ranjan, R.B.A.: A toolkit for modeling and simulation of cloud computing environments and evaluation of resource provisioning algorithms (2011)
16. Dauphin, Y.N., de Vries, H., Chung, J., Bengio, Y.: Rmsprop and equilibrated adaptive learning rates for non-convex optimization. arXiv: Learning (2015)

An Immune Clone Particle Swarm Optimization Algorithm for Sparse Representation of Hyperspectral Images

Li Wang$^{(\boxtimes)}$, Wei Wang, and Boni Liu

Xi'an Aeronautical University, Xi'an 710077, Shaanxi, China

Abstract. The sparse representation of hyperspectral images can reduce the amount of data and facilitate image classification and interpretation processing. An immune clone particle swarm optimization algorithm (ICPSO) to achieve sparse representation of hyperspectral images is proposed in this paper. The main idea of the algorithm is to use the evolutionary process of particle swarm to simulate the atomic matching process of the orthogonal chasing algorithm to improve the diversity and efficiency of atom selection. Further, according to the clonal selection theory of biological immunology, immune cloning, cloning mutation and cloning selection operators are used to expand the local search range, fully maintain the diversity of the population, improve the convergence speed and avoid the premature convergence. Sparse representation experiments are carried out on hyperspectral images using proposed ICPSO to verify the performance of the algorithm. Compared with the orthogonal matching pursuit algorithm, the proposed algorithm can improve the reconstruction accuracy as well as the computing efficiency.

Keywords: Hyperspectral image · Immune clone · Particle swarm algorithm · Reconstruction · Sparse representation

1 Introduction

Containing abundant spatial geometric information and spectral feature information, hyperspectral images (HSIs) [1] are suitable for terrain reconnaissance [2], target detection and recognition [3, 4], classification [5, 6]. The development of hyperspectral imaging spectrometer [7–9] and the research of hyperspectral image interpretation [10–12] have become the focus of attention. The expanding application fields require hyperspectral images to provide more detailed target information. The higher the spatial and spectral resolution is, the higher the challenge to the system's data storage and transmission capabilities.

Effective sparse representation could capture the main features of the signal, which leads to achieve a small amount of data for signal description. The basic idea of sparse representation is that, from the basic functions set of the signal projection, only a small number of the basic functions could be extracted to represent the original signal with little

© ICST Institute for Computer Sciences, Social Informatics and Telecommunications Engineering 2021
Published by Springer Nature Switzerland AG 2021. All Rights Reserved
X. Wang et al. (Eds.): AICON 2021, LNICST 396, pp. 593–611, 2021.
https://doi.org/10.1007/978-3-030-90196-7_51

distortion [13, 14]. Sparse representation model requires that in the signal expansion, the coefficients of most of the basic functions are zero, and only a few basic functions have large non-zero coefficients. Its applications include image classification [15], signal de-noising [16], object detection [17], and face recognition [18]. Applying the signal sparse decomposition theory to hyperspectral images to obtain sparse representations, can greatly reduce the amount of data and achieve further classification and interpretation of hyperspectral images.

A typical way to obtain such signal sparse representation is the orthogonal matching pursuit (OMP) algorithm [19, 20]. OMP, an iterative greedy algorithm, chooses the best atom from the dictionary to match the signal, thereby achieving high reconstruction accuracy. Hyperspectral image features are complex, and redundant dictionaries can be used to obtain good sparse representations, but the computation time of OMP is unbearable under the existing computing conditions. Instead, the evolutionary algorithms [21, 22] could be used to achieve the sparse representation.

This paper proposes an immune clone particle swarm algorithm to achieve sparse representation of hyperspectral images to overcome the problem of low calculation efficiency of OMP algorithm. The main idea is: utilize particle swarm optimization (Particle Swarm Optimization, PSO) to simulate the atomic matching process of OMP, which can improve the search process of the optimal atom; further, introduce the immune clone algorithm to increase the diversity of the population and increase the convergence rate, and ultimately improve the efficiency of sparse representation. Four classic hyperspectral images are used to test the effectiveness of the proposed algorithm.

The remainder of this paper is organized as follows. In Sect. 2, the sparse decomposition process using OMP and the basic PSO algorithm are described. And then in Sect. 3, the principle of the proposed Immune Clone Particle Swarm Algorithm (ICPSO) are presented, included four aspects, namely initial Particle production, Immune cloning operator, cloning mutation operator, cloning selection operator, particle updating operator. Moreover, the implementation process of proposed algorithm is also introduced in this section. Next in Sect. 4, experimental results are shown and analyzed. Finally, in Sect. 5, some concluding remarks are made.

2   Principles of OMP and PSO

2.1   Sparse Representation

The signal sparse representation model based on redundant dictionary is expressed as:

$$\min \|\theta\|_0 \quad s.t. \quad x = \Phi\theta \tag{1}$$

Where, $x \in R^N$ is the original signal, $\Phi \in R^{N \times M}$ is the redundant dictionary, and $\theta \in R^M$ is the sparse coefficient vector. Each column in Φ is called as an atom. In sparse representation, there are two issues needed to be solved: 1) construct the redundant dictionary Φ, and 2) solve the optimal function in Eq. (1) to obtain the sparse coefficient vector θ. In the proposed algorithm, Gabor dictionary [23, 24] is used to be the sparse basis for hyperspectral images, and its generating function is expressed as,

$$g_\gamma(n) = \frac{1}{\sqrt{s}} e^{-\pi \left(\frac{n-u}{s}\right)^2} \cos(\upsilon n + \varphi) \tag{2}$$

Where, $n = 0, 1, ..., N$, $\gamma = (s, u, \upsilon, \varphi)$ is the time-frequency parameter vector. The variation range is: $1 \leq s \leq N$, $1 \leq u \leq N$, $0 \leq \upsilon \leq 2\pi$, $0 \leq \varphi \leq 2\pi$. After the discretization of the time-frequency parameters, the number of atoms in the Gabor dictionary is $M = 52(N \log_2 N + N - 1)$.

2.2 OMP Algorithm

Solving signal sparse representation under a redundant dictionary is a NP-hard problem. There does not exist known polynomial time algorithm to solve this optimization problem, a sub-optimal approximation method is needed. The basic idea of OMP for sparse representation is to find the optimal atoms that can linearly represent the original signal in the redundant dictionary through continuous iteration. When the residual between the original signal and the represented signal is continuously reduced, an approximate linear representation of the original signal can be obtained.

Specifically, through continuous iteration, OMP selects some optimal atoms from the dictionary $\boldsymbol{\Phi}$, these atoms make up the set of the true signal. The implementation process of OMP is summarized as follows:

Step 1: Initializition: iterative number $k = 1$, residual $\boldsymbol{r}_0 = \boldsymbol{x}$, index collection of optimal atoms $\Lambda_0 = []$.
Step 2: Select the index of optimal atom: The selected atom needs to meet the principle of maximum relevance, therefore, we need to traversal all the atoms in dictionary $\boldsymbol{\Phi}$, compute the relevance and sort them,

$$\lambda_k = \arg\max_l |\langle \boldsymbol{r}_{k-1}, \boldsymbol{\Phi}_l \rangle| \tag{3}$$

Where, $\boldsymbol{\Phi}_l$ is l-th column of $\boldsymbol{\Phi}$.
Step 3: Update index collection: Add the optimal atom index to the collection, $\Lambda_k = \Lambda_{k-1} \cup \lambda_k$.
Step 4: Update residual: Use the searched best atoms to linearly represent the signal and calculate the residual,

$$\boldsymbol{r}_k = \boldsymbol{x} - \boldsymbol{\Phi}_{\Lambda_k} \left(\boldsymbol{\Phi}_{\Lambda_k}^{\mathrm{T}} \boldsymbol{\Phi}_{\Lambda_k} \right)^{-1} \boldsymbol{\Phi}_{\Lambda_k}^{\mathrm{T}} \boldsymbol{x} \tag{4}$$

Where, $\boldsymbol{\Phi}_{\Lambda_k}$ represents the sub-matrix constructed by the atoms indexed by Λ_k.
Step 5: Determine whether the maximum iteration number K is satisfied, if not then $k = k + 1$, repeat Step 2–Step 4, else stop iteration.

In other words, the maximum iteration number in OMP is the number of optimal atoms to represent the original signal. The original signal $\boldsymbol{x}$ could be represented using the K optimal atoms indexed by Λ_K. The sparse coefficient vector is,

$$\hat{\boldsymbol{\theta}} = \left(\boldsymbol{\Phi}_{\Lambda_K}^{\mathrm{T}} \boldsymbol{\Phi}_{\Lambda_K} \right)^{-1} \boldsymbol{\Phi}_{\Lambda_K}^{\mathrm{T}} \boldsymbol{x} \tag{5}$$

Where, $\boldsymbol{\Phi}_{\Lambda_K}$ represents the sub-matrix consisting of column vectors in $\boldsymbol{\Phi}$ indexed by Λ_K.

Use these optimal atoms to linearly represent the signal and the reconstructed signal is expressed as:

$$\hat{x} = \boldsymbol{\Phi}_{\Lambda_K} \hat{\boldsymbol{\theta}} \tag{6}$$

2.3 Particle Swarm Optimization

The particle swarm optimization algorithm treats the potential solution of the optimization problem as a particle in the search space without mass [25, 26]. The particle has a certain flying speed and position. Assume that the dimensional of search space is L, the population $A = (A_1, A_2, ..., A_i, ..., A_Q)$ contains Q particles, where the i th particle represents its position in the search space and is represented as a vector $A_i = (a_{i1}, a_{i2}, ..., a_{il}, ..., a_{iL})$, $i = 1, 2, ..., Q$, $l = 1, 2, ..., L$. The velocity of the i th particle is $V_i = (v_{i1}, v_{i2}, ..., v_{il}, ..., v_{iL})$, the individual extremum is $P_{besti} = (P_{i1}, P_{i2}, ..., P_{il}, ..., P_{iL})$ and the population extremum is $G_{best} = (G_1, G_2, ..., G_l, ..., G_L)$.

Particles update their speed and position by tracking individual extremes and group extremes,

$$v_{il}^t = w v_{il}^{t-1} + c_1 r_1 \left(P_{il}^{t-1} - a_{il}^{t-1}\right) + c_2 r_2 \left(G_l^{t-1} - a_{il}^{t-1}\right) \tag{7}$$

$$a_{il}^t = a_{il}^{t-1} + v_{il}^t \tag{8}$$

Where, t is the current evolution generation, w is the inertia weights, c_1 and c_2 are non-negative constants, r_1 and r_2 are random numbers distributed in the interval $[0, 1]$.

Particle swarm algorithm can use individual experience information and population experience information to adjust its state. The advantage of the algorithm is the fast convergence, but the disadvantage is that the particles easily fall into local extremes and cannot be rid of them, which limits the search range of the particles and reduces the search efficiency. Clonal selection [27, 28] is an important theory of biological immune system theory. Compared with the evolutionary algorithm, the clone selection algorithm can increase the speed of convergence whereas expanding the local search range, and maintain the diversity of the population through cloning, mutation, selection, etc., thereby improving the performance of the particle swarm algorithm. For the reason that, combining immune clone with particle swarm algorithm, an immune clone particle swarm optimization (ICPSO) algorithm for sparse representation is proposed in this paper.

3   Proposed ICPSO Algorithm for Sparse Representation

In this section, the details about the proposed ICPSO are presented. First of all, the optimization problem and initial particle production in the proposed ICPSO are described. And then, the four operators in the proposed algorithm, including the immune cloning operator, cloning mutation operator, cloning selection operator and particle updating operator are designed. Finally, the implementation process is summarized.

3.1 Optimization Problem and Initial Particle Production

The main framework of the proposed algorithm is based on the OMP algorithm, that is, the sparse representation is completed in an iterative way. In its iteration, the proposed ICPSO use the particle evolution to find one optimal atom, then updates the optimal atom set, updates the residuals, and finally uses the found optimal atoms to sparsely approximate the original signal.

The core idea of ICPSO is using particle evolution to simulate the atom matching process of OMP. Particularly, ICPSO does not need generate dictionary in advance, whereas particles expressed by position, velocity and fitness value are used to represent the atoms. According to the generation principle of Gabor atoms, the search space dimension of our optimization problem is $L = 4$. The initial population is denoted as $A = \left(a_1, a_2, ..., a_Q\right)$, where Q is the population size. The initial position of the i th particle is $a_i = \left(a_{i1}, a_{i2}, a_{i3}, a_{i4}\right)$, and each component is corresponding to the time-frequency parameter vector in Gabor dictionary.

The principle of maximum correlation is used to find the optimal atoms; therefore, the fitness value for i th particle can be described as,

$$f(a_i) = \left|\langle r_{k-1}, g_{a_i}\rangle\right| \tag{9}$$

$$g_{a_i}(n) = \frac{1}{\sqrt{a_{i1}}} e^{-\pi\left(\frac{n-a_{i2}}{a_{i1}}\right)^2} \cos(a_{i3}n + a_{i4}) \tag{10}$$

Where, g_{a_i} is the corresponding atom generated by particle a_i.

The optimization problem of the algorithm ICPSO can be summarized as,

$$\max\{f(a): a \in (s, u, \upsilon, \varphi)\} \tag{11}$$

If the initial population is randomly generated, the individual cannot be representative, which is not conducive to searching for the global best. We expect that the initial individuals can be dispersed as evenly as possible over the entire feasible solution space, so that the algorithm can search uniformly over the entire feasible solution space. Here we use chaotic logic mapping to generate a set of particles as the initial population $A^0 = \left(a_1^0, a_2^0, ..., a_Q^0\right)$. Set the optimal position of the i th particle as $P_{besti} = a_i^0$, and the extreme value of the initial population to $G_{best} = \max_{a_i^0} f(a_i^0)$, $i = 1, 2, ..., Q$. The initial velocity of the particles is $v_i^0 = (v_{i1}^0, v_{i2}^0, v_{i3}^0, v_{i4}^0)$. The positions and velocities are updated by the following four operators.

3.2 ICPSO Operators

Immune Cloning Operator. For the current population $A(t-1)$, we perform immune cloning operations on it, that is,

$$\vartheta(A(t-1)) = \left(\vartheta(a_1); \vartheta(a_2); ...; \vartheta(a_Q)\right) \tag{12}$$

Where, $\vartheta(a_i)$ is the clone of a_i. The clone number is defined as,

$$C_i = C\frac{f(a_i)}{\sum_{i=1}^{Q}f(a_i)}, i = 1, 2, ..., Q \tag{13}$$

Where, C is the clone constant.

After Immune cloning operator, the population turns to,

$$A'(t-1) = \left(A; A_1'; A_2'; ...; A_Q'\right) \tag{14}$$

Where, $A_i' = \left(a_{i1}; a_{i2}; ...; a_{iC_i-1}\right), a_{iq} = a_i, q = 1, 2, ..., C_i - 1.$

Cloning Mutation Operator. In order to promote the exchange of useful information between individuals and improve the uniformity of the individual solution of the offspring, a cloning mutation operator is used to generate representative offspring individuals. During this process, in order to retain the original information of the population, the mutation operator is only applied to clone population $\vartheta(a_i)$. Specify mutation probability P_m, for each component of the particle, generates a random number p_m between 0 and 1. If $p_m < P_m$, then the corresponding component would be re-selected as one number from its variant range, otherwise the component would not change. Mutated individuals are indicated by d_i and the population is denoted as $D(t-1)$.

Cloning Selection Operator. The clone selection operator selects excellent individuals from the progeny of the cloned mutations of the particles, thereby forming a new population. Calculate the fitness of the current population, and calculate the fitness of all the offspring that have been cloned and mutated.

If there exists the outstanding mutation particle which satisfies the following two conditions,

$$b = \max\{f(a_{iq})|q = 1, 2, ..., C_i - 1\} \tag{15}$$

$$f(a_i) < f(b) \quad a_i \in A(t-1) \tag{16}$$

Then particle b is chosen to replace the parent particle a_i to update the population.

Particle Updating Operator. Define the speed and position update operators are,

$$v_i(t) = wv_i(t-1) + c_1r_1\left(P_{besti}(t-1) - a_i(t-1)\right) + c_2r_2\left(G_{best}(t-1) - a_i(t-1)\right) \tag{17}$$

$$a_i(t) = a_i(t-1) + v_i(t) \tag{18}$$

The inertia weight w adopts a linear differential decreasing strategy [29], expressed as,

$$w(t) = w_{max} - \frac{(w_{max} - w_{min})}{T^2}t \tag{19}$$

Where, T is the maximum evolution algebra. In the early stage of algorithm evolution, the decreasing trend of w is slow, and the global search ability is strong, which is benefit for finding good particles. In the later stage of algorithm evolution, the decreasing trend of w is accelerated, which can improve the convergence speed of the algorithm. After the above operators, the tth population would be evolved to the $t+1$th generation population.

3.3 Implementation Process of ICPSO

Combining the clonal selection theory of the immune system with the particle swarm optimization algorithm of advanced evolution theory, an immune clone particle swarm optimization algorithm is proposed to solve the sparse representation problem. The block diagram of the proposed algorithm is depicted in Fig. 1, and the implementation process is summarized as follows.

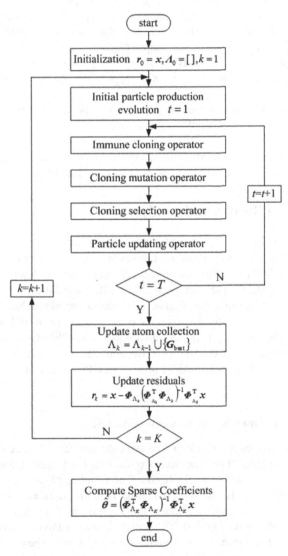

Fig. 1. Block diagram of proposed algorithm.

Step 1: Algorithm initialization, iterative number $k = 1$, residual $r_0 = x$, optimal atom collection $\Lambda_0 = []$.

Step 2: Initial particle production: Initialize the particle population to A^0, calculate the fitness of the particles. Determine P_{besti} and G_{best}, and set the evolution algebra to $t = 1$.

Step 3: Utilizing immune cloning operator to obtain a cloned population $A'(t - 1)$ using (12)–(14).

Step 4: Utilizing cloning mutation operator to obtain the mutated population $D(t - 1)$.

Step 5: Utilizing cloning selection operator to obtain $\overline{A}(t - 1)$ using (15)–(16).

Step 6: According to particle updating operator, update speed and position of particles to obtain $A(t)$, calculate the new fitness function, and updating P_{besti} and G_{best}.

Step 7: Check whether the maximum evolution algebra T is reached. If not then let $t = t + 1$ and repeat Step 3–Step 6, else output G_{best}.

Step 8: Update atom collection with G_{best}, $\Lambda_k = \Lambda_{k-1} \cup G_{best}$.

Step 9: Update residuals using (4), here Φ_{Λ_k} represents the dictionary consisting of atoms in Λ_k.

Step 10: Check whether the maximum iteration number K is satisfied, if then stop iteration. Else let $k = k + 1$, repeat Step 2–Step 9.

Sparsely represent the original signal using the optimal atom obtained by ICPSO and the reconstructed signal could be expressed using (5) and (6).

4   Experimental Results and Analysis

In order to evaluate the performance of the proposed algorithm, some experimental results and analysis on four hyperspectral images are carried out in this section. At the beginning, utilize OMP algorithm for sparse representation to determine the number of optimal atoms. Next, the parameters, including the population size and maximum evolution algebra, number of optimal atoms, for proposed algorithm ICPSO are discussed. And then, the comparison between the proposed algorithm ICPSO and standard OMP algorithm is shown, using peak signal-to-noise ratio (PSNR), structural similarity (SSIM) [30] and runtime to assess the performance. The hardware and software environments for these experiments are: AMD quad-core CPU, 3.80 GHz, 16G memory and Matlab2012b.

4.1   Hyperspectral Datasets and Evaluation Metrics

Four hyperspectral images were selected to evaluate the performance of the proposed sparse representation algorithm. The first two datasets are Cuprite1 and Cuprite2 collected by AVIRIS with a total of 224 bands. The number of available bands is 188, excluded the abnormal bands and all zero bands. The third dataset is Indian Pines collected by AVIRIS with a total of 220 bands. After removing the water absorption band, the number of available bands is 200. The fourth dataset is Pavia University collected by ROSIS with a total of 115 bands. Removing the noisy bands, the number of available bands is 103.

Based on the above analysis, the computational complexity of OMP algorithm has high relevance with the atoms in redundant dictionary, and the number of atoms is greatly increasing with the length of signal. Taking into account the computation efficiency, the hyperspectral images are processing block by block. Given consideration to accuracy and efficiency, the block size is set as 16 in the following experiments. Without loss of generality, the Indian Pines is spatially cropped to 128 * 128 and the other datasets are cropped to 256 * 256. The hyperspectral image is represented by a two-dimensional matrix $X \in R^{N_p \times N_\lambda}$, where, $X = [x_1, x_2, ..., x_b, ..., x_{N_\lambda}]$, x_b is the vectorized representation of the b th band image, N_p is the pixels of a single band image, and N_λ represents the band number. The original image of the 50th band is shown in Fig. 2.

Two metrics are adopted to evaluate the reconstruction accuracy of the proposed algorithm, PSNR and SSIM between the reconstructed image and the original image. The PSNR measured in dB is defined as,

$$\text{PSNR}(x, \hat{x}) = 20 \log_{10} \frac{\max(x)}{\sqrt{\text{MSE}(x, \hat{x})}} \tag{20}$$

Where, x and $\hat{x}$ are the original and reconstructed image, $\max(x)$ is the peak value of x, $\text{MSE}(x, \hat{x})$ is the mean squared error,

$$\text{MSE}(x, \hat{x}) = \frac{1}{N} \|x - \hat{x}\|_2^2 \tag{21}$$

The SSIM between x and $\hat{x}$ is defined as,

$$\text{SSIM}(x, \hat{x}) = \frac{(2\mu_1\mu_2 + C_1)(2\sigma_{12} + C_2)}{(\mu_1^2 + \mu_2^2 + C_1)(\sigma_1^2 + \sigma_2^2 + C_2)} \tag{22}$$

Where, μ_1 and μ_2 are the mean values of x and $\hat{x}$, σ_1 and σ_2 are the standard deviation values of x and $\hat{x}$, σ_{12} represents the correlation coefficient between x and $\hat{x}$, C_1 and C_2 are constants related to the dynamic range of the pixel values. The details for these parameters can refer to [30].

4.2 Parameter Selection for OMP

Analysis from the implementation process of OMP, one atom is increased into the optimal atom collection every iteration; that is, the number of iterations is the number of optimal atoms. The accuracy of the reconstructed signal is decided by the optimal atoms. There is no doubt that the number of optimal atoms K would have significant effect on performance of OMP. In this part, experiments on the 50th band images using OMP with different K are presented. The atom number is varied from 1 to 100 at the interval of one. The reconstructed images are represented by the optimal K atoms. The PSNR and relative change between two iterations are shown in Fig. 3.

It is not surprising that, with the increase of the atom number, the reconstructed PSNR is increasing as well. We noticed that the PSNR is not keeping increasing with the atom number. When the atom number increases to 50, PSNR would tend to be smooth and has little oscillation. The relative change between two adjacent iterations, shown in Fig. 3(b), drops quickly when the iteration starts. With the iteration progresses, the relative change descends slowly and almost tends to be stable after 50 iterations. Therefore, we can draw such a conclusion that the number of optimal atoms of OMP algorithm could be set as $K = 50$ with good reconstruction performance.

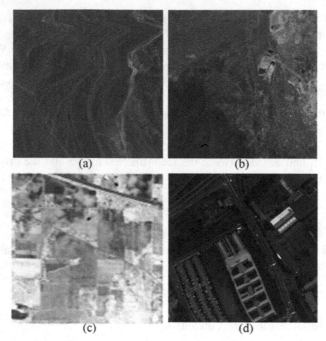

Fig. 2. Original 50th images of four datasets. (a) Cuprite1; (b) Cuprite2; (c) Indian Pines; (d) Pavia University.

4.3 Parameter Selection for ICPSO

In the implementation process of proposed ICPSO algorithm, the maximum evolution algebra T, the population size Q and the optimal atom number K would have significance on the performance. In this part, experiments on the 50th band images using ICPSO with different parameters are presented. The maximum evolution algebra T and the population size Q are varied from 5 to 50 at the interval of 5. The optimal atom number K is varied from 10 to 100 at the interval of 10. In addition, the clone constant C and mutation probability P_m are set as $C = 15$ and $P_m = 0.2$. The reconstructed images are represented by the optimal K atoms. Considering the randomness of ICPSO algorithm, the simulation would run 10 times under the same parameter to obtain the average value. The PSNR changes with different parameters for Cuprite1 and Indian Pines are shown in Fig. 4 and Fig. 5, respectively.

When the optimal atom number K is fixed at 100, the PSNR changes with maximum evolution algebra T and population size Q is shown in Fig. 4(a). Seen from the figure, when the maximum evolution algebra T increases, the variation of PSNR is not obviously, whereas the variation of PSNR with increasing of population size Q is more significant. When the population size reaches 30, the PSNR tends stable. Through this comparison, we can say that population size has more importance on the PSNR than that of maximum evolution algebra.

When the population size Q is fixed at 30, the PSNR changes with the maximum evolution algebra T and optimal atom number K is shown in Fig. 4(b). With the increase

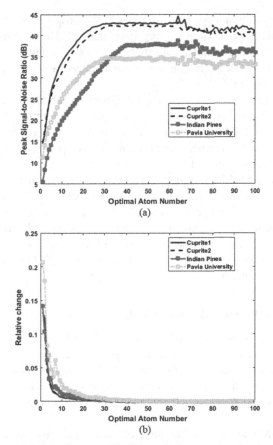

Fig. 3. The PSNR and relative change with different atom number for four band images using OMP. (a) PSNR; (b) Relative change.

of optimal atom number, the reconstructed PSNR would gradually be improved. However, the maximum evolution algebra has little effect on the PSNR. The result can further confirm the truth that the maximum evolution algebra has little effect of on reconstructed PSNR.

To further analyze the impact of maximum evolution algebra on PSNR, the results of maximum evolution algebra varied from 1 to 5 is given in Fig. 4(c). The optimal atom number is 100 and the PSNR is changed with population size. Seen from these curves, the effect of evolution algebra on PSNR is really very weak. Particularly, when the population size is greater than 30, several curves are cross together. This could further verify that we can set the parameter T to the lowest level without loss of reconstruction performance.

The analysis of Fig. 5 is similar with that of Fig. 4, therefore, we can draw a conclusion that the optimal atom number has the largest influence on the reconstructed PSNR, followed by population size, and the maximum evolution algebra has the smallest. We can also find that when population size is greater than 30, the PSNR has little increase.

Even if maximum evolution algebra is as low as 1, the proposed ICPSO could achieve good performance when population size is greater than 30. The other two hyperspectral images have the similar results and are able to reach the same conclusion. Based on these experimental results, we set the maximum evolution algebra $T = 1$ and $Q = 30$ in the proposed ICPSO algorithm.

After the population size and maximum evolution algebra are determined, experiments are carried out on four hyperspectral images to determine the optimal atoms number in proposed ICPSO. Results on the 50th band images using proposed ICPSO with different optimal atom number K are presented. The optimal atom number is varied from 10 to 100 at the interval of 10. The reconstructed images are represented by the optimal K atoms. The SSIM and relative change between two iterations are shown in Fig. 6. With the increase of the atom number, the reconstructed SSIM is increasing as well, whereas the relative change decreases. Due to the uncertainty of evolution algorithm, the SSIM and relative change are not a smooth process. However, with the help of the three immune cloning operators, the proposed ICPSO still converges quickly and finally tends stable. Thence, the optimal atom number in ICPSO is set as $K = 100$ in the following experiments.

4.4 Comparison Between OMP and ICPSO

In this subsection, the comparison between standard OMP algorithm and the proposed ICPSO algorithm is presented. The four hyperspectral datasets are sparse represented using the optimal atoms searched by OMP and ICPSO, respectively. The reconstructed PSNR, SSIM and computation time are used to evaluate the performance. The optimal atom number in OMP is $K = 50$. The parameters in ICPSO are $Q = 30$, $T = 1$ and $K = 100$.

The PSNR, SSIM and runtime (the three parameters are averaged on all bands) are shown in Table 1. Seen from the table, the PSNR of proposed ICPSO is about 1–2 dB higher than that of OMP. Moreover, the SSIM of two algorithms could both reach 0.97 or higher, which demonstrates that the optimal atoms searched by the two algorithms could describe the structure of the images very well. This fully states that by searching optimal atoms using the biological evolution manner, the proposed ICPSO could achieve better reconstruction accuracy than that of OMP. The immune cloning operators, which maintain the diversity of population, allow the algorithm converging to a good optimal solution.

The computation efficiency of these two algorithms is analyzed. The runtime shown in Table 1 is the average computation time consumed by one band. The OMP algorithm needs to traversal all the atoms in the redundant dictionary to find one optimal atom. In our experiments, the atoms in the Gabor dictionary are 119756 when the signal length is 256. Therefore, the OMP algorithm needs to complete 5987800 inner product operators to find 50 atoms. Whereas in the proposed ICPSO algorithm, in its iteration, it needs to complete immune cloning, cloning mutation, cloning selection and updating operator of 30 particles. Although the proposed ICPSO requires 100 iterations, the evolution process of ICPSO is still faster than that of OMP.

The comparison between the reconstructed image and the original image using OMP and proposed ICPSO are shown in Fig. 7 and Fig. 8. The 50th band results of Cuprite2 and

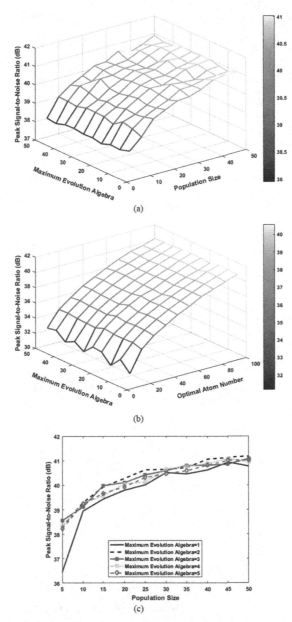

Fig. 4. The PSNR changes with different parameters for Cuprite1. (a) PSNR changes with evolution algebra and population size with optimal atom number fixed at 100; (b) PSNR changes with evolution algebra and optimal atom number with population size fixed at 30; (c) PSNR changes with population size, when optimal atom number is fixed at 100.

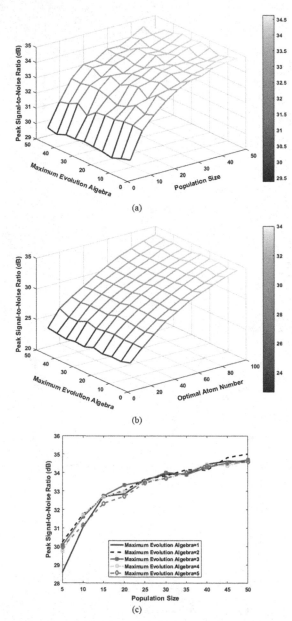

Fig. 5. The PSNR changes with different parameters for Indian Pines. (a) PSNR changes with evolution algebra and population size with optimal atom number fixed at 100; (b) PSNR changes with evolution algebra and optimal atom number with population size fixed at 30; (c) PSNR changes with population size, when optimal atom number is fixed at 100.

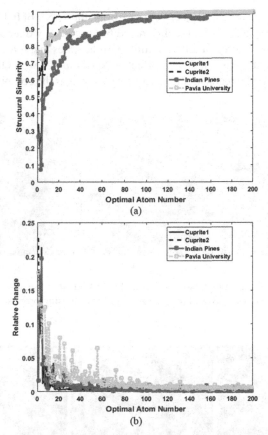

Fig. 6. The SSIM and relative change with different atom number for four band images using ICPSO. (a) SSIM; (b) Relative change.

Table 1. Comparison between OMP and proposed ICPSO.

Hyperspectral datasets	Algorithm	PSNR/dB	SSIM	Runtime/s
Cuprite1	OMP	40.2079	0.9792	372.81
	ICPSO	41.9437	0.9870	108.17
Cuprite2	OMP	39.6879	0.9722	379.93
	ICPSO	41.8877	0.9842	125.05
Indian Pines	OMP	31.8922	0.9787	93.47
	ICPSO	32.8223	0.9836	26.57
Pavia University	OMP	39.0706	0.9717	375.68
	ICPSO	40.0297	0.9778	113.21

Pavia University are given here. Objectively speaking, the PSNR of ICPSO is higher than that of OMP. From the naked eye, the difference between the two reconstructed images and the original image is very small. This fully demonstrates that the atoms searched by ICPSO can represent the original images effectively. Compared with OMP, the proposed ICPSO could improve the reconstruction accuracy as well as the computation efficiency.

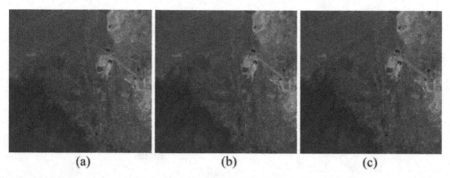

Fig. 7. The 50th band image comparison of Cuprite2. (a) Original image, (b) reconstructed image using OMP, PSNR = 33.5874 dB, and (c) reconstructed image using proposed ICPSO, PSNR = 34.6696 dB.

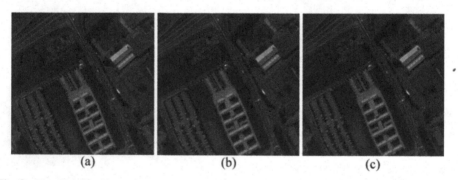

Fig. 8. The 50th band image comparison of Pavia University. (a) Original image, (b) reconstructed image using OMP, PSNR = 39.6655 dB, and (c) reconstructed image using proposed ICPSO, PSNR = 40.1998 dB.

5 Conclusion

Combining immune cloning and evolutionary theory, an immune clone particle swarm optimization algorithm (ICPSO) for sparse representation of hyperspectral images is proposed. Based on the OMP algorithm, particle position and velocity updating is used to simulate the process of searching optimal atoms. The idea of immune cloning is introduced, with immune cloning, cloning mutation, and cloning selection operators on the particle population, to prompt the particle population converging quickly to the optimal solution. We discussed the effects of optimal atoms number, population size and maximum evolutionary algebra on the performance of the algorithm through experiments, and determined the parameters for OMP and ICPSO. The reconstructed images are represented by the optimal atoms searched by OMP and ICPSO, reconstructed PSNR, SSIM and runtime are compared. The results carried on four hyperspectral datasets could demonstrate that the proposed ICPSO could find the optimal atoms to sparse represent the original images. Compared with OMP algorithm, the proposed ICPSO has 1–2 dB higher PSNR and SSIM than that of OMP, whereas consume less time. In summary, ICPSO algorithm could improve the reconstruction accuracy as well as computation efficiency for sparse representation of hyperspectral images.

Acknowledgments. This work was supported by the National Natural Science Foundation of China under grant number 61901350, Aeronautical Science Foundation of China under grant number 2019ZH0T7001, and Science Research Foundation of Xi'an Aeronautical University under grant number 2019KY0208.

References

1. Chang, C.: A review of virtual dimensionality for hyperspectral imagery. IEEE J. Sel. Top. Appl. Earth Obs. Remote Sens. **11**(4), 1285–1305 (2018). https://doi.org/10.1109/JSTARS. 2017.2782706
2. Das, S., Jain, L., Das, A.: Deep learning for military image captioning. In: 2018 21st International Conference on Information Fusion (FUSION), Cambridge, pp. 2165–2171 (2018). https://doi.org/10.23919/ICIF.2018.8455321
3. Niu, Y., Wang, B.: Extracting target spectrum for hyperspectral target detection: an adaptive weighted learning method using a self-completed background dictionary. IEEE Trans. Geosci. Remote Sens. **55**(3), 1604–1617 (2017). https://doi.org/10.1109/TGRS.2016.2628085
4. Pan, L., Li, H., Li, W., Chen, X., Wu, G., Du, Q.: Discriminant analysis of hyperspectral imagery using fast kernel sparse and low-rank graph. IEEE Trans. Geosci. Remote Sens. **55**(11), 6085–6098 (2017). https://doi.org/10.1109/TGRS.2017.2720584
5. AlSuwaidi, A., Grieve, B., Yin, H.: Feature-ensemble-based novelty detection for analyzing plant hyperspectral datasets. IEEE J. Sel. Top. Appl. Earth Obs. Remote Sens. **11**(4), 1041–1055 (2018). https://doi.org/10.1109/JSTARS.2017.2788426
6. Pan, L., Li, H., Meng, H., Li, W., Du, Q., Emery, W.J.: Hyperspectral image classification via low-rank and sparse representation with spectral consistency constraint. IEEE Geosci. Remote Sens. Lett. **14**(11), 2117–2121 (2017). https://doi.org/10.1109/LGRS.2017.2753401
7. Picone, D., Dolet, A., Gousset, S., Voisin, D., Mura, M.D., Le Coarer, E.: Characterisation of a snapshot Fourier transform imaging spectrometer based on an array of fabry-perot interferometers. In: ICASSP 2020 - 2020 IEEE International Conference on Acoustics, Speech and Signal Processing (ICASSP), Barcelona, Spain, pp. 1529–1533 (2020). https://doi.org/10.1109/ICASSP40776.2020.9053032
8. Uto, K., Seki, H., Saito, G., Kosugi, Y., Komatsu, T.: Measurement of a coastal area by a hyperspectral imager using an optical fiber bundle, a swing mirror and compact spectrometers. In: 2016 8th Workshop on Hyperspectral Image and Signal Processing: Evolution in Remote Sensing (WHISPERS), Los Angeles, CA, pp. 1–4 (2016). https://doi.org/10.1109/WHISPERS.2016.8071670
9. Uto, K., Seki, H., Saito, G., Kosugi, Y., Komatsu, T.: Development of hyperspectral imaging system using optical fiber bundle and swing mirror. In: 2015 7th Workshop on Hyperspectral Image and Signal Processing: Evolution in Remote Sensing (WHISPERS), Tokyo, pp. 1–4 (2015). https://doi.org/10.1109/WHISPERS.2015.8075489

10. Fang, L., He, N., Li, S., Plaza, A.J., Plaza, J.: A new spatial-spectral feature extraction method for hyperspectral images using local covariance matrix representation. IEEE Trans. Geosci. Remote Sens. **56**(6), 3534–3546 (2018). https://doi.org/10.1109/TGRS.2018.2801387

11. Zhang, X., Huang, W., Wang, Q., Li, X.: SSR-NET: spatial-spectral reconstruction network for hyperspectral and multispectral image fusion. IEEE Trans. Geosci. Remote Sens. https://doi.org/10.1109/TGRS.2020.3018732

12. Sun, L., Wu, F., He, C., Zhan, T., Liu, W., Zhang, D.: Weighted collaborative sparse and L1/2 low-rank regularizations with superpixel segmentation for hyperspectral unmixing. IEEE Geosci. Remote Sens. Lett. https://doi.org/10.1109/LGRS.2020.3019427

13. Mallat, S.G., Zhang, Z.: Matching pursuits with time-frequency dictionaries. IEEE Trans. Sig. Process. **41**(12), 3397–3415 (1993). https://doi.org/10.1109/78.258082

14. Zayyani, H., Babaie-Zadeh, M., Jutten, C.: Bayesian Pursuit algorithm for sparse representation. In: 2009 IEEE International Conference on Acoustics, Speech and Signal Processing, Taipei, pp. 1549–1552 (2009). https://doi.org/10.1109/ICASSP.2009.4959892

15. Yang, W., Peng, J., Sun, W., Du, Q.: Log-euclidean kernel-based joint sparse representation for hyperspectral image classification. IEEE J. Sel. Top. Appl. Earth Obs. Remote Sens. **12**(12), 5023–5034 (2019). https://doi.org/10.1109/JSTARS.2019.2952408

16. Song, X., Wu, L., Hao, H.: Hyperspectral image denoising base on adaptive sparse representation. In: 2018 IEEE Third International Conference on Data Science in Cyberspace (DSC), Guangzhou, pp. 735–739 (2018). https://doi.org/10.1109/DSC.2018.00117

17. Yao, L., Du, X.: Identification of underwater targets based on sparse representation. IEEE Access **8**, 215–228 (2020). https://doi.org/10.1109/ACCESS.2019.2962005

18. Tan, S., Sun, X., Chan, W., Qu, L., Shao, L.: Robust face recognition with kernelized locality-sensitive group sparsity representation. IEEE Trans. Image Process. **26**(10), 4661–4668 (2017). https://doi.org/10.1109/TIP.2017.2716180

19. Kulkarni, A., Mohsenin, T.: Low overhead architectures for OMP compressive sensing reconstruction algorithm. IEEE Trans. Circ. Syst. I Regul. Pap. **64**(6), 1468–1480 (2017). https://doi.org/10.1109/TCSI.2017.2648854

20. Tian, Y., Wang, Z.: An adaptive orthogonal matching pursuit algorithm based on redundancy dictionary. In: 2013 10th International Conference on Fuzzy Systems and Knowledge Discovery (FSKD), Shenyang, pp. 578–582 (2013). https://doi.org/10.1109/FSKD.2013.6816263

21. Shivagunde, S., Biswas, M.: Saliency guided image super-resolution using PSO and MLP based interpolation in wavelet domain. In: 2019 International Conference on Communication and Electronics Systems (ICCES), Coimbatore, India, pp. 613–620 (2019). https://doi.org/10.1109/ICCES45898.2019.9002042

22. Wang, R., Wu, Y., Shen, M., Cao, W.: Sparse representation for color image based on geometric algebra. In: 2018 IEEE International Conference on Multimedia and Expo (ICME), San Diego, CA, pp. 1–6 (2018). https://doi.org/10.1109/ICME.2018.8486524

23. Chardon, G., Necciari, T., Balazs, P.: Perceptual matching pursuit with Gabor dictionaries and time-frequency masking. In: 2014 IEEE International Conference on Acoustics, Speech and Signal Processing (ICASSP), Florence, pp. 3102–3106 (2014). https://doi.org/10.1109/ICASSP.2014.6854171

24. Jia, S., Hu, J., Tang, G., Shen, L., Deng, L.: Gabor feature based dictionary fusion for hyperspectral imagery classification. In: 2015 IEEE International Geoscience and Remote Sensing Symposium (IGARSS), Milan, pp. 433–436 (2015). https://doi.org/10.1109/IGARSS.2015.7325793

25. Guo, H., Li, B., Li, W., Qiao, F., Rong, X., Li, Y.: Local coupled extreme learning machine based on particle swarm optimization. Algorithms **11**(11), 174 (2018). https://doi.org/10.3390/a11110174

26. Shen, Y.: Research on swarm size of multi-swarm particle swarm optimization algorithm. In: 2018 IEEE 4th International Conference on Computer and Communications (ICCC), Chengdu, China, pp. 2243–2247 (2018). https://doi.org/10.1109/CompComm.2018.8781013
27. Yang, Z., Chen, L., Liu, S., Liu, Z., Chen, Q., Li, H.: Coverage control strategy based on multi-objective optimization of immune clone in wireless sensor networks. In: 2018 Ninth International Conference on Intelligent Control and Information Processing (ICICIP), Wanzhou, pp. 79–85 (2018). https://doi.org/10.1109/ICICIP.2018.8606691
28. Li, L., Lin, W., Lin, Q., Ming, Z.: Balancing convergence and diversity in multiobjective immune algorithm. In: 2020 12th International Conference on Advanced Computational Intelligence (ICACI), Dali, China, pp. 102–109 (2020). https://doi.org/10.1109/ICACI49185.2020.9177787
29. Dai, H., Chen, D., Zheng, S.: Effects of random values for particle swarm optimization algorithm. Algorithms 11(2), 23 (2018). https://doi.org/10.3390/a11020023
30. Wang, L., Feng, Y., Gao, Y., Wang, Z., He, M.: Compressed sensing reconstruction of hyperspectral images based on spectral unmixing. IEEE J. Sel. Top. Appl. Earth Obs. Remote Sens. 11(4), 1266–1284 (2018). https://doi.org/10.1109/JSTARS.2017.2787483

Research of a New Type Oil-Pan Forming Process

Wang Gaozhi[1], Xu Fucheng[1], Wang Shoujie[1], Zhang Jianxing[1], and Li Jin[2(✉)] (iD)

[1] Weichai Heavy Machinery Co., Ltd., Weifang 261000, China
wanggaoz@weichaihm.com
[2] State Key Laboratory of Integrated Service Networks, Xidian University, Xi'an 710071, China

Abstract. The technologic characteristics of the main oil-pan were analyzed with the aid of stamping molding analysis software. The structure, the working process and trying process of dies for drawing the main oil-pan were introduced; The technologic characteristics of the vice oil-pan were analyzed; The welding technologic characteristics of the main oil-pan and vice oil-pan were analyzed; The production process of the oil-pan were introduced.

Keywords: Oil-pan · Drawing · Welding

1 Introduction

The oil pan belongs to the automobile covering parts, which was a long box shaped drawing part with relatively complex shape and it's also a stamping part with high challenge. Usually, soft steel with good tensile properties was used as drawing material. The oil pan parts introduced in this paper adopt 2 mm thick ultra-deep drawing cold-rolled steel plate DC06. The material was an ultra-low-carbon steel which characterized with good surface quality, high dimensional accuracy, superior processing and welding performance in cold state, excellent deep drawing performance and has been widely used in the automotive industry. In recent years, how to increase the capacity of oil pan has become the research direction of various automobile companies due to the increasing demand of consumers for the oil change cycle. This paper introduces a production process of oil pan based on the combination of drawing and welding to increase the capacity of oil pan.

This work was supported in part by the National Natural Science Foundation of China under Grants 61801363 and 62071364.

X. Wang et al. (Eds.): AICON 2021, LNICST 396, pp. 612–620, 2021.
https://doi.org/10.1007/978-3-030-90196-7_52

2   Forming of Main Oil Sump

Through the comprehensive analysis of the parts structure and operating requirement, the process flow of the parts was preliminary determinate as follows: blanking - drawing (times not determined) - shaping - edge cutting, punching bottom hole - flanging - punching side hole (drilling side hole). Due to the absence of difficulties for blanking, shaping, edge cutting, bottom punching, flanging and other processes in the actual production, the drawing process will only be been studied in-depth research in this paper.

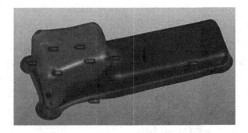

Fig. 1. Variation of oil pan thickness.

2.1   Process Analysis of Drawing

Through the comprehensive analysis of the parts structure and operating requirement, the process flow of the parts was preliminary determinate as follows: blanking - drawing (times not determined) - shaping - edge cutting, punching bottom hole - flanging - punching side hole (drilling side hole). Due to the absence of difficulties for blanking, shaping, edge cutting, bottom punching, flanging and other processes in the actual production, the drawing process will only be been studied in-depth research in this paper.

2.2   Process Analysis of Drawing

Surface scratches and creases were not allowed in the main sump. The flatness of the flange was required to be no more than 1 mm and can be matched with the engine seal to prevent oil leakage. One end of the main oil pan shell shows a dovetail shape, with a deep depth of 310 mm; The bottom was in the form of steps, with a shallow depth of 90 mm. In order to ensure the capacity of the oil pan and prevent the interference between the end face and the internal oil pump of the engine, the slope of the drawing mold on each side of the deep end was only 1. The Autoform forming software was employed for the formability analysis and structure optimization. After optimization, the thinning coefficient of the main oil pan thickness should not exceed the performance index of DC06-2.0 which can be considered to meet the requirements.

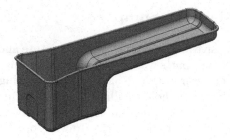

Fig. 2. Shape drawing of oil sump.

As can be seen from the simulation analysis figure (Fig. 1), the thinning of the bottom fillet exceeds the design requirements of the oil pan, which was mainly caused by the small fillet of the punch and can be improved by grinding the fillet of the punch in the process of mold verification to meet the requirements of the product. The actual shape after forming was shown in Fig. 2.

2.3   Process Analysis of Drawing

Due to the main oil sump drawing depth of 310 mm and width of 270 mm, the relative height was calculated by box drawing forming of calculation formula and methods: relative height = depth of oil pan/width of oil pan = 0.87, which was far greater than the maximum relative height of 0.589 achieved by one-time drawing of the box parts. In this respect, the drawing die of the main oil pan was designed according to two-time drawing forming.

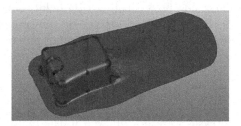

Fig. 3. One-time pull-out limit diagram.

The boundary conditions were set to analyze the oil pan formability according to the simulation analysis of the stamping analysis software combined with the current situation of the company's equipment and materials, including drawing, stress and strain, dangerous sections, etc., which can be properly compensated in the mold design. According to the comprehensive analysis, in the process of primary drawing and secondary drawing, the fracture was prone to occur at the transition of the fillet corner at the end of the oil pan (Fig. 3 and Fig. 4), and

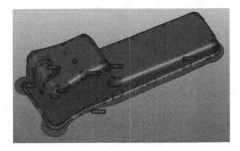

Fig. 4. Two-time pull-out limit diagram.

the stress exceeds the material strength limit. Due to the deviation between the software simulation and the actual operation, the two-time drawing scheme can be determined to be feasible.

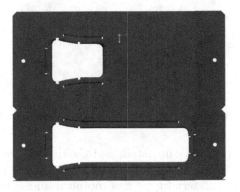

Fig. 5. Position diagram of drawbead.

The mold adopts circular drawing bead, which was distributed around the straight-line section, and there was no drawing bead at the transition part of the rounded corner. The structure and position of the final tendons were shown in Fig. 5. As the side shape of the main oil pan was strictly required by the welding procedure, the gap between the punch and concave dies was reduced as much as possible and preliminarily determined to be 1.1t in order to reduce the deformation degree of the oil pan after drawing forming. In the subsequent die test process, the height and clearance of drawing beading, the clearance of convex, concave dies and local fillet corners were adjusted appropriately according to the state of the die and the drawing situation, so that it can be successfully drawn and consistent. The mold structure was shown in Fig. 6.

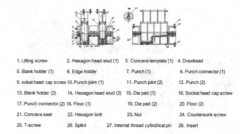

1. Lifting screw	2. Hexagon head stud (1)	3. Concave template (1)	4. Drawbead
5. Blank holder (1)	6. Edge holder	7. Punch (1)	8. Punch connector (1)
9. soket head cap screw	10. Punch joint (1)	11. Punch joint (2)	12. Punch (2)
13. Blank holder (2)	14. Hexagon head stud (2)	15. Die pad (1)	16. Socket head cap screw
17. Punch connector (2)	18. Floor (1)	19. Die pad (2)	20. Floor (2)
21. Concave seat	22. Hexagon bolt	23. Nut	24. Countersunk screw
25. T-screw	26. Splint	27. Internal thread cylindrical pin	28. Insert

Fig. 6. Diagram of drawing die structure.

2.4   The Working Process of the Mold and the Verification of Drawing Die

Fig. 7. Diagram of material structure.

The blank type of oil pan was calculated, and the size of sheet material required for drawing was preliminarily determined by the stamping analysis software. As shown in Fig. 7, the material type was modified and optimized in the mold verification process.

Mould Verification Process. Because of many uncertain factors in the drawing process, the verification of drawing die for deep oil pan is a very difficult job. So much practical experience is required, not only the drawing of hydraulic press and the sealing pressure need to be adjusted. It is also necessary to grind the convex and concave molds of the mold itself, and a certain lubrication method is required.

First of all, a trial drawing was carried out for a drawing, only a certain amount of drawing oil was applied to the surface of the template and the sheet, and serious cracking occured after drawing. The final drawing result was shown in Fig. 8, by adjusting the sealing force of the four corners of the blank holder and grinding the drawbead. The friction of the material flow was reduced by grinding, adjusting the corners of the convex and concave molds and the gap between the convex and concave molds, what's more, laying plastic film to increase lubrication, and adjusting the blank holder pressure. After many adjustment tests, the cracks were eliminated and good results had been achieved.

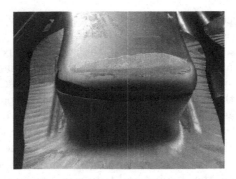

Fig. 8. The graph of one-time drawing breakage.

Secondly, trial drawing was performed on the secondary drawing die. To reach the final shape of the product, the secondary drawing was to draw 90 mm again on the basis of the primary drawing. It was relatively easy to form due to the shallow drawing depth. Whatever, there were also many problems in the extension process. During the verification process, only a certain amount of drawing oil was applied to the surface of the template and the sheet material. Serious cracks occurred at the fillet of the bottom of the oil pan and the sealing surface after drawing. The friction of the material flow during the molding process was reduced by matching the size of the round corners of the convex and concave dies with one and two pulls, and maintaining the gap between the convex and concave molds, grinding the round corners of the convex and concave molds, as well as spreading plastic film to increase the lubrication. As shown in Fig. 9, the secondary drawing was completed while no cracks appeared.

Fig. 9. The graph of drawing.

3   The Forming of Auxiliary Oil Pan

Since the drawing depth of the auxiliary oil pan is relatively shallow, the deepest part is only 94 mm. It has a shape of square box, and it is easy to form. There is no difficulty in production. Therefore, this paper only analyzes its requirements and process characteristics.

In order to increase the amount of oil in the sump, an auxiliary oil sump was added on both sides of the main oil sump. Since the auxiliary oil sump on the main oil sump was a spatially curved shape, in order to closely fit the main and auxiliary oil sumps, the joint surface of the auxiliary oil pan was designed to have the same shape as the side surface of the main oil pan. In order to facilitate welding, a suitable size flange edge should be reserved for the joint surface of the auxiliary oil pan. Due to the deviation of the size of the part after forming from the theoretical size, the position should be adjusted at all four sides of the auxiliary oil pan during the shaping and trimming process, so as to ensure the flange edge of the auxiliary oil pan.

4   The Welding of Main and Auxiliary Oil Pan

The auxiliary oil pan needed to be welded to the side of the main oil pan after the main and auxiliary oil pans were separately formed. The welding seam of the new oil pan was three-dimensional and irregular, and the total length of the welding seam was more than two meters. The DC06 drawn plate used in the shell contains very low carbon content while the plate was thin, so that manual welding cannot guarantee the welding strength of the parts, and it is difficult to meet the appearance quality requirements. In order to reduce the leakage rate after welding of the oil pan, improve the welding quality and appearance aesthetics, it is necessary to introduce and apply a robot welding system to complete the welding according to the application requirements of the oil pan. The use of robot welding has higher requirements for the size consistency of the oil pan and the joint surface gap, which should not be greater than 2 mm, otherwise the welding will be broken or unable to be welded during welding. The operation process of the robot is shown in Fig. 10.

During the welding process of the main and auxiliary oil pans, it was found that the gap between the parts of the joint surface was greater than 2 mm due to mold grinding, springback after drawing, etc., which also resulted in a low pass rate of one-time welding. In order to solve this problem, measures such as welding and repairing the mold in the area with a large gap, reinforcing the joint surface of the main and auxiliary oil pans, and expanding the shape of the mold center have been adopted to reduce the gap between the convex and concave molds. The maximum joint gap was only 1 mm with all these measures. After the welding was completed, it is necessary to conduct an air tightness test on the oil pan in order to check the tightness of the weld.

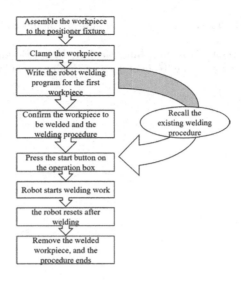

Fig. 10. The operation process of the robot.

5   Conclusion

The new diesel engine oil pan was designed in the case of the limited installation space. The oil storage capacity should be increased, if it cannot be stamped and formed at one time. While the stamping and welding forming scheme not only meets the design requirements, but also meets the application requirements. The development and research of the new oil pan process was the new breakthrough in drawing technology and welding technology. It not only reached a leading level in related fields and made important contributions to the improvement of market competitiveness of the company, but also created significant economic and social benefit.

References

1. Xue, Q.: Stamping Die Design Structure Atlas. Chemical Industry Press, Beijing (2005)
2. Wu, Y.: Stretch forming process and die design of engine oil tank bottom shell. Mold Ind. **2**(5), 99–110 (2002)
3. Xiao, X., Wang, X.: China Die & Mould Design Contest, vol. III. Jiangxi Science and Technology Press, Jiangxi (2003)
4. Xiong, N., Shi, Q.: Design of Cold Stamping Die. Science Press, Beijing (2000)
5. Xiaowen, T.: Practical Manual of Principles, Skills and Combat Cases of Auto Form. Hubei Science and Technology Press, Wuhan (2013)
6. Li, D.: Modern Mold Design Method. China Machine Press, Beijing (2004)
7. Zhou, H.: Welding Technique. China Machine Press, Beijing (2013)

8. Welding Society of Chinese society of Mechanical Engineering: Welding manual. China Machine Press (2015)
9. Klaus, M.: Diesel Engine Manual. China Machine Press, Beijing (2017)
10. Sun, F.: Mould Manufacturing Technology and Equipment. China Machine Press, Beijing (1983)

Author Index

Printed in the United States
by Baker & Taylor Publisher Services